It Can’t Last Forever

Canadian Unit, Formation, and Command Histories

Units – regiments, corps, squadrons, and ships – form the foundation of the Canadian military. This new series from Wilfrid Laurier University Press critically explores the organizational, personal, societal, and cultural themes of those units by blending traditional operational history with innovative approaches in military scholarship.

It Can't Last Forever

The 19th Battalion and the Canadian Corps in the First World War

David Campbell

WILFRID LAURIER UNIVERSITY PRESS
www.wlupress.wlu.ca

LAURIER
Inspiring Lives.

Wilfrid Laurier University Press acknowledges the support of the Canada Council for the Arts for our publishing program. We acknowledge the financial support of the Government of Canada through the Canada Book Fund for our publishing activities. This work was supported by the Research Support Fund.

Canada | Canada Council for the Arts | Conseil des arts du Canada | ONTARIO ARTS COUNCIL | CONSEIL DES ARTS DE L'ONTARIO | an Ontario government agency | un organisme du gouvernement de l'Ontario

Library and Archives Canada Cataloguing in Publication

Campbell, David, 1972–, author
It can't last forever : the 19th Battalion and the Canadian Corps in the First World War / David Campbell.

(Canadian unit, formation, and command histories)
Includes bibliographical references and index.
Issued in print and electronic formats.
ISBN 978-1-77112-236-8 (hardback).—ISBN 978-1-77112-253-5 (PDF).—
ISBN 978-1-77112-254-2 (EPUB)

1. Canada. Canadian Army. Battalion, 19th. 2. World War, 1914–1918—Regimental histories—Canada. 3. World War, 1914–1918—Campaigns—France. I. Title. II. Series: Canadian unit, formation, and command histories

D547.C2C19 2017 940.4'1271 C2016-906815-3
C2016-906816-1

Front cover: Canadians on their way to pay Fritz a visit. July, 1917 (LAC PA-001415).
Cover, text, and map design by Mike Bechthold.

Published by Wilfrid Laurier University Press
Waterloo, Ontario, Canada
www.wlupress.wlu.ca

This book is printed on FSC® certified paper and is certified Ecologo. It contains post-consumer fibre, is processed chlorine free, and is manufactured using biogas energy.

Printed in Canada

Contents

List of Maps

Abbreviations

AA	assistant adjutant
ADMS	Assistant Director of Medical Services
ADS	advanced dressing station
AO	Archives of Ontario
APM	Assistant Provost Marshal
ASH	Argyll and Sutherland Highlanders
BEF	British Expeditionary Force
CAMC	Canadian Army Medical Corps
CCS	casualty clearing station
CE	Canadian Engineers
CEF	Canadian Expeditionary Force
CFA	Canadian Field Artillery
CMGC	Canadian Machine gun Corps
CNE	Canadian National Exhibition
CO	commanding officer
CSM	company sergeant major
CT	communication trench
CWM	Canadian War Museum
DCM	Distinguished Conduct Medal
DCM	district court martial
DHH	Directorate of History and Heritage
DSO	Distinguished Service Order
FGCM	field general court martial
FOO	forward observation officer
FP 1	Field Punishment no. 1
FP 2	Field Punishment no. 2
GCM	general court martial
GHQ	general headquarters
GMA	Glenbow Museum Archives
GOC	general officer commanding

GOCRA	general officer commanding Royal Artillery
GSO	general staff officer
IWM	Imperial War Museum
LAC	Library and Archives Canada
LOB	left out of battle
mc	Military Cross
MO	medical officer
MUA	McMaster University Archives
NCO	non-commissioned officer
NSA	Nova Scotia Archives
OC	officer commanding
PRO	Public Record Office
QMG	Quartermaster General
RAP	regimental aid post
RCHA	Royal Canadian Horse Artillery
RCM	regimental court martial
RFA	Royal Field Artillery
RFC	Royal Flying Corps
RG	record group
RQMS	regimental quartermaster sergeant
RSM	regimental sergeant-major
SBR	small box respirator
SIW	self-inflicted wounds
WO	War Office

Her Majesty Queen Elizabeth II
Colonel-in-Chief
The Argyll and Sutherland Highlanders of Canada (Princess Louise's)
Windsor Castle, March 2017

The image of Her Majesty Queen Elizabeth II is reproduced courtesy of Ian Macdonald (photographer).
Her Majesty wears the Regimental brooch presented to her upon her appointment in 1950.

On 22 October 2014, Cpl. Nathan Cirillo was murdered while standing vigil as part of the Ceremonial Guard at the National War Memorial and the Tomb of the Unknown Soldier in Ottawa. The tragic loss of Cpl. Cirillo exemplifies the spirit of service and sacrifice that unites members of the Argyll and Sutherland Highlanders of Canada with the men of the 19th Battalion, CEF. (With respect and gratitude to the family of Cpl. Nathan Cirillo and to artist Bruce MacKinnon)

Battle Honours of the 19th Battalion

"Mount Sorrel" **"Somme, 1916, 1918"**

"Flers-Courcelette" "Thiepval"

"Ancre Heights" **"Arras, 1917, 1918"**

"Vimy, 1917" "Hill 70" **"Ypres, 1917"**

"Passchendaele" **"Amiens"** "Scarpe, 1918"

"Drocourt-Quéant" **"Hindenburg Line"**

"Canal du Nord" "Cambrai, 1918"

"Pursuit to Mons" **"France and Flanders, 1915-1918"**

Note: Boldfaced Battle Honours are those which appear on the colours of the Argyll and Sutherland Highlanders of Canada (Princess Louise's)

Foreword

"I just thought they'd always be here!" I remember the words vividly; they were spoken in the early 1990s by LCol Colin MacKay, CD, who had commanded the battalion in the 1960s; his father LCol Ernest MacKay commanded in the 1920s; Ernie MacKay was an original 91st officer, a 19th Battalion officer, and ended the war as a brevet major. Colin had been contemplating the forthcoming publication of the Regiment's third historical publication, *Black Yesterdays the Argylls' War* (1996) and grew rueful that something similar had not been done for the 19th.

I knew exactly what he was thinking – a grand opportunity had been lost. Aside from *Black Yesterdays*, the Regiment had published two previous books: *Historical Records of The Argyll and Sutherland Highlanders of Canada (Princess Louise's) formerly 91st Regiment Canadian Highlanders Canada Militia 1903–1928* [Hamilton, 1928] and *The Argyll and Sutherland Highlanders of Canada* [Hamilton, 1953]. The 1928 and 1953 books were celebratory and marked the occasions of the Regiment's 25th and 50th anniversaries. The first was a compilation by a committee and the second comprised eleven chapters; the first and the last were lists written by officers of the Regiment and the other nine, covering the Second World War, were written by Maj. Hugh N. Maclean.

In 1987, Capt. Sam Chapman, one of our Second War veterans, gave a memorable Toast to Fallen Comrades in which he mentioned our history "written in blood." Yet the history of the Regiment's First World War battalion, the 19th, was sadly missing. The 19th Battalion Association had planned one; some work was done; the decades passed and nothing came of it. For the Regiment's centennial in 2003, the planning committee made the 19th's history a major goal. The Chairman, Col. Alan Earp, OC, himself one of our Second War veterans, endorsed the decision enthusiastically. After some discussion, the committee approached David Campbell, then on the verge of defending his doctoral thesis on the 2nd Division, CEF, of which the 19th was a part. We made him a proposition; he agreed; and in a few years we had a manuscript – a good manuscript.

There was, however, no money for publication and the next step awaited the anniversaries commemorating the First World War and our next Regimental fundraising campaign. Douglas Hunter, QC, took on the task of seeing the manuscript through the editing process; I am certain, at points, Dave Campbell also thought "it can't last forever." Doug's enthusiasm for the project, for the manuscript, for the 19th, and for the author has been evident every step of the long way. We are grateful for his assiduous effort at every stage.

As Chairman of the Argyll Regimental Foundation, I congratulate Dr. Campbell whose skill as a scholar and a writer leap from every page of this remarkable book. The 19th has finally found its historian. And now LCol MacKay can rest easy!

— Col. R.D. Kennedy, CD
Chairman of the Argyll Regimental Foundation

Preface

It seems difficult to imagine now, but there was a time when I had not heard of the 19th Battalion of the Canadian Expeditionary Force (CEF). During my youth I could name only a small number of Canadian military units that served overseas between 1914 and 1918. As my interest in the history of the First World War grew, the 19th Battalion became, to me, just one of the 260 numbered infantry battalions recruited for the CEF. However, it had the distinction of being one of the limited number of such units (forty-six in all)[1] to see front-line service as part of the Canadian Corps. Although some of these units have had their stories published over the years (some more than once), the 19th Battalion had the dubious distinction of never having been the subject of a detailed historical account.[2]

My own knowledge of the 19th Battalion grew considerably during the course of research for my doctoral dissertation on the 2nd Division of the Canadian Corps. The 19th was one of twelve infantry battalions that constituted the majority of the division's personnel, and I quickly grew familiar with the broad contours of the unit's origins in 1914 and its experiences on the battlefields of France and Belgium from September 1915 through November 1918. But this familiarity was set mainly within the broader context of the unit's parent formations, the 4th Infantry Brigade and, most especially, the 2nd Division itself – the primary focus of my study.

It was through my work on the 2nd Division that my name came to the attention of Dr. Robert Fraser, the regimental historian of The Argyll and Sutherland Highlanders of Canada (Princess Louise's), the reserve unit in the Canadian Army that perpetuates the historical legacy of the 19th Battalion. As part of a broader program commemorating the Argylls' rich heritage, a history of the 19th Battalion was proposed and Robert contacted me to enquire whether I would be interested in taking on the project. Although I had no personal connection with the Argylls or the 19th Battalion, my knowledge of the battalion's parent formations made me a viable candidate for the job.

As a graduate student enticed by the prospects of payment and publication, I met with Robert, and, during the first of many congenial discussions to follow, I decided to accept the challenge of becoming the 19th Battalion's historian. It was a task that was rendered a bit more complex by my ongoing dissertation work. But with the two projects being essentially complementary, I quickly found that the in-depth research I began on the 19th Battalion proved extremely useful for various elements of my larger divisional study. Although working on these projects simultaneously slowed my progress on both, in the end I had a richer fund of battalion-level evidence that served the finished dissertation extremely well. When it came time to begin drafting the manuscript for the 19th Battalion's story, the broader context for the battalion's experiences at home and abroad was already mapped out for me in the dissertation.

Researching the 19th Battalion's story was made easier in one sense by the extensive collection of records generated by the unit and many of its individual members. I knew already from my dissertation research that the 19th Battalion had kept one of the most complete and extensive war diaries[3] that I had ever come across. The depth of detail in most of the daily entries was exceeded only by the voluminous appendices of orders, reports, summaries, field messages, and maps that accompanied each monthly volume of the war diary. In terms of the documentary evidence, the war diary became the backbone for the manuscript that developed. These records were augmented by additional official files concerning the battalion in the collections of Library and Archives Canada, the Directorate of History and Heritage of the Department of National Defence, and the Canadian War Museum, all in Ottawa.

However, what really made the 19th Battalion's story come to life for me were the personal records, such as letters, diaries, and interviews, as well as photographs found in archival repositories in Ottawa, Toronto (the Archives of Ontario), Calgary (the Glenbow Archives), and Hamilton (the archives of McMaster University and the archives of The Argyll and Sutherland Highlanders). These collections, in addition to some published personal accounts, provide the human heart of the 19th Battalion's story. The most vivid of these published accounts is Bruce Cane's *It Made You Think of Home: The Haunting Journal of Deward Barnes, Canadian Expeditionary Force: 1916–1919* (2004), and I am grateful to Bruce and to his publisher, Dundurn Press, for their generosity in allowing me to quote extensively from the book. After reading through such material, my initial lack of connection with the battalion was completely transformed into a strong sense of personal investment in its history and in the stories of its members.

Many of these personal stories came from the archives of The Argyll and Sutherland Highlanders and the Canadian War Museum, both of which feature wonderful collections of material generated by 19th Battalion veterans during the postwar decades. These include newsletters from the 19th Battalion Association, a group that endured into the early 1980s, and personal reminiscences that were compiled for an early attempt at a battalion history. The efforts of battalion veterans, such as Robert Spreckley, to produce a unit history decades earlier were by no means wasted, since much of the material they generated was of great assistance in preparing the present book.

Sadly, no veterans of the battalion remained for me to interview personally. However, I did have the honour of meeting and interviewing Mrs. Phyllis Douglas and her husband, Col. Ian Douglas. Mrs. Douglas's father was Lt.-Col. Lionel Millen, who commanded the 19th Battalion for much of the war. She and her husband were able to provide personal insights into the life of Lionel Millen and generously provided access to the extensive collection of letters that Millen wrote during the war to his mother and other family members at home in Hamilton.

The sheer volume and depth of available source material soon posed a challenge in terms of how to approach the manuscript itself. I could present a straightforward narrative account of modest length, spiced with occasional quotes and personal insights to maintain human interest. Or I could tell as complete a story as possible, often referencing events both weighty and routine as they occurred on a daily basis, sometimes presenting lengthy extracts from personal accounts, and anchoring the whole in the broader development of the 2nd Division and its parent formation, the Canadian Corps. The point of such an approach would be to fashion a memorial to the history of the 19th Battalion and the experiences of the individuals who served in it – a memorial that would serve not as mere hagiography but one that would address the problematic and difficult aspects of the battalion's history, as well as its achievements and the heroism of its members. In deciding upon this second approach, inspiration was provided by Robert Fraser's own regimental history, *Black Yesterdays: The Argylls' War*, which focuses on the Second World War and highlights the personal testimony of numerous veterans.[4]

In the course of researching and writing any work of history, an author happily racks up numerous debts of gratitude to those who have helped in some fashion. The entire project would not have occurred without the backing of the Argyll Regimental Foundation (ARF). In 2001–02 the ARF launched its commemorative campaign for the celebration of the Regiment's 100th anniversary in 2003. Many projects were considered and the history of the 19th Battalion was one of them. Among the battalion history's chief advocates was Col. Alan Earp: a scholar; a former president of Brock University; at that time the Regiment's honorary colonel and chair of the ARF; and an Argyll platoon commander (Pioneer Officer) during the Second World War. In addition to Col. Earp, I am extremely grateful for the support and enthusiasm of Col. Rick Kennedy (current Chair of the ARF, current honorary colonel of the Regiment, twice a former CO, and chair of the Regiment's World War I Committee). Col. Kennedy has been a steadfast supporter of the project from its inception, and he has, in so many ways, been crucial to the success of this effort. I am most grateful as well to Col. Geordie Elms (a member of the Regiment's World War I Committee and CO when the book project was launched); Col. Ron Foxcroft (former honorary colonel and supportive member of the ARF's Board of Directors); Honorary LCol. Glenn Gibson (a committed proponent of the project); Warrant Officer (retired) Colin Drake (curator and archivist of the Argyll Museum and Archives); and to LCol. Peter St. Denis (unit CO) and his predecessors in command of the Regiment for their support.

When the bulk of the research in Ottawa was conducted (now quite some time ago), Paul Marsden, Gregg McCooeye, and Tim Dubé at Library and Archives Canada (LAC) guided me through the structure and content of the various record and manuscript groups relating to the CEF. Tim Cook, now of the Canadian War Museum, was at that time working at LAC as well. In addition to the example he has set since then as a scholar and author, Tim has been a fount of information and encouragement. More recently, Lynn Lafontaine was extremely generous in helping facilitate timely reproduction of a great many photographs in LAC's extensive holdings.

At the Directorate of History and Heritage of the Department of National Defence, Stephen Harris and Bill Rawling oriented me to their important archival holdings and likewise provided plenty of advice and support during my visits. Carol Reid and Don Carrington of the library and archives at the Canadian War Museum located crucial documents in their collections and helped with copying the contents of some files that I did not have time to read on site. Other staff at the aforementioned institutions, at the Archives of Ontario, and the Glenbow Museum Archives, provided welcome assistance in accessing textual and visual material from their collections. At McMaster University, Gord Beck (Map Specialist, Lloyd Reeds Map Collection) and Renu Barrett (Archives and Research Collections) offered support with maps and granted access to a folio containing numerous photographs of people and places from the 19th Battalion's time in Canada and overseas.

A number of individuals and institutions were generous in granting permission to use various images. They include Christopher Lawson (photographer, for his photograph of the portrait of Major-General Robert Rennie, which hangs in the Officers' Mess of The Queen's Own Rifles of Canada); the 48th Highlanders Museum (for permission to reproduce a photograph of Major Armour Miller); Bruce MacKinnon (who approved the use of his editorial cartoon memorializing the death of Cpl. Nathan Cirillo); and Ian Macdonald (photographer, for his portrait of Her Majesty Queen Elizabeth II).

During the extended period in which the manuscript was drafted, I enjoyed regular communication with Bruce Cane, Fred Sherriff, and Kevin Shackleton, all of whom were immensely helpful with points of detail about the 19th Battalion, its personnel, and various other Ontario units in the militia and the CEF. Col. John Boileau and Chris McCreery provided timely advice on a last-minute question regarding honours and awards. Two anonymous reviewers took time to comment helpfully on an early draft of the manuscript, while Andrew Godefroy brought his scholarly expertise to bear in a careful review of the manuscript in more polished form. Along with his generous supporting comments, Andrew offered a number of valuable suggestions for further improvement.

Over the course of two trips to visit battlefields in France and Belgium, Jeremy Banning provided expert guidance and personal insight into one of the most important primary sources of all, the very ground over which men of the 19th Battalion fought and died a century ago. Fellow-travellers Des Leddin, Mark Sadler, and Richard Stevens provided not only good company on our battlefield excursions, but also their own insights into life in and behind the front lines on the Western Front. I am grateful as well for the support of the History departments at both Saint Mary's and Mount Saint Vincent Universities in helping to facilitate my battlefield studies while also keeping me gainfully employed.

As any novice author learns, editing and production of the manuscript into a finished book is an enormously involved process. These stages could not have been completed without the help and guidance of many individuals. First, I owe a tremendous debt of gratitude to Curtis Fahey, whose superlative editing skills made the manuscript a far better piece of work. I am extremely grateful as well to the staff at Wilfrid Laurier University Press for accepting the manuscript and for guiding me through the stages of publication. In this regard, special thanks are owed to Rob Kohlmeier (Managing Editor), Clare Hitchens (Marketing and Promotions), and most especially to Mike Bechthold (Production Coordinator). Not only did Mike express initial interest in the manuscript, he also provided much needed encouragement and direction through each phase of editing and production. And as any author who has worked with Mike knows well, his talents in map design add immeasurably to the value of any publication.

Finally, my highest thanks are owed to Robert Fraser, regimental historian of The Argyll and Sutherland Highlanders and Doug Hunter, of the Argyll Regimental Foundation. Robert set me on the path to uncover the 19th Battalion's history and provided invaluable support in countless ways through all phases of research, writing, and editing. Doug has been the prime mover in organizing the efforts that ultimately led to the manuscript's acceptance for publication, and he has laboured tirelessly to coordinate my own work on this project with the talents of many individuals already acknowledged. Both Robert and Doug helped uncover further sources of information on the 19th Battalion's history, and have in all ways kept the project moving toward completion. What I have done as an author could not have resulted in a finished book without their assistance, encouragement, good counsel, and above all, good humour. Of course, none of the individuals mentioned here bear any responsibility for remaining errors or imperfections in the book, which are mine alone.

On a personal level, I offer further thanks to my former PhD supervisor at the University of Calgary, Dr. Tim Travers, whose example of excellence in historical scholarship I can only hope to emulate. I am grateful to Wyn van der Schee for his friendship, for his encyclopedic knowledge of the history of the CEF and the Canadian Army in general, and for his generous gift of a set of 19th Battalion cap and collar badges. My parents, Greg and Maggie, and my brother Rob have also always been there for me and helped in more ways than they know. Finally, my greatest debt of gratitude and appreciation is to my wife, Trudy, and my sons, Matt and Mark, for keeping me (somewhat) sane and grounded in reality. Without their love and support there would be little point to anything else.

Notes

1 Forty-four of the numbered battalions plus the Royal Canadian Regiment and Princess Patricia's Canadian Light Infantry.

2 Of the four infantry battalions in the 4th Brigade, only the 20th Battalion boasted a full-scale published history until recent years. Now the story of the 21st Battalion has been addressed by Stephen Nichol, and the 18th Battalion has been covered by Sandy Antal and Kevin Shackleton in their extensive history of the regiment that perpetuates the battalion's legacy: the Essex and Kent Scottish Regiment. See D.J. Corrigall, *The History of the Twentieth Canadian Battalion (Central Ontario Regiment) Canadian Expeditionary Force in the Great War, 1914–1918* (Toronto: Stone and Cox, 1935); Stephen J. Nichol, *Ordinary Heroes: Eastern Ontario's 21st Battalion C.E.F. in the Great War* (Almonte, ON: S.J. Nichol, 2008); Sandy Antal and Kevin R. Shackleton, *Duty Nobly Done: The Official History of the Essex and Kent Scottish Regiment* (Windsor, ON: Walkerville Publishing, 2006).

3 During the war, each unit kept an official record of its activities known as a war diary. In addition to the daily log of events, many unit diaries featured copies of orders, reports, maps, messages, and other ancillary documents that usually appeared in a series of appendices to each month's diary entries. Unit war diaries vary widely in the amount of detail found in their daily entries and in the volume of documents preserved in their appendices. This variation may be found from one unit to another, or from month to month within the war diary of an individual unit. Much depended on the interest and diligence of the unit officers who were assigned the task of maintaining the diary.

4 Robert Fraser, *Black Yesterdays: The Argylls' War* (Hamilton, ON: Argyll Regimental Foundation, 1996).

1

Recruiting and Mobilization: 1914–15

With a flurry of war declarations, the peace of Europe was shattered in late July and early August 1914. On 28 June the assassination of Archduke Franz Ferdinand, heir to the throne of the Austro-Hungarian Empire, ignited a diplomatic crisis that brought about war between two opposing international alliances. On one side was the alliance led by Germany and Austria-Hungary, on the other was the Entente of Russia, France, and Great Britain. But the conflict was not limited to the geographical confines of Europe, for each of the major powers also mobilized their imperial possessions. Although Canada was a self-governing Dominion within the British Empire, its foreign policy was still orchestrated by the British government. Thus, Canada soon found itself swept up in the maelstrom.[1]

During the heady days leading up to the conflict, there were many in Canada, even among those who paid attention to world events, who must have wondered what the assassination of an Austrian archduke had to do with the affairs of Britain, much less their own nation. Thousands more Canadians would have been largely oblivious to the diplomatic and military manoeuvrings of the rival alliances immediately preceding the opening shots of the "War to End All Wars." These Canadians were too busy seeing to their own, often uncertain, affairs. Indeed, the fine weather that marked the summer of 1914 belied the anxiety in which a significant portion of the Canadian population lived, for at that time Canada was sliding into the most serious economic depression since the 1890s.[2]

Left: Major-General Sam Hughes. His October 1915 promotion was backdated to 1912. (LAC C-002468) Right: The Right Honourable Sir Robert Laird Borden. (LAC C-000694)

Distracted as many Canadians were, steadily increasing numbers took notice of the news from Europe during the twilight hours of peace. In the final days of July, crowds regularly gathered outside newspaper offices and in public squares of the large cities, anxious to hear the latest developments. When the German armies struck through neutral Belgium in an attempt to knock France out of the war, Britain, long pledged by treaty to uphold Belgian neutrality, joined the struggle alongside France and Russia. When Britain declared war on 4 August, Canada, along with the rest of the British Empire, was automatically included among the belligerents.

Although the outbreak of hostilities touched off a wave of enthusiasm among thousands of Canadians, there probably was nobody in the country more excited at the prospect of war than Colonel Samuel Hughes. Hughes was the mercurial Member of Parliament for Victoria and Haliburton, who served as Canada's militia and defence minister in the cabinet of Sir Robert Borden, the Conservative prime minister. With respect to military matters, Hughes was at heart a romantic who dreamed of leading Canadian troops to victory in a struggle with imperial Germany – a struggle he had anticipated for some time.[3]

A committed exponent of what historians have termed the "militia myth," Hughes took every opportunity to extol the virtues and promote the interests of Canada's volunteer amateur soldiers.[4] However, he often did this at the expense of the tiny Canadian permanent force. Professional soldiers – Canadian, British, or otherwise – were viewed by Hughes and his ilk as hidebound and imbued with less "common sense" than their amateur counterparts. Since being appointed to his portfolio in 1911, "Drill Hall Sam" had pumped unprecedented amounts of money into the militia, filling out establishments and improving training facilities.[5] He also saw to it that large numbers of militia units were put through their collective paces and trained en masse. During the summer of 1914, when more than 59,000 men were in training across the country, Hughes ordered a mixed force of over 10,000 militiamen to assemble at Petawawa, Ontario, where they carried out combined-arms manoeuvres "which more closely achieved active service conditions than any held in Canada since the Fenian disturbances half a century before."[6] Thus, the Dominion appeared to be as well prepared as it ever had been to field a military force in support of an imperial war effort. Appearances, however, were somewhat deceiving.

At first glance, the established strength of Canada's land forces in the summer of 1914 seemed impressive (at least when compared to previous years), with 3,110 in the permanent force and 74,213 in the militia. But actual strengths were, in fact, lower.[7] Moreover, there was no clear legal authority to send militia units on active duty beyond Canadian borders. Therefore, "only volunteers, as distinct from the Dominion's forces," would be acceptable for an overseas expeditionary force.[8] This legal sticking point virtually ensured that any Canadian overseas force would be comprised of composite units, or entirely new ones, with the officers and other ranks being assembled only during mobilization. The cohesion of established militia regiments would be virtually absent in the expeditionary force, and developing that cohesion in the latter would take time. Lacking a large standing army or a European-style system of universal military service, Canada did not have a sizable pool of military men who were fully trained and ready for service in a foreign land.

Between 1911 and 1914, mobilization plans had been drawn up by British officers serving on the Canadian staff, but these would remain essentially unused. The minister of militia, with his characteristic disdain for the ideas of professional soldiers, dismissed these plans on the hazy grounds that they were "devoid of all military merit."[9] In assembling the First Canadian Contingent for overseas service, Hughes bypassed the existing mobilization schemes as well as the established hierarchies in the regional divisions and districts in which all military forces in Canada were organized.[10] Instead, on the night of 6 August, he issued telegrams directly to each militia unit in the country, instructing their commanders to prepare "descriptive rolls" of volunteers, which were to be forwarded to militia headquarters in Ottawa. From these rolls, men for the contingent would be selected. Regimental commanders would then be informed of the number of men required from their respective units, and once these had been assembled, the men were to proceed to the new camp that was being constructed at Valcartier, Quebec. Over the following weeks, amid a confusing barrage of often contradictory orders that spewed forth from Ottawa, Hughes's mobilization arrangements underwent a number of modifications. Eventually, most militia commanders simply sent as many men as they could to Valcartier, which soon quartered more than 32,000 eager volunteers. It was there that selection for the expeditionary force would take place, with the chosen officers and men in the infantry being formed into composite numbered battalions, many of these representing a particular region of the country.[11] Infantry battalions in the First Contingent would be numbered from 1 through 17.

Hughes persistently interfered in the appointment of officers and in the organization of the contingent. But whatever criticism or praise may be heaped upon his actions and his choices, his energy was unfailing, and he was unquestionably the driving force behind the entire enterprise. Despite all the early disorder, 30,617 troops of the First Contingent of the Canadian Expeditionary Force (CEF) were successfully shipped to England beginning on 1 October 1914.[12] Most of them were organized into a division of almost 18,000 men, which, after a miserable period of training on Salisbury Plain in England, finally proceeded to France in February 1915.[13]

All in all, Canada had done remarkably well so far. Six months had elapsed between Hughes's "call to arms" and the point at which the 1st Canadian Division was dispatched to the front, having been trained and equipped. This feat compared favourably with the 8.7 months on average that it took the British to ready their Territorial divisions for war.[14] The accomplishment was all the more remarkable given the astonishingly minimal experience that the Canadians had in organizing higher army formations, compounded with Hughes's chaotic, ad hoc mobilization arrangements.

Raising the 19th Battalion

On 6 October 1914, only a few days after the First Canadian Contingent had set sail for England, the Canadian government offered "to place and maintain in the field a second overseas contingent of twenty thousand men."[15] The following day, anticipating a positive response from the imperial authorities in London, Canada set in motion plans to raise the new contingent. Britain cabled its official approval on 31 October, suggesting that the troops of the Second Contingent be organized into a 2nd Canadian Division.[16]

In raising the new contingent, Sam Hughes dispensed with the dramatic, centralized concentration of troops that had marked the organization of the First Contingent. He apparently had become convinced that "more satisfactory results" might be gained by mobilizing and training the Second Contingent at a local level.[17] Units would be allotted by quota to regional division and district commands throughout the country, the commanders of which would be put squarely in charge of recruiting, quartering, and training activities within their jurisdictions.[18] Although at heart Hughes might have preferred to organize the new contingent at Valcartier, as had been done with the previous one, that camp simply was not equipped with suitable quarters to accommodate thousands of men in the rapidly approaching winter season. In fact, there was no suitable winter accommodation in Canada for even a brigade-sized force.[19] The excitement of mobilization would now be spread among numerous centres across the country as the administrative machinery in divisional areas and military districts kicked into high gear, translating Ottawa's vision for the new contingent into reality.

It was amid this swirl of renewed activity that the order from Ottawa authorizing the mobilization of the 19th Battalion was issued, probably on 19 October. The following day, Lieutenant-Colonel J.I. McLaren received his appointment as commanding officer (CO) by wire from the headquarters of the 2nd Divisional Area in Toronto.[20] John Inglis McLaren, or "John I." as he was popularly known, was a man of considerable experience in the realms of business, politics, and the military. Born on 2 September 1865 in Goderich, Canada West, he was educated in Guelph and Hamilton. After working as an office boy in a wholesale grocery firm, he formed the Hamilton Coffee and Spice Company in 1888, in partnership with his older brother William. His military service began later, when he helped organize Hamilton's 91st Regiment (Canadian Highlanders) in 1903. That same year, he was gazetted captain in this unit, rising to the rank of senior major in 1909 and to lieutenant-colonel in command of the unit on 2 April 1912.[21]

Despite his amateur background, McLaren cut a sufficiently impressive military figure. At six feet in height, and with the confidence in administration and personnel management that came from years of business experience, McLaren did not have to work hard to impress his personality upon his subordinates. He was a keen sportsman and a first-class shot with a rifle; indeed, he had competed in the British army's annual musketry competition at Bisley in 1911 and was a past president of the Dominion of Canada Rifle Association.[22] In addition to his commercial and military endeavours, McLaren involved himself in politics, serving as alderman in the city of Hamilton in 1907 and 1908 and as mayor in 1909 and 1910. Although he had done well at the municipal level, his attempt to enter federal politics was thwarted during the 1911 federal election, when he ran as a Liberal candidate to the House of Commons and was defeated.[23] With his wide-ranging interests and the variety of offices he held, it is little wonder that on his attestation paper for the CEF McLaren identified his trade or calling as "Gentleman."[24] It also is worth noting that McLaren's appointment to a command in the CEF shows that Hughes, as militia minister, did not dispense favours solely to Conservative Party supporters.[25]

In August, before the order came to mobilize the 19th Battalion, McLaren and his second-in-command, Major William R. Turnbull, had appeared before Major-General François-Louis Lessard (General Officer Commanding [GOC], 2nd Divisional Area) in Toronto and offered the 91st Regiment for overseas service in response to Hughes's original "call to arms." Evidently unaware or heedless of the policy favouring composite units over established militia regiments, the two officers were disappointed by Lessard's inability to accept the offer. However,

Officers of the 19th Battalion who had served in the 91st Regiment. From left to right: Lt. F.L. Henderson, Lt. H.C. Hatch, Lt. E.G. MacKay, Maj. W.R. Turnbull, Lt.-Col. J.I. McLaren, Capt. L.H. Millen, Lt. W.H. McLaren, Lt. D.L. Wilson, Lt. H.D. Fearman. (ASH, Officers' Mess)

as a consolation, they were ordered to begin enlisting men for service in the new overseas units. By 22 August, the 91st had dispatched its own first contingent of volunteers, consisting of 5 officers and 151 other ranks, to Valcartier, where they were incorporated into the 16th Battalion (Canadian Scottish).[26] On receiving his appointment in October to command the 19th Battalion,[27] McLaren relinquished command of the 91st Regiment and immediately set about drawing up a list of suitable candidates to occupy staff positions in his new unit.

It is not surprising that McLaren's old unit, the 91st Regiment, was well represented among the members of the battalion staff. These included the 19th Battalion's second-in-command, Maj. Turnbull; the quartermaster, Lt. D.L. Wilson; the transport officer, Lt. H.C. Hatch; and the signalling officer, Lt. H.D. Fearman. Of the remaining staff assembled for the 19th Battalion, Maj. F.C. McCordick transferred from the 19th (Lincoln) Regiment in St Catharines; the adjutant, Lt. T. Morrison, arrived from the 13th Royal Regiment of Hamilton; and the paymaster, Lt. C.S. Patterson, came from the 19th Regiment as well. The original medical officer was Lt. G.W. Anderson of the Canadian Army Medical Corps (CAMC).[28]

McLaren's second-in-command, Major William Robert Turnbull, was born in Hamilton on 9 January 1865. Like McLaren, he was a businessman, and on his CEF attestation papers identified himself as a merchant and manufacturer. His interest in military matters had drawn him to earlier service with two of Hamilton's established militia infantry regiments. His first three years were spent with the 13th Regiment, the following eleven with the 91st Regiment. A fair-haired man of average height, Turnbull had been one of the original officers of the 91st, serving as a captain alongside John I. in 1903 and rising to the rank of major in 1910.[29] Turnbull's services as second-in-command of the 91st Regiment evidently were good enough that McLaren picked him to carry on in the same capacity in the new 19th Battalion. It was his job to understudy McLaren in all aspects of battalion command; should anything happen to the commanding officer, Turnbull would be next in line to replace him.[30]

Manpower and Mobilization

Personnel for the 19th Battalion were drawn from, and recruited by, a variety of existing militia regiments throughout central Ontario. Starting on 20 October 1914, companies were raised locally by the contributing regiments, and since the initial fervour of war enthusiasm had not yet cooled, recruiting officers had no trouble filling their quotas. In Lt.-Col. McLaren's hometown of Hamilton, men continued to flock to the colours, and by 6 November detachments from both of the city's contributing infantry regiments (the 13th and 91st) were assembled and ready to depart for Toronto. There, they would be concentrated with other companies from Toronto, Brantford, Sault Ste. Marie, and St. Catharines to form the 19th Battalion.

To merit inclusion among the ranks of the Second Contingent, volunteers had to meet the same criteria as those required of First Contingent recruits. Individuals

Recruiting poster for the 91st Regiment, one of the units contributing officers and men to the 19th Battalion. (ASH, Regimental Collection)

had to be between the ages of eighteen and forty-five and physically fit for service in the field. No doubt, there were some underage and overage individuals who succeeded in bluffing their way past the recruiters and examining physicians. Nevertheless, a small sample of twenty-seven other ranks taken from the 19th Battalion's published nominal roll in 1915 revealed an average age of twenty-five years. Other requirements that candidates had to meet included a minimum height of 5 feet 3 inches and a minimum chest measurement of 33½ inches. Recruiters preferred unmarried men and men with previous military experience, but this did not preclude acceptance of married men, with or without children.[31]

Once the contributing militia regiments had assembled their quotas of recruits, the various detachments proceeded from local points of concentration to Toronto for mobilization and basic training. The departure scene for the troops in Hamilton was mirrored in spirit, if not in detail, in the other communities outside Toronto that furnished men for service in the 19th Battalion. Cheering crowds lined the streets through which the troops paraded on their way to board the waiting railcars. At the Grand Trunk Railway Station in Hamilton, nearly 5,000 people thronged to catch a last glimpse of the second wave of local boys who marched off to war. As the men of the 13th and 91st Regiments filed into their assigned cars, the expected eastbound train approached, bearing the detachment from the 19th Regiment. The *Hamilton Herald* reported that "a hearty cheer" greeted the men of St. Catharines, "for the Nineteenth is not unknown in Hamilton, and many recognized friends wearing the scarlet coat, whom they had last seen at Niagara camp" during summer training exercises. The train paused to pick up the cars bearing the Hamilton contingent, while emotional family members said their goodbyes. As the *Herald* reported in the unabashedly jingoistic language of the day:

> The band struck up Tipperary … Partings were many, and some were touching … A party of pretty girls … shook hands with all the troops within reach and distributed packages of cigarettes to the men … Finally the cars containing the Thirteenth Royals and the Highlanders was attached to the Toronto train and the band struck up the Maple Leaf. The crowds cheered and cheered again. Then as Tipperary struck up afresh the train slowly moved out of the station and … swung away … bound for the mobilization camp at Toronto.[32]

Upon arrival in Toronto on 6 November, the various contingents that were slated to form the 19th Battalion proceeded to the grounds of the Canadian National Exhibition (CNE), where they joined companies of Torontonians to complete the initial concentration of battalion personnel.[33] Although it would appear that the battalion's entire strength was drawn from existing members of the various contributing militia units, in fact over half of the 1,105 other ranks listed in the unit's original nominal roll claimed no previous affiliation with any particular unit or branch of the military.[34] At war's outbreak, 420 men already had some military experience. The remaining 685 did not claim any form of prior military service. Because records do not indicate that hundreds of men were discharged from the battalion and were replaced by new personnel, we must assume that a large proportion of the men supplied by each contributing militia unit to the 19th Battalion were recent recruits who had joined those units within the previous three months. On the other hand, each of the forty-two officers listed on the 1915 nominal roll claimed earlier service in a unit or branch of the Canadian forces.[35]

Even though 59.7 percent of all ranks listed in the 1915 nominal roll did not claim previous military service, the 40.3 percent who did represented a slightly higher percentage of experienced personnel than was found in the entire population of the CEF between 1914 and 1918.[36] This was because recruits boasting some measure of previous service tended to be in greater supply during 1914 and early 1915 than in subsequent periods. Yet even among those who claimed some form of prior service, experience levels could vary widely. Some men had spent years with a particular unit, while others had only the briefest and most superficial of introductions to military life – either at an urban armoury or drill hall, or during an annual militia summer camp, which usually lasted around two weeks.

Most of the senior battalion and company officers were men of some experience, and in 1914 a few had more than a decade of militia service behind them. For the most part, the majors and captains of the 19th Battalion already held their ranks as such in their own militia units. Some, such as future battalion commanders Maj. W.R. Turnbull and Capt. Lionel H. Millen, had held these ranks for several years before the war. The experience levels of junior officers, however, were much more variable. Although some boasted several years of militia service, in a number of cases much of that service had been in the other ranks. The vast majority of the lieutenants had received their commissions either shortly before or just after the war broke out. Thus some of these subalterns had to sit before a Board of Examination on 9 November 1914 in order to qualify for their rank.[37] Men volunteered for a variety of reasons. For many during the summer and autumn of 1914, financial concerns loomed large. For those who were down on their luck as a result of the recent economic slump, a private soldier's pay ($1.10 per day) and the prospect of regular meals were highly appealing incentives. As historian John Herd Thompson perceptively put it, "'hungerscription' proved one of the CEF's most effective recruiting sergeants."[38]

Another instant attraction was the chance of free passage to the British Isles, which many of the men still viewed as home. Among the other ranks listed on the 1915 nominal roll, 529 men were born in England, 160 in Scotland, 52 in Ireland, 8 in Wales, 1 in the Orkney Islands, and 5 in the Channel Islands – a total of 755 out of 1,105 other ranks. Just under 30 percent of the other ranks (322 in all) were born in Canada[39] – a proportion that mirrored the number of Canadian-born men who had departed Canada with the First Canadian Contingent.[40]

Officers of the 19th Battalion (photo taken in Toronto later in 1915). (CWM 19830277-001)

But when we examine the addresses of next of kin as listed on the 1915 nominal roll, we find that ties to Canada were stronger than those indicated merely by place of birth. Of the 1,105 other ranks on the nominal roll, 676 – more than double the number of Canadian-born – provided a Canadian address (in almost all cases an Ontario one) for their next of kin.[41] Although much is usually made about the predominantly "British" character of the CEF, particularly during the early years of the war, familial ties with Canada were much stronger than might appear at first, when only the other ranks' places of birth are considered.[42] As well, familial ties *within* the battalion were strong for a few of the men, for the 1915 nominal roll contains sixteen possible pairs of brothers.[43]

Whereas the majority of other ranks were not Canadian-born, virtually all of the officers were. Only three of the forty-two officers on the original nominal roll claimed birth outside Canada (one in England, one in Ireland, and one in the Channel Islands). In addition, only one officer listed a non-Canadian address for his next of kin, and only two did so for non-Ontario addresses within Canada. Hamilton and Toronto were the dominant locations given for officers' next of kin; these two cities were identified by thirteen and sixteen officers, respectively.[44]

It is not surprising that the officers were overwhelmingly Canadian-born, given that most officers in the 19th Battalion, in common with their comrades throughout

the CEF, tended to be drawn from the upper and middle classes of society. Frequently, they were men with professional, managerial, or mercantile backgrounds, or students engaged in some form of post-secondary education. Owing to the relative stability and comfort of their upbringing, they or their parents had less inclination to move from one country to another than did many among the other ranks. An exception was Capt. Lionel Millen, who was born in London, England, in 1876 and moved with his family to Hamilton when he was seventeen. But like most of his peers, Millen was an experienced businessman and militia officer by 1914. In the pre-war period, he had established a successful importing business with his brother while finding time to indulge his keen interest in military life. After serving in the ranks of the 13th Royal Regiment, he joined the 91st Regiment in 1904 and was commissioned a lieutenant. He received his captaincy in 1910, and before the 19th Battalion's departure from Canada, he would be promoted to major and placed in command of D Company.[45]

Aside from reasons of economic hardship or sentimental desire to return to the British Isles, many officers and other ranks were motivated to enlist by sheer patriotic sentiment, or by desires to break free from the patterns of their everyday lives, experience new sensations, and see different parts of the world. Some no doubt fled to the army to escape various personal commitments, while others found themselves hustled into uniform through social or peer pressure. Some of those who had seen service in earlier conflicts such as the South African War, and who were not left embittered by their experiences, felt a surge of excitement in heading off to

D Company, 19th Battalion, Toronto, 1915. (LAC e010932321)

war again. Whatever the individual motives, there was no lack of volunteers when recruiting began for units of the Second Canadian Contingent. Thousands of men had failed for various reasons to gain a place in the First Contingent and so jumped at the chance to join the Second. Thus, infantry battalions recruiting everywhere, from Nova Scotia to Vancouver Island, found little difficulty in filling their ranks. In fact, large numbers of would-be recruits continued to be turned away, for it was still so early in the war that unit vacancies were being filled only by the fittest, the most experienced, the luckiest, or those with the best social and political connections.

Battalion Organization

The infantry battalion was a fundamental combat unit in the British and Canadian orders of battle; it also served important administrative and social functions. Under battalion auspices, men were trained for combat, fed, paid, clothed, granted leave, medically treated, given spiritual guidance, and provided opportunities for recreation. Thus the battalion "figured largely in the lives of most infantrymen, since it was large enough to minister for their basic needs, yet not so large as to seem impersonal; on the contrary, all officers, and most N.C.O.s and private soldiers of a battalion knew each other by sight at least."[46] Because of this, a battalion had the potential to develop into a relatively close-knit community – one with its own social dynamic that was generated by the interplay of shared experience and the unique personalities of its individual members.

Each battalion contained between thirty and thirty-five officers and roughly 1,000 other ranks, but official establishments were rarely maintained, especially once a unit began suffering casualties.[47] In accordance with pre-war Canadian

establishments, the personnel were divided among a battalion headquarters detachment and eight rifle companies. This was the fashion in which battalions in both the First and Second Contingents were organized initially. But after the First Contingent arrived in England, the British War Office ordered that it conform to a four-company arrangement, which doubled the size of the individual companies. This was in keeping with the latest British establishment, which had been adopted on 1 January 1914. British battalion organization then was finally in line with that of other European armies (particularly the French and German), which already had embraced the use of four strong companies per battalion, as opposed to a larger number of weaker ones. The new battalions of the Second Canadian Contingent received the order to adopt this system on 10 December 1914. By 4 January 1915, the changeover had been completed in the 19th Battalion, which then consisted of four rifle companies plus a headquarters company.[48]

The headquarters company was composed of the battalion commander and his administrative staff, along with transport, medical, and signals personnel, a small complement of pioneers for construction duties, and a machine-gun section. This left around 900 men in the rifle companies. Each of the rifle companies was sub divided into four platoons, and a platoon was made up of four sections of between ten and fourteen men each. A battalion thus contained sixteen platoons and sixty-four sections within its four rifle companies. The battalion's machine-gun section consisted of eighteen men, equipped with two Colt machine guns. This establishment later would be doubled to thirty-five all ranks and four machine guns.[49]

Commissioned officers commanded companies and platoons, while sections were led by non-commissioned officers (NCOs). A company was commanded by a

No. 1 Company, 19th Battalion. Considering the date of the change in company organization and designation, either the company in this photo is misnamed or the photo is misdated. (LAC e010932633)

major or, more commonly, a captain, while a platoon was led by a subaltern (either a full lieutenant or a second-lieutenant). The platoon commander was assisted by a second-in-command – usually a senior NCO known as the platoon sergeant. During operational service, when high casualty rates among subalterns left platoons bereft of commissioned officers, the platoon sergeant frequently assumed the mantle of command, with the second sergeant in the platoon assisting him. Finally, each section was headed by a corporal.[50] The entire unit was commanded by a lieutenant-colonel, who was assisted by a second-in-command with the rank of major.

A machine-gun section in training, armed with a Colt-Browning M1895 machine gun and Ross service rifles. Most troops referred to the machine gun simply as "the Colt." (LAC PA-004916)

"You're in the Army Now": Quarters, Equipment, and Training

The officers and other ranks of the 19th Battalion shared the facilities at the CNE, which became known as Exhibition Camp, with troops from other units. These included the 20th Battalion, the 5th Canadian Field Ambulance, the 4th Canadian Mounted Rifles, units of the 2nd Divisional Artillery, and the 2nd Divisional Train.

Officers of the 19th Battalion were quartered with their 20th Battalion counterparts in the Applied Arts Building, and in part of the ground floor of the Women's Building, which also contained the senior NCOs' quarters and mess. The rest of the other ranks were allotted quarters in the Government Building. Battalion headquarters was located in the Women's Restaurant, while the officers of all units shared a large mess in the Administrative Block.[51]

One veteran other rank recalled the pervasive odour of disinfectant that dominated the atmosphere in the Government Building. On first viewing his new accommodations, he likened them to a "combination of jail and hospital."[52] "We were quartered in what was known as the old government building," stated veteran Ed Youngman, "right inside the Dufferin Street entrance" of Exhibition Park. The engineers "had built bunks and there was eight to a section, four slept down below and four slept above … The fellow that slept directly under me … was among the first men who were killed in the trenches when we arrived there."[53] At the first lights out on 6 November, the novelty of barrack life immediately wore thin for some.

Queuing up for mess call at Exhibition Camp. (MUA RC 0835)

Fred Stitt remembered "yells of 'open the windows,' 'close the windows.' Guys on top layer [bunk] not bad off; on the lower deck the overhead creaks, cracks and groans of new wood were the accompaniment to snores in many keys from all over that huge bedroom. Reveille was a relief."[54]

If the accommodations seemed somewhat makeshift at first, the officers made an impressive show "in their neat, well cut uniforms and Sam Browne belts with sword attached."[55] But the same could not be said of the other ranks. According to R.H. (Harry) Neil, "when the first Battalion parade was held on a brisk November morning at the Exhibition Grounds in Toronto, to the experienced critical eye, it must have appeared a somewhat nondescript outfit in the ill-fitting uniforms of their respective militia units."[56] In taking the measure of his new comrades on 6 November 1914, Fred Stitt beheld "Coxy's Army uniforms everywhere, part khaki, part dress, part civie, even Christie hats and button boots."[57] J. Howard Jarvis of St. Catharines, who arrived with the contingent of men from the 19th Regiment, wrote after the war: "Well do I remember our arrival on November 6th, 1914, at Exhibition Grounds … in our red tunics and blue trousers with the red stripe. Jack Buller told me we looked like a bunch of farmers. Nevertheless we could drill. Farmers make good soldiers."[58]

The other ranks' appearance improved dramatically with the issue of new khaki uniforms beginning on 9 November.[59] The remainder of their kit trickled in during the succeeding weeks and consisted mainly of outdated equipment – the best and most up-to-date gear had been sent overseas with the First Contingent. Holdalls, gloves, belts, and ammunition pouches were issued during the week of 15 November, but not until the second week of December were all companies completely outfitted with Oliver equipment.[60] The latter consisted of a complex assortment of leather shoulder straps, pouches, packs, and belt, and was designed to carry the soldier's food, clothing, and ammunition. It had been condemned years earlier during the South African War as "uncomfortable, awkward, and unable to carry a soldier's basic needs."[61] But for the time being, it was all that was available to the troops of the Second Contingent. "It was most ungodly … terrible stuff," complained Fred Stitt.[62]

Rifles were issued during the week of 22 November, when the men received Short Ross Mk. II rifles along with bayonets. These were subsequently replaced by the newer Long Ross Mk. III rifles on 30 December.[63] Developed by Scottish businessman Sir Charles Ross, and based upon the Model 1890 Austrian Mannlicher rifle design, the Ross rifle was adopted by the Canadian government in 1902 and manufactured in a purpose-built factory near the Plains of Abraham at Quebec. Although it proved to be a wonderfully accurate target rifle, the Ross was a "temperamental" weapon that was prone to jamming during rapid firing or when its mechanism was exposed to dirt. It also did not work well with British cartridges, which, according to Sir Charles, were not manufactured as precisely as the Austrian and American ammunition he had employed when his weapon was first designed and tested.[64]

The defects remained essentially unresolved, even though numerous modifications were made in the various marks of the rifle that were manufactured up to 1914. Nevertheless, based largely upon the weapon's accuracy (under ideal conditions), and the fact that he had been a member of the committee that originally

Troops at Exhibition Camp trying to put together their Oliver equipment. (MUA RC 0835)

Ed Youngman, Bill Welling, "Tex" Adams, Bill Cook, Wally MacLennan, and [first name unknown] Winlock. (MUA RC 0835)

recommended its adoption, the militia minister, Sam Hughes, became the Ross rifle's most public and ardent champion. A "prisoner of his own enthusiasm for it," Hughes extolled the weapon as "the most perfect military rifle in every sense in the World today."[65] Despite the minister's unshakable faith in the Ross rifle, it would not pass the brutal test of combat on the Western Front, as the troops of the 1st Canadian Division found to their frustration during the Second Battle of Ypres in the spring of 1915. Yet Hughes's formidable political power ensured that the men of the 19th Battalion, and their comrades in other units of the 2nd Canadian Division, would take the Ross rifle into combat, even after the 1st Canadian Division had been rearmed with the more robust British-made Lee-Enfield rifle. But all that lay in the future.

From day one, all ranks were put through their paces by drill instructors who sometimes knew scarcely more than the men they ordered around. Even officers familiar with parade ground routine, such as McLaren, found handling raw recruits somewhat challenging. To one sergeant major, McLaren complained, "Every time I say 'stand easy,' down they flop."[66] Later, in May 1915, during an inspection by Sam Hughes, McLaren tried in vain to organize the men in a hollow-square formation in order to hear an address by the minister. According to veteran Ted Lang, Hughes, sensing McLaren's "dilemma, came to his rescue with a kindly 'Just break ranks, Colonel, and close up.'" According to Lang, "'Sam' addressed us as the '19th Regiment' which added a further touch of pride to our esprit de corps."[67]

Although the largely inexperienced other ranks were a handful, McLaren had to iron out a few rough edges of his own. For all his experience in the spheres of business, politics, and the militia, and despite his demonstrated skills in marksmanship with a rifle, McLaren apparently was not accomplished in the art of equitation. Ed Youngman, who was well versed in handling horses, was appointed McLaren's groom and was asked to ensure that the horse that had been selected for the colonel was of a quiet temperament. In accordance with the CO's instructions, Youngman paraded the horse through the noisiest parts of the Exhibition Camp to ensure that the animal would not startle easily. After getting the horse used to the din of artillery batteries practising their trade, Youngman was ordered to take the animal on walks through the nearby streets to get it accustomed to the noise of passing streetcars.[68]

Basic training, if it did little ultimately to prepare the men of the 19th for the harsh business of fighting on the Western Front, at least served to socialize them to army life. "Oh we had all sorts of training from foot drill right up to musketry … and bayonet fighting," recalled Fred Stitt. "We also had night maneuvers up through [the] northern part of Toronto at night time when it was good and dirty and mucky and wet and snowy and freezing … And they were hard nights and they taught us

Ed Youngman with "Danny," Lt.-Col. McLaren's mount. According to the photo's original caption, Danny was the "first horse taken on strength" of the 19th Battalion. (MUA RC 0835)

Morning roll call at Exhibition Camp, Toronto. (MUA RC 0835)

that being a soldier wasn't going to be all honey and butter."[69] Indeed, immediately after their arrival at Exhibition Camp, the men of the 19th Battalion plunged into a strict schedule of training and routine, which was organized initially as follows: reveille – 6:00 AM; breakfast – 7:30 AM; first drill – 9:00–10:45 AM; second drill – 11:00 AM–12:30 PM; dinner – 1:00 PM; third drill – 2:00–3:30 PM; fourth drill – 3:45–5:00 PM; tea – 5:30 PM; guard mounting – 6:30 PM; retreat – 7:30 PM; first post – 9:30 PM; last post – 10:00 PM; lights out – 10:15 PM[70] At the first morning roll call, a number of men were somewhat casual in their attitudes towards punctuality. "Quite a few had the impression any old time would do," claimed Fred Stitt. "In 'A' company this gave Colour-Sgt Pete Merson the opportunity to commence one of his boring addresses on the subject 'you're in the Army now.' These always finished up with the silly quote 'transgressors will be shot.'"[71]

Both officers and other ranks did an hour of physical training each day and one hour each of musketry and bayonet fighting on alternate days. Work in the latter two subjects would soon increase during early 1915 to daily frequency. The rudiments of musketry, such as sighting, trigger pressing, and charger loading, were practised first on the parade ground, while indoor firing exercises were carried out under the CNE's grandstand during the winter with .22 calibre target rifles. Troops in specialist positions, such as signallers, machine gunners, and scouts, also required time to learn the tactics and technologies of their particular trades.[72]

As the men's individual skills improved, the daily drill sessions were structured to include plenty of work in squad, platoon, company, and extended order drill. In addition, company commanders regularly lectured their men on such topics as the conduct of an advance, the handling of rear guards, and the establishment of outposts. NCOs in particular were lectured on administration, interior economy, discipline, and military law. Even senior officers benefited from occasional lectures by instructional staff from camp and divisional headquarters on a variety of administrative and tactical issues, because some of them were still relatively new to their duties.[73]

Among the more irksome and exhausting features of training were the regular company and battalion route marches. The former were daily events, while the latter were held one to three times a week and could cover between six and twelve miles. Marching and musketry were combined beginning on 8 March 1915 as each company in succession marched approximately ten miles to the firing ranges at Long Branch. Shooting was carried out in the afternoons, after which company personnel would camp out overnight at the ranges. The following morning would see more target practice, and after lunch the company would march back to Exhibition Camp. By 8 April, the battalion had completed its musketry course, each man having fired twenty to thirty-five rounds per day during his time on the range.[74]

While repetitive exercises, such as thrusting bayonets into the vitals of straw-filled dummies, continued to occupy a significant part of the training curriculum, as the winter and spring of 1915 wore on, increasing amounts of time were devoted to unit manoeuvres at locations in and around Toronto, such as High Park, Cedarvale, Leaside, and along the Don Valley. In these exercises the men put their training to the test, both as individuals and as a collective, carrying out offensive and defensive tactical scenarios that pitted companies against one another, or occasionally the entire battalion against another unit, such as the 20th Battalion.

Some of the larger tactical exercises were organized by the staff of the Divisional Area and included most of the infantry, mounted, and artillery units from the Exhibition Camp. Many of the other ranks who took part in these schemes

Officers of the 19th Battalion and their mounts, Exhibition Camp, 1915. At the centre are Lt.-Col. McLaren and his horse Danny. This image was provided by the family of Lt. Herbert D. Fearman, the officer on the far left.

believed they were more for the benefit of the senior officers. To the rank and file, the exercises "only meant marches, halts, more marches and more halts, officers galloping here and there, groups standing seriously studying maps. Mystic words such as 'outposts,' 'advanced guards,' etc., were wafted towards them, until, after being told to 'attack,' 'lie down,' and 'get up' they were marched back to barracks thoroughly wearied, sadder but decidedly not wiser men."[75] With the hindsight gained through harsh experience in France and Belgium, Fred Stitt later dismissed much of the tactical instruction in Canada as "Good Boer War thinking."[76] These exercises also revealed the inexperience, if not the inventiveness, of some of the junior officers. Mortimer Sturgeon recalled one incident along the Humber River during a night exercise that called for the use of stealth tactics. One of the lieutenants issued a curious order to retire, which ran along the lines of, "No. 6 platoon, about turn, quick crawl."[77]

Discipline and Esprit de Corps

In assessing Lt.-Col. McLaren, Ed Youngman declared that "if there was one man that was responsible for the true esprit de corps of the 19th Battalion, it was he." Youngman argued that even miscreants whom McLaren ordered confined to the guardroom could scarcely bear any ill feeling towards him once they were released, because at heart they knew they had been dealt with fairly and justly. There doubtless was some exaggeration in this claim. Nevertheless, at a reunion in 1938, when Youngman asked McLaren what the secret of his popularity had been, the elderly colonel replied, "Well, Youngman, underneath all the military discipline I always realized that I was dealing with men."[78]

This attitude to discipline was common among militia COs in the pre-war period. It had long been the tradition in the Canadian militia that stern punishments were not normally employed, for it was reasoned that volunteers who felt themselves ill-used by their officers simply would not choose to re-enlist once their periods of service had expired.[79] In addition, the complex social relations among officers and other ranks may have encouraged the establishment of a more relaxed disciplinary climate among Canadian troops. In many cases, both officers and other ranks within a militia unit had known one another personally in civil life; some even may have been related by blood or by marriage. This made it difficult to uphold the British military tradition of maintaining a social gulf between officers and other ranks, a tradition that, in theory, was supposed to make it easier for officers to enforce discipline and administer punishment according to regulations.[80]

The somewhat freer disciplinary spirit among Canadian soldiers, combined with the relative proximity of Toronto's attractions, contributed to the prevalence of certain types of offences among the troops stationed at Exhibition Camp – most notably, absence without leave and drunkenness. Within the 19th Battalion alone, almost 290 incidents of absence without leave were recorded between 1 December

Above: Most men could find some relief from the discipline of military life through harmless off-duty fun. Harvey Wright, Keith Lyon, Harold Stitt, and Ed Youngman clowning around at Exhibition Camp, Toronto. (MUA RC 0835)

Right: Regimental Sergeant Major William Witthun. (ASH, Regimental Archives)

1914 and 31 March 1915.[81] The most common punishment for minor cases of short-term absence was simple forfeiture of pay, while men who dared to indulge in longer stretches of unauthorized time away from their duties received varying terms of detention. A stint in the guardhouse generally awaited those convicted of other serious offences, such as flagrant disobedience, insubordination, or striking a superior officer.[82] As for the incorrigible minority who proved stubbornly resistant to the demands of military discipline, the simplest solution was found to be discharge from the unit.

After inspecting the 19th Battalion at the end of January 1915, a Board of Officers charged with reporting back to the secretary of the Militia Council noted that "large numbers of men have been discharged from this Regiment for various causes. Minor offences appear to have been numerous." But officials in Ottawa were assured that "from careful inquiries made, the discipline is improving and undesirables are being weeded out."[83] The report gave no indication as to what "large numbers" meant in terms of actual numbers of men discharged. However, according to battalion records, between 1 December 1914 and 31 March 1915, around fifty-five other ranks had been struck off the battalion's strength as being "unsuitable" or "undesirable." During the same period, around 325 breaches of discipline occurred, for which individuals received punishment.[84] These figures appear to have been well below the average observed in other units; some Ontario battalions reported

Pipes and drums leading the 19th Battalion out of the gate at Exhibition Camp, February 1915. (LAC PA-061260)

a 10 percent wastage of manpower through discharges stemming from misbehaviour.[85] Although the men of the 19th Battalion were not always paragons of military virtue, from a comparative standpoint they do appear to have been reasonably well disciplined. In the opinion of the Board of Officers, Lt.-Col. McLaren's efforts to enhance the quality of discipline were made easier by the work of the regimental sergeant major, William Witthun, whom they judged to be "a capable man and a good disciplinarian."[86]

Some of the men's restless energy, which no doubt led to many of the disciplinary infractions, could be channelled into more productive ends that also fostered the development of unit pride. Competition among units and sub-units was one means through which the men's initiative and efforts could be directed towards endeavours that encouraged corporate discipline, excellence in performance, and group solidarity. A contest among companies for the best march time from Long Branch to Exhibition Camp was one example of such activity.[87] Competition with troops outside the 19th Battalion also existed, and a friendly rivalry grew between the 19th and 20th Battalions during their sojourn at Exhibition Camp. Another element of the battalion that eventually would play a significant role in promoting cohesion and raising spirits was the pipe band, which was supplied by personnel from the 91st Regiment and led initially by Pipe-Sgt. Alexander McKenzie.[88] However, the beneficial effect of the pipe band was not immediately evident, for it appears that some of the pipers had not yet mastered their art, and one veteran's reminiscences do not indicate universal appreciation of the musicians' efforts to hone their skills. Fred Stitt recalled some cacophonous practices in a certain part of the Government Building that came to be known as the "Pipers' grotto." According to Stitt: "It was a huge building that old Government Building but in no part of it were you immune to the peculiar dirge of the chanters, several of 'em going at once and all different tunes – if they *were* tunes."[89] By comparison, Stitt and his friends observed "with some envy the Twentieth Battalion entering the Camp after a route march with their good brass band in front."[90] But the grass was not as green on the other side of the barrack yard as Stitt had presumed. As much as he disliked the skirling and screeching of the practising pipers, Stitt admitted that "we were somewhat consoled when we looked across to the Horticultural Building and heard the 20th Battalion brass horns going oompah, oompah, etc. etc." during their own practice sessions. In fact, Stitt declared that "as time went on we became very fond of our Pipes and Drums." Indeed, the 19th Battalion would be well served musically, not only by their pipes and drums but also by their own brass band. Although not mentioned as often as the pipes and drums, the brass band likely expanded from an original core of buglers who were with the unit from its earliest days.

Another source of collective amusement was supplied by a black bear cub, which was christened "Henri." The little bear had been sent to Capt. Edward H. Newman for the express purpose of becoming battalion mascot, and many in the unit quickly regarded him as a cherished "pet." Ptes. Danny Ryan and Fred Hardman were among those charged with handling young Henri, and they soon found the bear to be admirably suited for handling certain "extra" duties beyond his emblematic status. Specifically, it was found that Henri proved ideal for hazing new

Buglers of the 19th Battalion at Exhibition Camp, November 1914. (LAC PA-061329)

recruits who were as yet unaware of the mascot's existence. Hardman remembered one particularly memorable case:

> The Boys were troubled about a new recruit who could not stand the quick change from sheets to blankets and had brought his own sheets and a pillow with case. On top of this he was well supplied with cold creams, face lotions and what not. Naturally a lot of the boys couldn't take it and the bear was called into action. While said recruit … was sleeping, [Henri] was led in and forced to crawl on the bed of the offending party. Imagine being awoke from a deep sleep to gaze into the face of a real live bear. Within a few days our recruit was away and soon forgotten.[91]

But despite the entertainment Henri provided for all ranks, he did not retain his manageable size for long. Before the battalion embarked for England, the bear was left in the care of the Toronto zoo.[92]

Inspections and Embarkation

Throughout the winter of 1914–15 the 19th Battalion was visited, reviewed, or inspected on numerous occasions by public and military figures, including the governor general, the Duke of Connaught; the prime minister, Sir Robert Borden; the lieutenant-governor of Ontario, John S. Hendrie; and the GOC, 4th Infantry Brigade of the Second Contingent, Col. Septimus Denison. Visits by state officials essentially were social occasions, whereas inspections by senior military officials were events of greater import for the administration of the battalion, for it was on these occasions that the efficiency of its officers and other ranks was assessed.

The Board of Officers that reported to the secretary of the Militia Council in Ottawa delivered its findings on the general efficiency of the 19th Battalion on 29 January 1915. It judged all battalion accommodations at Exhibition Camp to be clean, sanitary, and suitable for the various purposes for which they were being used. The copious indoor space allowed for continuation of training, even during the prevailing conditions of heavy snow that existed at that time. Training in physical and company drill, bayonet exercises, and instruction in the principles of musketry and machine gunnery were judged to be satisfactory. However, it was felt that more experience was wanted by the headquarters staff in the tactical handling of the battalion.

Each officer was closely scrutinized with regard to his qualifications, background, and fitness to carry out assigned duties. With only a few exceptions, the officers were found to be satisfactory and it was recommended that most be confirmed in their ranks by the minister of militia-in-council. It was noted that some "of the lieutenants have not yet had much experience but all show a great desire to improve – are steady – working hard and with more training should make good [*sic*]. There seems to be an honest desire among the offices to loyally support the C.O. who appears to have the confidence of all ranks."[93]

On 25 February, the Inspector General, Maj.-Gen. F.L. Lessard (former GOC of the 2nd Divisional Area), echoed the earlier favourable appraisal of the Board of Officers regarding the 19th Battalion's efficiency. Lessard found that both Lt.-Col. McLaren and Maj. Turnbull appeared well suited for their positions. He judged McLaren to be "popular with his officers and men, a good disciplinarian – he is keen, tactful, and has good common sense," while the remaining officers and the NCOs were considered to be efficient and worthy of their positions. "This in my opinion is the best regiment I have inspected yet," Lessard declared. "The interior economy of the regiment is excellent and there exists a good esprit de corps ... The men are in excellent physical condition [and] great care has been taken in the training of the section commanders."[94]

During the same month, and continuing into the next, there were occasional outbreaks of illness that afflicted a number of officers and other ranks. Isolated cases of mumps appeared, but of more pressing concern was the increasing prevalence of pneumonia, which medical staff worked to keep in check among the men crowded in their barracks. Despite their efforts, an "epidemic" of pneumonia swept through Exhibition Camp during the first week of February, during which one member of the 19th Battalion died.[95] The most serious alarm was caused by several cases of cerebrospinal meningitis, which quickly resulted in two deaths during the third week of February. As reported by McLaren, "extreme measures" were taken to counteract the disease. Aside from increased efforts at sanitation, two officers and forty-four other ranks were isolated in the Inglis Building for observation and five confirmed carriers were isolated at the Old General Hospital. By mid-March, virtually all of the individuals under observation had returned to duty and the outbreak was effectively under control. However, the carriers remained under isolation in hospital, and by the end of March two more men had succumbed.[96] In general, regular medical examinations and a series of inoculations administered at intervals throughout the fall and winter months of 1914–15 kept fatalities from disease to a minimum.

On 10 April, by invitation of the City Council, the 19th Battalion paid a special visit to the Hamilton "for the edification of the citizens and to help stimulate recruiting." Charles Henderson recalled: "The day before the big event, there was intense preparation. Shoes were shined, buttons polished, bayonets burnished so that they sparkled in the sun; and the Officers' Sam Browne belts were given an extra touch of the old elbow grease." After boarding the steamship *Macassa* at the Yonge Street dock at 9:00 AM, the troops disembarked at 12:15 PM in Hamilton. For many in the battalion, the visit was a homecoming and a chance to show families and friends something of their increasingly refined military deportment.[97] According to Henderson, once the men of the 19th had arrived in Hamilton,

The 19th Battalion on parade, Exhibition Camp, 1915. (CWM 19830277-002)

the first item on the program was lunch. The Ladies Auxiliary provided a wonderful meal in the Armouries, and it did not take long for 1,000 hungry infantrymen to do full justice to it. There were speeches of welcome, and other festivities, and then the troops were given a couple of hours off, before the main event of the visit – receiving the Freedom of the City, and the march through the streets with bayonets at the fix.

But soon, Henderson added,

the great day was over, and the Battalion boarded the [*Macassa*] for the return trip to Exhibition Camp. In the gathering dusk on the quiet waters of Lake Ontario, snatches of song could be heard, and in some secluded corner a piper was softly piping a lament.

> It was sobering to reflect that before many days were over the Battalion would be on the way to join their comrades on the Western Front.[98]

Throughout the rest of April, the battalion continued its regular program of drilling, marching, and weapons training, spiced with weekly tactical exercises and "sham" battles. By around "the beginning of May," the men were growing somewhat restless as rumours of troop movements "for points of embarkation spread through the barracks, one being that the 4th C.M.R.s and the Artillery were to leave before the 19th and 20th Battalions."[99] The 19th Battalion would not be kept waiting for much longer, however. On the morning of 12 May, battalion personnel were ordered to evacuate the Government Building and prepare for departure from Exhibition Camp to the port of embarkation for overseas service. At 6:30 PM the battalion's 41 officers and 1,096 other ranks[100] assembled and marched to Exhibition Siding, where they immediately boarded two trains for Montreal.[101] Of the departure from Toronto, Cpl. Harry Adie wrote: "As usual under these now somewhat common circumstances there were many touching scenes just before the trains pulled out, as mother, sweetheart and child said what for some might be the last good-bye. However, with Tipperary, Are We Downhearted and the Gang's All Here, the spirits of the men were soon as buoyant as ever as we realized that at last we were really on our way."[102] "They are fit and ready and will give a good account of themselves," declared an enthusiastic McLaren to a group of well-wishers from Hamilton, who had come to Toronto to see the battalion off.[103]

The journey to Montreal would be an overnight one. As the trains carrying the battalion steamed away from the bustle of Toronto and into the countryside, the lengthening hours of daylight allowed the men a final glimpse of Ontario. The sun was going down, not only upon the surrounding landscape but also upon the last lingering geographic ties that the men still had with their civilian lives. As darkness fell and the trains swayed along towards the distant Montreal docks, many men must have looked forward to the future with a mixture of excitement and nervous apprehension. At last they were on their way to take full part in what was, to them, the defining event of their generation. The lengthening casualty lists that were posted and published throughout Toronto and all parts of the Dominion during the previous weeks must have given the men of the 19th Battalion some sober pause, and good reason to presume that the conflict they were about to join was not some mere "boy's own" adventure. The very recent sufferings of their comrades in the 1st Canadian Division under the German gas clouds at Ypres furnished a grim warning to those who still cultivated romantic notions about the nature of war and provided an ominous foretaste of things to come.

2

Training in England: May–September 1915

On 13 May the two trains carrying the 19th Battalion finally reached Montreal. Upon detraining during a heavy rain, the men were assembled at the berth of the RMS *Scandinavian*, and by 7:45 AM all ranks had settled into their assigned quarters. The ship slipped out into the St. Lawrence at 11 AM to the sound of cheering crowds and booming horns from surrounding vessels. The 19th Battalion was on its way at last.[1]

Traffic on the river was busy, necessitating extreme caution and resulting in relatively slow progress. On reaching Rimouski the following morning, the ship offloaded the last shipment of mail and then struck out into the Gulf of St. Lawrence. Although the voyage had barely begun and the weather was still fine, some of the more sensitive "landlubbers" aboard were beginning to suffer from seasickness.[2] On 15 May, Lt.-Col. McLaren instituted daily parades at 10:00 AM, which included a complete inspection of the ship and the men's berths. At 12:30 PM, as the *Scandinavian* surged onward into the grey North Atlantic, she passed within sight of Cape Race, Newfoundland, and the battalion finally bid farewell to North America.

The deep ocean swells took hold of the vessel, and increasing numbers of men succumbed to bouts of seasickness of varying violence and duration. Practically all of the 257 men reporting sick on 15 May were suffering from *mal de mer*. Yet this did not prevent the execution of boat drills at 4:00 PM, during which all personnel had to wear lifebelts and practise assembling at their assigned lifeboats – an activity that would be carried on at regular intervals for the remainder of the voyage.[3] After passing Cape Race, the *Scandinavian* veered south before finally turning east towards England. According to Pte. H.W. Hunt, this was done "to avoid both the Montreal and New York boats." Indeed, the ship was "steering a long course for Plymouth, avoiding as much as possible the regular trade routes," which might have attracted the most attention from prowling German submarines.[4] Radio silence was maintained as well, although the ship's wireless operator occasionally picked up stray messages intended for other vessels, which sometimes included war news as well as American and National League baseball scores.

After losing sight of Newfoundland's rugged shore, the *Scandinavian* passed within two miles of the spot where the *Titanic* had gone down in 1912, which drew considerable interest among the passengers.[5] Yet, sobering as thoughts of the *Titanic* tragedy were, another, much more recent, maritime disaster would have been uppermost in the minds of most 19th Battalion personnel. Just over a week earlier, on 7 May, the Cunard liner *Lusitania* had been torpedoed by a German U-boat off the south coast of Ireland. Some 1,200 lives had been lost, many of them women and children. If the Germans had little compunction about torpedoing a vessel with so many civilians aboard, how much more eager would they have been to sink the *Scandinavian*, with its complement of fighting men on their way to the front lines?

But for many Canadians who had not yet found their sea legs, the trials of life on the *Scandinavian*'s pitching decks grew more wearisome than their fear of enemy submarines. According to Pte. Gladstone Ghent of the battalion's machine-gun section, "the ship rolled all the way across, and we had some time trying to keep our meals down. Often you would hear the remark, 'If only a torpedo would hit this ship!' But we mostly hoped it would not."[6] In a letter to the *Hamilton Spectator* under the pseudonym "Omar," Cpl. Harry Adie told a similar tale of his comrades' woes: "Saturday, May 15, 1915. Quite a rough sea to-day and judging from the far-away expression on some of the faces the men are beginning to realize it. Cpl. Roy Matheson, one of the early victims, casually remarks how different things taste going up and down."[7]

Not everyone was stricken by seasickness, and some appear to have enjoyed their transatlantic passage. One of the latter was Pte. Hunt. "Day after day went by," he wrote. "We had physical drill at 6:45; inspection at 10 and semaphore at 1:45. The whole three took about 1½ hours, so it was easy. Combine this with excellent grub, and an excellent bunk. All was O.K., and I'm glad to say that I was not sick a minute."[8] The commander of D Company, Maj. Lionel Millen, likewise admitted little personal discomfort during the voyage. This probably owed in part to his previous experience in crossing the Atlantic as a teenager. Writing to his mother on 22 May, Millen explained: "The trip across has been rather uneventful. We traveled somewhat off the regular course, we only passed about 5 or 6 boats … Was not sick at all and there was not as much as you might expect, though some had pretty bad spells … I ate big meals every day and the eats were good."[9]

Efforts were made to satisfy all ranks' need for comfort and entertainment. A concert was held in the men's forward dining room on the evening of 17 May,[10] and on the following evening, according to Harry Adie, "the sergeants held a dance on the promenade deck – strictly stag, as the nearest thing to petticoats on this ship is Pipe-Sergeant MacKenzie and his kiltie band."[11] Even more engaging were the sporting events that were organized periodically for officers and other ranks, which further stimulated the competitive spirit evidenced during the battalion's sojourn at Exhibition Camp. All ranks came together, however, in cheering for Pte. Brooks of D Company in a boxing match with one of the ship's stokers.[12]

Along with the need to keep the men's spirits up was the importance of preventing their martial skills from becoming rusty during the ocean crossing. This was especially true for some of the more technical specialist personnel, such as the machine gunners. One of them, Pte. Ghent, described the measures taken to keep up with their training:

> We started target practice with our machine gun from the stern by throwing empty barrels and boxes overboard. We did so well that the guns were ordered mounted fore and aft when we entered the danger zone. We were on the lookout for periscopes, but did not see any … We got one scare … when the lookout reported something suspicious on our port quarter. It turned out to be two whales out taking the air. Put a whale side by side with a submarine, and it's pretty hard to tell them apart at a distance.[13]

By noon on Friday, 21 May, the *Scandinavian* was sailing some 220 miles off the south coast of Ireland and making straight for the centre of the English Channel. The mood aboard ship grew noticeably more tense as they entered the war zone – or "danger zone" as termed by Ghent – around the British Isles.[14] According to Charles Henderson, "what the Germans did not know" was that two of the men on board were prize-winning marksmen, "who could be counted on to drill a hole in the periscope of any submarine that came too close."[15] Even so, the *Scandinavian* and all aboard her would have stood next to no chance if caught in the sights of a vigilant U-boat skipper. Rifles and machine guns provided paltry protection, and the only defence the ship could put up at night was one of partial concealment. According to Maj. Turnbull, precautions had been "taken nightly against showing any but the deck lights, other windows and port holes being covered by screens, towels, brown paper etc."[16] Still more protective measures were taken. Ted Lang recalled that after breakfast on 21 May all battalion personnel were mustered and "informed that we were to don life belts and keep them on permanently for the balance of the voyage as we were now in waters within which enemy submarines were operating. Needless to say there wasn't any joking about it, and as the hours passed we became more apprehensive."[17]

"Our escort." This photo was presumably taken from the deck of the RMS *Scandinavian* and depicts one of the two destroyers (HMS *Linnet* or HMS *Lawford*) that escorted the ship into port at Plymouth. (MUA RC 0835)

Only a naval escort could have provided any real sense of security as the ship neared the south coast of England. Fortunately, such assistance quickly came to hand. As H.W. Hunt recorded: "Just about 6 [PM] our bunch in the bow saw two little black specks on the horizon, and almost before you could say Jack Robinson two little destroyers came up and turned almost in their own lengths. Then 150 yards on each side of us we saw small, but you can bet, tough specimens of the British navy, and how we did cheer."[18] HMS *Linnet* and HMS *Lawford* took up position to starboard and port respectively, while the 19th Battalion's buglers and pipe band were assembled on deck and struck up a lively series of musical selections in honour of their escorts. But despite the air of jubilation and relief, security measures were not relaxed. Increasing numbers of armed observation pickets were posted around the ship, and arrangements were made to keep the vessel in total darkness once night fell.

The "Old Country"

The 22nd of May dawned calm and clear as the *Scandinavian* steamed towards port, still attended by her naval escort. Shortly before 10:00 AM, she entered Plymouth Sound. Despite the eagerness of all ranks to place their feet back on terra firma, the tides were not favourable for transporting the men and equipment ashore and orders were received to prepare to disembark on the following morning. In the meantime, time was found for recreation. Some officers were ferried ashore to tour the numerous historic sites in the vicinity, and in the evening one last concert was held on the *Scandinavian*'s deck and an exchange of songs occurred between the men of the 19th Battalion and the Royal Naval cadets stationed on nearby training ships.[19]

The Canadian troops were struck by the beauty of the surrounding English countryside, which made an especially vivid impression on those who had never seen it before. In his letter to the *Hamilton Spectator*, Harry Adie confessed: "I can now understand a little of the Englishman's enthusiasm for the land of his birth. The mystery is, not that they love it, but that they leave it. The country here is a perfect picture with its rolling lands beginning with a gradual slope right at the water's edge and divided on the hillsides in the distance by dark green hawthorn hedges against the lighter background of the sea-green fields."[20] Another soldier, Charles Henderson, remarked: "When we left Toronto the trees were still without leaves, and the landscape was dull. Going into Plymouth the bright green hills surrounding the city were a welcome sight from our ship."[21]

Reveille sounded at 5:00 AM on Sunday, 23 May, and final preparations for disembarkation were undertaken by all ranks. At 6:00 AM the tender *Sir Walter Raleigh* pulled up alongside the *Scandinavian* and made ready to receive the battalion's baggage and equipment. Between 8:30 and 10:00 AM the battalion personnel were ferried in two successive sections by the tender *Sir Francis Drake* to the Mill Bay docks.[22] "Everyone cheered as we passed along the river," remarked Gladstone Ghent of the reception received from the local population. "The warmth of the welcome made one's blood tingle."[23]

In short order, the troops were loaded onto waiting trains. The relatively diminutive size of the engines and carriages amused many Canadians, who were accustomed to the larger vehicles more commonly used in North America.[24] Their destination was Westenhanger Station, Kent, which was reached later that evening after a pleasant journey through southern England, including the suburbs of London. Maj. Millen, like many born Englishmen, felt a surge of emotion in returning to the land of his youth. "The country was a perfect picture all the way," he wrote to his mother in Hamilton. "Especially so in Devon. I tell you when I first saw it there was a lump in my throat and moisture in my eyes and I was glad I was on this job."[25] At a few of the stops that were made en route, some of the more eager among the 19th Battalion wrote their names on the hardtack biscuits that were included in their rations and passed them through the railcar windows as souvenirs to the bevies of smiling women lining the station platforms.

Despite the idyllic quality of the countryside and the impressive vastness of metropolitan London, many of the 19th Battalion boys quickly realized they were no longer in a part of the world where "the war" was a mere abstraction. With its much closer proximity to the Western Front in Europe, life in England had assumed a sense of urgency that had not been generated in far-off Canada. Numerous churches observed along the train route were seen flying Red Cross flags, indicating

Map 1 – United Kingdom

that they were now being used as hospitals for the wounded. "Any misgivings that the war might be over before we arrived were now dispelled," remarked Charles Henderson.[26] Ted Lang likewise remembered that "after leaving Clapham Junction behind, we passed a Red Cross train carrying wounded from the battlefields. That really, in Shakespeare's words, gave us pause."[27] Harry Adie noted how "the whole country seemed to be practically depleted of men, almost every physically-fit male being with the colors somewhere. A man not in uniform is regarded here with suspicion – almost contempt – and the feeling is so intense that civilian clothes require an explanation, if not an apology."[28]

When the battalion detrained at Westenhanger, its equipment was loaded onto transports and the men marched two miles to the camp of the 4th Canadian Infantry Brigade at West Sandling, where both supper and sleeping quarters awaited them.[29] "Here the Advance Party of our Battalion soon had us sorted out to our respective huts," related Ted Lang, "where we were served steaming mugs of hot tea and, would you believe it, slabs of English sultana cake!"[30]

Training Camp

West Sandling Camp was located in the Shorncliffe area not far from the English Channel, and its facilities were much more inviting than those the troops of the First Canadian Contingent had endured on Salisbury Plain during the previous winter. Moreover, the men of the Second Contingent were not faced with the prospect of training during the bleak English winter.

Other ranks were accommodated in single-room clapboard huts, each containing thirty-two men. Officers were typically granted a little more privacy, their huts being divided into rooms, each of which was shared by three individuals. Along with living quarters, the camp contained offices, stables, storage areas, and a sizable parade ground.[31] To add a taste of home to their new surroundings, the men gave familiar names to many of the buildings and pathways throughout the camp. The area allotted to D Company, which comprised a great many men from Hamilton, was situated "at the corner of King and James streets, one of their huts bearing the placard "the Connaught Hotel."[32] Overall, the accommodations at Sandling were rated "very fine" by veteran Fred Stitt. Writing from his new quarters in the camp, Pte. Ghent remarked: "Just 12 days ago we left Toronto, and here we are comfortably settled in camp. West Sandling is just nine miles from Folkestone and five miles from Shorncliffe, and is as pretty a place as one could wish for. The sun started to shine on our first drill, and we consider it a good omen. Everyone is glad we are here."[33]

Thus began the serious business of training. Although efforts had been made aboard ship to maintain the men's physical conditioning, it was imperative that the work begun in Canada be resumed and intensified, especially in the realm of tactical training. All ranks in each section, platoon, and company had to learn how to perform effectively as a collective force, and the officers needed to sharpen their leadership skills. All ranks in the 19th Battalion had to function as a discrete unit; they also had to learn how to work effectively within the higher formations to which they would belong. It was in England that these formations – the 4th Canadian Infantry Brigade and the 2nd Canadian Division – were finally organized.

The 4th Infantry Brigade was an "all-Ontario" formation containing the 18th Battalion (mobilized at London), the 19th and 20th Battalions (both mobilized at

Fred Stitt, Fred Tate, and Bill Welling at West Sandling. (MUA RC 0835)

Toronto), and the 21st Battalion (mobilized at Kingston). It was commanded initially by Col. Septimus Denison, of the well-known Toronto military family. Denison, however, was not in the best of health,[34] and he would be replaced on 25 June by Brigadier-General Lord Brooke. Lord Brooke was an English officer who had seen service in Canada before the war. He had made a favourable impression on Sam Hughes, whose approval was needed for all principal command appointments in the contingent.

At West Sandling, the four battalions of the 4th Brigade were finally concentrated, each occupying a quadrant of the brigade camp. Nearby were situated the camps of the 5th and 6th Infantry Brigades, which, together with the 4th Brigade, would form the infantry component of the 2nd Canadian Division. The 5th Brigade contained two units from Quebec – the 22nd Battalion (later nicknamed the "Vandoos"), which was composed mainly of French-speaking volunteers, and the 24th Battalion, an English-speaking unit recruited primarily from Montreal. The 5th Brigade's other two units hailed from the Maritimes – the 25th Battalion from Nova Scotia and the 26th Battalion from New Brunswick. The 6th Brigade was made up of units from each of the western Canadian provinces: the 27th Battalion from Manitoba; the 28th Battalion from Saskatchewan; the 29th Battalion from British Columbia; and the 31st Battalion from Alberta. These three infantry brigades, along with brigades of field artillery, companies of engineering troops, mounted, motor-machine gun, and signals units, supply and ammunition columns, and the 4th, 5th, and 6th Canadian Field Ambulances, would comprise the 2nd Canadian Division, a force containing approximately 19,800 all ranks, under the command of Maj.-Gen. Samuel Steele, of North-West Mounted Police fame.[35]

Under the direction of divisional and brigade staffs, Lt.-Col. McLaren and his officers drew up training syllabi and prepared all ranks of the 19th Battalion for a strenuous course of practical and theoretical instruction. Until mid-July much of the daily routine was given over to physical drill, bayonet fighting, musketry, route marching, and elementary company and battalion tactical exercises. "There will soon be nothing left of me if I keep on running," wrote John Mochrie to his father later that summer. "I'm down to 144½ pounds, but still feel good."[36]

With respect to musketry, special emphasis was devoted to "rapid manipulation" of the rifle, and the men were expected to load and fire "fifteen aimed shots to the minute before [being] considered fit" to proceed to more advanced musketry instruction.[37] Whether the men experienced difficulties with their Ross rifles jamming under rapid-fire conditions on the ranges is not clear.[38] Some of their compatriots in the 1st Canadian Division already were extremely frustrated with the weapon because of reported jamming during the bitter Second Battle of Ypres in late April and early May. As Andrew Iarocci has demonstrated in his history of the 1st Division, comments on the rifle's weaknesses were not as prevalent in operational reports dating from April 1915 as they would be in later reports and in postwar accounts. Yet if postwar narratives exaggerated the Ross rifle's failings during the Second Battle of Ypres (when lack of ammunition and artillery support were greater problems), the reality of its weaknesses belied the glowing panegyrics regarding the weapon's virtues that were served up to 2nd Canadian Division troops in England.[39] Special lecturers claimed that "experience has shown that [the] Ross rifle is [the] best service rifle at the front."[40] In any event, by the time the battalion had completed its musketry course on the ranges at Hythe, 15 men had achieved marksman status, 136 were ranked as first-class shots, 488 had attained second-class standing, and 272 were rated third class.[41]

The overall training regimen thus far did not differ dramatically from what had been done in Canada; however, it featured more specialized instruction in reconnaissance and patrolling, map reading, and grenade (or "bomb") throwing, which had become very prevalent in fighting along the Western Front. Special classes were established to instruct the men in the use of grenades. "Reports from the front indicate that this is a very important branch of the work," remarked Maj. Turnbull, "and eventually every man in the Battalion is to receive instruction in making, lighting and throwing bombs."[42] In addition, some officers and other ranks were selected to attend advanced courses in bayonet fighting, musketry, machine gunnery, and signal work. These courses, which usually lasted from one to three weeks, gave students additional practice in these subjects. This enabled the students to assume

German infantry in an early trench. (LAC C-006531)

increased leadership responsibilities or instructional duties after returning to their battalion.[43]

While traditional training exercises continued, the absence of winter weather and the battalion's presence in more open country permitted an increased emphasis on fieldwork, especially the tactics of trench warfare. During late 1914, the desperate attempts of Allied and German armies to outflank each other in France and Belgium had ended in failure. The battle lines then solidified into an increasingly complex system of opposing trenches and field fortifications stretching some 470 miles from the Belgian coast to the Swiss frontier. Protecting these trenches were thick belts of barbed wire and a formidable array of firepower, including machine guns, artillery, and infantrymen's rifles. Fighting along Europe's Western Front thus assumed a siege-like quality, with British, French, and Belgian forces working to break the defensive lines protecting the Germans' recently conquered territories in Belgium and northeastern France.[44]

In an effort to ready themselves for this semi-subterranean campaign, companies of the 19th Battalion constructed trench systems on nearby Tolsford Hill, where they also weaved intricate barbed-wire barriers under the watchful gaze of battle-hardened British and Canadian instructors. Once excavated, these trenches became the scene of various offensive and defensive exercises, as companies practised patrolling and carried out mock attacks by day and night.[45]

From the middle of July onward, greater amounts of time were devoted to more advanced and larger-scale tactical schemes, first at brigade and then at divisional levels. The unit diary of the 20th Battalion was unusually forthright in its admission that "many mistakes were made," especially during the initial exercises, "but a great deal of useful information was gained therefrom."[46] During one of the brigade exercises conducted in the first week of August, Lt.-Col. McLaren was placed in command of the brigade advance guard, which was composed of his own battalion, a section of field artillery, a detachment from the 5th Field Ambulance, and two "imaginary" cavalry squadrons.[47] Records are not clear regarding the quality of McLaren's performance or that of his battalion. However, Col. H. De Prée, the divisional chief of staff (known as the GSO1, or General Staff Officer, Grade 1), offered some criticisms of the work done by the brigades, noting that overall, the information passed back to superior headquarters "was not all that it should be, either in accuracy or clearness of expression." Positions, once occupied by advancing troops, had not been consolidated in a timely or vigorous fashion, and the timing of some attacks was not properly synchronized among the various units participating.[48]

On 14 August the 19th Battalion played a leading role in a brigade attack near Dymchurch against their comrades in the 5th Infantry Brigade. McLaren's men launched a frontal attack on a very wide front in order to give their opponents the impression that they were a much larger force. "This was entirely successful," wrote Maj. Turnbull, "as the enemy mistook us for three battalions." Meanwhile, the 18th, 20th, and 21st Battalions executed a flank attack, crossing a canal on pontoons constructed by engineering troops. Brig.-Gen. Lord Brooke congratulated McLaren on the success of the day's operations and expressed "his high appreciation of the part taken by the 19th Battalion in the holding attack which so materially assisted in the complete success of our Brigade, notwithstanding that they were required to work without a noon-day lunch and without sufficient sleep."[49] Fortitude in the face of hunger and exhaustion would become an everyday requirement of McLaren's men once they reached the front.

In August, even larger exercises were carried out by the entire 2nd Canadian Division, and, as with the brigade-level tactical schemes, results were mixed. Many of the difficulties that arose stemmed from the usual problems of timeliness and accuracy in communication and in the coordination of numerous units and arms. As Capt. Andrew Macphail of the 6th Field Ambulance pronounced: "The main trouble was that some of the Brigade Headquarters forgot that we were operating under Divisional Orders, and neglected to transmit those orders, with the result that the various units did not know their places."[50]

Division and brigade commanders and staffs derived the most benefit from formation-level exercises, since this sort of training tested their leadership and administrative skills and indicated where improvements were needed. Battalion and company commanders likewise profited from the larger operational schemes, and these "dress rehearsals" were supplemented by "tactical schemes without troops," in which small groups of senior officers were presented with operational scenarios requiring them to formulate solutions and draw up the kinds of orders they would issue if such situations were encountered in reality.[51]

Overall, although the training received in England was of higher quality and utility than that carried out in Canada, many other ranks took a dim view of it, especially after they had gained practical experience in soldiering at the front. Commenting in retrospect, Pte. Donald Fraser of the 31st Battalion concluded: "When I think of it, our training was decidedly amateurish and impractical. It consisted mainly of route marches and alignment movements. Our musketry course amounted to nothing; we had only half an idea about the handling of bombs. We were perfectly ignorant regarding rifle grenades. But in due time we learned from Fritz what bombs, rifle grenades, trench mortars and machine guns really were."[52]

Recreation and Discipline

Life in England for the men of the 19th Battalion was not occupied solely by relentless training. Sporting activities were organized and encouraged by senior officers, who viewed them as a "healthy" alternative to other popular recreational pursuits such as gambling or consorting with local women. The competitive spirit that had developed among all ranks in Toronto had not diminished, and, more often than not, the men of the 19th emerged the victors in athletic meets and soccer or baseball matches against competitors from the other units of the 4th Brigade.[53]

A certain amount of leisure time was built into the weekly training regimens. Weekdays were dominated by drills, tactical schemes, marches, lectures, and other work, but on most Saturdays such activities were limited to the morning hours, the remainder of the day being declared a "half holiday." Sunday mornings were given over to church parades, during which the men broke up into their respective denominations, each group attending divine service under the charge of an officer. As for the remainder of the day, the men appear to have been left to their own devices. However, their freedom to explore the surrounding countryside was curtailed to some degree by the policy of placing certain areas, such as Dover, "out of bounds," with consequent disciplinary penalties for trespassers.[54]

The proximity of West Sandling Camp to the Channel coast afforded a grandstand seat for viewing naval operations, especially from the summit of the surrounding hills. For example, on 10 August a British trawler, which was observed sweeping for mines off Hythe, "was struck by a torpedo from a German submarine and though badly damaged succeeded in reaching port with the assistance of two British destroyers."[55] Additional excitement, and occasional anxiety, was generated by the relative frequency of aerial activity in the vicinity of the Canadian encampment. British aircraft were a common sight, and several German Zeppelins passed over or near the camps on their nighttime forays over southern England.[56]

Periods of leave were granted: around one-third of the 19th Battalion's personnel were given six days of furlough on 27 May, and a second detachment of similar size received it on 2 June.[57] Many among the Canadian troops who were born in the United Kingdom visited family and old friends, while the city of London naturally proved an irresistible attraction for officers and other ranks alike. For some, the temptation to overstay one's furlough or weekend pass was impossible to resist. Indeed, the incidence of absence without leave rose sharply during the 19th Battalion's stay in England. Whereas 290 cases of absenteeism were reported in Canada between 1 December 1914 and 31 March 1915, some 484 cases cropped up between 6 June and 14 September 1915.[58] The problem reached its height during the months of August and September 1915, which saw 149 and 145 cases respectively, ranging from a few hours in duration to several days.[59]

This was in keeping with an overall rise in the incidence of minor offences – a common trend among most Canadian units after arriving in England. Such behaviour may have stemmed from the natural boisterousness of men from the British Isles who had returned to their native land, or of men from Canada who were experiencing the excitement of their first trip abroad. However, some incidents of indiscipline among Canadian troops were more serious than others. One such case was the large-scale rioting that was precipitated in Folkestone by men of the 2nd Canadian Division on Saturday, 5 June. The uproar resulted from the troops' anger at local business owners, who allegedly had taken advantage of some Canadians' ignorance of the English monetary system by cheating them in sales transactions and currency exchanges. It took military and civil authorities two and a half hours to quell the affair, and over seventy arrests were made. The division's assistant provost marshal (APM), Maj. Arthur M. Jarvis, concluded that personnel from the 20th, 24th, and 25th Battalions were the most prominent offenders. But Jarvis's caveat that "practically every unit was represented" among the rioters raises the possibility that some 19th Battalion men were involved too – although battalion records are not clear on this point.[60]

Offences committed by Canadians were on the increase; that said, the decay of discipline within the 19th Battalion ultimately did not get out of hand, probably because Lt.-Col. McLaren and his company commanders took an increasingly firm stance in their approach to punishment.[61] The necessities of wartime service overseas encouraged the gradual abandonment of the more easygoing disciplinary ethos that had prevailed in Canada, and measures that were more in line with the full force of British military law were adopted. Under the King's Regulations, battalion commanders (such as McLaren) were empowered to give out punishments of up to twenty-eight days of detention or field punishment, while a court martial, which would be convened to try more serious cases, could award up to three months.[62] "Field Punishment no. 2," (FP 2) which came into regular use among Canadian troops in England, entailed "a note in the pay book, pay forfeit, sleeping under guard and the performance of such fatigues and pack drills as could be crammed into the day. All the while the offender would be on a diet of water and biscuit. Worse, he would not be allowed to smoke" for the duration of his punishment,[63] and he could be placed in irons, if necessary, to prevent escape. Later, after

Hatch (battalion transport officer) and C.E. Kilmer.[77] They would rejoin the rest of the battalion in France.

At 6:40 PM on 14 September, the 19th Battalion began the nine-mile march from West Sandling to the docks at Folkestone, with Lt.-Col. McLaren, Maj. Turnbull, and Capt. Morrison leading the column. Strict nighttime march procedure was followed, with all lights extinguished and all ranks ordered to maintain silence. The dominant sound came from the steady tramp of almost a thousand pairs of boots on the hard-surface roads that wound through the hills on the south coast of England. This march was no easy feat, for the men were burdened with between 60 and 85 pounds of equipment, including 120 rounds of ammunition. It was "a load to test the endurance of the strongest man in the Battalion," wrote Harry Adie. Moreover, they were expected to complete the march in two and a half hours.[78] "My most unforgettable experience in the 1914–18 War was, strange to say, not in the field of battle, but on the march to the troopship at Folkestone from Sandling Camp," confessed Ted Lang. One of Lang's comrades, Charlie Worthington, "a good-natured gangling lad of English parents," became so exhausted that he was unable to continue. Lang was told by a platoon sergeant to look after Worthington, and together they started marching again once the young Englishmen was sufficiently recovered. Soon, however, Worthington "was showing signs of collapsing again. This kept up for some time and I could see visions of the ship steaming away without us … luckily … a wine-merchant's 'dogcart' hove in sight and I hailed the driver, and appealed to his sense of patriotism. The upshot was that Charlie and I drove to the docks behind a spanking sorrel in time to be the last of the troops to board the transport."[79]

Lang and Worthington were fortunate in securing the ride, for they likely never would have reached the Folkestone docks in time before their comrades sailed. "With wonderful precision, every detail for transportation" had been prearranged, wrote Harry Adie. Shortly after the battalion's arrival at the berth of the SS *Queen*, "the men were huddled together in every available inch of space" on the vessel.[80] Sharing the transport with them was Maj.-Gen. Richard Turner, the new GOC, 2nd Canadian Division, and his headquarters staff.[81] The passage across the Channel was to be handled in the same manner as the night march, with no lights, no smoking, and as little noise as possible. All ranks braced themselves for yet another, albeit shorter, voyage. Since the weather in the Channel was rough that night, the familiar pangs of seasickness would soon revisit many a veteran of the transatlantic crossing. Instead of dwelling upon the trials that awaited them in France and Flanders, most men simply concentrated on surviving the crossing to the French port of Boulogne.

3

Life in the Trenches: September–December 1915

The English Channel was alive with activity during the nights between 13 and 17 September as units of the 2nd Canadian Division were ferried across to France. Hot, humid weather on the night of 14–15 September combined with choppy seas to make the trip an uncomfortable affair for the men of the 19th Battalion aboard the SS *Queen*. But they did not feel as isolated as they had during their voyage across the Atlantic. Nearby were transports carrying the other units of the 4th Infantry Brigade, as well as swift destroyer escorts of the Royal Navy, which zigzagged at breakneck speed through the crashing waves, ever on the alert for marauding enemy submarines.[1]

The *Queen* reached Boulogne at 2:45 AM on 15 September, and no time was wasted in disembarking all ranks. The men formed up along the quay and marched inland, en route to the front lines in Belgium near the border with France. The firmness of French cobblestone roads under the men's feet provided a marked contrast to the rolling decks of the ship. After a quick breather at nearby Ostrohove Camp, the men slogged on to the railway station at Pont-de-Briques. There, they met the train carrying the 19th Battalion's advance party, which had departed West Sandling on 12 September. The battalion was now reunited, and the troops who had just arrived from Boulogne subsequently piled into the waiting boxcars, on the sides of which was scrawled a phrase that would become all too familiar: "Hommes 40, Chevaux 8."[2]

The train steamed through the countryside of northern France and by 5:00 PM had reached the town of St-Omer, where it disgorged its weary human cargo. Within two hours of its arrival, the 19th Battalion was on the march yet again, tramping towards the battlefront through the villages of Arques, Fort Rouge, and Eblinghem; finally, at half past midnight, the men pitched camp outside Wallon-Cappel. This march, carried out at the end of a long day and with full equipment, had stretched the troops' endurance to the limit. Exhausted men lightened their loads, tossing aside extra pairs of boots, spare shirts, underwear, brushes, and other items of kit. These were strewn along the roadside for miles, to the benefit of scavenging civilians. It was also during this trek that Lt.-Col. McLaren made a remark that would become a classic among 19th Battalion veterans. In response to grumbling overheard early in the march, McLaren tried to buck up the men with an encouraging "Only five hundred yards further, boys." "Well it was a darn long 500 yards," recalled one veteran. Pte. Felix Cullen, a native of Sault Ste. Marie, estimated it was more like seventeen miles.[3]

On 16 September they marched through Caestre to Godewaersvelde, where they halted and bivouacked among four adjacent farms. All during the war, the hospitality of the adult occupants of such farms ranged from warm generosity to sullen indifference. However, local children usually could be counted on for a smile.[4] They remained in bivouac through 18 September, getting a much-needed respite from marching but little real rest, owing to the intermittent thundering of the nearby heavy artillery. On the 17th they were inspected by Lt.-Gen. Sir Edwin Alderson, the commander of the recently created Canadian Corps, who was accompanied by his two division commanders: Maj.-Gens. Arthur Currie and Richard Turner of the 1st and 2nd Canadian Divisions.[5]

Canadian and British authorities had decided earlier that the two Canadian divisions should operate together as a distinct Canadian Corps within the British order of battle. Alderson, the professional British officer who hitherto had served as GOC, 1st Canadian Division, had been selected to command the new corps. Arthur Currie, who had made a good name for himself as commander of the 2nd Canadian Infantry Brigade, succeeded Alderson at the head of the 1st Division. On 13 September, just before the balance of the 2nd Canadian Division arrived in France, Canadian Corps headquarters opened at Bailleul, in northern France near the Belgian border. By the end of the month, the corps, with its two divisions, corps troops, and attached units, would contain 37,876 officers and other ranks.[6]

During his inspection, Alderson made a point of complimenting McLaren on the smart appearance of his men and delivered a short "pep talk" to the assembled ranks.[7] The corps commander had decided that the men needed a few extra words of encouragement, for they were not going to get the "breaking-in" period usually experienced by troops that were new to fighting on the Western Front.[8] Instead, the 2nd Canadian Division would be thrown into action immediately, relieving the

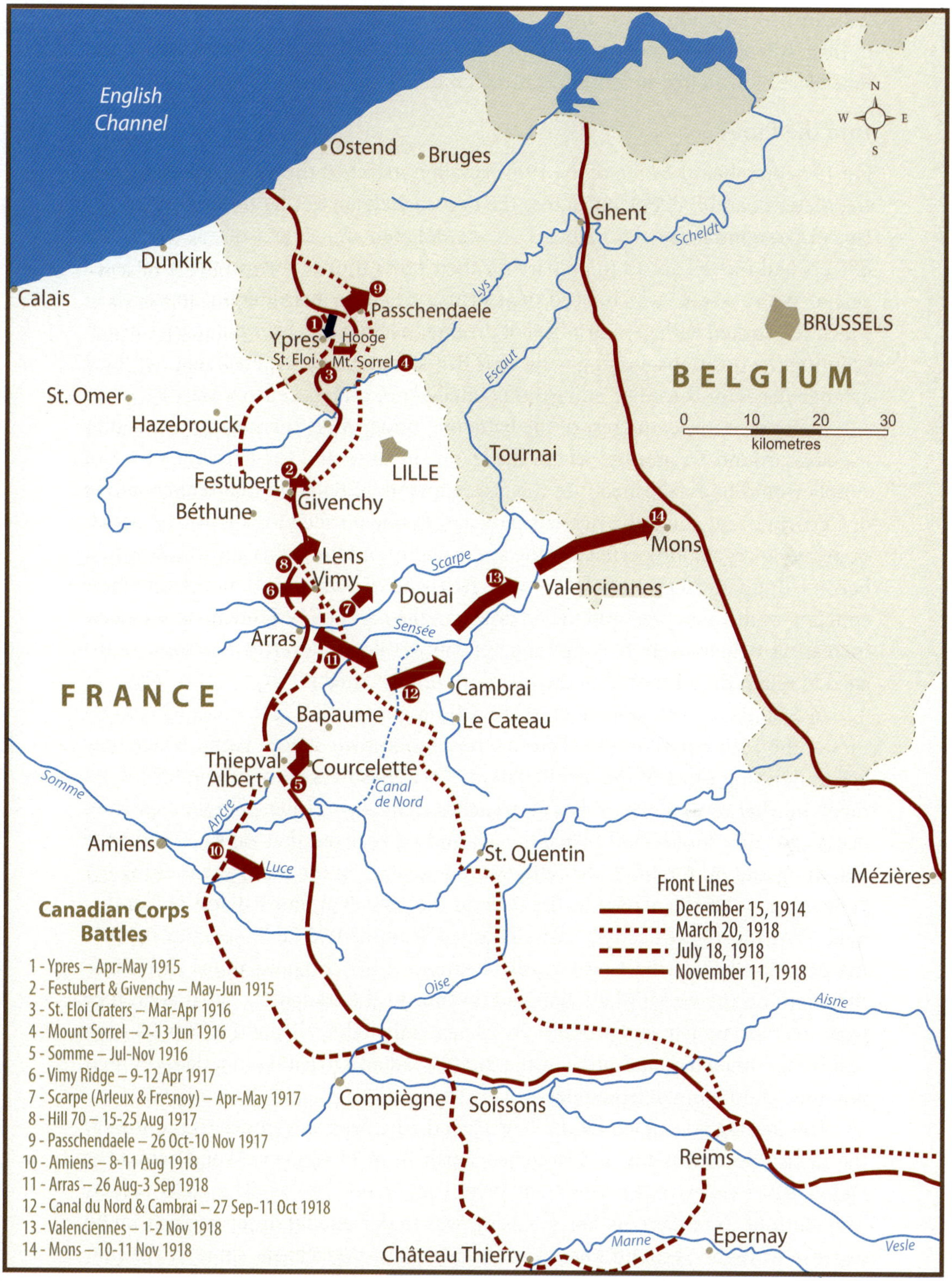

Map 2 – Operations of the CEF 1915–1919

28th British Division in the front lines of the Kemmel sector. The 28th Division, in turn, was slated to move south for the upcoming British offensive, which would take place along a five-mile front centred on the French village of Loos.[9]

Into the Lines

On 19 September, the men of the 19th Battalion marched through Thieshouk, Fletre, Meterin, and Bailleul and across the Franco-Belgian border to the Belgian village of Dranoutre. The day before, Lt.-Col. McLaren and a party of fourteen other officers had moved ahead to prepare for their unit's tour of duty in the front lines east of Wulverghem, which faced the German defences guarding the approach to Messines. Tasked with getting a "feel of the line," as Fred Stitt later put it, they began scouting the positions, liaising with their British counterparts, finalizing logistical arrangements for the relief, and gaining intelligence on local enemy activity.[10]

In the meantime, the rest of the battalion, under Maj. Turnbull, proceeded to the area around Dranoutre, where the transport lines and the battalion's base of supply would be established.[11] In the last remnants of Belgium that remained free of German occupation, the rich farmlands had gone untilled for a year. The stench of decaying vegetation permeated the atmosphere, and the sights and smells would become dramatically worse closer to the front-line trenches.[12] Of more immediate concern, as the men prepared to bed down on the night of 19 September, was their increasing vulnerability to long-range enemy artillery. Nevertheless, some managed to retain their bravado in the first flush of real danger.

At 5:30 PM on 20 September, the machine-gun section and A and C companies of the 19th Battalion marched to a position known as R.E. Farm, where they began relieving units of the 3rd Battalion, Royal Fusiliers (City of London) Regiment, in what was known as the "D" trenches. Ted Lang recalled: "In the silence an occasional rifle shot would pierce the air, and we realized that we were in for the real thing and no foolin'."[13] The relief was completed on the following evening (21 September) with the arrival in the lines of the 19th Battalion's B and D Companies.[14] "We must have been pretty well trained," commented Ed Youngman, because the outgoing CO of the Royal Fusiliers extended his congratulations to Lt.-Col. McLaren "on the way his battalion had taken over the trenches … as though they were veterans; we felt very proud."[15] By 23 September, the relief of the 28th Division had been completed, and units of the 2nd Canadian Division embarked on their first tour of duty in the front lines.

The frontage occupied by the new Canadian Corps was under the control of the British Second Army and stretched north from Ploegsteert Wood across the Douve River valley to the Vierstraat-Wytschaete road. The whole area, which lay just south of the infamous Ypres Salient, was under enemy observation from an expanse of higher ground known as the Messines-Wytschaete spur. In the portion of the line held by the Canadian Corps, the 1st Canadian Division occupied the right sector and the 2nd Canadian Division the left. The southern part of the 2nd Canadian Division's sector was held by the 4th Infantry Brigade. Facing 2nd Canadian Division, "at distances varying from 500 down to only a few yards," were regiments of the 3rd and 4th Royal Bavarian Infantry Divisions, II Royal Bavarian Army Corps.[16]

Fortunately, no casualties were sustained during the 19th Battalion's first twenty-four hours in the front lines. But this state of affairs would not last, and the battalion reported its first casualty on 22 September; Pte. Charles Kisby received shrapnel wounds in the arm and chest. His injury was avenged by the battalion snipers, who reported "five Germans bagged" on the same day.[17]

Saturday, 25 September, saw the opening of the British offensive at Loos, which was part of a much larger coordinated attack with the French. The French Second and Fourth Armies, striking north from Champagne, along with the French Tenth and British First Armies, pushing east from Artois, attempted to pinch out a large German-held salient between the Aisne and Scarpe rivers. The Canadians, who were situated north of these main efforts, did not play a direct role in the British portion of the attack. However, they did orchestrate some diversionary demonstrations designed to confuse the enemy as to the scale and direction of the British advance. At dawn the 1st and 2nd Canadian Divisions executed a sham gas attack along a 10,000-yard front by setting alight some 6,000 oat sacks and sandbags filled with a mixture of damp straw and sulphur. Although the demonstration drew some retaliatory artillery fire and provoked the opposing Bavarians to initiate a gas alert, it was not taken seriously enough to influence the course of operations to the south, which ultimately failed.[18]

The Canadians were lucky to be left on the outskirts of the offensive. For the troops involved in the main British effort against Loos, the battle proved to be long and bloody. In all, 60,000 casualties were sustained between 25 September and 4 November, when the offensive finally ground to a halt. During the same period, the French and Germans suffered even more – around 200,000 and 150,000 casualties respectively. For the British armies on the Western Front, the failure at Loos brought an end to major operations during 1915. It also ended the career of their commander-in-chief, Sir John French. He was replaced in December by Sir Douglas Haig, former GOC, First Army.[19]

In the meantime, the 19th Battalion concluded its first tour in the D trenches, being relieved by companies of the 18th Battalion on 27–28 September. McLaren's men now moved into bivouac at Wood Camp, where they would remain until 3 October.[20] According to one veteran, the battalion's first tour had passed "uneventfully enough as far as casualties were concerned ... and the boys had a chance to get accustomed to the idea of being in the front line."[21] Although casualties had been light, there had been some losses. Maj. Millen reported:

> D Company have had 4 wounded since coming into [the] trenches. First a man was loading a revolver and it went off wounding one of our own boys through the leg. Next we had a man shot through [the] cheek in a sniping box. Then another man against orders kept looking over [the] parapet and firing in the daytime and he got a bullet through the cheek. The last got his face cut from broken glass from a periscope that had been hit.[22]

These incidents served as a clear warning to officers that they needed to get a firm grip on their men in order to minimize the occurrence of such injuries, especially those due to carelessness and disobedience. Evidently some personnel still viewed the war as the great "game" depicted in contemporary propaganda. Even Millen's letter to his mother on 28 September betrays a rather lighthearted perspective on the battalion's initial experience in the lines. According to Millen, "this trench life is not so very serious. We eat pretty well, get mail out to trenches every night, so are not quite as far away from the world as one might think." Whether Millen was painting an overly rosy picture of events to soothe his mother's nerves is not certain. The tone of his correspondence would grow less cheery over time as conditions in the lines worsened and the burden of command became heavier. Indeed, the burdens of command and sacrifice would weigh heavier still when the 19th Battalion reported its first fatal casualty in the trenches. On the night of 3 October Pte. George W. Durrand was killed when a bullet struck him in the right temple.[23]

On 8 October, the fifth day of its second tour in the D trenches, the 19th Battalion was relieved by companies of the 2nd Battalion, 1st Canadian Division. The following day, it moved into brigade reserve at Ridgewood, one mile behind the front line. Over the next five days the men trained, carried out various work details, and prepared for the unit's next tour. This would be in the M and N trenches, on the southern extremity of the Ypres Salient, northeast of the village of Vierstraat.[24] The new position, which they would occupy on the evening of 14 October, would prove much less comfortable and far more dangerous than the D trenches. As the loss of Pte. Durrand already demonstrated, the "game" in which so many men had been anxious to take part was proving more deadly than they had imagined. Ed Youngman remembered that before their arrival at the front, "we not only read the papers we also talked to the boys who were wounded who came back … and we were positive that we knew what we were going to face. Well, we were absolutely wrong, because no matter what they said, it was many, many times different and worse in many aspects than anything we had conceived."[25]

Life in the Trenches

Much of the horror stemmed from the troglodyte world of the trenches inhabited by the combatants. A newspaper article likely authored by Harry Adie admitted that "it would be difficult and probably unwise to describe these maze-like lanes which have become the homes of thousands of present-day cave-dwellers … The

A view of Vierstraat from the M and N Trenches. (MUA RC 0835)

shriek of the rifle, the rattle of the machine gun and the boom of the grenades is incessant, punctuated by the ear-splitting roar of the shells fired by the trench mortars and artillery of both sides."[26]

The use of trenches in warfare was nothing new, but the scale of their employment during the First World War was something unprecedented.[27] In the British-held sectors in Flanders and northern France, the trenches tended to be eight to ten feet in depth and six feet or more in width. The forward portion of the trench, which faced the enemy, was shielded by a thick parapet of earth, sandbags, timber, and whatever other materials came to hand. It also featured a low ledge, or "fire step," employed most often by sentries or by entire units when "standing-to" to counter a potential attack. The rear portion of the trench, termed the parados, was constructed in similar fashion, but without the fire step. Although the interior walls of the trench were sometimes revetted with sandbags, timber, or sheets of corrugated metal, they might still dissolve or crumble in the face of heavy rainfall or enemy shelling. Steps were taken to keep the floor of the trench somewhat dry by digging drainage channels leading to sumps. These drains were covered by walkways made from loose planks or wooden ladder-like assemblages known as "duckboards."[28] All too often, such efforts proved futile, particularly in low-lying sectors during wet weather. Sometimes men were forced to struggle through sodden trenches submerged to their knees – or even their waists – in water and gluey mud. Where the water table was particularly high, as in much of Flanders, trenches sometimes could not be sunk into the ground more than a couple of feet. Instead, the parapets and parados were built up with heaps of sandbags, usually filled with earth or clay, to a thickness of twenty feet or more at the base and roughly ten feet at the top. These breastworks were augmented by occasional concrete-reinforced strong points, designed to protect valuable command and observation posts as well as machine gun and mortar emplacements.[29]

Although disparities in terrain and variations in construction methods meant that British, French, and German trench systems could differ somewhat in design, they all served as bases for offensive and defensive action, as sources of protective cover, and as routes of communication and supply. In general, the trench systems in British sectors comprised three parallel lines: front, support, and reserve. The front line itself often consisted of a forward fire trench close behind which was a command trench. The former was the main forward line of defence, while the latter contained dugout shelters and latrines. Both were linked by numerous short connecting trenches. In addition, small sap trenches usually were dug out from the fire trench, extending twenty or thirty yards towards enemy lines. When viewed from the air, these saps, constructed at intervals along the length of the fire trench, looked "like suckers sprouting from a gnarled branch." They terminated in small, isolated positions that served as observation or early-warning posts. It is estimated that it took 450 men six hours to dig 250 yards of a front-line trench system.[30]

The support line, located anywhere from 70 to as much as 500 yards behind the front line, accommodated the support troops for the front-line garrisons and featured deeper dugouts for command, communication, cooking, and medical facilities. Finally, the reserve line, situated 400 to 600 yards behind the support trench, quartered the units that reinforced the front and support lines. The front, support, and reserve lines were, in turn, connected at regular intervals by communication trenches through which passed personnel and supplies (e.g., food, ammunition, and construction material) and in which were laid telephone cables linking brigade and battalion headquarters in the rear with company headquarters and observation posts to the fore.[31]

Most trenches were not built in continuous straight lines but rather zigzagged in a "saw-tooth" or crenellated fashion. This prevented enemy intruders or artillery from firing down the entire length of the trench (enfilade fire) and inflicting maximum damage. Mutually supporting strongpoints also were established in the areas between the front, support, and reserve lines. These redoubts often contained machine-gun or trench-mortar emplacements and were manned by varying numbers depending on their size. Farther to the rear of the reserve trenches, and generally out of range of enemy small-arms fire, were the artillery lines, which furnished the heaviest measures of both defensive and offensive firepower.[32]

Dugouts of varying size, mostly situated in the command, support, and reserve trenches, provided living quarters for officers and other ranks and contained facilities such as company headquarters, cook houses, latrines, and medical-aid posts.

The smallest types of subterranean accommodation were "funk holes," excavated in the walls of some of the fire and command trenches, in which individual men could snatch a few moments of fitful sleep or find a modicum of shelter from the elements.[33] It should be noted, however, that not all living quarters or command and support facilities in the trenches were dugout in nature. They could be established in existing cellars, mines, and caverns; or, in areas shielded by topography from direct enemy observation, above ground in abandoned dwellings and other civil structures, in purpose-built huts, tent complexes, or sandbagged enclosures.

Although sanitation measures were enforced in the lines (with varying degrees of success), the battlefield itself was littered with sufficient refuse and corpses to support huge populations of rats. These creatures, often reported to be "big as cats," invariably found their way into the men's dugouts and were the source of much annoyance, disgust, and, on occasion, dark comedy. Ted Lang recalled one enterprising rat that had taken up residence in his particular shelter in the M and N trenches at the end of 1915:

> This rat had much goods laid up against a possible famine, for his nest was well larded with a considerable quantity of stewed beef, hard tack, cheese, and the partly eaten carcass of a pheasant, all in various stages of putrefaction. Needless to say we made short shrift of this larder, rebuilt our "kennel" and had no more smells or prowling rats during the balance of our tour of duty on that front.[34]

Lang recalled another rat that had made off with a comrade's dental plate, inspiring a frantic hunt through the floorboards until the man's "store teeth" were successfully recovered.[35]

When doing a tour in the trenches, an infantry battalion's personnel usually were stationed in the front and support lines, and occasionally in the reserve line as well. Reserve positions, however, often were garrisoned by troops from another battalion, which functioned as the brigade reserve. Brigade staffs allocated portions of the line to battalions, but it was up to battalion headquarters to decide how their companies would be distributed. Sometimes they placed two companies in the front line with two in support; or perhaps two in the front line with one in support and one in reserve.[36]

The excavation of the trenches and the devastating effect of modern artillery on the surrounding landscape gave the Western Front a surreal atmosphere that would haunt many eyewitnesses to the end of their days. After a heavy bombardment, the terrain assumed a lunar quality, with shell holes and craters of differing size and depth pockmarking the surface of the earth. In some localities the skeletal remains of shattered trees stood silent sentry over a wasteland littered with the material detritus and human remains of earlier battles. In late November, during a fog-enshrouded daytime reconnaissance of the ground in front of their trenches, some 19th Battalion men "discovered the bodies of ten Frenchmen with rifles by their sides and bayonets fixed. On one of the bodies Lt. William Vincent Carey found a diary dating from the commencement of the war to what likely was the date of the man's death.[37]

The disconcerting ambiance of the battlefield was accentuated at night, when sounds and sights assumed an even more ethereal quality, especially under the pale glow of the signal flares, or "star shells," which periodically lit the sky. Remembering his first trip in the lines, Fred Stitt said that the discharge of a rifle was "an eerie sort of a sound. At night the sound of a rifle shot, or a series of rifle shots sounds awesome ... And it reverberates [and] echoes from various corners and in the midst of this you can see in a distance the star shelling [flares] going up in a huge arch and lighting up the terrain for a few hundred feet."[38]

The most desolate and forbidding part of this wasteland was the space between the opposing front-line trenches, which became known as "no man's land." This strip of ground ran the length of the Western Front, and its width ranged from a few yards to a mile or more. In locations such as the D trenches, where the opposing fire trenches were situated less than fifty yards apart, the danger from small arms, and particularly from grenades, increased. However, this was offset somewhat by a marked reduction in shellfire. "Our position is rather close to the German lines," Maj. Millen wrote on 21 September, "but this is rather an advantage as we are not so likely to be subject to artillery fire. The Germans being afraid of shells falling short and going into their own lines."[39]

Although the breadth of no man's land often varied, it remained constant in the perils that it presented to any who entered it. Thick belts of barbed wire were the most common, and among the most formidable, obstacles facing both Allied and German infantry as they attempted to cross no man's land. These entanglements, usually a minimum of three feet in height and ten yards in depth, were erected about twenty yards in advance of the forward fire trench. The Germans, acting mainly in a defensive capacity to protect their conquests in Belgium and France, were especially diligent in constructing strong wire barriers in front of their positions. After the trench systems had become well established, belts of German wire often were fifty feet in depth – during the latter part of the war, sometimes 100 feet or more. Both sides often arranged their wire entanglements so that they channelled attackers into "killing zones" well covered by defending machine-gun posts, riflemen, and artillery.[40]

The lethality of modern small-arms and artillery fire made daylight movement above ground virtually suicidal in the face of vigilant snipers and artillery spotters. That is why inter-unit reliefs and other routine operations usually were performed at night. That the 19th Battalion's first entry to the front lines proceeded so smoothly was a credit to both the incoming and outgoing units, for the possibility of a mix-up in the maze-like network of trenches was increased by darkness. To minimize confusion, incoming officers needed to reconnoitre the positions to be occupied by their battalion, and outgoing units usually furnished guides to assist with the relief. These guides oriented newcomers not only to the position itself but also to the "tactical climate" of the sector, which included all intelligence regarding the behaviour of the local German garrisons and the nature of their defences.

Dawn and dusk were especially tense, for these were thought to be the most likely times for an attack to be launched. Troops were ordered to "stand-to" at the fire step with weapons at the ready, while sentries peered warily through camouflaged or armoured view slits and periscopes, watching for enemy incursions that rarely came. When it became apparent – usually after an hour of waiting – that no assault was forthcoming, those men not detailed for sentry duty were stood down for breakfast. Officers also were permitted to issue each individual a tot of rum, which, to those who partook of it, served as a soothing tonic after a cold or difficult night.[41] "I can tell you if Canada wants prohibition the army certainly wants its rum and I don't know what we would do without it in some of the bad weather," declared Maj. Millen.[42] Next came the daily routine of cleaning and inspecting rifles and other equipment. Once the officers were satisfied that all was correct and in good working order, most of the men not taking their turn at sentry duty were permitted to snatch whatever rest they could.[43]

During the previous hours of darkness, dry rations for the other ranks had been carried up to the front line in sandbags; tea and sugar were tied into separate corners of each bag and topped off with tins of jam, "bully beef" or Maconochie's meat and vegetable stew, and bread. The bags were labelled and addressed to specific platoons or sections of trench; this permitted the inclusion of mail for the men. Hot rations from the company field kitchens, such as porridge or stew, were hauled forward in "dixies" (metal cooking containers), old jam tins, or petrol cans, the latter of which were rinsed out, at least in theory. Unfortunately, by the time they reached their destination, their contents were usually anything but hot and sometimes tasted distinctly of gasoline. Water was transported in similar tins and purified with chloride of lime, which increased potability but, like the gasoline, did little to improve flavour. Officers' fare, not surprisingly, tended to be more savoury and plentiful than that of the other ranks and even in the trenches typically included "fresh meat, fish, fresh vegetables, salad, potted meats, cake, tinned fruit, cheese, dates or chocolate."[44] "You would be surprised at the meals that were served to us," admitted Maj. Millen. "Saturday night's dinner for instance was a portion of herring as a hors d'ouevre, then stew, welsh rabbit, and plum pudding. We indulged in afternoon tea."[45]

While rotating shifts of sentries kept watch throughout the day, the men played cards, ate their noon and evening meals, slept, and smoked. Smoking was such a universal habit that it has been called "the soldier's greatest pastime – in the trenches and out of them."[46] Far more accessible than rum, cigarettes "were part of the weekly rations; YMCA huts and canteens sold them cheaply; families and friends tucked them into parcels." Many chaplains enjoyed distributing them along with doses of spiritual comfort. Some men claimed to have smoked as many as fifty cigarettes a day as a matter of routine.[47] "I remember them in a package of ten," remarked Sid Smith of the 18th Battalion. "Sweet Caps yes, and Woodbines."[48]

When not enjoying a cigarette or getting a few badly needed moments of shut-eye themselves, the officers were busy planning nighttime reliefs, patrols, and working parties. Even during periods of relative quiet, a few incoming enemy artillery or mortar rounds ensured that there were enough repairs to do on one's own trenches and barbed wire to last the night – which was when the real work of trench warfare began. After evening stand-to, the number of sentries in the fire trench was increased from that employed during the day – from one sentry for every twelve men to one for every four – with reliefs every two to three hours. Wiring parties crept out in front of the fire trench, burdened down with stakes and rolls of barbed wire, and engaged in repairing or thickening the entanglements that protected their stretch of the line. At the same time, patrols of varying size were dispatched through concealed lanes in the barbed wire out into no man's land to gather information on the enemy's doings or, even better, to bring back a prisoner for interrogation. Next to patrol work, among the most hazardous duties was to be sent into one of the listening posts located at the head of one of the numerous saps that snaked out towards enemy lines. The two- or three-man teams occupying these posts had to endure hours of watching and listening, all the while knowing they were prime targets for enemy patrols.[49]

Although the officers were spared most of the backbreaking physical labour endured by the other ranks, they suffered the burden of responsibility for the proper functioning of their commands. They had to organize work parties, inspect the men, visit the sentries, maintain discipline, and lead their men on patrols or other operations against the enemy. Yet there were some moments of respite, however brief. On 28 September, Maj. Millen informed his mother, "Last night I laid down at 11:30 PM, up again at 2:00 AM, laid down again at 5:30 AM, up for breakfast, 8:15 AM. This gives you an idea of each night though the hours may vary."[50]

In addition to the myriad activities that demanded their attention, officers were afflicted by that natural corollary of executive authority: reams of paperwork. There were trench stores to be inventoried, casualty returns to be made, all manner of personnel issues to be dealt with and recorded, and reports on every conceivable subject to be written. The results of work parties' efforts, intelligence from patrols, scouts, and snipers, and patterns of enemy activity (or the lack thereof) all had to be noted and submitted to higher authority. But paperwork did not only flow up the chain of command. Subordinate officers also had to digest an unending stream of correspondence, memos, directives, and queries on matters both weighty and ephemeral, to say nothing of implementing routine and operational orders promulgated by their superiors.[51] It is not surprising that some officers simply broke down under the strain.

One method of limiting the stress placed on both officers and other ranks was to ensure that they did not spend inordinate stretches of time in the trenches. Of the roughly 20,000 men in a full-strength division, only about 2,000 were serving in the front line at any given time. In fact, a British veteran "reckoned a typical month as four days in the front line, four in support, eight in reserve and the remainder in rest."[52] But the length and frequency of periods spent "in the lines," "in reserve," and "in rest" could vary considerably and depended on context.[53] Between September 1915 and March 1916, it was the usual policy in the 2nd Canadian Division that battalions did six-day tours in the trenches, followed by six days in brigade reserve. Thereafter, another six days were spent in the trenches, followed by six days in divisional reserve. This schedule was modified for brief periods, such as during November, when the weather was so wet that trench tours were temporarily reduced to four days.[54] Many years after the war, Fred Stitt recalled these arrangements, noting that "it usually was a six day trip" in the trenches.[55] Another veteran, Deward Barnes, who would be posted to the 19th Battalion in April 1917, managed to calculate the amount of time he spent in and out of the lines during the final year and a half of the war. "As nearly as I can find out," Barnes stated, "just counting the trips in and out of the trenches and from one part of the line to another while with the 19th Battalion I was: In the trenches 248 days; in the front line 94 days; marched 882 miles, mostly at night; on the trains 91 hours. I was in France 18 months."[56]

Aside from the obvious influence of such factors as prudence, skill, and, above all, luck, there is no doubt that a man's chances of surviving long periods of time on active service owed much to the system by which troops were regularly rotated out of the combat zone and permitted some time to recuperate before the next tour. In addition, many long-serving veterans spent periods away from the front while recovering from wounds or illness or temporarily attached to other units.

Despite the care taken to ensure that most officers and men received regular breaks from front-line service, the strains and horrors of trench warfare could still inflict physical exhaustion and psychological trauma. During the First World War, the term "shell shock" emerged as a popular label to describe the condition of many traumatized soldiers. Deward Barnes argued after the war that "a man's nerves were never made to stand the shocks and concussions of shells, and sights and smells that go with War. I sincerely believe that the War has made me ten years older. It certainly has put my nerves on edge. My nerves are gone."[57]

Settling in for a Long, Wet Winter

On the evening of 14 October, the 19th Battalion's A and B Companies and machine-gun section relieved companies of the 18th Battalion in the front line, thus beginning a marathon four-and-a-half-month stint of thirteen successive tours in the dreary M and N trenches. As Fred Stitt noted, these tours would alternate with periods in brigade reserve at Ridgewood. In addition, the battalion would spend regular rotations in divisional reserve, farther back at La Clytte.[58]

For the most part, the M and N trenches scarcely deserved the appellation "trenches," for the high local water table prevented excavation of more than a few feet into the ground. Cover was provided by massive sandbagged breastworks, which were rotting and crumbling away by the time the 4th Brigade took possession of them. Much work was needed to restore these ramparts to a defensible state; the same was true of the wire, which "was so thin it hardly formed an obstacle."[59] During the month of November, the weather became so abysmally wet that ramparts, trenches, shelters, and dugouts regularly collapsed. Maj. Millen wrote on 7 November to his sister Gertie:

> Rain and mud, mud and rain, and then some more. I shall not forget for a long time the last day, slush or sticky mud up to your knees in the trenches, parapets giving way, and dugouts falling in. And when we were relieved and coming out at night time, raining and dark, through the narrow communication trenches ... Everybody was loaded with stuff ... The trench had caved in, in many places, and we stumbled and fell, and actually got ourselves covered with mud, picked ourselves up again, laughed, and on we trudged.[60]

In spite of Millen's upbeat description, such conditions probably resulted in more cursing than laughing.

A Herculean effort was needed to maintain the trenches in a defensible state. In the words of the historian of the 20th Battalion, "nothing stands out more clearly in the minds of those who endured the rigours of that first winter than the constant demand for working parties." Whether they were stationed in the trenches or in brigade reserve, the battalions of the 4th Brigade "had an average of two hundred men working each night, and on several occasions as many as six hundred. These parties were usually formed in groups of twenty-five, each under an officer, and detailed to different duties."[61] Parties from units in reserve sweated under the burden of supplies and equipment, which they carried forward to the troops occupying the trenches. In turn, work details from the trench garrisons hauled this materiel farther forward to where it was needed, stumbling through trenches in various states of disrepair. All units in the front lines and in brigade reserve set teams to work rebuilding dugouts and other shelters, shoring up damaged trenches and breastworks, constructing new defensive positions, weaving improved barbed-wire obstacles, and filling seemingly endless numbers of sandbags.[62]

The exhaustion brought on by such heavy labour was only accentuated by the prevailing muddy conditions, which sometimes demanded immense exertions in simply walking from one point to another. Yet Maj. Millen informed his sister on 7 November that it was "positively marvelous how cheerful the men are over all their difficulties and discomforts ... Don't imagine for a moment that because I write this we are grumbling or worrying. We are the happiest bunch you ever saw. We all know that some poor beggars are in worse shape than we are."[63]

Being an officer and thus largely exempt from the routine performance of labour tasks, it may have been easier for Millen to take an optimistic view of the other ranks' morale in these dismal conditions. But it is more likely that such heart-warming pronouncements were made to comfort correspondents at home and that Millen did not think it best to record the actual mood of most men in such circumstances. In reality, most of the troops regarded the constant employment on labour projects as at best a chronic nuisance and at worst a positive danger. At any rate, there was the very real risk that the troops might become worn out through overwork, and grumbling was more prevalent among the ranks than cheery whistling. Moreover, the time spent labouring was time taken away from improving the men's tactical training on both individual and collective levels. "Prior to the advent of the Labour Battalions on the Western Front," recalled Charles Henderson, "the infantryman was expected not only to fight his position, but to construct and maintain it as well."[64] This situation was later mitigated by the increasing employment of various types of labour and engineering units, including entrenching, pioneer, and, by 1918, engineer battalions, which assumed greater shares of the workload from 1916 onward.[65] In the meantime, Henderson and his comrades in the 19th Battalion would have to endure the drudgery throughout the winter of 1915–16.

When not engaged in the interminable labour projects, troops stationed in brigade reserve continued to drill and train, special attention being devoted to bombing techniques and to the use of anti-gas equipment. Training continued during periods in divisional reserve at La Clytte and featured the hated route marches that were supposed to improve the men's physical stamina. Time spent in divisional reserve also brought some measure of relief to all ranks in the form of bathing "parades," in which companies proceeded to bath facilities set up in prefabricated metal huts, or sometimes even in converted breweries, where men bobbed about in open vats of water. In the former type of bath facility, "rusty nozzles emitted a few minutes of warm water, stopped for men to soap themselves, and gushed a few more minutes of cold water, leaving the shivering men to dry themselves with a dirty towel or a flannel shirttail. Medical officers insisted that hot showers would be 'enervating.'"[66]

Maj. Millen reported that "all the men are taken to the baths when they come out of the trenches and also given a change of underclothing."[67] Laundries were usually attached to the baths, and the opportunity to obtain clean clothes came as a welcome relief for the men, most of whom were plagued by hordes of body lice, which infested their dirty uniforms. Yet the laundered garments often still contained louse larvae, burrowed into the seams, which would soon mature to torment the wearer again. During the men's off-hours, both in and out of the trenches, among the most popular pastimes was hunting down these vermin. Small groups would often gather around a lamp, strip down, and pick through their clothing, squashing the lice with their fingernails. The more adept also would run a candle along the seams of their shirts and trousers, which caused the blood ingested by a louse to coagulate, resulting in a "gratifying 'pop'" as the creature exploded. "Crumbing up," as this tactic became known, "was a highly social activity and took a couple of hours with much ribald comment and black humour."[68]

In addition to the hazards and annoyances brought on by enemy firepower, dismal weather, incessant labour projects, and vermin, troops at the front faced an additional health risk posed by the swampy conditions in which they lived and worked. Because men spent much of their time in the trenches or on work parties with their feet submerged in cold mud and water, they ran a high risk of developing a condition known as "trench foot." This ailment, which had been contracted by large numbers of British troops during the winter of 1914–15, was brought on by a reduction of blood circulation in the legs and feet caused by prolonged exposure to cold and water. Early symptoms included swelling and discoloration, followed by numbness or extreme pain. If left untreated, it resulted in a condition not unlike severe frostbite and could lead to gangrene and amputation of affected toes, or even of the entire foot.

It was found that the most effective methods of countering trench foot included smearing whale oil over the men's feet, loosening their puttees to maximize circulation, and ensuring that every man had regular changes of socks and, if possible, opportunities to remove their boots and dry their feet during each twenty-four-hour period in the lines. Also, limited numbers of rubber boots and hip waders were circulated among units as they took their turns in the lines. These measures proved to be so effective that, by mid-1915, the problem of trench foot had dramatically diminished. As a result, the British high command decreed that henceforth there would be no excuse for contracting the condition. Officers were held responsible for inspecting the state of their men's feet and seeing to it that sufficient protective measures were taken. In effect, the prevalence of trench foot within the ranks became one means by which a unit's discipline and efficiency were measured.[69]

Although not spotless, the 19th Battalion had a reasonably good early record in keeping trench foot incidence low, exhibiting only five cases between 15 October and 31 December 1915. On 25 November the 19th Battalion informed 4th Brigade headquarters that "officers commanding companies have inspected the men's feet and report that with the exception of about two men per company they are in good condition."[70]

Christmas at the Front

The members of the 19th Battalion had the good fortune to spend Christmas Day of 1915 in divisional reserve. This permitted them ample opportunity to indulge in some well-earned relaxation and festivity. "We had a very nice Xmas time," declared Maj. Millen:

> For dinner we had soup, roast chicken, potatoes and peas, Xmas pudding (which I, followed by all the others set on fire), Xmas cake, jelly, Camembert cheese, and tea, nuts and raisins, etc. etc. We had a party Xmas Eve, to which we invited 3 other Hamilton officers and had quite a nice time. Every one made a speech, mostly agreeing what a fine bunch we all were, especially "D" Company. We had champagne. This is not such an expensive luxury as it is in Canada.[71]

The other ranks, dining in less opulent fashion, depended to a great degree on the generosity of family and friends at home for their holiday treats. "Some of the boys had turkey," reported one veteran. But it was "of the canned variety, which had been sent in their parcels from the folks at home. Much fun being made regarding this, and plum and apple jam was transformed in imagination to the status of the good things we were accustomed to in the old days."[72] Others were not so fortunate as to receive even canned turkey. As Pte. Felix Cullen recorded in laconic fashion: "Xmas day and everything is quiet – hardly a gun firing. For dinner we had corn beef stew, boiled potatoes, hard tack bread, butter and tea. Some Xmas dinner."[73]

As 1915 drew to a close, the 19th Battalion was on the move again, out of divisional reserve and back to the M and N trenches, relieving the 18th Battalion on the evening of 28 December. In summing up the battalion's experience of trench warfare during the autumn, Maj. Millen claimed that "we are living within excitement, but without excitement." By 7 November he admitted that "things have really got down to a hum drum with us."[74] After being introduced so abruptly to trench warfare in late September, the battalion's personnel had acclimatized themselves to conditions in the trenches and to the conduct of trench warfare – to the extent that some, like Millen, came to regard the war as a rather tedious affair.

thereafter, ranging from twenty in December 1915 to eleven in March 1916.[3] In fact, throughout the war, during months in which it was not heavily engaged, the 19th Battalion would average around twenty-three battle casualties – somewhat less than Middlebrook's estimate.

Some of the wounded were not critical cases and did not require evacuation. Even a percentage of the more serious cases would recover and return to the battalion for active duty after a period of convalescence. During the war, nearly 90 per cent of wounded Canadians who received medical treatment survived and recovered either partly or completely from their injuries. The percentage of injured Canadians who returned to some form of duty probably matched the 82 percent of wounded British troops who did so, of whom 29 per cent returned to active service on the Western Front.[4]

After the war, Georges U. Francoeur of the 22nd Battalion maintained that "new men were always getting killed within a week and we always said that if they could go through the first ten days, they were alright."[5] Later in the war, new arrivals at the front would benefit greatly from the advice and example of surviving old hands. But in the unit's first months of trench duty, all personnel in the 19th Battalion were inexperienced, and this would have contributed to the higher numbers of casualties at that time, compared with other quiet months later in the war. Training was necessary, but nothing benefited all ranks more than practical experience.

Propaganda for the Home Front

The relative lack of large-scale operations did little to diminish the imagination of some soldier-correspondents such as the 19th Battalion's Harry Adie. Writing under his pseudonym, "Omar," Adie supplied local newspapers at home with vivid accounts of stirring deeds. On 3 October 1915, after completing only his first tour of duty in the D trenches, Adie wrote glowingly of the battalion's senior officers: McLaren was "everywhere during the heaviest attacks, directing, inspiring, encouraging, sharing every danger and every discomfort and lending by his own disregard of personal injury an incentive to the men under him"; Turnbull, a friend to everyone in the battalion, from "the smallest drummer boy up," was "also always in the thick of it, setting an example to the officers and men, sharing more of the personal danger than was absolutely necessary, but by his conduct, steadfastness and coolness winning the admiration of brave men"; Morrison was "in the true sense of the word, one of the 'biggest' men in Canada's army – cold, unemotional, a keen observer and strict disciplinarian."[6]

Adie's imagery, of officers "in the thick of it," heroically and personally leading their men through the "heaviest attacks," might have been appropriate for descriptions of the big British battle at Loos, but it bore scant relation to the realities of the 19th Battalion's first tour in the lines. His anachronistic reference to "the smallest drummer boy" seems calculated to evoke the romance of combat and military life from a bygone era. Moreover, this was not a war in which a battalion commander could carry out his duties most effectively by "leading from the front" in the style of the Napoleonic Wars.

A number of Adie's descriptions were published in newspapers such as the *Spectator* and the *Herald* back in Hamilton. If some readers at home were taken in by them, others sought confirmation from their family members and friends in the battalion. In response to his mother's queries about the reliability of "Omar's" reports, Lionel Millen offered a brutally candid appraisal:

> Say, that stuff in the *Spectator* signed 'Omar' is the most egotistical rot I ever saw ... Practically all the officers are disgusted with it. One would think we have been doing wonderful things, whereas so far all we have done is just routine stuff. As for the write ups on the Colonel and Major Turnbull ... words fail me, especially as regards the latter. The worst of it is they seem to like it. Let us hope some time they will be able to live up to these write ups.[7]

Later in December 1915, Millen reminded his mother: "'Omar' yes I know him, but don't you believe all the flowery stuff he writes."[8]

To what degree these reports may have sowed discord among the officers is difficult to determine. In any case, Millen's frank comments suggest that the performances of McLaren and Turnbull fell short not only of Adie's purple prose but also of realistic expectations. Millen offered no specific evidence to support his sentiment, and, to be fair to his superiors, they had only just come through their first experience in the lines when Adie drafted his tale of derring-do on 3 October; so a certain amount of shakiness on their part should not have been surprising. What is certain, however, is that Adie's communications to the press were composed with McLaren's full knowledge and, in some instances, at his behest. This clearly betrays McLaren's interest in self-promotion and may also indicate a desire to derive political capital from his military service.[9] Whatever their dubious merits, Adie's accounts of the 19th Battalion would soon cease, after he secured a transfer to the Royal Flying Corps (RFC) and obtained a commission. On 1 May 1916 he would die of wounds sustained during a reconnaissance flight over German lines.[10]

Tools of War

Although the death or serious injury of any individual was tragic, we have seen that the period between the autumn of 1915 and the spring of 1916 was not an especially dangerous time for the 19th Battalion. But was all really as quiet on the Western Front as the relatively low casualty rates imply? Sometimes, yes. But on other occasions, spasms of violence occurred that reminded all ranks of the deadly nature of the struggle. The ever-present threat of artillery – "the monstrous anger of the guns," as poet Wilfred Owen later put it – kept soldiers on both sides cowering in their trenches, fearful for their lives.[11] This is not to say that the troops endured constant heavy shelling over prolonged periods of time. During the early months of the war, all belligerent forces found that pre-war estimates of the quantities of guns and artillery shells required for a future conflict were inadequate, based as they were on hopes that the next great war in Europe would be short and decisive. It took time for domestic armaments industries to expand production so that output of weapons and ammunition gradually began to approach the phenomenal consumption levels observed since the beginning of hostilities. In the British armies, not until the middle of 1916 were stocks of artillery shells deemed sufficient for sustained offensive operations. By contrast, Germany's shell production had succeeded in meeting its artillery's needs by the spring of 1915.[12]

The shifting degrees of activity along different parts of the front sometimes permitted armies on both sides to reduce their ammunition expenditures in less active sectors in order to increase them in others where the pressure was more extreme. Season and climate also had an impact. With certain exceptions, such as the opening of the great German offensive at Verdun on 21 February 1916, the scale and intensity of operations tended to diminish during late autumn and winter. Increasingly wet and muddy conditions, frigid temperatures, and reduced hours of daylight conspired to hamper large-scale offensives until the return of better campaigning weather in the spring, summer, and early autumn months. It was fortunate for the 19th Battalion that it and the rest of the 2nd Canadian Division had arrived on the Western Front in the final quarter of 1915, for the decelerating tempo of operations made for an environment that was less consistently lethal for all ranks, and thus more conducive for gaining tactical experience.

Between October and December 1915, for example, the Germans fired anywhere from ten to thirty shrapnel and high-explosive shells per day into the trench lines occupied by 19th Battalion personnel. The level of this daily "hate" sometimes dropped to as few as four rounds of high explosive, as on 30 December.[13] The Germans subjected the 19th Battalion to similarly varying levels of punishment during the first three months of 1916, although the frequency of shelling in the M and N trenches was somewhat greater.

Although the rain of destruction was not constant, German artillery projectiles were formidable enough to inspire a variety of evocative nicknames, some of which betrayed a healthy respect for their hitting power. Among the more ubiquitous were the "whiz-bangs," lighter shells from field artillery such as the German 77 mm gun. Heavy gun or howitzer projectiles were sometimes referred to as "Jack Johnsons," after the famous heavyweight boxer; the name denoted their "punch." These weapons heralded their arrival with long, piercing shrieks, much like the ones so often heard decades later in war movies. The black smoke left by the burst of a heavy shell (such as a German 5.9-inch or 21 cm howitzer shell) was referred to as a "coal-box" or a "woolly bear."[14]

Then there were the mortars. These were short-barrelled weapons, usually muzzle-loaded and fired at a steep angle. Mortar rounds, although much easier to detect owing to their slower velocity, were greatly feared because, like howitzer shells, their steep trajectory permitted them to fall directly into a trench. Some of the larger ones could actually be seen with the naked eye as they arced lazily upward and then tumbled down onto the terrified occupants of the targeted position. The German varieties, known collectively as *Minenwerfers* (literally "mine throwers"), and as "minnies" by the British and Dominion troops, came in various sizes; the larger types were sometimes called "rum jars" or "flying pigs," while the smaller ones were known as "piss tins." The havoc these weapons could wreak was terrible. Large mortar projectiles filled with high explosive could create huge craters, and the concussion of their detonations sent debris and people flying in all directions. Mortar shells filled with shrapnel did hideous damage by spraying bits of scrap iron over a wide area. Survivors of such assaults reputedly had bits of old clocks and other domestic metal articles removed from their wounds.[15]

Perhaps the most fearful weapon, based largely on its novelty at this time, was gas. The Canadians had made their reputation as first-class troops through their dogged stand in the face of gas attacks during the Second Battle of Ypres in April 1915. Following the German lead, the Allies soon built up their own arsenal of chemical weapons. Although it did not prove to be a breakthrough weapon for either side on the Western Front, gas remained potent and terrifying, for its power lay as much in its ability to intimidate as in its capacity to maim and kill. Most sections of trench were equipped with various types of alarms (such as rattles, bells, gongs made from empty artillery shell cases, or klaxon horns) to be sounded by designated sentries should they perceive an odour of gas. The prevalence of false alarms added to the tension and exhaustion that pervaded the soldiers' daily lives at the front. This only accentuated the fear and discomfort brought on by real gas attacks, which increased in frequency to the end of the war.

During the spring and summer of 1915, the British quickly moved to develop a variety of protective measures to neutralize the effects of chlorine gas, which was the principle chemical agent employed by the Germans at that time. When troops of the 2nd Canadian Division arrived at the front, they were equipped first with the Hypo, or "smoke" helmet; in November 1915 this was replaced with the newer P-helmet (also known as the "tube helmet"). Both helmets were baggy protective hoods that had been pre-treated with special chemical solutions developed to neutralize the effects of gas. In the case of the P-helmet, an improved solution was used to counter the effects of phosgene, an even more lethal gas unleashed by the Germans in December. Although essential, these protective helmets were suffocating for the wearer, whose field of vision was seriously limited by easily fogged mica view windows or glass-covered eye holes.[16]

While anti-gas measures continued to develop, the British and Canadian infantry relied on the guns, howitzers, and mortars of their own artillery to exact vengeance on the Germans. The 60-pounder guns and 6-, 8-, and 9.2-inch howitzers of

Canadian gunners training with an 18-pounder field gun. (LAC PA 022712)

the Canadian Corps Heavy Artillery pounded enemy strongpoints and attempted to neutralize German artillery through counter-battery shoots, while the 18-pounder guns and 4.5-inch howitzers of the divisional field artillery brigades furnished closer support for infantry operations.[17] Canadian and other Allied forces had their own trench mortar units as well. Heavy and medium mortars were manned by divisional field artillery personnel, while light trench mortar batteries were formed in each infantry brigade. The rapid-firing 3-inch Stokes mortar was one of the more successful designs, and by June 1916 the Canadian light batteries were fully equipped with it.[18]

As for the ordinary infantryman, the high command viewed the rifle and bayonet as his chief weapons, with grenades and machine guns occupying subsidiary roles.[19] Nevertheless, grenades and machine guns were the weapons that afforded the heaviest firepower for the infantry, and grenades were embraced with particular enthusiasm by troops in the close-combat world of the trenches. It has been noted already that machine gunners formed their own specialist section within the battalion, owing largely to the technical skills required to operate their weapons. Personnel who displayed a particular aptitude in the use of grenades also would be grouped together in their own sections. But specialist sections were not limited to certain weapons groups. There were other subgroups within each infantry battalion that filled essential supporting roles such as communications and supply and transport.

Specialist Sections

Because of the technical nature of their tasks, specialist troops within a battalion sometimes assumed an elite air in comparison with their comrades in the rifle companies. Upon initial organization, infantry battalions contained specialist signals, pioneer, transport, medical, and machine-gun sections. All but the machine gunners were counted as part of the battalion headquarters establishment. Others, such as bombing and intelligence (or scouting) sections, were formed after mobilization, in response to needs that were recognized on the battlefield.

Lt. (later Maj.) Herbert D. Fearman was the 19th Battalion's original signals officer, and with the assistance of two NCOs he led a section of fifteen men.[20] Signallers employed a variety of communication methods and technologies, ranging from semaphore flags, signal lamps, and coloured rockets or flares, to portable field telephones. Their chief job was to keep battalion headquarters, the infantry companies, and the machine-gun section in touch with one another. They also cooperated with brigade-level signallers to keep the battalion in contact with brigade headquarters to the rear. In the event that artillery fire severed the telephone lines that were buried in the earth or strung along the walls of communication trenches, the battalion signallers resorted to other methods such as carrier pigeons or runners. The risks to both bird and man in carrying messages between headquarters were considerable during heavy shelling. Nevertheless, in an era without easily portable wireless radios, runners emerged as the most reliable form of communication when telephone lines were broken and conditions did not permit the use of visual techniques.[21]

During an attack, multiple communication methods were often used simultaneously in hopes that at least one of them would get the message through. The

19th Battalion headquarters runners. (MUA RC 0835)

(MO), assisted by two orderlies, oversaw the work of sixteen stretcher-bearers (four per rifle company) and five additional personnel attached from the Canadian Army Medical Corps (CAMC). The MO, himself attached from the CAMC, was responsible not only for the health of everyone in the battalion but also for sanitary arrangements (especially the provision of clean water) and for the training of stretcher-bearers. The bearers often were the first to treat a wounded man and were the ones who evacuated him to the unit's Regimental Aid Post (RAP), which usually was established at an accessible location (such as a dugout or cellar) in the second or third line of trenches. During battle, once a wounded man had been delivered to the RAP, the MO and his orderlies worked to stop any haemorrhaging and changed the field dressings that had been applied by the stretcher-bearers or by the wounded man himself. The RAP had not been designed for intensive surgical treatment or long-term recovery. Rather, its purpose was to stabilize a wounded man sufficiently for evacuation. After being evacuated by personnel from one of the divisional field ambulances, a casualty received more comprehensive treatment, including surgery if necessary, at either an Advanced Dressing Station (ADS) or still farther behind the lines at a Casualty Clearing Station (CCS).[25]

The original medical officer of the 19th Battalion was Lt. George W. Anderson, who had been attached for duty from the CAMC. But before the battalion left Canada, Capt. William Laurence Whittemore took over the position. Whittemore quickly displayed a talent for innovation. Before the battalion left England for the continent, Ed Youngman of the battalion transport section observed the doctor

Canadians training with a Colt machine gun. (LAC PA-004915)

Training with a Lewis automatic rifle. This photo was taken in Canada at Niagara Camp and shows one technique for steadying the weapon. They were usually equipped with bipods. (LAC PA-069844)

"pulling hairs out of one of my horse's tails, he was selecting these very long hairs, and I asked him why he was doing it, and he told me that he believed that if they were properly sterilized, they would make good suturing material."[26]

Within each infantry battalion, the signals, pioneer, transport, and medical sections occupied supporting roles for the troops who manned the rifle companies. The battalion machine-gun section, by contrast, was a distinct weapons group that cooperated with the rifle companies in combat. From an initial complement of two, the number of machine guns was increased during 1915, first to four and eventually to eight per battalion. By the time the latter increase was authorized for battalions throughout the British armies (in October 1915), a more portable type of gun – the Lewis automatic rifle – was coming into use. It would gradually replace the heavier, tripod-mounted Colt and Vickers guns with which battalion machine-gun sections had first been equipped.[27]

Along with the change in weaponry came a shift in machine-gun organization throughout the British armies. To give brigade headquarters greater control over the tactical deployment of machine-gun firepower, heavier weapons like the Vickers gun were gathered and formed into brigade machine-gun companies. The first of sixteen such companies was formed in the Canadian Corps in January 1916; each boasted sixteen heavy machine guns. Infantry battalions were to be equipped with the new Lewis guns, the establishment of which was set at eight, or two per

Testing a Vickers machine gun. (LAC PA-000635)

rifle company. That was the theory. In reality, the temperamental Colt, which had a tendency to jam, would continue to soldier on within Canadian brigade machine-gun companies and infantry battalions until they were replaced completely by more reliable Vickers guns in the former units by June 1916 and by Lewis guns in the latter during 1917.[28] Unfortunately, records from the 19th Battalion are unclear regarding how and precisely when these changes were implemented. According to battalion records, however, March 1917 was the last documented month in which two Colt guns remained in service with the battalion. Thereafter, only Lewis guns were employed.[29]

The 19th Battalion's machine-gun section comprised thirty-two rank and file, who were led initially by Lt. (later Capt.) Charles E. Kilmer of Toronto, who was assisted by two sergeants.[30] Kilmer was a former junior officer in the Queen's Own Rifles and an engineer by profession, which probably marked him as a suitable candidate for the command of such a technical section.[31] It was his job to advise Lt.-Col. McLaren on all matters related to the tactical use of machine guns and to ensure that all personnel and equipment in his section received the best possible care. Battalion machine-gun officers, such as Kilmer, were advised in no uncertain terms that "the machine gun problem is getting more important daily and the machine gun officer must never think for one moment that he knows it all."[32]

The significance of the machine gun to trench warfare can be grasped when one considers that, from the amount of frontage occupied by a Colt or Vickers gun (approximately two feet), a stream of firepower equivalent to some fifty rifles could spew forth. In terms of defensive firepower, one well-situated machine gun could stall an attacking battalion, and six guns could hold up an entire brigade. Similarly, a Lewis gunner, firing in short bursts, could emit as much lead as twenty to thirty riflemen.[33]

The machine gunners themselves certainly had no doubts about the power of their weapons, the technical know-how required to operate them, and their significance on the battlefield. This gave them a sense that they were a breed apart from the ordinary infantryman. The 19th Battalion's machine-gun section "prided itself on having a group of men of really very high mentality and physical prowess," declared Gladstone Ghent. "In fact 96% of us had either graduated or were in the process of getting some profession from a Canadian University at the time of our enlistment." In Ghent's view, the section's strongest attributes were exemplified by Alastir MacKenzie. A former heavyweight wrestling champion of the University of Toronto and a Canadian canoe singles champion of some years' standing, Mackenzie was "a born leader and a giant for work," capable of carrying "as much as two hundred pounds for over two miles of slippery trenches." Unfortunately, he was killed in action when his machine gun suffered a direct hit by a "flying pig."[34]

Two more specialist sections, of bombers and scouts, were added to the 19th Battalion's organization after mobilization. Although not originally part of the standard battalion establishment, these types of troops were proving essential to the conduct of trench warfare. Drawing on the experiences of formations already at the front, the 2nd Canadian Division ensured that its battalions adopted these new organizations before proceeding to France and Belgium.[35]

The hand grenade – or "bomb," as it was commonly referred to[36] – was not a widely used weapon in the British army when the war began, and indeed it had not been employed to a great degree in European warfare since the 1700s. Generally, grenades were employed as anti-personnel weapons, and were prized for the havoc they could wreak in a crowded trench or dugout. In a war where opposing troops rarely caught sight of each other, it was often easier to strike at an unseen enemy by lobbing a grenade on top of him than to wait for him to expose himself to rifle fire. Tests were conducted with a considerable number of manufactured grenade types until the advent in May 1915 of the "Mills bomb," which by the end of the year had largely replaced most other types in the British armies.[37] The Mills grenade was shaped like a large lemon, weighed around 20 ounces, and could be thrown roughly thirty yards. Although it is popularly believed that its segmented, pineapple-like surface was designed to scatter metal fragments, other sources maintain that the surface serrations merely facilitated an effective grip on the weapon.[38]

Another important innovation was the rifle grenade, of which the Hale no. 3 variety was the most common one in use by late 1915. The user attached the bomb to a 10-inch metal rod that was inserted down the barrel of a rifle, pulled the pin from the bomb, and then fired a blank cartridge. The bomb then flew some 175 yards and exploded on contact. With its dramatically better range than a hand-thrown type, the rifle grenade became a more attractive offensive weapon. However, its use caused a great deal of wear and tear on the barrel of a man's rifle, which tended to bulge and split over time. This problem was remedied by 1918, with the wider use of innovations such as cup dischargers for Mills grenades, which did away with rods.[39]

A battalion bombing section typically consisted of twenty to thirty men. Like the machine gunners, many bombers counted themselves among the elites of their unit.[40] Special bombing sections were sometimes formed within individual companies, and records indicate that the 19th Battalion employed bombing sections at both battalion and company levels.[41] The battalion bombing section was led by Lt. (later Lt.-Col.) Bertram O. Hooper, a banker from Hamilton who had joined the 19th Battalion through the 13th Royal Regiment.[42]

Skill in the use of grenades was viewed as a specialist attribute; even so, these weapons were important enough that all troops in the battalion were trained in

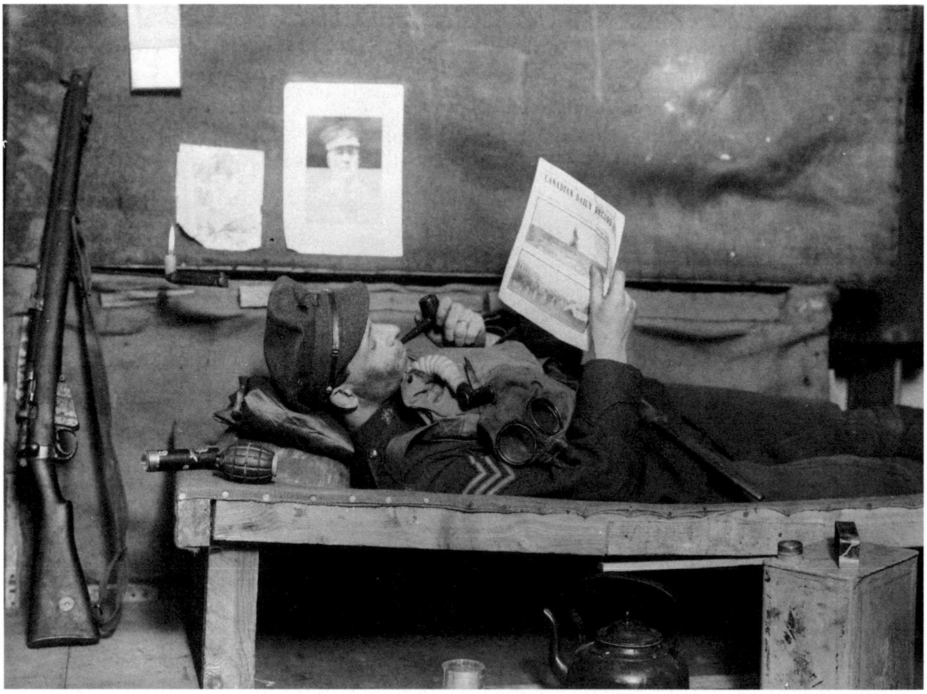

A sergeant enjoys a few minutes with the Canadian Daily Record. The photo was taken late in the war, in February 1918, but clearly shows a Mills grenade beside his pillow. (LAC PA-002507)

Rifle-grenade practice at Shorncliffe, England. Two lieutenants observe as soldiers fire rifle-grenades from modified Lee-Enfield rifles. (LAC PA-004745)

their use.[43] This broader level of training also served to identify those men who were especially talented grenade throwers, many of whom were subsequently transferred to the battalion bombing section. One man who was proficient in two specialties was Phil Collins, who was preparing to join the battalion signallers when his aptitude for throwing bombs led to his recruitment by Lt. Hooper's new bombing section, leaving Collins to marvel: "A Signaller one day and a Bomber the next! One never knew where one would end up in the army!"[44] Hooper's prerogative to select men already earmarked for other duties illustrates the emphasis placed on grenade work, as well as the "pecking order" that seems to have developed among specialist sections in the battalion. It seems that when claims to talented personnel were being staked, combatant sections like the bombers took precedence over support sections, such as the signallers.

Reconnaissance and intelligence work, often termed "scouting" in pre-war army parlance, emerged as another specialist province within the battalion. By 1915, groups of men were being organized in most battalions to carry out intelligence duties, such as patrol and observation work. In July, based largely on lessons learned in the field by the 1st Canadian Division, battalion intelligence sections (also known as "scout sections") were instituted throughout the 2nd Canadian Division while its personnel were still undergoing training in England. Initially, these sections had no fixed establishment, and in fact the Canadian Corps did not standardize the organization of battalion scout sections until 1918.[45]

The troops in most battalion scout sections were subdivided into various specialties. One subsection contained troops whose primary duty was to conduct nightly patrols in no man's land. They reconnoitred the state of the ground beyond the Canadian front line; they also served as security screens, protecting their comrades in the battalion's trench garrisons and work parties. Next were the listening-post men, who were situated just behind the patrols but usually in advance of the Canadian wire. They were positioned in isolated shell holes or at the heads of the small sap trenches that had been dug out into no man's land from the front-line trench. These men kept their eyes peeled and their ears open for any enemy activity and could communicate with sentries in the front-line trenches by means of tug lines. Farther back were trench observers and snipers, who carried out their work in shifts by day and night in carefully chosen positions within and behind the front line. A great deal of coordination was required among these various subsections so as to maximize security levels in their portion of the line.[46]

Scouts also played key roles before and during a full-scale attack. Immediately before an assault, they ensured that lanes were cut through the enemy's wire. During the battle itself, they carried out reconnaissance missions, guided troops to their objectives, liaised with neighbouring units, and helped the signallers maintain communications between the battle area and the rear. In the case of a successful attack, when the assault force had reached its objective the scouts then patrolled the battalion's newly captured frontage, providing a protective screen and working to determine the enemy's new dispositions.[47]

Like their comrades in the bombing section, members of the scout section had been specially selected. Required of them were qualities such as "fearlessness combined with discretion, and intelligence, craftiness, and quickness."[48] The commander of each scout section ensured that every man was intensively trained in map and compass reading, field sketching, report writing, the use of signalling equipment, and various patrolling techniques.[49] To compensate for the intensity of their training and for the risk and responsibility they were called to shoulder when in the trenches, scouts were to "be struck off other duties, working parties, parades, etc., during the period of their training, and during the time they are working as scouts, which is practically always."[50] A certain measure of resentment was to be expected from the rank and file of the rifle companies, who doubtless envied the privileges that were accorded scouts and the members of other specialist sections. However, as the hazards endured by many specialists became clearer, there probably were few riflemen who would have traded places with them.

Lt. (later Maj.) Sydney S. Burnham, a clerk from Toronto, was appointed to command the 19th Battalion's scout section, which consisted originally of nineteen other ranks. By May 1916, this number had expanded to twenty-four.[51] As the officer in charge of coordinating intelligence-gathering activities within the battalion, Burnham essentially functioned as his CO's "tactical 'eyes and ears.'" When the battalion was stationed in the trenches, it was his job to ensure that its entire frontage was covered with observation posts and snipers. He also was responsible for the organization, coordination, and debriefing of all patrols and for maintaining the accuracy of the battalion's map of no man's land. He had to liaise constantly with the company commanders in order to collect any intelligence gathered by company sentries or snipers. Finally, he had to collate all the intelligence data gleaned from the various specialists in his own section, and from those in the rifle companies, and submit reports to the staff captain in charge of intelligence at brigade headquarters. In essence, the officer in charge of the scout section was "the most informed officer on the terrain that lay in and outside a battalion commander's area of responsibility, and thus [was] key to any of the CO's command decisions on patrolling, raiding, preparing defensive contingency plans, etc."[52]

Patrolling and Raiding

Patrolling was a nightly activity that served a twofold purpose: it provided security for a battalion's positions; and it was a means of gathering intelligence, both on the state of no man's land and on activities in the German lines. In general, there were two types of patrols: reconnaissance and fighting. Troops like Fred Stitt also referred to these two types respectively as "stealth" and "battle" patrols.[53] The purpose of the former was to gather intelligence; of the latter, to drive off any German patrols or working parties, take prisoners for interrogation, or even attack and temporarily occupy an enemy position. In any case, the purpose of a fighting patrol was to inflict as much damage on the enemy as possible while protecting its own positions.

Most patrols carried out by the 19th Battalion during late 1915 and early 1916 focused on reconnaissance. Members of patrols removed all identifying papers and insignia from their pockets and uniforms, and to permit easy movement and minimize noise, they equipped themselves as lightly as possible. Often, they blackened their faces with grease, mud, or burnt cork, and they usually carried easily handled weapons such as pistols, knives, and makeshift clubs. They also carried grenades, but used them only when necessary to get out of a difficult situation. Because the goal was to gain useful intelligence, these types of patrols were not supposed to engage in combat unless attacked first. Each night, one or more patrols led by an officer or NCO (usually from the battalion or company scouts) would slip into no man's land and note the state of the German wire and any activity that could be seen or heard in front of and within enemy lines. Sentries in the Canadian trenches would be briefed on the movements of these patrols, which typically departed from one section of the front line and returned through another. Upon their return, patrol members would hoarsely whisper passwords to avoid being shot by a nervous sentry as they approached the parapet of their own trench.[54] Sentries sometimes did not receive word in time of a patrol's impending return, and such oversights could be fatal. In October 1915, Gladstone Ghent of the battalion machine-gun section almost shot one of his comrades on patrol. He would have killed the man had not his rifle failed to fire when he pulled the trigger, leading him to conclude that the soldier's survival was nothing short of a "miracle."[55]

The Germans also patrolled no man's land and sent wiring and other work parties out on a regular basis to maintain their defences. Yet direct encounters between 19th Battalion and German patrols did not occur to any appreciable degree during the winter of 1915–16. As one veteran recalled, "no man's land was patrolled each night by company scouts and although much activity was shown from the enemy trenches and artillery during the day the scouts never encountered any of their patrols. Their barbed wire defences were often examined as to condition and state of disrepair."[56] Nevertheless, unexpected encounters did occur, as happened on the night of 16 October 1915, when "two enemy working parties were seen when fog lifted. B Company opened with rapid fire and saw 3 Germans fall."[57]

Nerve-wracking as patrol work often was, the relative safety in which 19th Battalion scouts conducted their nocturnal forays tempted other curious members of the battalion to join them. That the scouts would entertain the notion of less experienced men joining them speaks to their confidence in the relative tranquility of no man's land at that time. One of these visitors was Allan Lynch, a battalion machine gunner, who could not resist the urge to experience no man's land first-hand. On the night in question, the patrol was ordered to fetch a sample of the German barbed wire. Lynch recalled:

> We chaps in the machine-gun section, for some reason or other, used to get an extra ration of rum and I'd just had mine before we crawled out into No Man's Land. There were about six of us in the patrol and we crawled along in Indian file, stopping every few yards to get our bearings and lie doggo straining our eyes to see if by chance there might be an enemy patrol out at the same time. On the second or third stop I dozed off and began to snore. A swift poke in the ribs had me wide awake and I heard one of the gang whisper "Keep quiet, you bl– – dy fool." Just before we reached Heinie's wire and were really lying doggo my rum ration took effect again and in no time flat I was

> snoring again. This time I got a swift kick in the pants and a whispered voice said "if you can't keep quiet, get to hell out of here." This really woke me up and soon we had a sample of Fritz's wire and were back in the safety of our own lines. Needless to say I wasn't very popular with the Scout section for a while![58]

Lynch's experience starkly demonstrated the wisdom of abstaining from such comforts as drink or cigarettes immediately before a patrol. A man who was groggy or given to fits of coughing was a menace to himself and his comrades. Nevertheless, over time, non-scouts within British and Canadian battalions increasingly shouldered the burden of patrol work. One practical reason for this had to do with the frequency with which it was carried out, and the consequent risk that the scouts would become exhausted. Another reason stemmed from the high command's desire that all ranks cultivate the proper "offensive spirit," which, it was argued, could be encouraged through taking part in activities such as patrols.[59]

Reconnaissance patrols varied in size, from a junior officer or NCO with one or two additional men to a platoon or more.[60] Although the 19th Battalion's records are not always clear regarding the size of every patrol, reports indicate that both small and larger groups were employed. Larger numbers were certainly used for more ambitious reconnaissance schemes, such as one carried out on the evening of 24 January 1916. One of the goals of this particular enterprise was to enter the German front line opposite Trench M2-5.

The group was led by Lts. Hooper and Burnham (the "Grenade" and "Patrol" officers) and consisted of Sgt. Jackson, Cpl. Derbyshire, Lance Cpls. Hoskin, McLean, Ransom, and Hutchison, and twelve other ranks.[61] They departed at 7:30 PM and divided into four separate parties. Two were stationed at positions in no man's land and probably functioned as covering parties. Meanwhile, Burnham and three men took up a position close to the German wire and just to the right of the point where Hooper and his party of two NCOs and three men made their way through the wire with the aid of a special mat flung over the entanglement. After crossing the wire, they proceeded to the German parapet and entered the front-line trench. This section was found to be unoccupied and contained a great deal of mud and water. Hooper and his men heard no voices and remained there for half an hour, exploring a little distance to their right and also some ten yards up a nearby communication trench.

Seeing nothing to be gained by remaining in this section, Hooper ordered his party out of the trench. Leaving two men on the parapet, he took the remaining three and proceeded to another point in the German front line, farther to the right of the section they had just vacated. As they approached this new section of trench, they heard the voices of sentries. They crept to get closer, but then the moon came out and Canadian troops positioned on the 19th Battalion's right flank started firing from their trenches. Deeming it unwise to proceed farther amidst this commotion,

Hooper decided to bring his party back the way they came. When they reached the men he had left at the German parapet, the two reported that a German had passed through the trench in front of them while Hooper and the others had been away. Unfortunately, the parapet was too wide for them to reach the man with the knobkerries they were sporting. In addition, they felt it unwise to use their grenades because they did not want to start a general fight without knowing where Hooper and the others were, for fear of getting them into trouble.

Although Hooper and his party did not reach their second objective, they were able to confirm that that part of the line was manned. By 10:00 PM all members of each party in the patrol had returned safely to their own lines. While this patrol may not in retrospect appear spectacular, it did mark the first recorded instance in which members of the 19th Battalion entered German lines. As such, for their work during this reconnaissance, Hooper would be awarded the Military Cross while Jackson and Hutchison would receive the Distinguished Conduct Medal (DCM).[62]

It should be noted that it was during late 1915 and early 1916 that the Canadian troops executed some of their first successful trench raids. Raids had evolved from patrolling, and throughout most of 1915 little distinction was made between the two activities. Raids, like patrols, were designed both to secure intelligence and to inflict damage on the enemy. However, as raiding developed, it began to differ from patrolling in terms of scale and in the increasing employment of supporting arms, such as artillery and trench mortars. Typically attired as for a patrol, albeit usually more heavily armed, the members of a raiding party would enter a section of the German trenches by surprise and there inflict as many casualties and as much damage as possible to key positions such as machine-gun nests, dugouts, mine shafts, and communication trenches. Grenades were the principal weapons in this sort of work. Having done their worst, the raiders would make a hasty getaway before the Germans could counterattack in strength, ideally carrying off one or more prisoners for intelligence purposes. As with patrols, the size of a raiding party varied according to the nature and scope of the objectives. Some smaller raids were carried out by groups of around ten men; larger enterprises could employ 200 or even more. By 1917 and 1918, some very large raids could involve sizable parties from several battalions working in concert and striking at different targets in the enemy lines.[63]

It is not known exactly which unit carried out the first trench raid in the British armies on the Western Front.[64] We do know, however, that the trench raid as a "developed tactic" emerged on the night of 16–17 November 1915 when parties from the 1st Canadian Division successfully attacked German positions at La Petite Douve Farm. The raiders, supported by artillery and mortars, inflicted numerous casualties, captured a number of prisoners, and sustained only two casualties of their own.[65] Predictably, General Headquarters (GHQ) was elated with the results, and the favourable publicity it garnered encouraged similar efforts. As 1916 dawned, units in the 2nd Canadian Division moved quickly to establish their own reputations for raiding. The most successful of the early 2nd Division ventures occurred on the night of 30–31 January 1916, when parties from the 28th and 29th Battalions of the 6th Infantry Brigade successfully raided the German salient at Spanbroekmolen.

The increasing boldness of the 19th Battalion's patrol activities, as exemplified by events on the evening of 24 January, reflected the aggressive spirit that had taken root in the Canadian Corps and that found its outlet in raiding. The 19th Battalion did not conduct a full-scale raid of its own during early 1916, but it would have benefited from the lessons learned by other units. These included the need for careful planning and selection of personnel and equipment; the value of thorough scouting of the objective; the benefit of intensive rehearsal, often on training courses constructed to mimic enemy positions; and the importance of effective cooperation among the various arms and weapons groups involved (infantry, artillery, machine guns, trench mortars). Through such exploits as raids and patrols, and the routine of trench warfare, all ranks had the opportunity to gain practical experience in fighting.

Attitudes towards the Enemy

English-speaking troops often referred to the Germans both individually and collectively as "Fritz" or "Heinie," and somewhat less often as "Jerry," "Hun," and "Boche" (sometimes spelled "Bosche"). Very often the pronoun "he" or its objective and possessive cases were used in reference to the enemy. This accentuated the popular tendency to view the Germans as an undifferentiated mass, thus downplaying their individuality and hence, to some degree, their humanity.[66] Depending on the situation or the attitude of the individual user, these terms could express anything from grudging respect or admiration to hostility or outright hatred.

The British high command had planned no large-scale offensive operations for the winter of 1915–16. The orders and official rhetoric emanating from GHQ did, however, reflect a policy of continuous aggression, in order to deny the Germans any opportunity to rest and regroup from the fighting earlier in the year.[67] The major risk that accompanied hostile acts was that the understandably annoyed victims on the other side of no man's land would retaliate.

Whatever the official orders were, along some sectors of the Western Front informal or unspoken understandings developed between opposing troops that led to acts of aggression being carried out at reduced frequency or being ritualized to the point where the dangers to both sides were minimized. Some historians – most notably Tony Ashworth – have referred to this as the "live and let live" system of trench warfare.

Surviving records indicate that the 19th Battalion eschewed an explicit "live and let live" attitude, instead favouring a posture of consistent vigilance and hostility during late 1915 and early 1916. However, reports of amounts of small-arms ammunition expended by the battalion, which ranged from just over 500 to as many as 8,500 rounds per day,[68] provide no reliable means of gauging the effect of this firepower or, more important, the intent of 19th Battalion personnel. Be that as it may, we do know that during the battalion's tours in the trenches, nightly patrols monitored the situation in no man's land, while sentries kept watch and snipers plied their deadly trade; the latter reported over fifty Germans killed or wounded between 5 October 1915 and 31 March 1916.[69] We have noted already the absence of reported violent encounters between 19th Battalion and German patrols, but the degree to which patrols on either side may have practised avoidance behaviour may never be known. Although companies holding the front line did open fire on German work parties, they carried out no significant attacks or raids. Overall, the battalion's policy could be described as one of "aggressive defence."

It is not surprising that the 19th Battalion's official records report nothing in the way of attempts to communicate with the opposing German trench garrisons, since this kind of behaviour was strictly forbidden. If incidents involving their own men had occurred, battalion officers likely chose to omit them from the unit's war diary and associated reports. However, some accounts of German troops hailing the Canadians were recorded. Many Germans spoke either passable or excellent English, and significant numbers had lived and worked abroad throughout the English-speaking world – Canada included. Cpl. E.S. Richardson reported that during the 19th Battalion's very first tour in the trenches in September 1915, the opposing Germans would toss notes over to them in empty jam tins or "call over in very plain English and ask about different cities in Canada. Just how they came to know we were Canadians is a mystery," said Richardson, "but they did, and in fact know a whole lot more than we give them credit for."[70] The overtures from their opponents continued. On 27 September the 19th Battalion reported: "Much yelling from enemy lines last night inquiring for cigarettes and beer." That this probably was more in the line of a joke or some form of mockery on the Germans' part was shown later that same morning, when "at 11 AM they fired back into D 2 trenches the rod of one of our rifle grenades with a copy of the *Kriegsflugblatter* dated Lille Sept 22 attached."[71] The Germans also took opportunities to comment on the accuracy of Canadian musketry. On 5 October the 19th Battalion informed 4th Brigade headquarters that "at 10:15 PM last night a working party of 10 or 12 enemy was dispersed by our rifle fire. Immediately after our fire a voice was heard saying 'wrong direction no good.'"[72] Similarly, on 17 October, "one Bosche exposed himself on a couple of occasions and shouted and whistled to us. When fired upon he shouted back … and waved a pole with red disk."[73]

Yet the men of the 19th were not content to be the butts of German taunts and certainly gave as good as they got in the heckling department. William Poppelwell of A Company recounted an incident in which a four-foot rubber tube, with a cigarette holder complete with cigarette placed at one end, was used to trick German troops:

> One cigarette in the dark was hoisted on its stick up above the trench and the smoker sat down under cover on the firestep and kept the "fag" going through the rubber tube ... When Fritz saw the cigarette glow he naturally thought one of those dumb Canucks was forgetting himself, for bullets began to fly around, first in single shots and the cigarette was pulled down sharply so as not to invite suspicion too early. After a few seconds the cigarette was hoisted aloft again and more shots were fired at it. The boys in the bay began to enjoy the fun and while keeping well under cover kept the cigarette going up and down.[74]

Not all was "fun and games" between the opposing troops, and retaliatory measures often were taken by both sides for acts of violence. For example, on 30 November 1915 the 19th Battalion reported to the 4th Brigade that "for the past 3 days our companies have been very aggressive and ably supported by the artillery have kept the enemy very subdued. Retaliation today seems to prove that they must have had some damage or casualties."[75] Later, on 18 February, it was noted that "attitude of enemy, alert. A relief has taken place since our last tour and these [troops] are more aggressive and are willing to hand back everything we give."[76] This latter report underscores the significance of troop rotations, as well as the fact that activity levels within a given sector could change, depending on the character of the opposing units. Some men found these minor actions rather sporting. Wrote Maj. Millen on 19 February:

> We had a merry little bombing strafe with the Germans opposite one section of my trenches. He started it by chucking over some big bombs, we went back with our trench mortar gun and rifle grenades. We kept it up for about an hour and a half, each trying for the last word. We got it in the end. They did us no danger, whether we did any to them, we don't know. Can only hope we did.[77]

Most of the serious damage on both sides of no man's land was caused by artillery, which participated fully in the "tit for tat" nature of fighting during this period. On the whole, the 19th Battalion concluded that the Canadian artillery's response to episodes of German shelling was "very prompt."[78] But the ability of gunners to do more than merely answer their German counterparts was circumscribed by the limited quantities of ammunition available during 1915. This confined the Canadian artillery's activities mainly to "retaliatory measures" and engaging "targets of opportunity."[79] Moreover, while the effects of artillery fire were impressive from the visual and aural perspectives, its awesome destructive power was undercut by occasional inaccuracy. Remarked Millen in mid-October 1915:

> Some days are very quiet, others it's a perfect inferno of a row when the artillery are banging at one another. Of course we don't know just what damage our artillery are doing, but it seems a positive waste of theirs. The other day they dropped a bunch of big shells in rear of us that must have cost $8,000 to $10,000, with no more damage than making a water cart leak a little.[80]

However changeable the levels of violence may have been, the pressures of life on the Western Front were such that most men on both sides of no man's land would gladly have welcomed the end of hostilities. To be sure, now that they were in the middle of it, the men of the 19th Battalion were driven onward by a sense of duty to their comrades and by a determination to see the war through to a victorious conclusion. Yet few would have disagreed with the sentiment overheard in the German lines one night by a patrol from the 18th Battalion, which reported one German saying to another in English, "Say Bill, I wish we were back in Chicago."[81]

5

Trial by Fire: St-Eloi, April 1916

After the opposing Allied and German armies failed to gain a decisive advantage through manoeuvre in late 1914, the battlefront in France and Belgium congealed and both sides set about devising solutions to what has been termed the "riddle of the trenches."[1] The Germans, wisely trading a certain amount of space for tactical superiority, tended to establish their defensive positions on higher ground, which in many parts of Flanders rose only a few yards above the surrounding countryside. Yet even a minuscule advantage in height afforded an improvement in observation, especially for the artillery spotters, who directed the gunfire that dominated the fighting. The British, French, and Belgian armies, although often situated on lower ground, were determined to deny further territory to an invading force that already occupied most of Belgium and a significant portion of northeastern France. The Belgians and French were especially anxious to regain these lost territories, which in the French case were home to a good deal of the nation's industrial and mining resources. The British were similarly determined to maintain the security of the French Channel ports, the possession of which by the Germans would threaten the Royal Navy's dominance in the English Channel and the security of England itself. So the Allies deemed it vitally important to maintain their hold on key transport and communications centres near the front lines such as Ypres and Arras.[2]

The city of Ypres had additional symbolic importance for the British, for it was there that the surviving regulars of the original British Expeditionary Force (BEF) had made their successful stand in October and November 1914 – and died by the thousands in the process. However, the Germans had made better progress both north and south of the city, so that by the time the front had stabilized, Ypres stood at the base of a bulging salient jutting into German-occupied Belgium. German artillery could thus fire into British positions east of the city from three sides, making the salient a particularly deadly location in which to wage war. What was worse, as a result of the First and Second Battles of Ypres in 1914 and 1915, the Germans had also gained possession of most of the scythe-shaped swathe of higher ground overlooking the salient from the south and east. This afforded them advantages in observation and in the ability to screen the locations and movements of their own troops and guns from British ground observers. But the strategic and emotional importance the British attached to Ypres compelled them to maintain their grip on the salient for the remainder of the war, and contributed to the notion that ground must be held at all costs, no matter how disadvantageous it might be from a purely tactical standpoint.[3] This, then, was the operational environment in which the 19th Battalion, and the rest of the Canadian Corps, found itself in the spring of 1916. The imperative to retain territory was combined with the high command's policy of ceaseless aggression, so that the British armies would not lose their offensive spirit.

Battle for the Craters at St-Eloi: Strategic and Tactical Overview

Canadian involvement in the battle for several large mine craters near the tiny Belgian village of St-Eloi in April 1916 stemmed from the loss of British positions at a point in the Ypres Salient known as the Bluff on 14–15 February. The initial counterattacks to regain this lost territory met with little success, and at Second Army headquarters the decision was soon taken to exact retribution and carve off a slice of German-held ground at another point in the line. The position chosen for this retaliatory strike was the small German salient just south of British-held St-Eloi, some three miles south of the city of Ypres. In this sector the trenches ran in an east–west direction instead of the usual north–south configuration that typified much of the British-held portion of the Western Front. The diminutive salient near St-Eloi was around 600 yards wide and extended 100 yards north into British-occupied territory. The principal feature of this German position was a low artificial bank of rubble and earth called the Mound. Half an acre in area and originally thirty feet in height, the Mound had been reduced by shelling during the previous year. Nevertheless, it continued to afford the Germans an advantage in observation over the surrounding territory. For Gen. Sir Herbert Plumer, GOC Second Army, this was a position that was worth denying to the enemy, and he set about laying plans to capture the Mound while simultaneously working to recover the Bluff.[4]

The Bluff was recaptured on 2 March; even so, Plumer continued with his plan to seize the Mound. In fact, there already had been long-standing designs to deal with this position, as evidenced by the progress that had been made in

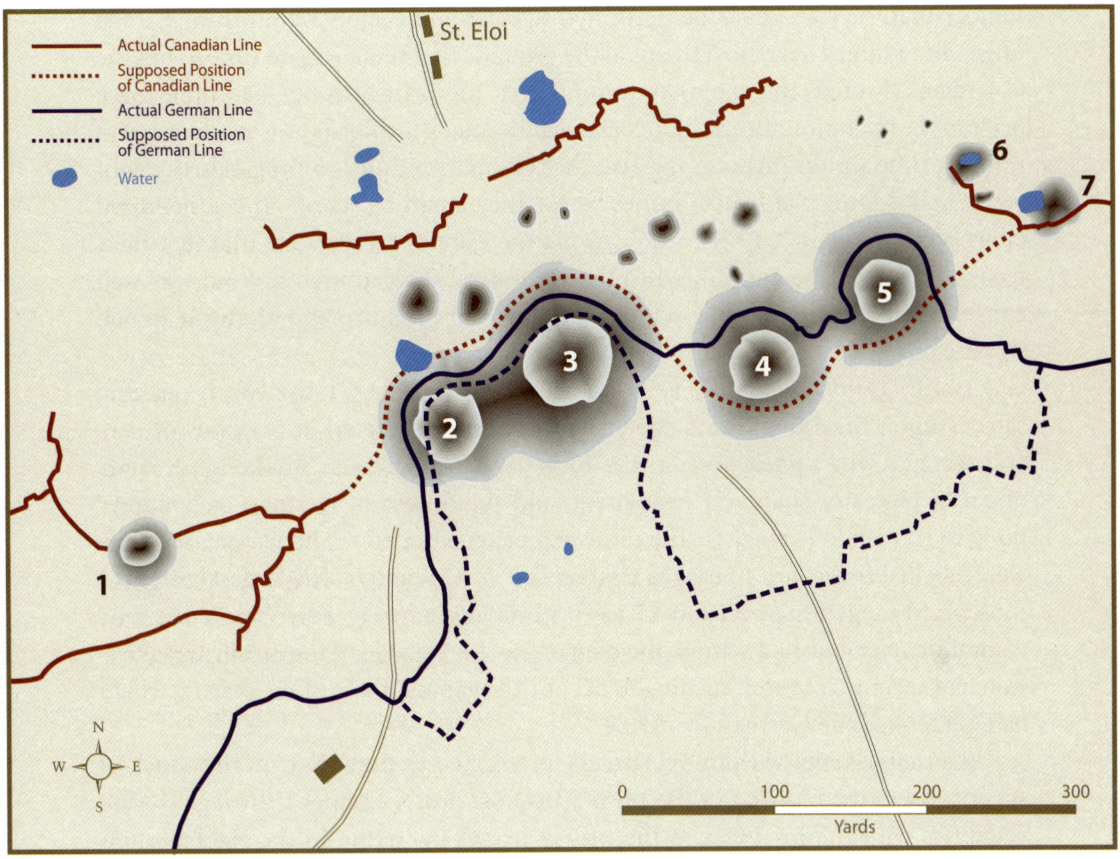

Map 3 – St-Eloi Craters.

underground mining operations in that vicinity since August 1915. The geology of the sector made mining possible, and three large shafts had been sunk well behind the British lines. These were pushed steadily forward throughout the autumn and winter months until they had reached the area directly under, and adjacent to, German positions on the Mound. By March 1916, six galleries had been excavated under the German lines, into which were packed immense quantities of ammonal, the individual charges ranging from 600 to 31,000 pounds. From west to east, these mines were numbered from 1 to 6, the distance between no. 1 and no. 6 being 600 yards – the width of the German salient itself.[5]

The 3rd Division of the British V Corps was detailed to assault and occupy the salient once the mines had been detonated. According to Plumer's plan, after the objective had been taken and consolidated by British troops, the Canadian Corps would move in, relieving V Corps and assigning the 2nd Canadian Division to occupy the already secured objective. Leery of the risks involved in a large-scale relief on what was sure to be an active battlefront, the commanders of both the Canadian Corps and the 2nd Canadian Division made strong representations to

Plumer that the Canadians be permitted to carry out the operation from start to finish. But Plumer overruled them on the grounds that there was no time to put the Canadians through the extensive training that the British troops had undergone prior to the operation. In addition, delaying the attack to afford the Canadians extra training time would increase the risk that German counter-mining efforts might locate and destroy the British mines before they could be set off. Thus, the initial effort was to remain a British show, while the Canadians were assured that their troops would not be committed to the relief until the captured ground was well consolidated and the fighting had settled down to the normal patterns of trench warfare.[6]

At 4:15 AM on 27 March, forty-one guns and howitzers loosed their opening salvoes upon the Mound and the six mines were detonated at intervals of several seconds. The upheaval from the mines was stupendous. Smoke, dust, clods of earth, pieces of shattered equipment, and the bodies of German troops were flung to tremendous heights. The mine explosions created six huge craters, which were labelled from west to east as Craters 1, 2, 3, 4, 5, and 6. The largest craters (2 through 5) ranged in size from 45 to 70 yards in diameter.[7] Even before the dust from the explosions had settled, the men of the 9th Brigade of the 3rd British Division had sprung to action, rushing to occupy the gaping maws of the craters, which had obliterated the German front line.[8]

Their efforts met with initial success, predicated as they were on the shock of surprise from the blowing of the mines. In short order, Craters 1 through 3 were occupied, with minimal loss to the British troops operating in the right portion of the assault. On the left, however, it was a different story, for one of the British units had been checked temporarily in its advance by German machine-gun fire, which reaped a heavy toll, particularly among the officers. Even so, the troops on the left struggled forward, through a violent German counter-bombardment, and eventually reported that they had reached positions south of Craters 4 and 5. This proved to be an error. What they had done instead was occupy Crater 6 and an older depression later named Crater 7. Neither side held Craters 4 and 5, and for the next three days a dangerous gap existed in the new British line – a gap that was finally exploited by the Germans on 30 April, when they slipped troops into Crater 5 and began fortifying it. Through a combination of ground and aerial reconnaissance, the British also eventually figured out the situation, and on the same day that the Germans occupied Crater 5, the British moved into Crater 4 and established a machine-gun post.[9]

This confusion resulted mainly from what was termed the "changing landscape" of the battlefield at St-Eloi. The blowing of the mines had radically altered the once-familiar landscape of the sector containing the former German salient. Much of the Mound itself had been blown away and replaced by Crater 3. Meanwhile, both British and German artillery continued to churn up the surrounding terrain, which

One of the mine craters at St. Eloi. The photo was taken in 1919, but the landscape is still scarred from the terrible struggles of 1916. (LAC C-043979)

already had been ravaged by months of bombardment and earlier mining activities. In fact, some thirty-three mines and thirty-one camouflets already had been blown in a mere 10-acre area in this sector during the previous year. Even officers who had been familiar with the ground in this area now found it extremely difficult to orient themselves. Still worse, the huge mine explosions and attendant artillery bombardments on 27 March had disrupted the local drainage systems, creating a boggy moonscape of water-filled ditches, shell holes, and craters.[10] These conditions were exacerbated by rainy weather that compounded the drainage problem. The ground had taken on a porridge-like consistency, and the leaden and rain-swept skies had made aerial reconnaissance more difficult during the period when the gap existed in the new British line. On 29 March the weather improved enough for aircraft to go aloft, and observers took several "very good photographs of the mine craters" at St-Eloi that assisted efforts to assess the situation. As well, the fact that units of the British left and right flanks were not in touch with each other encouraged greater efforts at scouting on the ground, the results of which provided commanders with an increasingly accurate picture of the situation in Craters 4 and 5.[11]

After the British had discerned the truth of their dispositions among the craters, it took several more days of ferocious fighting before the Germans were finally ejected from their positions in Crater 5 on 3 April. By now, the battalions of the 3rd British Division, which had been rotated in and out of action since 27 March, were so horribly exhausted and depleted that the British Second Army had to dispense with the original plan, which had been to delay the 3rd's relief until the objective had been properly consolidated and the front settled down to a state of normal trench warfare. As a result, the Canadians were sent in ahead of schedule to take over a sector that barely had been secured and that still required consolidation. Moreover, there remained the possibility that the Germans would launch a counterattack in full force in order to retake the lost positions. The senior Canadian commanders had feared they would face this sort of situation. But all Maj.-Gen. Turner could do was steel his 2nd Canadian Division for a stint of hard work and peril the likes of which it had never faced before. The first troops sent in by Turner were those of Brig.-Gen. H.D.B. Ketchen's 6th Brigade.[12]

On the night of 3–4 April, Ketchen's men slogged forward through the desolate bog to relieve the shattered British units holding the crater sector. Pte. Donald Fraser of the 31st Battalion recalled an exchange between one of the incoming Canadians and a departing, distraught Englishman. "Cheer up! Don't be downhearted!" the Canadian urged. "You'll be downhearted," whispered the Tommy, "when you see what's up there; I have lost my best chums."[13] By noon on 4 April, Canadian Corps headquarters had taken formal control over the crater sector. This was the first time that an entire British corps had ever been relieved by another on an active battlefront.[14]

That day, Turner made a personal reconnaissance of the frontage for which his division was now responsible, and he was deeply disturbed by what he saw. There was no continuous front line at all in the area taken over by Ketchen's brigade – only a series of disconnected slit trenches, old German fire trenches, drains, and water-filled shell holes just south of the craters. But the worst feature was the absence of a communication trench through the centre of the crater sector, for this would seriously impede movement between the forward positions and those to the rear. Instead, troops would have to make their way around the flanks of the craters, and the four central craters (nos. 2, 3, 4, and 5) had been blown so close together that they effectively barred direct movement between the front and the rear. And even if the positions taken over by Turner's men had been relatively secure, they were under direct observation by German artillery spotters operating on the Wytschaete Ridge farther to the south, which left them exceedingly vulnerable to massed enemy artillery fire. The artillery formations supporting the Canadians enjoyed no comparable advantage in observation and were still subject to shell-rationing requirements. This fact alone calls into question the wisdom of the entire operation as conceived by Second Army headquarters.[15]

In the pre-dawn hours of 4 April, the men of the 6th Brigade, assisted by large parties from the 4th and 5th Brigades, the 2nd Canadian Pioneer Battalion, and engineering troops, began toiling feverishly in the gruel-like ground to construct a continuous defensive line on the southern slopes of the craters. Writing of the miserable conditions the Canadians endured, Lord Beaverbrook noted that "as men splashed from shell hole to shell hole – and the surface of the earth consisted of nothing else – they sank up to the armpits and could find no grip for their feet. One of the strongest men in the 2nd Division declared that after sixty yards of this work he was incapable of going further."[16] Moreover, the mud not only limited effective movement around the battlefield but also clogged the men's Ross rifles, often rendering them useless precisely when they were most needed.

The consolidation efforts were brought to an abrupt halt when battalions of the German 46th Reserve Division unleashed the anticipated counterattack in the early morning hours of 6 April. Beginning at 3:30 AM, a savage artillery bombardment rained down on the 6th Brigade men, blasting many of them out of their unfinished positions. Valiant and self-sacrificial assistance was offered by parties of Lewis gunners from all four battalions of the 5th Brigade, who had relieved their counterparts from the 6th Brigade earlier that night. Nevertheless, most of the Canadian positions in the crater sector were overpowered. Even the barrage from the British artillery batteries supporting the 2nd Canadian Division could do little to stem the attack, for the German infantry filtered through the maelstrom in small parties, employing tactics practised earlier at Verdun. They deployed inside the British barrage, drove back the surviving Canadians, and occupied Craters 2 through 5. Ketchen ordered immediate counterattacks, and later that morning word filtered back to brigade and division headquarters that parties from the 28th and 31st Battalions had retaken craters 4 and 5. But this proved to be inaccurate. In reality, the Canadians had only repeated the error made earlier by the British in mistaking Craters 6 and 7 for Craters 4 and 5. The misconception would persist for the next ten days, when successive attempts by the 6th, 4th, and 5th Brigades to recover Craters 2 and 3 were predicated upon the incorrect premise that Craters 4 and 5 were in Canadian hands. This led to faulty coordination of the Canadian infantry's efforts to advance from the flanks of Craters 2 through 5, to a regrettable absence of Canadian artillery fire on German positions around Craters 4 and 5, and to heavy losses for the 2nd Canadian Division. Poor weather hampered aerial observation from 8 April onward. It was not until 16 April that aerial photos revealed the awful truth of the situation.[17]

The 19th Battalion played its full share in this ill-starred operation, which was the 2nd Division's first real baptism of fire. Lt.-Col. McLaren's officers and other ranks acquitted themselves well in this, their first pitched battle, but they too had failed to perceive the truth of the Canadians' situation in the craters. It is to the 19th Battalion's particular part in the fight at St-Eloi that we now turn.

The 19th Battalion at St-Eloi

During February and March, the main efforts of the Second Army were directed towards retaking the Bluff and planning the assault at St-Eloi. Meanwhile, the

Canadian Corps continued to occupy the sectors immediately south of the Ypres Salient, between Ploegsteert and the trenches northeast of Vierstraat (a distance of some six miles). On 17 February the Canadians assisted the British by taking over an additional 700 yards of trenches, which brought them to the outskirts of St-Eloi.[18] These new positions comprised the O and P trenches, which adjoined the 19th Battalion's familiar haunt since 14 October 1915 – the M and N trenches.

After completing its thirteenth tour in the M and N trenches on 27 February, the 19th Battalion moved back to divisional reserve at La Clytte, ostensibly for eight days of well-earned rest. Soon, however, the battalion was ordered to make ready to move at fifteen minutes' notice. This period of alert lasted from 7:30 AM on 1 March to 11:30 AM on 3 March, while the British recommenced their counterattack on the Bluff. The Canadian Corps, on the southern flank of these efforts, assisted by simulating attacks of its own, employing smoke bombs and artillery bombardments and having the infantry stage noisy demonstrations – complete with cheering – in their own front-line trenches.[19]

On 5 March the 19th Battalion was rotated out of divisional reserve and relieved the 18th Battalion in the left sub-section of the P trenches, south of the village of Voormezeele. Two companies were situated in the front line, with one in support and one in reserve at Ridgewood. Following this first six-day tour, the entire battalion was relieved and sent back for a brief rest at Ridgewood. It then returned to the P trenches for a second tour of five days before being relieved on 22 March by British troops of the 8th Battalion, East Yorkshire Regiment (8th Brigade, 3rd British Division). The 19th Battalion once more returned to divisional reserve at La Clytte, where it remained for the next six days. At 9 PM on 26 March, the battalion stood-to and remained on alert throughout the following day while the 3rd British Division executed its assault at St-Eloi. The concussion and noise of the mine explosions in the early morning of 27 March must have been indescribable at La Clytte, for the blasts could be felt as far away as Folkestone in southern England.[20]

While the first phase of the battle for the craters raged, the 19th Battalion returned to the front lines on 28 March, this time relieving the 18th Battalion in the familiar M and N trenches. On 4 April its place in the line was taken over by the 9th Battalion, Durham Light Infantry, as the British V and Canadian Corps began exchanging fronts. The 19th Battalion then proceeded back to brigade reserve at Ridgewood, where it was relieved the following day by the 8th Battalion, Durham Light Infantry, and moved to a position called Camp E near the town of Reninghelst.[21]

At noon on 4 April, the Canadian Corps assumed control over the crater sector at St-Eloi, having completed its relief of V Corps. The principal feature of this exchange was the relief of the hard-pressed 3rd British Division by the 2nd Canadian Division, whose 6th Infantry Brigade took over the precarious positions in the crater sector. In the meantime, the remaining infantry brigades of the 2nd

Canadian Division were moved into positions from which they could furnish support and prepare to relieve their comrades in the front line.

In the early afternoon of 6 April, the 19th Battalion departed Camp E and marched to a field near the position known as Canada Huts. Earlier that morning, the Germans had launched their counterattack to retake the crater sector, and the 6th Brigade was suffering a severe mauling at the hands of enemy artillery and infantry. But the German artillery was pounding not only the Canadian forward positions. From their observation posts on the Wytschaete Ridge, German gunners were able to home in on targets well behind the Canadian front lines, and their heavy long-range guns did considerable damage throughout the day. Around 4:00 PM, the area around Canada Huts was heavily shelled, and the 19th Battalion suffered four casualties. Having endured the worst of the bombardment, the battalion remained in this vicinity until 11:30 PM, when it was ordered forward to Scottish Wood and Voormezeele. The 4th Brigade was working to relieve the battered remnants of Ketchen's 6th Brigade, and by noon on 7 April the former had taken control of the front line.[22]

The 4th Brigade was now under the command of Brig.-Gen. Robert Rennie, who had replaced Lord Brooke on 17 November 1915. Rennie, a Toronto businessman and militia officer, had until then commanded the 3rd Battalion in the 1st Canadian Division. In Canada, his family ran a well-known seed distribution company; hence, some of his men gave him the nickname "Bird-seed Rennie."[23] In the estimation of 19th Battalion veteran Joe O'Neill, Rennie "was really a marvelous Brigadier ... You perhaps wouldn't call him a colourful character, but he was efficient."[24] As a result, Rennie would retain his position at the head of the 4th Brigade until almost the end of the war. But for all his competence and experience, the utter chaos of the fighting at St-Eloi would prove too much for him – and his superiors – to handle. It did not help at all that he had inherited his predecessor's misconception concerning the actual location and status of Craters 4 and 5.

On reaching Voormezeele on 7 April, the 19th Battalion was ordered to move to Camp A, where it remained until 9 PM, at which time it finally was given the word to relieve the exhausted 31st Battalion in the front lines. The positions taken over by the 19th Battalion on 7–8 April stretched from Trench 18 to the Ypres-Comines Canal. B Company occupied trenches 18 to 20. This sub-section included what was thought to be Craters 4 and 5 but actually were Craters 6 and 7. C Company manned the line from Trench 21 to a point halfway to the canal, while D Company occupied the remaining stretch of trenches as far as the canal itself. In support was A Company, which was tasked with supplying carrying parties, mainly for B Company. The latter would be the hardest pressed of the 19th Battalion's four companies, occupying as it did the left portion of the crater sector. As a result, on 9 April, A and B companies would exchange positions, with A taking over Trenches 18 to 20 and B moving back to support. On the 19th Battalion's right, facing the central portion of the crater sector (Trenches 14 through 17), was the 18th Battalion from its own brigade. The 1st Battalion of the 1st Canadian Division took up positions to the left, on the other side of the canal. The 21st Battalion was placed to the right of the 18th Battalion, holding the P trenches through to Crater 1 (also known as Trenches 9 through 13), while the 20th Battalion stood ready in reserve at Scottish Wood and Dickebusch.[25]

Even in the best of conditions it took time and considerable organizational effort for one battalion to relieve another in the front lines. At St-Eloi the confusing nature of the terrain, the indescribably muddy conditions, which severely hampered movement of men and supplies, and the severity of German bombardments, which effectively restricted movement to nighttime (making it even harder for men to find their way about), all conspired to prolong the 19th Battalion's relief of 31st Battalion for over twenty-four hours. Fresh platoons of Ontarians filed into the scattered and extended positions held by the exhausted surviving Albertans, who staggered back through the glutinous muck and the gauntlet of German fire to reserve positions. Not until 11:35 PM on 8 April was the relief finally completed.[26]

While elements of the 19th Battalion trickled into their new positions, Brig.-Gen. Rennie ordered an assault on Craters 2 and 3. A party from the 21st Battalion was ordered to attack Crater 2; parties from the 18th and 19th Battalions were to attack what was believed to be Crater 3 but actually was Crater 5. This confusion resulted from misperceptions at all command levels as to the craters' identities and locations. Looking southwest from their positions in what they had been told was Crater 4 (but was actually Crater 6), the 19th Battalion men thought they were viewing the lip of Crater 3, but it was really Crater 5.

Lt.-Col. Ernest S. Wigle, CO of the 18th Battalion, was placed in overall command of the attack, which began at midnight, 8–9 April. The 19th Battalion contributed fifty bombers to the effort, as well as fifty more men to serve as a working party. On the left, the 21st Battalion's assault on Crater 2 was checked by heavy German artillery, machine-gun, and rifle fire. Meanwhile, things seemed to be going better initially with the 18th and 19th Battalions' attack on what they thought was Crater 3. The parties from both units worked their way forward until they found themselves at the edge of a large depression, or crater, with a considerable pool of water at the bottom. Having no previous experience of the ground in the crater sector, they assumed they had arrived at their objective. At 1:43 AM the 18th Battalion reported to 4th Brigade headquarters that it had reached the northern edge of Crater 3.[27]

Later, however, Lt. Bertram Hooper, leading the 19th Battalion bombers, reported that groups from both units had been forced to fall back in the face of severe bombing and heavy rifle fire from German troops, who seemed to be occupying a trench behind the crater's southern edge. When the ruckus had died down, the work party from the 18th Battalion was ordered forward to occupy and consolidate the area reached earlier by the bombers, since it did not appear that the Germans occupied the forward portion of the crater itself. Later, Hooper was sent out to locate the work party and discovered that the party had not reached the spot on the crater lip that the bombers originally reconnoitred. Instead, it had taken up position in some fragments of an old trench some distance to the north and east of the crater. It was extremely difficult for anyone to maintain their bearings in the crater sector that night, for a heavy mist covered the ground, which compounded the confusion generated by the sodden and grotesquely pitted terrain. Hooper reported the turn of events to Lt.-Col. Wigle, who ordered him and his men to return to their own headquarters. Day was breaking, and owing to the German artillery's dominance of the sector during daylight, there was little that could be done until the following night.[28]

The 4th Brigade ordered that operations be resumed on the night of 9–10 April in order to capture Crater 2 and strengthen the position at what was believed to be Crater 3. Once again, the 19th Battalion was detailed to assist the 18th Battalion in efforts at "Crater 3," this time by supplying a bombing party of eleven men led by Lt. Hooper to operate on the eastern side of the crater and protect the work of the consolidation parties detailed to occupy its lip. Given the uncertainty of the situation, and growing suspicions that German troops might now be occupying the crater itself, Hooper was charged with leading a preliminary officers' patrol to clarify matters. The patrol succeeded in reaching the point occupied by the 18th Battalion work party on the previous night, and the decision was made to summon the bombing and work parties from their assembly point on the northern outskirts of St-Eloi village. However, before this could be done, a Stokes mortar that had been detailed to support the operation opened fire prematurely, and this precipitated a rain of retaliatory bombing and artillery fire from the Germans that effectively put an end to the night's proceedings. Hooper and his party lay trapped in the bombardment, scrambling for what little cover they could find in the remnants of the old trench. The firestorm kept up throughout the night until dawn, when the beleaguered patrol made its way back to the assembly point near St-Eloi, with Hooper himself helping to evacuate three wounded men.[29]

That same night, reports of the 21st Battalion's efforts against Crater 2 sounded more favourable; bombing parties had apparently established themselves on the northern side of that crater. In the meantime, the 19th Battalion had maintained garrisons in what was believed to be Craters 4 and 5, and since the night of 8–9 April it had been working to strengthen the trench connecting the two depressions. During daylight hours, these two craters were held with thirty men each – a number that was increased to sixty at night. Lts. Hamilton Cassels and Archibald W. Macdonald initially were placed in charge of the parties in Craters 4 and 5, respectively. On the second night (9–10 April), Cassels was relieved by Lt. Harry B. Pepler and Macdonald was relieved by Lt. Russell B. Thomson.[30]

To the staffs at 4th Brigade and 2nd Canadian Division headquarters, it appeared that the position held by the 6th Brigade before the German counterattack was gradually being re-established.[31] Even though the position occupied by the 18th Battalion work party on the night of 8–9 April was not believed by Lt. Hooper and others to be on the actual lip of Crater 3, it must have been considered close enough for all concerned to suppose that the northern rim of the crater was reasonably secure. In any case, events would not bear out this optimistic appraisal of the situation. On the morning of 11 April, engineer officers sent up to help oversee consolidation efforts in front of what was supposed to be Crater 3 determined that the old trench occupied by 18th Battalion personnel was in fact just north of an older crater and was seventy-five yards north of Crater 3 (actually Crater 5).[32] Exactly why the officers and men of the 18th and 19th Battalions were unable to determine this for themselves is not clear, although Hooper's report to McLaren regarding the events of 8–10 April indicates that both he and Sgt. Jackson of the 19th Battalion bombing party suspected that the depression they had skirted on the night of 8–9 April might not in fact be Crater 3. Moreover, similar reconnaissance work had determined that the 21st Battalion was not occupying the northern rim of Crater 2. Like the 18th Battalion, the 21st Battalion troops had stumbled into a smaller crater in front of the objective. The closest position they held to Crater 2 was a bombing post at Point 96, "a grenade throw" from the crater.[33]

On 11 April, the Canadian Corps commander, Lt.-Gen. Alderson, sheepishly reported to Gen. Plumer at Second Army headquarters:

> It is evident that officers have reconnoitered the northern lips of Craters 2 and 3 but that the parties subsequently detailed to hold these points have not reached them, neither did the R.E. [Royal Engineers] parties detailed for work therein last night. The party to hold Crater 3 is evidently the party in the trench 75 yards short of it ... The whole place is a mass of craters and enormous shell holes full of water and mud, and movement is very difficult, and it is certain from the C.O's accounts that troops after falling from one hole into another do not know where they are. The holes are very deep and the men looking up against the sky line think they have reached the craters when they have not.[34]

Maj.-Gen. Turner, acutely aware of how badly this confusion reflected on the competence of his subordinates and himself, was anxious to renew efforts to seize Craters 2 and 3 once and for all. But he met with protests from the battalion commanders of the 4th Brigade, who pointed out that their men were exhausted and that most of the personnel in their bombing sections were casualties. As a consequence, Brig.-Gen. David Watson's 5th Infantry Brigade was ordered to prepare to relieve Rennie's formation on the night of 11–12 April.[35]

The 19th Battalion's exertions in the crater sector would soon end, but not before the men endured a stiff bombing assault by the Germans, accompanied by a violent artillery bombardment, in the early morning hours of 11 April. They held on tenaciously and ultimately repelled attacks on Craters 4 and 5 (actually 6 and 7). But the strain had been terrible, and Maj. Morrison, commanding A Company, sent word back to Lt.-Col. McLaren requesting that the projected relief be expedited as soon as possible. The "men appear very much shaken," he reported. "I am in [a] bad way personally from shell shock but trust relief will take place."[36]

Fred Stitt later recalled his own harrowing experience:

> I stopped a piece of five nine shell ... Two chaps behind me were blown to pieces ... Captain Eddy who was our Platoon commander he was hit badly in the face ... One of our platoon Sergeants was badly hit in the wrist and elbow, and the other Sergeant, the second Sergeant of the platoon, Fred Steel, he was hit in the face ... If memory serves, this Number 1 Platoon of which I was a member left a Lance Corporal and six men in that position to hold on. The rest of us were evacuated, wounded, with also two killed.[37]

According to one veteran, who probably was writing of the events on 11 April, so bad was the bombardment along the frontage held by C Company that its men were forced to pull back, temporarily leaving a gap in the line. It is unclear whether this action was sanctioned by Lt.-Col. McLaren and how long the gap was allowed to remain. In any case, according to the unnamed veteran, the men of No. 1 Platoon, to the immediate right of C Company, followed suit in withdrawing from their portion of the line. Both these parties were ordered back to their posts by McLaren, who declared that the position was of vital tactical importance and had to be held "at all costs."[38] Hold they did, and on 12 April the 19th Battalion began handing its positions over to the 26th Battalion, the relief being completed at 12:15 AM on the following morning. The 19th spent the next nine and a half days in divisional reserve.[39]

On 16 April, the weather, which had been dismal for several days, cleared just enough for aerial reconnaissance to be conducted over the crater sector at St-Eloi. The resulting photos came as a shock to senior officers at corps and division headquarters, for they revealed the inaccuracy of previous reports regarding the location of Canadian positions in the craters. For the past ten days, Maj.-Gen. Turner and his staff had been labouring under the assumption that their men held all but Craters 2 and 3 – sources in the front lines had repeatedly told them as much. Yet these latest aerial photos made it obvious that German trenches encompassed Craters 2 through 5; only now did the Canadians realize that instead of occupying Craters 4 and 5, they had actually installed themselves in Crater 6 and an older pit referred to as Crater 7. Aerial photos of the craters had been taken earlier, on 8 April; why the corps and divisional staffs had not been able to determine the actual situation from these images is not clear. Captain Duncan E. Macintyre, at that time the 6th Brigade's chief intelligence officer, claimed that the quality of the 8 April photos was "rather poor," which may have contributed to the error. Macintyre added that "a better understanding of airplane photography, which showed crater 7

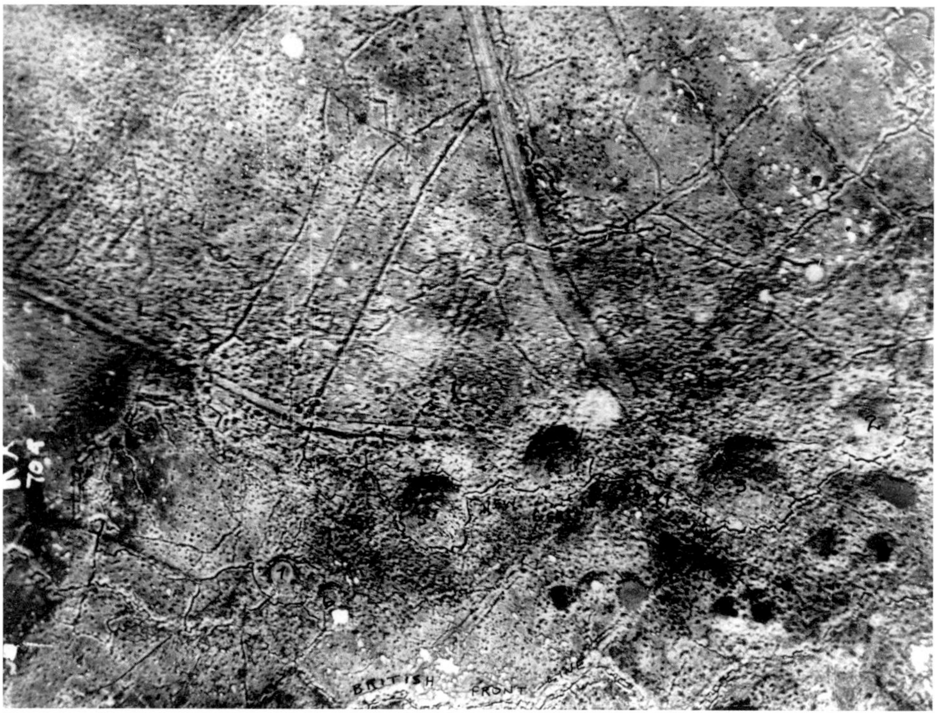

An aerial photo taken on 16 April 1916 of the craters at St. Eloi. The terrain has been reduced to a muddy moonscape. (LAC PA-004394)

to be half full of water while the others were comparatively dry, would have saved a lot of trouble, but at that time few of our officers had ever seen air photos and knew little about the reading of them."[40] More likely, staff officers examining the 8 April aerial photos had mistaken the German positions for their own, having repeatedly received reports from front-line units that Craters 4 and 5 were in their hands.[41] In any case, all efforts to recover Craters 2 and 3 came to a crashing halt as division, corps, and army staffs took stock of the situation and initiated inquiries to discover what had gone wrong.

Some factors were self-evident. The 2nd Canadian Division had been rushed into action on 4 April without an opportunity to prepare or to gather adequate intelligence, and it had been thrust onto an active battlefront in defensive positions that hardly deserved the name, so battered and fragmentary were they. Ketchen's 6th Brigade had worked hard to make the position tenable, but the Germans had launched their devastating counterattack on 6 April before that work could be completed and the men could gain a firm understanding of the terrain. Thus, the odds were stacked terribly against the Canadians. After the battle, McLaren echoed the view of other Canadian senior officers when he asserted that in trench warfare "the heaviest casualties come in consolidating positions after they are taken, and not in the taking of them."[42]

For his part, Lt.-Gen. Alderson pointed out that on 4 April it was "only fair to say that the line was taken over in the dark, no one knew the ground or the craters, and that the mud and water was waist high."[43] Even officers from the 3rd British Division, who had attempted to orient the Canadians to their new positions, found themselves utterly confused by the shattered and swampy landscape.[44] Throughout the battle, the men were unable to make sense of the terrain by night, even with the aid of luminous compasses and rudimentary maps, because in the dark each crater or shell hole looked like the next.[45]

Compounding the confusion was the physical exhaustion induced by struggling through the deep mud that covered much of the battlefield – mud that rivalled, if not eclipsed, what the Canadians would encounter later at Passchendaele. Such exertion disrupted the men's sense of distance regarding the amount of ground they traversed, which would have adversely affected their ability to judge where they were. Even if the ground had been relatively dry, movement by daylight was virtually impossible because of the deadly accuracy and intensity of German artillery barrages, which were directed by observers enjoying a clear view of the whole sector from atop the Wytschaete Ridge. Besides destroying defensive positions and killing and maiming men, the bombardments seriously hamstrung Canadian operations by frequently disrupting communication links and preventing daylight reconnaissance. The punishment the German gunners inflicted on the 2nd Canadian Division was extraordinary. In his appraisal of the bombardments that preceded the German counterattack on 6 April, a British artillery officer who had spent the previous year in the Ypres Salient described the intensity of the shelling at St-Eloi as "far greater than he had hitherto experienced."[46] Harry Neil went even further, arguing after the war that "at no time during the balance of the war did the 19th [Battalion] undergo such concentrated artillery pounding as at St. Eloi."[47] In summing up the debacle, D.E. Macintyre described the operation as "like poking a stick into a well-organized hornet's nest."[48]

The day after the 19th Battalion arrived in divisional reserve at Reninghelst, an exhausted Maj. Lionel Millen wrote to his mother: "I still have a bit of a tired feeling but probably after another good night's rest I will be feeling as fine as silk."[49] In fact, there would be little rest for the officers, given the considerable job that faced them in reorganizing their battered units and compiling reports on operations and the condition of their men. But amidst the tedium of paperwork, there was an opportunity for the officers to take stock of the many individual acts of heroism and outstanding devotion to duty they had witnessed during the previous week. Having come through their first real trial by fire, McLaren and his senior officers must have been proud of how their troops had acquitted themselves. During and after the 19th Battalion's tour in the crater sector, reports made to 4th Brigade headquarters highlighted the deeds of a number of individual officers and other ranks, of which a selection are presented here. They illustrate the heroic efforts and feats of endurance displayed by members of the battalion under the worst conditions they had yet faced.

Among the officers, Lts. Thomson, Macdonald, Pepler, and Cassels were lauded for their steadfastness in commanding the garrisons of Craters 4 and 5 (actually Craters 6 and 7). Majs. William W. Moors and Gordon F. Morrison were praised for their "conspicuous gallantry in command of companies" holding the craters "on the nights of April 8–9th and 10–11th respectively," as well as for their work in overseeing a detached telephone station that maintained communication between the forward positions and battalion headquarters back near Voormezeele.Lts. Burnham and Hooper (Military Cross [MC]) were singled out for their skill and fearlessness in directing patrols, scouting efforts, and the movements of work and bombing parties, as well as for their devotion in assisting with the evacuation of wounded. Many of the NCOs, such as Lance Sgt. L. Jackson (DCM) and Lance Cpls. G.A. McLean and J.M. Wardlaw, displayed exemplary coolness and leadership, often taking charge of small groups of men and carrying them through extremely difficult circumstances, such as holding various positions of tactical importance for extended periods and repelling German attacks. From 8 to 12 April, Lt. Herbert D. Fearman, in charge of the signals section, maintained communication links with the craters, "frequently passing through the enemy's barrage to repair and lay wire." In this work he was assisted greatly by numerous other ranks, including Pte. H.E. McLean, who "ventured forth eight times to repair breaks in the wire." Unfortunately, on his ninth sortie, "he was severely wounded." During the intervals when phone lines were cut, individuals like Ptes. Richard Ratcliffe and Edwin Trendell risked their lives as runners, carrying messages to and from detached forward positions under heavy fire, while guides such as Lance Cpl. W.C. Holtum helped many others find their way through the maelstrom.

The work of the machine gunners was vital in ensuring the security of the line occupied by the 19th Battalion. Ptes. D.C. Ballantine, A. Dunnigan, H.W. Sharpe, and W. Hull "volunteered to occupy a greatly exposed position with a machine gun. They stayed at their post [for] 70 hours," presumably without relief. In addition, after the crew of another machine gun had been wiped out by an enemy bombardment, Cpl. A.F. Lynch went out under "very heavy fire" and dragged the gun in, saving it for further use.

Finally, there were countless acts of selflessness in assisting others. To give but a few examples, Pte. C. Hagan carried Pte. Hoffman, who was wounded in both legs, to a place of safety 500 yards away. Lance Cpl. S. Bishop and Pte. E.D. Schwann (DCM) volunteered on 9 April "to carry food and water in broad daylight to the garrison of a crater which had been cut off 48 hours. They were held up by the enemy's intense barrage but succeeded in getting through at dusk." On the night of 11 April, Ptes. W. Heyburn and N.P. Stewart "crossed 400 yards of shell swept trench to render assistance to wounded men and to guide them back to safety." Likewise, Ptes.

L.M. Goodfellow and R.W. Ward, and stretcher-bearers W.C. Scott, G.H. Hughes, L.H. Moss, F.G. Thompson, and G.F. Arum, braved the worst of conditions to assist numerous wounded men.[50]

Meanwhile, as much as the men of 19th Battalion needed time to rest in divisional reserve after their ordeal in the craters had ended on 12–13 April, the situation at St-Eloi demanded that they supply a large work party of 3 officers and 400 other ranks on 17 April. This aroused some sarcastic comment from the still exhausted troops, but everyone knew that the position in front of the craters would not be improved without strenuous efforts. From 14 to 21 April, the 2nd Canadian Division continuously employed large numbers of men from its reserve units in rebuilding support and reserve trenches. This was in addition to the work being done by battalions stationed in the front line. On any given night, anywhere from 900 to 2,000 infantry were set to work, along with two companies from the 2nd Canadian Pioneer Battalion and two companies of Canadian Engineers. Despite these efforts, Maj.-Gen. Turner was disappointed with the results, which suffered greatly from the effects of the all-seeing German artillery and from the awkward handling of large groups of men over very broken and muddy ground. With so many men at work in a comparatively small area, the German gunners inflicted heavy casualties on the trench garrisons and work parties. Eventually, it was concluded that smaller work parties were preferable, for they caused less congestion and confusion in the communication trenches, were easier for the officers to handle, and consequently performed more work.[51]

At 2:00 PM on 22 April, the 19th Battalion left divisional reserve and made its way back to the front lines, once more relieving a 6th Brigade unit (this time the 28th Battalion) in Trenches 19 to 28 in front of St-Eloi. The relief was completed by 1:20 AM the next morning. C Company took up position in the left sub-section of the firing line, with D Company on the right and A and B Companies in battalion reserve. Increasingly warm conditions provided relief from the recent cold and wet weather, but the German artillery continued intermittent "strafes" of the Canadian lines. The companies in the line exchanged places with those in reserve on 25 April. Two days later the battalion completed this tour, being relieved by the 27th Battalion.

The Fallout from the Crater Fight

The fight for the craters at St-Eloi ended just before the 19th Battalion returned to the trenches on 22 April. On the evening of 19 April, a German raiding party, supported by a fierce artillery bombardment, drove the dazed defenders from the luckless 6th Brigade out of Craters 6 and 7. Subsequent reconnaissance efforts determined that retaking these two craters was impractical. They were completely untenable in daylight and were dominated by German positions in the much larger Crater 5. By dawn the next day, counterattack plans had been shelved. Ketchen's

Two views of Crater 4, St-Eloi. Viewing the site today, it is difficult to imagine the carnage that occurred here in March and April 1916. (Author's collection, 2015)

men were now ordered to consolidate their existing positions just north of the craters. Although German shelling continued to reap a grim toll on the Canadians for the rest of the month, the battle at St-Eloi was effectively over. Few who survived the fighting could recall it later without a shudder of dread. "It was a horrible place, St. Eloi," pronounced Fred Stitt.[52]

In the end, the Germans recovered all the ground they had lost on 27 March. They had suffered fewer than 483 casualties since their counterattack on 6 April.[53] The 2nd Canadian Division fared far worse, sustaining 1,953 casualties during the month of April, 125 of which were men from the 19th Battalion. Of these 125 casualties, 29 other ranks were killed and 3 officers and 85 other ranks were wounded by enemy fire. The remaining one officer and seven other ranks were wounded or injured in various accidental circumstances. The battalion suffered more than half its casualties (69 all ranks) on 10–11 April, ten of these as a result of "friendly fire" when three 18-pounder artillery shells landed short in Trench 26 early on the morning of 10 April.[54] In one month, the 19th Battalion had suffered only twenty-five fewer battle casualties than it had sustained during the entire period from September 1915 through to the end of March 1916.

Albeit on a much smaller scale, the hell of St-Eloi rivalled the inferno of Verdun, which was also raging at that time. But whereas the action at St-Eloi lasted a mere, but murderous, twenty-four days,[55] the "mincing machine" of Verdun would continue to rumble until December. Senior Canadian officers must have derived some comfort, however minuscule, from the French commander-in-chief, General Joseph Joffre, who "spontaneously thanked General Plumer for the operations" at St-Eloi, which, he said, were "an appreciable help to the French operations at Verdun."[56] In truth, because of its limited scale, it is unlikely that the battle at St-Eloi, savage as it was, had any notable impact on German efforts at Verdun. The fight for the craters did, however, have serious consequences for the Canadian command structure.

The dust at 2nd Canadian Division and Canadian Corps headquarters had not yet settled from the news of the crater misidentification on 16 April when a round of inquiries began in order to determine what had gone wrong and who was most responsible.[57] In his assessment, written on 18 April, Lt.-Gen. Alderson pointed to the events of 3–6 April as the root of the problem. The exhaustion of the 3rd British Division had forced the high command to commit the 2nd Canadian Division to the fray before the crater sector had been properly consolidated. It had been the 6th Brigade's misfortune to fall victim to an all-out German counterattack on 6 April before it had a chance to put up an effective defence, and in their initial attempt to recover the craters, Brig.-Gen. Ketchen's men had erroneously reported that they had captured Craters 4 and 5 when they actually had occupied Craters 6 and 7. All subsequent ground reconnaissance efforts were based on this premise, with the result that the error was not recognized until weather conditions permitted the taking of clear aerial photos of the craters on 16 April. "To sum up the situation," reported Alderson to Gen. Plumer, "I can only say that I think these troops were put into a very difficult situation and were heavily attacked before they had time to consolidate or make themselves acquainted with the ground." Yet, although he acknowledged the impact of cruel necessity and ill fortune, as well as the bewildering terrain and the pernicious influence of weather, Alderson was not prepared to let his Canadian subordinates off the hook. He asserted that they "did not … acquit themselves as creditably as I had hoped for … I am of opinion that it should not have taken 10 days for the Division concerned to have ascertained the exact situation of its troops, and the responsibility for the forwarding of inaccurate information during this period must rest with the 2nd Canadian Division."[58]

At Plumer's behest, Alderson identified the commander he believed was most to blame for the confusion – Brig.-Gen. Ketchen, whose 6th Brigade originally lost the craters and subsequently misidentified Craters 4 and 5 on 6 April. Alderson asked Maj.-Gen. Turner to submit an adverse report on Ketchen, but Turner stoutly refused, convinced as he was that the entire operation had been flawed from conception and that responsibility for it rested at higher levels. Alderson could not accept Turner's defiance, so he recommended that both Ketchen and Turner be removed from their commands. The squabble inevitably involved the commander-in-chief, Gen. Sir Douglas Haig, as well as Canada's general representative at the front, Sir Max Aitken (the future Lord Beaverbrook), who was a close confidant of Sir Sam Hughes. From his discussions with Aitken, Haig determined that the risk of a political row with the Canadian government was too great for him to approve of Turner's and Ketchen's dismissal, for both officers were well connected with the Canadian minister of militia, and Hughes wanted Turner in particular retained in his position. But keeping Turner on would be a clear slap in the face to Alderson, and in any case, it was impossible for Alderson and Turner to continue working with each other in light of recent events. Relations between the two had been strained ever since Turner's questionable showing as a brigade commander during the Second Battle of Ypres in 1915, and the disaster at St-Eloi brought the feud that had quietly simmered between the two commanders to a full boil.[59] As a solution to the command conundrum, Aitken and Haig decided that Alderson would have to be the one to go, and so, with the full approval of the Canadian government, it was arranged that Alderson be appointed Inspector General of Canadian forces in England, a post he would take up on 28 May 1916.[60]

During the battle for the craters at St-Eloi, the 19th Battalion had held its own. But its personnel must share in the collective responsibility for the confusion in identifying Craters 4 and 5. To be sure, they had inherited the misconception from the units they had relieved. Nevertheless, they had done no better than anyone else in recognizing that they actually were garrisoning Craters 6 and 7, as opposed to

Craters 4 and 5. As well, if the information from our unnamed veteran source is accurate, C Company's and No. 1 Platoon's temporary abandonment of their positions in the face of an admittedly horrendous German bombardment displayed a lapse in McLaren's ability to control events on his own frontage. It is true that McLaren's order to No. 1 Platoon to return to its position indicates that he regained control of the situation reasonably quickly, at least according to the anecdote. Be that as it may, the utter chaos of the fighting at St-Eloi left little scope for McLaren and his senior officers to exercise their own initiative or to keep a firm and constant grip on events in the most forward positions. Periodic breaks in telephone links left them dependent on runners for information, and the quagmire of the battlefield slowed the pace of movement – and information – to and from the front line. It was left mainly to the officers on the spot, such as Majs. Moors and Morrison, and most often to junior officers like Lts. Hooper and Burnham and those placed in charge of the crater garrisons, to direct their men as best they could. For the most part, this simply involved holding their positions in the face of heavy artillery bombardments and intermittent attacks from enemy infantry.

From 6 to 20 April, German infantry of the 46th Reserve Division, supported by overwhelming artillery firepower, seized and held the advantage at St-Eloi. Through their superior grasp of the terrain, these forces kept the 2nd Canadian Division off balance and consistently frustrated in its efforts to regain the mine craters. The subsequent loss of Craters 6 and 7, after the Canadians had properly identified the location of all the craters on 16 April, shows that even had Turner's men correctly identified their positions from the beginning, it may have made little difference with regard to their ability to recapture and hold the entire crater sector. The overwhelming dominance of the German artillery over the rather diminutive battlefield gave their troops a tremendous advantage, one that the Canadian and British artillery supporting Turner's division could not match, owing to limitations of observation and ammunition allotments. Still, correct identification of the St-Eloi craters might have saved some Canadian lives, for it would have permitted them to coordinate their offensive and defensive efforts more effectively. More important, it would have allowed Canadian and British gunners to devote some of their efforts to shelling German positions in and around the real Craters 4 and 5, which were thought to be in Canadian hands.

In the end, the entire operation had only a small chance of success because of its limited scope and the fact that the Germans enjoyed a decisive advantage in observation from the higher ground to the south. Putting out the eyes of the German spotters on the Wytschaete Ridge and suppressing their artillery through effective counter-battery action may have been the only ways to ensure the success of British and Canadian efforts at St-Eloi. Unfortunately, the logistical and technical capacity to do this would not come until later in the war.

6

"Trying the Nerves": May–July 1916

The chill, wet weather of April gradually gave way in May to sunnier and warmer conditions. But occasional rain showers and a high water table kept some sectors of the Western Front perpetually damp and muddy.[1] The 19th Battalion, weary from its work at St-Eloi, had been stationed in corps reserve at Reninghelst since 27 April and remained there through the first week of May. Pte. John F. Mould, a cook in A Company who recorded in vivid fashion his impressions of the events of the spring and summer of 1916, recalled that the first two nights in camp were not very restful, owing to two successive German gas attacks. "We felt very little effect from them, however," Mould wrote in his diary, "as the distance between us and 'Messines' [where] the attack was made was too far away to do any harm."[2] In addition, the men had recently received an improved type of gas mask termed the PH-helmet, which gave better protection against phosgene than the earlier P-helmet.[3] Following this initial annoyance, Mould noted that "splendid weather prevailed during the whole of our time here the men passing the time away with Football and other games, concerts were also arranged for the Battalion in the Y.M.C.A. Bands of other units also giving selections in Camp during the evening."[4]

On 8 May the 19th Battalion was called back to the trenches to relieve the 20th Battalion, beginning what would be a rather uneventful six-day tour in the "Left Sector" trenches between St-Eloi and the Ypres-Comines Canal. It would, in fact, be its only tour in the lines during May, something that no doubt pleased all

Left: Canadian soldier wearing a PH helmet, Shorncliffe, Kent, 1917. (LAC PA-056171)

Below: Cooks of the 19th Battalion, 1915. John Mould is seated on the far right. (AO F954, I0024379)

ranks, given the events of the previous month. But even a comparatively "quiet" tour exacted its toll in life and limb. Eleven casualties were sustained between 9 and 15 May, with three other ranks killed and eight wounded.[5] Although the opposing German troops made no offensive efforts, their artillery unleashed salvoes at Canadian lines at the slightest sign of movement during daylight.[6] As ever, the hours of darkness proved safer for work parties and patrolling. These ventures provoked occasional nervous responses from the Germans, who fired periodic machine-gun bursts across no man's land and hurled grenades into their own wire to discourage the Canadians from getting too close.[7]

At 11:45 PM on 15 May, the 26th Battalion completed its relief of the 19th Battalion and the latter unit proceeded back again to corps reserve at Camp D, Reninghelst. The usual rounds of inspections and drills were followed up by the regular demands for work parties, to which the battalion contributed as many as 8 officers and 400 other ranks on 18 and 20 May. According to Pte. Mould, even though the men must have been exhausted from their exertions, a general spirit of optimism prevailed throughout the unit, as if the men were making an extra effort to put the painful experiences of April behind them. He believed that

> no one would think their [*sic*] was any war on at all if they could have seen us any time marching to our Camps or even going in and out of the trenches everyone being quite happy and looking … the same way as they would when going on any ordinary walk in Canada. We all knew our lives were in danger most of the time so had to keep kind of jolly to forget about it.[8]

The attitudes of the officers helped establish this positive climate. "Don't think you will find a happier bunch of officers anywhere, than those in my company," declared Maj. Millen to his mother earlier that year. "It is always a case of poking fun at one another."[9]

On 23 May the 19th Battalion moved to Camp A at Reninghelst, relieving the 28th Battalion in divisional reserve. The following day, it was announced that "new steel helmets are being issued … It is expected that helmets for all ranks will shortly be complete and that each man will be held responsible for a helmet."[10] The round-brimmed Brodie pattern steel helmet (named for the engineer who designed it) had been adopted by the British army in October 1915. It took time, however, for production to supply sufficient quantities. In April 1916 there were enough available to equip only fifty men per company in the 2nd Canadian Division. Thus, the helmets were treated as trench stores, with units rotating out of the trenches handing them over to the units relieving them. But by late May, production had reached the stage where every man in the Canadian Corps could be issued a helmet, and by 3 June the "tin hat" would become part of their personal kit. Weighing two pounds and resembling an overturned washbasin, the helmet at first seemed to be a cumbersome nuisance to many soldiers. But a dramatic reduction in the frequency and severity of head wounds very shortly convinced them of its utility.[11]

The 19th Battalion remained at Reninghelst until the evening of 27 May, when it was transferred to Dickebusch, relieving the 21st Battalion. Upon arriving at Dickebusch, Pte. Mould noticed a great change in the state of the village. It had become a deserted ruin since they had last seen it in April. Part of the reason was

Top: Ernest Rapkin, Fred Tate, and Jack Ramsden. Ramsden sports the new "tin hat."
Above: Dickebusch Church. (MUA RC 0835)

that the area surrounding the village was now a hotbed of activity for British and Canadian artillery.[12]

Late in the day on 30 May, the 19th Battalion proceeded back to divisional reserve at Camp D, Reninghelst, after being relieved by the 29th Battalion.[13] During May 1916, the comparatively peaceful village of Reninghelst offered a stark contrast to the blasted rubble of Dickebusch. Maj. David J. Corrigall, a veteran of the 20th Battalion, penned an evocative description of conditions at Reninghelst during this period:

> In this quiet place one could at times almost forget the war. The pale green of the spring was giving new colour to the hedges and poplar trees, to the rolling hills and valleys of cultivated land and pasture. Smoke still came from the chimneys of houses whose

> owners worked in the fields about them and under the shadow of the windmill on a hill to the south of the village.

Still, the signs of war were everywhere: division headquarters billets, battalion camp huts, "motor transport columns, ordnance workshops, and supply depots … engineer dumps, railway sidings and artillery parks along the road to Ypres; horse lines, labour camps and salvage store, along the road to La Clytte."[14]

In addition to training regimens and sports and recreation, there were constant demands for working parties to improve the Canadian defences in the St-Eloi sector. On a daily basis, battalions stationed in divisional and corps reserve supplied parties ranging in size from sections to whole companies in order to assist the personnel of the engineering and labour units with excavating and improving new and existing trenches, dugouts, strongpoints, and communications links.[15] In addition, officers and other ranks from each infantry battalion, both individually and in small groups, were sent to various training schools and courses that had been established by brigade, division, corps, and army headquarters during the previous year. These training establishments provided more advanced instruction in various specialty subjects (such as the tactical employment of grenades, Lewis guns, and Stokes mortars); they also offered leadership training for junior officers and NCOs or for candidates deemed likely to be promoted to officer or NCO positions. Initially, corps and army schools had the primary responsibility for training selected officer and NCO candidates from the divisions under their authority. But as time went on, the divisions themselves assumed a greater share of this instruction (the 2nd Canadian Division began doing so in late 1915 and early 1916). In the meantime, advanced techniques in the engineering and weaponry of trench warfare were at the core of Canadian instructional programs at division and brigade levels.[16]

Some officers and other ranks saw time at a training school as a welcome change of pace from their daily routine. "You have no need to worry your head about my going to Trench Warfare School," Maj. Millen assured his mother. "To us it is a joke. It is just a school to teach trench building and protection, mostly under existing circumstances and conditions impracticable … All the officers are sent to courses at one time or another, and rather enjoy the change."[17] Millen's attitude notwithstanding, the corps, divisional, and brigade schools did serve a useful purpose. Because Canadian infantrymen would continue to receive the bulk of their training within their battalions, they needed quality instruction from their own junior officers and NCOs, whose teaching skills were, on the whole, improved by the training schools. This was important because training was a constant activity, and neither veterans nor newly arrived replacements were spared from it. Along with practical experience, training helped bring reinforcement personnel "up to speed" for service alongside the veterans. It also kept the "old sweats" on their toes, maintaining their own skills as well as the high level of discipline that officers and NCOs demanded

Canadians playing baseball. Baseball was one of the most popular sports among Canadian troops. (LAC PA-004155 & PA-001921)

and that the men usually derided. As had been largely the case in the autumn of 1915, battalion training syllabi during the spring of 1916 emphasized arms drill and inspections, bayonet fighting, musketry exercises (particularly rapid firing and readjustment of sights), the fitting and use of gas helmets, a half-hour to an hour of physical training per day, and various section, platoon, and company drills, both close order and tactical. Personnel in the specialist sections, such as the bombers, scouts, and machine gunners, received additional instruction in their respective areas of expertise under the watchful eye of their own officers.[18]

Recreation and Entertainment

Not every moment spent in reserve was given over to work parties, drill, and training courses. Time also was made in the daily routine for sports, recreation, and entertainment. Inter-company and inter-battalion sports matches were especially popular, and were encouraged by the high command as alternatives to other popular pursuits such as drinking, gambling, and consorting with prostitutes in the local towns and villages. Sports were promoted by officers as a means of providing "constructive recreation" and as a method for "imparting martial and moral virtues," such as esprit de corps, to the other ranks.[19] Football (soccer), basketball, track and field, boxing, and baseball (both indoor and outdoor varieties) were regularly played by the troops, especially from springtime through autumn. Officers were encouraged to take full part in these matches, and although they generally formed their own separate teams, they sometimes did play alongside the other ranks. On baseball teams, officers occasionally served as pitchers or catchers.[20] Lionel Millen was an enthusiastic participant and often pitched for his battalion's indoor baseball team. During the first week of May, when the 19th Battalion was stationed in corps reserve, Millen pitched two games, both of which his team won. "So you can see I am in pretty fair condition," he remarked to his mother.[21]

After a strenuous day on the training grounds or playing fields, many soldiers spent their evening off-duty hours relaxing or carousing in a local *estaminet*, which was a bar or café where the men gladly supplemented their monotonous army rations. Some *estaminets* were long-standing community establishments; others, especially in the zones immediately behind the front lines, were improvised affairs that had been set up by entrepreneurial proprietors in the front room of a farmhouse, an outbuilding, or a converted village shop. "Eggs and chips" (i.e., fried eggs and chunks of fried potato) were an *estaminet* staple and served as "a kind of early-twentieth-century fast food." As for liquid refreshment, hot tea or coffee was welcomed by tired men fresh from nights out on work detail. But beer and wine proved far more popular (even if occasionally watered down) and fuelled many a night of fun, raucous or otherwise.[22]

The *estaminet* has been remembered as "the focal point of a soldier's life out of the trenches," a venue in which "the men could feast … soothe their nerves with bottles of beer or 'van blong' [*vin blanc*], flirt with barmaids, and sing bawdy songs." In the postwar period, "it was a setting that came to symbolize much that was good about the soldiers' war. Indeed, if the symbols revered at unit reunions are any indication, the metaphor for the Great War was not mud, or barbed wire, or an endless row of headstones; it was the *estaminet* ... In short, the *estaminet* represented what the ex-soldier wanted to remember about his war experience."[23]

For those who were not keen on the boozing that typified *estaminet* culture, other diversions and entertainments were available, such as concert parties and cinemas. Concert parties were a form of amateur theatre put on by the soldiers themselves for the amusement of their comrades. Musical numbers and comedy sketches, with a strong vaudevillian flavour and sometimes featuring female impersonators, were the most popular presentations at these shows, which were organized by divisions, brigades, battalions, and other units. Some groups, especially the divisional concert parties, drew their talent from among the best singers, actors, and comedians in their respective formations. The most famous and enduring of the Canadian divisional troupes was the 3rd Division concert party, known as the "Dumbells," who after the war would enjoy tremendous success touring Canada, the United States, and England.[24] The 19th Battalion had its own concert party, but little information has survived about its composition, much less its formation, dissolution, and the frequency of its performances.[25]

Although not quite as beloved as the concert parties, cinemas and gambling also provided entertainment to large numbers of troops. By 1916, many British and Dominion divisions were running their own cinemas, and among the attractions, no film star proved more popular than Charlie Chaplin. The 2nd Canadian Division's cinema, operating out of a rented barn, was already established by the summer of 1916. In July alone, attendance reached 25,040 all ranks, with box office receipts totalling 6,522.50 francs.[26] With regard to gambling, Crown and Anchor was among the more popular games of chance, along with various card games. The thrill of risk and the joys of reward were all the more sweet because of the army's official proscriptions against gambling. Crown and Anchor was specifically forbidden in all areas occupied by the Canadian Corps. But in spite of regulations, enterprising men usually found ways to set up a game.[27]

Of all soldiers' pastimes, letter writing was the most personal and, sometimes, the most poignant, especially when the correspondence was directed to loved ones at home. That said, the other ranks could not post their thoughts with complete privacy. Under the security regulations, personal mail had to be read by censors in order to prevent the transmission of information (such as troop movements) that might be useful to the enemy should it become more widely known. One of a company or platoon commander's regular duties was to read through all outgoing letters from his men and censor any information deemed unsuitable for public consumption. "The men in the company write lots of letters," admitted Maj. Millen, "but before they are sealed, my officers have to censor them, quite a job, some are very amusing."[28] Expressing a sentiment common among Canadian officers, Capt. Robert N. Clements of the 25th Battalion admitted that most of the letters they read "were very much of a pattern. After reading a dozen or more the job became routine, something to be cleared up as soon as possible." To give the men some modicum of privacy, at least from their own officers, they were issued special "green envelopes" on a periodic basis. This meant that the censoring officer would not be from the writer's own unit but from another command – usually one of the base establishments.[29]

Although honour-bound not to divulge the contents of a man's letter to others, officers took notice when "once in awhile a real gem came along." As Clements

Bringing up mail from a dugout, September 1918. (LAC PA-003211)

during a meeting with Hughes in which Byng was subjected to a lengthy discourse on how best to handle Canadian troops, the minister concluded with the assurance that he was "never wrong." At Byng's immediate retort, "What a damn dull life you must have had, Minister!," even Hughes himself was reduced to fits of laughter.[37]

In time, Byng made an equally good impression on many of the Canadian rank and file. Ted Lang recalled that

> in the latter part of May 1916 one of the chaps in my platoon casually mentioned to me that he heard we had a new Corps Commander by the name of Julian Byng. The news meant nothing to us at the time as we had never heard of him. Little did we realize then that in less than a year we were to idolize him as the man who planned and carried out the capture of Vimy Ridge, bringing fame to the Canadian Corps throughout the British Empire.

Lang added that shortly after the capture of Vimy,

> General Byng inspected our Battalion. Broad of shoulder but tapering down to carefully gaitered legs, he seemed to look down on us from a great height and, to me at any rate, the blistering sun of the Khyber Pass in North-West India had left an indelible tan on his strong face. He moved slowly along our ranks asking an occasional question at intervals. His star was certainly in the ascendant at that time, but he took it all in his stride.[38]

But, popular and pragmatic as he was, Byng was still a "brass hat," and his rank represented the force of military authority against which many volunteers chafed. As tiresome as formal inspections were for most men, some revelled in their occasional success in "putting one over" on their superiors. Harry James, originally of the 19th Battalion's No. 4 Platoon, remembered an inspection during which Byng

> passed down the line checking each man on various items … On coming to me he made no request, but just reached down and fingered the little pocket on the left inside flap of the bottom of the tunic. Satisfied that my field dressing was all present and correct he passed on, blissfully unaware that what he really felt was a pack of cards, a vital part of my stock-in-trade at all times. My sigh of relief was combined with the thought that the high and mighty can sometimes be fooled by the humble and meek.[39]

The "June Show": The Battle of Mont Sorrel

At the beginning of June 1916, the Canadian Corps held the southeastern portion of the Ypres Salient, now with three divisions in the line. The 3rd Canadian Division, which contained the 7th, 8th, and 9th Infantry Brigades, had been organized near the end of 1915 and was commanded by Maj.-Gen. Malcolm S. Mercer (formerly GOC 1st Infantry Brigade). By the latter part of March 1916, the new division was occupying the lines from a point one-third of a mile north of the tiny village of Hooge southward to the position known as Mont Sorrel. In June, this stretch of trenches comprised the left sector of the Canadian Corps' frontage and was one of the most dangerous on the Western Front. The 1st Canadian Division held the centre sector, which faced the important German-held feature known as Hill 60, while the 2nd Canadian Division held the right sector, from the Ypres-Comines railway to the trenches in front of St-Eloi. In all, the frontage occupied by the Canadian Corps stretched for five and a half miles.[40]

The 1st and 2nd Canadian Divisions had experienced traumatic baptisms of fire during the battles of Second Ypres and St-Eloi, and the first major operation involving the 3rd Canadian Division would be no less harrowing. The struggle would erupt on 2 June and become known as the Battle of Mont Sorrel. On the heels of one of the most vicious bombardments yet seen on the Western Front, troops of the XIII (Royal Württemberg) Army Corps advanced and seized roughly 1,000 yards of front from the 3rd Canadian Division. The German assault cost the Canadians not only the key heights of Mont Sorrel, Hill 61, and Hill 62, but also two of their most senior officers. Maj.-Gen. Mercer was killed during the bombardment, and Brig.-Gen. Victor Williams, GOC 8th Infantry Brigade, was wounded and taken prisoner. The attack was shocking in its intensity and was all the more horrifying for the Germans' use of flamethrowers, a weapon to which most Canadian troops had never before been exposed.[41] For Byng, it was a terrible beginning to his tenure as commander of the Canadian Corps. A bad situation was made even worse when the initial Canadian counterattack, which Byng rather hastily ordered on 3 June, was repulsed in bloody fashion. As a result, some who had gained a favourable early impression of their new corps commander may have found themselves suddenly questioning his ability. But, as the battle progressed, any doubts regarding Byng's skill would be laid to rest.

The 2nd Canadian Division was fortunate to be on the sidelines of the worst of the fighting on 2–3 June, although all units were on full alert, expecting that further German attacks were in the offing at any moment. The 19th Battalion was stationed in divisional reserve at Reninghelst when the Germans struck the 3rd Canadian Division on 2 June. On the following day, which saw the first desperate but unsuccessful Canadian counterattacks to retake the ground lost to the Germans, McLaren's men were kept in close billets, still in divisional reserve, and "held in readiness to move at 15 minutes notice." On 4 June the 19th Battalion was moved to Dickebusch, where it relieved the 29th Battalion of the 6th Infantry Brigade, and spent part of the next day in billets. However, McLaren soon received orders to relieve the 8th Battalion of the 2nd Infantry Brigade (1st Canadian Division) in the trenches.[42]

A stint in the trenches could hardly have seemed more dangerous than their billets at that time, for before the 19th Battalion men could vacate, German artillery found the range, and one of the houses they occupied received a direct hit. "It was in the afternoon when the heaviest of the shelling took place," reported Pte. John Mould, "one shell unfortunately for us, hitting one of the houses which our fellows occupied. This I am sorry to say accounted for another 14 of our Battalion, 4 being killed and 10 wounded. It is not very pleasant to witness such things as these and fairly upsets a man's nerves for the time being."[43]

The relief of the 8th Battalion commenced at 8:30 PM on 5 June and was completed by 12:30 AM. The 19th Battalion now found itself occupying the line from Trench 33 to the Ypres-Comines railway. This time, it was necessary for all companies to take up positions in the lines, A, B, C, and D Companies being disposed from left to right.[44] "The trenches which were situated in a large wood, formed a very strong position and one which would be very difficult to take from us," remarked Pte. Mould of A Company.[45] Later, in the course of a walk around parts of the line held by other companies of the battalion, Mould noticed that "the ground was literally lined with shell holes ... the trees which could also be seen for miles were cut right through the middle by shells their not being hardly a whole tree left standing. No doubt this district was the worst part of the whole line, the fighting which took place their [*sic*] being more severe than any part of the British front [*sic*]."[46] Nature itself was not the only casualty: strewn over the ravaged landscape was ample evidence of the human cost of earlier battles. The ground, churned up by successive bombardments, yielded a grisly harvest of corpses. One veteran remembered

> [the] bodies of dead Germans and Gordon Highlanders lying around and the odour was quite offensive. When attempting to put through a communication trench at night, we found some evidence of the fury of this battle when we came across a German and a Highlander locked in a death embrace. The Highlander had his fingers sunk deep into the throat of the German and the German had his arms wrapped around the Highlander and a knife sunk between the ribs.[47]

In support of the 19th Battalion on 6 June was one company of the 1st Battalion (1st Infantry Brigade). On the 19th Battalion's right flank were their comrades in the 18th Battalion, while men of the 5th Battalion (2nd Infantry Brigade) took up positions on the 19th Battalion's left flank.[48] The employment of troops from the 1st Canadian Division to serve as the 19th Battalion's support, and the 6th Infantry Brigade's movement (by order of corps headquarters) into the trenches around Hooge to relieve the exhausted remnants of the 7th Infantry Brigade, illustrates the extreme fluidity of the situation in the Canadian Corps sector. Units of different brigades and divisions served alongside and in direct support of one another as required by the ever-changing situation. Unfortunately for the men of the 6th Brigade, after having just barely settled into their new positions they would be hit hard yet again when the Germans blew four large mines in front of Hooge on 6 June. For Brig.-Gen. Ketchen, it must have seemed like St-Eloi all over again, except now it was the Germans who were blowing the mines. Two hundred yards of trench occupied by two companies from the 28th Battalion were obliterated in the blasts. The remnants of the 28th Battalion worked desperately with the 31st to throw back the German units advancing on the heels of the mine explosions, with the 27th and 29th Battalions fully committed in support. Ketchen's men tenaciously and successfully fought to maintain the integrity of their support positions, but the weight of the German advance was too much for the dazed survivors of the mine attack to handle, and they were compelled to withdraw from the front lines around Hooge.[49]

While these grim events unfolded on 6 June, the German artillery laid down a heavy drumfire along the Canadian lines, which exacted a considerable toll in casualties. On that day alone, the 19th Battalion saw four other ranks killed and two wounded.[50] And it was not only the German artillery that was active in the 2nd Canadian Division's sector. Although the 4th and 5th Brigades were situated well to the south of the 6th Brigade's trial at Hooge, the threat of more widespread German attacks appeared all the more likely when a raiding party assaulted positions known as Pollock and Bean trenches, held by the 18th Battalion.[51] The 19th Battalion immediately organized a party of bombers and sent them down the line to assist. But when the bombers arrived on the scene, they found that the 18th Battalion garrison had the situation well in hand. As the surviving German raiders retired, they were annihilated by Canadian artillery and trench mortar fire.[52] The fighting was especially ferocious in this sector because the Canadian and German trenches were so close together. Pte. Mould pointed out that "the distance across No Man's Land that separated us from the Germans was a matter of only 30 yds and both sides were able to drop bombs, rifle grenades, and trench mortars into each other's trenches quite easily."[53]

Duels between opposing artillery dominated the fighting along the Canadian front during the week of 2 June, with each side attempting to pummel the other into submission. Mould likened the noise of the shells whizzing overhead to "an express train going at full speed during the best part of its journey."[54] Mould reported that at 6:00 AM on 7 June, just after the Canadian artillery had opened up "a fierce and rapid shelling" of the German front line,

> the Huns retaliated … and between the two the whole place was nothing but a mass of bursting shells the deadly sound as they exploded and the awful vibration which followed, trying the nerves of every one around, quite a number having to be taken away with 'Shell Shock' … I was very lucky in not being hit myself as 2 pieces which landed at my feet just missed me by a matter of a few inches. All these narrow escapes are treated as a joke amongst the fellows. They generally passing it off with "You nearly got a 'Blighty' that time," this meaning a trip to England.[55]

Many men affected such sanguine attitudes as necessary coping mechanisms. Later that summer, Mould insisted that

> no one knew what was in store for them during their stay in the trenches and of course had to look on the bright side of everything. If ever a man had set his mind on what was going on around him he would have gone crazy as the bursting of shells would

> have played on his nerves that much that he would hardly have been able to move. I have seen some awful cases of "Shell Shock" and if possible I found something to occupy my mind during a heavy bombardment.[56]

But even amidst the mayhem, there could be curious, fleeting moments of beauty. Around 1:00 AM on 9 June, Mould was on duty and noticed that a lot of flares were being shot into the sky along the front lines. He later wrote:

> As I looked around on both sides, a fine sight met my eyes. For fully five minutes the sky was illuminated with a steady flow of light which enabled me to view the surrounding country for miles. As the light fell upon the Ruins of Ypres and into the Woods surrounding the Trenches I could not help but admire the lovely scene which stood before me. One by one the "Star Lights" fell to the ground, gradually hiding everything from view and leaving the whole place in complete darkness. The only thing then that disturbed the stillness of the night, being the heavy rains and the "Roar of the Guns" as they sent out a deadly fire into the German trenches.[57]

On 11 June, after what had been a rather harrowing tour in the trenches, the 19th Battalion was relieved by the 21st Battalion and moved into support, where it would remain until 17 June. During the 19th Battalion's time in support, the Canadian Corps launched its counterattack to regain the territory that was lost to the Germans on 2 June. The effort had been delayed until 13 June on account of poor weather and the setback at Hooge. In the meantime, an impressive array of artillery fire support had been assembled, much of it of very heavy calibre. Three battalions of the veteran 1st Canadian Division, under Maj.-Gen. Arthur Currie, were assigned the task of retaking the ground around Mont Sorrel, Hill 61, and Hill 62; simultaneously, a battalion attached from the 3rd Canadian Division would push into Sanctuary Wood to reclaim positions lost there.[58] Turner's 2nd Canadian Division was charged with securing both flanks of the assault, the 4th Brigade covering the right flank while the 9th Brigade, which had been placed temporarily under Turner's command, oversaw the left. The battered 6th Brigade remained in its positions near Hooge. These formations carried out various demonstrations and fended off local retaliatory strikes while the battalions from the 1st and 3rd Canadian Divisions swept forward behind a massive bombardment, successfully reached their objectives, and dug in.[59]

Faithful chronicler Pte. Mould, stationed with his company at a support position known as Bedford House, left an evocative description of these events as the Canadian attack commenced at 1:30 AM on 13 June:

> At 2 AM in the early hours of morning, the Canadians after a gallant charge through mud and rain regained the ground lost by us a few days ago. Not much difficulty was experienced in taking back the trenches this being mainly due to the fine work of our artillery during the last 4 days. Very little fight was put up by the Germans our boys capturing 153 prisoners and 4 officers.

Then German artillery retaliated:

> Hundreds of shells at lightning rapidity were sent over into the line occupied by our men this causing hundreds to be wounded from the shrapnel which fell all around the trenches. Our guns which were replying to the Germans very effectively from all parts of the line gradually silenced those of the enemy and at 4 AM hardly a sound could be heard all along the whole line.
>
> But the respite was short-lived:
>
> As soon as we got the news that the trenches were to be taken back every man had to be in readiness fully equipped and ready to move off at a minute's notice. As we were standing to we were subject to a very heavy shell fire from the enemy who were by all appearances trying to put some of our guns out of action. Several times they came very near their mark, the shells seeming to burst right in front of the guns. Some very brave work was accomplished by our artillery men during the bombardment[,] they sticking to their posts as if nothing was happening. The captain also giving his orders to fire whilst shells were bursting in all directions around him.[60]

Bedford House, Mould's vantage point, had an ADS staffed by field ambulance personnel. Here, Mould saw first-hand the terrible human cost of battle:

> I had not been there long when I heard the first ambulance wagon stop outside the Dressing Station with its first batch of wounded, this being the start of the saddest scene it had ever been my lot to witness. All through the day a steady stream of ambulances were bringing in wounded men … The condition of some of the poor fellows was too horrible to describe … A great number of them also suffered from "Shell Shock" most of these having been buried with shells during the heavy bombardment. German wounded were also brought here these numbering about 50 in all. Most of these were serious cases and were attended to with the same kindness as was shown to our own fellows. Speaking to some of the wounded they told me that they were proud to know that they had given the Huns all they asked for and that with a bit of luck would also get a good trip to "Blitey" [*sic*] (England). Wounded were still being brought in when night came, the men of the 1st Field Ambulance doing everything in their power to get the men away as soon as possible. At 10 PM the artillery on both sides began to get very active again and kept up a continual fire all through the night.[61]

The Canadians recovered much of the ground they had lost, but they had fared worse than their opponents in terms of casualties. All told, the Canadian Corps suffered over 8,000 casualties from the 2nd to the 14th of June; the Germans lost 5,765 during the same period.[62] Nevertheless, the Battle of Mont Sorrel was a key moment in the development of the Canadian Corps. Although many of the supporting artillery units were British, the counterattack of 13 June was the first large-scale "Canadian show" of the war, having been planned and executed entirely under the authority of Canadian Corps headquarters. The attack succeeded because sufficient time had been taken to assemble overwhelming artillery support,

Dugouts in the tortured landscape of the Ypres Salient, Summer 1916. (LAC PA-000086)

gather the necessary intelligence, and coordinate the infantry units involved. Byng was determined not to repeat the failure of 3 June, and he ensured that great care was taken in preparing the corps' plan of attack.

Clever use had been made of the artillery, which, in the days leading up to the assault, had identified and bombarded selected German strongpoints, alternating periods of intense fire with intervals of comparative calm. This left the Germans confused as to the timing of the operation. The Germans' uncertainty was further compounded by the early hour at which the Canadians launched their attack, the use of smokescreens that preceded the infantry, and a final intense artillery bombardment that effectively paralyzed much of their defensive capacity. The Canadian infantry also demonstrated a growing capacity to innovate. Some of the attacking units moved into no man's land before zero hour in a bid to avoid any retaliatory action from the German artillery.[63]

None of this is to say that the operation came off without a hitch. For instance, some overcrowding and confusion occurred among the infantry in the assembly areas. This caused temporary difficulties in moving the assault units forward and was exacerbated by the effects of rain and the attendant mud. Breakdowns in telephone communications as a result of shellfire also bedevilled Canadian efforts; but this was not a new problem, nor was it one that would be easily solved for the remainder of the war.[64] But in the end, the greater thoroughness in preparation that marked the successful Canadian counterattack at Mont Sorrel set the stage for the

Infantry resting in reserve trenches, June 1916. (LAC PA-000165)

deliberate, structured offensive style that would characterize Canadian operations in 1917 and 1918. The 19th Battalion and the rest of the 2nd Canadian Division served in auxiliary roles during this attack; even so, they would benefit from the lessons learned and the experience gained at Mont Sorrel.[65]

Business as Usual

After the fighting at Mont Sorrel settled down to a state of "normal trench warfare," the Canadians remained in the Ypres Salient and assumed a "stationary yet aggressive" posture.[66] On 17 June the 19th Battalion, which had been placed in support during the previous six days, relieved the 21st Battalion in the left sub-section of the 4th Brigade's frontage. For Pte. Mould, the ensuing tour "was for my part the most trying time I had ever experienced. Both day and night for the whole 6 days ... was one continual roar of shell fire ... Our total [casualties] for the week numbering around 60, of these 10 were killed whilst the others were badly wounded."[67]

On 23 June the 19th Battalion was relieved by the 21st and marched back to brigade reserve, settling for the following six days into a position named Micmac Camp. Then on the evening of 29 June, the men were rotated back to the front line, to the same trenches they had occupied during the previous tour.[68] On 1 July, the first Dominion Day they had spent in the trenches, traditional holiday activities were out of the question, but there was a fireworks display of sorts, courtesy of the Canadian artillery, which at noon unleashed three salvoes from all guns against the

Best G.S. limbered wagon competition, Canadian Corps Horse Show, 19 July 1916. It is not clear whether Lt. Hatch's section participated in this competition, but the image is probably typical of such events. (LAC PA-000245)

German lines.[69] But far greater – and grimmer – events were unfolding that day as General Haig launched his huge offensive at the Somme, which had been planned for some months past. Contemporary accounts from 19th Battalion members do not indicate that they were aware of the scale and nature of operations on 1 July. Certainly, no mention is made of the tragic outcome: the British assault divisions suffered 57,470 casualties, of which 19,240 were killed or died of wounds. The total number of casualties on that single day in fact exceeded the British army's combined losses in the Crimean War, the South African War, and the later conflict in Korea. Although some formations pushed ahead farther than others, notably in the southern sectors of the advance, in no case were any of the attacking divisions able to reach the objectives assigned to them.[70] It was fortunate for the Canadians that they were not involved in this disaster, although a battalion of infantry from the future province of Newfoundland was tragically decimated during its share of the 29th Division's attack. In time the Canadian Corps would become deeply embroiled at the Somme – but not before September, and only after undergoing a period of strenuous training.

On 4 July the 28th Battalion relieved the 19th in the trenches and the latter marched to Ontario Camp at Reninghelst for an eleven-day stint in divisional reserve. The rest of the 4th Brigade was also pulled out for a rest, its units having collectively endured thirty-five days of service in the lines, with many men not having had a chance to bathe for more than forty days.[71] During the 19th Battalion's time at Reninghelst, the usual full slate of physical, weapons, and tactical drills were administered by platoon officers and NCOs. Pte. Mould, who had recently returned to his company from hospital, where he recovered from a bout of influenza, noted that the battalion's work was the usual drudgery of "Physical Drill and Route Marches" but that the "weather was all that could be desired and their [*sic*] was all kinds of sports in which to pass the time away." The men took a keen interest in news of the "big push" at the Somme, and the propaganda machines of the day had already begun to place as positive a spin as possible on the grinding British offensive. Mould wrote that "great excitement was also seen in camp when the news came each day of the splendid British victories that were taking place in the Big Drive that had just commenced. The French and Russians were also performing great deeds and between the three the Huns were experiencing a pretty warm time."[72] Such naive optimism would not last out the summer.

During their time in reserve, the men of the 19th Battalion were subjected to a round of high-level inspections, first by Lt.-Gen. Byng on 7 July and then by Brig.-Gen. Rennie on the following day. Byng's inspection presumably was more low-key, as he made his rounds while the men were at work training and exercising. Rennie's inspection, by contrast, was a more formal affair, with the battalion being drawn up on parade for the occasion.[73] The inspections carried out on 8 July at the 4th Infantry Brigade's horse show at Reninghelst garnered far more interest from the ranks of the 19th Battalion, because their Transport Section under Lt. Hatch won the championship cup. The presence of Lt.-Gen. Byng, as well as Maj.-Gens. Turner and Lipsett (the new GOC 3rd Canadian Division), added to the lustre of "the most successful show in the Canadian Corps up to that time."[74]

On the evening of 15 July, the 19th Battalion returned to the trenches, this time in its old section in front of St-Eloi. Here the men spent the next sixteen days in Trenches 22 through 28, where they had relieved the 25th and 27th Battalions. This would be the longest single tour the battalion would undertake in the lines over the course of the war. Fortunately, the extended stint began quietly enough, with only sporadic shelling from artillery and mortars and some occasional bursts of heavy machine-gun fire to break the monotony.[75] The amenities in these trenches had improved greatly since the 19th Battalion last occupied them. Instead of sandbagged dugouts, the troops were now quartered in tunnels, which had been excavated at a depth of some forty feet, some of which could accommodate up to 200 men.

A Change of Command

An even bigger change for the battalion came on the morning of 18 July, when Lt.-Col. McLaren left for England en route to Canada, having been appointed to take command of a training brigade. The precise reasons for McLaren's recall are murky; the only specific one on record is Maj.-Gen. Turner's opinion that "John I" was too old for battlefield command. McLaren was not the only battalion commander in the 2nd Canadian Division about whom that pronouncement had been made. Lt.-Cols. I.R. Snider (27th Battalion), J.L. McAvity (26th Battalion), and E.S. Wigle (18th Battalion) also were considered by Turner to be somewhat "long in the tooth" for active service at the front and were likewise shuffled off to various training commands, either in England or Canada.[76] Whether Turner had additional grounds for replacing any of these officers is not yet clear, but certainly there was a wave of "housecleaning" throughout the 2nd Canadian Division in the wake of the failed operations at St-Eloi.[77]

Just before leaving, McLaren made a last tour of the front trenches, shaking hands, saying goodbye to all ranks, and offering to visit their friends and relations at home if any wished it.[78]

After arriving back in Hamilton at the end of July, he told reporters that

> there are many men from Hamilton at the front serving their country right now who are more worthy of honor than I am. If I had been a few years younger I would have kicked over the traces at coming home at the present time. We are now in a position where we know that we are on top in this game. After a few months' rest I hope that I can again join the boys at the front.[79]

This statement supports the notion that McLaren was recalled because of his age and diminishing stamina; it also implies that McLaren himself was not against the idea of returning home for a rest.

The question of McLaren's tactical competence is a difficult one to resolve. The fighting at St-Eloi was the most extensive and intense action experienced by the 19th Battalion during McLaren's time in command. But the exceedingly complex nature of that operation makes it a somewhat unfair forum in which to judge the capabilities of a commanding officer who at the time was a comparative novice when it came to leading men in a pitched battle. By April 1916, McLaren had been at the front for over six months and had fairly mastered the skills necessary to command a battalion during periods of relatively static trench warfare. Although leading a green battalion into the treacherous environment of the Western Front, and overseeing its gradual maturity into a unit that was efficient in holding the line, was an achievement worthy of some consideration, this may have been as far as McLaren's abilities went. The fact that Maj. Turnbull, who succeeded McLaren as commanding officer, was almost eight months *older* than McLaren leads one to suspect that McLaren's superiors were wary either of his tactical ability or of his capacity to stand further physical or mental strain.

It is conceivable that McLaren simply pushed himself too hard for his own good. J.H. Fitzgerald, a 19th Battalion veteran who returned home to Hamilton during the war (presumably to recover from wounds), recounted in the *Spectator* an occasion when both McLaren and Turnbull "took a sporting chance to visit the boys" in the firing line at great personal risk to themselves. According to Fitzgerald,

> The communicating trench [*sic*] had been washed away in places by recent floods, and it was impossible to gain the front line by this way, but this did not stop the colonel, who never missed visiting the firing line when the battalion was in action, and took the same chances and risks as the rest. We observed two figures coming across the fields, in full view of the Germans, and we all knew the terrible risks these two were taking … We even tried to signal them to turn back, but nothing doing; on they came, and made their objective, the firing-line, in safety. When we knew it was the colonel, along with Major Turnbull, who had risked their lives to see the boys, can you wonder at the boys feeling proud of such a noble commander![80]

Perhaps McLaren was brave to the point of foolhardiness – an undesirable trait in a commanding officer. Yet according to Fitzgerald's undated anecdote, the same criticism could be levelled at Maj. Turnbull. Possibly McLaren did such things more often than Turnbull; or perhaps the instance described by Fitzgerald occurred during one of the battalion's first tours in the trenches during 1915, when both officers were still inexperienced. In any event, it is strange that the two most senior officers in the battalion put themselves in such great danger at the same time. During the Battle of the Somme in 1916, stricter regulations would come into force, at least during battalion attacks: either the commanding officer or his second-in-command was required to remain behind, thereby ensuring continuity of command should one or the other become a casualty. In the end, setting aside reports that Turner had concerns about McLaren's age, the fact that Turnbull assumed McLaren's position as commanding officer despite being several months older leads one to conclude that "John I" was sent home because he was worn out, or because he had displayed some weakness in a faculty of command for which solid evidence has yet to be found.

Regarding his successor in command of the battalion, McLaren informed reporters at home that Turnbull "is as competent a commanding officer as there is with the Canadians. He has a good staff of officers and there is not an officer or man in the battalion who would not give his life, if necessary, for Major Turnbull."[81] Such glowing testimonials to Turnbull's ability were only to be expected in statements to the press and echo the effusive praise seen earlier in Harry Adie's dispatches to the Hamilton papers. But if Turnbull initially had failed to live up to expectations, as Lionel Millen implied in a letter to his mother in November 1915 (see Chapter 4), he evidently developed into a competent leader and administrator, or at least competent enough to be accepted by Brig.-Gen. Rennie and Maj.-Gen. Turner as a suitable replacement for McLaren. Later in the autumn of 1916, Millen would admit that he and Turnbull "get along fine together," which may not say anything about Turnbull's quality as a commanding officer but suggests that Millen's opinion of Turnbull had improved over time. At the very least, Millen respected Turnbull sufficiently that they were able to work together effectively.[82]

Indeed, Turnbull's ability to deal with a potentially difficult tactical situation was highlighted by the 19th Battalion's performance on the evening of 25 July, when the Germans exploded a mine under positions held by 1st Canadian Division troops in the Bluff sector. The Germans' action had been anticipated; steps had already been taken to evacuate or reduce the garrisons in the positions most likely to be mined, and supporting artillery and machine-gun units throughout the sector and on either flank had been placed on alert to stop any German advance. When the expected mine explosion occurred at around 9:50 PM, casualties among the infantry were minimal and Canadian artillery laid down a heavy barrage on the German front line. At the same time, machine gunners, including those of the 19th Battalion on the south bank of the Ypres-Comines Canal, swept the ground east of the smoking mine crater, aiding the artillery in keeping the German infantry pinned down in their trenches while troops from the 1st Canadian Division moved to secure the new crater. The Canadians maintained their firm grip on the Bluff, and Maj.-Gen. Currie expressed his gratitude for the prompt action of the 19th Battalion's machine guns in lending support to the 1st Canadian Division.[83] It was an auspicious beginning to Turnbull's tenure as commanding officer. But before the end of July, his battalion would distinguish itself in a far greater feat.

7

A Daylight Coup and Departing Belgium: 29 July–August 1916

Near the end of the 19th Battalion's marathon tour in the trenches from 16 to 31 July 1916 came an event often spoken of in subsequent years – the battalion's trench raid on the morning of 29 July. As noted earlier, by late 1915 aggressive patrols had evolved into highly organized trench raids carried out under cloak of darkness. These types of activities marked the first two principal styles of offensive trench warfare as practised by the Canadians. With its assault on the morning of 29 July 1916, the 19th Battalion inaugurated a third style – the daylight raid.[1]

During the first week of July, Gen. Plumer paid a visit to 2nd Canadian Division headquarters and "expressed the wish that everything possible would be done to keep the enemy in a nervous frame of mind." With this prompt, Maj.-Gen. Turner and his brigadiers encouraged their battalions to design and carry out "minor enterprises, raids, etc. … as much as possible, not only with a view to keeping the enemy on the alert, but also to obtain identifications, which are always required." These instructions were duly noted and passed down to company commanders in the 19th Battalion on 7 July.

Once the Canadians had recovered sufficiently from the stress of heavy fighting at St-Eloi and Mont Sorrel, they set about fulfilling the high command's wishes with a vengeance. The 2nd Canadian Division alone planned around twenty-five raids and offensive patrol enterprises between 27 June and 15 August, of which twenty-two were carried out. Eleven of these exploits were rated by divisional headquarters as partly or completely successful in their efforts to penetrate German lines, inflict casualties, secure prisoners or identifications, and damage or destroy defensive positions such as machine-gun nests. The remaining operations were thwarted by a variety of factors including enemy vigilance, the presence of barbed-wire obstacles that were stronger than anticipated, or the brightness of moonlit nights when utter darkness was required for movement across no man's land.[2] It was in this climate of accelerated offensive activity that the 19th Battalion decided to mount its own raiding effort.

On the night of 20–21 July, just over a week before the 19th Battalion launched its raid, some excitement occurred that served as an effective warm-up for the raid itself. A patrol led by Lt. Owen S. Dunn, proceeding towards German lines along an old abandoned shallow trench that stretched across much of no man's land, encountered an enemy patrol of three men heading towards them. Dunn quickly drew his revolver and fired, wounding one of them. Shortly afterwards, following an exchange of grenades between the Germans and Canadians, Dunn found the soldier he had shot. The German was carried back to the Canadian front lines, from where he was bundled off to headquarters for interrogation. He proved to be a member of Infantry Regiment 124 of the 27th Infantry Division (2nd Royal Württemberg), XIII (Royal Württemberg) Army Corps.[3]

Planning the Venture

Meanwhile, preparations for a full-scale raid were in high gear within the 19th Battalion. The patrol encounter buoyed the spirits of everyone in the unit. The upcoming raid would be the only offensive operation executed by the battalion during the summer of 1916. Its purpose was twofold: to confirm the identity of the German unit stationed opposite them; and to locate evidence of enemy equipment and facilities for employing gas along that section of the front. Although the patrol encounter of 20–21 July had yielded a useful identification, the possibility that the Germans would soon rotate their units meant that such intelligence needed frequent updating.

While the motivation for the raid is clear enough from surviving documents, it is more difficult to determine who the principal architect of the raid was and who first made the audacious suggestion of attacking in daylight – something that previous raiding parties had not dared to do. A post-armistice article in the *Hamilton Spectator* recounting the raid, which by then had become a key event in 19th Battalion lore, claimed that Lt.-Col. Turnbull planned the venture, while a commemorative history of the 4th Infantry Brigade reported that Lts. Hooper and Burnham were the organizers.[4] One suspects that the "dynamic duo" of Hooper and Burnham was most responsible. As members of the raiding party itself, they certainly would have been instrumental in designing the operation.

Whoever the principal organizer was, the project would never have come off without Turnbull's sanction. Since raiding had until then always been a nocturnal activity, Turnbull would have needed a great deal of courage and confidence in his subordinate officers to lend his support to such a novel idea as a daylight assault. According to the *Spectator*, he "placed his proposition before his superior officers, but they were unfavorable to the venture, believing that it was too risky."[5] Finally, reported the *Spectator*, Lt.-Gen. Byng "was acquainted with the project." Evidently intrigued by it, "he shook hands with Col. Turnbull and wished him good luck."[6]

One vital factor that gave the 19th Battalion officers the necessary assurance that their idea could work was the terrain along their particular sub-section of the front. A number of old trenches and ditches criss-crossed no man's land in front of the battalion, and at that time they were reasonably dry and afforded wonderful cover for small teams of men to crawl or scurry across. The rest of the ground was somewhat uneven, much of it broken pastureland and a series of hollows. This also furnished decent cover for crawling or for a covering party to lie prone and monitor events.[7]

The raid was scheduled for the morning of 29 July. During the week leading up to the event, careful scouting of no man's land and the proposed entry point in the German line was carried out by parties led by Lts. Burnham and Hooper.[8] This reconnaissance showed that conditions for the raid continued to appear favourable, and on 28 July final orders and instructions were issued.

The entire operation would involve four officers and thirty-four other ranks from the 19th Battalion, supported by machine gunners from the 20th Battalion and the 4th Brigade Machine-Gun Company, as well as five field batteries from "Stewart's Group" of the divisional artillery.[9] The raiding party itself, consisting of eighteen other ranks, would be commanded by Capt. Charles Kilmer, the battalion machine-gun officer, assisted by Lt. Harry Pepler, a platoon commander from A Company. They were to crawl up the old trench used by Lt. Dunn's patrol on the night of 20–21 July. This trench, often referred to as a "ditch" in the post-action reports, cut across no man's land towards the point selected for entry into the German front-line trench. The raiders then would proceed through a gap cut in the German wire on the previous night. Once in the enemy trench they were to break up into three smaller groups, one moving twenty yards to the left of the entry point, the other twenty yards to the right, and the third to remain in the centre. All groups were to bomb dugouts and note any evidence of gas equipment or the presence of mine shafts. Only the centre group was charged with securing prisoners for intelligence purposes. Both Kilmer and Pepler would remain with the centre group to

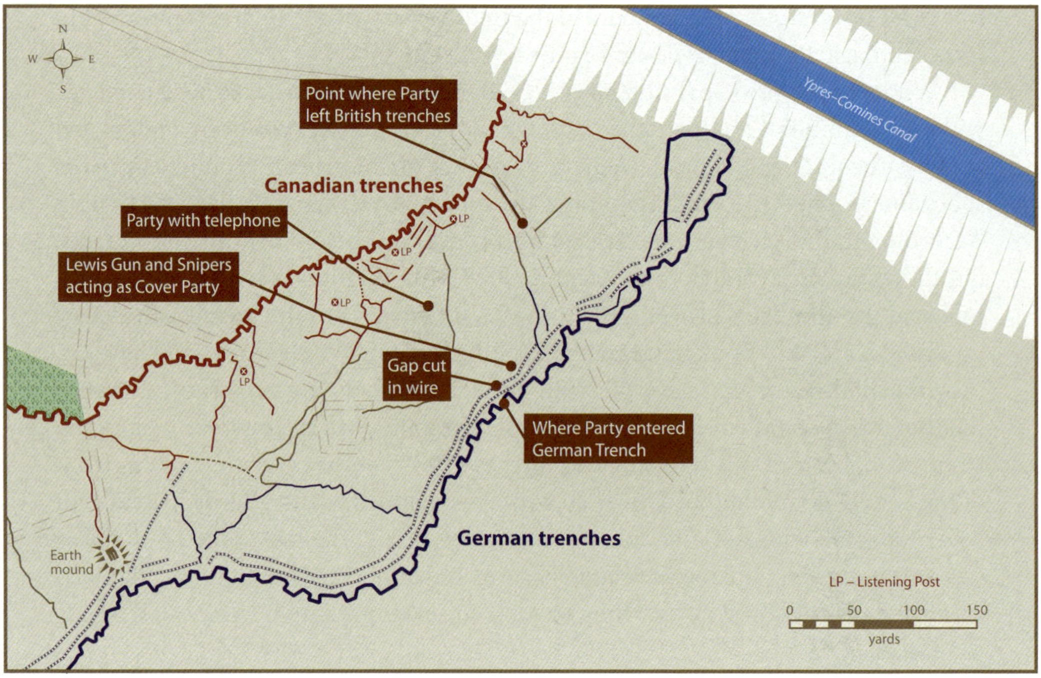

Map 4 – Daylight Trench Raid, 29 July 1916.

direct the operation and to give the signal to withdraw after the groups had been in the enemy trench for no more than five minutes.[10]

The raiders would be supported by two other parties. The first, under the command of Burnham, consisted of three bombers, four snipers, and one Lewis gun team of two men. They would remain at the head of the old trench used to reach the German wire and would provide cover for the raiders during both the assault and the retirement. The second party, under Hooper's command, comprised seven other ranks, including scout Sgt. Edwin Trendell and a telephone operator. One of their jobs was to occupy the rear portion of the old trench, near the Canadian front line, and help evacuate wounded men and prisoners during the raiders' withdrawal. But most important, they were to maintain telephone communication with the forward observation officer (FOO) from the artillery, who was stationed in the Canadian front line, and provide instructions for additional artillery fire support, if needed. Hooper and the telephone operator were to take up their position some 100 yards beyond the Canadian parapet.[11]

All officers and NCOs were instructed to carry two grenades; six men of the raiding party and two men of the covering party were to carry four additional grenades (six in total). The rest of the other ranks in the raiding party would carry rifles, bayonets, and fifteen rounds of ammunition. They would travel lightly, taking little or no additional equipment, except for four wire cutters and two seven-yard-long mats. The mats would be used in case the men detailed to cut the wire on the previous night were unable to complete their work. In that event, the mats would be flung over the top of any remaining uncut German wire, compressing it downward and creating a crude bridge over which the raiders could scramble.[12]

The 19th Battalion machine-gun section would traverse the flanks of the raiders' point of entry in the German parapet. At the same time, the 4th Brigade machine-gun company would enfilade enemy positions to the left of the 19th Battalion's subsection of the front, while the machine-gun section of the 20th Battalion enfiladed positions to the right. The supporting artillery batteries, along with medium and light mortar units, would open fire on the German front line to the right and left of the point of entry, as well as on German support trenches and nearby machine-gun emplacements. The signal for the bombardment to commence would be given only after the raiding party entered the German front line.[13]

Into the Breach

Through the night of 28–29 July, Ptes. Norman A. Wheadon and Cecil J. Rule performed the nerve-wracking work of cutting their way through the formidable web of barbed wire that masked the point in the enemy parapet selected for the raiders' entry into the German front-line trench. As they went about their task, the clipping sound of their heavy wire cutters was masked by fusillades of machine-gun fire that played along the length of the German parapet.[14] In the meantime, the raiding, covering, and rear parties steeled themselves for the dangerous work ahead. It was broad daylight when they finally left their own lines by way of a tunnel through their own parapet that led to a listening post. They then moved into the shallow abandoned trench that cut across no man's land towards a point near the gap in the enemy wire cut by Wheadon and Rule.

Members of the rear party took up their positions closer to Canadian lines, Lt. Hooper and the signaller with his telephone making ready to call in the artillery barrage at the right moment. The raiding and covering parties had the farthest to go, crawling in single file 120 yards through the abandoned trench and reaching a point within forty-five yards of the German parapet. The raiders then left the cover of the trench and rushed headlong towards the wire, hoping that the cutters had accomplished their task. Fortunately, Wheadon and Rule had done a superlative job. After dropping his mat, Lance Cpl. Wilfred Wilson "made for the trench getting on to the parapet where I drew my revolver and fired at three or four Germans who were running down the trench." It was 8:55 AM.[15]

Immediately, one group consisting of Sgt. John Holk and five men darted to the left, while a second group of five men led by Cpl. Harold Brisbin rushed to the right. Capt. Kilmer, Lt. Pepler, and Cpl Allen Lynch, along with five additional men, remained in the centre to anchor the operation and support the two flanking parties. According to Holk, the trenches were

> in first class condition and very deep, I should say about 8 feet. The sentry in the bay ran to the left and he did not see us until we looked over the parapet. He had no rifle or equipment on when we saw him. He ran into a dug-out and we threw a bomb in after him, and by the sounds we judged there were six or more men in it. The next bay also had a dug-out and Pte Montgomery threw two bombs in it, a lot of yelling issued from this dug-out.[16]

Montgomery reported that

> on jumping the parapet I saw a German almost in front of me … I threw a bomb without pulling the pin, which struck him in the back. He was so close, that had I pulled the pin, it would have endangered my companions and myself. He ran on about a bay and a half and turned to the right into a dug-out. I threw a bomb and they started squealing. Just then a bullet whizzed past me and looking up I saw three men about fifteen yards away, with what looked like a machine gun. Pte. Livingstone threw a bomb which went wide. I threw one which went right into the bay and exploded. I saw a gas box similar to ours about one bay to the right of where the machine gun was.[17]

Pte. Walter Nettleton also noticed "wooden boxes similar to our own Gas tank boxes," as well as a communication trench up which he threw several bombs.[18]

At the same time, Cpl. Brisbin "got into the trench and turned to the right and went two bays, passing two dug-outs," into each of which he threw a grenade. According to Brisbin, he and his group "then threw bombs at long distance up the trench, gradually shortening the range, in this way driving the enemy toward us. Going around the bay, one German dived for a dug-out and L/Cpl Dinsmore shot him. Two more men were encountered, one a sniper at his post. The sniper was shot and the other got away."[19]

Recalling his part in the action, Lance Cpl. Richard Dinsmore stated: "In the second dug-out a German made a dive from the bay to it, and I fired at him catching him in the backside." Moving on to the next bay, Dinsmore encountered the sniper mentioned by Brisbin: "He yelled so I fired. He looked at me so I fired again. After this he passed me his rifle through the door, butt first. I judged this as a token of surrender … [But] he refused to get over the parapet and L/Cpl Wilson finished him … No signs of gas were in evidence. No signs of mining were seen."[20]

But Pte. Cecil Stephenson did notice another wooden box in the German trench that resembled the ones used in the British and Canadian lines for holding gas cylinders. He then

> turned to the right around [a] traverse and saw four of the enemy. One ran into a snipers box and I fired at him. The other three ran along the trench, I fired my revolver at the man in the snipers box, who had at first put his hands up, and then made a grab for his rifle. I think I killed him as he fell into a heap … [He] appeared to be about 35 years of age, with close cropped beard.[21]

Pte. George Pattenden claimed that, as he jumped into the German trench, he "saw two large boxes about the same as our gas tank boxes but wide." Left to guard a communication trench, he "saw a German running into the next bay and L/Cpl Dinsmore shot him."[22]

Meanwhile, members of the centre group quickly surveyed the situation, assisted with efforts on both flanks, and made some interesting discoveries of their own. Lance Cpl. Fred Willoughby reported that he "entered the trench and turned to the right and found a dug-out in the centre of the bay. Five bombs were thrown into this dug-out, one by Captain Kilmer and one by each man. The enemy in the dug-out squealed like pigs."[23] Pte. William Tapp "saw a passage leading back into the parados" of the German trench "with a dug-out on either side, which we bombed. I was put on guard over the entrances." As the smoke from the grenades dissipated from the dugouts, Tapp noticed at least three bodies. Although the Germans appeared dead, the Canadian was not about to take any chances. "On getting word to leave," said Tapp, "I looked into one dug-out and saw two men lying on the floor. I pumped a bullet into each man. I then looked into the other and saw a man lying and also shot him."[24]

So far, this frenzy of action had lasted a mere three to four minutes, during which at least eight Germans were shot and four large dugouts, which were believed to be "crowded with Huns," were bombed. As their allotted time in the enemy trench was running out, Capt. Kilmer and Lt. Pepler agreed that it was time to get going and gave the signal to all groups to retire. The raiders speedily evacuated the position in an orderly fashion, but as the last group commenced its departure, a sizable body of German reinforcements were observed making their way down the communication trench. Several of these reinforcements took up position in a bombing post situated off the communication trench within bombing range of the firing line. From there, they flung a large number of bombs at the retreating Canadians, which resulted in several casualties. But these injuries were "mostly slight, with the exception of Captain Kilmer, Lieutenant Pepler, and Sergeant Holk, who sustained shrapnel wounds."[25]

Kilmer was the last to leave the German trench, and he followed the rest of his party back towards the abandoned trench. Although wounded himself, Holk had helped Pepler over the German parapet and back to the trench, noting along the way that Kilmer had "already got out and was running for the ditch." When Holk and Pepler made it to the head of the trench, they met Lance Cpl. Wilson, who "stated that Captain Kilmer was in a shell hole." Pepler was sent back immediately for medical treatment. Holk remained "at [the] ditch-head as long as possible, but owing to wounds in my leg," he later remarked, "I had to crawl in."[26] Kilmer, suffering from the effects of shrapnel and a fractured ankle, had made it only as far as a shell hole around eight yards from the German wire.[27]

The rest of the raiding party made it safely back to Canadian lines under covering fire from the supporting artillery batteries and the rifles and Lewis gun of Lt. Burnham's party. As soon as the raiders began departing the German front line, all batteries in Stewart's Group commenced firing as per instructions to cover the withdrawal. German machine-gun emplacements in the vicinity had been accurately located and were suppressed by the bombardment.[28] "The excellent support of our artillery assisted greatly in the success of the enterprise and in lessening possible casualties," reported Maj. F. Logie Armstrong of the 4th Brigade staff. The artillery fire had been very efficiently directed by Lt. Dillon, the FOO for the 17th Battery, who was stationed in the Canadian front-line trench during the raid and who relayed the command to open fire from Hooper's rear party.[29]

Burnham's covering party also ensured that the German reinforcements kept their heads down as the raiders made their way back to Canadian lines. The snipers stationed in no man's land claimed four hits on enemy soldiers who dared to look over their own parapet. Meanwhile, members of Hooper's rear party helped evacuate all members of the raiding party, taking particular care to assist the wounded.[30] In this work, other members of the 19th Battalion also rendered valuable service. Pte. Joseph Newton, a scout who had not accompanied the raiding party, took up a position in Trench 28 and helped the raiders back into Canadian lines. Newton later reported that "Mr. Pepler came in wounded, and I carried him on my back toward the Estaminet Lane C.T. [communication trench] for about four bays. I put him on the fire step and then heard that Captain Kilmer was not back, but was out in No Man's Land wounded."[31]

Saving Capt. Kilmer

The severity of Kilmer's injuries was not known, and because he was still so close to German lines, the likelihood that he would be killed or captured was very high. Joe Newton decided that he would attempt a rescue and made his way down the abandoned trench, where he encountered Lt. Burnham. "I told Mr. Burnham that I was going out to try and bring Captain Kilmer in," Newton later recounted, "and he told me it was all right but to be careful."[32]

It was shortly before 11 AM when Lt T.H. O'Brien, an FOO for the 19th Battery, "was informed that a party of two men were going to attempt a rescue of Capt Kilmer … and that the artillery would cover the rescuers."[33] Lt. Dillon was again put in charge of covering fire and was told that Lance Cpl. Wilson and Pte. Newton would signal Burnham when they were prepared to make their dash to the point where they believed Kilmer was lying. Burnham would then relay this signal to Dillon, who, in turn, would initiate (presumably by telephone) a covering bombardment from the 17th Battery. In order to get Burnham's signal, which evidently was visual in nature, Dillon would have to move out into no man's land and take up a position that left him dangerously exposed to enemy rifle and machine-gun fire.[34]

At around 11:05 AM, after all participants had taken up their positions, Wilson and Newton signalled their readiness to go. A few moments later the artillery laid down a brisk barrage of covering fire.[35] According to Newton,

> L/Cpl Wilson and I decided that on the second burst of artillery fire we would jump up and run for it. We ran in the open for 75 yards to the shell hole which was beside the enemy wire. [There] we found Captain Kilmer with his face down and his head towards the enemy. We had decided to each grab an arm and run with him back to the ditch. I shook Captain Kilmer and called him by name. He appeared to be dazed.[36]

Seeing that Kilmer's ankle and leg were badly injured, Wilson very gently tried to pick up the officer, who suddenly revived and implored his rescuers to "hurry up." "I'm afraid of hurting your leg sir," explained Wilson. But Kilmer insisted that all three of them get a move on, hissing, "Damn the leg, get the rest of me in."[37] "We each took an arm and dragged him along back to the ditch," said Newton. "Here we were met by Sergt Trendell, L/Cpl Dinsmore and Pte Livingstone, who brought Captain Kilmer in."[38]

The trip back to the abandoned trench might have entailed certain death for Newton, Wilson, and Kilmer had it not been for the skilful direction of the covering artillery by Lt. Dillon. The screen of flying metal paralyzed the German trench garrison, preventing it from firing on the Canadians as they made their way back. According to Lt.-Col. John S. Stewart, commanding the artillery group supporting the 19th Battalion, Dillon also noticed a machine gun "firing from the German trenches [that] was being engaged by the Sniper gun of the 26th Battery and upon receiving a correction of '5 minutes' from Lieut Dillon this gun succeeded in securing a direct hit on this M.G."[39]

"Splendid Arrangement"

It had been an outstanding morning's work by all concerned.[40] An estimated forty to fifty Germans had been killed or wounded, and although no prisoners had been secured, the raiders had managed to confirm that Württembergers were still holding the line. The raiders had gathered useful intelligence on the depth and design of the German trenches, as well as the presence of suspected gas-cylinder boxes and a trench mortar emplacement. At least two enemy machine-gun posts had been put out of action by the raiders and by the supporting bombardment during Capt. Kilmer's rescue. The cost to the Canadians had been relatively light, with between five and eight casualties claimed in various reports, the injuries to Holk, Pepler, and Kilmer being the most serious. Although the three men's wounds were believed to be "not of a dangerous character,"[41] Kilmer's leg was in a very bad state and required immediate medical attention.

Fortunately, the battalion MO, Capt. W.L. Whittemore, was on hand. Whittemore dressed Kilmer's shattered leg and stabilized it sufficiently for the officer to be

Top: Snapshot from the M and N Trenches. The original caption reads: "That's Heinie over there." Above: Fred Stitt and Ernie Cook taking a break in the M and N trenches. (MUA RC 0835)

10 August. "We are now in the part of the line we were most of the Winter. New Headquarters have been built since we were here last and we are most comfortable. I personally have never had such accommodation before. You can therefore guess I am not keen on Bill Turnbull hurrying back."[54]

Two days later, on 12 August, the 19th Battalion was treated to an artillery demonstration against German positions opposite Trenches N3 and N4. The purpose of the exercise was to show how closely the infantry could advance to an objective behind the cover of an artillery barrage without suffering casualties from the barrage itself.[55] Another spectacular artillery demonstration was carried out on the afternoon of the 14th, during a visit paid to the Canadian Corps by King George V and the Prince of Wales. While the royal entourage watched, 6-inch howitzers and field guns from the Canadian Corps Heavy Artillery, the 2nd Canadian Divisional Artillery, and a Belgian battery bombarded German positions in the St-Eloi sector. The downside to this display came in the form of stiff German retaliation, which struck the 4th Infantry Brigade's positions at Bois-Carré and along the front line.[56]

It was not a good day to be stirring up trouble with the Germans, for their general attitude was reported to be "more aggressive than usual."[57] Just before noon, the 19th Battalion's trenches were knocked about by "trench mortars, rum jars and whiz bangs," which succeeded in blowing in sections of the parapet in Trenches N2 and N2A and scoring a direct hit on a dugout. A sharp response from Canadian heavy trench mortars and artillery eventually put a stop to these barrages. But the "hate" resumed once again in the afternoon, when German lines opposite Trenches M1 to M3 were bombarded. This aroused the wrath of the German gunners, and the 19th Battalion's support and reserve lines were peppered with shells, while their front line was showered with high explosives and whiz-bangs. As a result of these strafes, Maj. William W. Moors (OC B Company) and Lt. Charles W. Hoare were killed, and Maj. John R. Biscoe and one other rank were wounded. "Every man in the battalion felt the loss of Major Moors very keenly," remarked Pte. John Mould, "he having been with us right from the beginning."[58]

There was little time to mourn, however, for on 15 August the 19th Battalion was charged with executing a "dummy raid" against the Hollandscheschuur Farm and Bois Quarante salients. This operation would be in support of an actual raid attempt by the 21st Battalion, operating on the 19th Battalion's left flank. In addition, the "dummy raid" was to inflict as many casualties on the Germans as possible by drawing their support troops into their front line and then subjecting them to intense artillery fire.[59]

The 19th Battalion's share of the operation commenced at 3:45 AM, when the German barbed wire was vigorously shaken at three designated points by means of strong wires strung across no man's land from Canadian lines and attached to the entanglements. This provoked the Germans to hurl grenades into their own wire. One minute after the commotion started, supporting Canadian artillery and Stokes mortars opened fire on selected targets along the enemy front-line and support positions. The Germans responded to this abuse with a bombardment of their own, but many of these shells dropped short into their own front line at Hollandscheschuur Farm.[60]

While the 19th Battalion effort was rated a success, the 21st Battalion raid was aborted owing to the brightness of the moonlit night, which rendered concealment on the approach to the enemy's wire virtually impossible.[61] The 19th Battalion's

Top: Holding the line in the M and N trenches. Appearing in the photo are "Paddy" Smyth, unidentified man, Bob Ford, Harold Stitt, "Tommy" Adkins, and Charlie Williams.
Above: Freddie White taking aim in the M and N trenches. (MUA RC 0835)

Fred Tate and [first name unknown] Cissereno in the M and N trenches. (MUA RC 0835)

tour in the lines concluded later in the day on 15 August, when it was relieved by the 46th Battalion from the newly arrived 4th Canadian Division. Amidst the stress and activity of the final two days of their tour, the 19th Battalion had taken under its wing the green troops from A Company of the 46th Battalion, who were attached for forty-eight hours of trench warfare instruction before taking over the line themselves.[62]

Back to La Clytte and divisional reserve trudged the weary men from Ontario. Over the following two days the usual program of training and drilling cut short their ambitions for sustained relaxation. Then a visit on 18 August by Sir Sam Hughes subjected the 19th Battalion to a generally unwanted flurry of activity, as officers fussed over arrangements for the formal inspection and march-past, ensuring that all ranks and every inch of their encampment were spic and span. Adding insult to injury was yet another inspection on the following day, this time by Brig. Gen. Rennie. Commenting on the annoyance that Hughes's inspection entailed for the rank and file, Capt. Andrew Macphail, a medical officer with the 6th Field Ambulance, and a well-known physician, author, and social critic in civilian life, declared that "all ranks resent the impertinence of being called out to be observed by a man who has no standing in the B.E.F. Many of these men have just come from the trenches and require sleep and rest."[63] Maj. Millen also was sympathetic to the men's sensibilities and tended to take a dim view of prolonged or unnecessary ceremonial events. He argued that a good officer should never "bugger about" with the men,[64] and informed his mother that "these inspections don't appeal to us very strongly."[65]

Farewell to the Ross Rifle

If some 19th Battalion men were fed up with the whims of politicians and "brass hats," perhaps their opinions softened on 20 August, when all ranks were ordered to turn in their Ross rifles in exchange for Lee-Enfield rifles. Persistent complaints about the Ross's unreliability – and especially its tendency to jam – had prompted the wholesale rearming of the 1st Canadian Division in June 1915; but political pressure, emanating mainly from the Canadian militia minister, kept the Ross in service in the 2nd and 3rd Canadian Divisions through the first half of 1916. Complaints about the Ross rifle continued in the latter two divisions throughout the winter and spring of 1916, as did clandestine efforts to procure Lee-Enfields (often from dead British troops in no man's land) even in the face of official proscriptions against such activities. Matters came to a head in May 1916 when Lt.-Gen. Alderson, in one of his last acts as corps commander, launched an inquiry to ascertain both the incidence with which the Ross rifle malfunctioned and the level of confidence the men had in the weapon.[66]

The 3rd Canadian Division submitted reports that uniformly condemned the Ross rifle; however, the 2nd Canadian Division was split on the issue. In all, there were forty-eight infantry companies in the division, commanded by forty-eight officers. Twenty-two of these company commanders reported that their men were generally satisfied with the Ross; twenty-three others reported that there was little or no confidence in it. The responses of the remaining three company commanders were ambiguous, either claiming a perfect split of opinion among the other ranks or simply offering no clear support or condemnation of the weapon.[67] There is some evidence that Maj.-Gen. Turner exerted pressure on his subordinates to submit favourable reports, anxious as he was to retain the favour of Sir Sam Hughes, who was among the strongest boosters of the Ross.[68] If such influence did exist, then it is to the credit of Maj. Turnbull – who was acting batallion commander in McLaren's absence – that he faithfully reported the opinion of the majority in his battalion, which clearly favoured the Lee-Enfield over the Ross.[69]

Of the four company commanders in the 19th Battalion at that time, Maj. G.F. Morrison of A Company submitted the most extensive and damning critique of the Ross:

> The men complain that the barrel is too long ... All ranks are desirous of being equipped with the Lee Enfield. On an inspection recently 18 men were found to have Lee Enfield Rifles in their possession. These were immediately replaced by Ross Rifles much to their disgust. The Snipers speak well of its accuracy. With regard to the men being in possession of Lee Enfield Rifles the Ross was discarded by them because of jams, it being impossible to clean them in the craters [at St-Eloi], and the Lee Enfields

> picked up by them apparently having laid there for considerable time but were found to work very satisfactory [*sic*].[70]

Maj. Moors of B Company was more succinct in his criticism of the Ross but likewise condemned it, reporting that "on several instances the bolt has jammed ... and it was found impossible to open same until the barrel had cooled. The rifles at the time were perfectly clean. The majority of the men have no confidence in the rifle due to above reasons and also to the fact that it is too long for being carried slung over the shoulder in narrow trenches."[71]

With such obviously negative conclusions from Turnbull, Morrison, and Moors, it is curious that Capt. F.J. Buchanan, then commanding C Company, and Maj. Millen of D Company were both vague in their responses. With respect to Alderson's key question regarding the men's confidence in the Ross rifle, Buchanan stated simply that "about 50 % have, remainder prefer the Lee Enfield owing to its shortness and bolt action."[72] Millen, by contrast, ascribed recent incidents of rifle jams in his company to defective ammunition "marked U.S.A. which on account of narrow rims would not extract." Amazingly, while Millen claimed that his "men have confidence in the [Ross] rifle," he had to admit that "the majority prefer the Lee Enfield," giving no clear reasons why. Moreover, he concluded that some of the Ross's malfunctions could be explained by mishandling. "In rapid fire men are apt not to draw back the bolt far enough to properly extract the empty shell," Millen argued, adding that, in closing the bolt, the men often did not "drive it home far enough."[73]

The results of Alderson's inquiry were forwarded to British GHQ for review, and Gen. Haig recommended that the 2nd and 3rd Canadian Divisions be rearmed with the Lee-Enfield. On 6 June the Canadian government announced its willingness to accept the commander-in-chief's judgment, and by 21 June the Army Council had declared its approval of the change. It took two further months for the actual exchange to be effected; the men of the 19th Battalion received their new Lee-Enfields on 20 August. By the end of August, the 2nd and 3rd Canadian Divisions had been fully rearmed; the recently arrived 4th Canadian Division followed suit during September. Thereafter, almost all Canadian troops in France carried the Lee-Enfield, except for some snipers, who continued to favour the Ross for its accuracy as a target weapon.[74]

On the Move

The withdrawal of the Ross rifle was the most memorable aspect of the 19th Battalion's period in divisional reserve from 16 to 23 August. The rest of the time was taken up by the usual round of drills, parades, and lectures. By now, most of the men knew that their familiar routine in and out of the lines in Belgium was coming to an end. Talk of a great offensive to the south had been in the wind throughout

The original caption for this photo from M and N trenches identifies the soldier simply as "Martin" and further adds: "Note Ross Rifle." (MUA RC 0835)

the 4th Brigade since early August, when a memo was sent to battalion commanders announcing an impending move to the Somme before the end of the month.[75] "There was no doubt in our minds that we were getting prepared for something big," recounted one veteran. "New issues were made to all ranks for all deficiencies of kit. Various men were sent away for short periods of special instruction in all branches of the service, especially Lewis machine guns."[76]

Those who were sick of serving in and near the Ypres Salient saw transfer to the Somme battlefront as a welcome change and were "happy in the thought that at last we were going to go after Fritz instead of sitting still and taking what he was able to hand us."[77] But there were others who viewed the move with a shudder of apprehension. If some among the high command and the journalistic community remained hopeful of a decisive victory at the Somme, the ever-lengthening casualty lists made it clear that the British armies were not yet achieving a major breakthrough.[78] This meant that the Germans were making an extremely tough fight of it, which always entailed a heavy price in life and limb.

All ranks of the 19th Battalion knew that their debut in the "big show" was at hand when the order came through on 23 August for the 2nd Canadian Division to withdraw from the lines and proceed to the Second Army Training Area near St-Omer.[79] At 5:40 AM the following day, the 19th Battalion marched from Ontario Camp near Reninghelst and began its trek to the appointed training area. The march was completed in stages over the course of the following four days. The troops were allowed rest halts of ten minutes' duration every hour, so as not to wear them out, and two pipers from the battalion pipe band were placed at the head of each company. Their job was to furnish tunes lively enough to keep up the men's spirits and their rate of march.[80]

On 28 August the 19th Battalion, at a strength of 29 officers and 858 other ranks, marched into the Second Army Training Area, where the men began settling into their assigned billets in the village of Nordausques. They were reinforced by an additional draft of eighty-three other ranks, who arrived the same day.[81] For many in the battalion, the march had been excruciating. Heavy rain on 26 August had soaked the men's packs, making them "feel twice as heavy," according to Pte. Mould. In spite of the provision for periodic rests, Mould and his exhausted comrades "passed scores of men who had dropped out on the road and by the time we had finished our journey we could hardly walk! We happened to get into a good billet however and were not long before we were resting our tired limbs."[82]

The events of the previous year had gradually changed the make-up of the 19th Battalion, and many of the old originals who were left must have wondered how much longer the unit they had known since their time at the Exhibition Camp in Toronto would survive. As one veteran put it, some comrades already had "paid the supreme price; others casualties to Blighty and the Base; many had transferred to Corps and Divisional units. A number of our officers had been promoted from the ranks, many going to other units, the Flying Corps, and Imperial Battalions. New faces were now beginning to outnumber the old ones."[83] There was something to this claim, for the battalion had received 24 officers and 734 other ranks as reinforcements between 2 November 1915 and 28 August 1916 – well over half its established strength.[84] From a purely numerical standpoint, these reinforcements more than made up for the total casualties sustained between 15 September 1915 and 25 August 1916, which amounted to 16 officers and 534 other ranks (of whom

3 officers and 126 other ranks were killed).[85] The great majority of these casualties were wounded or injured, and a percentage of them would eventually return to service with their comrades in the battalion. But, as noted above, there were other officers and men who were transferred out of the 19th Battalion to different units or to staff duties, and the services of many of these would be lost to the battalion for the balance of the war.

Such constant shifts in the battalion's personnel composition resulted in a very real sense of dislocation, which was experienced both by veterans and by reinforcements. Many veterans learned to cope with the loss of old friends by assuming a positive and outgoing demeanour ("keeping jolly," as Pte. John Mould would have put it) and by striking up new friendships with reinforcement personnel; meanwhile, reinforcements had to prepare to "dive in" and "learn the ropes." Those who could not adapt stood a higher chance of becoming physical or emotional casualties themselves.

In any case, the men of the 19th Battalion could take heart in the fact that their battalion was well equipped and up to strength, with a significant proportion of experienced officers and other ranks who had survived months of fighting in the hellish Ypres Salient. The old battalion may have changed since its arrival in France, but it had also matured and now appeared ready for the challenges that faced it in the weeks to come. What nobody realized was just how suddenly and how drastically the face of their battalion would change yet again over the course of the coming month.

8

Preparing for Battle: 28 August–15 September 1916

Having established its billets at Nordausques on 28 August, the 19th Battalion embarked on a seven-day course of intensive training, the first three days of which focused specifically on the familiar skill sets of musketry and bombing while also highlighting various facets of communication. Getting information back and forth between forward platoons and companies and battalion headquarters to the rear would be a key component in the success of any battalion attack – especially if the fighting became more open and fluid than in the comparatively static conditions on the Ypres Salient.[1] Regrettably, the training was made more difficult by the execrable weather that dominated the initial days. On 29 August, having marched the three miles from their billets to the training grounds, the men were put through six hours of bayonet and platoon drills in the pouring rain. But greater sense prevailed the following day, as officers decided to scrub the day's outdoor training regimen amidst the continuing downpour; the men were permitted some hours of leisure before better weather saw the resumption of drilling on 31 August.[2]

Once the men brushed up on their individual skills, the first three days of September were given over to more advanced exercises, such as trench attacks. All ranks also attended lectures on various topics, such as methods of assault and consolidation, how to attack trenches and advance to limited objectives, and how to attack under cover of heavy artillery and machine-gun barrages. There even was some rudimentary instruction on how infantry could communicate with aircraft by means of visual signals.[3]

Senior Canadian commanders and staffs had been following reports of the fighting at the Somme as closely as they had been able and were determined to see that the troops were well trained and ready for some intense fighting. One of the greatest challenges for any attacking unit was the loss of leadership that occurred in the event of heavy casualties among the officers. To minimize this problem, Lt.-Gen. Byng insisted that all ranks in each attacking company be thoroughly instructed as to their objectives and duties, as well as the tactics required to achieve their goals. In some battalions he personally supervised training schemes. Eventually he had companies practising attacks under the command of one of their sergeants (or even a corporal); sometimes an entire battalion was placed under the command of a lieutenant. "The effect of this, we'd never seen anything like it before," remarked Capt. J.F. McKay of the 28th Battalion. "It had the effect of just electrifying every man in that whole show because he felt, well I've got to listen to my instructions, because I may have to take over and carry on."[4]

In tandem with this emphasis on devolution of command and responsibility, there was a growing appreciation of the importance of small-unit tactics – something that already was spreading throughout the British armies on the Western Front. Having studied reports of the fighting at the Somme from British and Australian formations, Maj.-Gen. Turner pointed out that "the necessity for decentralization has been clearly marked" and that "training must be systematic: it must start with the smallest unit and work gradually upwards. At least 4 days must be allotted to section, platoon and company training." Battalions were exhorted to ensure that specialist troops such as bombers, machine gunners, and scouts take full part in company and battalion exercises and not train in isolation from their comrades in the rifle companies.[5]

This was a step in the right direction, for small-unit tactics within rifle companies would not be effective without the close cooperation of the battalion's heavier specialist sections. Unfortunately, this thinking was not carried far enough, and further experience at the Somme would demonstrate to many British and Canadian officers that true flexibility and the full tactical potential of small units would not be realized until the various infantry weapons (rifles, bayonets, Lewis guns, hand and rifle grenades) were effectively coordinated at the lowest levels within a battalion – in platoons and sections. For this to occur, a structural reorganization of the battalion would need to take place, but this would not come about until the winter of 1916–17.

Another impediment to true flexibility among the Canadian infantry at the Somme had to do with how successive linear wave formations were employed during attacks.[6] GHQ's overall philosophy was that sheer weight of numbers was required to breach enemy trench lines. According to a training document issued by GHQ in May, "in many instances experience has shown that to capture a hostile trench a single line of men has usually failed, two lines have generally failed but sometimes succeeded, three lines have generally succeeded but sometimes failed, and four or more lines have usually succeeded."[7] The emphasis on line-abreast troop deployments in each successive attacking wave also reflected the high command's belief before the opening of the Somme offensive that most officers and NCOs (especially those in the New Army[8] and Dominion divisions raised after the war's outbreak) did not yet have enough experience and skill to retain control over more dispersed troop formations during confusing and unexpected situations on the battlefield. Frontal assaults in which platoon members were arrayed side by side were, in theory, easier for novice officers to control than more fluid attacks in which a platoon's constituent sections manoeuvred independently against an objective's flanks. But as the battle of the Somme progressed and all ranks gained more experience, this assumption gradually began to weaken, especially within some formations such as the 5th British Division, which placed increasing emphasis on small-unit firepower and manoeuvre.[9] Indeed, even on 1 July some British formations, especially in the southern sectors of the attack, had arrayed their infantry in small groups instead of in strictly linear fashion. There was an overarching trend in GHQ's directives towards encouraging the use of linear dispositions in 1916; however, the high command left it to individual commanders to design their own tactical formations to suit the particular situations they faced. Consequently, the most consistent thing about British infantry tactics was their inconsistency in practice, especially among different divisions and even among different brigades and battalions within divisions.[10]

The Canadian training program in late August and early September thus reflected a gradual but incomplete shift towards increasingly fluid small-unit fire and movement tactics. Although trust in the initiative and tactical competence of junior officers and other ranks had increased, as evidenced by the training scenarios employed by Lt.-Gen. Byng, there remained an overall reliance on comparatively rigid linear infantry dispositions within the Canadian Corps. This dependence was reinforced by the prevailing artillery tactics of the day, which were equally linear in nature and predicated on the employment of creeping barrages.

A creeping barrage was, in essence, a "barrier" of artillery fire (usually of shrapnel) that moved, or "crept," ahead of the advancing infantry. Such a barrage served to screen the infantry's movement across no man's land and to suppress the enemy's defensive capability. By the time a creeping barrage had moved beyond an enemy trench, the attacking infantry were, ideally, in a position to rush the enemy parapet before the defenders could take up their firing positions and fight back. Moving barrages had been employed to varying degrees during the opening phase of the

Somme offensive and perhaps even earlier. However, these earlier barrages tended to "jump" from one line of enemy trenches to the next, covering wide expanses of ground in a single bound and making it virtually impossible for the infantry to keep up. As the Somme offensive ground on, it became more widely accepted that a creeping barrage would be more useful if its "creeps," or lifts, were timed more slowly, rolling forward approximately 100 yards ahead of the attacking troops at a rate of 100 yards every three to five minutes. This would enable the infantry to follow more closely, or "hug" the barrage, thereby maximizing its protective capacity.[11]

As September dawned, units of the 2nd Canadian Division took advantage of what little time they had left for training before they were thrust into active operations at the Somme. Areas of ground were taped off to represent enemy trenches, and units practised their movements over these taped courses. The use of long strips of white "tape" positioned on the ground with stakes to denote the outline of enemy trenches and strong points was not a new concept in the British armies, or even in the 19th Battalion itself, for as early as 27 December 1915 the battalion had practised company attacks over a small taped course.[12]

Following Byng's lead, unit commanders ensured that casualties among officers and NCOs were simulated during practice attacks, in order to foster initiative among all ranks.[13] Manoeuvres were conducted on the training grounds, first with sections, then with platoons and companies, and finally with entire battalions and brigades.[14] Practice assaults on dummy trenches introduced the other ranks to the concept of advancing behind an artillery barrage, which on the training fields was "represented by men carrying flags, who moved in bounds on timed programmes to indicate the area on which the shells would fall."[15]

March to the Somme

This phase of training came to an end on 4 September, when units of the 2nd Canadian Division began their journey to the Somme battlefront, the 19th Battalion marching from Nordausques to Audruicq. The 19th and the rest of the Canadian Corps were slated to join the British Reserve Army, which was operating between the Ancre and Somme rivers. The march did not begin nicely, however, for after the men departed Nordausques at 2:00 PM, the heavens opened and, according to Pte. Mould, "it was not more than 15 minutes before every man was soaked to the skin." There was some relief when they arrived at Audruicq and found that the next part of their journey would be by train. By the time the time the train pulled out at around 7:00 PM, fully 30 officers and 946 other ranks had been loaded; the battalion was now virtually up to full strength.[16]

Although the journey by train was a break from the usual process of foot slogging, the trip was not without its discomforts for the tired and soaked men crammed into boxcars bearing the ubiquitous legend, "hommes 40, cheveaux 8." The trip was not a long one, however, and by 2:00 AM the following morning the men had reached their destination at Auxi-le-Chateau, where they detrained, loosened up their sore and damp limbs, and marched six miles to the village of Agenville, some thirty-five miles from the battle line, where they went into billets.[17] On 6 September they set out on the march again, passing through Bonneville, Teutencourt, and Vadencourt until they finally reached the town of Albert, near the zone of operations, on 9 September. There, they bivouacked at a position known as the Brickfields, on the western outskirts of the town.[18] The rumble of artillery that had been clearly audible along the march during the previous days now became thunderous – the front line was now less than four miles away. The Canadians had entered a beehive of activity around Albert. Columns of troops from all parts of the empire were on the move to and from the trenches and reserve camps, kicking up clouds of dust as they tramped along the packed roadways, competing for space with transport wagons, motor trucks, ambulances, staff cars, and messengers whizzing along on motorcycles. Overhead was the constant drone of aircraft – slower, heavier two-seaters flying reconnaissance and artillery-spotting sorties, and swifter, nimble fighters charged with protecting the observers and driving enemy craft from the sky.[19]

Once they had set up their rough little shelters, the men were issued a significant element of their uniforms: divisional patches. These were 2-by 3-inch pieces

Louie West, Hugh Riley, Jimmie Wild, and Bob O'Connell. Three of the men are clearly sporting their divisional patches. (MUA RC 0835)

of coloured cloth that they sewed onto their tunic sleeves near the shoulders. Each division was assigned an identifying colour: red for a member of the 1st Canadian Division, blue for the 2nd, and grey for the 3rd. Troops of the 4th Canadian Division, which was still serving in the British Second Army, would sport green patches. Additional small patches were issued to be sewn above the divisional patches. The colour and shape of these signified the wearer's membership in a particular brigade and battalion within the division. Thus, members of the 19th Battalion sported a green semicircle over their blue divisional shoulder patches. The scout and bombing sections within the battalion also received distinctive emblems, the scouts sporting a "north point" of blue cloth and the bombers a one-and-one-half-inch-wide green band on their left forearm.[20]

The following morning, 10 September, saw the parading of all ranks for divine service. "Almost to a man the troops attended confirmation service, knowing it would be the last for a great many of us," remembered a veteran from No. 4 Platoon, whom we will refer to as "Pte. Smith."[21] Later that afternoon, the 4th Infantry Brigade would begin relieving the 1st Brigade in the front lines of the sector assigned to the Canadian Corps. The 19th Battalion would be the first in the brigade to take possession of the front line, with the 21st Battalion in the support trenches and the 18th and 20th Battalions in brigade reserve at the Brickfields and Albert, respectively. To the 19th's left would be the 29th Battalion of the 6th Infantry Brigade, with British troops of the 27th Battalion, Northumberland Fusiliers, 103rd Brigade, to its right.[22]

The Canadians were now serving in Gen. Sir Hubert Gough's Reserve Army, which had assumed control over operations in the northern portion of the Somme battlefront. In the southern portion, British operations were being carried out by Gen. Sir Henry Rawlinson's Fourth Army. As the 19th Battalion settled into its new, and very dangerous, positions, the commanders and staffs at the 4th Brigade and 2nd Canadian Division headquarters finalized plans for their formations' parts in the impending offensive, which would become known as the Battle of Flers-Courcelette. The battle, which would rage along the roughly ten miles of front between Thiepval to the west and Combles to the east, took its name from two villages situated three miles apart that were among the principal British objectives. On 15 September, three corps of Rawlinson's Fourth Army would deliver the main thrust, towards the villages of Morval and Flers, while Gough's Reserve Army would secure Rawlinson's left flank by attacking Courcelette and capturing observation positions beyond it. The Canadian Corps was charged with carrying out the Reserve Army's thrust against Courcelette; British II Corps would assault German positions south of Thiepval. If, as Gen. Sir Douglas Haig hoped, the offensive succeeded in breaking through the formidable German defences known as the Third Position, which lay just south and west of Flers and to the northeast of Courcelette, an opportunity might open for the British Cavalry Corps to pour

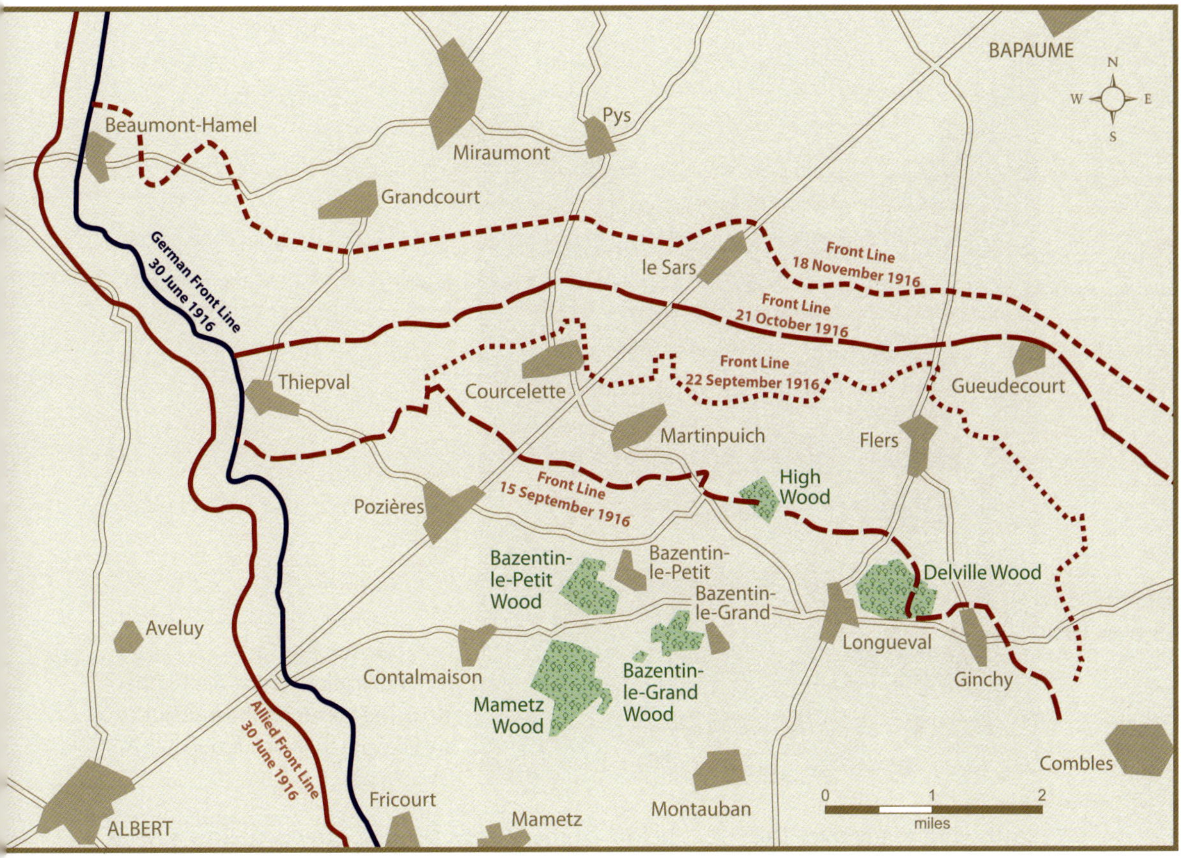

Map 5 – The Somme.

through the breach and seize Bapaume as a prelude to rolling up the remaining German defences on the Western Front. Wildly optimistic as this vision was, hopes for success rode high on the strength of two significant factors that the British high command trusted would give their troops a decisive advantage: the use of creeping barrages on a massive scale, and an entirely new type of weapon, the tank.[23]

Into the Cauldron

At 2:00 PM on 10 September, the 19th Battalion left the Brickfields and started off for the firing line. "Everyone was quite cheerful when we marched off," remarked Pte. Mould, "although we knew at the time that we were going to take part in some of the fiercest fighting that had taken place during the war."[24] As they passed through Albert, the men saw ample evidence of the destruction wrought by the earlier phases of the Battle of the Somme. Perhaps the most famous "casualty" was a gilded statue of the Virgin Mary holding aloft the infant Christ that crowned the steeple of the basilica of Notre-Dame-des-Brébières. The basilica had been hit by shellfire earlier in the war, and the statue was now tipped off its pedestal and suspended at

Canadian troops in a communication trench, September 1916. The men look cheerful but are keeping their heads down. (LAC PA-000723)

a dizzying angle over the street below. Some troops passing directly below saw in the statue's precarious attitude a welcome sign of benediction as they made their way towards the front line. Ted Lang would recall the strong belief among the local people that on the day the statue "toppled to the ground the war would end."[25]

From Albert the men also could see in the distance the white lines of trenches dug out of the chalk over which the great battles of 1 July had raged. When they reached the open country outside the town, they were overwhelmed by the desolation of the landscape. "No growth of any live vegetation was to be seen," reported "Pte. Smith." Instead, as far as the eye could see were "stunted, shell-torn trees, shell holes everywhere, only the odd cellar indicating where there had once been a prosperous village." When they reached the reserve trenches near Contalmaison, Pte. Mould was struck by how difficult the fighting must have been for the units that had seized those positions: "As I looked around and noticed the strong fortifications I began to wonder however such a place could have been captured. So great praise must be given to all the Brave Lads who took part in gaining such a fine position and one which seemed almost impossible to penetrate."[26]

The landscape in this area was dominated by the Pozières Ridge, most of which had been secured recently at great cost by Australian and British troops. Possession of the village of Pozières, near the highest point of the ridge, afforded the Reserve

Army a favourable vantage point for launching attacks towards Courcelette and Thiepval while at the same time sheltering the massive concentrations of Allied artillery that were drawn up on low ground to the south and west. The ridge also effectively screened the movements of the numerous formations that were concentrating for the upcoming attack.[27]

On the evening of 10 September the 19th Battalion relieved the exhausted troops of the 2nd Battalion in the front-line trenches. Pte. Mould admitted that "on nearing our destination we came across dead Germans everywhere and … it fairly made my blood run cold."[28] Troops of the 1st Canadian Division had been in the line since 3 September and had expended great effort and many lives in gaining additional ground from which the offensive would commence on 15 September. "The previous night the 1st Brigade had attacked in the sector which we [took] over, capturing a new front line," stated "Pte. Smith," and "it was quite apparent that we would have to stand some severe counter-attacks in order to hold these gains."[29]

Maj. Morrison, still in command during Lt.-Col. Turnbull's absence, had garrisoned his front line with nine platoons from A, B, and C Companies, placing an

Front-line trench, September 1916. The sentry in the background keeps watch with a periscope while a comrade snatches a few moments of rest on the firestep. (LAC PA-000587)

additional three in support. D Company, which was somewhat weaker in strength than its sister companies, stood by in battalion reserve. Each man in the lines had taken with him two Mills bombs, two sandbags, and two extra bandoliers of small-arms ammunition. Also, half the battalion's bombers had been dispatched to the front line, with the remainder standing by at battalion headquarters, along with the forty-strong scout section. Extra firepower was afforded by eight of the Lewis guns, which were disposed along the front line, while two Colt heavy machine guns were disposed on either flank. An additional two Colts, as well as a Vickers heavy machine gun, were kept in readiness at battalion headquarters.[30]

The infantry in the fire trenches were broken up into sections of fours, reported Pte. Mould, "this being done to give each man a rest from looking over the parapet." Mould took his turn first, keeping

> a steady watch across No Mans Land for any sign of movement by the enemy ... The first thing I noticed was that [the Germans] held a very strong position on the top of a large ridge ... Directly in front of the ridge was a Sunken Road in which was situated a Sugar Factory this being a good strong point for the Huns and one which they used for massing troops. Their front line did not extend back this far however, they occupying one which they had managed to make after being driven out of the one we occupied then. It was not more than 80 yards from us.[31]

A mere three hours after the men of the 19th assumed control of the front line, they began repelling attacks by German assault parties about thirty-five-strong each, which attempted to rush a trench block that the 19th was charged with protecting. The Germans were driven back by determined fusillades of rifle and machine-gun fire. This boded well for the Canadians, but it was only the briefest of overtures to what was yet to come.[32] Throughout 11 September, both Canadian and German troops laboured to consolidate and improve their front-line positions, the opposing fire trenches in the 19th Battalion's sub-section being a little less than 150 yards apart. All day, Morrison's men were harassed by vigilant enemy snipers operating out of the strongly fortified sugar factory, while the German gunners laid on a continuous barrage of the Canadian front lines with shrapnel, high explosive, and lachrymatory shells. The latter chemical ordnance, although not lethal like chlorine or phosgene, would have sent all ranks scurrying to don their protective masks.[33]

The casualties mounted. In its first twenty-four hours at the Somme, the 19th Battalion lost twelve other ranks killed and twelve wounded. Two officers also were wounded – Lt. William H.S. Richardson and Capt. W. Laurence Whittemore, the battalion medical officer. The loss or injury of any man was a tragedy, but it seemed an especially hard blow for the 19th to be deprived of its trusted medical officer just when he would be needed most. Whittemore would survive his wounds but would not return to the unit. The battalion would be serviced by a number of temporary medical officers until the permanent appointment of Capt. Herbert C. Allison on 8 November.[34]

Canadian troops sheltering in a communication trench, September 1916. (LAC PA-000758)

Meanwhile, Canadian gunners reaped a grim harvest of death among the German trench garrisons. Regular bombardments were unleashed, and it was hoped they would soften up the enemy defences enough to facilitate the great advance that was scheduled to take place in a few short days. Amidst such torrents of firepower, the 19th Battalion rotated its companies between front-line and reserve positions, all the while carrying out the principal task to which it had been assigned, which was, to prepare positions from which the upcoming advance would be launched. This involved digging a number of saps to a distance of at least fifty yards in advance of the present Canadian fire trench. These were then to be connected, forming a new forward trench from which the attacking battalions would depart at the commencement of the assault on 15 September. By the pre-dawn hours of 12 September, five saps had been pushed out the required distance in front of the 19th's firing line and linked up. In addition, part of a trench crossing the Bapaume road was successfully reclaimed. Three other saps were attempted but remained as yet unfinished owing to the intensity of the German bombardment, which did its utmost to hamper the Canadians' efforts.[35]

Although 12 September "was a day of heavy shelling on both sides," there was, according to "Pte. Smith," "no active trench fighting." However, the skies above the 19th Battalion's trenches were humming with activity, and at one point the men's attention was diverted from digging to a dramatic aerial duel directly overhead. "We could see quite plain that it was a fight to the death," wrote Pte. Mould. The British pilot emerged the victor, and all ranks watched as the German plane plummeted in a wreath of flame, "just immediately behind" the 19th Battalion's front line. Mould declared that "it was a fearful sight to witness and also a terrible death[,] both machine and aviator being burnt beyond recognition." The Germans at once "started to shell the vicinity where the plane landed," stated "Pte. Smith," "so that we could not secure any evidence of it. However, some of our boys dared the flames and shelling to secure souvenirs."[36]

Through sheer stamina and the determination of the men, the remaining saps neared completion on 13 September, as artillery on both sides pounded opposing positions and wily snipers increased their personal scores at the expense of the unwary or unlucky. Reliefs, usually welcome events for platoons working the front lines, became perilous adventures because the communication trenches through which parties proceeded were prime targets for the enemy artillery. Mould's trek to the rear at 9:00 PM was especially miserable:

> I shall always have in mind the journey through the trenches that night. The mud was over our shoe tops and the rain was beating down worse than ever. By the time we reached the reserve Lines we all looked as if we had been rolled in a mud heap. Most of this was caused by us having to drop down in it to escape the Shrapnel that was flying all around us. I think it was more luck than anything that we all managed to get out in safety we reaching our destination at 11 PM at night.[37]

Maj. Morrison dispatched patrols to cover his battalion's front and to protect the sappers and digging parties that were working feverishly to complete the jumping-off positions. The Germans, meanwhile, were doing their utmost to strengthen their own defences, observers on each side catching sight of the other's work details. But even in the midst of the ruthlessness of total war, brief incidents of humanitarianism seeped through, as when German stretcher-bearers, operating under a white flag, were allowed a short respite to retrieve their wounded. Finally, on 14 September – the eve of the offensive – word was sent back to 19th Battalion headquarters that the jumping-off positions were virtually complete. The only exception was a short stretch of linking trench between two of the saps, which could not be completed owing to the extremely short proximity between Canadian and German positions at that particular point – a mere fifteen yards.[38]

While the Germans collected their wounded, the 19th Battalion had more than enough casualties of its own to tend to. Between 12 and 14 September, the battalion lost an additional 23 other ranks killed and a staggering 105 wounded. The officer cadre also was whittled down. Capts. Thomas A. Baxter, Gershom H. Carpenter, and Frederick L. Henderson, and Lts. Hamilton Cassels, Huson M. Harman, and Sydney Burnham, were all wounded. Like those of "Doc" Whittemore, the services of Burnham, the redoubtable patrol officer, who was then in command of B Company, would be sorely missed during the upcoming operations. Fortunately, he would recover and return to the battalion on 26 November – with the rank of captain. His "partner in crime," Lt. Bert Hooper, had also departed, although not by reason of enemy action. Hooper had left a month earlier, on 1 August, when he was seconded for service with the Divisional School.[39]

Although the losses were disheartening and the labour exhausting, it was still a momentous time, not only for the men of the 19th Battalion but also for the entire division. They had not yet participated in a large-scale offensive, and after a year of acting primarily in a defensive capacity in and near the Ypres Salient, they were anxious to give a good account of themselves. Maj.-Gen. Turner was active throughout the day on 14 September, visiting battalions during the morning and speaking of the work that lay ahead of them while reminding them of the hardships they already had endured over the previous year. In the evening, he indulged his well-known habit of conducting personal tours of the front lines and paid a visit to the parties of the 19th Battalion, which had just finished digging the jumping-off trenches for their comrades in the 4th Brigade. Turner chatted with individuals and did his best to project an air of geniality, even borrowing a pipe of tobacco from one of the men in No. 4 Platoon. In sympathy for their ordeal and for the casualties they had suffered in the process, Turner promised to pull them out later that night. His empathy increased as a result of his own experience. Just as Turner departed from the front line, the Germans unleashed a heavy bombardment that forced him to jump shell holes and "run for it to get out."[40]

Plan of Attack

The 15th of September, the day of the attack, marked the first anniversary of the 2nd Canadian Division's arrival in France. In the pre-dawn hours, the bracing temperatures heightened the nerves of everyone in the assault units of the 2nd Canadian Division as they, and the rest of the attacking formations in the British Fourth and Reserve Armies, prepared for the largest, most concerted assault since 1 July.

The Canadian Corps would employ its 2nd and 3rd Divisions on a 2,200-yard front. The 2nd Canadian Division, mounting the main effort along the Albert–Bapaume road, would attack on a two-brigade front, with the Westerners of Brig.-Gen. Ketchen's 6th Brigade on the left and the Ontarians of Brig.-Gen. Rennie's 4th Brigade on the right. Supporting them, to Ketchen's left, would be the 8th Infantry Brigade of the 3rd Canadian Division; the 15th British Division would operate along Rennie's right flank. In the divisional instructions for the attack, issued on 8 September, Turner had recommended that the 4th Brigade attack on a three-battalion front. Accordingly, Rennie ordered the 21st, 20th, and 18th Battalions to take up the left, centre, and right sub-sections respectively, with the 19th Battalion in support. Given the exertions that Maj. Morrison's men had been put through up to that time, there was no question that they would be employed as the supporting unit for the attack. In addition, the 24th Battalion was detached from the 5th Brigade, which was in divisional reserve and temporarily placed under Rennie's command for use in brigade reserve.[41]

The 2nd Canadian Division's objective on 15 September was a strip of German-held territory ranging in depth from 1,000 yards on the right to around 400 yards

The devastating effect of artillery on the approaches to Courcelette. The ruins of the village itself can be seen on the horizon, under heavy shellfire. (LAC PA-000772)

on the left, with the objectives stretching in front of the village of Courcelette. These included Candy Trench, which was a line running northwest from the village of Martinpuich; roughly 1,500 yards of Sugar Trench, which cut across Candy Trench; and the fortified ruins of the sugar factory, the daunting strongpoint observed earlier by Pte. Mould. This edifice, along with many of the intact buildings in Courcelette itself, was heavily fortified and bristled with machine guns. In addition, the village was honeycombed with cellars, dugouts, and galleries that furnished ample protection for large numbers of defending troops, which belonged to the 45th Reserve Division of the Guard Reserve Corps. To the 2nd Division's left, the 8th Infantry Brigade of the 3rd Canadian Division would advance some 400 yards and provide flank protection. During the 2nd Division's part in the attack, Rennie's 4th Brigade would have the farthest to advance. Because it occupied the right portion of the division's sector, the 4th Brigade would have to cover the full 1,000 yards, hence the advisability of employing three battalions in the attack. To help the infantry achieve its objectives, 64 heavy and 234 field pieces were assembled for fire support – an unprecedented number of guns for a Canadian operation.[42]

The attacking infantry would advance in successive waves behind the first large-scale creeping barrage ever fired by the Canadian artillery. Four minutes before zero hour – 6:24 AM for the 4th Brigade – the 18-pounders of the supporting field artillery batteries would open fire with shrapnel on a barrage line fifty yards in front of the German front trench and hold there for one minute. At 6:21 AM (three minutes before zero hour), the barrage would lift to the German front-line trench and hold there until zero hour, whereupon the barrage would lift 100 yards farther at the same time as the infantry began its advance. Thereafter, the barrage was scheduled to lift 100 yards every three minutes until it covered the infantry's final objective line. There it would pause for six minutes before moving on in three more lifts of three minutes each to the final barrage line, which linked the villages of Courcelette and Martinpuich – a total of 3,000 yards from the infantry's jumping-off trenches.[43]

Extra fire support would come from the 1st Canadian Motor Machine Gun Brigade, along with machine guns from the 4th, 6th, and 9th Canadian Machine Gun Companies, all operating under the command of Lt.-Col. Raymond Brutinel (commanding the 1st Canadian Motor Machine Gun Brigade). The machine gunners were to furnish additional cover for the advance with barrages of indirect fire, along with occasional concentrations of fire upon selected enemy strongpoints. Other machine-gun detachments would move forward with the infantry, garrison hastily constructed strongpoints, and offer protection against the expected enemy counterattacks.[44]

Additional, and much more novel, support for the attack would be provided by a section of tanks – a new type of weapon that would see its battlefield debut on 15 September. Of the forty-nine operable tanks available at that time, only seven were allotted to the Reserve Army, the rest being earmarked for the main effort mounted by the British Fourth Army. However, the Reserve Army's entire complement of seven tanks had been assigned to assist the 2nd Canadian Division. One of these tanks would be kept in reserve, leaving the remaining six to accompany the infantry. Three tanks would advance in support of each of the division's two attacking brigades. The three assigned to assist the 4th Brigade were to proceed directly along the Albert–Bapaume road towards the sugar factory, providing close support for the infantry along the way. Once the infantry had gained its objectives, the tanks were to proceed back to their assembly point, where they would be rearmed, refuelled, and made ready for further operations if necessary.[45] It was hoped that these armoured, lozenge-shaped, caterpillar-tracked behemoths would prove instrumental in eliminating any German strongpoints that the artillery barrage had not destroyed; but the high command was not willing to stake the success of the entire operation on their performance. Operational orders for the offensive stipulated that the tanks were to "conform to the infantry advance," and that if the tanks proved unable to keep up with the infantry, then "the latter will not wait for them."[46] Suspicion on this score was well founded, for the twenty-eight-ton tanks had a top speed of only 3.7 miles per hour on optimum terrain. On a scarred and pitted battlefield, they moved scarcely faster than a half a mile per hour.[47]

In accordance with the operational orders issued by 4th Brigade headquarters, the infantry assault would be delivered in a series of waves against a line running

Two views of a British Mark I tank armed with shielded Vickers machine guns and equipped with a distinctive wheeled steering tail. The tail would not be used on later models. (LAC PA-001358 & PA-001357)

along Candy Trench. Thus the area covered by the brigade would include the heavily fortified sugar factory. Each of the attacking battalions in the 4th Brigade would be disposed in five waves advancing on a three-platoon front. Each wave would be separated by an interval of 50 yards, except for the fourth and fifth waves, the latter following the former at a distance of 100 yards. Far from being left out of the advance, the 19th Battalion, acting in support, would see many of its men advancing just behind the first wave of attackers. According to the plan, the 19th Battalion would contribute twelve platoons, which would serve as intermediate waves between the first and second waves of the attacking battalions. The first intermediate wave of nine platoons would follow ten yards behind the first wave of attackers, three platoons being assigned to each of the three attacking battalions. Also, three additional platoons from the 19th Battalion would form a second intermediate wave to follow ten yards behind the first intermediate wave supporting the left attacking unit – the 21st Battalion.[48]

The job of the first intermediate wave in support of all three attacking battalions was to mop up any remaining resistance along the German front line while the successive attacking waves proceeded forward towards the objective along Candy Trench and just beyond the sugar factory. The men in the second intermediate wave, supporting the 21st Battalion on the left, were to move forward to a position known as Sunken Road, where they too would serve as moppers-up. The remaining four platoons of the 19th Battalion would follow up the fifth wave of the attacking battalions. Three of these platoons (one following the fifth wave of each of the three attacking battalions) would serve as carrying and consolidating parties for the troops occupying the former German front line. An additional platoon following the fifth wave of the 21st Battalion would act as a carrying and consolidation party for the Sunken Road.[49]

Final Preparations

The assembly was not without its difficulties. The day before the attack, while the personnel of the 19th Battalion prepared to take up their positions in the intermediate and follow-up waves, an accident injured a dozen men, including the battalion's redoubtable pipe major, Charles Dunbar. Pte. Mould witnessed it but luckily was not among the two officers and ten other ranks who were wounded. According to Mould,

> as we were receiving our Bombs, a sand bag containing about 100 of them suddenly flew in all directions. We knew in a second that some of the pins must have came loose thus causing them to explode. We all got safely away except the men I have mentioned, they getting some nasty wounds with the shrapnel … This left us with no officers again [and] we had to get more before we could take over the trenches.[50]

"Pte. Smith" also wrote about the episode, claiming that it was a "box of bombs" that had exploded. He related how he

> followed Pipe Major Dunbar into the advanced dressing station and, according to the Y.M.C.A. Officer to whom the Pipe Major had given his beloved stick and was willing to give everything else he had, he was the maddest and most disappointed man in the whole Canadian Corps as his heart had been set on piping the 19th over the top.[51]

There also was some disorder as each battalion in the brigade moved forward in the pre-dawn hours of 15 September through crowded communication trenches.

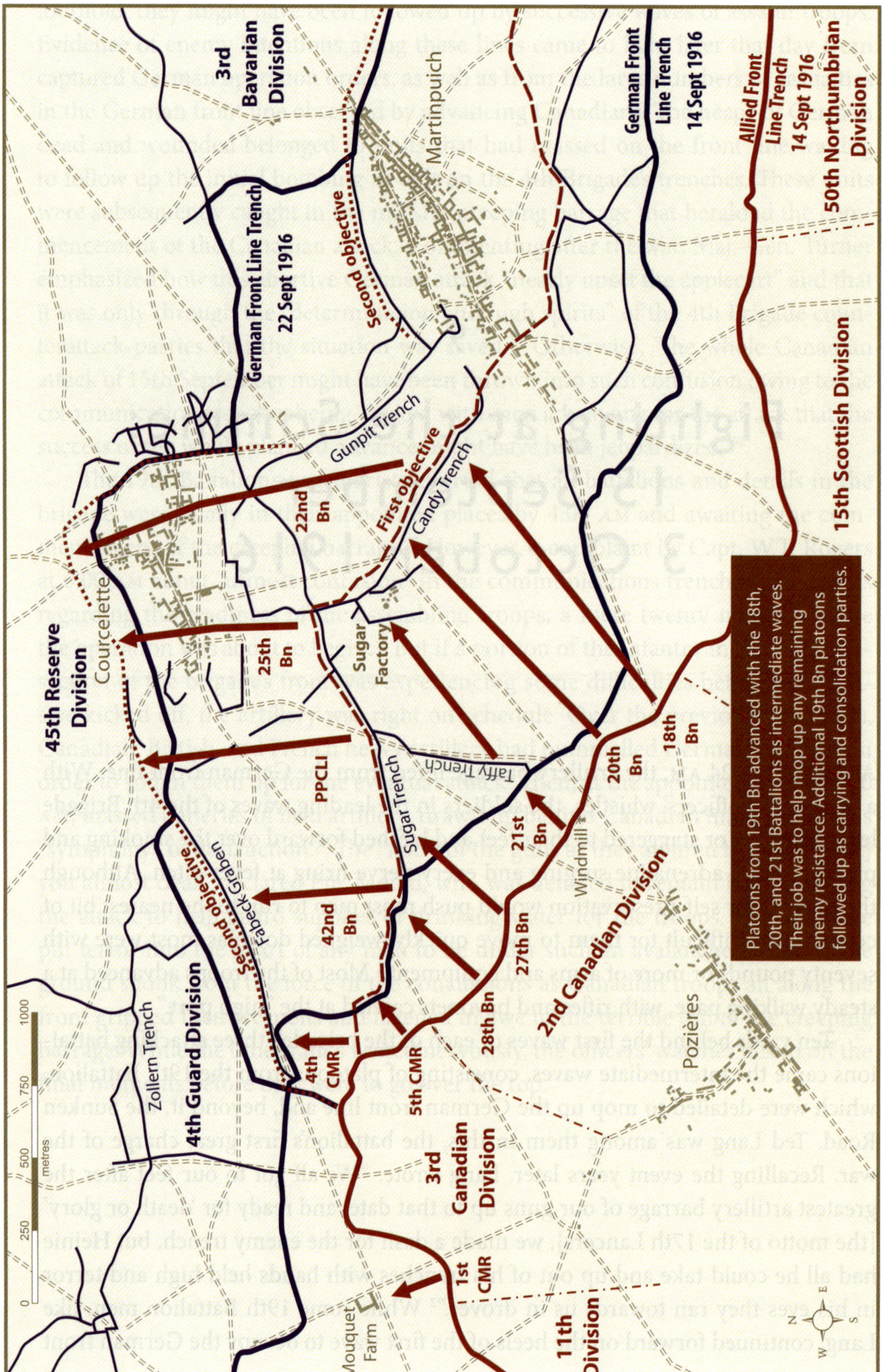

Map 6 – The Somme – Courcelette.

Ground over which 4th Brigade advanced on the morning of 15 September 1916. The direction of the advance was right to left. (Author's collection, 2015)

A view of Courcelette taken from the remains of the windmill at Pozières. Elements of the 4th and 6th Brigades advanced across this open ground on the morning of 15 September 1916. (Author's collection, 2015)

line, others busily rounded up the dazed and terrified prisoners. One of Pte. John Mould's friends, who went over the top that day, later claimed that

> he had never seen a finer sight in his life than he witnessed that morning. He told me that the earth for miles seemed to open up with nothing else but Canadian soldiers, all bent on the one object – that of capturing the German trenches. He said no one could

> have faced such a charge as that and it was like child's play getting into their front line[,] no sooner did they see our men climbing the parapet than up went their hands and out of their mouths came the word "Comrad."[3]

The numbers of German prisoners, at first a trickle, became a flood as the morning wore on. By day's end, over 300 would pass through the hands of the 19th Battalion, among them six officers.[4]

By 6:35 AM the 4th Brigade had secured the German front-line trench. The troops of the leading wave pressed on, carrying another "intermediate" trench situated from 100 to 250 yards behind the front line and around 500 yards south of the sugar factory.[5] The creeping barrage, which was moving steadily onward in its scheduled 100-yard lifts, had crushed enemy resistance in the front line. Heaps of dead and wounded Germans lay strewn throughout the trench, making for a gruesome and pitiful sight for moppers-up like Ted Lang, whose job was to secure and consolidate the position. Lang wrote:

> Nothing [was] in the trench directly in my path but dead Germans ... and one live one lying on his back and dying in extreme agony. And then something happened I have never forgotten. A young fellow who had just joined the 19th a few days previously in a draft from England and assigned to my section, born in Russia, knelt down beside the dying German, unhooked his own water bottle, drew the stopper and poured some water into the poor fellow's mouth. On the instant he [the German] breathed his last. Then he [the "young fellow"] helped me swing the dead Heinies out of our bit of trench and await further orders.[6]

German bodies in the blasted remnants of a trench captured by the Canadians on 15 September 1916. (LAC PA-000639)

Looking across the Albert–Bapaume road toward Martinpuich on the horizon. The 4th Brigade's objectives along Candy Trench lay across the field, stretching from the road to the edge of Martinpuich. (Author's collection, 2015)

In the meantime, the attack continued with almost irresistible force. But farther along the Canadian path of advance, stubborn pockets of resistance were increasingly encountered, especially along the 4th Brigade's left flank and throughout the 6th Brigade's section. The shock of surprise, the ferocity of the creeping barrage, and the close proximity of the opposing front trenches had placed the survivors in the German front line at an insurmountable disadvantage, making it virtually impossible for them to mount any effective resistance; but German troops in positions farther to the rear had more time to react. Although they must have been terrified by the approach of the creeping barrage, the extra minutes they had to prepare themselves probably allowed some of them to secure cover from the passing "storm of steel." Those Germans who did survive the bombardment now emerged from their shelters in isolated shell holes or stretches of trench to pour frontal or enfilade fire into the ranks of the advancing Canadians. The first-wave troops in some of the attacking battalions suffered many casualties, but successive waves eventually wore down and eliminated the remaining enemy strongpoints.[7]

While sporadic resistance from the German infantry could be dealt with, the German artillery was another matter. Three minutes after the attack began, German gunners commenced their own barrage, which would harry the Canadians throughout their advance.[8] Nevertheless, the attack maintained its overall cohesion, and the 4th and 6th Brigades moved forward to the second principal German line of resistance – the intersecting trenches code-named Sugar Trench and Candy Trench. By just after 7 AM the 4th Brigade had secured its objectives along

"Candy"; the 6th Brigade reported likewise from "Sugar" some forty minutes later.[9] The climax of the 4th Brigade's effort had come with the battle for the fortified sugar factory, which lay within the 21st Battalion's path of advance. It had been expected that the fight for the sugar factory would be fierce, and with that in mind, arrangements had been made to bring down a concentrated bombardment of heavy artillery on the factory and surrounding area. This succeeded in crushing a good part of the opposition at the strongpoint, especially from the usually steadfast German machine gunners. As soon as the bombardment lifted, infantry from the 21st Battalion rushed the factory from three sides and took possession of it, capturing 125 prisoners in the bargain.[10]

As for the 19th Battalion, Lt. A.W. Macdonald (of B Company), commanding the three platoons of the first intermediate wave supporting the 21st Battalion, reported reaching what he called the German "second line" at 7:04 AM. This would have been the "intermediate" trench located just beyond the German front line. To the right of Macdonald's men in this captured trench were those of Lt. Arthur W. Ellis (of C Company), leading the three platoons of the intermediate wave supporting the 20th Battalion.[11] Six minutes later, at 7:10 AM, Lt. James A. Linton (of A Company) reported that his three platoons of the second intermediate wave supporting the 21st Battalion had reached and consolidated their assigned position along the Sunken Road. He and his men were now working to construct shelters

View from what was German-held territory on the morning of 15 September 1916. This photo was taken close to where the sugar factory was located, looking back along the Albert–Bapaume road towards Pozières. The 4th Brigade's jumping-off positions are roughly along the horizon, extending from the left side of the photo across the road and continuing along the horizon behind the trees in the middle distance. 4th Brigade troops advanced parallel with, and on both sides of, the road. (Author's collection, 2015)

for the wounded while simultaneously providing support for the 31st Battalion of the 6th Brigade, which was advancing along their left flank.[12] Later, at 8:40 AM, Capt. William T. Rogers (of D Company), in charge of the three platoons of the intermediate wave supporting the 18th Battalion, reported that they had achieved their objective and were digging in along the "intermediate" trench. Rogers had found himself in command that morning after Capt. William H. McLaren was lost early in the attack.[13]

After all objectives along the 4th Brigade's front had been secured, the work of consolidating the new Canadian positions along Candy Trench and just beyond the sugar factory went into full swing. This kept up through the remainder of the day and was made no easier by persistent German shelling. All of the consolidation parties from the 19th Battalion had a rough time of it, but the platoons on the left under Lt A.W. Macdonald were particularly hard pressed. "Have been crumped out of original position and have moved the remainder of my men to communication trench running forward from D. Company lines where I await further orders," reported Macdonald to Maj. Morrison back at battalion headquarters. Macdonald concluded grimly: "Old line untenable. We are badly in need of parties to carry out wounded who are in terrible shape."[14]

The shelling not only made life miserably perilous for the consolidating parties but also compounded difficulties with communications. Because of the extreme vulnerability of exposed telephone lines, all messages to and from battalion headquarters had to be carried by runners, who, according to the battalion's after-action report, "certainly had their work cut out for them and did much toward the success of the day in getting the required information into Headquarters. This work was all done under heavy shell fire, and though they lost one killed and two wounded [they] won their place in the Battalion as heroes."[15] Heroes they may have been, but the inevitable time lag that came with using runners during a battle made it impossible for commanding officers to exert any sort of immediate control over the course of the fighting.

By 2:20 PM, Macdonald and his men evidently had reached the end of their tethers as a result of being bashed about by enemy artillery. Once more he sent word back to Maj. Morrison: "I have just set [*sic*] you a message saying we have been blown out of our original position into communication trench running towards sugar factory. We shall watch our old line and take it over as soon as shelling slackens. Our casualties are very serious and I repeat that it will ease our minds to know when relief will take [place]."[16] With all of his platoons engaged in carrying supplies forward and making good the captured German front-line and intermediate trenches, there was little Morrison could do until the entire battalion was relieved by order of brigade headquarters. "Hold on to your position," was the only response he could give Macdonald. But he added the following hopeful message: "The 5th Brigade will be going over you shortly. They are going to advance."[17]

Top: Desolate vista from a sunken road outside the ruins of Courcelette. The original archival caption titles this image "The Road to Death." (LAC PA-000712) Above: "The Road to Death" in 2015. (Author's collection)

Difficult as it might have been for Macdonald and his men to believe, the morning's operations had gone extremely well from the perspective of division and corps headquarters. By afternoon, the attacking units from the 4th and 6th Brigades had managed to set up a number of strongpoints manned by Lewis gunners well forward of the morning's objectives. Offensive patrols and advance posts were pushed ahead onto "Gun Pit Road," and some even reached the southern outskirts of the village of Courcelette itself. The reports these patrols sent back encouraged Lt.-Gen. Byng to order an immediate continuation of the attack, which would involve the capture of Courcelette.[18] Maj.-Gen. Turner thus ordered his remaining brigade, the 5th, to prepare for action.

At around 5 PM, the 22nd, 25th, and 26th Battalions of Brig.-Gen. A.H. Macdonell's 5th Infantry Brigade passed through the 19th Battalion's positions on their way to capture Courcelette.[19] By 6:45 PM, after a gruelling advance through stiff German bombardments and deadly bayonet clashes in the village, Macdonell's men had achieved their objectives and Courcelette was in Canadian hands.[20] From their assembly point in the reserve area, the troops of 5th Brigade had crossed two miles of open ground in broad daylight and, with the help of a creeping barrage, fought their way through Courcelette until they reached their objective line along the northern and eastern outskirts of the village.[21]

Assessing the Outcome

By the standards of the war to date, the Canadian achievement on 15 September had been a remarkable one. The 2nd Canadian Division had captured Courcelette, while to its left, the 3rd Canadian Division had secured significant portions of the German position known as Fabeck Graben. But such deeds had exacted a price in human life. Among the 19th Battalion's other ranks, around 250 were killed or wounded that day. As for the officers, Lts. Maurice F. Wilkes and A.W. Macdonald were killed in action. Having held out as long as he could, the unfortunate

Dressing wounded in a trench during the battle at Courcelette, 15 September 1916. (LAC PA-000909)

A British Mark I tank emerging from smoke. (LAC PA-001009)

Macdonald died at his post around 3:00 PM, likely as a result of shellfire. Also, Capt. W.H. McLaren was still missing and believed killed, and Capt. C.S. Patterson (the battalion's paymaster) and Lts. William R. McGie and Everest B. Gandier were wounded.[22]

During the morning attack, some casualties among the first-wave troops from the other three battalions in the brigade may have resulted from "friendly fire," which cut down those who, out of enthusiasm or inexperience, had "hugged" the creeping barrage too closely. Exactly how many perished or were injured in this manner is impossible to ascertain. Since the platoons from the 19th Battalion had been assigned to the intermediate waves, the danger posed by the creeping barrage should have been minimal for them. Most 19th Battalion casualties were inflicted by retaliatory German bombardments, which raked the parties of men attempting to hold and consolidate captured ground. "They always try to take [their trenches] back again, if possible," asserted Pte. Mould, "or if not they shell the line unmercifully. It was here that we got most of our casualties, the bombardment during the day being terrible … It was awful to see shocking sights that were being taken to hospital and all around did what they could to give a helping hand."[23]

A few survivors believed that the morning's death toll might have been worse if not for the presence of the tanks. Even the 19th Battalion's after-action report on the day's operations made a great deal of their presence. "The tanks played a very important part in the attack," the report asserted, the author concluding (rather inelegantly) that these machines "were greatly to blame for the final victory."[24] Yet of the six tanks that had been assigned to the 2nd Canadian Division, all but two were knocked out of action shortly after they rolled forward from their assembly positions at zero hour.[25] One of the three machines supporting the 4th Brigade broke down before it had even crossed the front line, and another bellied down in the mud of no man's land. The sole remaining tank with the 4th Brigade was left lumbering alone along the Albert–Bapaume road, well behind the leading waves of infantry. But even this single machine, slow and ungainly as it was, made a vivid impression on all who saw it. Magnus Macintyre Hood of the 24th Battalion was serving in a carrying party bringing up ammunition and grenades to the 21st Battalion near the sugar factory. According to Hood, once his party had reached the 21st Battalion men, they watched this tank "pass ahead and go right up to the walls of the refinery, its guns blazing. It seemed to lean against one of the walls which collapsed and the monster tore into the fort, while we could see the Germans streaming out behind it offering an excellent target to the riflemen in the shell holes."[26]

Although Hood's description might lead one to believe that the tank played a pivotal role in the capture of the sugar factory, in fact the tank did not arrive on the scene until almost a full hour after the factory had been bombarded by the artillery and seized by the infantry. Neither Brig.-Gen. Rennie nor Lt.-Col. Elmer Jones (CO 21st Battalion) mentioned tank support in their reports on the capture of the sugar factory. Even the tank crews themselves made no claim in their after-action reports to have played a key role in neutralizing this important strongpoint.[27] Being a member of a carrying party from a reserve battalion, Hood would have arrived on the scene considerably later than the personnel from the assault battalions. Consequently, he probably misinterpreted some mopping-up work by the tank as being the actual capture of the factory. By way of contrast, a veteran of the 21st Battalion expressed a decidedly more cynical view of the tanks' role on 15 September. In his opinion, the tanks "were a fluke; they didn't amount to anything. They didn't go

A British Mark I tank with damaged wheeled steering tail. (LAC PA-000968)

very far ... they bogged down. They got caught in the old trenches, you know, and they tipped over ... it was all muddy, you know, and they weren't a success."[28]

As was the case for the 4th Brigade, a single surviving tank had moved forward behind the 6th Brigade's assault troops, and those Germans who were directly in the path of the armoured leviathans had a dramatically different opinion of their effectiveness. Some surrendered at the tanks' approach or fled in terror. Others stood their ground, only to be mowed down by fire from the tanks' guns. The 19th Battalion reported that the "Germans turned and ran from these awkward looking beasts who spit M.G. fire at them, and fired 6 pound shells into their trenches besides squashing their M.G. emplacements." The same report quoted a captured German battalion commander, who was said to have exclaimed that the use of such weapons "was 'not war but slaughter.'" The report's author smugly informed his readers that the officer "was promptly reminded of Gas and Zepplins [*sic*]."[29] In the end, the Canadian high command decided that the tank experiment had succeeded, albeit in a very limited fashion. Maj.-Gen. Turner concluded that the tanks' main role in the future would be in mopping-up operations, while Lt.-Gen. Byng declared more bluntly that "tanks are a useful accessory to the infantry, but nothing more."[30]

An accessory, perhaps, but one that presented extremely trying conditions for the crews that operated them. Ed Youngman described an opportunity he had to experience battle inside a tank:

> It was hot, it was in September, and these men [the tank crew] just worked with a little pair of shorts, puttees and boots, not another thing on them. I had full battle dress except my rifle, it was on the mule, and I was only there ten minutes when I wished I had never got in it, on account of the terrific heat. So after going, oh four or five hundred yards, I noticed that there was a lot of noise, seemed to be bumping and banging and I noticed that the back vent was open about a foot or fifteen inches and there was some cool air coming in there and when the lieutenant wasn't watching I hoisted myself and I went out through that and fell head first to the ground and was glad – that's the only time I was ever in a tank and I was damn glad to get out of it. When I laid there on the ground trying to get my senses I knew what the banging was – old Jerry was trying – throwing everything from a forty-five Colt to a five point nine [at the tank]. I got out of there quickly.[31]

For the Germans, the tanks were not the only source of "frightfulness" during the attack. Leaving aside the considerable numbers of prisoners taken, many troops from the 2nd Canadian Division displayed a ruthless attitude towards their opponents at Courcelette. Some Canadians killed German troops out of hand, even, in some cases, after the Germans had expressed a desire to surrender. This was done for a variety of reasons, which included revenge for the punishment the Canadians had taken from the Germans during their time in the Ypres Salient; fears of German treachery (stories abounded of Germans feigning surrender only to ambush and kill their would-be captors); the inherent risks involved in dealing with dugouts full of Germans; and possible encouragement from officers.[32] Lt.-Col. Elmer Jones admitted later that "on our advancing, some of the enemy offered to surrender but in most cases these men were bayonetted by our advancing troops."[33] Even Maj.-Gen. Turner was aware of the pent-up hostility in his men, and he wrote in his diary on 18 September that "the men were not looking for prisoners, and considered a dead German was the best."[34] Although there is anecdotal evidence that some officers encouraged their men to take no prisoners on 15 September 1916, it is not surprising that no such instructions have yet been found in official orders or documents.[35]

In the end, the choice of whether or not to take prisoners was an individual one, subject to the particulars of the situation and the personal inclinations of each soldier. Certainly, for all of the instances of Canadian ruthlessness at Courcelette, there also were acts of charity towards injured opponents, as evidenced by Ted Lang's companion, who shared his water bottle with a dying German. Yet it is important to remember, as historian Tim Cook has pointed out, that "while soldiers generally felt sympathy for fellow sufferers, the Western Front often left soldiers with two choices: kill or be killed. The Great War soldier was as much an executioner as he was a victim."[36]

On 15 September the British Fourth and Reserve Armies had advanced to an average depth of a mile along a six-mile front and captured the fortified villages of Flers, Martinpuich, and Courcelette. This amounted to more than twice the amount of territory gained on 1 July for around half the cost in casualties. But although the German defences had buckled, they were by no means breached. German reinforcements poured into the battle area to shore up their position and prevent a breakthrough, especially in the Flers sector. At the same time, the momentum of the attacking Allied forces had been sapped by casualties, fatigue, and the inevitable disorganization that resulted when units went forward without the benefit of real-time communication with their commanding officers. The latter problem would bedevil infantry units in all armies throughout the war and would not be solved until the later development of truly portable two-way radios.[37]

Although the offensive mounted on 15 September did not succeed in attaining either its immediate objective of capturing Bapaume or its broader, entirely unrealistic goal of destabilizing the entire German position on the Western Front, the British commander-in-chief, Gen. Haig, was encouraged by the progress made on the opening day. On 17 September he wrote to Gen. Gough at Reserve Army headquarters, stating that "the capture by your troops of the Sucerie, Courcelette, and Mouquet Farm, besides several miles of enemy's trenches during the last three days is a fine performance of which all ranks may well be proud. I congratulate you all warmly."[38]

There was no time permitted to bask in the glow of even this modest success. Plans had already been laid for the continuation of the offensive, which, in the Reserve Army's sector, would be aimed principally at the village of Thiepval and its namesake ridge. In the meantime, the 19th Battalion had been in the forefront of the action since 10 September and was sorely in need of a rest by sunset on the 15th. Fortunately, respite was not long in coming: orders came through just after midnight that the battalion was to withdraw from the line and march back to bivouac in brigade reserve, around half a mile to the rear.[39] However, it was not a simple process to collect the scattered elements of the battalion, occupying as they did positions that were dispersed across the breadth of the section held by the brigade. The battalion after-action report stated that "it was a hard task the runners had before them to go out in the rain over that churned up ground and locate a platoon then about ten men] dug in a few shell holes, and guide them in. Carrying in the wounded was an act deserving great credit."[40]

The battalion remained in reserve on 16 September, when it stood by in support of the 5th Brigade. Parties also were dispatched to carry out the grim task of gathering and burying the dead. Those who were not detailed for this duty were scarcely more comfortable, however, for they had little in the way of shelter from the increasingly cold and wet weather. It was an especially trying time for those who were at the breaking point, both physically and mentally, because of the recent operations. As their nerves gradually relaxed from the prolonged excitement and panic that had dominated their lives over the previous days, many men fell into a profound state of lethargy. Some seemed almost to age before their comrades' eyes. A bit of hot food and the knowledge that they had won a significant victory were, according to the battalion report, "the only things which kept them going."[41]

On 17 September the 19th and the other battalions of the 4th Brigade were moved back to the Brickfields near Albert, and from there the brigade marched, in the rain, still farther back, to a reinforcement camp at Val de Maison, where they arrived on 19 September. By then, the entire division had been pulled out of the line and placed in corps reserve, and all ranks had had time to reflect on the price of their latest efforts. By their best reckoning, the total casualties in the 19th Battalion from 10 to 17 September had been 15 officers and 313 other ranks. Two officers and 58 other ranks had been killed, 12 officers and 220 other ranks had been wounded, and one officer and 35 other ranks were missing. In addition, 27 other ranks were listed as being sick.[42] Their comrades throughout the 2nd Canadian Division and the rest of the Canadian Corps also had suffered heavily in their shares of the offensive. By 22 September, the Canadian Corps counted 7,230 casualties.[43]

It was in a mixed atmosphere of relief, sorrow, and overwhelming exhaustion that Lt.-Col. Turnbull found his battalion when he returned from his convalescence, arriving at Val de Maison on 20 September. The Canadians had made their greatest advance of the war to date; the failure at St-Eloi had been avenged. True, many old faces were now absent from the regimental family, some temporarily, a few others permanently. Yet new blood was infused immediately into the depleted battalion, when ninety-five other ranks arrived as reinforcements on 16 September, and a further twenty-seven other ranks three days later. And on 23–24 September, six new officers came to occupy some of the empty seats in the mess.[44]

Second Tour at the Somme

Having moved as far back as the village of Berteaucourt on 21 September, the 19th Battalion enjoyed a brief rest on the following day before making its way forward again through the reserve area, billeting again in Val de Maison and Vadencourt and arriving once more at the Brickfields on 25 September. Here the troops of the 4th Brigade were again assembled, and that evening they marched to bivouac in Tara Valley. They, and the rest of the 2nd Canadian Division, now prepared for their second tour of duty at the Somme.[45] It would be as gruelling as their first.

The Germans were grimly contesting the loss of every bit of territory, and through incessant bombardments and fierce infantry counterattacks, had made the 2nd Canadian Division pay dearly for its gains before it was relieved on 18 September. Now, after only six days in reserve, the division was sent back into the fray before its ranks were fully rested and replenished. Gens. Haig and Gough were determined to capitalize on the accomplishments of 15 September, and the Reserve Army now commenced its assault against German positions along Thiepval Ridge, to the northwest of Courcelette. This task was allotted primarily to the British II and Canadian Corps. Among the principal objectives for the Canadians were the German positions code-named Zollern, Hessian, Kenora, and Regina trenches. The Canadian Corps would attack with two divisions, the 1st on the left and the 2nd on the right.[46] The fighting commenced on 26 September and was a savage see-saw affair. On the following day, the 2nd and 3rd Brigades of the 1st Canadian Division finally secured the portions of Zollern and Hessian trenches assigned to the Canadians. But the eastern end of Kenora Trench, which had been captured by the 3rd Brigade on the 26th, was retaken by the Germans on the 27th. The 6th Brigade conducted the 2nd Canadian Division's share of the attack striking at German front-line positions to the north and northeast of Courcelette. The 29th Battalion on the right of the 6th Brigade's front managed to reach its objectives, but only limited progress was made by the 31st Battalion on the left. These difficulties were mitigated on the night of 26–27 September, when the German troops opposing the 2nd Canadian Division withdrew to stronger defences in Regina Trench. This allowed the 6th Brigade to advance its positions and push patrols forward on 27 September with comparatively less difficulty than on the previous day. The 28th Battalion managed to gain ground west of the Bapaume Road, while the 27th and 29th Battalions dispatched patrols along either side of the Dyke Road, reconnoitring the

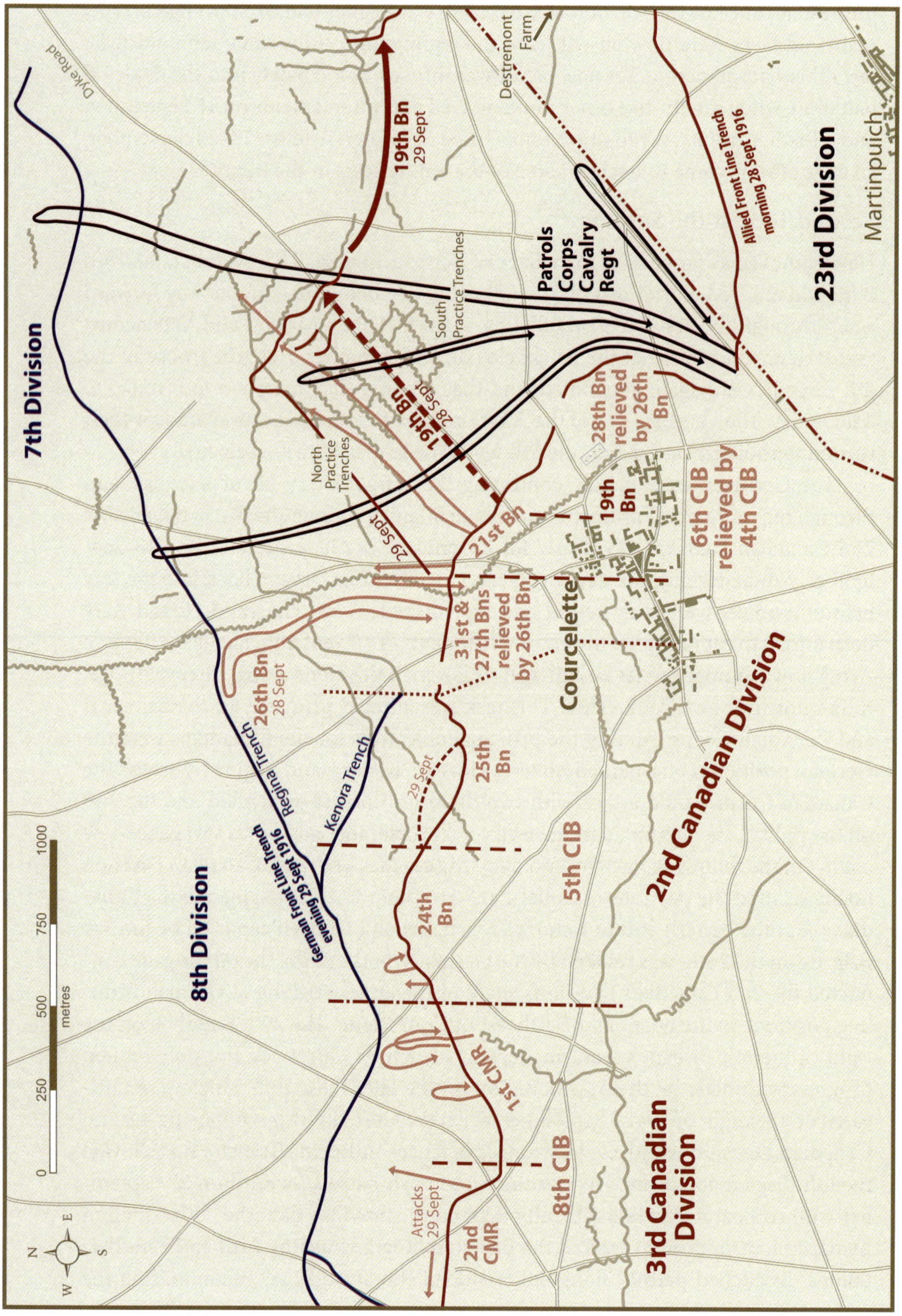

Map 7 – The Somme – Thiepval Ridge.

north and south practice trenches, which had been abandoned by the enemy.[47] The Battle of Thiepval Ridge petered out on 28 September with two of the principal Canadian objectives – Regina and Kenora trenches – still untaken. But it had set the stage for the 19th Battalion's second eventful tour at the Somme.

Earlier, on 26 September, the 4th Brigade had been attached briefly to the 1st Canadian Division during the initial stages of the fighting for Thiepval Ridge. The brigade was held in readiness to operate along the 1st Division's left flank, but the situation permitted its return to the 2nd Canadian Division on 27 September. The 19th Battalion was held in reserve in Sausage Valley and Chalk Pits on 26–27 September and was then ordered to march to Gun Pit Road near Courcelette. There, Lt.-Col. Turnbull would receive further instructions from Brig.-Gen. Ketchen of the 6th Brigade, under whose command the battalion would be placed temporarily.[48] Upon reaching his destination at about 3:00 AM on 28 September, Turnbull telephoned Ketchen, who informed him that recent patrols had detected very few Germans ahead of Canadian positions. Division headquarters wanted to capitalize on this development, so the 19th Battalion was to move out "into the open to the North East of Courcelette and go on until held up, and then dig in and hold their ground as best they could." Turnbull realized that this was "practically open fighting," something that the battalion as yet had no experience in. When he asked Ketchen what protection his battalion would have on its flanks, Ketchen flatly informed him that there would be none, adding, "You must provide your own."[49]

This was hardly encouraging, but there was little that Turnbull could do. Summoning his officers, he explained the situation to them and placed Capt. Harry Hatch, now in command of C Company, in charge of the operation. Assisting Hatch would be the battalion adjutant, Lt. Herbert Fearman, who would manage the telephone link back to battalion headquarters. The officers permitted their men some time to rest while they set about drawing up their plans and collecting all possible information from the 6th Brigade about the nature of the ground and the enemy positions ahead of them. As one report put it, "this was a task which needed very careful handling because to send a whole battalion of men forward a mile without any protection on their flanks meant almost certain death unless skillfully handled."[50]

Yet, although they had no flank protection, the troops of the 19th Battalion would not be operating entirely alone. A Canadian cavalry patrol of two officers and twenty other ranks was ordered to proceed from a point on the Pozières–Bapaume Road near the junction with Gun Pit Road and cut across country towards the village of Pys, passing just west of the notorious German strongpoint known as Destremont Farm. Before the cavalry was to set off at 5:30 AM, word came down from brigade that Destremont Farm had been captured by British troops of the 23rd Division, which cheered all ranks, especially those of the cavalry patrol. The optimistic atmosphere would not last long, however, for shortly after the cavalry set out in extended order, it was fired upon by snipers and machine guns from the direction of Destremont Farm. One trooper was killed, two were wounded, and six horses were lost by the time the patrol was forced to fall back. This regrettable turn of events was reported to 6th Brigade headquarters, which informed Turnbull that his battalion should still proceed as planned.[51]

At 6:00 AM on 28 September, a patrol led by Lt. O.S. Dunn (patrol officer) was ordered to move out ahead of the battalion and, if possible, make contact with the forward elements of the 23rd Division. A telephone operator was sent with them, his job being to keep Hatch abreast of any developments as they moved towards the German lines that stretched between the distant villages of Le Sars and Pys. At 7:00 AM, the rest of the battalion, led by Hatch at the head of C Company, completed its assembly and moved out in a mixed formation. Hatch's company was followed by D Company, under Capt. W.T. Rogers, B Company, under Lt. J. Linton, and A Company, led by Lt. A.W. Ellis.[52]

John Mould, who had been held back from the advance for other duties on 15 September, had just been promoted to corporal and was now given his chance to face the enemy. His diary provides the most detailed personal record available of the 19th Battalion's operations during its second tour at the Somme. As the men advanced to their assembly point through the ruins of Courcelette, Mould was chilled by the spectacle that lay before him:

> Whilst passing down the Courcelette Road to a point where we had to make the advance a sight met our eyes which would have upset the nerves of anyone. This village which was only captured a few days previous by the Canadians was strongly held by the Germans and naturally their [*sic*] were a large number of casualties on either side. Every yard along the road their [*sic*] were dead bodies lying in all positions some of them being awful to look upon. A cold feeling seemed to run through my body as I stepped over some of them and my thoughts at once went to their dear ones whom they had left behind.[53]

The 19th Battalion moved forward with its right flank situated along the Dyke Road. After advancing roughly 500 yards, the troops reached the abandoned practice trenches.[54] Lt. Dunn then reported back over the telephone that he and his patrol were 1,000 yards ahead and being fired upon by enemy snipers from the direction of the Le Sars Trench. Moreover, they had found no trace of the 23rd Division, and they confirmed that Destremont Farm remained in enemy hands. Capt. Hatch then decided to recall the patrol. After taking stock of the situation, he ordered all companies to advance a further 500 yards to a point where they reportedly would find a depression in the ground. Once there, they could take advantage of the cover afforded by the topography, extend their frontage, and dig in.[55]

As the men of the 19th covered the remaining 500 yards to the appointed position, their ranks were lacerated by bursts of machine-gun and rifle fire, which grew more deadly as they neared their destination. Fortunately, once they had reached the designated area, the undulating ground and the presence of numerous shell holes gave them some cover. But they had to work quickly to dig a viable trench in order to gain more complete protection from the bullets that whizzed about them. Wrote Cpl. Mould:

> We had quite a number of casualties in the last stage of the advance, I myself being rather fortunate in getting away with a clear skin. We had just started to dig with our entrenching tools when one poor fellow who was on the right side of me was killed instantly. Another fellow who was also working on my left being wounded at the same time. I shall never forget my feelings when this happened and it took me several minutes before I came to my proper senses again.[56]

When the last platoons arrived on the scene, the situation became even more dangerous as the Germans loosed salvoes of whiz-bangs along the Dyke Road. Until that point, the German artillery had been relatively quiet, which was a blessing for Mould and his comrades. Mould wondered why the enemy artillery had not been more active earlier, in view of the fact that he could see numerous German observation balloons in the distance. He surmised that, because their advance had been made without an accompanying artillery barrage, this had surprised the Germans and made it difficult for them to follow the battalion's movements.[57]

The men kept on digging for their lives. The Germans, increasingly wise to the situation, shelled them more heavily as the day wore on. By the afternoon, a front and support trench had been excavated, but the barrage had already killed and wounded a number of men. Lt. Linton of B Company had his arm broken, and Lt. Gidley, in charge of C Company while Capt. Hatch was in overall command of the operation, was knocked temporarily unconscious by a "heavy piece of mud" thrown up by the explosion of a shell. Linton and Gidley were succeeded by Lts. J.R. Goodman and Samuel H. Johnston respectively. Admitted Cpl. Mould:

> I had a very close call myself during this bombardment, a shell bursting within 2 yards of w[h]ere I was digging. I never knew a thing for a few minutes the force of the explosion sending me quite silly. It was an awful experience and one which I hoped would not happen again. After about 5 hours of this terrible anxiety things became much quieter. So we were able to proceed with our work of digging more quicker than before. Keeping hard at it during the night, we had by the morning completed 3 lines of trenches and also consolidated them good enough to protect the Battalion from machine gun fire and shrapnel.[58]

Although it had not advanced as far as Destremont Farm, the 19th Battalion managed to secure a position to the west of it and roughly 400 yards north of the practice trenches. The men had advanced 1,000 yards beyond their starting point that morning and were sheltered in newly constructed front, support, and reserve trenches. Also, additional protective trenches had been dug at right angles along both flanks of their position, and posts for Lewis gun teams and bombers had been

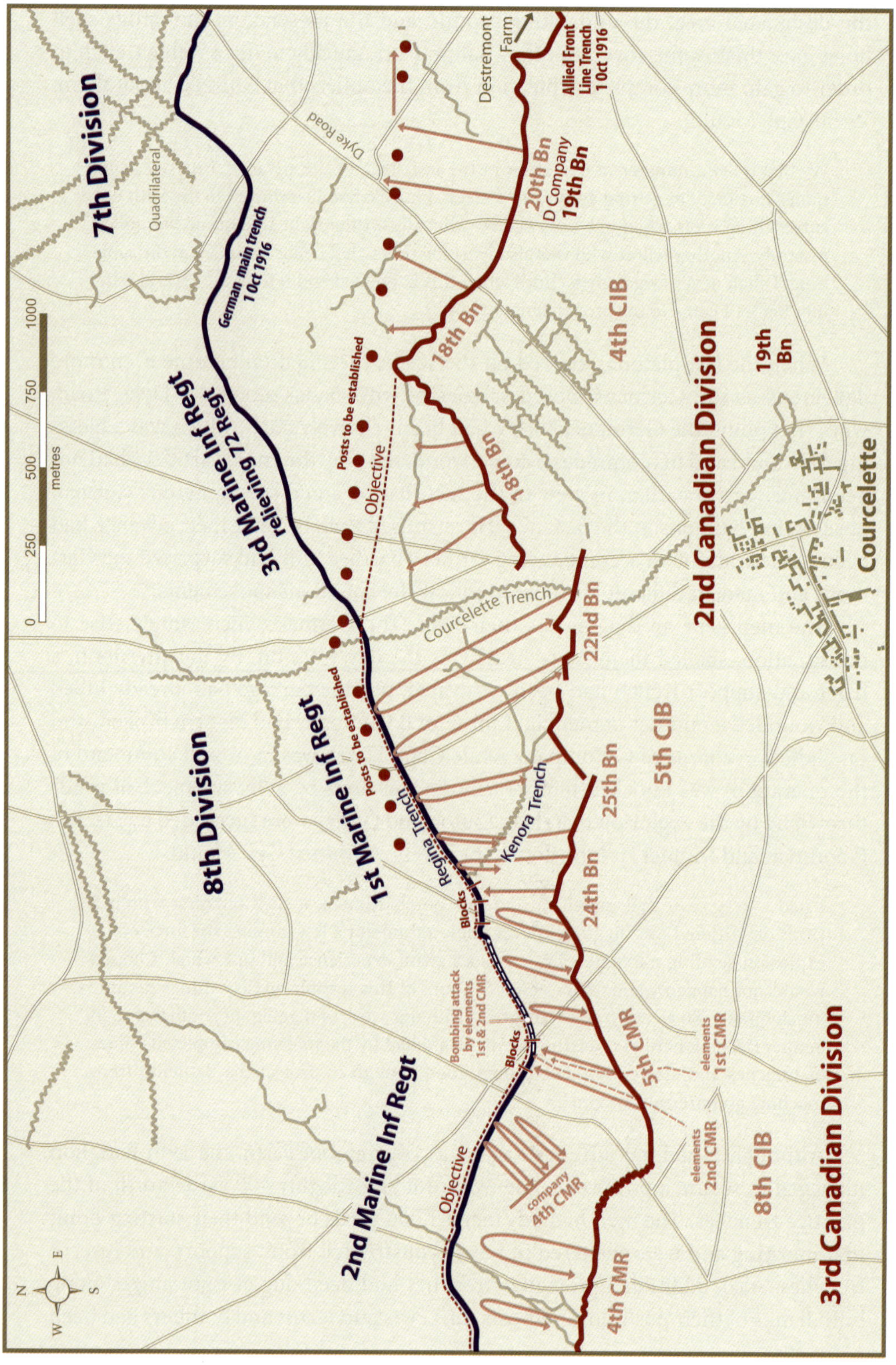

Map 8 – The Somme – Ancre Heights.

set up. A telephone link was established with battalion headquarters, but after artillery fire severed it, runners were used to maintain communications. On several occasions, British aircraft flew over the 19th Battalion's trenches, signalling with klaxon horns for the infantry to identify its new positions. The troops obliged by lighting coloured flares, the position of which the airmen noted on their maps. These maps and accompanying explanatory notes were then delivered to headquarters in weighted message bags at designated drop points, thus keeping battalion and brigade commanders informed about the location of their units.[59]

All ranks in the 19th Battalion worked steadily throughout the day to consolidate their positions in the face of continuous machine-gun fire, their efforts earning the praise of both Maj.-Gen. Turner and Brig.-Gen. Rennie.[60] The situation thus appeared reasonably favourable on the right portion of the 2nd Canadian Division's sector. Unfortunately, things had not gone so well on the left, where patrols from the 5th Brigade were bloodily repulsed when they attempted to enter Regina Trench, a position that was well manned and strongly wired.[61]

On the night of 28–29 September, the 4th Brigade relieved the 6th Brigade in the right portion of the division's sector and the 19th Battalion reverted to the control of its parent formation. The 21st Battalion, which had been moved forward the previous day, took up positions on the 19th Battalion's left flank, while the 20th and 18th Battalions were in support and reserve. Throughout the day on 29 September, work continued on improving existing positions while new bombing and Lewis gun posts were established 150 to 200 yards in advance of the front line.[62] The weather did not make the work any easier. Heavy rain fell during the day, transforming the newly dug trenches into ditches filled with gluey muck. "Food had also been very scarce up till now," stated Cpl. Mould, "and it was also very hard to get water this being the greatest need of all. At times the men were simply parched, and when water did come we went at it like wolves."[63]

Earlier in the morning on 29 September, Maj. C.M. Hoare-Ruthven of the 2nd Canadian Division staff had made his way into the 19th Battalion's trenches. He was reported to have been "highly satisfied with the great progress the 19th had made." According to a battalion report, "he realized the very dangerous position the battalion was in and gave orders we were not to go further forward."[64] But this order was modified after word came through shortly after 11:00 AM that British troops from the 23rd Division had finally taken possession of Destremont Farm. C Company was now detailed to establish a line of posts and maintain communication between the battalion's right flank and the British positions about 1,000 yards away at the farm.[65]

In the meantime, the Germans set about avenging the loss of Destremont Farm by shelling the neighbouring sectors throughout the day. This took its inevitable toll on all units in the 4th Brigade. On the night of 29–30 September, the intensity of the bombardments diminished, although the weather remained rainy and miserable. "When morning came," Cpl. Mould reported, the men were "very cold" and so were

> thankful for the issue of rum that was given out to us a short time after. Things were much about the same as regards artillery activity, we coming in for a fierce shelling during the day. It was nothing compared with what our guns sent over though, and I often wondered however they [the Germans] were able to live through it … It was 5 days now since we had seen rest and when the order came that we were to be relieved that night we were more pleased than ever.[66]

On the night of 30 September–1 October, the 19th Battalion was relieved by the 20th Battalion in the right sub-section of the 4th Brigade's line. Turnbull's men finally moved back into support along Gun Pit Road and Sugar Trench. But the relief was short-lived for D Company, which was sent back to the front lines to assist the 20th Battalion, whose front was rather extended and difficult to hold with the numbers at its disposal. All ranks involved in this turnaround were in an understandably black mood while heading back to the trenches. But they managed to subdue their frustration and overcome their exhaustion just enough to carry out their orders and dig themselves into new positions.[67]

The 20th and 18th Battalions made advances of their own on 1 October in support of the 5th Brigade's ill-fated effort against Regina Trench. This date saw the opening of what became known as the Battle of the Ancre Heights, which would drag on until 11 November. The two units from 4th Brigade started out at 3:15 PM, were able to make some headway east of the East Miraumont Road, in spite of periodic bursts of machine-gun fire from defending troops of the German 72nd Regiment, which was in the midst of a relief by the 3rd Marine Regiment. It was fortunate timing for the 4th Brigade's advance, and the troops managed to gain an additional 400 yards of ground on the flanks of the brigade's frontage, thereby straightening out its front line. The 4th Brigade's right flank was secured by the 23rd British Division, which mounted an attack at the same time and successfully maintained contact with the Canadians on its left.[68]

By contrast, the 5th Brigade's attack on Regina Trench was an utter disaster. The 24th, 25th, and 22nd Battalions went over the top at 3:15 PM and encountered masses of uncut barbed-wire obstacles, an intense artillery barrage, and heavy rifle and machine-gun fire from fresh troops of the Germans' 1st Marine Infantry Regiment. Operating with dismally depleted units, the 5th Brigade went from a total trench strength of 1,717 all ranks on 27 September to only 773 effective combatants on 2 October – less than a single battalion's worth. Before the attack was launched, Maj.-Gen. Turner had protested against it, but pressure from Reserve Army headquarters forced it to go ahead, with predictably tragic results.[69]

As these events unfolded, the bulk of the 19th Battalion remained in support at Gun Pit Road and Candy Trench. D Company, however, was in the lines and temporarily under the tactical control of the 20th Battalion. On 2 October the men of

D Company were set to work digging a new position from a point 200 yards north of Destremont Farm to a point approximately 200 yards to the northwest, where they linked up with the advance trench that had been dug by the 19th Battalion on 28 September. Meanwhile, their comrades back in support, far from being left idle, furnished work parties at night.[70]

From 30 September, when the bulk of the battalion had moved into support, until 3 October, the men had to contend not only with a shortage of water but also, reported Cpl. Mould, with "very little food" and incessant rain. On the 1st, Mould witnessed the "fiercest bombardment I had yet heard," followed by "British troops" (most likely from the 23rd Division) charging ahead to capture three lines of trenches, "one of the finest sights I have ever seen during the war." Then, on the afternoon of the 3rd, "word came around that we were to be relieved sometime during the night and … we were all thankful once more to get away from the scene of action."[71] His hopes were fulfilled. On the night of 3–4 October, A, B, and C Companies of the 19th Battalion were relieved in their support positions by the 52nd Battalion (3rd Canadian Division), after which they moved back to Usna Valley. At the same time, D Company, along with the 20th Battalion, was relieved in the front lines by the 21st Battalion. D Company proceeded back to Usna Valley as well, where it rejoined the rest of the 19th Battalion.[72]

But the Somme battlefield had some vicious parting shots to offer the 19th Battalion just as it set out for a rest in reserve. As Mould proceeded with his company out of the support trenches,

> a shell without the slightest warning to anyone burst within 2 yards of our party. All I knew at the time was that their [*sic*] was a terrific explosion and I [found] myself lying in a shell hole, I being thrown off my feet by the force of the explosion. Dirt flew over me from all directions but lucky for me their [*sic*] was no shrapnel amongst it. Thinking of my own safety and that their [*sic*] might be more shells [to] follow, I rushed through the smoke and dropped into a trench a few yards further on.

One officer lay killed and four other ranks wounded. Mould recounted what happened next:

> I did my best in helping the wounded and after a time we found stretchers with which we carried them to the dressing station. Long shall I remember the hard time we had in getting them their [*sic*][,] it was pitch dark at the time and to find the dressing station seemed out of the question. Over shell holes through trenches we carried and lifted the wounded men till we could hardly stand[,] finally finding the place we wanted after about 2 hours search. We had another 6 miles to walk to our destination [Usna Valley] and how we ever got through this walk I cannot say. Through water and thick clay and occasionally falling in shell holes we looked a fine specimen of human beings by the time we arrived at our resting place. I had been through some rough times up till this, but never did I experience such a terrible time that we had to go through on this occasion.

Mould and his comrades, after "a good feed and a hot drink of tea," then resumed marching, this time to the village of Bouzincourt, twenty-five miles from their starting point.[73] They reached their destination in mid-afternoon on 4 October and would remain there for the best part of two days getting some much-needed rest in billets.

As Turnbull's men proceeded into reserve, so too did the rest of the 2nd Canadian Division, its units being relieved in the lines by those of the 3rd Canadian Division. Much to the relief of all ranks, the division's second tour at the Somme was its last. During the first ten days of October, its constituent units began marching to a new sector of the front near the foot of the infamous height known as Vimy Ridge. Once there, the division came under the control of Gen. Sir Henry Horne's First Army. The 1st and 3rd Canadian Divisions would continue the fight at the Somme until mid-October, when they were relieved by the 4th Canadian Division, recently arrived from the Ypres Salient. The 1st and 3rd Canadian Divisions then proceeded to the First Army area and reunited with the 2nd Division, leaving Maj.-Gen. David Watson's 4th Canadian Division with the grim task of completing the Canadian phase of operations in the Battle of the Somme. It was Watson's men who finally captured Regina Trench – that "ditch of evil memory" – on 11 November. A week later, on 18 November, they also seized Desire Trench, their final major objective. The latter date saw the official termination of the Battle of the Somme, a "battle" that actually was a campaign comprised of several successive major operations. By the time the offensive finally ground to a tortuous halt in the late autumn rain and mud, all four Canadian divisions plus associated corps troops had suffered a staggering 24,029 casualties, all ranks.[74]

The Impact of the Somme

The 19th Battalion's second tour at the Somme, while arduous to the extreme, was not nearly as costly as its first. It was reckoned that from 25 September to 3 October, 1 officer and 12 other ranks were killed, 3 officers and 84 other ranks were wounded, and 3 other ranks were missing. An additional 29 other ranks had fallen sick over the same period.[75] The combined losses from both tours were far more sobering. It is estimated that in less than a month, from 10 September to 3 October, the battalion suffered battle casualties to the tune of 19 officers and 412 other ranks. This was a shocking loss rate for such a short span of time, especially in view of the fact that the battalion casualties during the *entire* period from 15 September 1915 to the end of August 1916 amounted to approximately 16 officers and 534 other ranks.[76]

For the 19th Battalion, for the Canadian Corps, for the British and French armies involved, and for the Germans, the Somme was indeed every bit the "bloodbath" that has been popularly portrayed. Disturbing as the casualty figures for the 19th Battalion were, they were the losses from just one of scores of individual units whose ranks had been decimated by the battle. In all, there had been 419,654 British casualties at the Somme between 1 July and 20 November 1916, 127,751 of whom were killed. The French suffered 204,253 casualties in the Somme offensive, bringing a total of 623,907 Allied casualties. German losses have been a bone of contention among historians; the figures quoted usually range from 465,000 to 600,000.[77] In their history of the campaign, Robin Prior and Trevor Wilson argue that German losses were far lower. Citing evidence furnished by the German *Reichsarchiv* to Winston Churchill in the 1920s, they estimate that the Kaiser's armies suffered "a total of 230,000" casualties against the British at the Somme.[78]

The Germans had passed two-thirds of their divisions on the Western Front through the fighting at the Somme,[79] and the effect of such hard pounding was compounded by the impact of the continuing struggle at Verdun. Indeed, the merciless *Materialschlachten* ("battles of material") at Verdun and the Somme, which pitted human flesh against munitions and machines, saw the loss of many of the German army's effective small-unit leaders.[80] Gary Sheffield suggests that as a result, German casualties, while perhaps fewer than the Allies' in numerical terms, were more serious for their having contained such a huge percentage of seasoned troops, especially officers and NCOs. He quotes a number of contemporary observations from sources such as Capt. Hans von Hentig of the Guard Reserve Division, who claimed that the Somme was "the muddy grave of the German field army," and Crown Prince Rupprecht of Bavaria, who declared that "what remained of the old first-class peace-trained German infantry had been expended on the battlefield."[81]

But Sheffield also argues that the "British Army was a far more effective instrument of war in November 1916 than it had been in July. In contrast to the Germans, the British lost mainly inexperienced troops, while the survivors had, in a strictly military sense, benefited greatly from the experience." Of the fifty-six infantry divisions in the BEF at that time, fifty-three had been rotated through the battle, meaning that virtually the entire strength of the British armies on the Western Front had some experience of the fighting. "British morale remained good," Sheffield maintains, "although the enthusiasm of the summer had been replaced by grim determination."[82]

In truth, the German army, although shaken, was far from broken by the Somme, and remained as determined to prevail as the British. It could not have been apparent to contemporary observers that the Battle of the Somme was, for the Allies and for the British in particular, the seedbed of eventual victory in 1918 that some modern commentators, writing with the benefit of hindsight, claim it to be.[83] To be sure, the Somme served as a very large, very bloody school for the BEF, and especially for the inexperienced New Army divisions that were raised in Britain by Lord Kitchener after the war's outbreak. But confusion among the British high command as to whether the offensive's purpose was one of attrition (based on "bite and hold" tactics) or breakthrough resulted in an inconsistent operational design that kept various phases of the offensive – and ultimately the offensive as a whole – running for longer than they should have, especially in the face of deteriorating weather in the autumn.[84] Hew Strachan offers a balanced assessment when he claims that at the Somme "the learning process which the British army's high command was passing through did pay dividends in 1918, but its route there need not have been so sanguinary."[85]

In mid-October, Maj. Lionel Millen wearily informed his mother:

> We are now through with the Somme for which we are all duly thankful. It has been a costly tour for us, some of my best pals gone. Poor Bill McLaren's wife, I have had a couple of letters from her. The old battalion is all changed. I am now 2nd in command, Gordon Morrison being given command of the 18th Battalion. Naturally I am glad, as it means no more living in front line trenches for me.[86]

Near the end of the month, Millen told his father that

> the spirit of the boys was wonderful after what they had been through. I tell you it's a hard, hard game and I hope the day is not very distant when it will all be over. So many of our best and finest [are] going.[87]

While Millen expressed a discernible tinge of optimism in his letter, Fred Stitt reported years later that he and others had adopted an air of pessimism and grim resignation. In Stitt's view, after months of fighting in the trenches,

> you became professional soldiers and that was all there was to it, you had to face that fact. There was very little conversation about what we would do when we got back to civil life. The mere idea of civil life didn't enter into our heads anymore … this thing was going on and on forever.[88]

10

A "Most Uneventful Tour": October 1916–March 1917

The year 1916 had been a severe testing time for the Canadian Corps. The 2nd and 3rd Canadian Divisions received bloody baptisms of fire in their first major operations at St-Eloi and Mont Sorrel. The 4th Canadian Division arrived at the front in August and would cut its operational teeth in the Battle of the Somme. The Somme was the awful proving ground where the Canadians survived their first extended series of large-scale attacks, their most notable successes being the capture of Courcelette on 15 September and the storming of Regina Trench on 11 November. But if the fighting at the Somme left the Canadians feeling exhausted and embittered, it at least spurred many to rethink the ways in which their forces were organized, trained, and handled in combat. In retrospect, the Somme battles were hideously wasteful affairs, prolonged far past the point where the men's sacrifices were worth the degree of advantage gained over the enemy. The German army, although mauled and deprived of countless experienced veterans, remained powerful and set to work revising its defensive arrangements – devising new doctrines for its troops and designing new fortified defence systems from which it would operate with deadly effect.

The Canadians, too, began reorganizing and retraining their units, based largely on lessons and conclusions drawn from serious analysis of the fighting at the Somme. The need to refine and improve organizations and methods was made all the more pressing by the corps' assignment to capture, in the spring of 1917, one of the most formidable German defence systems on the Western Front: Vimy Ridge.

Holding the Line and Rebuilding the Battalion

From the bloodstained fields of Picardy, the 2nd Canadian Division began moving in October to the industrial region of Artois, where they settled into the trenches of the Calonne sector, northwest of Vimy Ridge. The Canadian Corps assumed control of the right sector of Gen. Sir Henry Horne's First Army front. By the end of October the 1st, 2nd, and 3rd Canadian Divisions occupied a ten-mile stretch of front extending from positions two miles north of Arras to a point two miles northwest of Lens.[1]

After leaving the Somme battlefields, the men of the 19th Battalion proceeded to the new front, making their way to Hersin, where they took a brief rest and prepared to enter the lines in the Calonne sector. Cpl John Mould noted that "it was fine to get to one of these places after going through some hard fighting, as it helped to put new life into us and also to forget the hardships we had been subject to."[2]

The 19th Battalion was back in the front lines again on 17 October, in the Calonne I Section of trenches. There it stayed until 23 October, when it was relieved by the 21st Battalion. The 19th then moved into brigade support in the ruined village of Calonne, settling into billets just before 1:00 PM.[3] The next day, Maj. Millen wrote the following to his mother: "Just fancy two years ago today since we joined up. I certainly hope that it will all be over before another year comes around."[4] Millen and his men had just completed the first of eight successive tours in the trenches at Calonne, a stretch of duty that would take them through mid-January 1917. For the rest of 1916 and early 1917, the general pattern of activity in the lines was one of low-level hostility punctuated by periods of excitement and terror. Such periods were marked by occasional exchanges of artillery and mortar fire, constant patrolling, and frequent trench raids along the Canadian Corps' front. Nevertheless, Sgt. R.H. Neil described the three-month period at Calonne as "the most uneventful tour of front line duty" in the 19th Battalion's history.[5]

This was a good thing, for it gave the unit a chance to recuperate from the heavy fighting at the Somme, where its numbers had shrivelled from 976 to 501 all ranks between 4 September and 2 October 1916. This deficit was largely remedied by 24 officers and over 400 other ranks who joined the 19th Battalion between 16 September and 11 December. In addition, at least six experienced NCOs in the battalion were granted commissions.[6] By now, the various accents of the British Isles that identified many original volunteers of 1914 and early 1915 had begun to fade in the 19th Battalion and the rest of the Canadian Corps. Conversations became increasingly dominated by the flatter vocal tones of the predominantly Canadian-born reinforcements.[7]

Reconstituting the battalion and assimilating these reinforcements became a major priority. The task was made more manageable by a policy adopted by the Canadian Corps earlier in the Somme campaign, which ensured that the full strength of any infantry battalion was not sent into battle at any one time. A certain percentage of officers and other ranks were kept back in order to form a nucleus of experienced personnel around which the unit could re-form in the event of heavy casualties. If the worst were to happen, the survivors of the battle and those held back from it would be left to impart their skills and experience to the drafts of new troops sent up to reinforce them. Those officers and other ranks who were retained in reserve during an operation were referred to as "Left Out of Battle," or LOB. The precise numbers of men designated as LOB might vary from formation to formation over time. But typically, either the battalion CO or the second-in-command would remain out of harm's way, as would two of the company commanders, several platoon sergeants, a proportion of specialist troops, and some ordinary riflemen.[8]

The job of integrating new reinforcements and rebuilding the 19th Battalion's command and social structure was aided by the comparatively low casualty rates during its tours of duty in the Calonne sector. From 17 October 1916 to 19 January 1917 (the final day of the battalion's eighth tour in the sector), the sum total of battle casualties and accidental injuries was 60 other ranks (including 17 men killed), with no losses among the officers. There also were 112 reported cases of sickness in the same period.[9] Some of those who were wounded or ill would have remained at duty owing to the minor nature of their conditions, while a notable proportion of those evacuated – perhaps as high as 29 percent – would have returned to the unit after a period of convalescence.[10] The relative stability of the battalion's roster gave veterans and newcomers the time to become familiar with one another and to learn how to work effectively together.

However, one departure from the 19th Battalion during this time period is worthy of note. Faithful chronicler John Mould left the battalion on the morning of 20 November 1916 after fourteen months of service in the trenches. During the Battle of the Somme, Mould had suffered a degree of hearing loss, and as he put it, "I got that bad at times that I could not hear my name being called on parade." But if he was no longer fit for duty at the front, he was still able to work in some capacity behind the lines. Thus, it was arranged for him to transfer to the 2nd Canadian Division School, where he would resume his work as a cook. Subsequent medical boards would confirm his unfitness for front-line duty, and he would serve out the remainder of the war in various labour units before returning home to his wife Edith in St. Catharines.[11]

For every departing veteran like Mould, there was a new face to fill the void. Pte. John Gaetz, a twenty-two-year-old farmer from Red Deer, Alberta, whose first

Figure 10.1 John and Edith Mould. (AO F 954, I0024378)

tour in the lines with the 19th Battalion was in December 1916, later marvelled at his own ability to cope with life at the front:

> Being neither too old or too young[,] I have been impressed time and time again that a man should be mature for front line work out here, and yet not old enough to reach the stage where one is susceptible to Rhuematics and complaints which are caused by exposure … This is where the too young find it hard in not getting sleep … I've got now so as I can get along on very little sleep and at the same time march all day. I was never more free from colds than I am now and never sick. I can make a good meal out of hard tack, cheese, tea and a cigarette.[12]

Some Lessons of the Somme

The slower pace of operations during the last two months of 1916 gave the Canadian Corps the opportunity to analyze the experience of fighting at the Somme. This gave rise to organizational and tactical reforms that, when examined in retrospect, would shape the character of Canadian operations for the remainder of the war. After-action reports from all levels of command were rigorously studied, and frank opinions were solicited from subordinate commanders by their superiors.

Right: John Raymond Gaetz (photo taken later in 1918). (GMA NA-2214-11)
Below: A gunner writing an early Christmas greeting ("I am the Hun's Father Christmas") on the mounting of a 9.2-inch heavy howitzer, November 1916. (LAC PA-000938)

Brigade and division headquarters collected reports and suggestions from lower units and submitted their own analyses to corps headquarters for study. Taking into account the multitude of opinions generated by this process, corps, division, and brigade commanders and staffs worked together to evaluate existing procedures and address any problems. New ideas were then disseminated throughout the Canadian Corps by means of corps, divisional, and brigade training schools, as well as through senior officers' conferences and courses. This sort of institutionalized and collaborative learning process ultimately underpinned future Canadian successes on the battlefield during the First World War.[13]

As part of this process, Canadian Corps headquarters circulated a questionnaire on 3 November 1916 to each division, brigade, and battalion commander requesting their views on a variety of topics, including labour and preparatory work, the organization of attacks, and the operation of command, communications, liaison, weapons, and equipment. Based on his battalion's experiences at the Somme, Lt.-Col. Turnbull recommended that units holding the line before an attack be withdrawn and only fresh troops used for the assault.[14] On the important question of whether it was best for the first wave of attackers to proceed directly to the final objective, Turnbull maintained that they should indeed do so. If they did not, the following waves "when they see the first wave stop, think they have gained their objective and their Officers have difficulty in getting the men to advance to their second objective."[15] This was not a prescient recommendation, for the Canadian Corps eventually chose to adopt a "leapfrog" approach in organizing its assaults. According to this system, the first waves of attacking troops, which would bear the brunt of the fighting, would halt at the initial objective and consolidate; fresher waves of troops would then pass through them to seize more distant objectives.[16]

In response to corps headquarters' question about the possible benefits of instituting a standard attack drill among the infantry, Turnbull decided that it would be "desirable" but "should not be of a hard and fast nature" – the implication being that officers and men needed to be flexible in their approaches to unexpected tactical problems. Turnbull recommended that any drills involve "general ideas" only and be "practiced over real trenches as near like those to be attacked as possible." Although modern historians tend to comment favorably on the Canadian Corps' use of taped training courses for tactical rehearsals, Turnbull pointed out the limitation of this approach, believing that the troops could not get a real sense of what to expect in an attack unless they were moving over ground that was broken and excavated in similar fashion to that over which they would be advancing. "Trenches marked out by tapes are absolutely useless for this purpose," he asserted.[17] Despite such strident reservations, taped courses would continue to form a major part of the Canadians' training repertoire. No doubt the French farmers, on whose lands the training courses were laid out, disliked having their properties dug up any more than was necessary.

Turnbull also advised that, given the uncertain quality of battlefield communication, the brigade commander "should be as near the front as possible. He then has a better chance of understanding the situation" (the implication here was that Brig.-Gen. Rennie was out of touch with events). Similarly, he declared that battalion commanders "should be in [the] front line when attack is launched." However, Turnbull realized that even this expedient was limited in its impact, for "once the attack is launched," he maintained, "control passes out of the hands of all above the platoon commander."[18] This was an important conclusion, for it underscored the key role of the most junior officers during battle. It also anticipated important reforms that would reshape the structure of infantry platoons throughout the corps during December 1916 and January 1917. These changes came about largely through the leadership of Lt.-Gen. Byng and his chief of staff, Brig.-Gen. P.P. de B. Radcliffe. Together, they would help establish an improved platoon organization that would empower junior officers, encourage greater initiative among the other ranks, and facilitate more effective, and fluid, fire and movement tactics.

Senior Officer Training

While these reforms were gestating, Byng further stimulated discussion on matters of policy, procedure, doctrine, and tactics while also encouraging the development of productive working relationships among his commanding officers. He accomplished this through a series of week-long courses for battalion commanders and seconds-in-command, which were held at Canadian Corps headquarters beginning in November 1916.[19]

Instruction in each course was based on a combination of classroom lectures and practical demonstrations, or tactical exercises without troops, which were carried out during excursions in the field. The content essentially blended recent experience of trench warfare with pre-war theories dealing with more open forms of fighting. It emphasized such topics as the drafting of clear and effective orders, the actions of advanced guards, how to attack a village, and methods of organizing and consolidating a captured position.[20]

Through these courses, Byng was able to encourage greater methodological uniformity throughout the corps. In addition, Byng went out of his way to take part in each of the courses, lecturing to attendees and occasionally dining with them. By doing this, he got to know his battalion commanders and their understudies on professional and personal levels, just as they became better acquainted with him and with one another.[21] Such direct contact also would have allowed Byng to form his own judgments regarding the qualities and capabilities of his senior battalion officers. Whether it was explicitly intended or not, the courses may have helped identify effective and weak officers.[22]

Maj. Lionel Millen of the 19th Battalion attended the first of these commanding officers' courses, which ran from 15 to 19 November. With him were two other officers from the 2nd Canadian Division, along with six officers from the 1st and 3rd Canadian Divisions. After returning from the course, Millen wrote to his mother: "I think I told you that I was going to a course at the Canadian Corps Hdqrs. Well I enjoyed it immensely … I fancy I did as well as the average."[23]

Lt.-Col. Turnbull attended the second such course, from 20 to 26 November. He did not record his thoughts on the experience, and it is not known how he performed compared to the other attendees. The fact that Turnbull's tenure as battalion commander effectively ended less than a month later may have had nothing to do with his showing at the commanding officers' course. Indeed, as press reports suggest, it probably owed more to exhaustion or ill health stemming from the wound he had sustained in his foot earlier that summer. In any event, on 17 December Turnbull departed the battalion for a period of extended leave and Millen took over command the following day.[24]

On 20 December, Millen wrote his mother:

> I am not occupying my old dugout or cellar, but the C.O.'s as I am acting that at present. The C.O. left a couple of days ago on a 30 days special leave, and if possible will get it extended so as to get to Canada. Strictly between ourselves, if he gets back that far he is going to try and stay. So there is a possibility yet that I may be a Lt. Col.[25]

These comments imply that Turnbull was prepared to give up his command willingly, although when he arrived back in Hamilton on 6 January he publicly expressed his hope (in similar fashion to McLaren before him) that the sojourn at home would "render him more fit to once again resume his duties overseas."[26] To his credit, Turnbull had overseen his battalion's notable success in the innovative daylight raid of 29 July, and there is little to criticize in his handling of the battalion during its second tour of duty at the Somme. He seems to have performed as effectively as any battalion commander during the frustrating and bloody series of operations that followed the capture of Courcelette.

In the end, it is probable that Turnbull, like McLaren, was worn out by his time at the front. Millen, on the other hand, thoroughly enjoyed his role as battalion commander. "You know that at present I am C.O. of this battalion," he informed his sister on 5 January 1917, "and I like the job. It made Xmas a busy but a happy day for me visiting everybody in that capacity. Between ourselves I wish Col. Turnbull would take a notion and could arrange not to come back, meaning of course that authorities higher up would give me his job."[27] Millen did not have long to wait, for Turnbull would be retained in Canada and placed in command of the Welland Canal Field Force as of 7 February.[28] Official confirmation of Millen's position as commanding officer of the 19th Battalion would come through later in April 1917, with his promotion to lieutenant-colonel being backdated to 18 December 1916. Millen must have found this satisfying, for in previous correspondence he had doubted that he would ever advance very far in the brigade. "As far as further

Major H.C. Hatch, DSO. (LAC PA-007337)

promotion is concerned, I do not think there is very much chance for me," he had written on 3 December 1916. "I do not think I am a prime favorite with the Brigadier, and we feel one has to be to get on with him ... The lack of regard might be mutual between us anyway."[29] Millen's dislike of certain military formalities, such as inspections, would not have endeared him to Brig.-Gen. Rennie, who indulged in them regularly. But whatever the depth of Millen's indifference, Rennie was not averse to Millen's promotion. Rennie was evidently confident in Millen's ability, if not his enthusiasm for pomp and ceremony.

Emerging as senior major and second-in-command of the battalion was Harry Hatch, who had performed well, first as battalion transport officer and then in command of C Company at the Somme. Promoted major in October,[30] the youthful Hatch was very popular with fellow officers and other ranks alike. "He is a great boy," Millen wrote enthusiastically. "His take off on different people is great. It is a real treat to listen to him talk and have him around."[31] Hatch would assume command of the battalion on a number of occasions in 1917 and 1918, during periods when Millen was temporarily absent for reasons such as illness or leave. Joe O'Neill, a junior officer who was posted to the 19th Battalion later in November 1917, declared that "the boys fairly adored" Hatch. "He was strictly a front line officer ... we were never in the front lines at night, that he didn't go down to No Mans Land."[32]

Sir Sam Hughes arrives in France for a visit to the front, August 1916. (LAC PA-000704)

The 19th Battalion was by no means the only unit in the Canadian Corps to undergo a change in command in the aftermath of the Battle of the Somme. Between 15 October 1916 and 1 April 1917, one division, two brigades, and fifteen battalions (the 19th included) would see their commanders promoted, transferred, or posted out of the corps altogether. To a large degree, these shifts were made possible by the reduction of overt political influence in the matter of promotions and appointments within the Canadian Corps. The minister of militia, Sir Sam Hughes, had always insisted on his right to control or approve promotions, which severely undercut the ability of brigade, division, and corps commanders to advance those whom they felt were most suitable to fill command or staff vacancies. When Hughes refused to cooperate with Prime Minister Sir Robert Borden's efforts to reform the chaotic organization and administration of Canada's overseas military forces (especially those in England), Borden demanded his resignation on 9 November 1916. With Hughes's departure, Byng and his subordinate commanders found themselves free to promote officers on the basis of demonstrated talent. This marked a crucial step in the development of the Canadian Corps' efficiency.[33]

Reorganizing and Training

The increasing emphasis on meritocracy within the Canadian Corps coincided with, and partly propelled, a series of organizational and technical reforms during the winter of 1916–17. This period became, arguably, the single most important one in the evolution of the Canadian Corps as an effective fighting formation. The impetus for change came from lessons learned at the Somme and from British and French formations. In addition, during early 1917, the Canadian divisions finally were treated to extended periods out of the lines. Much of this time was devoted to intensive tactical training. When they moved back into the lines, each division also stepped up its efforts in patrolling and raiding. These activities served as a prelude to the Canadians' next big assignment, the capture of Vimy Ridge.

Within the Canadian Corps, and the British armies as a whole, some of the most important post-Somme reforms involved the artillery. Utilization of scientific counter-battery techniques such as flash spotting and sound ranging, increased attention to the calibration of guns, and application of intelligence gained from aerial observation and other sources, enabled Canadian and British gunners to suppress or destroy German artillery batteries with greater precision than ever before. Also, the new "instantaneous" 106-fuse permitted artillery shells to explode on contact before burying themselves in the ground – a development that brought improvements in the artillery's ability to blast paths through enemy wire.[34]

During the winter of 1917 the number of heavy machine guns per division rose to sixty-four. These weapons gradually came into their own as an intermediate arm between the artillery and the infantry. With the growing prominence of Lewis guns in direct support of the infantry, heavy machine guns were used increasingly in the consolidation and defence of captured ground and offensively through provision of indirect barrage fire. This technique relied on mass machine-gun firepower against a designated area to suppress enemy trench garrisons and harass their rear areas, supplementing the work of the artillery.[35]

For the infantry, the most significant reform during this period was the restructuring of battalions to facilitate more effective platoon tactics. The big change came with the elimination of separate specialist sections of Lewis gunners, bombers, and rifle grenadiers, which typically had been attached to company or battalion headquarters. The detachment of personnel to form these specialist sections had reduced platoon strength from approximately fifty rank and file to a mere twenty or so riflemen. It had also fostered the growth of "a sort of class consciousness … in which the ordinary riflemen were seen (by the specialists) as the lowest of the low." With the reintegration of specialist personnel, each platoon now featured a proportion of all the major infantry weapons – rifles, Lewis guns, hand grenades,

Members of a platoon carry out a practice attack, England, 1917. (LAC PA-022652)

and rifle grenades. This was aided by an eventual increase in the number of Lewis guns, to the tune of sixteen per battalion, or one for each platoon, thus dramatically improving the firepower that a platoon commander could bring to bear. His small command had thus become a viable tactical unit.[36]

On 27 December 1916, Lt.-Gen. Byng's chief of staff, Brig.-Gen. Radcliffe, issued the orders instituting the new platoon organization throughout the Canadian Corps. This focus on platoons and small-unit tactics was nothing new, nor was it uniquely Canadian. German practice favoured devolution of responsibility for tactics to junior officers and their NCOs, while British experience at the Somme and French efforts at Verdun confirmed the need for greater emphasis on platoon and section tactics. Indeed, small-unit fire and movement tactics had been prevalent in much pre-war British Army training.[37] The new platoon organization made these tactics potentially more effective, by integrating all of the major infantry weapons groups.

Divisions in the Canadian Corps were permitted to experiment with the distribution of weapons and personnel among the four sections of each infantry platoon. The 2nd Canadian Division decided to pattern its platoon organization along the lines suggested by corps headquarters on 27 December. Thus each platoon had two sections combining riflemen and rifle grenadiers, one bombing section, and one Lewis gun section, for a total platoon strength of one officer and forty-nine other ranks. By mid-January 1917 the process of reorganization within the division had already begun; it was overseen by a new GOC.[38] Maj.-Gen. Henry Burstall had

Above: Lt.-Gen. Richard Turner, VC (GOC, 2nd Canadian Division, August 1915–November 1916). (LAC PA-007941)
Right: Maj.-Gen. Henry Burstall (GOC, 2nd Canadian Division, December 1916–May 1919). (LAC PA-002276)

taken over the 2nd Division on 15 December 1916, after Maj.-Gen. Turner was promoted to command all Canadian troops stationed in England. A gunner by trade, Burstall was a Canadian permanent force officer who had served with distinction during the war as GOCRA 1st Canadian Division, and then as GOCRA Canadian Corps. But Burstall was by no means preoccupied solely with artillery matters. While he set about learning his new role and responsibilities as division commander, he threw himself into the work of implementing Byng's infantry reforms and overseeing the training program through which they were tested.[39]

The 2nd Division trained during a three-week period commencing on 20 January, when the formation moved into corps reserve. The previous day, the men of the 19th Battalion had completed their eighth successive tour in the Calonne sector since mid-October. After their relief in the trenches they marched to billets in the village of Maisnil-lès-Ruitz, where they would be quartered for the next ten days.

There, on 21 January, Lt.-Col. Millen oversaw the reorganization of his platoons in accordance with the directives issued by division and corps headquarters.[40]

Once personnel had been reallocated, Millen's men began the first stage of their training program, focusing on usual subjects such as physical, section, platoon, and company drills, rifle exercises, and bayonet fighting. This ten-day program was rounded off on 29 January with the first efforts to put the new platoons through their paces in a series of practice attacks.[41]

The 19th Battalion departed Maisnil-lès-Ruitz on 30 January and marched to new billets at Marles-les-Mines, where it remained for the next eleven days. Training continued with physical and weapons drills in the mornings and tactical exercises for platoons in the afternoons. In keeping with the recommendations of British GHQ, they practised a standard two-line attack formation.[42] Each platoon was led by Nos. 1 and 2 sections (each of riflemen and rifle grenadiers), followed by a second line featuring the Lewis gunners of No. 3 section and the bombers of No. 4 section.[43] It was not expected that standard attack formations would apply equally well to all circumstances. But it was hoped that they would serve as useful aids, especially for novice platoon commanders as they trained their men and led them into battle.[44] Training platoon commanders and their men to advance in a standardized formation was acceptable, but only to a point. Officers and other ranks needed to be flexible in order to meet the challenges posed by different types of ground and different enemy defences.

To ensure that platoons would continue to function even after heavy casualties, Lt.-Gen. Byng insisted that every man be trained "to act in case of necessity as a specialist, i.e. as a bomber, rifle grenadier, or Lewis gunner." In the 19th Battalion, Lt.-Col. Millen further emphasized the need for enterprise and command continuity, warning each platoon commander and NCO that he would be required to know "every detail in connection with his unit, the names of his men, the names of the Seniors," so that in the event of the platoon commander or senior NCOs becoming casualties, "the next senior man knows that he takes hold and the other men must know who they will look upon as their senior."[45] It would seem obvious that officers and other ranks should master such details, but in view of the recent platoon reorganization, and with the battalion strength back up to its pre-Somme level of 40 officers and 937 other ranks, there was much work to be done on these lines.[46]

While the men trained, they were experiencing the harshest European winter in twenty-two years. It is said that portions of a man's hot rations would freeze before he had the chance to finish eating them from his mess tin.[47] The frigid conditions continued into early February, chilling even Pte. John Gaetz, who was well accustomed to crisp western Canadian winters. He wrote on 4 February:

> It has been quite cold for the last two weeks without a break or thaw and we are glad to be out of the trenches. The day we arrived in our new billets [at Marles-les-Mines]

> we were put in a barn with half the roof off and part of the walls down. It was a pretty cold place. Another fellow and myself went to a nearby mine and got a couple of sand bags of coal. By punching a few holes in an old bucket with our bayonets we were able to have a fire which although didn't make the place much warmer was good for heating up our food and was pleasant to sit around and hear some of the old timers relate experiences.

Things improved once the men left the barn for more comfortable billets:

> In the evenings we go out into the village which is teeming with estaminets … where you can get coffee, eggs and chips, stout and Bass [a brand of English beer]. These places have tables and are well lighted and are a good place to read, smoke, and sup a little ale … Tonight I am sitting in a chair and writing at a table[,] quite a luxury.[48]

To the Thélus Sector

The time for such modest luxuries was drawing to a close, as was the 19th Battalion's extended period in reserve. On 10 February the battalion vacated its billets in Marles-les-Mines and began marching to the Thélus sector, arriving in brigade reserve on 12 February. Battalion headquarters was established at Maison Blanche, and companies took up positions in support of the battalions in the line, furnishing daily work parties.[49]

Millen's men got their first taste of the lines in this sector on 19 February when they relieved the 21st Battalion in the left sub-section of the brigade frontage. Conditions were about as quiet here as they had been in the Calonne sector, but they would not remain that way. The German-held village of Thélus was, in fact, located on the western slope of Vimy Ridge, which had been assigned to the Canadian Corps as its objective in the next major British offensive, scheduled to commence in April. Long-range planning for this operation had begun in November 1916, and by mid-January 1917 Gen. Horne (GOC First Army) had informed Lt.-Gen. Byng that the Canadians were to capture the entire crest of the ridge. This was a daunting task that would require the combined efforts of all four Canadian divisions.[50]

Dominating the western edge of the German-occupied Douai Plain, the main portion of Vimy Ridge stretched for roughly four miles northwest from Farbus Wood to a point just west of the village of Givenchy-en-Gohelle. The Canadians faced the ridge's western approaches, which rose in a gentle slope towards two heights situated on its opposite ends – Hill 135 towards the southeastern end, and Hill 145 at the northwestern end. The latter point was the highest on the ridge, at 475 feet above sea level. East of the crest, the ridge dropped precipitously, and at its foot were thick woods and a series of small villages, including Farbus, Vimy, and Petit-Vimy. Strategically, Vimy Ridge overlooked the cities of Lens to the north, Douai to the east, and Arras to the south. Possession of the ridge had helped the Germans secure their grip on the Lens coalfields and the industrial area of Lille.

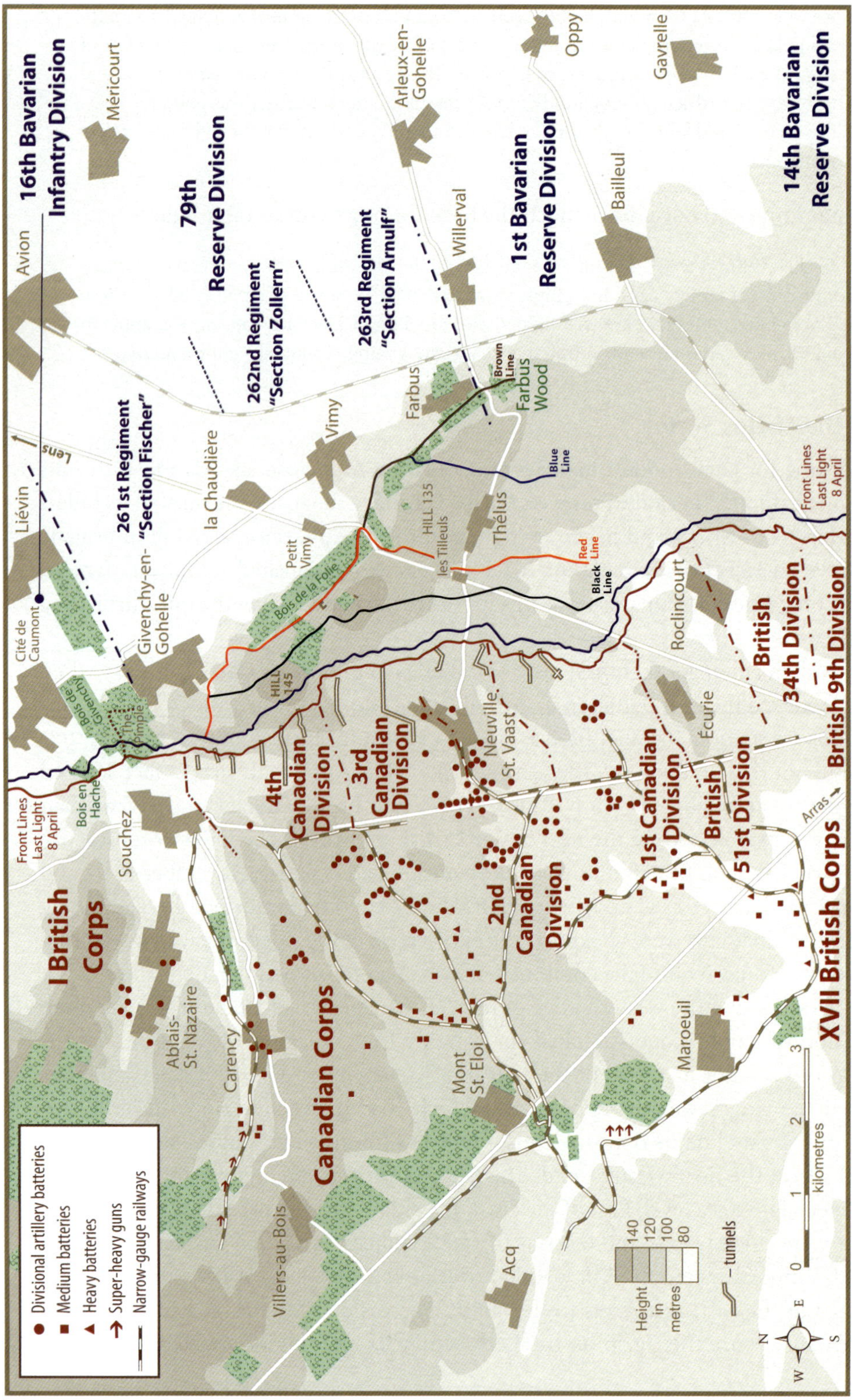

Map 9 – Vimy Ridge.

Moreover, it shielded the northern flank of the formidable new defensive line that the Germans were constructing – the *Siegfriedstellung*, more popularly known to the Allies as the Hindenburg Line. Thus, Vimy was one of the key positions on the Western Front and had been the scene of terrible fighting since its capture by the Germans in 1914. During that year, and in 1915, the French had failed in several attempts to retake the ridge, incurring a fearsome toll of over 150,000 casualties. Then, in March 1916, the British assumed control of the sector. Although they succeeded in counteracting German mining operations in the area, they did not make headway against the ridge itself.[51] Although sometimes minimized in postwar Canadian accounts, these earlier French and British efforts were instrumental in seizing and securing positions that put the Canadians within achievable striking distance of the ridge's crest.

Nevertheless, German defences on the ridge remained formidable. Parts of no man's land and sections of the opposing front lines featured huge craters dating from earlier episodes of mine warfare in 1915 and 1916. In their own sectors, the Germans had created "a dense network of trenches, tunnels, concrete emplacements, wire, and dugouts," one of which was so big that it could shelter a battalion. The forward defensive zone on the western slopes boasted three successive trench lines, and an equally well-defended zone lay just beyond the crest. West of the crest, hills, scattered farmsteads, and the villages of Thélus and Les Tilleuls were strongly fortified, while the woods at the foot of the eastern slopes afforded excellent cover for batteries of artillery and mortars. In short, Vimy Ridge was a tough nut for any army to crack. Its defenders, the troops of the 1st Bavarian Reserve Infantry Division, the 16th Bavarian Infantry Division, and the 79th Prussian Reserve Infantry Division of Generaloberst Ludwig von Falkenhausen's 6th Army, were confident in their ability to hold it – so confident, in fact, that they were not terribly concerned that the design of their defences was already out of date. During late 1916 and early 1917, the Germans had developed a new defensive scheme, but the fortifications of Vimy had not been updated accordingly.[52]

Like the Allies, the Germans had been appalled by their losses at the Somme. This prompted them to search for more effective ways to defend their positions and conserve manpower. Instead of fighting to the last man from clearly delineated, heavily manned trench lines (as they had often done at the Somme), the Germans decided to distribute their forces in greater depth and in looser order. The hallmark of their new system of defence-in-depth was its organization into successive outpost, battle, and rear zones, which collectively might extend six to eight miles in depth. This system was designed to defeat an enemy attack by drawing it into an elaborate defensive network and then smashing it with a well-timed counterattack.

Dispersed forces in the more thinly manned outpost zone would employ flanking machine-gun and rifle fire to shatter the cohesion of an enemy assault. Stronger garrisons in the main battle zone, operating from successive trench lines and mutually supporting strongpoints, would absorb the worst of the enemy attack, ideally blunting it and rendering it vulnerable to specially trained *Eingriefdivisionen* (counterattack divisions). These divisions were positioned in the rear battle zone and tasked with crushing whatever remained of an Allied force mired in the main battle zone. Finally, there was the rear zone, which served as the assembly area for the counterattack divisions and also featured most of the heavy artillery positions.

By surrendering ground in the outpost zone and the forward portion of the main battle zone, the Germans hoped to draw an attacking force deeper into the main battle zone beyond the support of its own field artillery. There, the attackers could be defeated by divisions defending the outpost and main battle zones, or by counterattack divisions held ready in reserve. When the attacking Allied forces were defeated or driven back, the Germans could then retake the ground they had yielded in the main battle and outpost zones. The system was highly flexible and depended heavily on the decentralization of command to company officers and NCOs, especially in the more dispersed defences of the forward zones.[53]

The philosophy of elastic defence-in-depth had been implemented in many German sectors of the Western Front, especially along the new Hindenburg Line. But the heights of Vimy Ridge, with its steep, wooded eastern slopes, made it far more difficult to implement the design in that particular sector. Counterattacking up those slopes could be suicidal if an enemy force gained the crest of the ridge. As well, the northern part of the ridge was simply too narrow to accommodate deep outpost and battle zones. Also, it was deemed unwise to position counterattack forces within easy reach of the ridge, for if an enemy managed to seize the eastern face of the crest and bring up artillery, they would completely dominate the plain below. Reserves would have to be held at a safe distance beyond the range of any enemy guns that might be positioned along the ridge. But this situation did not overly concern the Germans: although the ridge's defences were not of the latest design, they remained strong and had defeated all previous Allied attempts to break them. There seemed little reason to doubt their effectiveness in future attacks.[54]

As the men of the 19th Battalion shivered in their frosty but still reasonably dry trenches, they must have viewed the opposing lines with a sense of foreboding. "This area was one of the most bitterly fought over in France," remarked Maj. Duncan E. Macintyre at 4th Brigade headquarters:

> I found it terribly torn up and depressing. It seemed incredible that anyone could have passed this way during action and lived to tell of it. The ground was littered with dud shells and bombs, helmets, rusty rifles and bayonets and, most gruesome of all, skeletons. What had once been a young and healthy man was now a skull and a few bones, some rags, leather and buttons, and sometimes the remnants of a French soldier's baggy red trousers. What a brilliant target for a German rifleman![55]

The vista grew even more depressing as the weather warmed and frost began to seep out of the tortured ground. The white chalk soil turned into "a thick soupy consistency when wet," and soon the trenches were awash in a sticky grey gruel.[56] "This together with the rains certainly make a mess," complained John Gaetz in late February. "However we are pretty well supplied with rubber boots and … when the weather and trenches are bad such as they are now we do not stay in [them] as long."[57]

Patrolling and Raiding

By the eve of the attack at Vimy Ridge, which eventually was scheduled for 9 April (Easter Monday), ground conditions would improve somewhat and anxieties about tackling the vaunted German positions would diminish, if only slightly. During the weeks of pre-battle preparation, the men's confidence would be bolstered by a combination of intensive training, aggressive patrolling and raiding, and, most important, the application of massive artillery firepower to soften up the enemy defences.

While the commanders and staffs at corps, division, and brigade headquarters drew up operational plans, the 19th Battalion played its part in the infantry's principal tasks before launching the attack: gathering intelligence, wearing the Germans down, and gaining ascendancy over no man's land. This was done through the usual methods of patrolling and raiding. Although raids were sometimes costly in terms of casualties, they did yield valuable information on the topography of no man's land, the state of enemy front-line defences, and the identity of opposing German units. They also gave the Canadians some opportunity to practise and experiment with small-unit tactics under actual battle conditions.

From the end of October 1916 to 1 April 1917, the Canadian Corps launched some sixty raids against German positions along the Calonne and Vimy fronts.[58] One of the largest and most spectacular efforts was carried out by the 20th and 21st Battalions in the Calonne sector on the morning of 17 January; it was a well-planned operation during which over 100 German prisoners were captured.[59] On 20 March, during its third tour in the Thélus sector trenches, the 19th Battalion carried out its first and only full-scale raid during this period. It was a complex operation involving four officers and sixty-three other ranks divided into seven parties. As with most raids, its purpose was to secure prisoners, identify opposing units, inflict casualties, and damage or destroy enemy positions. Three of the raiding parties were detailed to attack the German front line. One party would operate along the right portion of the targeted stretch of trench, another would attack the centre, and the third would take care of the left. There were two "CT" (communication trench) parties, one on the right and the other on the left. Their job was to proceed up the two targeted German CTs, bombing and destroying any dugouts they encountered. A covering party would provide close support with rifle grenade barrages, while a control party would direct the artillery fire support over a buzzer system. The whole operation would last no longer than fifteen minutes.

At 4:54 AM on 20 March, the guns of the 27th Battery, CFA, opened fire on the German front line opposite the raiders' assembly positions in "Observation Line" and "Pulpit Sap." Four minutes later, the front-line parties leapt into the German trench, just after the barrage lifted 100 yards farther to pound the enemy support positions and isolate the targeted trenches. The parties assigned to the right and left portions of the front line rushed in opposite directions from the point of entry, bombing as they went. Both parties discovered dugouts with occupants equally reluctant to emerge. These shelters, along with their residents, were promptly destroyed with Stokes charges, made from converted mortar rounds. After bombing sentry and machine-gun positions, each party then established defensive blocks at predetermined positions just beyond the points where the front line intersected with the right and left CTs.[60]

In the meantime, the parties assaulting the CTs dashed to their respective positions, bombing dugouts as they went. The right CT party had a notable success in their capture of five Germans from a dugout farther up the trench. The dazed prisoners were quickly sent back to the front line, where they were taken in hand by members of the centre front-line party.[61]

After the raiders had done their worst, the signal to withdraw sounded at 5:13 AM. The officer in charge of the centre front-line party gave several blasts of a horn brought along for the purpose. Within two minutes, the front line and CT parties, prisoners in tow, scrambled out of the German lines and scurried over to "Pulpit Sap," where they made their way back through Canadian lines to their appointed meeting point in Elbe Trench. The prisoners were immediately dispatched to the advance brigade headquarters for interrogation. After the assault parties came the covering and control parties. The former had been stationed in Edinburgh Crater, where, with fusillades of rifle grenades and sniper fire, they pinned down the German garrison of a small, strongly defended salient facing the crater. The control party was the last to scuttle back to safety. Its officer was responsible for signalling the artillery to lift its barrage back to the German front-line trench once the assault parties completed their withdrawal.[62]

Lt.-Col. Millen and his superiors were overjoyed with the results of the operation. In just over fifteen minutes the raiders had destroyed a number of dugouts with their occupants, captured five unwounded prisoners, and identified the unit facing them – the 263rd Reserve Infantry Regiment. Moreover, the cost in casualties, for the number of men involved, had been remarkably small. Three other ranks – Sgt. J. Reynolds, Pte. C.A. Horner, and Pte. G. Anning – were slightly wounded. In addition to praising his infantry, Millen was quick to pay tribute to the supporting artillery and Stokes mortars (the latter had been detailed to bombard a nearby German strongpoint known as "Sheba's Breast"). He also applauded the efforts of the 4th Canadian Machine Gun Company, which "placed a splendid M.G. barrage on the back country" behind the German front line. Four days later, when he and his men were stationed in reserve, Millen enthused in a letter to his mother: "The good old battalion had rather a wonderful tour last trip … I am proud, proud, proud of my – yes my – boys, and others higher up have also expressed their appreciation … Yes, though I often wish I was out of it, I don't think I can bring myself to quit until the game is over. Let us pray it won't be long."[63]

But the Germans were not just passive victims of Canadian aggression. The 19th Battalion alone reported three raids on its own positions, on 21 December 1916, 5 March, and 21 March 1917. The first was the most serious, with ten to twelve Germans entering the 19th Battalion's positions at a point between Trenches 228 and 229 in the Calonne sector. The Germans did not remain long, however, staying for only one or two minutes before being driven off. "I am confident we caused casualties," Millen reported. "Whatever the objective of the raid, it was defeated, and they gained absolutely no identification." Unfortunately, the action resulted in the deaths of two other ranks and the wounding of four more.[64] Neither of the German raids in March managed to get as far as the 19th Battalion's front line in the Thélus sector, the enemy parties being driven off with considerable losses.[65]

The 19th Battalion's third tour in the trenches of the Thélus sector came to an end on 21 March, when it was relieved by the 18th Battalion. Lt.-Col. Millen's men then moved into huts in the Bois-des-Alleux, where they remained in divisional reserve until 25 March. On that day the rest of the 4th Brigade joined them in the same wooded area, having been relieved in the lines and concentrated for training purposes. Now they would begin work in grim earnest, preparing for their parts in the upcoming assault on Vimy Ridge.[66] "Now that Spring is here, the days are getting longer," Pte. Gaetz informed his father, "and of course with the spring comes expectations of action. The guns as you see in the papers are barking and coughing more frequently. I should think that every active soldier in France now is ready to go over the bags if called upon because it is the only way to finish it."[67]

11

"An Easter Gift" – Vimy Ridge: 25 March–9 April 1917

In spite of the central place Vimy Ridge occupies in Canadian memory of the First World War, its assault was a subsidiary operation designed to support larger British and French offensives to the south. The new French commander-in-chief, Gen. Robert Nivelle, had orchestrated an ambitious scheme with French and British forces attacking the southern and northern portions of a great German-held salient between Soissons and Arras. A massive French advance over the Chemin des Dames Ridge, in the southern part of this salient, was intended to link up with a combined French and British effort in the north, aimed at the city of Cambrai. If these two forces converged, they would envelop a large portion of the German armies on the Western Front.[1]

But Nivelle's grand design was upset by the Germans' skilful withdrawal from much of the targeted salient between 15 and 18 March and their subsequent re-establishment along the *Siegfriedstellung*, better known to the Allies as the Hindenburg Line. With this withdrawal, the Germans shortened their frontage between Arras and Soissons by as much as one-third and released thirteen divisions to their reserve strength. Moreover, they eliminated the possibility of trapping a large part of their army in the former salient. The Germans retained their positions along the Chemin des Dames Ridge, leaving one of Nivelle's key objectives intact, but his larger strategic goal of envelopment was nullified. Additionally, the combined French and British advance to Cambrai would now become an exclusively British

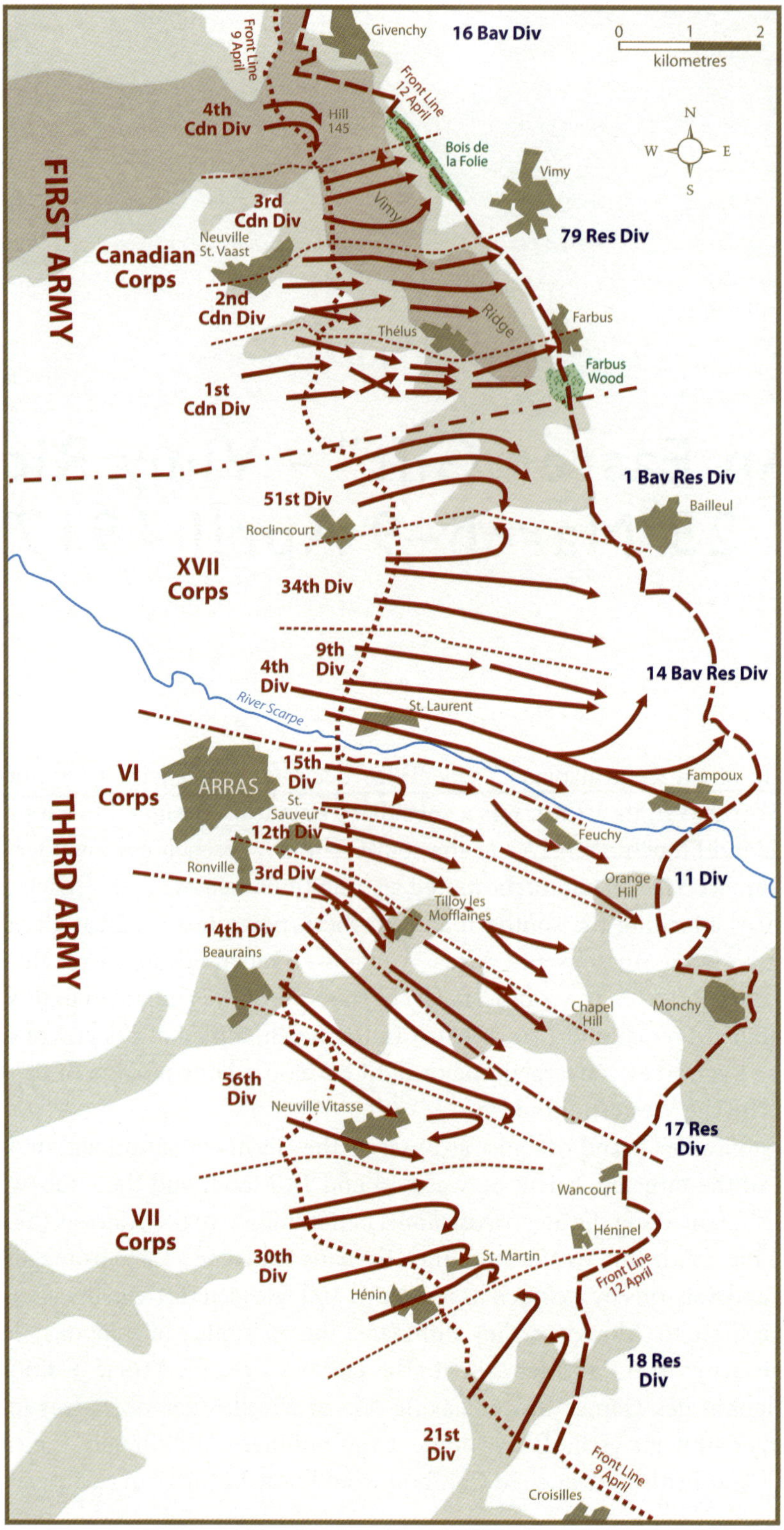

Map 10 – Battle of Arras, 1917.

affair, as the German withdrawal and scorched-earth tactics had devastated the territory over which the French would advance. There would be no time for them to construct new lines of supply and communication before the offensive, which was scheduled to begin in April. Thus, it was left to British Third Army, under Gen. Sir Edmund Allenby, to take Cambrai. Gen. Sir Hubert Gough's Fifth Army would secure Allenby's southern flank while Gen. Sir Henry Horne's First Army took care of the northern flank, which was threatened by the Germans' dominant position on Vimy Ridge.[2] The entire series of British attacks would become known collectively as the Battle of Arras.

The battle for Vimy Ridge would involve nothing in the way of complex manoeuvres on a grand scale. Like many battles on the Western Front both before and after, it would be a frontal assault. What differentiated it from earlier Canadian attacks was the care with which it was planned and the detail of the preparations. The general scheme drawn up by Lt.-Gen. Byng and his staff at corps headquarters was simple in its broad outlines, but it required a high degree of coordination among the forces involved. All four divisions of the corps would advance shoulder to shoulder along a frontage of roughly 7,000 yards in order to seize the ridge. Because the opposing front lines angled away from the ridge as one proceeded from northwest to southeast, the Canadian zone of attack would be roughly triangular in shape. The 1st Canadian Division, in the southern sector, would have the farthest distance to cover (around 4,000 yards), over comparatively easy ground. The 4th Canadian Division, in the northernmost sector, would have the shortest distance to advance (just under 1,000 yards) but would face the steepest terrain and some of the strongest German defences. The 19th Battalion's parent formation, the 2nd Canadian Division, would advance along the 1st Division's left flank, traversing around 3,000 yards of German-held territory before reaching its objective. Although the 2nd Division would jump off from a frontage of approximately 1,400 yards, its sector would widen considerably along the path of advance to a 2,000-yard front along its final objective.[3]

For each division, the attack would comprise a series of bounds to successive objective lines, the first two of which would be assaulted by all four divisions. The first objective, termed the Black Line on the operation maps, lay an average distance of 750 yards from the Canadian front line. The second objective, the Red Line, ran northwards along a portion of the German trench called the *Zwischenstellung*. It then continued along another line known as *Turko Graben* before turning northwest at the Bois-de-la-Folie. From there, it ran beyond the eastern crest of the ridge towards the village of Givenchy-en-Gohelle. The Red Line would be the final objective line for the 4th and 3rd Canadian Divisions, in the left half of the corps' sector. On the right, the 2nd and 1st Divisions, with more ground to cover, each would have to make two more bounds, to the Blue and Brown lines. In the 2nd Division's sector, the area between the Red and Blue lines included the village of

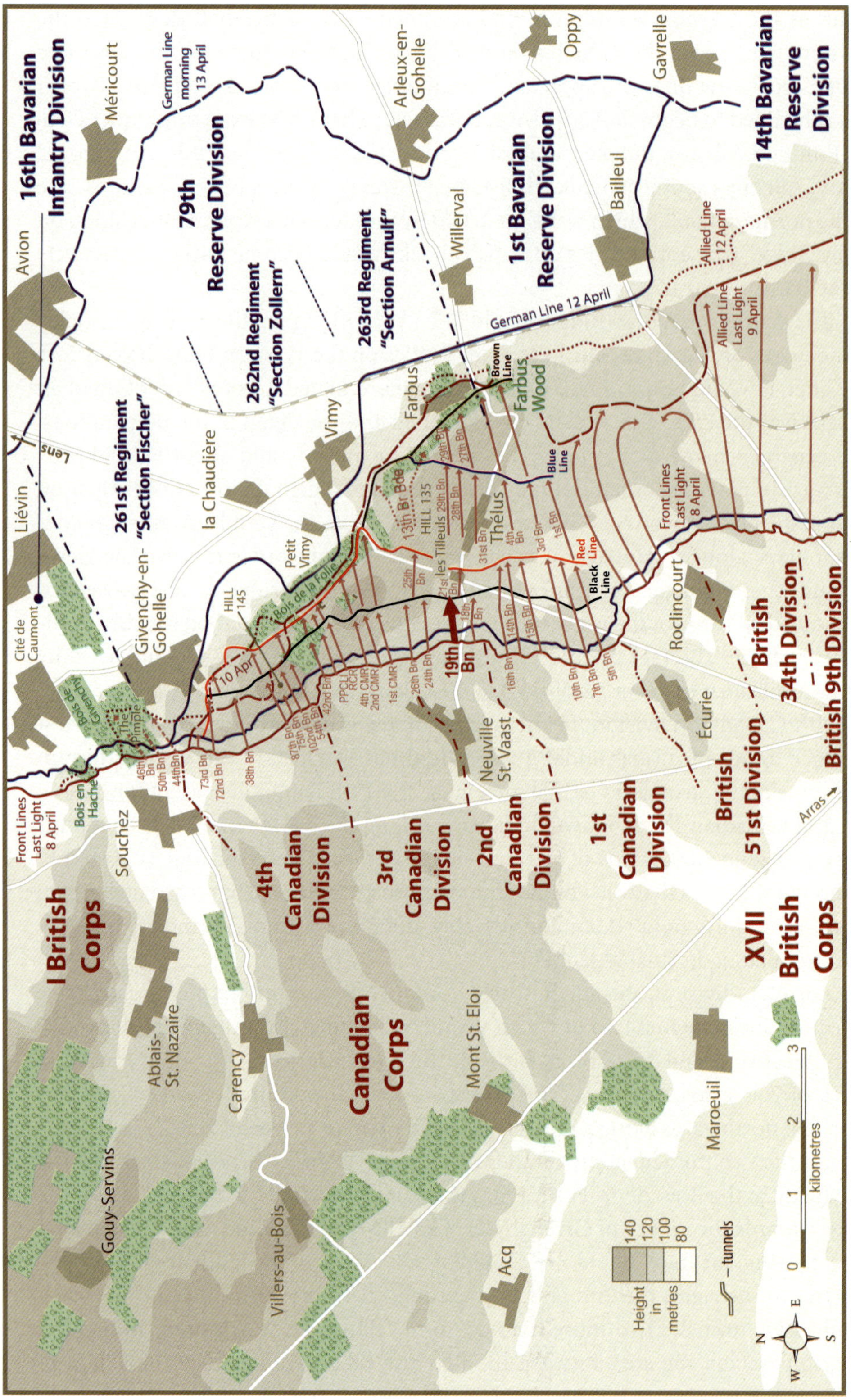

Map 11 – Battle of Vimy Ridge.

Thélus and the height known as Hill 135. The final objective, the Brown Line, ran through the woods along the steeper eastern slope of the ridge, overlooking the villages of Farbus and Vimy.[4] These objectives would be captured according to a strict timetable. Starting at 5:30 AM on "Z-day," which eventually was fixed for 9 April,[5] the infantry would advance behind a creeping barrage, which was scheduled to lift 100 yards every three minutes. As each of the colour-coded objective lines was taken, the barrage would pause while follow-up units organized themselves to push on for the next phase of the attack. If all went according to plan, the Canadians would be in full possession of Vimy Ridge by 1:18 PM.[6]

Leading off the 2nd Canadian Division's attack would be the 5th Brigade on the left and the 4th Brigade on the right, both advancing through the German-occupied area east of the Canadian-held village of Neuville-Saint-Vaast. The men of the 19th Battalion would have the honour of being in the first wave, advancing alongside their comrades in the 18th Battalion. The portion of the Black Line along the German trenches known as the *Zwolfer* and *Zwischen Stellungen* would be their final objective. There they would halt and dig in while their comrades in the 21st Battalion leapfrogged ahead to continue the attack to the Red Line, which would be the limit of the 4th and 5th Brigade's respective advances. It would be left to the division's reserve forces to take the Blue and Brown lines. However, because the 2nd Division's frontage widened significantly as it approached the Brown Line, more manpower would be needed than the division's only remaining infantry brigade (the 6th) could supply. To solve this problem, additional support would be furnished by the 13th Infantry Brigade, temporarily attached from the 5th British Division. The 6th Brigade would take up the advance to the Blue and Brown lines on the right, after forming up along the portion of the Red Line captured by the 4th Brigade. Meanwhile, the British troops of the 13th Brigade would strike out from the ground captured earlier by the 5th Brigade.[7]

As Tim Cook correctly points out, the British infantry would fight effectively within the Canadian Corps' "operational envelope, proving that the British training was not very different from that of the Canadians."[8] Indeed, contrary to popular assumptions that Canadian preparations for this battle were unique in their rationale and thoroughness, they were very much in line with policy, doctrine, and training employed by the British Army. Before the Battle of Arras, both British and Canadian infantry had been carefully rehearsed in practice attacks based on the platoon-oriented tactics that had been refined during the winter.[9]

The preparatory stages for the attack at Vimy began in January and intensified as the weeks wore on. Eventually, 983 artillery pieces (field and heavy guns and howitzers, as well as medium and heavy trench mortars) were assembled from Canadian, British, Australian, and other Dominion formations to support the attack. On 20 March they began a systematic bombardment of the ridge in order to reduce its defences. The preliminary artillery program, an important component of

For all the cover afforded by tunnels and caverns, there was no concealing from the Germans that the Canadians intended to assault Vimy. The scale of the preparatory measures was too vast to go unnoticed, even when much of the work was carried out at night. But the Canadians did what they could to keep their opponents in the dark as to the precise time of the attack. During the week leading up to Z-day, Canadian gunners fired numerous creeping barrages against German positions. Because creeping barrages usually meant an attack was imminent, the Germans eventually got used to the frequent false alarms and "became somewhat careless about the prompt manning of the trenches" when the barrages ceased.[14]

Although vital for misleading the enemy, such deceptions were of secondary importance compared to the principal tasks of destruction and interdiction carried out by Canadian and British field and heavy artillery batteries during the week before the attack. The gunners maintained a constant drumfire in order to blast gaps in the Germans' barbed wire, smash their trenches and strongpoints, suppress and destroy their artillery, and disrupt their supply and communication routes. In this latter task, the corps' heavy machine-gun units also rendered valuable service, employing indirect barrage-fire techniques to shower targeted portions of the German rear areas with streams of bullets, making it exceedingly difficult for ration parties to bring food up to the hungry and dazed troops in the German front lines. In the three weeks preceding the Canadian advance, more than a million artillery shells and countless quantities of small arms ammunition rained down on the slopes of Vimy Ridge and the countryside beyond it, churning the landscape into a scarcely habitable wilderness. There was little wonder, after the Canadian and British gunners stepped up their efforts on 2 April, that Germans in this sector referred to the ensuing seven days as "The Week of Suffering."[15]

Training and Assembly

As the logistical arrangements were laboriously carried out and the artillery embarked in earnest on its campaign of destruction, the Canadian infantry engaged in a final, intense period of preliminary training for the attack. For the men of the 19th Battalion, this began near Maisnil-Bouche, where they carried out assault exercises at platoon, company, and battalion levels from 27 to 31 March. Unfortunately for Lt.-Col. Millen, he would miss much of this key training period owing to a nasty flare-up of bronchitis, which forced his temporary evacuation to hospital from 27 March until 6 April, when he finally returned to the unit. In his stead, Maj. Hatch commanded the battalion.

The practice attacks were carried out over a gently sloping open field that had been requisitioned near the Château-de-la-Haie. There, a training course was established, with tapes laid out to represent the positions of German trenches and strongpoints east of Neuville-Saint-Vaast.[16] "Over these tapes we put the men again and again," remarked the brigade major, D.E. Macintyre, "first by platoons and then by increasing numbers, until the day came when the entire brigade carried out the exercise together, one battalion following another in line, everyone walking, the officers timing the advance by their watches and the men with their rifles at the high port, bayonets fixed, ready to shoot or lunge."[17] Harry Neil of the 19th Battalion similarly observed that "practice at the model entrenchments, carefully prepared from aerial reconnaissance, seemed unending. But Sir Julian Byng, the Corps' commander, was leaving nothing to chance."[18] Other ranks were given highly detailed briefings on their units' objectives and the tactics required to capture them. In addition, "every officer and N.C.O. was given a small large-scale map, plotted from aeroplane photographs which showed their own front and indicated all obstacles" and points of resistance. These maps and aerial photographs "were studied with unusual care, since everybody was interested in knowing all probable obstructions."[19]

Besides all of this, a detailed scale model of the terrain and German positions along Vimy Ridge was constructed at First Army headquarters, and parties of Canadian officers and other ranks were transported there to view and study its features. The corps commander himself occasionally would turn up at these sessions, chatting with the men and dispensing advice. "Make sure that every man knows his task," Byng instructed his officers and NCOs. "Explain it to him again and again. Encourage him to ask questions."[20] This would ensure that subordinates could step in and assume the roles of their superiors in case the latter were killed or wounded.[21]

After a brief break from dress rehearsals on Sunday, 1 April, which was marked by intermittent rain and sleet, the 19th Battalion was back at it again the following day, when it carried out a battalion-level practice attack in the morning and then participated in a brigade-level exercise later in the afternoon. But the weather in the succeeding days remained uncooperative. Plans to continue with brigade exercises were put on hold on 3 April, owing to a nasty blizzard on the previous night that blanketed the countryside with snow, obscuring the taped course and preventing outdoor training. Instead, Maj. Hatch set the men to work cleaning their kit and further discussing their plans for the upcoming offensive.[22]

On Wednesday, 4 April, most men in the 19th Battalion continued their activities of the previous day. However, the men of Nos. 1 and 3 Platoons, along with six scouts, all of whom were placed under the command of Lt. W.J. Wright, moved forward to the support trenches in the right sub-section of the Thélus sector. There, they came under the orders of the 20th Battalion and were detailed to prepare jumping-off trenches and cut lanes through the barbed wire in front of this section of the Canadian front line.[23]

The next morning, 5 April, their comrades in the rest of the battalion recommenced training in earnest. That day they also paraded to a gas hut established by the divisional gas school, where all ranks were put through an equipment test. The

An infantryman wearing a small box respirator, March 1917. (LAC PA-000928)

previous November, all ranks had been issued a new type of gas protection called the small box respirator (SBR), which was a major improvement over previous gas masks. The SBR was lighter, more comfortable, and able to protect against higher concentrations of gas. It consisted of a satchel suspended on the soldier's chest. Inside the satchel was a metal container that served as a filter. Contaminated air was drawn in through a valve at the bottom of the satchel; this air was then filtered by chemically treated granules that had been sealed inside the metal container. The purified air could then be inhaled through a rubber tube that connected the satchel with a mouthpiece in the mask itself. This mask gave full facial coverage and had two large, glassed, circular eyeholes, as well as an interior nose clip to prevent the wearer from breathing anything but the filtered air flowing into the mouthpiece. Instruction in the proper use of the SBR was taken in hand by the battalion gas officer, who was assisted by a gas NCO in each of the battalion's four companies. They worked to ensure that all ranks were well versed in the prescribed anti-gas drills and procedures.[24]

Later that afternoon the 19th Battalion cooperated with the 18th and 20th Battalions in carrying out another brigade-level exercise. This one simulated the advance on their assigned portions of the Black Line at Vimy Ridge. This time, the troops practised their movements while carrying the same loads they would be bearing during the attack itself. Some progress had been made in reducing the infantry's burden since 1916. Instead of staggering under sixty to eighty pounds of clothing and equipment as he had at the Somme, the average infantryman at Vimy could walk briskly or perhaps even jog for short spurts while lugging approximately forty pounds of gear. This included his rifle, 120 rounds of ammunition, bayonet, grenades, entrenching tool, gas mask, water bottle, minimal rations, and a waterproof groundsheet. However, some individuals would be more heavily loaded with extra items such as signal flares, wire cutters, and protective gloves, or equipment for consolidation, such as empty sandbags, picks, and shovels.[25]

While their comrades sweated on the training grounds, the men in Nos. 1 and 3 Platoons toiled on at the front, digging and improving the 19th Battalion's jumping-off positions. If there were any members of these two platoons who were veterans of the attack at Courcelette, they must have grumbled and cursed at being put through the same sort of exhausting preliminary work yet again.[26]

Good Friday, 6 April, saw Lt.-Col. Millen's return to the battalion from hospital and the official announcement that the Canadian attack at Vimy would be made on 9 April.[27] It also saw the formal entry of the United States into the conflict on the side of the Allies, a development of immense significance for the war's eventual outcome. That morning, all ranks of the 19th Battalion who were stationed in the training area attended morning lectures by their company commanders, who reminded them of their unit's role in the upcoming attack. Church services were held during the afternoon, and many men must have prayed for their own and their friends' safety in the deadly days ahead.

At the same time, the scouts and men of Nos. 1 and 3 Platoons were concentrating their energies on preparing the unit's assembly positions for the attack. Also, Maj. Russell B. Thomson (nicknamed "Punk" by his fellow officers) was sent to an observation post in the ruins of Neuville-Saint-Vaast, from which he observed the state of the German barbed wire. He sent back the encouraging message that all wire appeared to be well cut along the battalion's front.[28] The artillery, employing shells equipped with the new 106-fuse, which exploded on contact and was more effective in destroying barbed-wire entanglements, was doing its job well.

The artillery's effectiveness stemmed from more than just improved technology. Intelligence regarding the enemy's defences was the real key to the gunners' overall success. This knowledge was gained through frequent scouting and raiding efforts on the ground as well as ceaseless aerial reconnaissance.[29] As the offensive drew near, the skies above Vimy Ridge and the surrounding sectors grew increasingly violent, and casualties among RFC personnel mounted during what became known as "Bloody April." The aerial battlefield above Vimy was the stage for numerous deadly clashes between Allied and German squadrons. The constant activity of British reconnaissance and artillery-spotting aircraft made the sector a favourite hunting ground for Manfred von Richthofen – Germany's famed "Red Baron." Fighting hard to fend off the German squadrons were scores of Allied fighter pilots, including Canada's Billy Bishop.[30]

On 7 April, back on the ground, work continued as before for all platoons, both at the front and in the training area. The following day, Easter Sunday, was the final day before the attack and as such was a major day of preparation. By 1:00 PM the 19th Battalion had assembled on its parade ground, with the troops equipped in battle order and drawn up in two main sections. First were those assigned to take part in the attack, who constituted the majority of the battalion's personnel – 21 officers and 664 other ranks. This group moved into bivouac at 2:10 PM in the Boix-des-Alleux. The remaining members of the battalion, who were designated LOB, were moved to McKenzie Camp, where they would stay during the battle. Later that evening, at 7:00 PM, Lt.-Col. Millen led the attacking platoons forward to occupy their positions in the front line, and battalion headquarters and a report centre were set up in the protective confines of Zivy Cave.[31] "My memory wanders back to the night of April 8th at Vimy Ridge," Pte. Art Clymer later wrote. "We left the Battalion headquarters to take up our position in an old French trench ahead of our own front line as a jumping off trench. As we left, our Commanding Officer, Lt.-Col. Millen, shook hands with us and wished us God speed."[32]

At Vimy, it was the 19th Battalion's turn to be in the forefront of the assault, operating along the 4th Brigade's left sub-section while the 18th Battalion took up the right. The 21st Battalion would be held in reserve during the initial phase of the attack and would become the brigade's vanguard once the 18th and 19th Battalions had achieved their objectives. As had been the case at Courcelette, mopping-up duties for the attacking battalions would be carried out by parties from another unit – in this case, the 20th Battalion. Although some officers had criticized such arrangements weeks earlier in their assessment of operations at the Somme, this time it was hoped that confusion would be minimized, if not eliminated, by giving the mopping-up parties "a definite mode of procedure and sphere of action." According to Maj. D.J. Corrigall, "they were to disarm and send back prisoners, clear the dugouts of their occupants and collect maps, documents and material."[33]

Each of the attacking battalions would operate on a three-company front, with each attacking company, in turn, being on a one-platoon front and formed up to a depth of three waves. By this time in the Canadian Corps, the word "wave" no longer meant a line of soldiers moving forward as on parade, but referred to those units that left the trenches at the same given moment."[34] Assigned to the left portion of the 19th Battalion's attack was D Company under Maj. Russell Thomson, which would lead off with No. 13 Platoon, followed by No. 14 and 16 platoons. In the centre was B Company, commanded by Lt. Robert H. Bliss, with No. 6, 7, and 8 Platoons, while on the right was C Company, led by Maj. Charles E. Sinclair, which fielded No. 9, 11, and 12 platoons. Following up the 19th Battalion's three attacking companies was A Company, with, from left to right, No. 3, 2, and 1 platoons functioning as battalion reserve under Maj. Arthur Ellis. Each platoon of the attacking companies would be disposed in two successive lines, presumably in keeping with the standard platoon formation employed during training exercises earlier in the winter. The sections in No. 3, 2, and 1 Platoons would advance in what was termed "artillery formation." This meant that the men in each section would advance in column instead of in line, with the four sections of each platoon moving together in a diamond configuration. This provided greater dispersal of personnel and some reduction of the danger posed by enemy artillery fire. The fourth platoon of each company contained those men who were designated LOB and held back at McKenzie Camp.[35]

The 19th Battalion's objectives for the morning of 9 April would be, first, the German front-line trench, next, the German support line, and, finally, the enemy positions along the Black Line, which, in the 19th Battalion's sub-section, ran along the trench system known as *Zwischenstellung*. The 19th and 18th Battalions would halt and consolidate along the Black Line while the 21st Battalion pushed ahead to capture the Red Line, running along the *Turko Graben* and a small portion of the *Zwischenstellung*. After securing the Red Line, the 21st Battalion would dig in and the battalions of the 6th Brigade would continue ahead, passing through the 4th Brigade and advancing from the Red Line to capture first the Blue Line and then the Brown Line in cooperation with British troops from the 13th Brigade operating on their left.[36]

In the frosty pre-dawn hours of Easter Monday, some 35,000 men in the leading and reserve waves filed into their assembly positions along the Canadian Corps front.[37] Opposing them were no more than 10,000 troops from the 1st Bavarian Reserve, 79th Prussian Reserve, and 16th Bavarian Divisions.[38] At 4:40 AM, the assaulting platoons of the 19th Battalion were in position and ready to go. By all appearances, the weather seemed as though it might be fine, albeit cold, for the coming day. But as the men's watches ticked off the minutes before zero hour, the skies became increasingly overcast and the icy winds began to whip up sleet and flurries of snow. On the plus side, the wind was at the Canadians' backs and in the Germans' faces, while the frigid temperatures had hardened the mud somewhat, giving the men better footing – at least, according to the Canadian official historian. Harry Neil remembered the terrain at Vimy differently: "It was a snowy and bitterly cold Easter Monday and the mud between our positions and the top of the Ridge had the consistency of glue."[39]

As Maj. D.J. Corrigall of the 20th Battalion later recalled,

> while we watched the minutes pass, we thought of the thousands of others lying as we were, ready to leap forward, of the waiting trench-mortar and machine-gun crews, of gunners standing by to fire, of the airmen "tuning up" for flight, of the services in rear already moving supplies forward, and of the staff of many formations preparing for developments. We wondered if they felt as nervous as we did.[40]

The 19th Battalion officers, like D Company's Maj. Russell Thomson, quietly moved up and down the line, offering a pat on the back, a handshake, and some final words of encouragement to their men. "Major Thompson [*sic*] was to lead

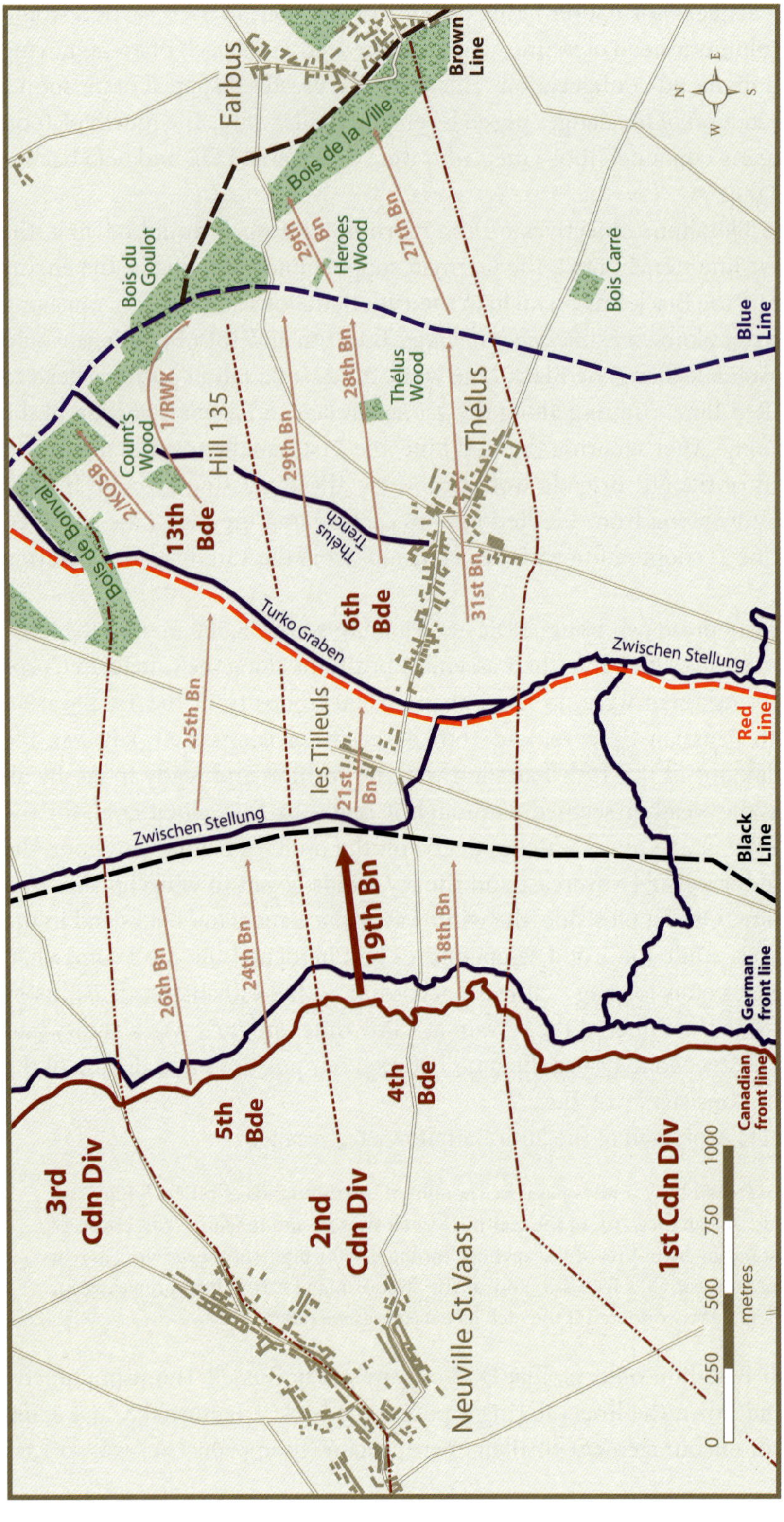

Map 12 – Battle of Vimy Ridge – the 2nd Canadian Division's sector.

the battalion on this attack," recalled Pte. Art Clymer. "Just before the zero hour, [he] … crawled along the trench to wish us all good luck."[41]

Over the Top

At precisely 5:30 AM, 9 April 1917, the artillery opened up with a stupendous barrage and the infantry rose from trenches or filed out of assembly tunnels and trudged across the bleak, sleet-swept no man's land towards the German front line. As at the Somme, the troops followed a lethal curtain of bursting shrapnel shells – a creeping barrage – that pounded and rolled over German positions like a tidal wave of fire and flying metal.[42]

Closely following (or "hugging") the barrage had its risks, for the occasional shell might fall short and thereby endanger the attackers. But the men had been trained rigorously to keep within roughly sixty-five yards of the barrage "in order to make the final rush when the shells lifted off to their next objective" at the rate of 100 yards every three minutes. The whole process took "nerves of steel," for if the infantry fell too far behind the barrage they would be at the mercy of any Germans who had managed to survive the maelstrom.[43] With words that could well describe the experience of most Canadian infantry in the initial advance that morning, Maj. D.J. Corrigall of the 20th Battalion set the scene as the troops went over the top on the heels of the barrage:

> We scrambled forth, our accoutrements jangling and our rifles, with bayonets fixed, at "high port." Across "No Man's Land," walking, running and jumping, we followed the whitish-grey puffs, which lifted every four minutes [*sic*] as they advanced; we passed through the enemy's wire and jumped into his trenches, pulled ourselves out of these and went on, the attacking waves continuing to follow the barrage while we, the "moppers," broke off at prearranged points to search the trenches and dugouts.[44]

As soon as the Canadian and British artillery commenced its destructive work, there occurred a strangely captivating spectacle as hundreds of SOS rockets shot up from the German front line along the length of the ridge. The signal flares arced lazily upward and then spiralled down to earth, while those who fired them waited anxiously for a response from the German artillery that never came.[45] During the pre-battle bombardments, the Canadian counter-battery organization under Lt.-Col. Andrew McNaughton had done its work well, neutralizing 83 per cent of known enemy guns and depriving the Germans of one of their principal means of resistance.[46] In the first seven minutes of the attack there was almost no German artillery retaliation. When it did commence, the fire was "noticeably weak and uncertain," falling first on the Canadian front line and then upon the Germans' own captured forward positions.[47] Throughout the attack, Canadian and British gunners continued bombarding the German rear areas, laying down a series of standing barrages beyond the creeping barrage, which destroyed or suppressed numerous

Ground over which the 19th Battalion advanced at Vimy, in the vicinity of their jumping-off line on 9 April 1917. They would have advanced towards the hedge and trees on the horizon. Photo taken along the road leading from Neuville-Saint-Vaast to Thélus, opposite Zivy Crater Cemetery. (Author's collection, 2015)

Canadian infantry advancing through German wire entanglements on Vimy Ridge. Some of the explosions appear to be later additions to the original image. Such doctoring of photos was done for dramatic effect. (LAC PA-001087)

German strongpoints, dugouts, machine-gun nests, and mortar emplacements. The torrent of artillery unleashed upon the Germans that morning was made even deadlier by an accompanying hail of fire that spewed forth from 150 heavy machine guns employing long-range indirect-fire tactics. These weapons deluged crossroads, communication trenches, and close-support artillery positions with approximately seven million bullets.[48]

But if the German artillery measures were largely frustrated, scattered groups of soldiers who survived the creeping barrage made their inevitable appearance and exacted fierce retribution on the attacking waves of Canadian infantry. Resistance in the 2nd Canadian Division's sector came mainly from troops of the 79th Reserve Division.[49] For the 19th Battalion, the Battle of Vimy Ridge would be no light-hearted cakewalk, and little did the unfortunate Maj. Russell Thomson realize that, as he wished his men good luck during the last moments before zero hour, he was also bidding them a final farewell. According to Pte. Art Clymer, Thomson was cut down almost immediately, being "among the first killed as we went over the top." True to their training, other men quickly assumed the leadership roles of those who were killed. "I recall how Lieut. Herbert very coolly halted us," Clymer stated, "as the enemy were throwing their hand grenades – potato mashers. [Herbert] called for the rifle grenadiers to get into action. This silenced the enemy and we advanced to our objective."[50] In Clymer's brief vignette, we can discern fleeting glimpses of the new infantry platoon organization in action, and apparently working effectively.

German machine gunners also made their destructive presence known, especially in the left portion of the 4th Brigade's path of advance, along which the 19th Battalion had the misfortune to be operating. Machine guns in a position known as Balloon Trench proved especially troublesome, temporarily checking the unit's advance, inflicting casualties, and forcing a considerable number of troops to dive for cover. While the survivors remained pinned down, flanking parties, including moppers-up from B Company of the 20th Battalion, worked their way around both sides of the position and destroyed the machine guns with volleys of rifle grenades. By 6 AM the 19th Battalion had resumed its advance.[51]

Other scattered parties of Germans, who had survived the creeping barrage and witnessed the annihilation of their machine-gun crews, quickly lost their will to resist. As the Canadians moved resolutely forward across the smoking and pitted ground, which now became increasingly slippery from snow and slush, they

Rounding up German prisoners, April 1917. (LAC PA-001128)

A tank crossing the German front line at Vimy. (LAC PA-002253)

encountered the dazed denizens of various dugouts and strongpoints who were sufficiently demoralized that they threw up their hands in surrender.[52]

At 6:07 AM Lt. Edwin Trendell, the officer in charge of the 19th Battalion's advanced report centre, informed Lt.-Col. Millen that the men had succeeded in reaching all of the unit's assigned portion of the Black Line. All the while, low-flying contact patrol aircraft darted over the position, observed the Canadians' progress, and relayed the good news back to division and corps headquarters. While the assault parties began clearing debris and reclaiming the shattered enemy trenches, the troops of the 21st Battalion filtered through their positions at 6:40 AM and commenced their own phase of the attack, advancing to capture their allotted section of the Red Line and taking the tiny hamlet of Les Tilleuls in the process.[53]

As the din of the creeping barrage rolled steadily eastward, the men of the 19th Battalion suddenly heard the growling of motors and the clanking of metal. Lifting their heads from their labours, they caught sight of four of the eight tanks assigned to take part in the 2nd Canadian Division's attack. The armoured leviathans crawled laboriously over the grotesquely scarred terrain, lumbering over slime-filled shell holes and ditches some 400 yards beyond the 19th Battalion's left flank. Corps headquarters had allocated all the tanks placed at its disposal to the 2nd Division's sector of the attack because it was feared that the German garrisons of Les Tilleuls, Thélus, and Farbus would put up a stiff fight from their shelters in the cellars and ruins of these small villages. The tanks, it was felt, could render additional needed support. It was a good theory; however, none of the machines caught up with the attacking infantry that morning. Each of them came to a wallowing halt in the mud and craters on the ridge's western slope and did not even make it as far as the Black Line. Fortunately, the division's assault would progress well enough that the tanks' absence would not prove detrimental to its overall success.[54]

Canadian infantry advancing past one of the tanks mired on the battlefield at Vimy Ridge. (LAC PA-001496)

One of the tanks used in the Vimy Ridge advance. Although not effective in this particular attack, their imposing bulk demonstrates the importance of such machines when used en masse in later operations (such as at Cambrai and Amiens during late 1917 and 1918). (LAC PA-001503)

Indeed, the advance continued on schedule. With the Red Line breached by 7:15 AM, the 4th Brigade's part in the forefront of the attack soon came to an end. Later that morning, at around 9:00 AM, units of the 6th Brigade passed through the 4th Brigade's positions, forming up on the Red Line a half-hour later to continue the advance to the Blue and Brown lines. As the men from western Canada pressed onward towards the Blue Line, they captured the village of Thélus, which had been

Even in defeat, still imposing: a captured German machine-gun emplacement in the village of Thélus, April 1917. (LAC PA-000882)

The remains of a German machine-gun position in Thélus. (LAC PA-001122)

reduced by the artillery to little more than a smoking pile of rubble. After occupying the Blue Line just to the east, they paused for an hour and a half to regroup and rotate fresh units into position to continue the advance. When the barrage swept on once more, the infantry pushed forward over the low crest of the ridge, taking out German machine-gun crews with rifle grenades – a weapon that had proven its worth in eminent fashion that morning.

By pure coincidence, just as many of the Canadians crested the ridge, the weather broke and the sun briefly shone through the gloom, transfiguring the vista

Canadians advancing over the crest of Vimy Ridge, (LAC PA-001046)

Captured German first line and Canadians on the crest of Vimy Ridge advancing on the German third-line trench. (LAC PA-001113)

beyond the eastern scarp. There, stretched out before them, lay the comparatively unspoiled landscape of the Douai plain, while immediately below them, along the wooded eastern slopes of the ridge itself, groups of Germans scurried eastward in headlong retreat. There was scant time to admire the view, however, for the 6th Brigade still had one more objective to take. With the 2/King's Own Scottish Borderers and the 1/Royal West Kents surging forward on their left, the Manitobans and British Columbians of the 27th and 29th Battalions dashed down the eastern slope. Whooping and yelling, they charged the first line of German field artillery batteries in the Bois-de-la-Ville, where they bayoneted or captured those among the gun crews who dared to stand their ground. At 1:55 PM the Brown Line was secured along the 2nd Canadian Division's front.[55] The efforts of the 1st and 3rd Canadian Divisions on either flank also met with success, and the bulk of Vimy Ridge lay in Canadian hands on the first day of the attack. Only on the far left were serious delays encountered by the 4th Canadian Division, which fought an especially savage battle to seize Hill 145 and another height to the north, code-named

Canadians consolidating their positions on Vimy Ridge, April 1917. (LAC PA-001052)

Men of the 19th Battalion consolidating their new positions on Vimy Ridge. The fighting has moved far enough ahead that a few men can take a brief break from their labours to pose for the camera. The original archival reference for this image states, "Man in foreground is private Valentine Townsend." Townsend enlisted with the 123rd Battalion in Toronto in 1915 and was transferred to the 19th Battalion. He would survive the war and pass away at the age of 69 on 28 April 1959 in Clinton, Ontario, the community where he was born. (LAC PA-001085)

the Pimple. The latter position would finally capitulate on 12 April, after the spilling of much blood on both sides.[56]

For the remainder of 9 April, consolidation efforts continued at full pace along the positions already captured, amidst desultory shelling from some German batteries well beyond the ridge that still were able to put up a fight. That afternoon, as clouds and sleet once more settled over the battlefield, the 19th Battalion's foremost positions were at the Black Line along the *Zwischenstellung*. Situated from left to right along this line were D, B, and C Companies, with one platoon of A Company still attached to each as a reserve force. As soon as it was deemed safe to do so, battalion headquarters moved forward from Zivy Cave and re-established itself in the German support line. Lt.-Col. Millen had a great deal to be proud of in the conduct of his men. In addition to the territory seized, the 19th Battalion had captured five machine guns, five German "Fish Tail Bomb Carriers," two light trench mortars, and at least 120 prisoners.[57] It was an outstanding morning's work by all ranks.

Many of those who came through physically unscathed would write glowing letters home, describing the emotion, if not the tactical details, of the moment. Later in April, Pte. John Gaetz informed his mother: "By this time no news will have been good news, and you will be pleased to know that I came through the recent operations alright. The latter I know will have been made well known in Canada. It was certainly a great experience and one I will not forget shortly. The Canadians will have still more to be proud of now."[58] Nor could Lt.-Col. Millen contain his satisfaction in a letter he wrote a week after the battle: "My dear Mother … You of course know we have been in a scrap … The whole thing was absolutely wonderful, every one did fine work … Of course I am not permitted to go into details but it was certainly a wonderful feeling to be living in places that had been held by the enemy for years and to walk over ground that had been barred to us."[59] Although Vimy proved to be a great victory for the Canadians, it was by no means a bloodless one. In fact, the opening day of the attack was not only the single bloodiest day of the war for the Canadians but also "the bloodiest in all of Canadian military history," with 7,707 casualties occurring on 9 April and the early part of 10 April.[60] Altogether, between 9 and 14 April (the official dates of the battle), the Canadian Corps would suffer 10,602 casualties, 3,598 of them fatal. German casualties at Vimy have not been calculated specifically, but when combined with the 4,000 known prisoners captured, they probably approximated the total sustained by the Canadians. In any case, it is safe to assume that German losses were much higher than the Canadians' as a proportion of the numbers of troops involved in the battle.[61] As ever, many of the wounded, whether on the victorious side or the vanquished, suffered horribly. "I did not know until days afterward the result of this battle, as I was seriously wounded in the morning by machine gun fire," wrote Cpl. Charles Henderson years after the war:

Wounded men waiting to be loaded onto a light railway. Vimy Ridge, April 1917. (LAC PA-001034)

> I crawled into an old trench for shelter, but could not go further because my hip was shattered and a hole [was] blown in my bladder. The Germans were firing gas shells at this location, and I had to bury my face in the mud for protection, as I had lost my gas mask when I was struck down. I heard another soldier moaning around a turn in the trench, but I could not move to help him. After many hours I was found by stretcher-bearers, who bandaged my wound and lifted me out of the trench. They then ordered some German prisoners to carry me back behind the lines, but the enemy shelling became heavier, and the prisoners dropped me and ran for protection. I was eventually taken to a field dressing station for emergency treatment, and then to a Field Hospital.[62]

During the battle, casualties were cleared by battalion stretcher-bearers, assisted by additional men specially trained and detailed from the infantry companies. [63] As for the dead, there was nothing that survivors could do but mourn and wait for the burial parties to collect the bodies. No longer were men simply interred where they fell, as had often been the case. In keeping with recently adopted policy, corpses now were removed from the battlefield and laid to rest in pre-arranged cemeteries.[64] In the interim, officers and other ranks moving back and forth over the captured ground in the course of their duties came upon many heartbreaking sights. "We were going over the Ridge and I saw one of the saddest things that I have ever seen in my life," remarked Ed Youngman, who was as busy as ever with his work in the battalion transport section, hauling ammunition forward to his comrades on 9 April. He recounted how a team of horses pulling an artillery gun "got a direct hit with a shell" and how the wounded driver, on seeing two of his horses "intertwined in death," opted not to go back and thereby possibly save himself but instead "crawled between his – his beloved horses – laid his head on one of the cheeks and just died with them."[65] Then there was Maj. D.E. Macintyre, the chief staff officer of the 4th Brigade, who came across the body of one officer he had known personally, Maj. Russell Thomson:

> In No Man's Land I recognized an officer of the 19th Battalion with whom I had enjoyed dinner a short time before the battle, and with whom I had played basketball in Canada. He lay in that awkward humpbacked posture I had so often observed in the dead, made more conspicuous by the heavy pack on his back as though the load had been too heavy and he had stumbled and fallen face down, his knees buckled under him, his hands spread before him. A gallant officer who died leading his men.[66]

Thomson had been a popular officer, and his death came as a sad blow for his friends in the battalion. "Poor Punk Thomson," wrote Lt.-Col. Millen. "I am glad he never knew what struck him. I went out myself with some other officers and found his body, and we were able to give him a proper burial in a regular cemetery."[67]

While the bodies of many of the Canadian dead were relatively intact, having fallen victim to machine-gun fire or grenade fragments,[68] some of the Germans were found in a hideously mangled state, having been torn apart by the merciless artillery barrage. Writing after the war of his experiences at Vimy, Maj. Macintyre recalled that

> the first dead German I saw was spread-eagled against the parados, or back wall, of his trench, arms flung out as though crucified. Where his head had been was a red pulp

Light railway truck with wounded on board. Prisoners often were pressed into service moving the wounded to safety. (LAC PA-001022)

A Canadian camp at the foot of Vimy. In the foreground are several graves of fallen French soldiers, April 1917. (LAC PA-001148)

> like a crushed strawberry. Many of the dead lay as though sleeping without a mark of disfigurement and I am certain felt no pain, but others were disemboweled or with limbs shattered and clothing torn from their bodies by the blast of high explosives. The water in the shell holes was stained blood red.[69]

Yet amidst the carnage of battle at Vimy, there were deeds of selflessness and heroism displayed by combat and support personnel alike, the latter often forgotten in accounts that celebrate those who spearheaded the assault. In the 19th Battalion, heroes came in all sizes and from some of the least expected sources. One of them gave a much-needed helping hand to Ed Youngman, who found himself in dire straits just a few days after the Canadians stormed Vimy. In the midst of heavy shelling, Youngman was busy hauling water forward in two-gallon cans strapped to mules when one of the ropes holding the cans on his mule slipped. With the cans now under the mule's belly, the animal panicked, kicking the cans in frustration. "I tried to hold him," said Youngman, "but it was impossible."

> Now there was eighteen other mule drivers that went by me and they were scared, their faces were pale, they were frightened. I didn't blame [them] – they went right by me to get out of the shelling area. All but one fellow, we had … nicknamed him Lizzie years before, I don't know how he got that nickname, but he was a man who was very unkempt in his dress. He never kept his buttons polished, he was uneducated, he was

> the butt of all our jokes, and I am ashamed to say even today, but he was. I was bad as anybody, he came last about a hundred feet trailing the others and when he got opposite us he was the only little fellow who had the guts to say, "Can I help you Eddie?" He held my mule and his own, I don't know how he did it and I released the saddle and afterward, the shelling miraculously … slowed the minute I got the saddle off. Then I [rearranged the saddle and] put the water on and to even the thing up, he [Lizzie] carried one can under one arm and I carried the other and from that day on when anybody wanted to have a bit of quiet fun with Lizzie Banks it was okay with me, but when they went past a certain point I asked them to stop and I meant stop and I was ready to back it up with my fists, with my reputation … Lizzie Banks died last year and for me [he was] one of the bravest men [who] ever lived.[70]

"Lizzie" Banks was not the only man in the 19th Battalion whose reputation was redeemed by his actions at Vimy. According to Youngman, "there was a man wounded and one of the stretcher-bearers," who used the pseudonym of Robertson,

> decided that this man should have his arm amputated, it was almost amputated anyway. He took the razor out of his pocket, a straight razor, we did not have safety razors, and he made a first-class job of finishing amputating that arm, and he sewed it up with thread from his ordinary kit, and the man was put on a stretcher and he went right on through to casualty clearing.

Youngman explained that the men later learned that the stretcher-bearer's real name was Fred Presnail, but he had decided to keep it secret. "He belonged to a very fine prominent Canadian family" and "had been disbarred from [medical] practice in Canada because of the excessive use of drugs … But he had left his home town in Hamilton in disgrace and … just by a single thing he was restored to society again."[71]

The capture of Vimy Ridge has usually been viewed as a distinctly Canadian victory in which all four Canadian divisions operated together for the first time (albeit under a British corps commander, supported by British and other Dominion artillery[72] along with British infantry, and all in accordance with plans and orders drawn up by senior corps and divisional staff officers, many of whom were British). Nevertheless, some veterans and postwar commentators saw in this feat of arms, and in the sense of pride it engendered, the effective spiritual birth of an independent Canadian nation on the international stage.[73] For those who held such opinions, Vimy Ridge was the place where Canada essentially "discovered itself." For others, like "Lizzie" Banks and Fred Presnail, Vimy Ridge was something much more than a national experience; it was the place where they had found themselves.

Assessing the Achievement

Whatever its psychological and emotional impact on the collective psyche and nationalistic sentiment of Canadians, the Battle of Vimy Ridge saw the Canadian Corps come into its own as an internationally respected fighting force. The French

Blasted remains of the village of Farbus, on the eastern slopes of Vimy Ridge, April 1917. (LAC PA-001084)

press, surprised and excited by the news of the ridge's capture, hailed the victory as "an Easter gift from Canada to the French nation," while Britain's King George V proclaimed that "Canada will be proud that the taking of the coveted Vimy Ridge has fallen to the lot of her troops." The First Army commander, Gen. Sir Henry Horne, under whose aegis the attack had taken place, ascribed the victory to the soundness of the Canadians' plans, their "thoroughness of preparation, dash and determination in execution, and devotion to duty on the part of all concerned."[74]

Horne's assessment of the reasons for Canadian success was accurate, but only to a point: he did not account for certain tactical errors by the Germans. At Vimy, a combination of difficult topography on the ridge's eastern slopes, complacency regarding the strength of existing defences, and a certain level of conservatism on the part of Gen. Ludwig von Falkenhausen conspired to delay the implementation of the sort of defence-in-depth system that had been developed on other sectors of the German front. German reserve divisions, which would be called upon to counterattack any successful Allied incursions in the sector, were held well east of the ridge, around six hours' marching distance away. This kept them well out of range of any Allied artillery batteries that might be established along the crest of the ridge. Von Falkenhausen's decision had been a prudent one, so long as the assumption was correct that existing defence measures (and the ridge's natural features) rendered the German position impregnable, or at least strong enough to resist attack

Another view of the ruined village of Farbus captured by Canadians. (LAC PA-001097

until the distant reserves could be brought up. If this assumption proved wrong, as indeed it was by the overwhelming weight of Canadian shells and manpower, it spelled doom for German garrisons along the ridge itself, which were left without strong support close at hand when it was most needed.[75]

Altogether, the Germans had fielded no more than 10,000 men for the immediate defence of Vimy, while the Canadians had attacked them with around 35,000. The Canadians thus had an overwhelming advantage in numbers of men, as well as artillery shells, and they mobilized these resources in a highly orchestrated fashion against German defences that reflected, in their relative inflexibility, the forward defensive philosophy that had prevailed much of the time at the Somme in 1916. Such defences were exactly the type that the Canadian Corps had trained all winter to breach. However, the Canadians' own reliance upon artillery-dominated timetable tactics reflected a rigidity in operational planning that would have to be adapted in the future in the event that they came up against German positions that were defended in a more elastic fashion.[76]

To cope with such challenges, units like the 19th Battalion would need to continue refining their decentralized system of platoon-centred tactics. Only in this way could they hope to free themselves from heavy reliance on less mobile artillery resources and take the fight to the enemy with their own firepower. To be sure, clear evidence of real flexibility was displayed by the infantry battalions at Vimy, as when sections of rifle grenadiers or Lewis gunners outflanked and destroyed

A photo taken from Beehive Cemetery, near Willerval, looking back to the area around Farbus on the eastern slopes of Vimy Ridge. This view gives a nice impression of the flatness of much of the terrain east of Vimy Ridge and the degree to which the ridge dominated this ground. (Author's collection, 2015)

German strongpoints that had survived the artillery bombardments.[77] But many such obstacles had been located by ground and aerial reconnaissance before the battle, so the troops could prepare in advance to deal with these if they had to. To counter the unknowns posed by a dynamic system of defence-in-depth, fire and movement tactics would need to become so ingrained that the infantry would be able to execute them in battlefield situations that had not been rehearsed repeatedly over taped training courses. There was no magic formula for achieving such levels of expertise and improvisatory skill. It would require more time, more training, and more operational experience. In any case, the fact that Vimy Ridge was not won by artillery fire virtually on its own is proven in stark fashion by the magnitude of the casualties suffered by the infantry, who grimly fought their way forward behind the creeping barrage.

The German high command gained some solace from the notion that it was the older style of defences that had failed at Vimy. Still, it was a cold sort of comfort. "No one could have foreseen that the expected offensive would gain ground so quickly," wrote Crown Prince Rupprecht of Bavaria, the commander of the German army group responsible for Vimy. Realizing that it would be futile to attempt to storm the steep eastern face of Vimy Ridge in a counterattack, he resigned himself to the fact that the position was well and truly lost. On 10 April he ordered von Falkenhausen to withdraw his forces to the Oppy-Méricourt line and the Avion Switch, which guarded the southern and western suburbs of Lens, a move that was completed on the night of 12–13 April. By pulling back to a defensive position some two to three miles beyond the eastern slopes of the ridge, Rupprecht diminished the Canadians' newfound advantage in observation. He also quite literally levelled the playing field for the next phase of operations, for in order to follow up on their victory, the Canadians would have to come down from the heights of the ridge and meet the Germans on relatively equal terms with respect to terrain.[78]

The Canadians, meanwhile, would require several days to manage the back-breaking effort of moving their artillery batteries forward over a shattered landscape bereft of usable roads and covered with mud and shell holes. Only when the guns were within effective range of the Germans' new front-line positions could a continuation of the advance be contemplated. Herein lay the essential weakness of the set-piece tactics employed by Canadian and British forces. Reliance on artillery firepower to break into enemy positions did not facilitate the sort of rapid movement needed to exploit a "break-in" and convert it into a "breakthrough." In any case, no plans had been made by the British high command to fully exploit any Canadian success at Vimy. The operation was designed from the beginning to be a subsidiary one in support of the Third Army's offensive in the valley of the Scarpe, east of Arras. The Third Army, in turn, was acting mainly to support French General Robert Nivelle's grand offensive along the Ainse River, centred on the Chemin-des-Dames Ridge.[79] If the broader Anglo-French offensives failed to make any headway, then the Canadian victory at Vimy would have little more than a purely local impact.

Unfortunately, this is precisely what occurred. In the first phase of what became known as the Battle of Arras, Gen. Allenby's Third Army did not succeed in breaking through to Cambrai, nor did the Fifth Army make much progress in covering Allenby's right flank. Although the Third Army's initial territorial gains on 9 April were, in some instances, even more stunning than those at Vimy, its forward momentum steadily lost impetus as the Germans rushed forward fresh reserve divisions and strengthened their rear defences. German resistance grew fiercer and British casualties mounted alarmingly until the Battle of Arras finally petered out on 17 May. By that time, British and Dominion forces had suffered almost 159,000 casualties, which, over thirty-nine days of fighting, made for the heaviest daily casualty rate of all British offensives in the war – even heavier than had been suffered during the more infamous Battle of the Somme. The Germans fared little better: estimates of their losses ranged between 170,000 and 180,000 (including over 20,000 POWs). But their main lines of defence had held held firm.[80]

Worse still, the French were no more successful in their efforts farther to the south. The Nivelle offensive began on 16 April and ultimately proved to be a spectacularly tragic failure. Employing the tactics of defence-in-depth, relinquishing ground when necessary, and pulverizing attacking French divisions with overwhelming artillery fire and counterattack forces, the Germans wrought havoc among Nivelle's assault formations, which suffered approximately 134,000 casualties in the first ten days alone. By the time the battle reached its tortuous conclusion on 9 May, the French had gained little more than four miles of territory at horrifying cost. This failure, and the perceived callous disregard for human life displayed by the French high command, sparked a wave of mutinies that threatened to paralyze the French armies in the west. Restoring order and morale among the *poilus* would require the sacking of Nivelle and months of time, effort, and conciliation by the French high command. For the remainder of 1917, the British armies would have to shoulder the bulk of the burden on the Western Front – at least from an offensive standpoint.[81]

12

A Bloody Setback: 10 April–1 July 1917

After capturing and consolidating its portion of the Black Line at Vimy, the 19th Battalion advanced to positions along the Red Line on 10 April, where it relieved the 21st Battalion and a portion of the 5th Brigade. Lt.-Col. Millen's men now occupied a stretch of line from the 2nd Canadian Division's southern boundary north to a position known as *Cramer Haus*, which lay along *Turko Graben*. At the same time, battalion headquarters was shifted forward to Les Tilleuls Cave. In the line were D, C, and B Companies, each with one platoon of A Company still attached. They would occupy these positions through 12 April.[1]

On 13 April the 19th Battalion was relieved in the lines by the Nova Scotians of the 25th Battalion, and Millen's men moved back to a position known as Paynesley Tunnel. There, they were relieved again on the following day by troops of the 6th Brigade, who also relieved the remainder of the 4th Brigade. The latter formation was ordered into reserve on 14 April. The 19th Battalion marched back to Mont St-Eloi, where it took up billets in the village. By now the battalion had drawn up detailed casualty estimates for the period 9 to 14 April. Among the officers, Maj. Russell Thomson and Lt. Selby B. Longstreet were both killed in action, and Maj. Arthur Ellis died of his wounds. Six other officers – Lts. S.F. Wood, F.T. Wilson, E.A. Trendell, G. Johnston, A.G. Bennett, and A.R. Terhune – were wounded. As for the other ranks, the grim toll was 32 killed, 154 wounded, and 27 missing. An additional 15 other ranks were sick.[2]

Deward Barnes

During 14–15 April the battalion received an all-too-brief respite for reorganization and bathing before proceeding back to the trenches on 16 April to relieve the 22nd Battalion in support positions, which now were located in the vicinity of what had been the Canadian front-line system before 9 April. This they did, with a strength of 22 officers and 664 other ranks, the reserve platoon of each company being quartered in huts to the rear of Mont St-Eloi. This relief was completed by noon on 16 April, and the 19th Battalion spent the next several days in the support lines furnishing work and fatigue parties.[3]

From 1 to 16 April, the battalion received four junior officers and 133 other ranks as reinforcements, and it would be sent an additional 103 other ranks. This made up for the casualties sustained during the month. So far, the supply of reinforcements was keeping pace with operational losses.[4] One of these reinforcements was Pte. Deward Barnes, a Toronto native who had enlisted in the 180th Infantry Battalion (The Sportsmen) in February 1916. After arriving in England, this unit was absorbed by the 3rd Reserve Battalion, which trained and dispatched reinforcement drafts to the 4th and 19th Battalions, as well as to the 2nd and 4th Canadian Mounted Rifles. Barnes arrived at McKenzie Camp two days before the capture of Vimy Ridge. On 10 April he was posted to the Lewis gun section in No. 2 Platoon, A Company.[5] Barnes would keep a detailed personal diary that serves today as a vivid record of not only his own experiences but also those of the 19th Battalion.

On 17 April, while the battalion was situated in the support lines, Barnes was assigned to a work party that was detailed to fill in shell holes. The job was miserable, for the weather remained cold with intermittent snow and rain. But conditions were scarcely better in Barnes's dugout, mainly on account of the persistent vermin "We got back to Elk Trench," he wrote,

> and tried to sleep in dug-outs, but it was so lousy we had to get out and sleep in a trench full of mud. I had two rubber sheets, put one under me and one over. The rats were running over us all night. They didn't bother us, only you could hear and feel them running over your rubber sheet. This was an old trench, French, where they had battled nearly all through from the start of the war. Had been lost and retaken a few times and men had been blown to pieces, etc., then never found; the reason for so many rats.[6]

On the afternoon of 21 April the 19th Battalion moved farther forward to relieve the 28th Battalion in a position known as the "Observation Line," just east of Vimy Ridge. This relief was completed by 11:50 PM and the line consisted mainly of old gun pits. The Canadian trenches east of Vimy Ridge faced the Oppy-Méricourt line, to which the Germans had withdrawn on the night of 12–13 April. One of the main features of this new German front-line system was a pronounced salient that bulged out towards the Canadian lines. To engage the enemy "the British had to cross open fields largely devoid of cover."[7] Despite this disadvantage, Field Marshal Sir Douglas Haig insisted that his armies maintain pressure on the Germans both north and south of Arras in order to support the Nivelle offensive, which was launched on 16 April.[8] Canadian operations in this continuation of the larger Battle of Arras would begin later in the month, on 28 April, and focus on eliminating the loop of German trenches that jutted out in front of Arleux-en-Gohelle. The job would fall to Maj.-Gen. Currie's 1st Canadian Division.[9]

In the meantime, from 22 to 26 April, the 19th Battalion held its positions in the Observation Line. On 24 April some disruption was caused by German artillery, which bombarded the 19th Battalion's forward area with gas shells. The German gunners had also made life miserable for the Canadian artillery, transport, and supply personnel ever since the fighting moved out onto the flat expanse of the Douai Plain, for whenever units crested the ridge and proceeded down the eastern slopes towards the new battery lines or forward trenches, they were in full view of the German artillery spotters, who directed their batteries' fire with a vengeance and inflicted numerous casualties.[10]

But Lt.-Col. Millen's men held firm during the shelling and eventually were relieved by the 22nd Battalion on the afternoon of 26 April. After completing the relief at 11:15 PM the men marched back to a rest camp in corps reserve, where they were ordered to be ready to move at thirty minutes' notice, presumably because of the impending operations against the Arleux Loop. As it turned out, their services were not needed, for on 28 April the 1st Canadian Division succeeded not only in capturing the Arleux Loop but also in ejecting the German garrison of the village itself. This proved to be the only major accomplishment along the British front that day, for the thrusts to the south by divisions from the British First and Third Armies met with failure.[11]

Drilling, training, reorganization, and an inspection by Brig.-Gen. Rennie kept the 19th Battalion occupied during its time in corps reserve.[12] Yet the men still managed to find time to write to friends and families left behind in Canada. As always, the weather was a popular topic, and by the end of April it had finally taken a turn for the better. "It has almost been like camping out lately," wrote Pte. John Gaetz to his mother back in Alberta. And more than the weather had improved. Gaetz wrote that "there are bath houses, you know at every divisional headquarters where we get a bath and change of clothes every two weeks or so … The grub has never been more plentiful than the last few weeks. We get oranges now and again. Have often thought what a tremendous undertaking it all is. The transportation and distribution of everything."[13]

On 2 May, Gaetz and the rest of his comrades in the 19th Battalion passed out of corps reserve and moved forward to relieve the 28th Battalion in the support lines, where they formed part of the divisional reserve. Battalion headquarters was established at Paynesley Tunnel, with companies distributed among nearby dugouts and shelters. Maj. Hatch was now in charge of the battalion, it being his turn to lead the men into the trenches (at a strength of 19 officers and 664 other ranks), while Lt.-Col. Millen remained back in the transport lines.[14] "The battalion's rest is over," Millen informed his mother in a letter written on 3 May, in which he also referred to the "premier reputation" of the 19th.[15]

Under Hatch's watchful eye, Millen's men spent the next several days supplying work and carrying parties for various projects. Marauding German aircraft periodically harried the troops behind the front line. "These fast fighting planes are really wonderful the way they can dart, dive and climb," wrote Gaetz earlier, on 1 May. "Until recently our fast ones have been in the minority and Fritz has had an advantage over us."[16] The battalion had hardly settled into its support positions when, on 3 May, Pte. Barnes witnessed "Fritzie Red Devil planes [which] came over and fired all along [the] trench. We opened up with machine gun and rifle fire, but he got away. Our planes were not in it with his then for speed. He could make rings around ours."[17] The "Red Devil" was a common nickname given by Canadian infantry to Baron Manfred von Richthofen, whose red Albatros biplane was a familiar sight over the Vimy sector. Barnes likely extended the nickname to other German fighter pilots, who probably were members of von Richthofen's squadron, Jasta 11.

Several days later, on 7 May, Charles A. Gordon, who had recently joined the battalion in a reinforcement draft, witnessed "a plane swooping low, machine gun going, the boys hugging the ground, the flick of a wing and we counted our dead and wounded. Phil Collins, an original 19th Battalion man recently released from hospital[,] was carried away on a stretcher for the second time. We lost still more men on the way into the line." The aerial fighting of "Bloody April" had spilled over onto the ground war.[18]

Bloody Fresnoy

Tensions in the 19th Battalion rose still further on 3 May when all ranks in the trenches stood-to under orders to move at a moment's notice, owing to an attack that had just been launched by the 6th Brigade. The 6th was moving forward in order to protect the left flank of the 1st Brigade, whose task was to continue the advance from Arleux and breach the Oppy-Méricourt line along the western outskirts of the village of Fresnoy-en-Gohelle (often referred to, simply, as Fresnoy). Although the 6th Brigade was only partly successful in achieving its objectives, the troops of the 1st Brigade managed to force their way into and through Fresnoy. They then established a new front line some 250 yards east of the village, where they and their supporting artillery beat off two strong German counterattacks. On 5 May the 5th British Division, now serving in XIII Corps, relieved the 1st Canadian Division and took over the positions the Canadians had captured on 3 May. It was fully expected that the Germans would make further attempts to retake Fresnoy quickly, since it lay astride the important Oppy-Méricourt line and its environs provided good observation over the next great series of defensive lines, the Wotan system, which lay farther east.[19]

On 6 May the 4th Brigade took over the 2nd Canadian Division's entire front, relieving the 5th and 6th Brigades. On the following day, the 19th Battalion was ordered to relieve the 28th and 29th Battalions in the right sub-section of the brigade front, where it would occupy a stretch of trenches 1,200 yards in length. To its left would be the 18th Battalion and on its right flank would be the 95th Brigade (5th British Division), holding Fresnoy. After drawing up plans for his unit's dispositions, Maj. Hatch prepared to move his headquarters up to a point in the Arleux Loop, 600 yards behind the front line. Maintaining effective communication links would be extremely difficult in this stretch of the lines because heavy German shelling kept breaking the telephone wires, thus forcing battalion and company commanders to rely primarily on runners.[20]

The 19th Battalion would occupy the line on a three-company front: A Company under Maj. George T. Denison on the left, B Company under Lt. Huson Harman in the centre, and C Company under Lt. Samuel Johnston on the right, the latter having to link up with the British troops of the 12th Battalion, the Gloucestershire Regiment (12/Gloucestershire), on its right flank. The 19th Battalion's D Company would remain in support in the Arleux Loop under Capt. William Griesinger. In the forward area, Maj. Hatch would have under his command a total strength of 19 officers and 668 other ranks.[21]

This would be one of the worst trips in the line experienced by the 19th Battalion during the entire war. The trouble began as the battalion moved towards the

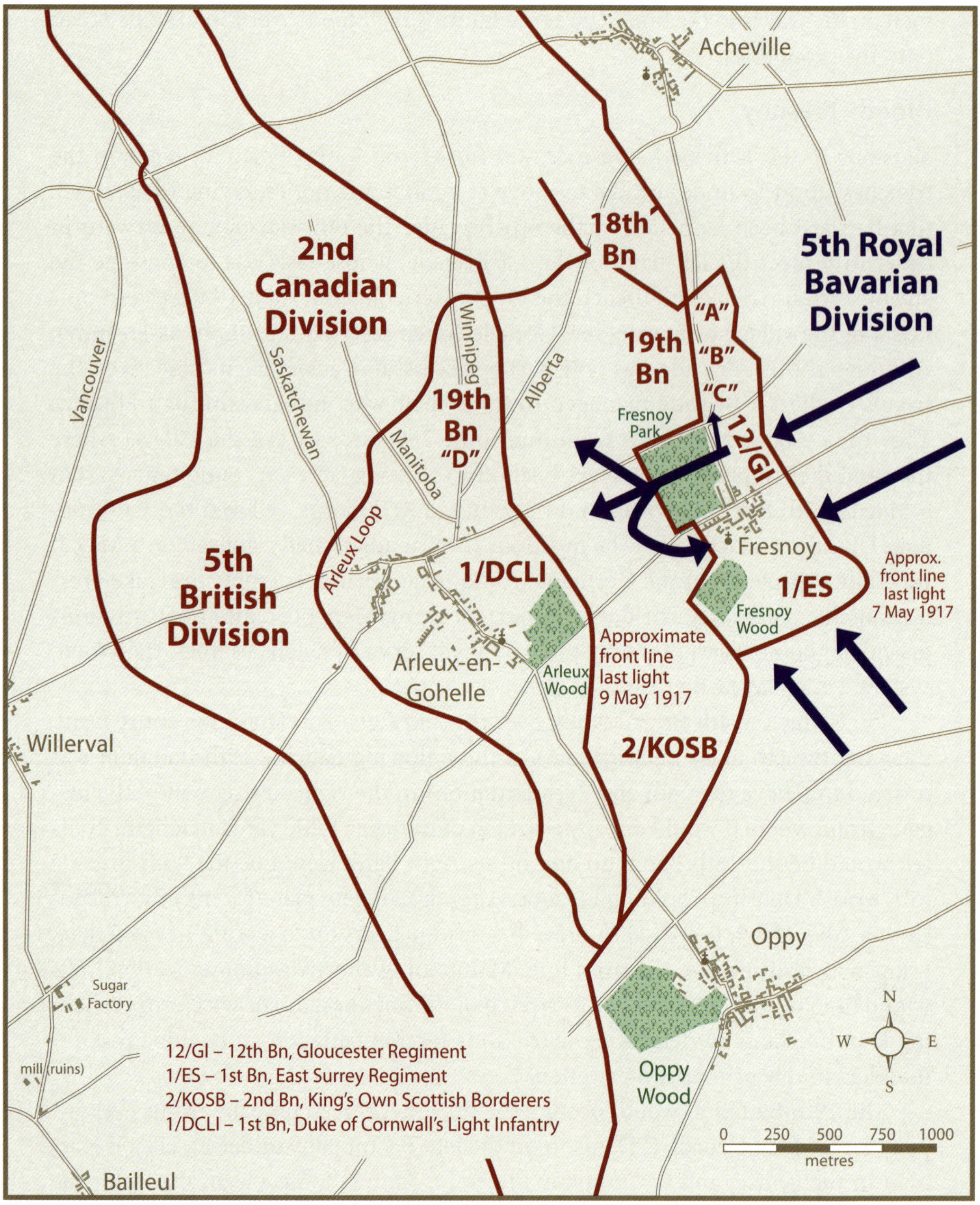

Map 13 – Fresnoy, 8 May 1917.

front line on the night of 7–8 May. "The famous Vimy Ridge had to be crossed," reported Maj. Herbert Fearman,

> and as we moved into the valley and out into the plain the order was passed along to put on our gas helmets. The Bosche was shelling the Railway embankment (near Farbus Wood) and all along the valley with gas shells. This was the first time that we had

> ever been through a gas cloud when relieving the front line, and the men (the majority of whom had not been long with us) behaved very coolly, and although there were shrapnel bursts accompanying the gas we reached the support line with only eight casualties.[22]

At 5:47 AM on 8 May, the Germans opened up a ferocious bombardment and the 5th Royal Bavarian Division launched an attack, the main weight of which fell upon the British battalions holding Fresnoy, the 12/Gloucestershire and 1/East Surrey. But at 3:45 AM, two hours before the main assault commenced, some of the German advance parties covering the assembly of the main force strayed too far forward and collided with the 19th Battalion's C Company while it was relieving the 29th Battalion. "This caught our men at a very great disadvantage," explained the battalion war diarist, "as this was a new part of the line." Worse still, the mist and rain that dominated the sector at that time prevented the artillery from seeing the SOS signals sent up from the Canadian front line. Even if they had been able to see the signal flares, many batteries would have been unable to respond, for some guns had been destroyed by preliminary bombardments and casualties from gas were extremely heavy among the artillery personnel that morning.[23] "The shelling was terrible," complained Pte. Deward Barnes, recalling in his diary the period just before the German advance guards struck C Company's lines:

> It made you think of home. Our corporal told us not to be afraid ... The rain never stopped. The trenches were all caving in and puddles of mud and water. We were soaked through hours ago and thick with mud. We watched. We knew they were coming and fear had left me by that time. My eyes must have been half out of my head from excitement. Finally, about 4:00 AM or just about daybreak, one of the boys says, "There they are." I couldn't see them just then and finally I saw one within a stone's throw away and then dozens of them. The front line of the Germans had been skirmishing and in the distance there were four lines of Germans. You could not see between them.[24]

It was "a battle to be remembered," wrote Charles Gordon of No. 11 Platoon. "One gray wave, then another, then again another ... On they came as tireless as the waves of old Lake Ontario on a stormy day." There was no shortage of targets for the Canadians, for according to Gordon, "it was impossible to miss hitting some of them, as they came over no man's land all bunched together. It was very costly for both sides."[25]

Almost immediately after the fighting broke out, Lt. Johnston was wounded and the command of C Company fell to Lt. Harold E. Bridge, who noticed that some German troops had managed to infiltrate his unit's position and were now threatening their rear. Because of this disturbing turn of events, Bridge ordered his men to fall back to a trench roughly 100 yards behind their original front line, where they made another stand. Fighting alongside them were three Lewis gun crews from B Company of the 29th Battalion, which had remained behind to assist when the marauding Germans interrupted the battalion relief. Barnes remembered

Bridge's fateful order: "Well boys, we are done, do your duty and fight to the finish." The men scarcely needed the formal encouragement, for they were battling for their very survival. "We stuck," wrote Barnes, "fear had left us. I was never so cool before. I did not bayonet any, but some did. The Germans were behind us, some killed just as they were about to get into our trenches, some sitting on top of our trenches dead, but looked alive. They were Bavarians ... and the finest men I had seen. None looked under 6 feet, and big ... We hung on."[26]

Charles Gordon also was in the thick of it with the other beleaguered members of C Company. "I can still recall the picture of that fight," he remarked after the war. "My bombs breaking as they should, a dozen or more, but it was of no use. I felt giddy, the sky whirled above me, then I lost my grip on life. Darkness ... sleep." By the time Gordon regained consciousness, his position had been overrun by the Germans. Wounded in the left thigh and arm, he lay stranded in a shell hole for two days and nights before being picked up by a German stretcher party. He spent the rest of the war as a prisoner.[27]

Despite his best efforts to save the situation, Lt. Bridge was wounded and knocked unconscious,[28] while C Company was split. One of its platoons, under Lt. Frank G. Lawson, became separated in the mêlée and fell back along with elements of the Gloucesters to the right. Sources are unclear as to the precise chronology of events, but it would seem that by this point, the Bavarians' main assault against the British at Fresnoy had already begun. The Gloucesters, on the 19th Battalion's right flank, fell back under the irresistible weight of the enemy attack, taking Lt. Lawson's platoon with them. Lt. Thomas J. Lynott now took charge of what remained of C Company's other two platoons. Seeing that continued German pressure was threatening to cut them off from the rest of the battalion, he ordered his men to fall back into B Company's front. B Company already had gone through a rough time of its own, the Germans having obtained a lodgment in its section of the trenches earlier that morning. But the invaders were shortly turfed out of this position by a swift counterattack, and, by the time Lynott had arrived with his two platoons, B Company had regained effective control of its original frontage and dispatched runners to battalion headquarters to keep them apprised of the situation.[29]

In the meantime, the Germans, with overwhelming artillery support and hordes of infantry, continued to push back the British troops on the 19th Battalion's right flank, leaving the Canadians exposed to deadly enfilade fire. Moreover, the enemy was now firmly ensconced in the front-line trench originally held by C Company. At this point, D Company, in battalion support, was thrown into the fray, having been ordered by Maj. Hatch to counterattack and retake the line originally held by C Company. "The Support Company went about their work in a most satisfactory manner," reported Maj. Fearman. They worked their way down the front line through the trenches still held by A and B Companies and "attacked the enemy on the flank, capturing three unwounded prisoners and killing a number of

Bosches with bombs and bayonets. The enemy, surprised at our fast counterattack [which was] launched about 1½ hours after the bombardment of our line, rushed out of the trench, leaving us in possession of our complete front line which we had taken over."[30]

Word of these developments was sent to the officer commanding the Gloucesters. It was requested that they likewise counterattack in order to restore the situation on the 19th Battalion's right flank. But the British troops had been practically annihilated during their withdrawal from Fresnoy, and the officer commanding the Gloucesters claimed that he had only about 130 men left. Therefore, it was impossible for him to assist. Fortunately, troops of the 4th Canadian Machine Gun Company arrived on the scene and bought the 19th Battalion some additional time by beating back parties of Germans attempting to work their way around the battalion's right flank. But this was only a temporary respite. When word reached the 19th Battalion at 1:30 PM on 8 May that the Gloucesters could offer no support on the right, the extreme precariousness of the situation compelled the Canadians to pull back again so that they could link up with British troops situated farther back in Winnipeg Road. This was one of a series of sunken roads that ran roughly north to south and were integrated into the Canadian and British defensive system. From west to east, these roads were named "Vancouver," Saskatchewan," "Manitoba," "Winnipeg," and "Alberta." The latter three intersected with the Arleux Loop. Besides withdrawing to Winnipeg Road, Maj. Hatch saw to it that his troops maintained a series of outposts and patrols in Alberta Road, approximately 350 yards ahead. But the eventual restoration of a continuous front with the British did not make things any easier for the 19th Battalion in terms of casualties. As the war diarist noted grimly, "our casualties while in the Winnipeg Road were heavy on account of that position being considerably outflanked." Because the 19th Battalion now sat in a pronounced salient, German gunners were having a field day, shelling Canadian positions from three sides.[31] The impact of the bombardment on groups of men huddled in the sunken road and in other nearby positions was hideous, and the wet weather turned the ground into a quagmire, making it even more difficult for exhausted and terrified men to move. "In the front line you miss most of the shells," reported Pte. Barnes,

> but back farther it was terrible, hundreds of dead were lying on the part we saw alone. There were hands sticking out of the mud and just faces. Some looked peaceful and others out of shape. The sight was terrible. It was that sticky clay. Every time you would go to lift your foot it would stick, and then stick to the other. You would sink to the tops of your boots in mud, trying not to step on faces, etc. And nothing to eat, no sleep, excited and dead tired, and trying to get back as fast as you can. It was hell.[32]

The men of the 19th Battalion caught their collective breath the next day, on 9 May, when they reorganized their front-line garrison into two companies. D

Canadians in a support trench, May 1917. (LAC PA-001168)

Company continued to serve as such, but the remnants of A, B, and C Companies in the front line were formed into a composite company, temporarily referred to as "B" Company. This expedient served until the battalion was relieved later that night, the positions along Winnipeg Road then being held by the 18th Battalion (which had moved in along the 19th Battalion's left flank earlier that morning) and the 20th Battalion. When this relief was completed the newly organized composite "B" Company moved back to Saskatchewan Road, while D Company withdrew into support for the 18th Battalion. There they remained for four days, sheltered in a series of dreary dugouts and funkholes, furnishing wiring parties for the new support and reserve lines that were being consolidated.[33]

A hastily organized British counterattack on the early morning of 9 May had failed to regain the positions at Fresnoy. Efforts by the 4th Brigade to protect the British left flank proved no more successful. Later that afternoon, the whole enterprise was called off and a new front line was established between Arleux and Fresnoy. In the view of the Canadian official historian, "the loss of Fresnoy, after it had been held for more than three days, was a serious setback – both because a hard-gained position of advantage had been sacrificed, and because of the blow to the morale of the British troops."[34] There certainly had been no shame in the 19th Battalion's conduct throughout this ordeal. It had, in fact, acquitted itself extremely well. It had been attacked during the course of a relief, in a part of the lines with which its personnel were not yet familiar, and its rapid response to restore the situation met with initial success. This was thwarted, however, by the untenable nature of the battalion's position after the Germans captured Fresnoy and drove back the forces on its right flank. The butcher's bill for this brief, but horrific, front-line tour provides stark testimony to the battalion's determination, endurance, and spirit of self-sacrifice. Total casualties were 11 officers and 225 other ranks, many of whom were "killed outright with shrapnel" during several savage bombardments.[35] Included among the losses was the first significant number of prisoners taken from the battalion. Postwar records indicate that 2 officers and 17 other ranks from the 19th Battalion were captured by the Germans on 8–9 May. One of the officers and nine of the other ranks taken prisoner had already been wounded, like the unfortunate Charles Gordon. The fact that no comparably large number of men was taken prisoner from the 19th Battalion at any other time in the war testifies to the chaos, ferocity, and close-quarters nature of the fighting near Fresnoy.[36]

On 13 May the 19th Battalion was relieved of its duties in the support lines by the 26th Battalion and moved back to divisional reserve near Mont St-Eloi, where Lt.-Col. Millen probably resumed command of his unit, although records are not explicit on that point. There it stayed in camp for the next six days. As the exhausted other ranks drilled and the surviving officers set about restoring their shattered companies, some time was wisely given over to recreational activities in order to calm rattled nerves and boost sagging spirits.[37] "We have just come out of the line," wrote a weary Pte. Gaetz to his mother:

> By George! It was a hot trip we had too. We got a pretty good shaking up … I am sorry to say that I have lost pretty nearly all my friends who were in the gun section since the drive. I am glad though that they were only wounded and hear from them in England (or Blighty as we say), quite often … There are quite a number of troops and units camped about here and with the fine weather the different bands are busy. Every afternoon and evening there are concerts.[38]

Morale and esprit de corps could also be enhanced by games and sporting events, and some games earned their popularity in part because of the accessibility of the equipment needed to play them. Gaetz noted that "now that longer days are here with fine weather there are games of baseball, foot ball and lacrosse played in our billeting ground. Another common game which we play a good deal is 'horse shoe.' The horse shoes are easier to get than the other sporting goods."[39]

On the morning of 19 May, spit and polish was the order of the day as the battalion assembled for inspection by the corps commander, Lt.-Gen. Byng, after which there was a formal march-past led by the battalion pipe band.[40] This event proved to be the grand finale of the battalion's time in reserve, for later that afternoon the 19th moved back towards the front lines, stopping first in the divisional support area, where it relieved the 29th Battalion. Battalion headquarters set up shop in Paynesley Tunnel, as it had earlier on 2 May. Companies again settled into nearby dugouts and shelters, from which work parties were dispatched regularly to carry out various construction and maintenance tasks in the lines.[41] Men like

Left: Memorial to the 19th Battalion's fight at Fresnoy. (The Argyll and Sutherland Highlanders of Canada)

Below: Official unveiling of the 19th Battalion's memorial at Fresnoy-en-Gohelle by representatives of the Argyll and Sutherland Highlanders of Canada and the local commune and department, 17 May 2015. (The Argyll and Sutherland Highlanders of Canada)

Pte. Gaetz, who presumably belonged to one of the Lewis gun sections, also spent plenty of time simply keeping their weapons and equipment clean and in working order. He informed his brother:

> We have had a rather heavy rain which has made things pretty muddy. It is very hard to keep your rifle clean and in good working order. We have to be still more particular with our machine gun and ammunition. In these guns both ammunition and gun must be quite clean or you are almost sure to have trouble. Sometimes when in the line we have to clean it 3 or 4 times a day when the weather is bad. From where I am sitting I can count about twenty German balloons strung out behind their lines and just behind

> me are about the same number of ours. Men sit in baskets attached to these balloons and observe. Sometimes on a very windy day they break the cable and drift away out of sight, or sometimes an aeroplane may shoot out of the clouds just above and fire on it, setting the balloon on fire. The men in the basket have parachutes which they can come down in, in case anything happens to the balloon.[42]

Then, on 26 May, it was back to the front lines for the 19th Battalion, which again relieved British Columbia's 29th. This time the battalion went in on a two-company frontage, D Company taking up the right position and B Company the left. A Company moved into support in Winnipeg Road (which instantly conjured up evil memories for survivors of the Fresnoy fight), while C Company sat in reserve in Saskatchewan Road. The quoted strength of the battalion on this date, according to the war diary, was 13 officers and 477 other ranks.[43]

This would prove to be a brief tour in the front lines, for the 19th Battalion men were relieved late in the day on 29 May by their comrades of the 20th Battalion, the former marching back after midnight into brigade reserve along the railway embankment near Farbus at the foot of the eastern slope of Vimy Ridge.[44] There, Lt.-Col. Millen basked in accommodations that he found especially comfortable, but he was even more pleased at the prospect of his men receiving an extended period of rest from their travails.[45]

The battalion languished for a mere three days before moving again – not back to the front line, but farther to the rear into divisional support around the familiar environs of Paynesley Tunnel and Zivy Cave. This was not their final destination, however. Shortly before 1:00 AM on the morning of 2 June, Millen's men headed back to camp near Mont St-Eloi. From there, they moved on 3 June with the rest of the 4th Brigade back to the Barlin Training Ground and were billeted in the nearby town of Verdrel. There they would remain until 3 July, finally getting some long-term respite from duty in the trenches while they reorganized, drilled, and trained.[46]

New Plans and a New Corps Commander

On 7 May, Field Marshal Sir Douglas Haig revealed to his army commanders his plans for the coming months. Instead of continuing to aim his heaviest blows along the Arras front, Haig had decided to shift the main axis of attack north to Messines and Ypres. There, the offensive would be renewed in early June with a huge attack at Messines Ridge. This would kick off a series of concerted drives intended to break the German position in Flanders, clear the Belgian coast, and effect a great strategic victory in Western Europe. The liberation of German-occupied Channel ports, such as Ostend and Zeebrugge, which served as bases for marauding U-boats, and the elimination of German air bases near the coast, from which formations of heavy bombers ranged over southern England, were additional concerns proffered by the Royal Navy and the Royal Flying Corps. But Haig's main object remained,

Lt.-Gen. Sir Arthur Currie (LAC PA-001606)

simply, the achievement of a decisive victory – that most elusive prize on the Western Front. As for the other British-held sectors, further operations in places such as Arras, Vimy, and Lens would divert enemy attention from the main British effort in Flanders and also from the French armies, which were desperately trying to quell the waves of mutinies that erupted during the failed Nivelle offensive.[47]

On 7 June the first stage of Haig's Flanders offensive began when Gen. Sir Herbert Plumer's Second Army launched its attack at Messines, the main feature of which was the detonation of nineteen massive mines laid under the German lines at key points stretching between Hill 60 in the north and Ploegsteert Wood in the south. By the standards of the Western Front it was an outstanding success, with all of the first day's objectives captured on schedule. By the time the battle concluded on 14 June, Plumer's forces had advanced two and a half miles and eliminated "German domination of the Ypres Salient from the south."[48] The situation appeared very favourable to proceed with subsequent stages of the Flanders offensive, which would become known to history as the Third Battle of Ypres. One of

Haig's objectives in his planned sweep to the Channel coast was a small village that sat on a barely perceptible ridge northeast of Ypres. The name of that village was Passchendaele.

South of Flanders, the British First Army would not sit idly by, holding the line while the main offensive raged. To support the efforts of his forces in the north, Haig ordered Gen. Horne to pin down as many German formations facing him as possible, draw in their reserves, and prevent them from moving troops north to oppose British attacks in Belgium. One way to achieve these ends was to attack and capture the city of Lens and its environs. The Germans would never countenance the loss of such a key industrial and mining centre and would be compelled to devote prodigious quantities of men and material resources to its recapture.[49]

The Canadian Corps would play a leading role in the fulfillment of First Army's mission during the upcoming offensive, and it would do so with a new commander. On 8 June, the day after the British attack at Messines commenced, Lt.-Gen. Sir Julian Byng was promoted to command the Third Army. Although the Canadians were sorry to see him go, the disappointment felt upon losing a trusted commander was softened by the news that command of the corps would go to one of their own – Maj.-Gen. Arthur Currie.[50]

A successful pre-war militia officer, Currie had performed well in the CEF, first as commander of the 2nd Infantry Brigade and then as GOC 1st Canadian Division. Although his double chin and tall, pear-shaped physique did not make him the "very model of a modern major-general" in a physical sense, his keen intellect, attention to detail, and professional commitment had marked him out in the eyes of his superiors as a good prospect for high command. Hard experience had taught Currie that success in modern industrial warfare required careful planning and efficient management of men and material. With his executive style of leadership, Currie encouraged discussion and debate among his staff and subordinate commanders. He reached his decisions after carefully considering the best available information and advice. He worked tirelessly to improve the tactics and organization of the troops under his command, adopted good ideas wherever he found them (whether from Canadian, British, or French sources), and paid close attention to German tactics and methods. He also cared deeply about the welfare of the ordinary troops and constantly sought better ways to use the power of artillery and other technologies to conserve the lives of his men.[51] Although it is often remarked that Currie's relative lack of charisma made him an uninspiring commander from the other ranks' perspective, his emphasis on the practicalities of soldiering did appeal to some. For example, Ted Lang of the 19th Battalion recalled an inspection during which Currie

> gave us a short talk on the importance of promptly obeying the orders of the senior officer or N.C.O. present, or in the event of all the officers and N.C.O's being casualties,

> then we must take our orders without question from the "oldest soldier" [not in age, but in length of service with the platoon]. It was a refreshing change from some of the 'Top Brass' inspections I had experienced on earlier occasions.[52]

Currie assumed command of the Canadian Corps on 9 June, his place at the head of the 1st Canadian Division being taken by Archibald Cameron Macdonell, the former GOC 7th Infantry Brigade. Within the 2nd Canadian Division, Maj.-Gen. Henry Burstall remained at the helm at division headquarters, and would do so to the end of the war. Brig.-Gen. Rennie retained his command of the 4th Brigade, having proven his ability and steadiness in that capacity since the autumn of 1915.[53]

Lt.-Gen. Currie would have less than a month to settle into his new position before receiving word from the First Army on 7 July that the Canadians had been assigned to capture Lens.[54] This would be no easy task. The city, with its ruined suburbs and nearby mining installations, would provide an ideal battleground for the defending Germans. Any offensive effort against Lens was bound to be a bitter and costly affair. It was well that before taking up this formidable task, the 19th Battalion and other units of the Canadian Corps had ample opportunity to replenish their ranks and train.

Fresh Faces

After the heavy fighting of April and May, the 2nd Canadian Division was withdrawn to reserve for an extended period of rest and training. The thirty days (from 3 June to 3 July) spent by the 19th Battalion at the brigade training grounds at Verdrel could not have come at a better time, given the recent mauling the unit had received at Fresnoy. During the month of May, Lt.-Col. Millen had lost 32 other ranks killed, 117 wounded, and 89 missing. As for his officers, six had been killed in action, two had died of wounds, two were wounded, and one was reported missing and probably killed.[55]

Reinforcements had been exceedingly slow in coming to the unit throughout May. Although twelve junior officers arrived, which made good the heavy losses in commissioned ranks that month, only forty-eight other ranks were taken on strength.[56] But the situation dramatically changed for the better in June, when a total of 352 other ranks were taken on strength in various drafts, the majority (299) arriving on 12 June. An additional thirteen officers also were taken on strength.[57] Most of these reinforcements came from battalions that had been recruited in Canada during 1915 and 1916 but that were deemed surplus to establishments after arriving in England. This was due to the fact that the strength of the Canadian Corps was effectively frozen at four divisions, each with its twelve infantry battalions plus other arms and support units. With the exception of two battalion substitutions that occurred in 3rd and 4th Canadian Divisions during 1917, there would be no wholesale addition of new battalions to the Canadian order of battle in France. The only thing to do with surplus units in England was have them supply reinforcements to the front-line units of the corps.

Most of the surplus battalions in England were absorbed into training units called reserve battalions. These reserve battalions often took in personnel from units that had been recruited in a certain geographic region and then dispatched drafts of reinforcements to units at the front that hailed from the same area. For example, in January 1917 the 120th City of Hamilton Battalion was absorbed by the 2nd Reserve Battalion, which was affiliated with the Central Ontario Regiment. The 2nd Reserve Battalion, in turn, later was absorbed by the 3rd Reserve Battalion (Central Ontario affiliation), which supplied drafts of reinforcements to the 4th and 19th Battalions and to the 2nd and 4th Canadian Mounted Rifles Battalions in France.[58]

To ensure that new men were able to function in existing section and platoon teams, a great deal of effort was spent on drilling and training reinforcements and veterans together. Tactical training, such as practice attacks by sections, platoons, and companies, benefited the veterans as much as the new men, for not only did the veterans' existing skills require constant practice, but they also had to learn how to work with their new comrades. Officers who were new to the unit badly needed the opportunity to socialize themselves to unit culture and procedure and, most important, to get to know the men under their command. This latter point was driven home in vivid fashion to a young lieutenant named Joe O'Neill, who joined the 19th Battalion later in November 1917. O'Neill was posted to a new platoon just before the battalion was inspected by Lt.-Gen. Currie. The subaltern's glib attempts at feigning sufficient knowledge of his men did not impress the corps commander. "Well I must admit," O'Neill confessed,

> at that time, I guess he recognized that I was just a young smart alec officer who was the product of Bexhill, the officer training school [in England], where we thought we knew just about everything that was to be known. So I suppose he recognized me as such, so he started to ask questions, [such as] who is this man. Well in typical fashion I gave him a name, never saw the man before, but that didn't matter, and what did he do. Well this man was a farmer, and John Jones was a motor mechanic and so on. Currie went down the line a little piece and instead of doing the usual stunt of just taking your word for it, he came back and he started to ask these boys their names, and what they were. Of course the men told the truth, and my names were all fictitious. So the General, he called all the junior officers together and he started to give them a lecture on the duties, the real job of a junior officer. Well I think he held me up as one of the horrible examples of what a junior officer should not be. Well he dressed me down from top to bottom, and he pointed out that the real job of a junior officer was to know his men, to understand them. To work with them and to understand their problems, and to make them understand that he was their natural leader. Above all things, it was up to that officer to know the men personally, and know that ... one man would react to kindness

> and another man you had to crowd a bit and so on. But we had to get to understand our men … I just stood there and took the calling down, oh brother …
>
> Well at that time I must say I hated him … But … I soon came to understand that the man was right, that one of the most interesting things in life was to know and really like the boys … and understand them and know their problems, and be their natural leader. I must say I never enjoyed anything more in my life … I began to think that this real calling down, the worst calling down I ever had in my life, was one of the best things [that] ever happened to me.[59]

Training and Athletics

In preparation for the extended period of training that was planned for the month of June, 2nd Canadian Division headquarters drew up a training program and issued it to subordinate commands during late May. It was a three-week regimen similar in focus to the training exercises carried out during January and February. The first week concentrated mainly on physical drill and individual proficiency with arms and equipment, such as rifle, bayonet, and gas mask. The second week highlighted the tactical training of sections and platoons in the attack, one of the features of which would be "simple schemes to bring out the principles of co-operation of the various weapons with which the Platoon is armed." While many of the drills and exercises carried out in the first two weeks were continued in the third week, the tactical training of companies in the attack was finally added in this stage of the program.[60]

The first week of training also saw some reorganization in the structure of infantry platoons throughout the 2nd Canadian Division. In accordance with divisional orders, each battalion reorganized its platoons to conform to the structure outlined in the British training manual S.S. 143, *Instructions for the Training of Platoons for Offensive Action, 1917*, which had been issued by the War Office earlier in February. Whereas Nos. 1 and 2 sections in each platoon in the division previously contained a mixture of riflemen and rifle grenadiers, No. 1 Section now was composed entirely of riflemen and Number 2 Section contained only rifle grenadiers. The reasons for this switch are not entirely clear. Perhaps it was discovered during the fighting in April and May that combining riflemen and rifle grenadiers in two sections was not as effective as anticipated and that better results might be obtained by separating them into their own homogenous sections. Whatever the case, division headquarters took care to remind battalions that flexibility was paramount in platoon tactics, the disposition of each section being dependent on the platoon's specific mission and the nature of the terrain over which it advanced.[61]

Of course, training and changes to platoon structure were not always uppermost on the men's minds during this period. Reflecting the soldier's traditional and understandable preoccupation with food, Pte. Barnes penned critical comments in his journal on the state of his rations. "During the whole rest," he wrote, "our rations were bad, we did not see much bread and when we did it was twelve to fifteen men on a small loaf (a thin slice for a day). We mostly had hardtack. Of course there were canteens around and if you had any money and were lucky enough to get in line before the biscuits were gone you were all right."[62] The battalion's senior officers fared much better in the gastronomical department. Writing to his mother on 11 June, Lt.-Col. Millen enthused that he was

> having a great time at present. You know we are out for several weeks rest and it is great. My billet is most comfy, a chateau with a fine garden. We have headquarters mess here also, 8 of us, and we are living. Real cream on our porage [*sic*], and butter that comes from the cow, not made of other fats, as we have most of the time. I imagine the people in England would envy us the meals we have now. We are putting on a little bit of swank too, our mess waiter dressed in a white coat with brass buttons. On the sideboard is almost everything necessary in the drink line. At meal times he will say to me "What do you care to drink sir." "A sherry and bitters please Cooper" or a beer or Scotch and soda or Collins as the case may be. There is always a jug of lemonade waiting should you come in dry and thirsty. Nothing like living well when you can. I am getting some exercise now, riding and baseball playing.[63]

Sporting events were, at least, one aspect of life that all ranks could enjoy in equal measure. Sports did much to liven the routine of training and inspections,

Lt.-Col. Lionel Millen. (ASH, Argyll Regimental Foundation)

and a series of elimination contests were held leading up to the divisional competitions on 23 June. The 19th Battalion held its contests on 13 June, with the winners going on to compete in the 4th Brigade competitions five days later, where they did rather well. Lt. Gordon Applegath won the 100-yard dash for officers, and the battalion team won the 440-yard open-relay race. Ptes. Flick and Davey placed first and second in the mule race, while Ptes. Hopkins and Dear did likewise in the obstacle race. Much to Millen's satisfaction, the officers' team won the indoor baseball match, and in the ever-popular boxing bouts, Pte. Teddy Mallett won the 133-lb.-and-under class while Pte. Jock Fisher emerged the champion in the 160- lb.-and-under class.[64]

At the 2nd Canadian Divisional Athletic Meet, held at Hersin-Coupigny, the 19th Battalion was represented in outstanding fashion, winning more prizes than any other single unit in competition. The battalion teams placed second in both the one-mile open-relay race and the officers' indoor baseball final, and Ptes. Allen and Hopkins both placed second in the one-mile race and the obstacle race, respectively. However, Pte. Boyd took top honours in the mule race, and in boxing the battalion displayed a marked dominance. Ptes. Mallett and Fisher both emerged as divisional champions in their weight classes, while Pte. Bell placed second in the 120-lb.-and-under class.[65]

An additional week of training rounded out the battalion's time in reserve until the end of June. This also was prime time for high-level inspections, and the battalion was in especially good shape now that it had been reinforced and the men were rested, bathed, and trained. On 28 June, Millen formed up his men for review by Maj.-Gen. Burstall. "We have just had an inspection by our divisional commander," wrote Pte John Gaetz two days after the affair. "The Colonel says he never saw the battalion in better condition than it is just now. I think the change has done every one good."[66]

On Sunday, 1 July, all ranks paraded to the sporting field at Coupigny, where they attended services in honour of the fiftieth anniversary of Canadian Confederation. Two days later, the lengthy break from trench duty finally came to an end when the battalion, led by its pipe band, marched to billets at nearby Marqueffles Farm. There they stayed in divisional reserve for the next five days, carrying out platoon and company training.[67]

13

"The Worst Ever": July–August 1917 and the Battle for Hill 70

On 8 July, Lt.-Col. Millen received orders to move the battalion to Fosse 10, located between Bully and Hersin, where the men would stay in scattered billets, still in divisional reserve.[1] Two days later, on 10 July, the 19th Battalion was ordered up to the front lines to relieve the 24th Battalion in the right sub-section of the Lens sector. With his battalion now well up to strength, Millen took 24 officers and 665 other ranks into the lines, the fourth platoon of each company remaining behind at Noulette Wood training camp under the command of Maj. Hatch. By 9:00 PM, preparations were complete, and the troops marched towards the front line, where they completed the relief by 2:30 AM.[2]

The 19th Battalion was in the line for only two days, at which point it was relieved by the 27th Battalion on the early morning of 13 July. The battalion moved back to brigade reserve at Maroc, where the men remained for three days, quartered in cellars and furnishing work and fatigue parties.

On 16 July they returned to the same trenches they had vacated only three days earlier. They relieved the 29th Battalion in the pre-dawn hours of 17 July and began a tour of more standard duration – seven days. Pte. Deward Barnes noted that the situation between the opposing troops was "very quiet even though the Germans are one hundred yards away."[3]

The 19th Battalion on the march. The original archival caption states: "Canadians on their way to pay Fritz a visit. July, 1917." (LAC PA-001415)

The midsummer nights were sultry, but also short, so extra efforts were made by Canadian units to exploit the hours of darkness by carrying out construction and patrol work among the blasted ruins of the Lens suburbs. Writing with perceptible irony, the 20th Battalion's Maj. D.J. Corrigall described the general tenor of routine night duties in the front lines at that time:

> Seeing more of the nights than of the days, we were familiar with the night life of nature and rejoiced in the companionship of rats, bats, June-bugs and moths. On patrol it would be perfectly still for a time, then a breeze rustling through the grass would make the shattered rafters of the ruined houses creak and groan. When there was a moon, the weird shadows kept us continually "seeing things." During these queer nights angle iron posts could be seen forming fours, patrolling, advancing, et cetera. Imagination ruled the nights.[4]

The 1st and 2nd Canadian Divisions by now had assumed control of three miles of the line stretching northward from the Souchez River to a point just northeast of Loos. South of the Souchez, holding the line in the Avion–Méricourt sector, was the 3rd Canadian Division. The Canadian Corps had received instructions from the First Army to launch a frontal attack on the town of Lens, but this scheme did not sit well with Lt.-Gen. Currie. Because Lens was dominated by Hill 70 to the north and Sallaumines Hill to the southeast, this would leave his attacking divisions dangerously exposed to German observation and artillery fire. Even if they could capture Lens, the prospect of holding it seemed remote so long as the Germans held the the high ground. On 10 July, at a conference of corps commanders presided over by Gen. Horne, Currie made his opinions known and convinced his superiors that Hill 70 should be the principal objective. Possession of this hill would give Canadian observers a view over a wide expanse of German-held territory, including Lens. Currie reasoned that the Germans' positions would be so threatened by Canadian possession of Hill 70 that they would be forced to launch strong counterattacks in order to regain it. If all went as Currie planned, his gunners would cut the advancing divisions to pieces before they could effectively come to grips with his own men. In preparation for the impending attack, Currie launched a series of raids and bombardments directed mainly against Lens itself to mislead the enemy as to the Canadian Corps' precise objective. He hoped to conquer Hill 70 by the end of July; as it turned out, the weather would prove uncooperative and the assault would be delayed until mid-August.[5]

Preparing for Action

As corps headquarters finalized its scheme for the capture of Hill 70, the divisions slated to make the assault – the 1st and 2nd – set about training their troops for the operation. The 29th Battalion relieved the 19th Battalion in the lines on 23 July, and Lt.-Col. Millen's men moved back to positions in divisional reserve at Fosse 10. For the next thirteen days, they trained and conducted platoon and company drills on a special practice course established at Marqueffles Farm. Some practice attacks

Original archival caption: "Just like their Summer House at home. July, 1917." (LAC PA-001468)

were held at dawn, in light conditions similar to those in which the troops would be fighting. Individual companies were put through their paces; then each of the assaulting battalions was exercised, until the day came when the entire 4th Brigade trained en masse over the course. Lt.-Gen. Currie, accompanied by Gen. Horne, arrived on 27 July to observe the troops practising various tactical scenarios over the training field. By that time, according to the 20th Battalion's Maj. D.J. Corrigall, the men had "rehearsed the plan repeatedly until every method had been tried and tested."[6]

Despite the officers' enthusiasm for the training program, the other ranks had mixed feelings about how well prepared they would be for the attack. Pte. Barnes would later offer some critical appraisal of training activities:

> Passed hundreds of guns in the bushes and on the sides of roads. Getting ready and laced for Hill 70 Battle. Thousands of machine guns on that front. The next few days we practiced over tapes … Practising an advance over tapes proved a failure, the tapes were laid out as streets and buildings according to area maps and named before you got there. Each man was supposed to know what street or lane to go down when the real thing came (all bosh).[7]

Others, however, were more in agreement with Corrigall. "One realizes what a wonderful organization this is," wrote William Morgan, an infantryman in the 24th Battalion. "We even know the names of the streets we are to march up and the actual houses we are to mop up."[8]

During the final days of July and early August, heavy rains interfered with much of the outdoor training. Officers attempted to compensate by delivering lectures to their men,[9] and no doubt the tenets of fire and movement, as practised on the training grounds, featured largely in these talks. This final training session came to an end for the 19th Battalion on the evening of 5 August, when the unit began relieving the 31st Battalion in the front-line trenches of the Laurent sector, the relief being completed by 1:15 AM the following morning. According to the war diary, Lt.-Col. Millen sent his battalion into the lines at "full strength" – 28 officers and 805 other ranks.[10]

Immediately, Millen set his officers to work organizing patrols and pushing out eleven advance posts beyond the front-line fire trench. These posts varied in size and housed garrisons of between three and eight other ranks from B and D Companies. Although work parties and advance post garrisons encountered heavy enemy machine-gun and artillery fire, their efforts were not seriously disrupted, and miraculously, only one man was slightly wounded.[11] The situation remained much the same on 7 August, when Pte. Barnes noted that, while there had been "all kinds of machine guns and always plenty of shelling," there had been "few casualties so far." Perhaps the strength of the positions inhabited by the Canadians and the Germans accounted for this, for many trenches cut through ruined cellars and buildings, which provided strong and ample cover. "French cellars [are] built for war," Barnes observed, with their "arched brick roofs. You could see whole towns right down to the ground but half the cellars would be good and still standing. The whole country in fact was built for war, crooked sunken roads, etc." Nevertheless, there was one weapon against which no stone or brick wall could provide a complete shield, and that was gas. In the same journal entry, Barnes admitted that they had been "gassed all day," but the fact that there were "few casualties" indicates that the Germans must have employed a type of gas (such as chlorine, phosgene, or diphosgene) with which the Canadians were already familiar. The Germans had not yet exposed them to the newest weapon in their arsenal, which was the cause of great concern among the Allied armies. It was a new type of chemical agent, known colloquially as mustard gas.[12]

Mustard gas had made its operational debut only recently, when the Germans introduced it in the Ypres Salient in mid-July. Unlike previous agents, which dissipated relatively quickly, mustard was a persistent gas that could contaminate soil and clothing for a considerable period of time after contact. When delivered by an exploding artillery shell, the concentrated gas "was scattered over the ground or anybody nearby, where it slowly evaporated." It also was much harder for the men to detect than earlier gases (such as chlorine), which had an almost immediate effect and which usually had to be delivered in heavy concentrations. By contrast, the initial effects of mustard gas often were little more than a slight tickle in the nose and throat, a sudden desire to sneeze, and a faint smell reminiscent of mustard. But this comparatively benign overture gave way hours later to the development of terrible blisters on contaminated areas of skin, severe swelling and inflammation of the eyes, and violent vomiting. Blindness – temporary or permanent – could set in, depending on the level of exposure, and if significant quantities of the agent were inhaled, the effect on the interior of the lungs was devastating and often fatal. Even a small number of shells filled with this insidious agent could contaminate a whole section of the front, which for days afterward would be rendered hazardous for habitation as the chemical lurked in the very earth in which the men crawled or burrowed. Thus, in addition to its obvious physical effects, mustard gas emerged as a potent psychological weapon. As historian Tim Cook points out, "not only did mustard gas kill, burn, and incapacitate, it also consigned the soldier to a permanent state of unease. With every puddle an imagined trap, with every patch of ground possibly containing a substance that burned and blinded men, it left the already exhausted and strained soldiers with no rest, physically and mentally, from the horrors of war."[13]

Based on information they received from British reports, Canadian commanders, gas officers, and NCOs did their best to help their men prepare for the inevitable encounter with mustard gas. Although it had been determined that proper use of the standard-issue small box respirator effectively protected a man's face and lungs from the gas, it would take discipline, frequent instruction, and hard experience before Canadian troops could really come to grips with this new weapon.[14]

Dimly aware of the new terrors that awaited them, the men of the 19th Battalion were happy to be relieved in the front lines once again, as elements of the 18th, 27th, and 31st Battalions replaced them in piecemeal fashion over a two-day period on 8–9 August. Millen's men marched back to billets in Fosse 10, where they alternately rested and carried out company and platoon drills for the next five days.[15] Although they did not yet know the exact time of the proposed attack on Hill 70, by now officers and other ranks were well acquainted with the tactical plans for the operation, which had been finalized in brigade and battalion orders between 29 and 31 July.[16]

According to the corps scheme, the main thrust against Hill 70 would be carried out by two divisions, the 1st Canadian Division advancing on the left and the 2nd Canadian Division on the right. Both divisions would launch their attacks along a combined frontage of around 4,000 yards and were expected to penetrate some 1,500 yards into territory held by the 26th and 165th Regiments of the German 7th Division. The Canadians' final objectives consisted of "a series of old German trenches which formed an arc around Hill 70's lower eastern slope, stretching for two miles" from Cité Ste-Elisabeth in the south to Bois Hugo in the north. These objectives, it was believed, were far enough forward to offer adequate protection for the artillery observation posts the Canadians planned to establish on the heights of Hill 70. From these vantage points, observers would direct a deadly drumfire on the assembly points and likely lines of advance of German counterattack forces. Lt.-Gen. Currie expected that once the battle was joined, the Germans would yield their foremost positions, hold their secondary line of trenches with machine guns, and then send in fresh formations to counterattack. This was the pattern of defence that Currie's plan of attack was designed to defeat.[17]

Maj.-Gen. Burstall and his staff decided that the 2nd Canadian Division's assault should be carried out on a frontage of two brigades. The 5th Brigade was selected for the left portion of the division attack; the 4th Brigade would take up the right; the 6th Brigade would be held in reserve. The 4th Brigade's jumping-off line would extend from "Cornwall Trench" to the church at Cité St-Edouard (a northern suburb of Lens), which made for a brigade frontage of 850 yards. The combined frontage of the 4th and 5th Brigades extended for some 1,700 yards.[18] Brig.-Gen. Rennie decided to employ three battalions in the 4th Brigade's assault. The 18th Battalion would operate on the right, the 21st in the centre, and the 20th on the left. The 19th Battalion, which deserved a break from the brunt of the action after its ordeal at Fresnoy, would be in support. However, one of its companies – C Company – would carry out mopping-up duties for the 20th Battalion during the attack. It was necessary to augment the 20th Battalion's strength because of the irregular shape of the 4th Brigade's zone of attack. The frontage along the brigade's objective line stood just over 500 yards from the jumping-off trenches along the right flank, but extended to 1,500 yards on the left, where the 20th Battalion's men were detailed to advance. Having a considerably greater distance to cover, they would need additional support.

Because the fighting in the 2nd Division's sector would take place in heavily built-up areas in the northern suburbs of Lens, the Germans had arranged their defences expecting that the Canadians would choose obvious routes of advance along existing streets and roads. Thus, they set up strong barricades across the main thoroughfares, which were well covered with machine-gun nests. But the Canadians, familiar with what lay ahead of them through aerial reconnaissance and a number of pre-battle raids, were careful not to fall into these killing zones. Instead of advancing down roadways as they had during practice attacks on the training grounds, commanding officers now instructed their units to avoid the roads and proceed forward "through gardens and other grounds to the rear of the houses," which after the pre-battle artillery bombardments were little more than shattered piles of rubble.[19]

For the 19th Battalion, the battle for Hill 70 would be an operation of some complexity, considering that a significant proportion of its troops would be under the temporary command of another unit. On 14 August, official notice came from brigade headquarters that zero hour would be at 4:25 AM the next day. After final preparations were made and all ranks reminded of their specific tasks, Lt.-Col. Millen received his orders to move his men into their assigned battle positions. By 9:30 PM all was ready, and the platoons began filtering into place. At 2:45 a.m, the assembly was complete, with the men of A Company taking up stations in Cockle and Colony trenches, while those of B and D Companies occupied a stretch of Corkscrew Trench along the southern outskirts of Cité St-Pierre. Although they were not participating in the initial attack, there were still important jobs for these support troops to carry out. For example, one platoon of B Company was detailed to provide carrying parties for the 20th and 21st Battalions; half of its personnel were to report to the 20th Battalion supply dump, the other half to 21st Battalion headquarters. The men of C Company, meanwhile, assumed their positions in Combat Trench, where they came under the temporary command of Lt.-Col. Herbert Rorke of the 20th Battalion.[20]

Capt. Ronald W. Catto was placed in charge of C Company for this operation. At his disposal were Nos. 9, 10, and 11 Platoons with their respective commanders, Lts. Arthur J. Duncan, Thomas Lynott, and Fred Cantlon. As his men steeled themselves for the difficult mopping-up work ahead of them, Catto detailed each platoon to follow one of the 20th Battalion's three waves of attackers.[21] Their job was an extremely important one, given the dispersed nature of German forward defences. It was impossible for the attacking troops to clear and secure every shell hole, crater, or dugout in their path and still maintain enough momentum to press

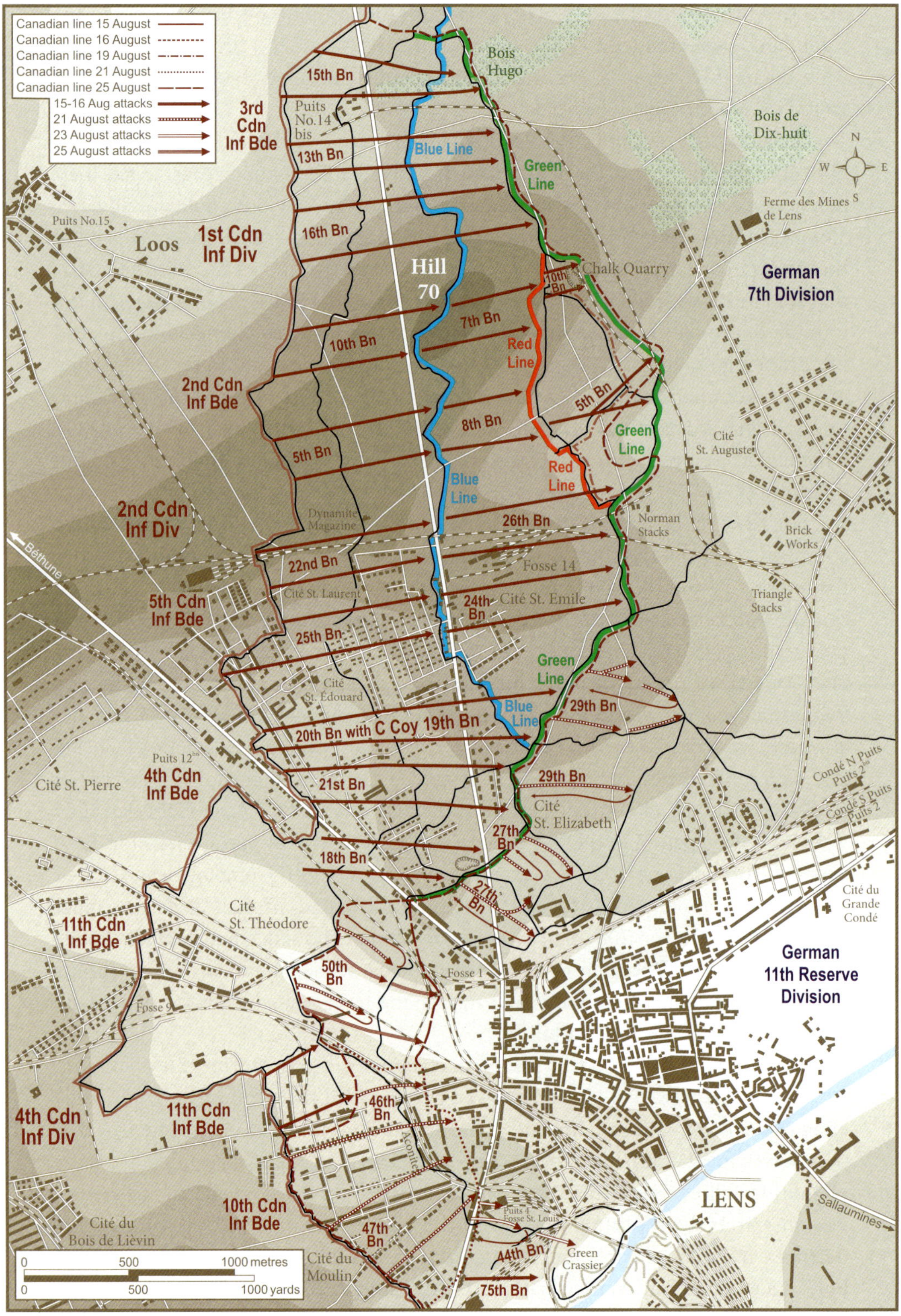

Map 14 – Hill 70 and Lens.

the attack forward to their objective. It was the job of the mopping-up forces, following closely behind, to secure the captured ground and ensure that no German stragglers emerged from cover to molest attacking Canadians from the rear.[22] Gone was the expectation that the artillery would leave little for the infantry to do beyond simply occupying blasted enemy trenches. The infantry would have to make full use of its own offensive capabilities. Only the synergistic effect of all arms working in concert could offer the best chance of success against a skilfully organized series of defensive positions.

Artillery and trench mortar batteries did, however, play a leading role in the period leading up to the attack, carrying out "a steady programme of wire-cutting, counter-battery work and gas shelling, which special companies of the Royal Engineers augmented by projecting drums of gas on Lens." By 15 August the town had been blanketed with deadly fumes from over 900 gas shells and some 3,500 drums. The Canadian counter-battery organization also had kicked into high gear, neutralizing around 40 of the estimated 102 German artillery batteries in the sector.[23]

On the day of the attack itself, nine brigades of field artillery would support the 1st and 2nd Canadian Divisions with a creeping barrage; meanwhile, 164 heavy guns and howitzers would lay down a series of jumping and standing barrages on known German strongpoints and communication centres farther to the rear. The gunners' work "would be supplemented by the fire of 160 machine guns," and machine-gun crews also would play a major role in consolidation. As soon as the infantry reached its objectives and the moppers-up were fully engaged in their tasks, forty-eight machine guns were to be brought forward as quickly as possible to support each of the attacking brigades. Each machine gun "would then become the center of a platoon strongpoint manned by at least 25 infantrymen." Speed was essential in this operation. Successive objective lines had to be captured and consolidated in time to meet anticipated enemy counterattacks.

"It was Hell!"

At 4:25 on the morning of 15 August, a storm of artillery burst forth and the troops rose from their trenches to follow the now-familiar creeping barrage as it rolled relentlessly over enemy trenches and scattered strongpoints. As punishing as the artillery was, the Canadians had an additional unpleasant surprise for their opponents: 500 drums of blazing oil, which they fired "at selected targets, to build up a smoke screen and demoralize the defenders."[24] Pte. Barnes thought it was "the greatest artillery fight I had ever seen. It was a beautiful sight of artillery duels (if you could take the horses out of it). The Germans, as well as us, always opened up immediately … Machine guns were as thick as could be."[25]

Indeed, the Germans, who had anticipated the attack, unleashed their own barrage just four minutes after the first Canadian guns opened fire. But the Canadian infantry successfully avoided much of the enemy artillery by forming up its assault

Canadians in an old German trench on Hill 70, August 1917. (LAC PA-001717)

waves in no man's land. Most of the German shells screeched over the Canadians' heads and burst behind them. According to the 20th Battalion's historian, Maj. Corrigall, "no difficulty was encountered in crossing enemy wire, due to the effective preliminary bombardments of our artillery." However, several German machine-gun nests spat forth a vicious fire, giving the attackers some trouble until small parties managed to rush and overcome them. "The advance was carried out as planned," reported Corrigall. "All opposition encountered was quickly overcome."[26]

But Capt. Catto, in charge of the mopping-up parties from the 19th Battalion, perceived the attack as being a bit more confused than portrayed by Corrigall. Catto noted that the assault waves became "somewhat disorganized and scattered," likely owing to the broken state of no man's land, the heavily built-up nature of the battlefield, and the dim light conditions at zero hour. It is not clear whether Catto was referring to the advancing troops from both the 20th and 19th Battalions or to just the progress of his own men. Whatever the case, when C Company's platoons had reached the German front line, the "platoon commanders, assisted by their N.C.O.s[,] energetically rallied their platoons and proceeded from then on in a more orderly manner to their respective areas and commenced their mopping up operations."[27]

As the 20th Battalion's attacking waves continued forward to their final objectives along Commotion Trench, Capt. Catto's men mopped up their assigned portion of ground, which stretched as far forward as the Lens–La Bassée Road. Lt. Duncan and No. 9 Platoon busied themselves clearing up the situation in the German front line, while almost 150 yards beyond, the other two platoons under Lts. Lynott and Cantlon did likewise, up to Cowley Trench. The remnants of the German garrison, having been bashed about by the artillery and then rolled over by the 20th Battalion's troops, generally offered little resistance, and this area was effectively mopped up by 7:00 AM.[28]

But one German dugout did present some problems. It sheltered a machine-gun and its crew, who, when ordered out by a party of 19th Battalion men, abruptly responded by hurling cylindrical stick grenades. The Canadians answered back with a bunch of Mills bombs, which persuaded the surviving holdouts that further resistance was futile. However, when the first of these Germans reached the dugout entrance, he suddenly refused to move any farther and was promptly shot for his defiance. The rest of the crew behind him then turned tail and ran back towards another exit in the rear of the dugout. Pte. Stanley Rootes, knowing where they were about to emerge, ran around the exterior of the position to catch them as they bolted outside. He was accompanied in this race by stretcher-bearer James Robertson, and the pair successfully "got the drop" on the fleeing Germans and took them prisoner.[29]

By 7:45 AM, Capt. Catto's men had effectively finished clearing out the 20th Battalion's zone up to the Lens–La Bassée Road, beyond which mopping-up activities

German machine-gun emplacement between Hill 70 and Lens. The photo was taken during September 1917. (LAC PA-003824)

German prisoners captured by Canadians on Hill 70, August 1917. (LAC PA-001344)

were carried out by personnel from the 20th Battalion's A and D Companies. In all, Catto's platoons had flushed out and captured seventy-two prisoners, including four officers, who were sent back to languish in prisoner compounds behind Canadian lines.

Successful as the operation was so far, it had been no cakewalk. Lts. Lynott and Duncan were wounded in action, but fortunately neither was injured seriously enough to prevent them from carrying out the remainder of their duties. Lynott nursed his wounded hand while directing his platoon's efforts, while Duncan, with the assistance of Lt. Cantlon, "energetically pursued the work of consolidation, sending out and caring for wounded and collecting prisoners for carrying parties."[30]

So far, events had unfolded as the Canadians hoped they would. Within twenty minutes of zero hour, the 1st and 2nd Canadian Divisions had taken the German front line and advanced 600 yards to capture their second main line of trenches, which snaked along the crest of Hill 70 and just beyond Cité St-Laurent and Cité St-Edouard. Over the course of the next twenty minutes, in the 4th Brigade's section, the 18th and 21st Battalions had occupied Chicory Trench and transformed it into a defensive flank facing the northern outskirts of Lens. Once this had been accomplished, the 20th Battalion resumed its advance through the rubble of Cité Ste-Elisabeth and captured Commotion Trench. On its left, battalions of the 5th Brigade had overrun Cité St-Emile and seized the enemy trench known as Nun's Alley. By 6:00 AM, both Canadian divisions had reached virtually all of their final objectives east and south of Hill 70, along what was code-named the Green Line.

A young German soldier being examined by a Canadian officer during the attack at Hill 70, August 1917. (LAC PA-001743)

Only one portion of the Green Line, facing the 7th and 8th Battalions of the 2nd Brigade, remained in German hands; it would not be taken until the following day. In the meantime, the Canadian artillery observers, engineers, and pioneer troops that followed in the wake of the infantry had set to work constructing observation posts and strongpoints, digging new communication trenches, reversing existing German trenches, and unrolling thickets of barbed wire.[31]

Captured ground which was 'No Man's Land', August 1917. The original caption for this photo reads: "The Boche attempt a counter-attack on Hill 70, but the Canadians drove them back." (LAC PA-001635)

Having achieved its immediate goals, the 19th Battalion's C Company set to work consolidating new positions in Contract and Counter trenches. Some of these positions came under heavy artillery fire, which prompted Capt. Catto to organize the excavation of a new stretch of trench. This was done by linking up and consolidating a series of shell holes, thus creating a new line extending from Counter Trench to a section of Contract Trench. The two existing systems were now linked. The new trench proved to be not only a more difficult target for the German gunners to hit but also a better vantage point facing German positions farther ahead. The Canadians, however, did not simply have to contend with enemy shelling. As in the days following the capture of Vimy Ridge, marauding German aircraft posed a constant threat from above. C Company's Lewis gunners put up a hail of fire that drove off one particularly persistent aviator.[32]

By 10:30 AM the German shelling had become so heavy that despite the improvements made to C Company's positions, most of the troops were forced to seek cover in cellars, dugouts, and funkholes for much of the day. By 5:30 PM, C Company had seen two of its members killed in action and thirteen wounded, including Lts. Lynott and Duncan, who finally returned to the rear for treatment after mopping-up was completed. There also were twelve missing men, but according to post-battle reports some of these men "afterwards turned up."[33]

The situation had been even hotter for the Canadian assault battalions occupying the foremost positions that day, for between 7:00 and 9:00 AM the German infantry carried out a series of determined but uncoordinated counterattacks. The overall failure of these initial German efforts stemmed from the Canadians' success in creating a "killing ground" east and south of Hill 70. Each German counterattack attempt was seen well ahead of time by ground and aerial observers, who called in crushing artillery barrages that broke up the attacks. Those Germans who survived the bombardment long enough to get within small arms range of Canadian lines were mowed down by steady streams of machine-gun and rifle fire.[34]

But as the morning wore on, the Germans threw more and more reserves into the fight, making good use of their remaining trench lines (such as Cinnabar Trench, facing the 4th Brigade's front) as springboards for their assaults. By noon, the Canadians faced at least fifteen German battalions from the 7th, 11th Reserve, 4th Guard, and 185th Divisions. For the most part, Canadian and British artillery continued to decimate these counterattack forces as they approached the front lines. But a few German units did manage to slip through the whirlwind of fire to engage in savage combat with Canadian troops. By now, ammunition was getting low in some sections of the Canadian lines, and many of the infantry were becoming exhausted from the relentless pounding. At 3:00 PM on the 4th Brigade front, German storming parties succeeded in retaking a good portion of Chicory Trench, which was held by the 18th and 21st Battalions. The 21st Battalion was hit especially hard, and the survivors reeled back towards Commotion Trench.[35]

In serious need of assistance, the 21st Battalion called upon the 19th Battalion's A Company for aid at 4:30 PM. This company, with three of its platoons under the command of Capt. Harold E. Goodman, was stationed in support trenches in Cité St-Pierre and had not been involved in the action. Now it would help deliver the counterattack to recapture Chicory Trench. Maj. A.P. Miller of the 21st Battalion soon arrived and led Capt. Goodman and his men towards the position through a heavy artillery barrage. Following Miller and Goodman through the storm of steel were Lt. James M. Bennett, in charge of No. 2 Platoon, Lt. A.J. Rankin, leading No. 3 Platoon, and Lt. Andrew Borrowman, at the head of No. 4 Platoon.[36] "We started under very heavy shelling," wrote Pte. Deward Barnes, who advanced with the rest of No. 2 Platoon's Lewis gun section:

> I don't know how any of us got there. We started to keep to the trenches and just got nicely started when six men in front of me got blown up. I was the next and missed it. We all got out of the trench and went overland. Trusting to Providence, we had to go anyway. We ran all the way regardless of shells. It was terrible then, the way men got cut up. My Number 1 gunner was killed, the corporal grabbed the gun. There were dozens killed and wounded – your pals going down around you – but you had to go on.
>
> After a hard run, and with our load of everything for an advance, we finally got to the line the 21st Battalion was holding, as they had lost the original objective. There were only half a dozen men holding the line [frontage] of a company. Weren't they glad to see us![37]

In short order, Maj. Miller delegated the platoons of A Company to their appointed tasks. Capt. Goodman, Lt. Rankin, and No. 3 Platoon were ordered to remain in support, while Lt. Borrowman and No. 4 Platoon were told to advance and occupy Chicory Trench from the Lens–La Bassée Road to the point where they would link up with the 18th Battalion on the right flank. Miller himself would lead Lt. Bennett and No. 2 Platoon in a rush against the portion of Chicory Trench from the Lens–La Bassée Road to the junction with Conductor Trench. This section of trench had been occupied by the 21st Battalion's C Company, which, tragically, had been practically wiped out in the fighting earlier that day.[38]

With a series of sharp, metallic clicks, the men of No. 2 Platoon fixed bayonets. Then Maj. Miller and Lt. Bennett led them "with the greatest dash" overland and across the road through heavy shelling and a hail of German rifle fire. They leapt into Chicory Trench, where the German defenders were thrown "into such disorder that they jumped out of the trench and retired overland," giving the Canadian Lewis gunners "an opportunity of exacting a heavy toll." So quickly had the Germans evacuated that they left behind wounded prisoners captured from the 21st Battalion's machine-gun section.[39] "[We were] yelling and shouting at them [the Germans]," reported Pte. Barnes. "They got frightened. Seeing reinforcements charging they scrambled back as fast as they could. Some jumped out of the trench so they could go faster. We killed a few with our rifles but did not have to bayonet any. We took the trench and the men dug in their positions as fast as possible."[40]

Maj. Miller immediately set out for 21st Battalion headquarters to inform them of the news and arrange for the relief of Lt. Bennett's platoon as quickly as possible. Before departing, he left Bennett with instructions for his men to hold the line, indicating generally where they should be able to link up with the 21st Battalion's D Company on their left flank. After Miller hurried off, Bennett set about making good his position with the scant resources at his command. Although he had only twenty-seven men to hold a 300-yard section of front, the officer set his exhausted men to work, posting his Lewis gun section at the junction of Conductor and Chicory trenches, establishing a bombing post thirty yards in advance of his line along the Lens-La Bassée Road, and distributing the remainder of his men between these two points.[41] Hunkered down in the advanced Lewis gun post, Pte. Barnes did what he could to make a defensible position for himself:

> It was hell! Heavy casualties and the trenches were all torn to pieces by shells. I picked out the best place I could see but a 21st fellow was right behind it with half his body shot away. It was the best spot, so I dug a hole [funkhole] in front of him and threw the dirt over him. Maybe he was never found. War is hell. I did not get his [identity] disc, hadn't time. The main thing is to dig in and get ready for an attack. We had to watch ourselves here … Only four men were left out of our section of eight, so we four men had to hold that post.[42]

Bennett's platoon quickly made contact with their comrades in No. 4 Platoon on the right, but attempts to link up with the 21st Battalion's D Company revealed a yawning 200-yard gap on the left flank. This gap was held by a single Stokes mortar crew of the 4th Brigade Trench Mortar Battery, under the command of a Lt. Wright. Bennett himself scurried over the desolate stretch of unoccupied ground and got in touch with a platoon of the 21st Battalion to the left of the gap. Finding only an NCO in charge, Bennett briefed him on the situation and then hustled off to find Wright and ensure that the mortar crew would be prepared to render all possible assistance if the Germans decided to make another local attack. Not until the next day (16 August) would Bennett's left flank be made more secure, when the 21st Battalion's B Company relieved its D Company. In the process, three outposts were established to cover the gap between the 21st Battalion troops and Bennett's men.[43]

Although no further counterattacks came on 15 August, Lt. Bennett and his men experienced considerable trouble from their own heavy artillery, which dropped a number of shells short, into Canadian positions, causing several casualties. A message was sent back to 21st Battalion headquarters to correct the gunners' range, but the problem was not fully rectified, for on the following day, Lt. Borrowman of No. 4 Platoon was killed by another "short." The unfortunate Borrowman had joined the 19th Battalion only two days earlier, and this had been his first tour in the front lines.[44]

On the evening of 15 August, Lt. Bennett ordered two runners to locate Capt. Goodman, but neither of these men returned, and records are unclear as to their fate. Darkness fell, and the tired, hungry, and thirsty men of A Company continued their strained vigil in Chicory Trench, waiting tensely through the night for whatever the Germans might have in store for them. No night attacks developed; however, the action resumed once more on the following morning, 16 August, when around 10:00 AM the Germans launched an attack up the Lens–La Bassée Road. This was "beaten back," according to one report, "mainly by the spirited efforts of … L/Cpl J. Dumaresque and his party of bombers; and a number of casualties inflicted." Joseph Dumaresque was wounded but remained at his post and in charge of his section until the enemy was driven off. Later that afternoon, the Germans again sallied forth, attempting another bombing raid against the hard-pressed A Company positions. This too, failed to make any appreciable headway. But even though the remaining Canadians grimly held their ground, some of them were breaking under the strain. As the anonymous author of one of A Company's after-action reports put it, with a candour uncharacteristic of such documents,

> one of our men (who from his actions appeared to be unhinged) jumped out of the trench, chased a German overland, caught him square in the back with a bomb and killed him. Instead of returning immediately as he could have done in comparative safety, he proceeded deliberately to search the body for souvenirs, and while doing so was sniped in the shoulder and leg. Two men attempted to get him in. One was

> wounded and the other killed. Pte. Brennan, who had previously done splendid work[,] then crawled out with the same object, but was instantly shot through the head. The cause of all this now began to wriggle about in an attempt to get in and was immediately riddled with m.g. bullets. A costly souvenir hunt.[45]

Lt. Bennett knew that his remaining troops would not be able to stand much more. At 5:00 PM he sent two more runners back to try and find Capt. Goodman and 21st Battalion headquarters. If they could not send up reinforcements, Bennett hoped they could at least send up some stretchers to help evacuate the wounded. But as with the runners dispatched on the previous evening, nothing more was heard from them. Bennett and the other survivors of A Company must have felt increasingly isolated and desperate. "No rations came that night and no word from anyone," he later wrote in his personal report. The best that could be done was to maintain contact with the troops on either flank. With Lt. Borrowman killed by "friendly fire," Sgt. O. Gower was left in charge of No. 4 Platoon on the right. Gower's command by this time amounted to little more than a section, with only fifteen men remaining. Nevertheless, they managed to establish machine-gun and bombing posts along the road and continued to stand fast. Later that night (16–17 August), it appeared that the Germans were massing for another attack. This prompted someone in the front line to send up an SOS flare, drawing a speedy, and presumably accurate, response from the artillery, which loosed a number of salvoes against the suspected concentration point. Whatever the enemy's original intentions, no attack was launched during the rest of the night.[46]

As 17 August dawned, the battered survivors of A Company could scarcely hold out for another day, especially if the Germans continued to press their assaults. "The situation," according to reports, "was rapidly becoming desperate and the men well nigh exhausted, having been nearly three days without food or water." With no word from his superiors, Lt. Bennett decided to take matters into his own hands and attempted to locate Capt. Goodman himself. Dashing through a "gauntlet of heavy machine gun fire," Bennett made his way to the rear and, much to his surprise, found that help already had arrived. It was C Company of the 19th Battalion, which had been ordered to move two of its platoons (Nos. 9 and 11) over to Commotion Trench on the morning of 16 August to provide further support for the 21st Battalion. Earlier in the night (16–17 August), No. 9 Platoon, led by Sgt. David Graham, had been moved forward to reinforce the remnants of No. 4 Platoon.

Cheered by this development, Bennett continued his search for Goodman. After a half-hour he finally gave up and hurried back to his men in the front line. On reaching his party he saw the very welcome sight of C Company's Capt. Catto, who had arrived with a runner, a guide, a sandbag full of bread, three cans of water, and the answer to the riddle of the missing Goodman. As the grateful survivors of No. 2 Platoon gobbled their bread and quenched their thirst, Catto explained how

Goodman, along with Lt. Rankin and acting CSM S.H. Robinson, had been evacuated to the rear after being gassed. Catto had learned where to find Nos. 2 and 4 Platoons from Maj. Miller of the 21st Battalion, and had brought up rations with all speed after being told that Bennett and his men had gone without supplies since moving forward on the 15th.

Fortified by food and drink, Bennett's men continued to hold on until 8:00 PM that evening, when Lt. A.E. Thompson of B Company, 19th Battalion, arrived on the scene with the good news that A and C Companies would be relieved later that night. These plans might have been upset shortly before midnight on 17 August, when it appeared that the Germans were preparing for yet another attack. However, the gunners supporting the Canadians laid down a barrage that kept the Germans from reaching the Canadian front line. The relief went ahead as planned, being almost complete by 2:00 AM. Just then, the Germans executed a heavy artillery bombardment of their own, which contained a high concentration of gas shells. The gas caused "a great deal of disorganization" among the outgoing troops of C Company, "the men being unable to see with their gas masks on in the dark. Many were gassed and several wounded, and it was not until late in the afternoon of the 18th that all the men had been accounted for in [Cité] St. Pierre."[47] Although battalion reports do not mention the type of chemical agent employed in the attack, this would have been the first occasion on which 19th Battalion personnel were exposed to mustard gas, the Germans having unleashed it against the Canadian Corps for the first time on the night of 17 August.[48]

One of those felled by mustard gas at Hill 70 was Edwin Adye, who already had injured his leg when he was caught in the open during the German barrage. "I got well out … into the very middle of a combined high explosive and mustard gas enemy barrage," Adye explained:

> I was blown up, I remember being up in the air, a most heavenly feeling. The silly thought flashed in my mind, well if this is Heaven, well this is OK. But when I landed with a thump, I knew it wasn't Heaven. Fortunately I didn't land on anything that hurt me. It was soft soil. And I finally found a trench. I didn't know which way it was going, but I staggered into it and got going. I finally found a small detachment of the medical corps who were looking after the wounded in a dugout. And … they saw that I was in pretty bad shape, so they took me down into a dugout. They didn't know of course but my clothes were soaked with liquid mustard gas from those exploding shells. This I learned later. They gave me some coffee and a drink of rum. And my back was badly splattered … they saw that I could walk however. They put me in charge of a group of walking wounded.

After shepherding the group of wounded men back to a casualty clearing station, Adye made his way back to 19th Battalion headquarters. Before long, the effects of the gas began to set in:

> I was dreadfully ill. In fact nearly passed out. And then up came a medical corporal, and began asking questions and discovered that I'd been through this barrage so he laid me on a stretcher and ticketed me and away I went ... Then at another casualty clearing station further back I remember we were being carried by German prisoners. And these were the first Germans that I had seen, to recognize as such ... And I'll never forget that lying there, half conscious, beginning to pain greatly, I looked at those fellows and I said to myself, "why they're just like we are." The same as us. And they carried us onto the little narrow gauge railway they'd built to take out wounded and bring in supplies and back I went. And I got to another dressing station where they did take my clothes off. Now not only were they contaminated but they were dreadfully lousy ... And the last thing I remember, for quite a long time[,] was they put the clothing under my head on another stretcher as a pillow. I summoned my regaining strength to push these clothes off the stretcher. And so that was the end of that for a while. And I was very, very ill ... Later on I was blind for two periods of three weeks; supposed to die but I didn't ... I never expected to see again ... And nobody would give me any information because mustard gas was so new this was one of the initial uses of it, and a lot of men were very badly burned and hurt at that time with the mustard gas ... The sight gradually returned ... The following March I was discharged from convalescence to Bramshott camp. To the 3rd Reserve Battalion.[49]

A Company also was savaged by the German bombardment on the night of 17–18 August, and its survivors were "badly scattered" in their attempts to avoid the plunging shells. There was little for poor Lt. Bennett to do but gather as many men as he could find and try to lead them back to relative safety. With only five men, Bennett reported back at his company's assigned position in Cité St-Pierre. Fortunately, other survivors from A Company straggled in by twos and threes over the course of the following day, 18 August. "Miracle to get through it all," concluded a shaken Pte. Barnes, "only seven left in No. 2 Platoon out of twenty-eight, dead all over. Tough game."

In the meantime, the units that relieved A and C Companies were in for a rough time of their own. These units were composite companies, made up of troops from the 19th Battalion's B and D Companies combined with LOB personnel recalled from reserve. These temporary units were referred to as No. 1 Composite Company and No. 2 Composite Company. They were commanded by Capts. Robert Bliss and James Linton, respectively, and had been created by Lt.-Col. Millen on 16 August because B and D Companies were extremely depleted in strength. Many of their personnel had been detached to supply fatigue and carrying parties to other units.[50]

The relieving units suffered some casualties from the same German bombardment that had harried the outgoing troops of A and C Companies. Then, at 4:00 AM on 18 August, yet another heavy bombardment pounded Chicory Trench and nearby Canadian positions. The shells fell at a furious rate for approximately twenty minutes before lifting to the support lines, at which time enemy infantry launched another attack. Capt. Linton reported that his men repelled the German assault "completely and without difficulty" along their portion of the front, their efforts being supported by a stiff artillery barrage from the Canadian guns. However, a party of sixteen Germans managed to force its way into a section of trench held by the 21st Battalion along No. 2 Composite Company's left flank. Upon learning this, Lt. William Waldrum of No. 14 Platoon "immediately organized a bombing party and supported by a barrage of rifle grenades worked up the trench and forced [the Germans] out before [they] had an opportunity to consolidate. Seeing that they could not stand, the remainder of [the German] party started back across No Man's Land but were caught by Lewis guns and snipers and none of [the] party succeeded in regaining [the] German line."[51] One German prisoner was captured – a member of a Saxon regiment. The Germans maintained their bombardment of Canadian support positions until 6:00 AM, after which activity levels diminished.[52] The remainder of 18 August passed in reasonably quiet fashion until the entire 19th Battalion was relieved later that evening by the 27th Battalion from the 6th Brigade. In the early morning hours of 19 August, Lt.-Col. Millen's worn-out men moved back to support positions in the old British front line along Edgware Road, where they caught their breath over the course of the next three days. This effectively brought to an end the 19th Battalion's active role in the battle for Hill 70.[53] From the battle's opening on 15 August to the day when Millen's men were finally relieved, the Canadian Corps beat back twenty-one German counterattacks.[54] Even historian John Swettenham's chillingly evocative characterization of the fighting from 15 to 18 August can impart only the vaguest impression of its ferocity:

> The resolute enemy stormed the Canadian parapets repeatedly, hurling grenades into the trenches and sweeping them with scorching flame. So impetuous were these assaults that many trenches were entered – a *mêlée* of shouting, lunging, wrestling men until one side or the other was ejected. But the Germans were not allowed to keep their gains. Where sections, heavily pressed, recoiled, our men would not be bested. They leapt back, cursing, to savage the enemy until he, in his turn, recoiled. So it continued for four days and three nights of infernal noise, with quiet passages made horrible by the screams and groans of wounded men."[55]

The butchery would not end on 18 August. For several more days the Canadians and Germans continued delivering thrusts and counter-thrusts at various portions of the line. But the Canadian Corps' grip on Hill 70 would not be broken.

The 19th Battalion was moved forward again to close support positions in Cité St-Pierre on 21 August, when the Canadian Corps commenced a series of bloody but ultimately unsuccessful attempts to push into the city of Lens itself. Fortunately, Millen's exhausted troops were relieved in the lines on the following day, this time by the 58th Battalion. The men of the 19th then moved back to Bouvigny Huts for the night, before marching out again on 23 August with the rest of the 4th Brigade, which was withdrawn from the lines for an extended rest period. The 19th

A stretcher-bearer party bringing up wounded from the German lines on Hill 70. August 1917. (LAC PA-001684)

Battalion was sent to billets in Villers-au-Bois, where it would stay for the next twenty-two days.

Savage as the fighting at Hill 70 was, it did not result in the 19th Battalion's heaviest losses in a major engagement to date. The battalion war diary for the month of August lists 2 officers (Lts. A. Borrowman and P.J.S. Laing) killed in action, along with 19 other ranks. Two more officers (Lts. A.J. Duncan and T.J. Lynott) and 101 other ranks were wounded, and 2 officers (Capt. H.E. Goodman and Lt. A.J. Rankin) and 4 other ranks were gassed. These numbers are somewhat lower than those found in postwar casualty records, which state that 8 officers and 182 other ranks were counted as casualties during the whole of August (see Appendix A), with most cases (7 officers and 106 other ranks) occurring between 15 and 18

August. The casualty statistics provided at the end of the August 1917 war diary text possibly reflect losses sustained only during the battalion's operations at Hill 70.[56]

These losses among the other ranks were offset by 136 reinforcements, which were taken on strength between 21 and 30 August. Since late July, ten officers also had arrived as reinforcements or were posted back to the 19th Battalion from other duties. Two of these were the unfortunate Lts. Borrowman and Laing.[57] It is probable that casualties in the 19th Battalion would have been greater had it been one of the principal attacking units at Hill 70. Compared to the 19th Battalion's 113 casualties, all ranks, between 15 and 18 August, the 18th, 20th, and 21st Battalions respectively sustained 171, 165, and 265 casualties, all ranks, during the same period.[58]

The battle's principal architect, Lt.-Gen. Currie, remarked afterward that the capture and retention of Hill 70 was "altogether the hardest battle in which the Corps has participated" to date. The battle for the hill and the ensuing operations against Lens cost the Canadian Corps 8,677 casualties. An additional 521 losses at other points along the Western Front during the same period brought a total of 9,198 casualties (killed, wounded, missing) between 15 and 25 August. In the

German prisoners captured at Hill 70 parade past a young child. The Germans do not appear to take much notice of their diminutive "reviewing officer." (LAC PA-001703)

process, the Canadians had mauled seven German divisions, inflicted an estimated 20,000 casualties, and upset the German high command's plans to relieve some of its worn-out formations opposing the main British offensive in Flanders. For their efforts, Currie's men had gained a useful territorial objective, and Hill 70, like Vimy Ridge, would remain in Allied hands for the rest of the war.[59] However, in the battle's immediate aftermath, success was a cold comfort for shaken survivors. Pte. Bob Gardner of the 21st Battalion described the fighting at Hill 70 as "the worst ever … Old Fritz had everything barricaded and armed … there were fights in cellars, dugouts, tunnels, and everywhere imaginable … I was buried [by exploding shells] five times in the four days that we were holding the new line."[60]

14

"A Dirty, Dirty Country": September–November 1917 and the Battle for Passchendaele

At Villers-au-Bois the 19th Battalion took up the familiar routine of training when out of the lines. Platoon and company drill, along with rifle-range practice, figured highly in the weekly training syllabi. "We have just come out of the line," Pte. John Gaetz informed his mother on 26 August, "and of course you will know from the papers that to be in the line these days, you are not idle. The weather has been fine lately[,] just what we want for 'our business.' It is much pleasanter both in the line and out."[1]

High-level inspections kept all ranks on their toes. On 27 August the entire 4th Brigade was assembled for inspection by the commander-in-chief himself, Field Marshal Haig. Four days later, on 31 August, Brig.-Gen. Rennie paid a visit to the battalion and delivered a short address to the assembled ranks praising them for the part they had played in the recent operations at Hill 70.[2] Gaetz proudly told his mother:

> You will perhaps be interested to know that the 4th Brigade that the 19th is in, stands very high in the Canadian Corps or the 1st Army [*sic*]. It is generally very successful in anything it undertakes and lately it has, as the brigadier told us today, 'Covered itself

Canadians who took part in the capture of Hill 70 marching past First Army commander General Sir Henry Horne. September 1917. (LAC PA-001833)

> with glory' and he referred to different congratulations he had received from those in the higher command. The officers and staff seem to be very capable and you always feel that there is never anything left undone. And everything [is] done to insure success with the least possible sacrifice.[3]

If Gaetz really meant what he wrote, and was not simply trying to present the best possible face to his anxious mother, then his words contradict the popular stereotype that trench soldiers held uniformly low opinions of the generals and their staffs.

A week later, on the evening of 7 September, Rennie organized a tattoo of massed bands from all four Canadian divisions, which Lt.-Gen. Currie and Maj.-Gen. Burstall attended. Another grand revue was held two days later, when the GOC First Army, Gen. Horne, attended a brigade church service, after which he reviewed the troops and presented decorations to officers and other ranks for their conduct in the August operations. Included among those receiving awards were four officers and nineteen other ranks from the 19th Battalion.[4]

Meanwhile, while some basked in the glow of public honours, other members of the battalion found themselves in a more reflective mood as the autumn season drew near. Gaetz wrote to his father:

> A trip out to the east country or down the river used to be a great anticipation. Some mornings just now are very similar to a fall morning in Alberta. The air is not quite so clear and raw but there is a brightness and freshness about it which is quite similar. The sound of the guns in the distance is very much the same as what you hear some early morning in the fall during shooting season.[5]

Sporting events and tactical competitions featured largely in the events of September, with the 19th Battalion holding its own sports day on 8 September, followed up by brigade games on the 12th. A more unique contest was held on 11 September: the 2nd Canadian Divisional Rifle Meet, which was a series of competitions designed to test individual marksmanship with rifle and revolver, as well as the tactical skills of individual platoons. The 19th Battalion's No. 11 Platoon placed third and qualified as one of three platoons to represent the division in the platoon competition at the Canadian Corps Rifle Meet, which was held at Pernes on 22 September.[6] As it turned out, No. 11 Platoon placed ninth out of twelve entries in the platoon match at the corps meet, while one of the other 2nd Canadian Division entries, a platoon from the 31st Battalion, took top honours and enjoyed bragging rights as "the best platoon in the whole of the Canadian Corps."[7] The platoon from the 19th Battalion had placed rather low in the corps competition; even so, Lt.-Col. Millen must have been proud to have one of his own make it all the way to the finals. Moreover, Millen had been accorded the singular honour of being placed in charge of the 2nd Canadian Division's entire slate of competitors at the corps rifle meet. Evidently, his organizational skills and keen sportsmanship had come to the notice of his superiors.

A lieutenant and a lance corporal conduct rifle inspections near a dugout, September 1917. (LAC PA-001864)

A mobile field kitchen in use during September 1917. One of the men is cleaning his Short Magazine Lee-Enfield rifle. The 2nd Canadian Division's distinctive symbol appears on the kitchen. (LAC PA-001931)

By 14 September it was back to the trenches again for the 4th Brigade, which was sent to relieve the 8th Brigade in the sector situated in front of the village of Vimy. The 19th Battalion was detailed to brigade support, with battalion headquarters, along with C and D Companies, being stationed in the Bois-de-la-Folie, while A Company was quartered in Paynesley Tunnel and B Company in the village of Vimy itself.[8] It was Maj. Hatch's turn to lead the battalion into the lines, which he did at a trench strength of 27 officers and 626 other ranks. While in brigade support, the 19th Battalion supplied numerous work parties ranging in size from 25 to well over 100 other ranks. They carried forward spools of barbed wire, dug a new section of front-line trench, and deepened and extended several existing support trenches. Fortunately, German activity levels were extremely low, and only one casualty was sustained during this period as a result of enemy action.[9]

On the night of 20–21 September, the units of the 4th Brigade marched back into divisional reserve after being relieved in the front lines by the 5th Brigade. The 19th Battalion moved into huts at Camblain-l'Abbé, where all ranks rested on the 21st. On 23 September, after the 19th and 20th Battalions held a combined church parade, both units were inspected by Maj.-Gen. Burstall. Training over a taped course commenced the next day, with C and D Companies conducting their exercises while A and B Companies carried on with specialist training. This arrangement was reversed on the following day, so that all companies had an opportunity to train on the course.[10] Possibly, this training was carried out for a projected

Canadian assault of Sallaumines Hill, just southeast of Lens. Unbeknownst to the troops, however, the Sallaumines project was merely a ruse, covering efforts to train them up for a planned offensive at Cambrai, which was to be launched by Gen. Byng's Third Army later in the autumn. The Cambrai scheme was top-secret, for it would involve the first use of tanks on a grand scale in a surprise attack. But as events turned out, the Canadian Corps would miss participating in this innovative offensive. Its service at Cambrai would be pre-empted by the requirements of the Flanders offensive.[11]

By 26 September it was the 4th Brigade's turn to move up into divisional support positions, where it replaced the 6th Brigade. As a result of this shift, the 19th Battalion relieved the 29th in Neuville-Saint-Vaast. Lt.-Col. Millen was in charge this time, Maj. Hatch presumably remaining out of the lines in charge of LOB personnel. The bulk of the battalion (at a trench strength of 32 officers and 746 other ranks) settled into billets in the dugouts and cellars that honeycombed the remnants of the village. As usual, a vigorous work program was carried out, with up to 150 men labouring by day on positions in the vicinity of their billets, and approximately 200 by night in and near the front lines, excavating trenches and helping to bury vital telephone cables. The Germans, again, were comparatively quiet. No casualties were reported among the work parties during the closing days of the month; nor did the 19th Battalion receive any reinforcements.

The 19th Battalion finally returned to front-line duty on 2 October, relieving the 27th Battalion of the 6th Brigade in the familiar sector in front of Vimy. Millen led his men into the line at a trench strength of 29 officers and 685 other ranks. Battalion headquarters was established in Canada Trench, as was C Company, which was assigned to battalion support. The men of A Company also were in support and were distributed between Canada and Kurton trenches, just to the right of Peggie Communication Trench. B and D Companies held the front line, known as Billie Burke Trench, with three platoons each, and both placed one platoon in company support in Teddie Gerrard Trench. An inter-company relief was carried out on the third day in the lines, with A Company relieving B Company and C relieving D. Patrols and nightly fatigue parties endured sporadic shelling, but no German parties were encountered in no man's land. Despite several unfortunate casualties (including three other ranks killed), the tour was reasonably quiet, with no major actions.[12]

In the early morning hours of 8 October, the 18th Battalion began a leisurely relief of the 19th; the latter's companies made their way back to Neuville-Saint-Vaast by 9 October. The following day, the men of the 19th were marched back farther to billets in Villers-au-Bois, where they carried out company and specialist training until 9:00 AM on 15 October. "We have just come out of the line," Millen reported earlier on 10 October,

> [and] it was a pretty dirty walk back, as we are getting some old chilly rains now, but of course it is tougher for those in the line … My little doggy is fast asleep on my knees he is a great pet; and I suppose you will say I spoil him as he always sleeps with me … I had him in the trenches with me this trip … I suppose by this time the leaves are falling fast, they have not started here yet – and the country is still quite green, it won't be long though before we also will be settling down for the Winter. I do hope it will be the last here.[13]

On 15 October the 19th Battalion was ordered to march to Diéval via Fresnicourt and Rebreuve, en route to a new front altogether. The troops departed Villers-au-Bois at 9:00 AM, reached their destination by 4:00 PM the same day, and were billeted in barns for the night. The next several days were occupied by tactical exercises, with a company scheme carried out on 18 October in the nearby fields being rated a particular success. This training stint was interrupted briefly on 20 October when Gen. Horne arrived to inspect units of the 4th Brigade and took the opportunity to bid "au revoir" to all ranks as they prepared to move up into Belgium for service in the Second Army. Overall, Horne had been more than pleased with the Canadians' efforts over the previous months. After expressing his great regret that the Canadians were leaving the First Army, he announced his hope that they would return to his command before long.[14]

Back to Flanders

The spectacular British coup at Messines in June had been only a preliminary operation for the main offensive in Flanders. Field Marshal Haig envisioned a massive drive involving the capture of the Passchendaele Ridge, seizure of the important communications centre of Roulers, and a final sweep to the Channel coast. To carry out this grand design, Haig shifted the axis of attack from Gen. Sir Herbert Plumer's Second Army (the victors at Messines) to Gen. Sir Hubert Gough's Fifth Army, trusting as he did that the aggressive Gough would achieve these goals more rapidly than the more methodical and deliberate Plumer. In the end, the choice was not a happy one, for Gough was not terribly familiar with Flanders and was inclined to set objectives for his infantry that were unrealistically distant. Moreover, Haig himself had muddied the waters by offering vague direction, leaving his subordinates unclear as to whether the methods employed in this offensive should entail a step-by-step advance or an attempt at a rapid and decisive breakthrough. In the end, the Fifth Army's efforts, commencing on 31 July and bedevilled by unusually wet weather, achieved only modest gains at a terrible cost in casualties. The tried and true methods of Plumer, employing the more conservative "bite and hold" style of attack (likewise used by the Canadians at Vimy and Hill 70), were brought in once more. Objectives would be kept strictly within artillery range so that infantry consolidating captured ground would be well supported by the gunners as they fended off German counterattacks. In other words, the attackers would "bite" into enemy-held territory only to a depth that they could defend or "hold" with their heaviest firepower assets – their artillery. As historian Ian Brown notes, it was not a "glamorous" way to wage war but it was relatively effective.[15]

By the end of August, Plumer had regained principal control of operations in Flanders, with Gough relegated to a supporting role. The Second Army, benefiting greatly from the return of drier weather, pulled off three successful advances during late September and early October. But abnormally heavy rains returned again, and this, combined with the drastic impact of massive artillery bombardments, overwhelmed and disrupted local drainage systems, transforming large parts of the low-lying battlefield into a veritable swamp. Even Plumer's tactics could not defeat nature, yet he persisted in attacking through October, with Haig's full support. By the middle of the month, even after hopes of achieving a breakthrough in Belgium had evaporated, capturing the village of Passchendaele – and, more important, the low ridge on which it sat – had become an end in itself. Haig reasoned that the ridge would be useful as a "jumping off place for the next BEF offensive in 1918." Accordingly, British, Australian, and New Zealand divisions were sent floundering forward through the horrible mire against dispersed German defences that were anchored by numerous mutually supporting concrete shelters, nicknamed "pillboxes" by the British. By 22 October, with the village of Passchendaele tantalizingly close, exhaustion set in among Plumer's attacking divisions. To salvage some measure of success before even worse winter weather set in, fresher formations would have to be thrown into the fight. So the Canadian Corps was summoned once more to the killing fields of Flanders.[16]

It was an assignment welcomed by no Canadian with past experience of the Ypres Salient, from the humblest private up to Lt.-Gen. Currie himself. Currie had been warned on 3 October that his corps would be moved to Flanders to take on the job of capturing Passchendaele, and although he protested vigorously against the assignment, Field Marshal Haig insisted that it had to be done. Fifty-one of the sixty divisions then serving in the British armies on the Western Front had already cycled through the offensive, and the Canadian divisions were among the only ones left that had not been committed. By Haig's reckoning, there had been far too much struggle and sacrifice to terminate the battle without at least capturing the higher ground around Passchendaele. The alternative was a withdrawal and the relinquishment of much hard-won ground. He also claimed that the attack was necessary to fix German attention on the British armies, which would give their French allies additional time to recover from their recent mutinies. Historians have vigorously criticized Haig's rationale. At the time, Currie could only bend to the field marshal's will after pressing his own objections as far as he could.[17]

Grimly predicting heavy losses, Currie began drawing up plans that he hoped would at least reduce the misery and casualties his troops would experience. Following in Plumer's footsteps, he demanded plenty of preparation time and proposed

Field Marshal Sir Douglas Haig and Lt.-Gen. Sir Arthur Currie (LAC PA-002497)

to capture Passchendaele village and ridge in a four-stage advance. The first two stages would be carried out by the 3rd and 4th Canadian Divisions on 26 and 30 October; the final two stages, which included the capture of Passchendaele itself and what remained of the ridge, would be taken care of by the 1st and 2nd Canadian Divisions on 6 and 10 November.[18] Canadian Corps headquarters moved up to the Ypres Salient, where it came under the command of Gen. Plumer's Second

The wasteland of mud at Passchendaele, November 1917. (LAC PA-040139)

Army, and assumed control of the sector formerly held by II Anzac Corps on 18 October. The 3rd and 4th Canadian Divisions moved into the front lines on 23 October; meanwhile, the 1st and 2nd Canadian Divisions began their own journey northward from the British First Army area.[19]

The sector taken over by the Canadian Corps was situated along the valley of the Stroombeek, between Gravenstafel Ridge to the west and the higher ground around Passchendaele to the east. It was bisected by the valley of the Ravebeek, a stream that emptied into the Stroombeek to the southwest. The Ravebeek was normally a watercourse of no consequence, but heavy rains and weeks of intense shelling had seriously disrupted its course, turning the surrounding area into a hellish bog, half a mile wide in some places.[20]

The troops of the 19th Battalion were still at Diéval when they were ordered to proceed to the trains that would carry them to Flanders. At midnight, 23–24 October, all ranks of the battalion hurriedly packed their kits and assembled for a march to Ligny-Saint-Flochel, where they boarded the waiting trains. The train carrying A, B, and C Companies departed at 3:30 AM and arrived at Caestre at 2:00 PM later that day. D Company left Ligny considerably later and was transported to Godewaeresvelde, where it met the rest of the battalion on the march from Caestre on 25 October. Fourteen months had passed since the 19th Battalion had tramped along the byways of Belgium, and surviving "old sweats" who had endured the operations of 1915 and 1916 "eagerly picked up and commented upon old landmarks" they remembered from dark days gone by. The battalion marched through the city of Ypres itself, proceeding in single file past the shattered spires of the medieval Cloth Hall and out through the Menin Gate to Potijze. Awestruck by the devastated countryside, the men looked upon their own unit as merely "a small part of the huge machinery of the offensive. Tents were pitched in an open field amongst the heavy batteries, and all ranks settled down for the first real sleep in some days."[21]

The battalion's first assignment was to furnish working parties for the 4th Canadian Division, which was taking part in the first phase of the Canadian Corps' attack. When not engaged in acutely exhausting work, such as carrying supplies and upgrading the roads over recently captured ground, Lt.-Col. Millen's men

Canadian troops laying duckboard paths across the swampy Passchendaele battlefield. (LAC PA-040127)

recovered their strength in tents and shelters at Potijze.[22] Working alongside countless labour parties from the 19th and other infantry battalions were numerous Canadian and British artillery, engineering, and pioneer troops, whose nerves and skills were pushed to the limit as they toiled ceaselessly over the quagmire before each phase of operations. They constructed plank roads, built wooden platforms on which artillery batteries could place their guns, and laid hundreds of yards of duckboard paths to give men, pack animals, and vehicles some semblance of solid footing amidst the deep stretches of mud. The work was both physically draining and extremely hazardous, owing to periods of intense shellfire from the German artillery that dominated the salient.[23]

Thrown into this miserable morass was Lt. Joe O'Neill, a fresh-faced young officer sent up from the Canadian Corps Reinforcement Camp to join the 19th Battalion on 1 November.[24] "When we were sent up there," O'Neill later remembered,

> the first job we had to do was … to build what they call, the plank road. See, the mud was so soft, that they couldn't get their guns up, and they had to build this big plank road to try to support guns and ammunition and so on … You couldn't walk across the country. They had to put down what we call bath mats. That is, they took pieces of two by four with slats across them, three inch slats or a piece one by four, and put these down as tracks … the Germans would concentrate on these tracks and on this old plank road that we had to build. Well they bounced some pretty heavy stuff off and blew them up and we'd have to put them back in again and so on.[25]

On 29 October, after the men had put in three hard days of this kind of work, the 19th Battalion was relieved by the 20th and made its way back to huts near Vlamertinghe. There they remained for the next four days, their time occupied by kit inspections and platoon drills. Meanwhile, the 3rd and 4th Canadian Divisions exhausted themselves carrying out the first two stages of the Canadian advance on 26 and 30 October. Parts of the battlefield over which they struggled were so difficult that the fighting sometimes resembled an amphibious operation. Moreover, the areas where the going was better were well covered by numerous concrete dugouts and shelters – the deadly German "pillboxes" – which were distributed in a checkerboard fashion to provide mutual support. Still, with the help of complex creeping barrages, the infantry inched its way forward, tackling pillboxes and other strongpoints with skilful platoon tactics. Some sections would use Lewis guns and rifle grenades to lay down covering fire while other sections worked their way around individual pillboxes and associated trench works to capture them from the flank and rear. But the cost in casualties was high and the fighting fierce, with the Canadians repelling a number of German counterattacks.[26]

Relief came, starting on the night of 2–3 November, when the 2nd Canadian Division arrived to replace the dog-tired units of the 4th Canadian Division in the right-hand portion of the Canadian Corps front. On the left, the 1st Canadian Division moved into the front lines, replacing the equally weary 3rd Canadian Division

A desolate vista of mud and German wire through which the Canadians had to advance at Passchendaele. (LAC PA-002167)

on 4 November.[27] Fortunately for the incoming divisions, their comrades in the outgoing formations had succeeded in advancing the front line to within achievable striking distance of Passchendaele itself, which was scheduled for capture on 6 November in the third stage of the corps' attack. The village was within the 2nd Canadian Division's assigned sector, and the honour of seizing it would go to the men of the 6th Brigade, supported on their right by one battalion of the 5th Brigade. This left the 4th Brigade with the dreary task of holding the front line and preparing jumping-off positions for the other two brigades during the days and nights leading up to the attack. Facing them would be fresh troops from the German 11th Division, which had moved into the line on 3 November between the Ypres–Roulers railway and the Mosselmarkt Road.[28]

On 2 November at 11:00 AM, the 19th Battalion departed Vlamertinghe, under orders to relieve the 78th Battalion in the right section of the 2nd Canadian Division's allotted frontage, just south of Passchendaele village. Because of the terrible state of the ground and the consequent difficulties in getting the men into their positions, the relief was not completed until later that night at 10:20 PM. Lt.-Col. Millen took command on this tour and brought into the lines with him 18 officers and 549 other ranks. In addition to the usual complement of LOB personnel who remained in billets during the tour, each battalion in the brigade was ordered to leave behind an additional 100 men in order to help evacuate the wounded – an exceptionally onerous task, given the hideously swampy nature of the battlefield.[29]

Once Millen's companies had reached the forward zone of the trenches, D and B Companies took up the right and left portions, respectively, of the battalion front, with C Company close behind in support and A Company in reserve. To Millen's left was the 21st Battalion, and to his right was the 9th Australian Battalion. Mercifully, no casualties were sustained during the relief, and the early part of the night remained comparatively quiet, at least as far as shelling was concerned. This gave Millen's men some opportunity to settle into their sodden positions.[30]

The dismal weather did nothing to brighten spirits. "This is sure some place for mud and rain, it is the limit," complained the 19th Battalion's Pte. Frederick McNulty.[31] "Up there it was just water, mud, rain all the time," remembered Joe O'Neill. "You lived in it, you slept in it, you just ate mud. You wiped a chunk of hardtack off on the seat of your pants and ate it, that kind of thing."[32] "Passchendaele was a terrible place," declared Pte. Deward Barnes:

> Rain all the time, mud, mud and quicksand. Roads had to be built on brush. Thousands of yards of trench mats [duckboards] to walk on, everything in the open. I never saw so many guns and disabled tanks. Packhorses would get into the mud and have to be [dug out] … Men had to be [dug out] that got off the mats in different places. There were few trenches. What there were, were half full of water. All you could do was sit up to your waist in water and sleep that way if you could. I never saw so many men drop from over exertion, big fellows some of them were too.[33]

Ed Youngman of the battalion transport section also had vivid memories of the treacherous "corduroy roads" that were laid over stretches of deep mud along the supply routes to the front lines. Some of these tracks were covered with planks; others were reinforced by bundles of sticks tied together (called fascines), which were laid in the muck like railway ties to provide some measure of footing. According to Youngman, walking on them

> was quite a trick, you had to watch or your foot would slip down between them. For a mule that was sharp-shod, it was quite a chore, and [one day] this mule [that] belonged to the 18th Battalion … lurched off the fascines into a shell hole. And before we came along they had did their best to pull him out when a couple of us came along and offered to pull him out, but the more that we pulled on him the worse it was and the poor thing kept sinking down, and down, inch by inch and we were frantic. We couldn't stop it and finally the officer, the transport officer of the 18th Battalion, decided there was only one thing to do. Rather than see the poor thing suffocated … [we had] to shoot him, and when his head was just above the mud the officer had pulled his revolver out of his holster and the mule turned his head and I will never forget the look on that poor brute's great big brown eyes when he looked at the officer and the officer shot him and then cried like a kid. Some of us too, I needn't talk about him, I had a lump in my throat about as big as a kitchen stove. It was those little things like that, you know, an animal you get very attached to them.[34]

Many men suffered a fate similar to that of the unfortunate mule. Horror stories abound in veterans' tales of the congestion encountered on the duckboard tracks and the men who slipped off them into the deadly deep slime of submerged shell holes. Sadly, there was little that could be done for many of them. The masses of men had to keep moving because the walkways were prime targets for the German artillery. L.R. Fennel remembered

> walking along and these wounded men hanging on to the end of the duckboards with their body about half submerged in mud, and some of these fellows [on the tracks] not knowing they were there would step on their fingers, you know, and the screams … It just haunts you. But – strict orders, you couldn't help them. You couldn't do a damn thing. You just had to keep going.[35]

R. Ferrie of the 31st Battalion remembered that "sometimes you would pass somewhere and the water would move a little and you would see men's heads bobbing up and down, drowned in sluices, whether they were wounded or killed first we don't know, and they had been there for some time."[36] Countless unburied bodies of men and animals were churned together with smashed and derelict equipment in soil that had been manured by generations of farmers. The entire mess produced a nauseating aroma. Cpl. Will Bird of the 42nd Battalion of the 3rd Canadian Division recalled "a sour smell of disinfectants, stale gas, sodden clothing, and a faint sickly odor of decay – the breath of the Salient."[37]

Ironically, the festering muck did have one redeeming virtue: it sometimes minimized the damage caused by enemy artillery. Ed Youngman remembered shells smacking into the mud and spawning "a geyser of dirty water … up in the air, about the size of a stovepipe or a little bigger."[38] "Those big shells," said Lt. Joe O'Neill,

> would light within 10, 15, 20 feet of you, and they would go down into the mud and make a hole not over two feet in diameter. They'd blow water and pieces of iron foundry up in the air. Then you'd hunch up underneath your … tin hat, and you'd get a rain of all those pieces of shrapnel on top of your hat, but you wouldn't be hurt … These shells were big enough to have simply blasted us clean off the earth, but on account of their weight and the soft mud, they went down so far it just felt like, as if someone hit you on top of the head with a rubber hammer, that was the extent of the damage you had.[39]

At 3:00 AM on 3 November, with the 19th Battalion already established in its positions on the extreme right of the Canadian Corps' line, scout officer Lt. Edwin A. Trendell began dispatching patrols to check the advance posts and to reconnoitre the Zonnebeke–Passchendaele Road. These patrols located what were believed to be German posts a mere 250 yards beyond the 19th Battalion's front line. Although "no definite outpost line could be seen," the appearance of German troops periodically dashing to and fro along stretches of ground in front of them indicated the presence of scattered forward defensive positions. Despite the increasingly close proximity of the opposing forces, the situation along the 19th Battalion's front remained quiet, with no stuttering German machine guns, no gaudy glare from signal rockets, and virtually no rifle fire to disturb the ominous tranquility.[40]

Suddenly, at around 4:40 AM, the "peace" was viciously broken. The Germans unleashed a "very heavy mixed barrage" of light and heavy artillery just in front of the 19th Battalion's front line. The air was shattered by the detonation of shrapnel shells, which spewed their deadly contents over the ground below. This barrage eventually fell back onto the front line itself, then gradually spread to the frontages of the flanking battalions, hovering over the fire trenches for approximately five minutes before rolling back to pummel the support positions. By this time, the dazed occupants of the front line could detect through the smoke and darkness "considerable movement" from the German infantry. Understandably alarmed, Millen's men quickly shot up an SOS flare, as did the units on either flank. Not content to rely solely on their artillery, whose response was "both prompt and effective," the infantry brought Lewis guns and rifles to bear, sweeping the ground in front of them with a withering fire that warded off any enemy designs on the 19th Battalion's frontage. But although their opponents had been held at bay, Millen's troops briefly had as much to fear from their own supporting guns as they did from the Germans – fifteen to twenty heavy shells fell short among their own lines. Fortunately, no casualties resulted from this.[41]

So far, except for this "friendly fire" incident, things had gone relatively well along the 19th Battalion's front. However, German storming parties had made a stronger impression on the flanking battalions. At 5:10 AM a portion of the 21st Battalion's right company had been driven back fifty yards by the leading wave of German assault troops. But the Canadians rapidly collected themselves, reorganized, and struck back with a decisive counterattack, driving the invaders out of the front line, taking eight prisoners, and re-establishing their original position. To the right of the 19th Bttalion, however, the Australians were experiencing greater difficulties.[42]

In response to reports that the Germans had broken into the 9th Australian Battalion's line, Millen moved his support company (C Company) to the right in order to offer the Australians some support; meanwhile, D Company, in the right portion of the 19th Battalion's front line, took steps to protect its flank. A busy day ensued, with Millen's front-line troops sniping any Germans who dared expose themselves while the Australians prepared their own counterattack. Operating without artillery support, the Australians reclaimed their original line "with very little difficulty" by 3:00 PM, capturing a number of prisoners in the bargain.[43]

Lt. Joe O'Neill in C Company had what he called a "grandstand seat" from which to observe the action that day. "We were in the extreme right of the Canadian Corps," he recalled years later,

> next to the Australians. Up till then the Australians and the Canadians hadn't been very good friends. In fact at one time if a Canadian and Australian met on the streets of London, there was a fight. But at this particular time some of the Aussie machine gunners were in our lines, and some of our fellows were next to theirs ... Well this particular morning the Germans put on an attack on the Aussies, and took a section of their line. Well our company was just back of where they were, and over on the left, and normally [the] Colonel would simply have ordered us to go in there and take it and help the Aussies, but due to [the hard feelings that occasionally arose between the troops of the two Dominions], he telephoned the Colonel of the Aussies, and told him that we'd take over part of their line, and give him enough men. That released enough of his men to put on an attack. So that it couldn't be said that the Canadians had to take the line off the Australians ... we were ordered out onto the face of this hill across in front of where the Hun was, we were up just high enough we were looking down at these Germans in this trench ... We had machine guns covering fire for the Aussies and we sat up there, and watched the Aussies put on an attack and drive the Hun out of this piece of trench.[44]

Later that night (3–4 November), after events had settled down, the 19th and 21st Battalions pushed their advance posts farther forward. They expected resistance from German infantry, but none was encountered. However, enemy gunners continued to bombard the 19th Battalion's forward, support, and reserve lines at regular intervals. The German artillery's efforts were aided greatly by the observation work of their own aviators, who enjoyed considerable local air superiority. Sometimes, though, quick thinking by an infantry officer could minimize the number of casualties inflicted on his men by artillery. According to Joe O'Neill, "for days the Germans had complete control of the skies ... There was a German plane come over, he wasn't, oh fifty, a hundred feet up, well you could see the buttons on his uniform we were so close. He leaned over the side of the plane and he waved at us and we waved at him, and he circled again," dropping smoke bombs. The company commander, Capt. M.C. Roberts of Hamilton, thought there was "something crooked here. They're not firing at us, they're letting us stay out here in the open." So he ordered his men to move back, over the brow of a hill. The German aircraft then dropped drums of oil on the hill, which artillery could then target, setting off an inferno that, said O'Neill, would have burnt the Canadians "to a crisp" if they had stayed in their original location. They owed their survival to Roberts's decision.[45]

The post was reoccupied later in the evening, and the situation remained stable until the 24th Battalion arrived to relieve the 19th that night (4–5 November). The 19th moved back to reserve positions, first in the Potijze area and then to huts at Brandhoek, a camp four miles west of Ypres.[46]

It had been a short but active front-line tour, and as ever, the price in casualties had been steep: 1 officer and 10 other ranks killed; 1 officer and 51 other ranks wounded; 7 other ranks gassed; and 1 other rank missing. Further incidents of Canadian heavy artillery shells dropping short had been reported before the

Lt. Edwin A. Trendell, MC & BAR, MM, MiD. (ASH, Regimental Collection)

battalion departed the front line, but the degree to which these may have been responsible for additional casualties is not clear.[47] Many of these "shorts" may not in fact have been Canadian shells at all. Numerous German artillery batteries, firing from either side of the Ypres Salient (and essentially from behind the forwardmost Canadian positions), were able to lob shells into the Canadian front lines from angles that made it seem to the infantrymen that their own guns were firing on them.[48]

An especially tough loss for the 19th Battalion during its initial tour at Passchendaele was Lt. Edwin Trendell, the battalion scout officer, who had been killed in action by machine-gun fire.[49] The battalion scouts had earned a reputation for skill and daring since the unit's early days at the front, and Trendell had carried on the tradition in admirable fashion, earning the Military Cross with bar for his bravery and devotion to duty in the field.[50] Looking back almost fifty years later, Joe O'Neill paid tribute to the remarkable audacity of Trendell and his scouts at Passchendale. He recounted that one night Trendell and a scout sergeant, Hamilton Clendining, crawled into what then passed as a company headquarters, the cellar of a destroyed house. After handing out German sausage they had stolen from a cook house in Passchendaele village, then still under German control, Trendell said that on leaving the village they were walking in a German trench when "we met about

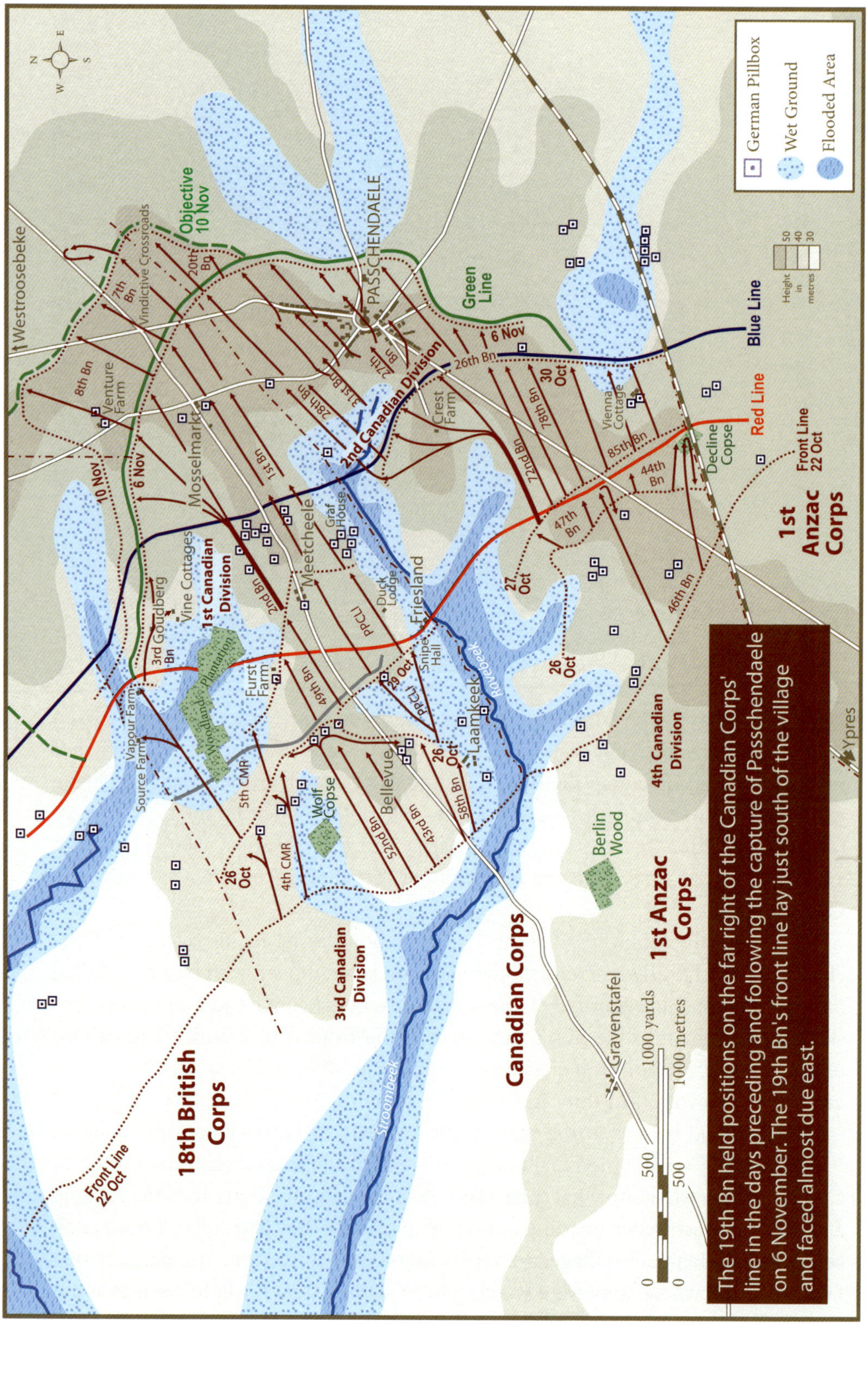

Map 15 – Passchendaele.

twenty Huns … well all we could do was squeeze over to the side of the trench and pull the Harris hats and they said Good-nok, and we said Good-nok [*sic*] and the whole bunch passed us and by that time we thought we better get out." But the story does not end happily. After leaving O'Neill and the others, "they found this German machine gun so they figured they'd take it." To quote O'Neill:

> While they were out there, the Germans decided to put on an attack … Of course our people shot up the S.O.S. … and there they were caught between the two barrages … As they tried to rush back somebody in this other battalion mistook Trendell for a German and shot him, they thought he was a German. But Glendening [*sic*], he got back all right, and Glendening was living in Toronto until recently. About a year ago he died, unfortunately, one of the grandest chaps that ever hit our battalion.[51]

Hamilton Clendining, a clerk in civil life who was born in Lisbellaw, County Fermanagh, Ireland, was an original member of the 19th Battalion, having enlisted in November 1914. His talents as a scout were widely known, and it was said that Brig.-Gen. Rennie himself occasionally summoned him to go out on special assignments. Clendining (who often went by his nickname, "Barney") was the natural choice to succeed Trendell as the 19th Battalion's scout officer, and he was commissioned as such at the end of December.[52]

The Fall of Passchendaele

On 6 November the 6th Brigade captured Passchendaele while the 1st Brigade advanced along its left flank to seize the neighbouring hamlet of Mosselmarkt. The taking of Passchendaele was the penultimate act in the long, agonizing Third Battle of Ypres, which had cost so many lives since it began on 31 July. Stretcher-bearer parties from the 19th Battalion were very busy that day helping to evacuate the wounded. Recalling the day's events, Pte. Deward Barnes later wrote:

> We carried out eight [wounded] that day and came back to tents at 11:30 PM. We had a long way to carry each one under shellfire, four to a stretcher … We could not keep to [the trench] mats, but had to go … sometimes a quarter of a mile out of our way. One fellow could slip in a little hole or sink in mud and let that end down. Some of the wounded were great, others moaned or yelled at each jar; it could not be helped. Often the four of us went through a big shell hole, water near the thighs. But we worked hard and did our best. It was rain and mud … Carrying the wounded out, most all we carried had parts of their faces shot away, some nearly all their face, as well as dozens of dead laying all around. Hundreds could get wounded and die in the mud, stuck with slight wounds. It is always a sickening sight to see them half-buried. But the mud saved many from getting hit by shells.[53]

While the stretcher-bearers struggled through the mud, the rest of the 19th Battalion spent three days reorganizing and drilling at Brandhoek. On 8 November the battalion was ordered back to the trenches where again it occupied the extreme right of the Canadian Corps' line. Lt.-Col. Millen once more led his men into the

Canadian stretcher-bearers carrying wounded along the duckboard paths at Passchendaele. (LAC PA-002367)

front line, this time at a trench strength of 22 officers and 560 other ranks. They relieved elements of the 24th and 25th Battalions and found the 18th Battalion taking up the positions to their left. To their right, once again, were the Australians. The relief, which was completed by 8:45 PM, was not without its problems. Earlier in the day, while moving forward, the 19th Battalion suffered several casualties from an enemy barrage. This mishap was attributed in part to the timing of the relief, which was carried out "too early in the afternoon," according to an after-action report.[54]

The Canadian front line had been extended just beyond Passchendaele, to the north and east, and was screened by a series of outposts. This was reinforced by a main line of resistance consisting of the old Canadian front-line trenches southwest of the village. Because of the conformation of the opposing trenches in this sector, the 19th Battalion's front-line positions lay just south of Passchendaele village and faced almost due east. A Company under Capt. John A. Harstone held the left portion of the battalion front, and C Company under Capt. R.W. Catto held the right. D Company, led by Capt. J.A. Linton, was in support, while B Company under Lt. C.R. Stillwell sat in reserve.[55]

The Canadian Corps' fourth and final advance in this offensive would be carried out on the morning of 10 November, mainly by battalions from the 2nd Brigade of the 1st Canadian Division. The objective was the remaining spur of Passchendaele Ridge to the north and east of Vindictive Crossroads. The 4th Brigade took up positions to the right of the 2nd Brigade, with the 19th Battalion on the 4th Brigade's far right, the 18th Battalion in the centre, the 20th Battalion on the left, and the 21st in support. The 4th Brigade's job was to anchor the right flank of the 2nd Brigade's assault. The 19th and 18th Battalions would remain where they were, while the 20th Battalion would pivot on its own right flank and advance its left flank some 800 yards in conformation with the movement of the 2nd Brigade troops to its immediate left.[56]

Sporadic shelling dominated the battlefield on 9 November. This continued until early the following morning, when the artillery opened fire and laid down the supporting barrage for the attack. The Germans responded in kind, and both sides lashed each other with torrents of shellfire throughout the duration of the morning's advance. By 8:00 AM, contact patrol aircraft were able to report good news: all targeted objectives had been captured. This was relayed immediately to those front-line units not directly engaged in the assault. But spirits soon were dampened, literally, by a heavy rain that "increased the amount of water in the trenches and shell holes until in some places the men were standing in water up to their thighs."[57]

The artillery bombardments continued for the rest of the day. By 2:30 PM, Capt. Catto, the senior officer in the 19th Battalion's front line, sent word back that the men in the forward trenches "were all in, and were not in good shape to withstand an attack." In response to Catto's request for reinforcements, brigade headquarters sent up detachments from the 21st Battalion, which reached the front lines at 5:30 PM and proceeded to relieve the 19th Battalion's A Company. B Company, which had been in reserve, also was moved forward and effected the relief of C Company in the right portion of the battalion front. D Company, in support, already was fully engaged, its personnel having been dispersed in small groups working as carrying parties or plugging gaps in the front line. It was in these dispositions that Millen's men continued to hold out for the rest of the day and night.[58]

The next day, 11 November, saw considerable improvement in the situation. The German artillery bombardments steadily diminished, and the weather gradually cleared. This gave the hard-pressed Canadian counter-battery organization greater opportunity to carry out its work, "with apparently good results" in silencing some of the German gun batteries. This trend continued through the following day, which facilitated the 19th Battalion's relief by the 54th Battalion, as scheduled.[59]

It was back to the Potijze area once more for Millen's men, who trudged over slippery duckboards and through thick sludge, taking care not to stumble into any waterlogged shell holes or craters. Observing the exhausted state of the men as they shambled back to their tents, Pte. Barnes noted that "when the boys came back from the line some gave out and fell as soon as they saw us, they could go no further. And nearly every one had to be carried. I never saw such feet, water-soaked and swollen."[60] During the four-day tour, the battalion had suffered eighty-one casualties, including one officer and eight other ranks who died of wounds.[61]

Before the Canadians embarked on their share of the operations at Passchendaele, Lt.-Gen. Currie had predicted that the battle would cost his corps 16,000

A wounded Canadian being taken to an aid post during the Battle of Passchendaele, November 1917. (LAC PA-002200)

casualties. His estimate was frighteningly accurate: by the time the Canadian Corps began pulling out of the Ypres Salient on 14 November, it had sustained 15,654 casualties.[62] Total losses in the British and German armies during the Third Battle of Ypres have been a matter of debate, but recent estimates fall in the neighbourhood of 271,000 British and 217,000 German between 31 July and 10 November.[63] Today it seems absurd to try to justify such prodigious expenditures of life and limb. But from the British perspective, during Gen. Plumer's successful advances in September and early October, the Second Army appeared to be on the threshold of a major victory in Flanders. To have halted the offensive while progress was being made would have seemed, at the time, utter folly. Yet the prospect of meaningful progress evaporated after 4 October, with the onset of dismally wet weather and increasingly unmanageable ground conditions. At that point, the offensive should have been brought to a halt, but neither Field Marshal Haig nor the British prime minister and his colleagues chose to take this step until the Passchendaele Ridge was secured. When the Canadians took the ridge, they paid dearly for an extended salient that grew precariously narrower the deeper it jutted into German-held territory. Far from providing a solid base of operations for future offensives, the position on Passchendaele Ridge proved untenable in the long run. Faced with an impending German offensive in the spring of 1918, Gen. Plumer, reluctantly

A wounded Canadian and wounded German share a light on the Passchendaele battlefield. (LAC PA-003683)

but wisely, chose to withdraw from the ridge without a fight and to take up more defensible positions.[64]

On 13 November the men of the 19th Battalion moved back to the Brandhoek area, where they stayed for the next two days at St. Lawrence Camp. Mercifully, no drill or training was on the agenda for these days, the time being devoted to pay parades, baths, reorganization, and, above all, rest. But the time for such luxury, however necessary, was fleeting. On 15 November they were on the march again, along with the rest of the corps, heading back to their old stomping grounds in the First Army area along the Lens–Vimy front. The battalion's destination was Villers-au-Bois, which it reached two days later, after riding the final leg of the journey in a convoy of lorries. As the vehicles wended their way through the countryside, "only men too old and boys too young to fight watched them go by. The women were in the fields working."[65]

Once the 19th Battalion reached Villers-au-Bois, the men moved into the huts of Suburban Camp, where they would remain for the following twelve days in divisional reserve.[66] "My dear Mother," a fatigued Lt.-Col. Millen wrote on 18 November:

> Here we are again back from where we left and not a dam bit sorry. It's a dirty, dirty country where we went but I do not think any of us regretted the experience, except of course for some of the good comrades we lost. Thought for awhile I might have to

> go sick myself, when I went up into the line the last time for 4 days I was feeling rather miserable and you can imagine that is no place for a sick man. My bronchitis had come back, but by taking care of myself I actually improved and now I am practically as right as can be ... So you think I have grown very fat. I suppose I am more so than when I left Canada, but really not very much so. I only weigh 5 or 6 lbs more and am in good condition.[67]

As he did in most of his letters, Millen downplayed the horrors that his men had experienced at Passchendaele. Nobody at home could possibly have comprehended such horrors anyway, and any attempts to express the truth of the situation would have intensified existing anxieties among family and friends. Far from having no regrets about their service at Passchendaele, the men of the 19th Battalion must have lamented every second of it.

15

Days of Uncertainty: November 1917–March 1918

On the battlefields of France and Flanders, the bloodletting of 1916 continued with a vengeance throughout 1917. For the British, initial successes in the battles of Arras and at Messines were overshadowed by tortuous progress and enormous casualties in the grinding struggle to capture Passchendaele. Catastrophic losses in the failed Nivelle offensive, coupled with poor service conditions, had driven elements of the French armies to open mutiny, as troops refused to mount further futile attacks. Fortunately, the French high command eventually succeeded in regaining control. But not until 1918 would France be able to bear the offensive mantle once more. To make matters worse, Russia's departure from the war (formalized on 3 March 1918), after months of revolutionary turmoil, released large numbers of German divisions for service in the west against weary Allied forces. However, the entry of the United States into the war on 6 April 1917 brought the promise of prodigious supplies of manpower and materiel for the Allied cause. But it would take time for the American war machine to lumber into high gear. Everyone knew that the reinforced German armies in the west would try to break the Allied position in France and Belgium before American forces could intervene in decisive strength.

Before 1917 drew to a close, a glimmer of hope for the future of British operations in the west came with the surprising success of Gen. Byng's Third Army at Cambrai, beginning on 20 November. The main features of this assault were the use en masse of 476 tanks along with predicted artillery barrages, both of which eliminated the need for a long preliminary bombardment that would have alerted the Germans to an impending attack. Tanks ploughed paths through the German wire for the infantry, and refinements in artillery calibration and target location allowed the gunners to hit enemy positions without firing preliminary ranging shots – a process called "registration" that invariably allowed the Germans to anticipate the attackers' intentions. Shelling targets based on map coordinates and without registration was known in gunners' parlance as "predicted fire." Specific targets, such as enemy artillery positions, machine-gun posts, and other strongpoints, could be hit with increasing accuracy and without warning.[1]

On the first day of the offensive at Cambrai, Byng's tanks and infantry forged ahead some five miles along a six-mile front. Those Germans who survived the initial assault fell back in stunned surprise. Bryn Hammond has argued that notwithstanding this armoured onslaught, the artillery was the real key to success.[2] But progress slowed, and by 30 November the Germans had delivered a powerful surprise counterattack, employing brief "hurricane" artillery bombardments, infiltration tactics by the infantry, and ground strikes by close-support aircraft. The British were thrown back, and the Germans were able to recover 75 percent of the ground they had lost over the previous ten days.

Ultimately, Cambrai left the British with few tangible territorial advantages. It did, however, provide valuable experience in the coordination of infantry, artillery, tanks, and aircraft. It also demonstrated that surprise on a large scale was still achievable on the Western Front. Unfortunately for the Allies, these lessons had also been learned all too well by the Germans. As for the Canadian Corps, Gen. Byng originally intended to include it in his attack at Cambrai. But Field Marshal Haig's determination to secure the Passchendaele Ridge before winter deprived the Canadians of the chance to participate in this innovative operation. Instead, Lt.-Gen. Currie and his subordinate commanders would have to digest the lessons of Cambrai at second-hand.[3]

Business as Usual

In mid-November 1917, while the British Third Army was making final preparations for its massive stroke at Cambrai, the 19th Battalion, along with the rest of the Canadian Corps, limped south from Ypres back to the familiar Lens–Vimy front. Restored to the First Army fold, the corps held its sectors with two divisions in the line and two in reserve, with rotations at regular intervals. The initial dispositions saw the 1st Canadian Division occupying the Lens sector and the 2nd Canadian Division at Méricourt. Facing them across no man's land were the 1st Guard Reserve Division on the German right and the 17th Infantry Division on the left. For the foreseeable future, both sides planned a program of "active defence, which meant, as far as the Germans were concerned, almost nightly raids. It was the familiar pattern of previous winters."[4]

Lt.-Col. Millen's men were sent to Villers-au-Bois on 17 November, where they stayed in divisional reserve for the next twelve days. After washing off the last of the fetid muck of the Ypres Salient, the troops resumed training. The weather remained reasonably fair until 24 November, when high winds whipped up during the day, giving way to bone-chilling rain after nightfall. By the evening of the 25th, temperatures had dipped further and snow had begun to fall.[5]

On 29 November the 19th Battalion finally returned to the trenches for a five-day tour, relieving the 20th Battalion in the front line of the Acheville sector. Taking command in the line this time was Maj. Herbert Fearman. Maj. Hatch, who usually alternated command in the line with Lt.-Col. Millen, was still away, attending a commanding officers' course at Aldershot.[6] The troops had been settled in their positions for a mere twelve hours when, at 3:00 AM on 30 November, a German raiding party stole across no man's land and forced its way into a portion of A Company's trenches, snatching one Canadian sentry and wounding another. Their mission accomplished, the intruders quickly made their way back to their own lines. The entire operation had lasted mere seconds. As soon as the troops in the adjoining posts realized what had happened, they opened fire on the retreating Germans, inflicting several casualties. In the meantime, a 19th Battalion patrol under Capt. John A. Harstone took off in pursuit of the raiders, and succeeded in capturing one of them before he could reach his own line. The score in prisoners thus stood even; even so, it was galling for the 19th Battalion to have lost a man in that manner. Canadian troops were accustomed to capturing prisoners, not being captured themselves.[7]

On 3 December the 19th Battalion was moved back to the support trenches, where it stayed for the next seven days. Over the previous month it had suffered a total of 159 casualties (4 officers, 155 other ranks), mainly during the operations at Passchendaele. Offsetting this was the arrival in November of 5 officers and 154 other ranks as reinforcements.[8] Among them was a returning veteran, Fred Stitt, who had been away from the battalion since being wounded at St-Eloi in April 1916. Stitt quickly learned that the battalion was not the same one that he had left:

> In my own Platoon Number 1, there were only three people … who had been there when I had been previously with the Platoon, and the remainder were all strangers. However they were such darn fine people that it didn't take us long to become acquainted and it's a peculiar thing. These boys had been in action for some time and had come from other units to the 19th as reinforcements. But as soon as they know that you … had been an original man with the unit, they perk up, they believe well here's somebody that knows the score you see, that sort of thing and they make you very welcome. Also your senior officers look for you, you weren't very long before they hung a lance stripe on me, and from there to a corporal, and in due course I became a sergeant.[9]

The Conscription Election

At this time, an extraordinary political battle was being fought on the Canadian home front. Prime Minister Sir Robert Borden had called a federal election in which conscription proved to be the major issue. Voluntary enlistment rates had fallen dramatically since mid-1916, and the prime minister concluded that the CEF's strength could only be maintained through the compulsory service of age-eligible men. Borden formed a new Union government in October 1917, which combined members of his own Conservative Party with Liberals who supported conscription. When the current parliamentary term expired, the government was forced back to the polls to seek a new mandate.

On 17 December, election day, a decisive majority of voters on the home front threw their support behind the Union government and its conscription policy. For the troops overseas, the polls had opened earlier, on 1 December, the 17th being the closing date for overseas voting. However, it was some time before these returns could be counted and officially issued. By March 1918, it had been revealed that over 90 per cent of military personnel on active service had voted for the Union government and its conscription platform. In the 19th Battalion, the war diarist stated simply that the unit polled 735 votes in the Dominion election during December. The exact date when voting was held was not given by the unit diarist, but Deward Barnes noted in his journal that he cast his vote for the Unionists on 7 December, during the week when the battalion was stationed in support. Given the overall result of the overseas vote, the vast majority of Barnes's comrades most likely voted in favour of conscription, as he had.[10]

The provisions of the Military Service Act, which had been passed by Borden's Conservative government at the end of August 1917, could now be implemented. Fears that reserves of manpower would run out due to declining voluntary enlistments in Canada began to diminish. But this came at a heavy social and political cost. The election campaign had exacerbated ethnic, linguistic, and regional tensions among Canadians, with many French and rural Canadians opposed to conscription. Also, while some women (those in the armed forces, and close relatives of serving soldiers) had been given the right to vote for the first time in a federal election, other Canadians (conscientious objectors and citizens born in enemy countries who were naturalized in Canada after 1902) had been stripped of that same right. It was the most bitterly contested federal election in Canadian history.

But from a purely military standpoint, there was little else that the Canadian government could have done to ensure the continuous reinforcement of its overseas forces. The influx of more than 24,000 conscripts would help maintain the Canadian Corps' viability as a fighting force. Had the war continued into 1919, as most experts at the time predicted, the conscripts would have proven absolutely essential to the corps' very survival.[11]

Canadian troops carrying rations and trench material up a communication trench to the front line. Note the anti-aircraft mounting for the Lewis gun. (LAC PA-002301)

Another "Break" for Training

It was back to the front line for the 19th Battalion on 10 December, as the men carried out another daytime relief in the Acheville sector. Three days later, on 13 December, a unique event occurred: the 19th Battalion's Lewis gunners shot down a low-flying German airplane. Unfortunately for the excited troops, they were unable to secure souvenirs from the stricken craft, since it had nosedived behind German lines.[12] This proved to be the highlight of a rather brief tour, for the 19th Battalion was relieved later that same day by the 21st Battalion. After filing out of the forward trenches, the men made their way back to Cellars Camp in Neuville-Saint-Vaast, where they moved into brigade reserve for the next six days.[13]

The 19th Battalion did not have to worry about being sent back to the front lines in the immediate future, for on 19 December the 4th Brigade was relieved in the Acheville sector and moved, along with the rest of the 2nd Canadian Division, to positions in corps reserve. There the troops commenced a period of training that would last until mid-January.[14] The 19th Battalion proceeded first to the village of Estrée-Cauchy (popularly known by the troops as "Extra Cushy"), where the troops spent the night before moving into billets at Westrehem, near their allotted training area, on 20 December.[15] The training directives issued by division headquarters

Troops moving back through the same communication trench. December, 1917 (LAC PA-002326)

were generally similar to those that had been issued for extended training periods since 1916. Training exercises would begin at section level in the first week and work up to company level by the third week. The battalion syllabus also called for plenty of work in basic drills (both physical and weapons), musketry, and technical training for the specialists in their respective areas (e.g., Lewis gunnery, scouting, signalling).[16]

Senior officers were mindful of lessons learned during the previous year's operations. Thus they realized that future battles might involve greater mobility and be less dependent on elaborate, static trench systems. The Canadians' own successes at Vimy, Hill 70, and Passchendaele had shown that a well-prepared, highly trained force employing overwhelming artillery firepower could break into even the most forbidding defensive positions; and the Third Army's initial success at Cambrai had demonstrated that a large-scale surprise attack was still possible on the Western Front. While conceding that prolonged periods of open warfare were unlikely, Canadian Corps headquarters advised all units to prepare for a phased style of fighting. The more fluid style of combat that might follow a successful "break-in" on a portion of the front would alternate with more familiar patterns of position warfare once the enemy retired to another defensive line farther to the rear.[17]

In response to corps and divisional inquiries about what could be learned from the previous year's operations, Lt.-Col. Millen and his officers replied in late November that the platoon organization instituted earlier in June was satisfactory for both tactical and administrative purposes. They agreed that the disposition for an attack on an organized trench system usually "should be a Company attacking on a platoon frontage with the resultant distribution in depth," to give it more driving power to break through enemy defences. In the event that an attack took on a "semi-open" character, moving beyond established trench systems and into areas of scattered strongpoints and defended shell holes, then "the first two waves" of attackers "should be extended, the rear wave advancing as far as the situation will permit in artillery formation." As for the actions of individual platoons against pillboxes or other strongpoints, of the sort that had been encountered at Passchendaele, Millen and his officers concluded, rather vaguely, that such positions "would have to be dealt with as the other factors of the situation warranted."[18] Since Millen's men had been used primarily in holding or support capacities at Passchendaele, they lacked the first-hand experience that other battalions had in tackling the formidable pillboxes. However, Millen's statement also implies a realization that the increasingly complex and occasionally dispersed nature of fighting required flexible methods. As useful as predetermined "normal attack dispositions" might be, the men would have to adapt to changing circumstances.

Millen was absent for part of the training period, having been granted a thirty-day leave as of 2 December. In the interim, Maj. Fearman took over, leading the battalion during its tours in and out of the lines during the first half of December and then overseeing the first week and a half of training in corps reserve. Maj. Hatch, on returning to the battalion from his commanding officers' course on 29 December, would take over command from Fearman.[19]

The men of the 19th got a break from drilling and training on 25 December, and, in accordance with usual practice, a special Christmas dinner was prepared for them. But despite the officers' best efforts, the event did not go off as well as the men hoped. "We had our Christmas dinner in a big tent with two long tables," wrote Deward Barnes.[20] "All we had that looked like Christmas was a small piece of pudding." Fred Stitt remembered that

> the Battalion erected a huge marquee tent and they built a field cooker emplacement at one end of it. That was a mistake. It was the 25th of December and a cold darn day and they had long back room tables the full length of the marquee. The plates were served at the cooker emplacement and passed down the table to the far end. By the time they got to the far end they were ice cold. Well … the day before they had sent half a dozen GS Wagons to Bethune … to get some beer. They had sent two gallon cans to put the beer in, the cans hadn't been swirled out and they had carried gasoline beforehand so that the beer tasted of gasoline. So I can safely say that was a wonderful Christmas, but it was the poorest Christmas dinner I had ever had in my life. It is rather a shame

> because the powers that be tried hard to make it a good Christmas. But we didn't do too bad and we managed to get a couple of bottles of champagne ... from an old estaminet keeper who didn't want to sell it to us in the first place, because he would rather have his champagne than money. He was making lots of money from the troops with gin blue and vin rouge and one thing and another and beer and he wanted to keep his champagne which was getting darn scarce in France at that time.[21]

Exactly how the boys acquired the champagne from the *estaminet* keeper is left to our imagination. In any case, the champagne seems to have made up for the less satisfying aspects of the day's proceedings.

It was a prime season for personnel either departing for, or returning from, periods of leave. Officers typically were allowed ten days of leave every three months; other ranks were eligible for only ten days per year. A small proportion of daily-leave allotments in the Canadian Corps were given over to "special leave" cases for more extended periods of time, often involving personal or family emergencies. Lt.-Col. Millen returned to the battalion after his month of leave on 3 January 1918. Why he was granted a full month is not clear, but it may have been for reasons of health or exhaustion.[22] Several days after his return, he informed his mother that he had arrived safely back with his unit "and naturally have been rather busy since."[23] Millen also received some good news when it was announced in the New Year's Honours List that both he and Maj. Hatch had been awarded the DSO for their devoted service to date.[24]

On 15 January the 4th Brigade began moving up towards the front line. The 19th Battalion's break had been a busy one on the chilly training fields and rifle ranges, but it had been safer than the front lines. There were plenty of newcomers in the ranks. By the end of December, 5 junior officers and 135 other ranks had joined the battalion from the Canadian Corps Reinforcement Camp. The battalion scout sergeant, Hamilton Clendining, had joined the officers' mess on 29 December, upon receiving his commission.[25]

Clendining was one of at least sixty-six men who were commissioned from the ranks in the 19th Battalion over the course of the war.[26] Joe O'Neill, who joined the battalion as a junior officer in November 1917, recalled the method by which promising candidates for commissions were selected from among the other ranks. According to him, battalions would be notified periodically about the number of candidates they were eligible to send to the Canadian Training School for Infantry Officers, which at that time was located at Bexhill in England. Upon receiving word of the appointed number of openings,

> an order would come to, say our company, [that] you have the right to send two men to school to qualify for officers ... Now what would happen would be this: the company commander would say, "Now look fellows, let's sit down after dinner and figure this out." The officers would sit down, the company officers, and of course everyone had his own ideas who he wanted to promote naturally ... Well finally we would agree, because

> you knew that whoever you suggested … was going to come back and stick his feet under the same table with you later on. He was going to have the next platoon to you in the line and you weren't taking any chances. You were going to have what you thought was the best man. Then when this was arranged the company commander would send for these men. Well [in] some cases boys didn't want to be promoted, didn't want it, others they did. The reason they didn't was this, that the percentage of the lieutenants killed was away out of all proportion higher than any other rank, and certainly a lot of boys didn't want it, didn't want to take a chance on it. But as a rule they did … Well these fellows then, they said, "Yes that would be fine, we'd be glad to have the promotion." They'd be sent to have an interview with the Colonel, from there they'd be sent to have an interview with the Brigadier, and from there they'd be sent to the divisional commander, General Burstall in our case. He'd have a talk with them, and if everybody was satisfied that this man looked all right, everybody agreed, which was usually the case … Those men [were] sent over to school in England, then they came back. They came back to your company, and they were officers sitting in the same mess with you and had a platoon right with you, right along side of you, so you weren't taking any chances.[27]

Interestingly enough, a similar collaborative system was used within companies for the promotion of NCOs.[28]

After departing the training grounds on 15 January, the 19th Battalion made its way back to the front along with the rest of the 2nd Canadian Division. An uneventful tour in the front lines of the Avion sector was followed by a period in divisional reserve. There the men engaged in some further training before moving up into the support lines on 8 February, this time in the vicinity of Méricourt. A week later, they were in the front lines once more.[29] During the remainder of February the battalion received more training time in divisional reserve near Château-de-la-Haie before moving up to the trenches in the Lens sector. Front-line tours of duty during this period were brief, usually lasting only four days. This was done likely to minimize the risk of men contracting conditions like trench foot in the cold, damp weather.[30]

If the tours of duty proved routine, matters in Lt.-Col. Millen's private life were not. His wife, Edith, had been suffering for some time from tuberculosis, and by early 1918 her condition had worsened. Millen applied for extended leave to return to Canada to be with her. His request was granted, and he temporarily relinquished command of the battalion to Maj. Hatch on 15 February. Millen would not return to the 19th Battalion until June. With this extended period of command came a temporary increase in rank for Hatch, who would assume the acting rank of lieutenant-colonel as of 3 March.[31]

Waiting for the Storm to Break

As March dawned, anticipation of a German offensive mounted steadily. Throughout the winter, while its divisions and brigades trained and rotated in and out of the lines, the Canadian Corps kept up a vigorous program of construction and

Canadian troops in trenches in the Lens sector. (LAC PA-002330)

consolidation to improve its defences in the region around Vimy Ridge. The ridge sat essentially in the centre of the British-held portion of the Western Front, and the territories to the west that were shielded by Canadian defences were of strategic importance. They featured vital coalfields and rail lines that were key components of the British army's transport and communication system.[32]

Accordingly, the Canadians planned and constructed a "deep defended area, consisting of successive defensive systems, roughly parallel to the general line of the Front and linked together by switch lines sited to protect both flanks … The whole area was compartmented in such a way that the loss of ground at any one point could be localized and would not cause a forced retirement from adjoining areas." During January, February, and March, some 250 miles of trenches, 300 miles of barbed-wire entanglements, and 200 tunnelled machine-gun emplacements were constructed behind the Canadian Corps' main front-line defensive system.[33]

The Canadian Corps was in comparatively good shape from the standpoint of manpower. The passage of conscription in the recent Canadian general election brought the promise of a steady supply of reinforcements. However, it would take considerable time for adequately trained conscripts to appear in large numbers.[34] To secure an ample supply of well-trained men as quickly as possible, Lt.-Gen. Currie persuaded the Canadian government to authorize the disbanding of the 5th

Canadian Division, which had been formed in early 1917 and was being held in England as a home defence force. The division was broken up on 9 February 1918, and personnel from its units were used to reinforce the Canadian Corps. At a time when shortages of reinforcements were forcing British divisions on the Western Front to downsize their infantry establishments from four battalions per brigade to three, the Canadian Corps was able to post an additional 100 men to each infantry battalion above their normal establishments; this was thanks in part to the sacrifice of the 5th Division. That division's contribution to the 19th Battalion consisted of 100 men from the 198th Battalion, a Toronto unit that had been absorbed in England by the 3rd Reserve Battalion following the breakup of its parent division. The 5th Division personnel made it possible for the Canadians to continue "overposting" their battalions until late August 1918.[35]

Strong as it was, the Canadian Corps was but a tiny fraction of the total Allied force on the Western Front – a force that by March 1918 was facing more Germans than ever. Having moved large numbers of troops to the west after the collapse of Russia, Germany now mustered 191 divisions in France and Belgium, while France and Britain and their allies deployed 175. But this disparity was less severe than these numbers suggest, since German divisions contained fewer men than French or British divisions. "[In] terms of absolute numbers the two sides were roughly equal: about 4 million soldiers."[36] This was still an extremely dangerous situation, because the Germans could concentrate overwhelming numbers against targeted portions of the Allied line. The German high command, under Gens. Paul von Hindenburg and Erich Ludendorff, did not intend to rest on the defensive and wait for fresh American manpower to reinvigorate the Allies. To have any hope of winning the war, they had to take the fight to the British and French before the Americans could bring their full strength to bear. The United States was still in the process of shifting its war effort into high gear, and it would not field a huge army in Europe until mid-1918.[37]

Following its relief in the front lines of the Lens sector on the night of 3–4 March, the 19th Battalion moved back, first to brigade support near Liéven, and then with the rest of 4th Brigade into reserve positions.[38] The battalion took up residence in Canada Camp at Château-de-la-Haie, where pay and bathing parades were followed by training and drilling until 11 March. Then the battalion moved to new billets at Noeux-les-Mines, still stationed in corps reserve, where training resumed again. On 14 March, Lt.-Col. Hatch received word that his battalion, along with the rest of the 4th Brigade, had passed into army reserve and had to be ready to move at twelve hours' notice. Anticipation of the German offensive was high, and all reserve formations made preparations to march at short notice to meet any sudden threat.[39]

A Disturbing Duty

One member of the battalion who would never march again was Pte. Harold Lodge, who was convicted by court martial on one count of desertion and two counts of attempted desertion. He was sentenced to death and shot by a firing squad on 13 March. Lodge was one of twenty-five Canadians who were executed during the First World War, and was the only member of the 19th Battalion to suffer this fate.[40]

Harold Lodge was born in Toronto and had worked as a driver before enlisting in the Canadian Engineers on 15 April 1915. Later that year, after shipping overseas to England, he was transferred to France, where in July 1916 he joined the ranks of the 19th Battalion. Aside from only "two trifling" breaches of discipline, his record was basically clean until the 19th Battalion moved into the lines at Passchendaele in early November 1917.[41]

On the night of 2–3 November, as his company made its way forward through the dark support trenches up to the front line, Pte. Lodge dropped out of the procession. He was noticed by his company commander, Capt. John Harstone, who hurried over to inform him that "no excuse would be taken for falling out and that he must reach the front line." Lodge's protest that he could "proceed no further" fell on deaf ears, for there appeared to be nothing physically wrong with him. After ordering him to proceed onward with his platoon, Harstone hurried off, noting that Lodge had shuffled back into the ranks and had rejoined the rear of his platoon. Later, when the acting platoon sergeant checked over the men to see that all was correct, he found no trace of Lodge. No one knew his whereabouts, nor did anyone admit seeing him depart. "It was very dark," explained Lance Cpl. George W.H. Finch, "and we were continually passing troops coming out of the line, it was impossible to distinguish features." In all likelihood, Lodge had surreptitiously snuck into the stream of outgoing troops and made his escape from duty in the lines. Exactly why he felt himself unable to carry on was a mystery at the time and remains so.[42]

A court of inquiry convened by Lt.-Col. Millen and presided over by Maj. Fearman at Villers-au-Bois on 24 November concluded that Lodge was indeed absent from 2 November, "but whether 'Absent without leave,' 'Killed' or 'Missing' it [was] impossible to say."[43] No more was heard of Lodge until he was spotted in Boulogne on 12 December and arrested on suspicion by military police. They found him dressed in the uniform of the British Red Cross Society and sporting corporal's chevrons. Little questioning was required before the police figured out he was not what he appeared to be, so he was bundled back to the 19th Battalion, where he was thrown promptly into the guardroom to await a court martial. Evidently anticipating that a court would show him no mercy, he escaped custody on 21 December and was on the run again, once more making for the English Channel and the port of Boulogne. His flight was facilitated by the negligence or collusion of one of his guards, who would get a court martial and six months' imprisonment with hard labour for his role in the escape. Lodge was arrested again on 7 January 1918 after being located "in the forepeak of a steamship about to sail."[44]

Ever more determined to escape, Lodge bolted yet again on 11 January, jumping from a moving train as he was being taken back to the 19th Battalion's guardroom. Three days later, he was located and again arrested in Boulogne. This time, there would be no escape for the desperate twenty-year-old. Lodge was tried by Field General Court Martial on 23 February for one count of desertion and two counts of attempted desertion. Maj. Hatch had assessed Lodge's previous fighting record as "excellent." Even so, his intent to desert had been so repeatedly blatant that, in accordance with military law and the perceived need to set a clear example to would-be imitators, the court sentenced him to be shot by firing squad. According to historian Andrew Godefroy, had Lodge "not attempted to escape custody, he may have received leniency from the court" on the strength of his previous record. Also, "it is uncertain why he tried to escape in the first place at all. He had not been charged when first confined, but perhaps fearing that he would be considered a deserter, he felt his chances were better on the run than in the court. Unfortunately he never had the chance to find out."[45] In her analysis of Canadian courts martial during the First World War, historian Teresa Iacobelli notes that Lodge presented one of "the worst cases" of a CEF member escaping from custody.[46]

The execution was scheduled for 13 March 1918, while the 19th Battalion was stationed in corps reserve at Noeux-les-Mines. Rumour had it that Lodge spent his final night on earth "quite happily, playing poker with his guards, whereas the officer who was detailed to command the firing squad [Lt. Albert R. Switzer] had a terrible night, threatening to become delirious more than once as the thought of his awful task seared him."[47] Another deeply reluctant participant in the affair was Pte. Deward Barnes, whose fears of being selected to join the firing party were unfortunately realized. In one of the few surviving eyewitness accounts of a Canadian execution during the First World War, Barnes described the grim proceedings:

> March 13, 1918: Woke up at 4:00 AM. I reported to the sergeant-major at 4:15 AM and then went to the Battalion Orderly Room at 4:30 AM to see Lieutenant Switzer. Two men [who had been selected the previous day as "spares"] were laid off, leaving only ten men and Sergeant Thatcher and Lieutenant Switzer. We went to the ranges where the execution took place. They had a curtain around, high enough that you could not see over, on a space of fifteen by fifteen yards with a drop curtain in front of the firing squad. By this time the whole battalion was lined up outside so as they could hear the shots and would learn a lesson about deserting. Guards were placed all around, with fixed bayonets, during the night. The officer (Lieutenant Switzer) had loaded the rifles and left them laying on the ground at our position. We got into position and were warned to fire straight, or we may have [to suffer] the same fate. The prisoner was taken out of a car (we saw him get out, with a black cap over his head and guarded) and placed on the other side of the curtain. After a while the Provost Marshall told us

> that the prisoner would not have anything to do with communion or the Church and all he asked is for us to shoot straight and make a good job of it. We took our positions, five kneeling and five standing behind; the sergeant on one side, and the Officer on the other to give orders. If we did not kill him, the Officer would have to. As soon as the curtain dropped (the prisoner was tied in a chair five paces away from us, a black cap over his head and big round disc over his heart) we got the order to fire. One blank and nine live rounds. It went off as one. I did not have the blank. The prisoner did not feel it. His body moved when we fired, then the curtain went up. That was the easiest way for an execution I had heard of. The firing squad only saw him for a few minutes. We went back to the Battalion Orderly Room and got a big tumbler of rum each, and went to our billets, ate, and went to bed. We had the rest of the day off. It was a job I never wanted.[48]

Lodge was the only member of the 19th Battalion who received a sentence of death for his disciplinary transgressions. According to the standards of the day, he was the architect of his own doom with his repeated attempts to escape. Whether his death served as an effective object lesson or deterrent to others in the 19th Battalion is impossible to determine without additional first-hand testimony. Although the crime of desertion was not rife within the 19th Battalion, records show that a steep rise in absence rates did occur in the battalion during December 1917 and January 1918, when Lodge had made his second and third attempts to desert. However, this problem gradually diminished during February and early March, before Lodge's execution, and petered out almost altogether in April, May, and June. The degree to which the virtual elimination of absenteeism in the latter three months resulted from men's fears of being charged with the more serious crime of desertion, or stemmed from the pressure of active operations during the German spring offensive, cannot be established. For a summary and analysis of offences and punishments in the 19th Battalion during the war, see Appendix B.

That carrying out the execution itself was a disturbing and repugnant duty is shown by the reactions of Lt. Switzer and Pte. Barnes. Also, the care taken to visually shield the men of the 19th Battalion from the spectacle of execution, while at the same time forming them up close enough to hear it, indicates a limited willingness on the part of the officers to expose the men to such a difficult "lesson." One gets the impression that the officers may not have fully approved of such extreme penalties but felt bound by the inexorable demands of military law to carry out the sentence on an individual whose actions had flown so deliberately in the face of discipline that they could not be ignored.

Ready for Anything

The 19th Battalion kept up an active training program during its time at Noeux-les-Mines. Within the rifle companies, there was some cross-training as well, with riflemen learning the basics of how to handle a Lewis gun and bombers gaining more experience with rifle grenades. Strict specialization within a platoon could be disadvantageous if, for example, most or all of the Lewis gun section was wiped out in an action.[49] Training was always a chore, but some veterans could appreciate it more in France, especially when compared to the dreariness of training in Canada and England. "Our life is certainly not as monotonous as the training in England or Canada," wrote John Gaetz to his mother, "... although when in the front line, especially these days of uncertainty, there is always more or less of a strain. But when out [of the front line] your training as I said before was not nearly as long or tedious and then there is more of a mutual spirit which makes things pleasanter."[50]

As of 20 March the 19th Battalion reported a trench strength of 28 officers and 783 other ranks. Presumably, this was the number of men available for immediate front-line duty and would not have included support personnel, such as members of the transport section, individuals temporarily absent at training courses, or those who were seconded for duties with other units, services, and staffs. Between 1 January and 31 March 1918 the 19th Battalion would take on 5 officers and 224 other ranks as reinforcements, while sustaining only 17 casualties among the other ranks, 3 of which were fatal. In addition, 3 officers and 160 other ranks were listed as sick during the same period. During the month of March alone, 24 men, who were reported as casualties, rejoined the battalion following their recovery.[51] In terms of available manpower, the battalion was in good shape and ready, in theory, for whatever challenges the future might hold.

16

"It Was Pretty Lively": 21 March–June 1918

On the morning of 21 March 1918, the long-awaited storm finally broke. On the heels of a ferocious five-hour bombardment, storming parties from among over seventy divisions of the German 2nd, 17th, and 18th Armies surged forward through a thick fog. They smashed into the defences held by twenty-six infantry divisions of the British Third and Fifth Armies positioned between Arras and La Fère. Units in the path of the German onslaught reeled under the weight of the assault, the brunt of which fell on Gen. Sir Hubert Gough's Fifth Army. The British had attempted to construct their own defences in depth over the course of the winter. But in Gough's sectors, along the old Somme battlefront, the work had not been completed by the time the Germans struck. Worse, his army was badly understrength, most British reserves having been sent to sectors farther north, which were deemed more vital and vulnerable. Field Marshal Haig had decided he could better afford to give ground in the Fifth Army's sectors than in the region stretching northward from Arras through Flanders. With far fewer troops than he wanted at his disposal, Haig had gambled that the worst of the German blow would fall outside the Fifth Army's domain. The Germans, however, were striking hardest where Haig was weakest, hoping to punch through and envelop the British armies while holding off any French forces that might try to intervene from the south.[1]

By its third day, the offensive, code-named *Michael* by the German high command and known in the popular press as the *Kaiserschlacht* ("Emperor's Battle"),

now attached to company headquarters. The precise reasons for this shift are not stated in surviving battalion records; however, it may have stemmed from existing LOB policy, coupled with the need to retain a certain number of men for labour parties on defensive positions behind the front lines. Whatever the reason, it was deemed preferable to organize all troops available for combat operations into three full-strength platoons per company instead of four weaker ones.[6]

If 19th Battalion records are not clear on the rationale for this shift, it was at least in keeping with similar experiments in company and platoon structure in other British and Canadian formations during late 1917 and early 1918. In his study of the 1st Canadian Division, Kenneth Radley notes that "some Imperial divisions went to a three-section platoon" and that the Canadian Corps also adopted this arrangement for a period of time. Some senior officers, including the commanders of the 1st and 3rd Canadian Divisions, were concerned that the platoon organization of 1917 would not continue to function effectively in the face of heavy casualties. Consequently, Canadian Corps headquarters allowed subordinate commanders to organize their platoons as they saw fit, as had been the case during the winter of 1916–17. Different solutions would be adopted throughout the corps. Not until May 1918 was a standardized platoon establishment instituted by corps headquarters.[7]

At mid-evening on 26 March the 19th Battalion was ordered to march again, this time to Bailleulval. The situation along the British Third Army front near Arras was still volatile. If the Germans ever managed to crash through a nearby section of the front, any battalion caught in the open on the march would be in very real danger of being cut to ribbons. Accordingly, Lt.-Col. Hatch did what he could to protect his unit while on the move, resorting to the time-honoured tactic of sending out flank and rearguard detachments to provide advance warning of any trouble.[8]

"We are going to march 'roughly ten miles' and [are] going straight into action," announced Hatch, just before his men moved out. Hatch, an officer who seems to have relished a good fight, undoubtedly intended to buck up the spirits of his men in this time of uncertainty. But the promise of immediate action at the end of a march probably had precisely the opposite effect. As for his comment on the length of the march, it proved to be wildly optimistic. One battalion veteran remarked later that "'roughly ten miles' became a catch phrase for a march of indeterminate length for long afterwards."[9] Moreover, by the time the men reached Bailleulval there was not enough accommodation for all of them, so they were forced to proceed on to Bailleulmont. Mercifully, after arriving in the early morning hours, they found enough shelter in the village for the entire battalion. Deward Barnes reckoned they had covered "about twenty-five miles – the longest forced march we had had getting from one front to another."[10] "We would have been far better off fighting the battle itself," complained Fred Stitt, "because that slugging in the forced march … it was terrific. We carried everything we owned on our backs. We had to scrounge for rations."[11] Such "scrounging" was done much to the chagrin of local villagers, who protested "the liberties taken with their farm products."[12]

The remainder of 27 March was spent taking a "well-earned rest." The relative calm was rudely broken on the following day when the Germans renewed their offensive against the Third Army's front. On 28 March, Gen. Ludendorff set Operation Mars in motion. This was an attempt to break through the British lines northeast of Arras and outflank the daunting defences around Vimy Ridge. This thrust was the most serious direct threat to the Canadian Corps' position along the Lens–Vimy front. A bad situation was made even worse by the fact that all four Canadian divisions were, at this point, either detached or under orders to be transferred from Lt.-Gen. Currie's control and scattered piecemeal among the reserve forces of various corps in the First and Third Armies. As it turned out, the hard-pressed British divisions in the front lines blunted and finally halted this latest German attack. Currie then took immediate steps to regain control of his own divisions. The 3rd and 4th Canadian Divisions were back under Currie's command by 30 March. A readjustment of corps boundaries would return the 1st Canadian Division to him on 8 April.[13]

Meanwhile, the 2nd Canadian Division remained under British control, having come under the command of VI Corps in Gen. Byng's Third Army on 28 March. The opening of another German offensive to the north (code-named *Georgette*) – this one against British positions along the Lys and Flanders fronts on 9 and 10 April – forced the British to abandon most of the ground they had gained at such appalling cost in the summer and autumn of 1917, including the Passchendaele Ridge. British reserves were being stretched increasingly thin, and this compelled Currie to cease agitating for the return of his 2nd Division. Maj.-Gen. Burstall's men, including those of the 19th Battalion, would stay with VI Corps for the time being.[14] The seriousness of the situation was underscored by Field Marshal Haig in his famous Order of the Day on 11 April. "There is no other course open to us but to fight it out!" he declared. "Every position must be held to the last man: there must be no retirement. With our backs to the wall, and believing in the justice of our cause, each one of us must fight on to the end. The safety of our homes and the freedom of mankind alike depend on the conduct of each one of us at this critical moment."[15] Such purple prose revealed the anxieties of the generals more than they built up the troops' morale.

Earlier, on 27 March, Lt.-Gen. Currie had issued an even more florid appeal to the Canadian Corps. It read in part: "To those who will fall I say, 'You will not die but step into immortality. Your mothers will not lament your fate but will be proud to have borne such sons. Your names will be revered forever and ever by your grateful country and God will take you unto Himself.'" When they were read out to units on parade, Currie's words often were dismissed or ridiculed by the men, who saw them simply as "hot air." Some commanders anticipated this reaction and chose not to read out the order at all.[16] On a copy of the order in the 19th Battalion's records, the paragraph commencing with the words "To those who will fall" is circled and beside it is handwritten, "leave out." Evidently, Lt.-Col. Hatch chose a middle path, reading out the order to his assembled men, probably on 28 March, but choosing to omit the passage most likely to offend their sensibilities.[17]

With British units standing fast in the front lines near Bailleulmont, Hatch and his men were ordered to new positions in the reserve line between Wailly and Ficheux. They reached their destination in the early morning of 29 March, moving into the trench system known as the Purple Line in support of their comrades in 20th Battalion. These moves were part of the 2nd Canadian Division's relief of the 3rd British Division, which was badly in need of rest after holding off determined German attacks. Upon completing the relief on 30 March, the 2nd Canadian Division now held the line on the left portion of VI Corps' front, about four miles south of Arras. The division's frontage extended northward from a point east of Boisleux-Saint-Marc approximately 6,000 yards to a point along the southern slopes of Telegraph Hill, not far from the German-occupied village of Neuville-Vitasse. By that time, the village was "a mere heap of ruins." To the Canadians' right were the Guards Division and the 32nd Division.[18]

The 19th Battalion took its turn in the firing line on 1 April, relieving the 20th Battalion in the right sub-section of the 4th Brigade's frontage, facing Neuville-Vitasse. This was the unit's first front-line tour since the opening of the German offensive on 21 March. It was not a bloodless relief: six casualties had been sustained on the way in, including one man killed. Except for occasional shelling, the following days were relatively quiet, giving the men some time to learn the local topography and German defences. This would change on 4 April when, in retaliation for the Canadians' nightly patrols, the Germans unleashed periodic barrages of artillery and machine-gun fire on the 19th Battalion's trenches.[19]

Not content with standing off and administering punishment from a distance, the Germans upped the ante by raiding 19th Battalion positions on the morning of 5 April. On the heels of a deadly salvo of "rum jars" and concentrated machine-gun barrages, a German raiding party some thirty-five strong split into three groups and assaulted the Canadian positions. Two of the groups managed to reach 19th Battalion advance posts and sap trenches; the third briefly gained a foothold in the front line. But determined Canadian bombing parties drove them back moments later, and the raiders quickly retired in disorder, leaving behind at least nine dead in the front line and strewn across no man's land. Fortunately for the 19th Battalion, only five other ranks were wounded. Corps, division, and brigade commanders lost no time in sending their congratulations for the good work in repelling the raid.[20]

No words of praise would have been as welcome as the sight of the 25th Battalion, which arrived later that day to relieve the 19th in the front line. The 19th Battalion was fortunate, not only because it suffered so few casualties from the enemy attack, but also because its parent formation had been scheduled for relief that same day. The men therefore had a chance to get some real rest immediately after the morning's exertions. Small in scale though the action had been, it was still a harrowing experience for those caught in the middle of it. Deward Barnes remembered a

> new man with us, a young fellow, Jim Latimer (who later on lost an eye). He had made a couple of trips but this was his worst. New men are not so afraid the first trip or two when it is quiet because they don't realize what damage can be done. Latimer used to laugh at the way some of the old timers and others would shake. This time poor Latimer was shaking like a leaf and as white as a ghost.[21]

Under such conditions, the steadiness of veterans like Barnes was essential for the cohesion of the battalion and the morale of its individual members.

"No Rest"

The 4th Brigade moved back into divisional reserve, and the troops of the 19th Battalion were assigned billets in Bailleulmont. On 9 April, the first anniversary of the Canadian victory at Vimy Ridge, and the first day of the German offensive along the Lys front, the 4th Brigade went back to the trenches to relieve the 6th Brigade near Boisleux-Saint-Marc. The 19th Battalion was detailed to the front line again, where it relieved the 28th Battalion in the right sub-section of the brigade front.[22]

The first five days of this week-long tour proceeded routinely enough, albeit with some persistent shelling during the night of 11–12 April. With German forces mounting renewed offensive efforts to the north, along the Lys River and in Flanders, the men in the front lines were nervous and expecting an attack at any time. On the sixth day of the tour, 14 April, the battalion suffered a serious loss with the wounding of its scout officer, Lt. Clendining, during a skirmish in no man's land. Clendining was leading a battle patrol of twenty other ranks in a raid on a German outpost when they were attacked by sixty to seventy Germans rushing to the aid of their comrades. Overwhelmed by numbers and grenades, the Canadians fell back with four wounded, Clendining among them. Fortunately they managed to reach safety without any further injuries, thanks to the covering fire of a nearby Lewis gun team. Clendining would survive his wound, but the battalion had lost his services as scout officer, a position that must have seemed somewhat cursed, given the unfortunate demise of Clendining's predecessor, Lt. Trendell, earlier at Passchendaele. More likely, it was the nature of the position to attract bold men who were unafraid to take personal risks.[23]

On the heels of this short, sharp action came an even more serious incident on 16 April. Two days earlier, the Guards Division had been relieved by the 2nd British Division in the centre sector of VI Corps' front. Whereas the units of the elite Guards Division consisted mainly of seasoned troops, those of the 2nd British

Division contained a large percentage of young recruits hurriedly brought up as reinforcements. It was not known how well these youths with little or no experience would perform in a crisis. Occupying as it did the far right of the 2nd Canadian Division's line, the 19th Battalion was in the best position to observe some of these troops as the 1st Battalion King's Liverpool Regiment took up station on its right flank.

At 9:20 AM the 19th Battalion received word that German raiders had struck part of the front line held by the Liverpools, some of whom were reported to have fled their posts while others stood fast and attempted to make a fight of it. In the tumult and confusion, the raiders forced their way into the trench, destabilizing the entire position and leaving the 19th Battalion's right flank essentially "in the air." Although the number of raiders was said to be small, this was not a situation that the pugnacious Lt.-Col. Hatch could tolerate. He ordered Capt. Maurice C. Roberts of A Company, whose right flank was in jeopardy, to send his support platoon down the British trench, clear out any Germans they encountered, and establish a block to protect their own battalion until the British could remedy the situation. The platoon, led by Lt. George B. Borthwick, advanced approximately 150 yards down the British trench, where they captured a machine gun and three prisoners, and set up their block, fortifying it with three abandoned Lewis guns.

By 11:45 AM, after receiving word of these developments, the Liverpools had dispatched a platoon to reoccupy their old front line. The 19th Battalion was asked to supply a reserve force. Two platoons from C Company were sent in, under cover of a supporting artillery barrage, and the Canadians kept watch at the block for any German movements in the Liverpools' front line. By mid-evening the British had finally regained complete control of their line, and Hatch was able to withdraw his men to their own positions. The cost of this minor action had been relatively heavy for the 19th Battalion. Lt. Borthwick and five other ranks were killed, and eight more other ranks were wounded. When Borthwick was killed by the blast of a German grenade, Lance Sgt. Thomas W. Thatcher and Sgt. Samuel Newell took charge and ably led the platoon for the rest of the day. Also singled out in post-action reports was stretcher-bearer James V. Nicholl, who "worked incessantly throughout the day, looking after his wounded."[24]

Once more, the men of the 19th Battalion were fortunate that their scheduled relief came through later that night. By the morning of 17 April they were resting in billets in Bretencourt. They were given the remainder of the day to recover from what had been a rather hectic tour. But there would be more action to come as the month wore on.[25] On 21 April Hatch's men were rotated forward to support positions. Three days later they were back in the front line, on the right section of the divisional front,where the opposing Germans remained aggressive. They fended off German patrols on the mornings of 26 and 27 April and repulsed a raid on A Company's positions on 28 April. Sniper Bert Sedore, who observed the retreating

Officers of the 19th Battalion, Neuville Vitasse, May 1918. Standing (l. to r.): D.E. Gerrard, V.K. Robertson, R.O. Spreckley, A.P. Fletcher, R. Shiell, J.W. Stewart, J.E. Johnson, [??] Moore, [J.A. or W.T.] McLaren, W.F. Smith, and [W.S. or H.] Herbert. Seated middle (l. to r.): J. O'Neill, R.H.L. Dinsmore, M.C. Roberts, G.H. Applegath, R.P. Saunders, H.C. Hatch, R.H. Bliss, W. Waldrum, J.A. Linton, L.H. MacLellan, A.O. Thompson, A.J. Duncan. Seated front (l. to r.) [A.E. or A.G.] Bell, G.A. Heffernan, A.F. Ogle, J.P. Fitzgerald, H.D. O'Donoghue. [A scrap book in McMaster University Archives features the same photo with a caption listing the surnames of the officers. First initials were determined from other battalion records. In cases where alternative initials are provided in brackets, it means more than one officer with that surname was serving in the battalion during May 1918.] (LAC PA-002702)

raiders from his isolated post, claimed five kills before the rest of the Germans reached safety.[26] This would have been good news for Hatch, but for the fact that three of his men were now missing and presumed captured by the Germans.[27] This sort of boldness and persistence on the part of the enemy was not something to which the 19th Battalion was accustomed. It was high time to take the fight back to the Germans, and what better way than by launching a raid of their own?

The venture, carried out in cooperation with the 21st Battalion, was a complex operation involving the coordinated efforts of four parties from the 19th Battalion alone. The target was the German outpost line in Neuville-Vitasse. Each raiding party was detailed to a specific initial objective, such as an outpost or a machine-gun nest, before moving on to the final objective, the sunken road running through Neuville-Vitasse. The raid commenced at precisely 2:00 AM on 29 April. With effective artillery support, the raiding parties engaged several German machine-gun nests, killing and dispersing their crews with bombs and bayonets. "On the whole, the Germans put up a poor fight," concluded the battalion war diarist, "numbers of them running away and being caught in our artillery barrage. All parties were back in our support line by 2:45 AM," along with six prisoners and two captured machine guns.[28]

Canadians digging reserve trenches, May 1918. (LAC PA-003802)

The raid was rated an outstanding success. No officers were wounded, and of the eleven other ranks who were, five were deemed only "slightly wounded," and the injuries suffered by two more were so minor that they remained at duty. Congratulations poured in from all quarters, including Gen. Byng. These kudos were followed up by the greater reward of a relief and a well-earned rest in billets at Basseux and Bailleulval.[29]

While the men may have needed a break, however brief, from their physical and mental exertions, the 19th Battalion remained unwilling to rest on its laurels. The unit demonstrated its willingness to experiment during a front-line tour just north and east of the hamlet of Boisleux-Saint-Marc. In the early morning hours of 15 May, Hatch's infantry cooperated with a Stokes mortar crew from the 4th Canadian Trench Mortar Battery, which accompanied two of their battle patrols. Each patrol moved forward and took up stations in different saps; meanwhile, the mortar crew sneaked into position some 400 yards ahead of the Canadian front line and opened fire on a German machine-gun post. Of the thirty Stokes rounds fired, fifteen scored direct hits. It was hoped that this would draw out an enemy patrol, which could then be ambushed by one or both of the battle patrols, the object being to inflict casualties and secure prisoners. The Germans wisely chose not to oblige the Canadians. But the mortar crew did silence the machine gun, and all ranks managed to return to their own lines with no casualties.[30]

Later that day, the 19th Battalion was relieved in the front lines by the 26th Battalion and moved back with the rest of the 4th Brigade into divisional reserve. The 19th was billeted in a camp at Bretencourt, where it remained for the next week.

The weather was perfect for training and recreation, with clear skies and temperatures that anticipated the rapidly approaching summer season.

Some reorganization was carried out at this time. On 18 May, Lt.-Col. Hatch ordered each company to reorganize itself on a four-platoon basis. As with the shift to a three-platoon structure earlier in March, the reason for this reversion to the original four-platoon arrangement is not clearly stated in battalion records. It likely stemmed from a desire for greater structural uniformity among different battalions, especially when adequate manpower was available. Indeed, the Canadian Corps that same month was implementing a standard platoon organization throughout its formations. From May through to the end of the war, Canadian platoons would consist of two sections of riflemen and rifle grenadiers and two sections of Lewis gunners. Although the 19th Battalion and its parent formations were still separated from the rest of the Canadian Corps, the reversion to a four-platoon company structure may have been intended to complement the corps' standardized organization of sections within each platoon. Under normal circumstances, infantry battalions would continue to organize themselves on the basis of four companies, each containing four platoons, each of which, in turn, featured four sections.[31]

Whatever the rationale for this change, Hatch's orders had been carried out by the time the battalion held its church parade on Sunday, 19 May, the day before it was drawn up for inspection by Lt.-Col. W. Rae, the general staff officer in charge of training at 2nd Canadian Division headquarters. Rae pronounced himself "very pleased with the appearance of the Battalion."[32] For the senior staff, a unit's efficiency was still measured as much by the quality of its discipline and turnout as by its tactical skill.

The sojourn in divisional reserve ended on 22 May, when the 4th Brigade relieved 6th Brigade in the left section of the divisional front, facing Neuville-Vitasse. The 19th Battalion returned again to the front line, taking over the right sub-section of the brigade front from the 27th Battalion. The battalion occupied the front line with three platoons per company and at a total strength of 23 officers and 612 other ranks. Those who were designated LOB from their companies – four officers and 105 other ranks in all – were left in billets at Bailleulval; an additional 3 officers and 86 other ranks were attached to a divisional work party and billeted at Wailly.

The German artillery was highly aggressive during this six-day tour in the front lines, especially after 25 May. The 19th Battalion's front and support lines were bombarded regularly by a variety of ordnance, including overhead shrapnel and gas shells. This made the men's lives more miserable than usual. Although the unit war diary reported only "slight" casualties during this period, postwar records indicate that the battalion's heaviest losses of the month came between 22 and 28 May. Of the 4 officers and 47 other ranks listed as casualties in May, 1 officer and 27 other ranks were killed or wounded during this tour alone.

The 20th Battalion relieved the 19th in the front lines on 28 May. The latter unit moved back into the right sub-section support area for the next six days. Just after midnight on 3 June, the battalion received a brief but grim reminder of its recent tour in the front lines when the support area was heavily bombarded with gas shells for about an hour. No casualties were reported, which indicates that security measures against gas were functioning well within the battalion, especially with regard to individual discipline in the proper use of respirators.[33] Later that same day, the 25th Battalion arrived to take over the support positions and the men of the 19th Battalion moved back with the rest of the 4th Brigade into divisional reserve, where they spent the next six days at Bellacourt. Afternoon sporting events were all the more popular during the continued run of fine warm weather. Even though the entire division was still separated from its normal parent formation, elimination contests were held to determine which teams and individuals would attend the upcoming Canadian Corps Sports Day, to be held on 1 July.[34]

On 9 June the 4th Brigade was ordered back to the lines to relieve the 6th Brigade in the right section of the divisional front, with the 19th Battalion detailed to replace the 28th Battalion in the brigade's right sub-section support lines. The troops were kept busy, and the tour proceeded quietly enough, with no noteworthy enemy activity.[35] Serving with the 19th Battalion at this time was Maj. Armour A. Miller, who had come up from the Canadian Corps Reinforcement Camp on 24 May and was attached to the battalion for a period of active service in the front lines. Until 28 February, Miller had been commanding officer of the 134th Battalion from Toronto, which was disbanded in England after the breakup of its parent formation, the 5th Canadian Division. Miller was not content to retain his lieutenant-colonelcy and return home without having seen any action. So, like many senior officers who found themselves without a command, he accepted a reduction in rank in exchange for the chance to do his bit at the front.[36] As it turned out, Miller seems to have fit in very well with the 19th Battalion, and like many officers and men, he took what opportunity he could to inform his family at home of what he saw and heard around him. To his wife, he wrote:

> The chief subject of conversation one hears is talking about the friends at home … and the fine times one is going to have after the beastly war is over. There is no spirit of discontent shown by the men either in their conversation or letters. On the other hand, [there is] a sincere confidence that we are winning and everything will finish all right but a lot of the older men in the Company are longing for their homes and families.

After describing the month's weather as "glorious" and offering some mild complaints about having to wear the same clothes all the time, he turned to the routines of an officer's life on the support lines:

> The irregular hours get me sometimes. We are up most of the nights and once in 3 or 4 nights I go out with a working party from the Company digging trenches anywhere

> from a mile or two away ... Stand-to at daybreak when everybody is on the alert and breakfast at 4 AM. Then sleep until noon and lunch at about 2:00. Then wash up and shave, write letters, or censor the men's letters, read a newspaper if there is one anywhere from 2 days to two months old. It does not matter whether it is from London or Calgary it is equally interesting. Supper at 9 PM and then routine over again.
>
> There is always a certain amount of [action] ... Someone starts a strafe and [then] all the guns start or occasionally a new gun starts away miles in rear. We get to know their different barks or the different tone of the shells as they go over. Some shriek like the souls of the damned and some like rustling maple trees and the big fellows like a railway train passing overhead. Then Heine plunks over a few and ... we have a laugh when we see them send a dozen in succession into a harmless field. Then some of our planes go over and Heine's archies go after them and the same with ours. So there is always something interesting going on.[37]

On 15 June, Lt.-Col. Hatch was ordered to move his men up into the front-line trenches, where they relieved the 18th Battalion in the brigade's right sub-section. Enemy activity again was minimal, in marked contrast to the battalion's previous front-line and support tours. Patrols actively scoured no man's land by night but detected scarcely a sign of their opponents. This period of relative calm was finally broken on 19 June, when German artillery proved more active than usual (likely in response to a raid carried out by the 16th Battalion, Lancashire Fusiliers, stationed on the 19th Battalion's right flank). This was followed up the next day by a successful joint raid carried out by the 20th and 21st Battalions from positions on the 19th Battalion's left. With the pace of raiding stepped up on both flanks, it was decided that the 19th Battalion should mount an effort of its own.[38]

The impulse for this raid, in terms of its timing, design, and objectives, probably came from the battalion itself – whether from Lt.-Col. Hatch or from one or more of his subordinates is not clear.[39] But it certainly was in keeping with the prevailing policy of maximum aggression in patrolling, sniping, machine gunnery, and capturing prisoners. Gen. Byng and British Third Army headquarters called for constant harassment of the Germans in order to gain intelligence and (it was hoped) dissuade them from further offensive efforts. As a result, Maj.-Gen. Burstall and his brigade commanders directed their battalions to give the Germans opposing them "no rest."[40]

There indeed would be little rest for either the 19th Battalion or the German troops opposite them in the pre-dawn hours of 21 June 1918. The raiders' objective was the German outpost line, the main feature of which was a trench that stretched southward from the Cojeul River (a tiny watercourse that ran eastward, just north of Boisleux-Saint-Marc) to a sunken road that led back towards the Canadian lines. The plan for the 19th Battalion raid was characteristically sophisticated, in keeping with the level of experience its veteran personnel had accrued. But it usually took more than determination, preparation, and a clever plan to bring off a successful

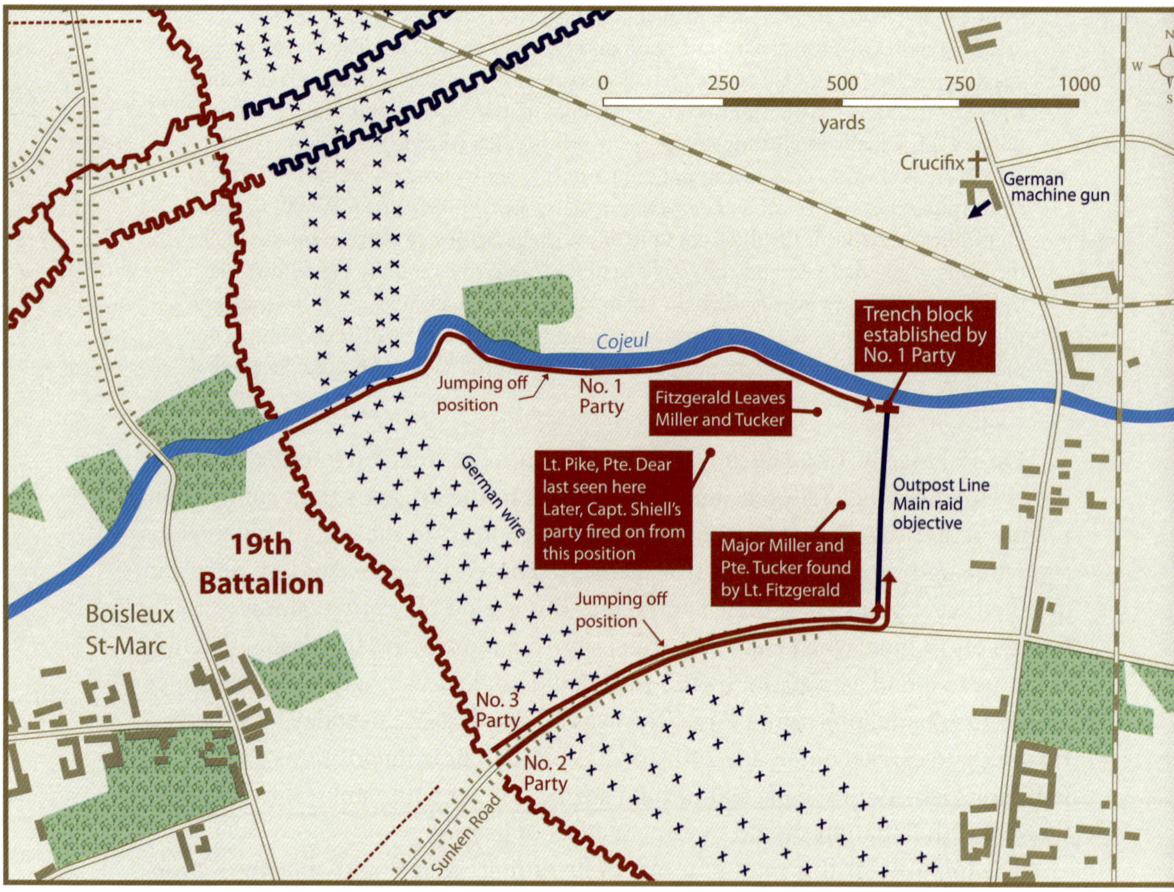

Map 17 – Trench raid, 21 June 1918.

raid. Luck was also needed. Unfortunately, for a number of men in the raiding party, their luck ran out that morning.

The operation was carried out by 5 officers and 110 other ranks from D Company, under the overall command of Lt, James A. McLaren. As was the case with most such ventures, the raiders were subdivided into various smaller parties, each of which had its own assignment. No. 1 party, consisting of thirty-three men from No. 13 Platoon, plus four battalion scouts, under the command of Lt. John R. Holk,[41] was ordered to proceed along the Cojeul River to the northern end of the targeted portion of the German outpost line and establish a block manned by riflemen and rifle grenadiers. Their job was to secure the flank and assist the other two parties in the collection of prisoners and the evacuation of wounded. Lt. James P. Fitzgerald led the thirty-two men of No. 15 Platoon that made up No. 2 party. They were detailed to move northeast along the sunken road until they reached the German trench. Upon doing so, they were to work their way north, behind this trench, driving the enemy garrison towards the river and the waiting arms of No. 1 party at the block. Maj. Armour Miller volunteered to command No. 3 party, which comprised thirty-four men of No. 16 Platoon. This group was ordered to proceed down the sunken road and then northward towards the river through the German trench, clearing it from the inside. Accompanying this party was the battalion scout officer, Lt. Walter F. Smith, and seven scouts, whose job was to move down the German trench to an adjoining hedge, along which they were to locate and clear a large dugout.[42]

The parties moved forward and by 1:30 AM were assembled at their jumping-off positions about halfway across no man's land. Each man was armed with two Mills bombs, 120 rounds of ammunition, and blackened bayonets. At zero hour, exactly ten minutes later, the supporting artillery laid down a box barrage, isolating the raiders' objectives, and each party dashed forward to carry out its assignment. No. 1 party, under Lt. Holk, encountered no resistance and easily established its block where the German trench met the riverbank. Holk and his men then took up their stations and kept watch for the approach of the other parties and any prisoners they swept before them.[43] Meanwhile, No. 2 party under Lt. Fitzgerald encountered heavier opposition from a German post. Three members of the stubborn little garrison of five were killed outright and the remaining two were taken in hand by Sgt. Alfred Curbishley, who hustled them north towards the block at the river. Along the way, Curbishly seems to have encountered another German concealed in a shell hole. Pte. Frederick Solvisburg of No. 3 party later reported witnessing Curbishley "battling with three Huns. One got out of a shell hole and the Sergeant grabbed him with his hands and both fired. The Sergeant staggered away and the Hun fell." Evidently unable to keep up with his two prisoners, Curbishley promptly shot them, rather than see them escape. Sgt. George Walley then came to Curbishley's aid, helping him back to Canadian lines and the nearest dressing station.[44]

At the same time, No. 3 party moved quickly but cautiously down the German trench, surprised to find no opposition. No. 2 party likewise encountered no further resistance behind the trench. Seeing that its task was complete, it made a break for the river. Around this time, four Germans were seen running from a hedge down the river, but they were caught in the Canadian barrage and presumed killed. The German artillery had opened up with a rather scattered retaliatory bombardment at two minutes after zero hour. At first, this did not seem to pose much of a threat to the raiders. Of more immediate concern for the Canadians was an enemy machine gun on the other side of the river, which sprayed the area with bullets.[45]

Lt. Fitzgerald paused to take account of his party members as they sped by on their way to the river. After most of them passed, he noticed two men farther behind, some twenty yards from a hedge near the German trench. One of them was clearly wounded and was being helped along by the other. The two figures suddenly stumbled and fell into a shell hole. Instead of following his own party, which already was making its way along the river back towards Canadian lines, Fitzgerald ran over to the shell hole to assist the other two men. When he reached them, he saw that the wounded man was Maj. Miller, the leader of No. 3 party, who was being helped along by Pte. George A. Tucker of Fitzgerald's own party. Miller had been wounded in the legs and stomach by shrapnel from an exploding shell, which apparently had also felled three other members of No. 3 party: Ptes. Alexander McPhail, Arthur W. Cane, and Harold S. White. After the raid, no trace was found of these three men, and they were presumed killed or taken prisoner.[46]

Fitzgerald and Tucker grabbed Miller, one on each side, and helped him along. They did not get very far before Miller collapsed, unable to stay on his feet. Fitzgerald then got down on all fours and Tucker hoisted the stricken Miller onto Fitzgerald's back. Acting as a "human stretcher," Fitzgerald hoped he could crawl far enough to get Miller to safety. Tucker crouched and moved alongside, helping to steady the major's body on the lieutenant's back. They moved by stages for approximately 175 yards before Miller finally lost the strength to cling to Fitzgerald's back and Tucker likewise became exhausted. The shelling and machine-gun fire increased in intensity, and Fitzgerald saw no other option but to position Miller under cover in a shell hole near the riverbank. Leaving Tucker to watch over the wounded major, Fitzgerald struck out for the Canadian lines to find more help in evacuating the two men he had just left behind.[47]

Within thirty minutes of zero hour, the remaining members of all three parties had made it back to the Canadian trenches. Everyone from No. 1 party was accounted for. But Maj. Miller and Ptes. McPhail, Cane, and White were missing from No. 3 party, while Lt. Fitzgerald and Ptes. Tucker and Charles C. Partridge were missing from No. 2 party. Fitzgerald and Tucker had stayed behind to assist Miller, and as for Partridge, he was last seen near the junction of the sunken road and the German trench. He had fallen in what appeared to be a thicket of barbed wire. In the ensuing tumult, his comrades lost track of him. It would never be learned what became of him.[48]

While those who had already returned safely to the Canadian trenches anxiously awaited word of their missing comrades, Lt. Fitzgerald struggled to bring back news of Miller and Tucker. He made it to the Cojeul River, which Joe O'Neill recalled as being

> a narrow river; in this country we'd call it a creek. Jimmy [Fitzgerald] managed to get into that river … The Germans got on him, and he was lying on his back under the water and just sticking his nose up and that's how he crawled on his back. When Jimmy got into us he was hardly able to stand. Frankly I thought he was almost dead, and he told us the story where Miller was and all the rest of it. Well one of our officers, a chap by the name of Abe Pike had been with Miller in Canada and he knew him, so he said "I'll take a party out and we'll find him."[49]

The exhausted Fitzgerald had delivered his news just after 3:00 AM. Right away, Lt. Abraham B. Pike, Sgt. Clifford D. Windsor, and Ptes. William B. Perry and Henry R. Dear of B Company set out to locate Miller and Tucker, based on Fitzgerald's general description of where he had left the two men. The four men crept along the Cojeul River, and when they reached a point near No. 1 party's jumping-off position for the raid earlier that morning, Pike ordered Windsor and Perry to sit tight and serve as a covering party while he and Dear forged ahead. Pike and Dear made it to a hedge about halfway between the German outpost line and the point where they left Windsor and Perry. Then they disappeared, never to be seen again. The only clue to their fate was the ominous sound of revolver shots that rang out just after they moved through the hedge.[50]

With the number of casualties and disappearances sustained so far, and Maj. Miller still lying wounded somewhere in or near German lines, the morning was shaping up to be a disaster for the 19th Battalion. After Pike and his party had been out for some time, another small group from B Company, made up of Capt. Robert Shiell, Lt. Arthur Duncan, and Pte. (acting Lance Cpl.) William H. Pace, set out to determine what was going on.[51] Pace was a company cook and former scout who had come up to the front line to observe the raid. When he heard of Miller's plight, he lobbied Lt. Joe O'Neill to be included in the rescue party.[52] Pace, Shiell, and Duncan reconnoitred the ground in front of the Canadian wire and eventually came upon Windsor and Perry, who told them about the disappearance of Pike and Dear. As the sun began to rise, no man's land became more dangerous for the five rescuers, who found themselves under increasingly heavy rifle and machine-gun fire from ahead and on both flanks. Since Shiell was not confident in his knowledge of the terrain farther ahead, he decided to go back to the Canadian lines, find Lt. Fitzgerald, and get a better sense of where Maj. Miller and Pte. Tucker were located.[53]

Putting his old scouting skills to good use, Pace pushed on ahead by himself, with Duncan, Windsor, and Perry following at a distance. He crept forward some 300 yards through heavy machine-gun fire and finally came upon the shell hole where Miller lay. The officer by now was in very bad shape, and Pace immediately re-dressed his wounds and called back to Duncan for assistance. "Between them," Shiell later wrote, "they were able to get the Colonel back to our lines in spite of machine gun fire and he had his wounds treated by the stretcher-bearer." (Shiell had served under Miller in the 134th Battalion and still referred to his former commanding officer by his old rank.)[54] O'Neill later recounted that to rescue Miller, "Bill [Pace] got down on his hands and knees and got Miller by the collar, and loaded him on his back. He crawled all the way through and across no man's land, and over to our line. How he did it is one of the freakish things." Even more astonishing is that according to O'Neill, Pace and Miller had gone that distance

Major Armour A. Miller
(48th Highlanders Museum)

under heavy fire without being hit: "I put my finger in 21 bullet holes in that man's [Pace's] clothes. He didn't have one single scratch. Seems unbelievable but it's true."[55] Whether O'Neill's story is true or not, the efforts of Pace and the others in finding and rescuing Miller stood out as a remarkable feat of bravery. O'Neill also stated that he recommended Pace for a VC or a DCM, but in the end all Pace received was a Military Medal, presumably because the story of his exploit seemed incredible.[56]

Miller had been found, but there was still more work to be done, for there was no sign of Pike and Dear; nor was Tucker, who had been left to care for Miller, anywhere to be found. So Lt. Duncan once more went out into no man's land, this time with Sgts. Clifford Windsor and Robert Hollidge, to look for the missing men. They moved quickly down the sunken road on the battalion's southern boundary and hunted northward along one of the hedges situated some distance in front of the German trench. Reaching a spot close to where Pike and Dear were last seen, the party called out their names but received no answer. Then they moved eastward, towards the area where Miller had been found, shouting Pike's name. The only response they received was some sniping fire from the Germans. Undaunted, Duncan and the two sergeants continued scouring no man's land, first in the area inside the hedge and then along the ground between the hedge and the Canadian wire, but to no avail. All they found were the bodies of a number of Germans who appeared to have been killed three or four days earlier. The three disappointed men returned to Canadian lines.[57]

Meanwhile, Miller's injuries were tended to by Capt. Herbert Allison, the battalion medical officer. Also in attendance was Lt. James McLaren, the officer commanding D Company and the overall commander of the morning raid. Miller was still able to talk and reported to both Allison and McLaren that he had either seen or heard Pike and another man (who would have been Dear) approach the shell hole in which he and Tucker were sheltered. Miller had then ordered Tucker to go out and meet Pike. But just as Tucker left the shell hole, Miller observed with dismay a party of ten Germans on the move in the same vicinity. Nobody came back to the shell hole, and Miller assumed that Tucker, Pike, and Dear had been captured. Given his extremely weakened condition, Miller was unable to give any further details. He died later that day at No. 3 Canadian Stationary Hospital at Doullens.[58]

The 19th Battalion had every reason to be frustrated with the results of its latest raiding effort: one officer dead from wounds (Maj. Miller), one other rank wounded (Sgt. Curbishley), and one officer and six other ranks missing and presumed dead or captured (Lt. Pike and Ptes. McPhail, Cane, White, Partridge, Dear, and Tucker). Of the seven missing men, it was determined later that that only White was killed in action, although his body was never recovered. The other six were taken prisoner. One of them, Tucker, died in captivity on 10 November 1918, the day before the armistice was declared.[59]

Pinpointing exactly what went wrong is difficult. The fact that the German trench was largely unoccupied when the raiders struck could indicate that the Canadians had misjudged the strength at which the position was held or that the Germans had expected the operation and pulled all but a skeleton garrison out of the area, leaving it to their artillery and nearby machine-gun nests to thwart the raiders. Also, the fact that a large dugout, which Lt. Smith and his scouts were supposed to clear out, "did not exist" at the location where it was supposed to be shows that the 19th Battalion's intelligence on the state of the German positions was not entirely accurate.[60] Nevertheless, Lt.-Col. Hatch concluded in his official report that "the operation throughout was skillfully planned and very well carried out."[61]

Hatch's comments might appear to be a disingenuous attempt to cover up possible failures and to place the best possible "spin" on a bad situation. But a consideration of the known facts leads to the conclusion that the operation was simply a victim of bad luck. Intelligence regarding the German positions may not have been perfect, but battlefield intelligence rarely ever is. The only element of the German defences that presented any challenge was the five-man post encountered by No. 2 party, but this was quickly cleared out and its garrison neutralized. The main features of the German outpost line were well enough known that all three parties were able to carry out their assignments and negotiate their way through the positions in the dark at high speed with little apparent difficulty. The real trouble

Opposite and above: Canadians coming out of the line after a raid. These three images were taken during 1917 in the vicinity of Avion. They effectively portray the exhaustion and relief felt by men who survived a raid. (LAC PA-001814, PA-001670, and PA-001669)

began when a shrapnel shell burst unfortunately close to No. 3 party, killing White, wounding Miller, and probably wounding McPhail and Cane. The attempts to help Miller resulted in the capture of three more men – Pike, Dear, and Tucker.

The raid was a failure, in terms of both the number of Germans captured, which was none, and the number of casualties sustained by the raiding party itself, which was nine.[62] The greater calamity for the 19th Battalion was the loss of its own men, and seven of the nine individuals who were killed, wounded, or taken prisoner met their fates either directly or indirectly as a result of the chance effect of a single shrapnel shell. It is unclear whether this shell was fired by German or Canadian gunners. Ralph Whitney, who served in No. 1 party during the raid, claimed after the war that "our own box barrage cooped us in and inflicted most of our casualties."[63] But according to Lt.-Col. Hatch, "our box barrage was very efficient and all ranks spoke in the highest praise of it."[64] Given the propensity for artillery rounds to fall short, it is perfectly possible that Miller and his men were victims of "friendly fire." It is also possible that the box barrage was laid down too close to the area targeted by the raiders (as Whitney implies), but this cannot be confirmed. In any case, if the artillery had erred, Hatch would have had every right to complain about it in his report. There were no constraints on him doing so. But he did not. Ever since the Battle of the Somme, Canadian infantry officers and other ranks had been more than willing to let their superiors know when their own guns were firing short. The simple fact is that raids, like any other military operation, were risky ventures. No matter how well they were planned, their success depended on a certain amount of luck. In the final analysis, luck was not with the 19th Battalion on the morning of 21 June 1918.

Returning to the Fold

As the 19th Battalion mourned its losses, orders came authorizing its relief by the 26th Battalion. The 4th Brigade was moved back to divisional reserve later in the day on 21 June, and the 19th Battalion trudged into billets at Bellacourt. The following day, Brig.-Gen. Rennie convened a meeting of all those involved in the raid to "investigate the circumstances under which one officer and six men were missing." There is no evidence of any official recriminations arising from this investigation, so Rennie appears to have been satisfied that the losses did not stem from negligence or poor leadership.[65]

That same day, 22 June, also saw Lt.-Col. Lionel Millen reassume command of the battalion following his extended leave to Canada. Although his wife Edith was still seriously ill, she was undergoing treatment and Millen evidently felt able to return to his battalion. He actually had arrived at the front several days earlier, while the 19th Battalion was embarking on its latest, ill-starred tour on the front lines,[66] and he immediately settled down to oversee his battalion's duties in the reserve area. Since the beginning of his absence in mid-February, a lot had happened to the battalion. But if his men were becoming weary from their exertions since the kickoff of the German offensives in March, at least Millen was fresh, having been spared the pressures of command during a stressful period. He saw to it that all ranks were afforded plenty of opportunity to unwind during their time in reserve; training activities were limited to the mornings; afternoons and evenings were given over to sports and other recreations.[67]

It had been an exhausting spring for the 19th Battalion and the rest of the 2nd Canadian Division, and a harrowing time for the Allied cause generally. Since 21 March, the Germans had launched ferocious blows against the British front astride the Somme and Lys rivers. But although they had dented the British line, the Germans had failed to achieve a breakthrough that would win the war for them. Instead, Gen. Ludendorff's forces had carved out two huge salients, which they would now have to defend. Subsequent offensives mounted against the French armies along the Aisne and Matz river fronts on 27 May and 9 June likewise produced dramatic early gains. But these efforts also ground to a halt in the face of increasingly effective resistance, buttressed by the rapidly growing American Expeditionary Force.[68]

By 25 June, the Germans held a front roughly 317 miles long, as opposed to the approximately 242 miles of line they had occupied on 20 March. They would make some further gains along the Marne later in mid-July, but these final successes would be short-lived; the French would be launching their own decisive counter-offensive on 18 July. Thus, although the series of offensives orchestrated by Ludendorff in 1918 resulted in the greatest territorial gains on the Western Front in the shortest span of time since 1914, in the end they left the German army weaker than ever. After suffering initial shocks and setbacks, the Allied forces fought back with growing tenacity so that the Germans paid dearly for their conquests. Between 21 March and mid-July, the Germans suffered between 800,000 and 1,000,000 casualties. The Allies had suffered equally heavily, losing around 900,000 men, but the Allies could cope far better with such losses, for they had much greater reserves of manpower than the Germans. By mid-summer, the German army in France and Belgium was stretched across a front that was much longer and more poorly defended than ever before. It would take time for them to construct new positions to match the strength of the ones that now sat far to their rear, such as the formidable Hindenburg Line. But with the Allies regrouping for an offensive of their own, time was what the Germans were running out of, even more quickly than men.[69]

During the last week of June, the long-awaited plans for the return of the 2nd Canadian Division to the Canadian Corps finally materialized, as brigades of the 3rd Canadian Division arrived to carry out the relief. On 28 June, the 19th Battalion moved to Habarcq, where they entered GHQ reserve and finally get a chance to enjoy some real rest. The following day being a Sunday, all ranks assembled for a brigade church parade. In attendance was N.W. Rowell, the president of the Canadian Privy Council, who was touring the front with Prime Minister Borden and other Canadian officials. After listening to an address by Rowell, the troops were dismissed. They later attended bath parades, not having had an opportunity to get cleaned up since moving into billets.[70]

Losses in the battalion had been somewhat lighter in June than during the previous two months, even factoring in the casualties sustained in the raid on 21 June. In all, 14 other ranks were killed in action, 1 officer and 6 other ranks died of wounds, 1 officer and 6 other ranks were missing, and 20 other ranks were wounded. Also, 2 officers and 22 other ranks were listed as sick or invalided to England. To make up for these losses, 6 officers and 69 other ranks joined the battalion that month as reinforcements, along with 37 returned veterans who completed their convalescence from injury or illness.[71]

During their three months of service outside the Canadian Corps in the lines near Arras, the 19th Battalion had sustained battle casualties amounting to 8 officers and 166 other ranks. In the same time frame, the 2nd Canadian Division as a whole suffered 2,767 casualties (120 officers and 2,647 other ranks) during its service in the Third Army with VI Corps. Considering that neither the entire division nor any of its units had been engaged in any protracted large-scale battles, these losses were considerable, especially when compared to those sustained by the other units and formations of the Canadian Corps, which collectively numbered approximately 185 officers and 2,556 other ranks.[72] The much lower casualty rate for the other Canadian divisions stemmed from the fact that, ever since 7 May, the Canadian Corps had been stationed in GHQ reserve in the First Army area, where its personnel rested, retrained, and reorganized. This aroused some resentment among members of the 2nd Canadian Division. Ed Youngman complained after the war that "even today ... you still hear [that] some of the men ... in the 2nd Division thought that we got a bit of a raw deal because the other three Canadian Divisions were taking it nice and easy while we were being pounded to bits on that front."[73]

But the 2nd Canadian Division also inflicted considerable punishment on its German opponents. During the division's ninety-two days in the line with VI Corps, its units executed twenty-seven raids and wore down the German 26th Reserve Division and 185th Infantry Division, reducing both, in Maj.-Gen. Burstall's words, to a "state of docility."[74] In short order, other troops were referring to Burstall's men as "master raiders."[75] "We started an aggressive campaign, for which the Canadians were more or less famous," remarked the 19th Battalion's Fred Stitt. In such raids, he explained,

> you ... do as much possible damage as there is to be done and kill as many men as you can, and bring back as many live ones as you can for interrogation. We harassed them continuously. It got so they expected a raid every night. That was one of the things [Gen. Byng] was pleased about, because of our aggressive attitude, although we were supposed to be the defending troops.[76]

Similarly, Joe O'Neill said that the "Germans were all hepped up with their enormous successes and they were all for widening their salient and going places ... It was up to us to put him in his place, because there was an unwritten rule in the Canadian Corps, everybody observed it, that we had to have control of no man's land." O'Neill also pointed out that the 2nd Canadian Division and the British divisions it was serving alongside were each "trying to outdo the other" in raiding and patrol exploits. "Well we had a lot of fun down there," O'Neill remarked years later, and with perceptible irony. "It was pretty lively."[77]

Although the 19th Battalion, like other units of the 2nd Canadian Division, was tired by the end of June, it was by no means worn out to the point of being ineffectual. It had not benefited from the extended phase of rest and training that units in the other Canadian divisions had enjoyed, but its experiences near Arras, mounting constant surveillance and battle patrols, launching two full-scale raids, and fending off a number of German raids, constituted a rigorous period of combat conditioning that may have toughened those who survived it with bodies and emotions intact. James Pedley, an officer from the 4th Battalion of the 1st Canadian Division, recalled visiting with a friend, Lt. Arthur Duncan of the 19th Battalion, after the latter unit had returned to the Canadian Corps. "Like the rest of the 19th crowd," Pedley observed, "Art was gaunt and hard, the result of hard line work. He looked well, though, and had not lost the capacity to enjoy himself in good company."[78] If Duncan was typical of the average battalion member, then it might be said that those experiences that hadn't killed them had made them stronger for the trials to come.

17

Prelude to Victory: July–7 August 1918

After a gruelling three-month stint of trench warfare in the Third Army, it was a relief for the men of the 19th Battalion and the rest of the 2nd Canadian Division to be out of the lines and back with the Canadian Corps. Little did they know, at the beginning of July 1918, that they were on the threshold of the longest and hardest period of sustained fighting in the entire war. The German spring offensives had already shaken the Western Front's deadlock; now the Allies, bolstered by growing American manpower, were preparing their great riposte.

Planning for the counterstroke was made easier by the appointment (earlier, on 26 March) of French general Ferdinand Foch as supreme commander of the Allied armies. Foch would help coordinate the efforts of the various national army groups, which remained under the authority of their respective commanders-in-chief (Douglas Haig for the British, Philippe Pétain for the French, and John J. Pershing for the Americans). Foch's broad aim was to execute rapid, concentrated, and successive blows against key German sectors along the Western Front, thereby confounding the movement of their reserves and threatening their lines of communication.[1] The Canadian Corps, and with it the 19th Battalion, would play a prominent part in carrying out this strategic vision.

Bigger and Stronger

The Canadian Corps had strengthened itself during the first half of 1918, absorbing reinforcements from England and reorganizing some of its arms and services.

Band entering the grounds at the Canadian Corps sports meet, 1 July 1918. (LAC PA-003160)

Lt.-Gen. Currie ordered the restructuring of engineering forces, creating strong engineering brigades in each of the four divisions. This improved the organization of engineering efforts within the corps; it also helped relieve infantry battalions of much routine labour.[2] The numbers of heavy machine guns in each division were increased, from sixty-four to ninety-six, allowing for the creation of new divisional machine-gun battalions.[3] And beginning in May, more Lewis guns were issued so that each infantry battalion would be equipped with thirty-six. This permitted a distribution of two Lewis guns to each platoon, plus four to battalion headquarters for anti-aircraft work. With these changes, the automatic firepower available to each platoon commander was doubled, and he could now deploy his platoon into two tactically viable half-platoons, each comprising a section of riflemen and rifle grenadiers and a section of Lewis gunners.[4] For the remainder of the war, the Canadian Corps would maintain this standardized platoon structure. On paper, a Canadian division, with twelve reinforced infantry battalions and a new machine-gun battalion, had more personnel and more automatic firepower than either a British or a German division. This gave the Canadians a clear advantage in striking capacity and endurance that would serve them extremely well in the hard campaigning to come.[5]

Training, Tactics, and Hijinks

On arriving at Habarcq on 28 June, the men of the 19th Battalion looked forward to the next two weeks of rest in GHQ reserve. The period was enlivened by a huge

Two aerial views of the Canadian Corps sports meet at Tincques, 1 July 1918.
(LAC PA-003227 and 003236)

The Duke of Connaught (left) and First Army GOC Sir Henry Horne. (LAC PA-001904)

Canadian Corps sports meet, held at the village of Tincques on 1 July. Almost 50,000 Canadians attended, along with a galaxy of senior officers and VIPs, among them the Duke of Connaught, Prime Minister Borden, and the American commander-in-chief, Gen. Pershing.[6] Although 19th Battalion men had no entries from their own unit to cheer for in the events on 1 July, their transport section did them proud several days later when they took top honours in the divisional horse show on 4 July and third place in the infantry transport competition at VI Corps' horse show on 11 July.[7]

Unfortunately, these happier events were soon overshadowed by the spectre of influenza, which reared its ugly head among the ranks of the 19th Battalion during early July. This was no ordinary bout of the flu but a deadly viral strain that may have originated in China during the winter of 1917–18.[8] It spread like wildfire around the globe, aided greatly by the mass movements of workers and military personnel from continent to continent.[9] By the time it mysteriously disappeared in 1919, influenza had claimed perhaps more than fifty million lives worldwide. It became known popularly as the "Spanish flu" because Spain was one of the first countries to widely publicize the outbreak.[10] In the 19th Battalion, Ralph Whitney remembered that "everybody [was] getting sick with flu, [but] they mostly got better in about 48 hours." He even claimed that it actually "killed no one" in his unit, although this would not remain the case later, in 1919.[11] Although over 45,000 Canadian soldiers would contract influenza, their mortality rate was relatively low – 776 deaths. As it turned out, the highest death rates among Canadians occurred on the home front, where there were an estimated 30–50,000 fatalities.[12]

Frightening as it was, the influenza outbreak did little to disrupt daily training activities among the able-bodied members of the 19th Battalion. Officers commanding companies and platoons were responsible for drawing up various tactical schemes,which their men then carried out on the training grounds. These schemes were submitted to the battalion orderly room on a daily basis for approval, which ensured that all units were working along similar lines and according to approved methods. The emphasis on practising more open forms of fighting, outside the familiar trench environment, had begun in late 1917 and now was stepped up.[13]

Canadian divisions other than the 2nd had been stationed in GHQ reserve since 7 May and had enjoyed a lengthy period of uninterrupted training during which they improved their proficiency in open-warfare tactics. Inspired by studies of German tactics and by *Notes on Recent Fighting*, which had recently been circulated by British GHQ, Lt.-Gen. Currie focused on increasing the mobility of all arms and their capacity to cooperate with one another.[14] While the 2nd Canadian Division was unable to commence training along these lines until July, in Maj.-Gen. Burstall's view the previous months of trench duty with British VI Corps had not been wasted. He argued that "the frequency of raids and patrols coupled with the experience gained in the outpost system of defence had given all ranks a great deal of confidence and had accustomed them to conditions approximating open warfare."[15]

But there was one realm in which the Canadian Corps as a whole arguably lagged: infantry–tank cooperation. The Canadians' prior experiences with tanks, at the Somme and at Vimy Ridge, had left them justifiably skeptical as to their value, especially when used in small numbers.[16] Nevertheless, Lt.-Gen. Currie and other Canadian officers realized they needed to keep abreast of new developments, and they closely studied reports on tank–infantry cooperation at Cambrai. Periodic training exercises with tanks during the winter and spring were stepped up during July, augmented with valuable information from other sources, such as the French infantry training school at Sautrecourt and the Australian Corps. The Australians in particular had taken a keen interest in infantry–tank tactics and demonstrated their prowess in dramatic fashion with a successful limited attack at Hamel on 4 July.[17] The 19th and 20th Battalions each spent time working with tanks on 10 and 11 July, and to increase the other ranks' interest in the machines, everyone was invited to take a ride on top of or inside one.[18] Although such exercises were vital, practical experience on the battlefield would be necessary, if only to instill real faith that the tanks could function effectively.

The 2nd Canadian Division was pulled out of GHQ reserve and made ready to relieve the 56th British Division in the Telegraph Hill sector, near Arras. After billeting first in Berneville, the 19th Battalion was ordered to brigade reserve in the city of Arras itself on 14 July. Companies were billeted along the rue d'Amiens, while battalion headquarters set up shop on the rue Chateauden. All daylight movement throughout the city was kept to a minimum, likely because of fears of German shelling.[19]

Contrary to the assertions of the battalion war diary, which described the time in Arras as "very quiet," elements of the 19th Battalion were uncharacteristically rowdy during this spell in reserve. According to G.D. Marshall, C Company found itself nicely quartered "in [a] mansion with wine-cellars conveniently attached." To soldiers weary from a rain-soaked march, this was just too good to be true, and the results were predictable. On 16 July, Marshall noted dryly: "Pilgrimages by the thirsty into the bowels of the earth. Bottles by the hundreds decorate our quarters. Peace lovers seek the sanctuary of the garret as night descends upon the ancient city. Reported that all of 'A' Company (the rowdies) under arrest."[20] One of the more restrained members of A Company was Deward Barnes, who seems to have observed much of the spree from the sidelines. "The boys got two hundred bottles of wine, all drunk all night long," he wrote. "The military police caught some … taking sacks home and one of them got away and ran to his billet and got his pistol. He went back and held the police up and the fellows got away."[21]

Naturally, the military police were not amused. The next day, Barnes reported, "the whole battalion had to parade … It was raining and we had to wear rubber sheets and caps. The military police went down each row and we had to open our coats up. They could not recognize any of the men, not one. The Colonel says he does not know what will happen now."[22] The extent of the damage incurred during these drunken follies can only be imagined, and the fallout continued for days afterward. As late as 26 July, muster parades were still being held to identify those whom G.D. Marshall termed the "wine-cellar culprits." Incredibly, considering the very public nature of the incident, the military police met with no success, which indicates that company or battalion officers were doing their best to hush up the incident.[23] It was no coincidence that the 19th Battalion quickly departed Arras on 18 July, having been relieved by the 13th Battalion of the 1st Canadian Division. With more than a few "swollen heads" among them, Millen's men trudged back to "Y" Huts, a camp located near Étrun, where they received orders to move back into GHQ reserve along with the rest of the 2nd Canadian Division.[24]

The 19th Battalion took up billets, first at Gouves and then in Ambrines, where they would remain from 23 to 29 July. Physical training, section and platoon drills, bayonet fighting, and route marching dominated the morning training regimen, along with tactical schemes for platoons. Additional attention was paid to essential skills such as musketry, Lewis gunnery, bombing, scouting, signal work, and gas discipline.[25] Gas warfare would remain a deadly reality for the rest of the conflict, and all ranks regularly practised rapid donning and adjustment of their respirators. Occasional surprise soundings of gas alarms heightened realism and kept all ranks on their toes.[26]

Junior officers and other ranks were not the only ones receiving rigorous instruction. On 27 July, Maj. Hatch assumed command of the battalion when Lt.-Col. Millen left to attend a six-day course at the First Army School along with eleven other officers. The exact nature of the course is not known, but presumably it was designed for commanding officers like Millen himself. "We all came down rather expecting it would be somewhat of a party," Millen admitted to his mother on 31 July, "but it is nothing of the sort, they are working us."[27]

Plans and Deceptions

By the summer of 1918, German offensive efforts, although showing no sign of ceasing altogether, were waning in the face of growing Allied strength. As of mid-June, the American Expeditionary Force in France was twenty divisions strong and still expanding at a rate of 250,000 men per month. For the Germans, the increasing Allied advantage in numbers was compounded by the nearly one million casualties they had suffered since 21 March.[28]

The Germans had to act fast before the situation swung irreversibly against them. But their attempt to force a decision in the west by launching an offensive against Paris on the Marne front, commencing on 15 July, did little more than create a pronounced salient that was vulnerable to Allied counterattack. The Allied blow fell quickly, beginning on 18 July, when the French Tenth and Sixth Armies (the former spearheaded by the US 1st and 2nd Divisions) drove the Germans back along the Marne. Tanks were employed en masse to great effect, and for the second time in the war (after the first Battle of the Marne in 1914), a jittery Parisian population was relieved of its fears of imminent siege. The French armies demonstrated decisively their material and moral recovery from the difficulties of 1917.[29]

With the Germans retreating from the Marne towards the Aisne River, the time had come for the British armies to launch their own offensive, the imperative for which became greater as German resistance stiffened and the French counter-offensive gradually lost steam before closing down in early August. Drawing from earlier experiences at Cambrai and more recent operations at Hamel, Field Marshal Haig's forces devised a scheme to drive the Germans back from their positions threatening the city of Amiens, which was a key Allied railway junction in the zone held by the British Fourth Army. Raiding and reconnaissance efforts in the sectors east of Amiens suggested that German defences there were poor in quality, making the area ripe for the picking. The architect of this offensive was the Fourth Army's commander, Gen. Sir Henry Rawlinson, who proposed an attack involving eleven divisions, including those of the Australian and Canadian Corps, which would spearhead the entire effort.[30]

The gifted Lt.-Gen. Sir John Monash, commander of the Australian Corps, "leapt at the suggestion" that his corps be paired with the Canadians, anxious as he was that his right flank be well secured in any proposed advance on the Villers-Bretonneux plateau, east of Amiens.[31] But at the time, the Canadians were serving with the First Army in the Arras sector. The Canadians by then had gained a formidable reputation as assault troops, which meant that if the Germans detected their sudden movement south to the Fourth Army's front, where the equally vaunted Australians also were concentrated, an impending attack was almost certain. For the enterprise to have any chance of success, the movement and preparation of the forces involved would have to be cloaked in absolute secrecy.

On 20 July, Canadian Corps headquarters received their first word about an impending offensive. The following day, Currie convened with Rawlinson, Monash, other top-level commanders, and chiefs of staff to discuss the proposed operation. Because of the need for strictest secrecy, Currie could not yet inform any of his officers (save for his most senior artillery commanders) of the plan or their objectives.[32] Even so, preparations needed to be made, and training needed to be conducted, so Currie cleverly proceeded with plans for an operation he had already envisioned against a position known as Orange Hill, east of Arras. The terrain there was favourable for tanks, so Currie was able to draw up training schemes and preliminary battle plans that approximated those his formations would actually use at Amiens. The subterfuge was maintained until 29 July, just before the corps was due to move to the Fourth Army's front. On that date, Currie informed his division commanders of their true destination and objectives, ordering them to keep this information to themselves for the time being.[33]

Foch insisted that the attack commence on 8 August in order to maintain pressure on the Germans. This left Currie and his division commanders with the immense challenge of transferring the 100,000-strong Canadian Corps some thirty miles south from their present positions around Arras without tipping off the Germans. They worked out a complex deception scheme that succeeded in confusing both the enemy and the rank and file of the Canadian Corps.[34] On 29 July the 27th Battalion and the 4th Canadian Mounted Rifles, along with some signals sections and two casualty-clearing stations, were sent in the opposite direction – north to Flanders and the British Second Army's zone. On arriving in Flanders, they were tasked with generating enough activity through small raids, patrols, and wireless traffic to convince the Germans that the Canadian Corps was moving north to retake Kemmel Hill. The ruse worked, and even among ordinary Canadian troops, "it became a question of which [attack] was for real, Orange Hill or Kemmel Hill?"[35]

The majority consensus among Canadian troops was that they would be sent north to Flanders. But when the main body of the Canadian Corps began to move by railway and bus, many men realized to their surprise that they were in fact headed south, away from Flanders. The 19th Battalion, still under the command of Maj. Hatch, began its journey in the pre-dawn hours of 30 July. After an eight-mile march to Petit-Houvin, the men boarded a train for the four-hour trip to Hangest-sur-Somme. Although not an immensely long journey, it was an uncomfortable one for most of the men. Deward Barnes complained that "they always put about ten too many in a car which meant you had no room to lay out or sit down properly … we were packed in worse than cattle."[36]

Although Hatch and his company commanders were not yet aware of the reason for the move south, they at least knew their destination before the battalion left Ambrines. Lt. Joe O'Neill, at that time in command of C Company, recalled the scene at battalion headquarters when he learned that the anticipated trip to Belgium was just a ruse:

> Well then, the night we were to take the train to move up into northern Belgium, our orders were definitely to fall in at twelve o'clock at night, and to march over to take the train. Just before, about an hour before … we were to fall in, the company commanders [were] summoned into battalion headquarters. The first thing was the [acting] Colonel gave us strict orders that we were not to tell anything to any other officer or to anybody about anything that was said in that room, under no consideration were we allowed to say anything. Then we pulled out our orders and then he started [to make] changes … we had complete operation orders for moving … down back of Amiens. Well it was a peculiar situation, because there were only the five company commanders and the Colonel, and the adjutant who knew in our battalion what was what. We got on the train and of course in the morning when we woke up, we were away down the Somme, the old Somme battlefields. All these boys, especially the old timers, they looked out the windows and they saw the name on a station, and oh if you could have heard their real old soldier stuff, about the blankety-blank staff that didn't know, that got us on the wrong train and shot us south when we should have been going north.[37]

After a brief rest following detrainment, Hatch led the battalion on a gruelling march to its final destination at Briquemesnil, in the Picquigny area, where the units of the 4th Brigade were ordered to concentrate.[38] On 1 August, the tired troops were ordered to hit the training fields and commence attack exercises in cooperation with Mark V heavy tanks from the 9th Tank Battalion. The 19th Battalion's war diarist declared that the exercise "clearly illustrated the co-operation between tanks and infantry in the attack," but did not offer any detail as to its design.[39] However, we know from various training instructions and descriptions from other units that in one type of textbook attack, infantry platoons could follow close behind the tanks, sheltered by their armoured bulk, while the tank gunners laid down a heavy suppressing fire. At an opportune moment, the infantry could then manoeuvre into position to take out an enemy strongpoint, or an anti-tank gun crew, while the tanks kept up their supporting fire.[40]

The 19th Battalion men must have performed well in their own exercise with the tanks on 1 August, for they were asked to perform a demonstration for the 18th and 21st Battalions before those units carried out their own training later that afternoon. "What particularly impressed everyone," remarked the 20th Battalion's historian, Maj. D.J. Corrigall, "was the ability of the latest types [of tanks] to overcome seemingly insurmountable obstacles."[41] But as impressive as the demonstrations were, they still gave the other ranks no idea as to when and where they might be used in any future operations. Moreover, all ranks were ordered in no uncertain terms to avoid talking about their unit's movements to any outsiders. As a reminder, a message boldly titled "keep your mouth shut" was pasted in every man's paybook.[42]

The veil of secrecy lifted one more level when on the afternoon of 1 August, Maj.-Gen. Burstall finally revealed the plan to his brigade commanders and their chiefs of staff.[43] On 3 August, Lt.-Col. Millen returned from his course and resumed command of the 19th Battalion. As had been the case with other officers who were away from their units during the move from Arras, Millen likely was shuttled to his battalion in a staff car supplied by GHQ and division headquarters, without his destination being revealed in advance or the reason for his unit's movement.[44] One can imagine his curiosity and his interest in the bustling atmosphere of his new surroundings. But he had no time to get accustomed to them, for on the same day that he returned, the battalion was ordered to march approximately fourteen miles to Cagny. After packing up and falling in, the men trudged out at 10:30 PM, reaching their destination at 3:00 AM.[45]

The exhausted men spent much of 4 August resting in tents and bivouacs just outside Cagny. But they were not allowed to remain for long. Later that afternoon, Millen was ordered to move the battalion into "a forward area in and near Bois d'Aquenne, west of Villers-Bretonneux." This they reached on 5 August, leaving their transport lines, LOB personnel, and rear details back at Cagny under the command of Maj. Hatch. By now, Millen had finally been brought up to speed on the situation. Brig.-Gen. Rennie had been given the go-ahead to inform his battalion commanders of the upcoming offensive, which he did at brigade headquarters on 4 August. As had been the case with every superior level of command, the unit COs were ordered to keep the information to themselves until given permission to divulge it to their subordinates.[46]

The General Plan and Opposing Forces

The operation would be carried out on 8 August by the British Fourth and French First Armies, with the main thrust occurring along a fourteen-mile stretch of front between Moreuil and Albert. Spearheading the operation would be the Australian and Canadian Corps, with the French XXXI and IX Corps advancing to cover the attack on the right and the British III Corps anchoring it on the left. In all, the Allies would pit twenty-one divisions against the German 2nd and 18th Armies, which mustered fourteen divisions in the battle area.[47]

As it was finally envisioned, the attack formed part of an overall scheme by Gen. Foch to secure important lateral railways running along the Allied front – such as the Paris–Amiens line – from direct German attack. But Field Marshal Haig altered the scope of the attack, expanding it from a comparatively limited operation to an attempt at a breakthrough. He insisted on 5 August that, if the attack progressed favourably, the Fourth Army should be prepared to push on to the line stretching between Chaulnes and Roye and then continue forward in the direction of Ham. Thus, at almost the last minute, Haig increased the scale of the attack, from an advance totalling seven miles in depth to one of approximately twenty-seven miles! Unrealistic as they were, Haig's optimistic goals did not derail the more limited and achievable plan for the first day of the attack. They would, however, have an effect on subsequent operations.[48]

The Canadian Corps was assigned to the extreme right of the Fourth Army, with the French XXXI Corps on their right flank. The Canadian start line would extend more than 8,500 yards from a point south of the village of Hourges northward to the Amiens–Chaulnes railway line. Just north of the railway ran the intercorps boundary with the Australians. There were three principal objective lines to be taken on the first day of the attack. The first and second objectives were known as the Green and Red lines; the third was identified on operation maps as the Blue Dotted Line. This third objective line stood roughly seven miles distant from the jumping-off positions on the Canadian Corps' left flank and ran along the old position known as the Outer Amiens Defence Line, which was Gen. Rawlinson's original final objective. But, due to Haig's influence, the Blue Dotted Line was not intended to be the stopping point for the attack. Instead, supporting cavalry and reserve infantry forces were supposed to push through and past it.[49]

Although they modified their orders to reflect Haig's wishes, Rawlinson and his staff continued to place more emphasis on the initial stage of the attack, up to the Blue Dotted Line – an emphasis with which Lt-Gen. Currie was in complete accord. According to Currie's plan, the Canadians would attack with three divisions in line, from south to north – the 3rd, the 1st, and the 2nd. The 1st and 2nd Canadian Divisions would advance towards the Blue Dotted Line in their respective sectors, along with elements of the 3rd Cavalry Division, which had been placed temporarily under Currie's command and would join the vanguard of the attack at the Red Line. On the corps right, where resistance was expected to be heavier, the 4th Canadian Division would advance from corps reserve and pass through the 3rd Canadian Division at the Red Line, where it would push ahead with the cavalry to take the Blue Dotted Line.[50]

In the 2nd Canadian Division's sector, Maj.-Gen. Burstall decided to attack on a single brigade front, employing his infantry brigades in relay fashion in order to take the three principal objective lines. To the 4th Brigade would fall the task of capturing the Green Line, after which the 5th Brigade would leapfrog past them to take the Red Line. If these first two stages proved successful, the 6th Brigade, in divisional reserve, would forge ahead to secure the Blue Dotted Line. The total depth of this advance was estimated at over 12,000 yards.[51]

The key element of the entire attack would be the artillery, which would open fire without heavy preliminary bombardments or registration. Supporting the French First and British Fourth Armies would be an incredible 2,166 field guns and howitzers, plus 1,510 heavy guns. Against this, the Germans could bring only around 530 guns to bear against the Fourth Army. From the massive array of Allied artillery, 646 field and heavy pieces would back the Canadian share of the operation. But not all gunners would remain in their usual firing positions well to the rear. One brigade of field artillery would move forward with each attacking division, leapfrogging its batteries forward to follow up the advance and, it was hoped, lending effective close-support firepower to the infantry while keeping the retreating enemy within range.[52]

The other vital elements operating at Amiens in concert with the infantry were the tanks, of which the Allies fielded 604 of all types. The Fourth Army boasted 324 Mark V heavy tanks and 96 medium tanks, the latter colloquially known as "Whippets." The 4th Tank Brigade was assigned to work with the Canadian Corps, and it furnished a tank battalion to each attacking division. The 1st, 2nd, and 3rd Canadian Divisions would each be supported by forty-two heavy tanks, while thirty-six would cooperate with the 4th Canadian Division. An individual section of tanks, consisting usually of three machines, was assigned to each attacking infantry battalion. In addition to the fighting tanks, supply tanks would support the advance, to the tune of about one per battalion. These machines would serve as "rolling storehouses," following up the attacking waves and conveying water, food, ammunition, fuel, tools, stakes, wire, and other essentials.[53]

Some 800 British aircraft were assigned to support the Fourth Army's ground attack, while the French assembled 1,349 aircraft along their First Army's front. Local German air power, at only 365 machines, was therefore vastly outnumbered. It is fortunate that persistent Allied air patrols, combined with overcast weather during the first week of August, minimized the activities of German reconnaissance flights over the Fourth Army's positions. As for the battle itself, direct aerial support for the Canadians would come from No. 5 Squadron of the Royal Air Force, which was tasked with dropping smoke and phosphorus bombs. These were intended to aid the artillery in laying down a protective smokescreen for the advancing infantry and tanks. In addition, the aircraft would perform contact patrol missions, locating the "continually changing and always indefinite line where the foremost troops were in conflict with the enemy."[54]

German defences facing the Fourth Army comprised "little more than three lines of trench, poorly wired and without good shelters."[55] But numerous small villages, many of which were ringed with orchards, provided "obvious defensive possibilities."[56] Rather than relying on massive field fortifications, the German defences in this region were based mainly on vast numbers of machine-gun nests scattered over the length and breadth of the front. Some of these machine guns had been placed on cleverly constructed platforms that could be lowered below ground level to hide them from view until they were needed. Defending this ground, from south to north, were troops of the 225th, 117th, and 41st Infantry Divisions of the German 2nd Army. These formations were rated by the army commander, Gen. Georg von der Marwitz, as "average" in calibre. The 2nd Army had suffered heavy losses during the spring offensives, and its strength had been further sapped by recent waves of influenza.[57]

Exhaustion, miscalculation, and complacency undermined the Germans' chances of checking the Allied attack at Amiens. When the Australians extended their front to the south, relieving elements of the French XXXI Corps during the first week of August, the German high command took this as a sign that no large-scale attack was immediately foreseeable in this sector from the British Fourth Army. How could it be, when the British and Australians appeared to be dissipating rather than concentrating their strength? Some German front-line units, detecting considerable levels of movement behind their opponents' lines, did suspect an attack in the offing, although its exact timing could not be determined. However, the high command dismissed reports of increased activity behind the Fourth Army front as the attendant ruckus that naturally followed the French relief and the side-stepping of the Australians. In fact, this Australian screen hid the massive buildup of Canadian troops.[58]

Final Orders and Preparations

On 6 August, a mere thirty-six hours before the attack was scheduled to commence, the Canadian infantry battalions received detailed operational orders from brigade headquarters. Junior officers were now informed about the impending assault, although even at this point they were warned not to share the information with the other ranks until they had moved closer to the front line and were well away from areas still accessible to civilians.[59] The 7th of August finally would see the issuance of the 19th Battalion's own detailed operation orders, based mainly on the schemes drawn up by division and brigade headquarters.[60]

The 2nd Canadian Division's attack would be led by two battalions of the 4th Brigade on a frontage of slightly more than 2,000 yards. Advancing on the right would be the 18th Battalion; the 19th Battalion had been selected to lead off on the left. The 21st Battalion would follow closely in support while the 20th Battalion stood ready in reserve. The chief object of the brigade was to capture the division's portion of the Green Line, which lay 500 yards east of the village of Marcelcave and almost three miles from the jumping-off line.[61] Brig.-Gen. Rennie's men would have the advantage of operating with full artillery support for most of its advance. The creeping barrage would commence at zero hour along a line 200 yards in front of the infantry's jumping-off line. It would move ahead of the troops in 100-yard lifts, most of which would occur at three-minute intervals for the first 1,000 yards. Thereafter, it would advance at a rate of 100 yards every four minutes until the limit of the 18-pounders' effective range for shrapnel was reached. "K" and "L" Batteries of No. 3 Company, 2nd Battalion, Canadian Machine Gun Corps, would cooperate by firing a barrage of their own along selected points in the path of advance.[62]

The village of Marcelcave, which presented the greatest and most obvious challenge to the attacking troops, fell squarely in the path of the 19th Battalion. Severe resistance was expected at this point, so it was decided that the support unit, the 21st Battalion, would cooperate with the 19th Battalion in eliminating all resistance in the village. Because Marcelcave lay beyond the effective range of most of the field artillery batteries, it would be subjected to a concentrated heavy artillery barrage for forty-five minutes. After that, the guns would lift to the final objective line and the infantry would rush the village from the north, west, and south. When the 18th, 19th, and 21st Battalions had secured both Marcelcave and their final objective along the Green Line, they were to stand fast and consolidate while the 5th Infantry Brigade passed through their positions to carry on the attack against the division's second objective, the Red Line.[63]

Additional support for the 4th Brigade would come from five sections of A and B Companies of the 14th Tank Battalion. This amounted to seventeen tanks in all, ten of which would operate with the 18th Battalion; the remaining seven would accompany the 19th Battalion. Those fighting along with the 19th Battalion were assigned to assist directly in the capture of Marcelcave. The 5th Brigade of the 2nd Canadian Divisional Artillery also was detailed to move ahead at zero hour and provide close-range artillery support for the infantry and tanks. "J" and "M" batteries of No. 3 Company, 2nd Battalion, CMGC, likewise were assigned to move forward and furnish covering fire once the infantry reached their objectives and began to dig in. Finally, four three-inch Stokes mortar crews of the 4th Canadian Trench Mortar Battery were allocated to the 19th Battalion, with two more assigned to the 21st Battalion and the remaining two in reserve with the 20th Battalion. Those supporting the 19th Battalion were charged with bombarding enemy machine-gun nests and a position known as Jaffa Trench for up to one and a half minutes after zero hour. Afterwards, they were to move forward and follow up the advancing infantry and tanks, bringing their guns into action as required.[64]

As for the infantry itself, Lt.-Col. Millen decided to organize the 19th Battalion's attack on a three-company front, with C Company operating on the right, A Company in the centre, and B Company on the left. D Company would remain in reserve. Battalion orders stipulated that each of the three assault companies would "attack with two platoons and one platoon in close support."[65] Presumably, this meant that each company would advance on a two-platoon frontage with the third platoon following closely behind. Each attacking company was in charge of mopping-up duties within its own assigned area, with D Company lending additional assistance in certain areas of the battlefield.[66]

Flexibility was the paramount concern when tackling enemy machine-gun nests and other strongpoints. Ideally, platoons and their constituent sections advanced by successive rushes, making intelligent use of ground and covering one another with the firepower of Lewis guns, rifles, and rifle grenades before engaging in close-quarter fighting with hand grenades and sometimes even bayonets. Imparting direction to this seemingly chaotic process required great skill and initiative on the part of junior officers and NCOs. The complexities increased when cooperation with other arms and weapons groups, such as tanks and heavy machine guns, was called for. The modern popular image of infantry mindlessly marching line-abreast into hails of machine-gun fire during all First World War battles is grossly unrealistic.

Although the continuing absence of suitably portable and reliable wireless communication technology prevented battalion and brigade headquarters from exerting any real influence on the infantry's movements once the attack began, every effort was still made to keep in contact with the fighting troops. The battalion signal section would see to it that each company went forward with a telephone; but this was a fragile system that depended on vulnerable cables, and it had to be supplemented by visual signalling equipment (such as flags and Lucas lamps) and runners. Also, attacking troops carried red flares to signal their position to contact patrol aircraft. The airmen would then relay information to division headquarters using weighted message bags at a prearranged "Dropping Station." Besides keeping in touch with battalion headquarters, all attacking companies were ordered to maintain contact with the units on either flank. While the 19th Battalion was advancing on the far left flank of the Canadian Corps, it detailed one platoon to advance north of the Amiens–Chaulnes railway line to keep in touch with the 26th Battalion of the Australian 7th Infantry Brigade.[67]

Of special importance would be the establishment of a forward report centre for the attacking battalion. There the officer in charge of the attack and the officer commanding the signals section would station themselves, along with signallers, scouts, and a number of runners. Attacking companies were to keep in touch with the report centre, which was charged with monitoring their progress and relaying information back to battalion headquarters by telephone, visual signals, or runners.

If the attack proved successful, battalion headquarters itself would move forward as soon as possible and establish itself at Marcelcave.[68]

Because of the need for secrecy, reconnaissance work in the forward areas by Canadian battalion scouts and officers had not been permitted until the final days before the attack. With opportunities for acquiring first-hand information highly restricted, all relevant information on topography and enemy dispositions was gathered and supplied by the Fourth Army, the Australians, the 2nd Canadian Division headquarters, and the RAF. In the end, although the ground on which the battalion would fight was new to them, Lt.-Col. Millen and his officers were provided with a good deal of information and accurate maps.[69] The need for prolonged training over taped courses mimicking the infantry's objectives "had fallen into discard," noted Fred Stitt.[70]

On 7 August, brigade headquarters finally issued a memo announcing zero hour, which was to be at 4:20 the following morning. As well, the other ranks were fully briefed on their tasks. As had been the case in the great set-piece attacks of 1917, Brig.-Gen. Rennie wanted all officers to ensure that every man fully understood his role and that of his section and platoon, so that if the officers and NCOs were killed or injured, the men themselves would know enough to carry out their mission.[71] Vivian E. Thompson of Toronto remembered the arrival of the battalion armourer that same day, "and all bayonet points were sharpened up as though some heavy sticking job was to be expected." After this grim ceremony at the grindstone, Thompson attended a very different sort of ritual, when he and other Catholic members of the battalion went to see their chaplain, Father Ewan J. Macdonald, to receive general absolution. With clean souls and keen bayonets, the men began their personal preparations for a battle from which some of them would never return. "Two of the lads of my company," Thompson remembered, "Clair Hagen and another lad, were last seen by me at this meeting [for general absolution], they being killed the next day. Another of our lads had a premonition of a similar fate as displayed when he got into a card game and lost, stating that it didn't matter as he would finish in this action."[72]

Feelings of grim resignation and fear were like old companions to many men in the final hours before an attack. Yet others exhibited a much more upbeat attitude in the days before moving up to their assembly points. Some sensed that they were on the threshold of a great turning point in the war. "A very interesting thing happened," observed Elmore Philpott, an artilleryman: "In the early years of the war the boys used to sing when they were going up to the line, but then they got in that sort of bleak blank period and nobody sang … [But] when our boys went up to that Amiens thing they all went up singing … There was a feeling in the air, the boys really believed that this was it."[73] Similarly, G.S. Rutherford of the 52nd Battalion recalled: "You had the feeling that everything was well planned, well organized … Everything seemed to go like clockwork and for the first time on your march you could hear the troops singing."[74] Little wonder that on the day before the attack, when Lt.-Gen. Currie observed a party of infantry belting out, "Hail, hail, the gang's all here; what the hell do we care now!" he exclaimed to one of his aides, "God help the Boche tomorrow!"[75]

At 10 PM on 7 August, the time for singing had passed and silence descended on the ranks. The four battalions of the 4th Brigade at last proceeded forward to their assembly positions immediately southeast of Villers-Bretonneux, from which they would relieve the 50th Australian Battalion in the front line later that night.[76] As Allied troops silently filed into their positions up and down the length of the front, the Germans still did not anticipate the horror that would be unleashed on them in a few short hours.[77]

Standard LOB procedure had come into effect earlier on 4 August, when each unit in the brigade was ordered to take forward no more than three complete platoons per company. Either the company commander or the second-in-command, and a due proportion of all specialists, were to remain out of action along with the fourth platoon. Orders stipulated that each platoon taking part in the attack be at a minimum strength of thirty-five other ranks.[78] Hedging his bets on the effectiveness of the tanks, Brig.-Gen. Rennie further advised his subordinates in no uncertain terms that "tanks are to be considered *aids* to the infantry. The attack must be pressed forward irrespective of any interruption in the progress of Tanks detailed to support the operation."[79]

At 3:20 AM – sixty minutes before zero hour – the 19th Battalion reported that all of its men were in position and ready for action. Even a last-minute tot of rum could not dull the tension racking every man while he waited in the darkness. As each Canadian division completed its assembly, it flashed the code word "Llandovery Castle," back to corps headquarters. The *Llandovery Castle* was a Canadian hospital ship that had been torpedoed by a German U-boat on 27 June. Of the 244 men and 14 nursing sisters aboard, only 24 were saved. What was worse, the U-boat crew had reportedly machine gunned many of the survivors as they struggled helplessly in the water. The Canadians had been enraged by this atrocity, and a desire to avenge the victims was widespread throughout the corps. Officers invoked the story during pre-battle "pep talks" to their men, seeking to whip up their fighting spirit. Brig.-Gen. George Tuxford, GOC 3rd Infantry Brigade, later admitted that he "gave instructions to the Brigade that the battle cry on the 8th of August should be 'Llandovery Castle,' and that that cry should be the last to ring in the ears of the Hun as the bayonet was driven home."[80] Even Lt.-Gen. Currie himself apparently encouraged his men to show no mercy to the Germans. Deward Barnes recounted that during Currie's review of the 19th Battalion on 12 July, "he said that we did not want any prisoners, which meant kill them all."[81]

Soon after the 19th Battalion moved into the scattered shell holes and small stretches of trench that lay along their start line, the Germans began to shell the area where the Australian and Canadian Corps had linked up. The bombardment hit the right portion of the Australian 7th Brigade and the left portion of the Canadian 4th Brigade – exactly where the men of the 19th Battalion had just settled in. There was nothing for the boys from Ontario, Queensland, and Tasmania to do but huddle under as much cover as they could get and simply wait it out. "Hell was let loose," remembered Vivian Thompson, "but I have no great idea of what went on as … we were at the bottom of a deep hole … When the guns first barked forth I can remember Red Conlin in the next hole calling for a shovel and start digging like the devil and that was the last I saw of him for that day."[82] "I was hit on the road going in," remarked Joe O'Neill, "so it was the biggest disappointment I ever had in my life. I had the company from about the first of June, and it was the first real attack." O'Neill was not gravely injured, but flying shrapnel broke his hand and his jaw and knocked out several teeth. It was off to Blighty for him, and command of C Company passed to Lt. A.P. Fletcher.[83]

Millen's companies suffered more casualties from this bombardment, which kept up "practically through to zero hour."[84] Deward Barnes was more candid, admitting in his journal that

> the Germans must have got wise, because we were not too quiet (it was dark and we were trying to keep in touch). His batteries opened up and he made an awful mess of us. A large number of us were wounded or killed. Some ran and stumbled into shell holes they could not see for the darkness. I ran too, but fell into a narrow trench. Some other fellows were in there too, so we waited there for the fire to stop.[85]

Compounding the disorienting effect of the bombardment, a dense mist began to form, so that within a few minutes many men could scarcely see farther than twenty yards in any direction.[86]

As countless synchronized watches ticked off the minutes to zero hour, and the men of the 19th Battalion continued to cringe under the falling German shells, a new sound pierced the gloom of the enveloping fog. It was the droning of a lone Handley-Page bomber cruising up and down the length of the front. The pilot was not out for a mere joyride and had been fortunate to get airborne at all, given the overcast conditions. His mission was to drown out the noise of the approaching armada of tanks, which, at twelve minutes before zero, began creeping forward from their starting points 1,000 yards behind the front line. The tank commanders ran their engines as quietly as possible, in second gear, while the Allied artillery kept up a sporadic, and very routine-sounding, gunfire – all of which combined with the aviator's efforts to create a sonic charade.[87] With the approach of the tanks, the curtain at last was ready to rise on the most spectacular Allied offensive effort to date. Little did anyone at the time suspect that it was, in fact, the kickoff to the final hundred days of the war.

18

The Battle of Amiens and Its Aftermath: 8–18 August 1918

The Battle of Amiens began, as so many others had before it, with a bang. At zero hour on 8 August, the Allied artillery thundered in unison and rained shells at a merciless rate upon the unsuspecting front-line garrisons of the German 2nd Army. "They had those guns for miles, wheel to wheel and one layer after another," remembered Joe O'Neill. "They were poked out through bushes, they were behind [and] under trees and they were covered."[1] Fred Stitt recalled the final moments before the barrage began, when he and his comrades crouched, tense and nervous, like coiled springs, waiting for the moment to go over: "We moved up quietly and at four twenty in the morning there was one gun went off away back some place, and then the whole sky lit up. I never saw anything like it in my life, that barrage on the 8th of August. You couldn't hear yourself think, and if you hadn't got your sense of direction you were done like a dinner."[2] "The shells came over our heads with an appalling shriek in the fog ahead," said Wilfred Macklin, "and we simply lit cigarettes, shouldered our rifles, and walked off after the shells."[3]

The "Black Day"

This was the first time that the 19th Battalion found itself in the vanguard of a major attack since the storming of Vimy Ridge. Capt. Robert Bliss was in overall charge

Three views of 60-pounder heavy field guns in action, Battle of Amiens. (LAC PA-002921, PA-002999, and LAC PA-002997)

of the assault, and he moved forward with his signal and scout personnel to set up the battalion report centre. From there, he could monitor the progress of the three advancing companies and report back to Lt.-Col. Millen at battalion headquarters, which was located in the railway embankment just east of Villers-Bretonneux. Along the battalion front, C Company, under the command of Lt. Aubrey Fletcher, struck out on the right; A Company, led by Lt. William S. Herbert, held the centre; and B Company, commanded by Capt. Gordon Applegath, advanced along the left. Behind them, waiting in reserve, was D Company under Lt. Thomas A. Allan.[4]

Aside from the din of the bombardment, men like Vivian Thompson quickly became aware of other sounds as they moved through the murk – the rattle of German machine guns and the whiz and chirp of their bullets. "I heard the first gun on our side go off," recalled Thompson. "After that gun I did not seem to be aware of the noise or the bursting of shells but only seemed concerned with machine guns which, despite the racket, seemed to be clearly distinguished. I can remember hearing them as they swung from right to left and from left to right and how I ducked each time they sounded just ahead."[5] It was, in theory, somewhat easier for the troops to dodge, weave, and run during this battle than in previous ones, for their kit had been modified to a new form termed "fighting order." This arrangement distributed the weight of their equipment more evenly and did away with some of the unnecessary burden borne in previous operations. Each man now carried a haversack, 250 rounds of ammunition (100 rounds of which were in bandoliers), a gas mask, two water bottles, "iron rations" (consisting of corned beef and biscuits), an entrenching tool, two Mills bombs, and two sandbags.[6]

As the pessimists feared, the morning mist, made thicker by the smoke of the barrage, caused a good deal of disorientation as the men set out to punch through the German forward defences. Sections frequently lost touch with one another, and small groups were taken in charge by the nearest officer, NCO, or ordinary man with enough initiative to assume the mantle of leadership. Officers were able to progress with the aid of compasses, but inevitably, some individuals lost their sense of direction. However, the noise of the bursting shells, which marked the location of the creeping barrage, must have given most attackers some sense of which way to proceed. Discerning friend from foe would be another problem altogether, and we are left to wonder how many unfortunate accidents occurred that morning along the Canadian front during the advance through the fog to the Green Line.[7]

As difficult as the Canadians and others found it to see their opponents, the German machine gunners found it equally hard to spot their attackers. Some machine-gun crews were overrun before they had a chance to fire a shot, while others were missed entirely by the first waves of attackers and had to be dealt with by follow-up platoons.[8] Along the Australian front to the Canadians' left, conditions were the same. According to Charles Bean, the Australian official historian,

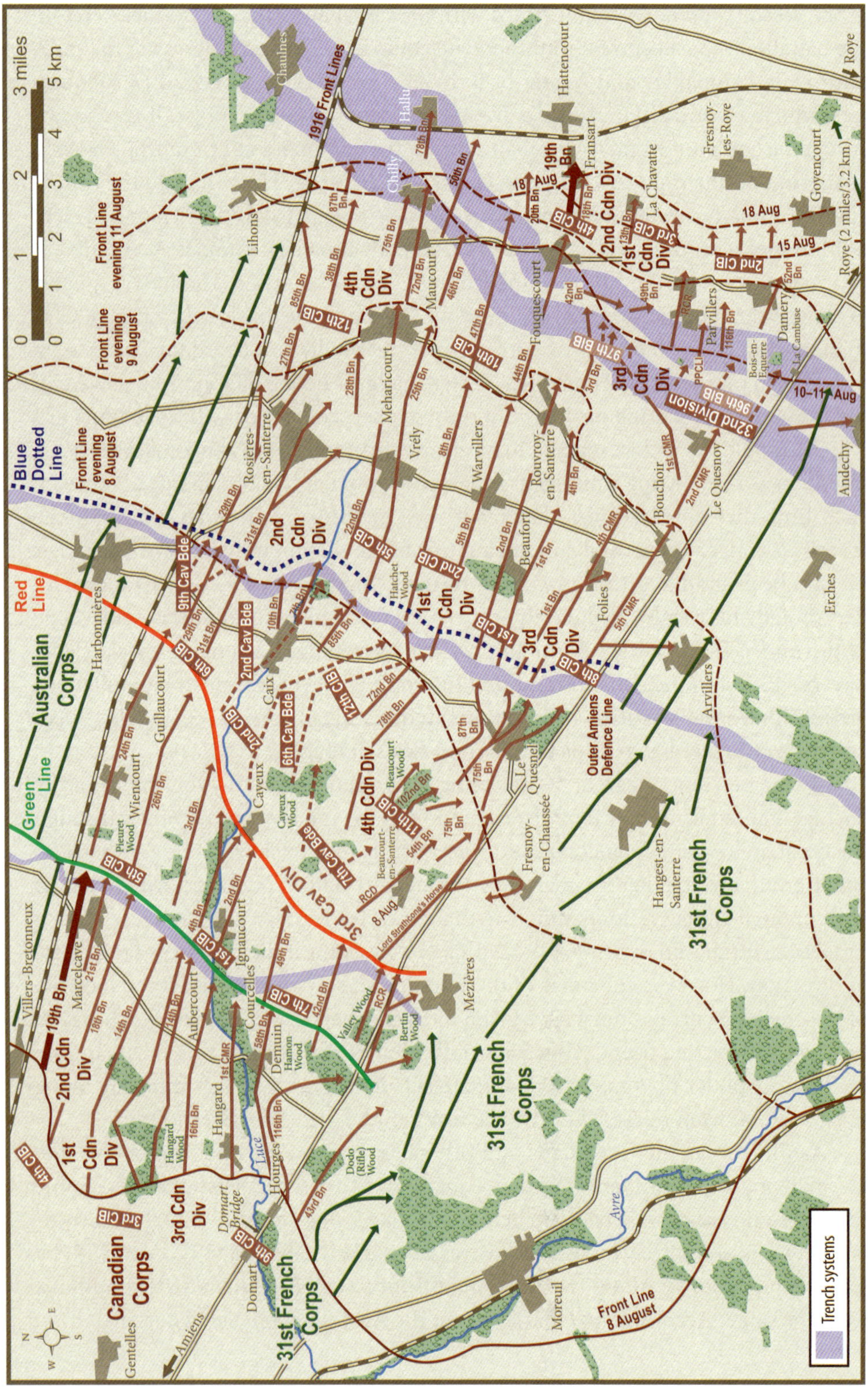

Map 18 – Amiens.

> German machine guns rattled out, heavily in places, mostly in the blank fog ahead, but sometimes on the flanks and occasionally in rear. Now and again an advancing party blundered straight upon a group of German machine gunners squatting, with scared faces, in a shell hole or small trench. Generally the crew would throw up its hands, sometimes after a few shots. Here and there a brave man kept his gun firing until rushed by someone from flank or rear and shot.[9]

Among the foremost German defensive positions, resistance generally was weaker. This was not surprising, considering that the troops there had the least amount of time to react before the attacking forces came to grips with them. "We got to their front line," reported Deward Barnes,

> and dozens of Germans put their hands up and said "mercy," "kamerad." Some got back [to our lines], but not all; we shot them down like dogs. We kept going and came to their support lines where we killed some more. By this time it was light but still very misty. You could not see ten feet in front of you for the mist. We had to go through a wheat field and we came upon some Germans hiding in the wheat. We kept on going and came to some more trenches. One trench had a rifle sticking up high with a man's cap on it. We put a Mills bomb in that trench. We later found the occupants all huddled in the corner – dead.
>
> We came to another bunch afraid to come out and did the same thing. It was getting quite light by now and the Germans came running at us, shouting "mercy" and "kamerad." One fellow made signs with his hands that he had a wife and family. Some of the fellows swore at him, then pointed back toward our lines. The Germans ran back and were shot in the backs.[10]

No clear evidence has been found yet that the men of the 19th Battalion were encouraged by their officers to execute cowering or surrendering Germans. In view of the hard feelings that many men nursed over the sinking of the *Llandovery Castle*, and the pre-battle harangues of some senior commanders like Lt.-Gen. Currie and the 3rd Brigade's Brig.-Gen. Tuxford, such cold-blooded actions may have been fairly common among the Canadians that morning. That said, live prisoners were taken in considerable numbers that day, although some of them were treated rather roughly by their Canadian captors. Vivian Thompson remembered meeting up

> with several of our fellows at a trench where they were hailing several of our noble enemy to come forth. One of these chaps had his arm in a sling and a newcomer to the scene got up on his tip toes, took a look, brought up his rifle and gave the wounded arm a vicious jab with the bayonet, over the heads of the crowd. Why in heck he should do that I never have been able to fathom. War is war but that seemed a bit thick to me.[11]

In a similar, and more fatal, vein, Deward Barnes recalled the actions of one of his comrades, Leonard Bell, who "wanted to say for sure that he killed a German and so he shot a prisoner point-blank. It worried him later though."[12] Once the morning's blood lust had worn off, some Canadians who committed such deeds came to regret them.

Prisoners captured by Canadians during the Battle of Amiens. (LAC PA-002891)

After the Canadians broke through the German front line, resistance in some locations gradually stiffened. The German defences along the approaches to Marcelcave were manned by troops of the 41st Division, and their positions, according to Maj.-Gen. Burstall, "consisted mainly of unconnected sections of trench with a little local wire entanglement. There was, however, one fairly continuous defensive line, well wired, about one thousand yards west of Marcelcave and there were some organized positions along the railway on our left flank."[13] These stronger positions on the left, especially Jaffa Trench, quickly posed difficulties for the men of the 19th Battalion's B Company, whose progress was stalled by heavy machine-gun fire. Lt. Allan Thompson (B Company) reported the delay to Capt. Bliss, who in turn sent a message back to battalion headquarters.[14]

Problems with Jaffa Trench had been anticipated from the beginning, and the position had been designated as a special target for the tanks of the 14th Tank Battalion and the Stokes mortar crews assigned to support the 19th Battalion. The mortars were supposed to bombard the trench for well over a minute after zero hour, but this plan had been quashed by the fog and smoke that masked the target. As for the tanks, Maj.-Gen. Burstall later reported that the nature of the ground in the 4th Brigade's assembly area had prevented them from forming up as close to the infantry's jumping-off line as planned. Moreover, what little visibility the tank crews had through the machines' view slits was obscured even further by the heavy fog, which also rendered useless the visual signalling system between tanks and infantry. As a consequence, the tanks had been unable to get under way until around 4:40 AM, some twenty minutes after the infantry had moved off. Their subsequent progress must have been slow, since they still had not caught up with the leading waves of troops by the time Capt. Bliss reported the check on B Company's progress at 5:47 AM.[15]

As soon as he sent word back to battalion headquarters, Bliss dashed from his report centre and set about organizing all the troops he could find in the vicinity of Jaffa Trench. According to the battalion's after-action report, he then coordinated a renewed assault on the position, which soon overcame all opposition. While justly lauding the leadership shown by Bliss, the report failed to mention the crucial assistance rendered by parties from the 21st Australian Battalion, two companies of which had been following up the leading waves of the 26th Australian Battalion in its advance along the north side of the Amiens–Chaulnes railway. The men of the 21st Australian Battalion had hooked up with those of the far left platoon of the 19th Battalion, whose job it was to maintain contact between the forces of the two sister dominions. As such, these Australian troops had also been caught up in the heavy fire emanating from Jaffa Trench, and their Lewis gunners played a prominent role in silencing the German machine gunners. In the process of helping clear the way, the Australians took ten prisoners, whom they immediately handed over to their Canadian comrades.[16]

With Jaffa Trench taken care of, the men of B Company were free to forge ahead again. But they had not gone far when the company's left flank again ran into stiff opposition. Lt. James L. Burton and Cpl. (Acting Sgt.) Robert Hollidge immediately rushed the offending machine-gun nest. Burton was swiftly cut down by a hail of bullets, but Hollidge somehow managed to keep going, unscathed, until he reached the position. Incredibly, the intrepid NCO killed the six-man garrison and seized the machine gun; he then turned the weapon around to open fire on a group of retreating Germans, inflicting "many casualties."[17]

Meanwhile, the two companies from the 21st Australian Battalion maintained their link with the 19th Battalion's left flank, and their Lewis gunners continued to pour a deadly fire against all points of opposition along the railway bank. As the advancing forces approached Marcelcave, one of the Australian officers, Lt. E.B. Mason, crossed the railway and moved over into Canadian territory to reconnoitre an enemy strongpoint in an orchard near Jean Rouxin Mill. He soon encountered a messenger sent by Capt. Bliss of the 19th Battalion requesting assistance in eliminating this obstacle, the garrison of which had been putting up a fierce resistance. Mason duly assembled a party of men and together they helped drive the Germans out of the orchard after a brutal bombing contest. Having rendered this valuable service, the Australians quickly moved ahead along the railway to cover the flank of the 26th Australian Battalion, which by then had managed to work its way north of Marcelcave.[18]

The ruins at Marcelcave bear stark witness to the bitter fighting on 8 August 1918. (LAC PA-004424)

As for the village itself, Marcelcave was pounded by a specially arranged heavy artillery bombardment. When this finally lifted, Capt. Bliss, together with Lt. Angus G. Bell of the 19th Battalion and Lt. W. Currie of the 21st Canadian Battalion, which had moved up from support, set about organizing the capture of the village. The fog had just begun to dissipate, and although it continued to linger, it was soon possible for the men to see upwards of 200 yards. With visibility much improved, parties from the 19th and 21st Battalions rushed Marcelcave from three sides, the 19th focusing mainly on the northern portion of the village. Prominent in the assault was the indomitable Acting Sgt. Hollidge, who "entered the town with a machine gun on his arm, firing down dugouts, cellars, up and down roads, etc."[19]

"We got to Marcelcave and took it alright," said Sgt. Fred Stitt, in charge of a Lewis gun section in A Company. "There was a little bit of street fighting because it hadn't been completely demolished, although it was an awful mess with artillery fire."[20] "I shouted down one cellar," Vivian Thompson explained,

> and on receiving no reply I got rid of one of my grenades which was the only bit of ammunition I set off in my whole time in France. From here I turned and saw a fine young [German] chap, with rimless nose glasses, come from a building. An officer gave him a good kick in the pants and sent him stumbling to the rear as I passed. I had not gone more than a few yards when I heard a report and on looking back I saw this German fall. Whether or not the officer had changed his mind and shot him, I cannot tell.[21]

Deward Barnes had made it to Marcelcave as well, and he left a brief but vivid description of the devastation wrought upon its defenders by both the heavy artillery and the charging infantry: "We could see Germans running back into the village," he stated. "We opened a sweeping fire on them. We continued forward and entered Marcelcave. I went down the main street while others took the side streets. There were German dead lying in the streets. We went through the town, firing into every house or store. We found a German [regimental] headquarters, but left it for those behind us to clean out."[22] Fred Stitt noted that "we found this German headquarters alright and after we got the red tabbed Generals up the stairs from this dugout we investigated this place and found the porridge warm on the table, that's how badly we surprised them. They didn't know the first thing about that attack, not the first thing." Although Stitt and his friends chose not to partake of the officers' breakfast, they helped themselves to whatever they found in the way of liquid refreshments. "Anything we found in water bottles we drank," he admitted, "which probably wasn't a good idea … but in this case being such a surprise there was no possibility of them trying to poison us or anything like that. We … captured quite a bit of stuff in bottles from the Germans, and it's not near as good as our own army rum."[23]

Parties of Australians also got in on the act. Elements of the 26th Australian Battalion, which had been held up by fire from the north end of Marcelcave, obtained the assistance of a tank and proceeded to attack the village. According to Charles Bean, the tank rumbled along the outskirts, firing its six-pound guns, "and then dived into the north of the village followed by the Australians." The tank and infantry worked their way through the northern edge of Marcelcave until they obtained a good view of the open country to the south and east. There, they observed German field guns positioned along Pieuret Wood, some distance beyond the Green Line on the Canadian front. The temptation to admire the view passed quickly after the guns opened fire on them, and in retaliation the Australians put to flight the crew of a 5.9-inch howitzer battery located in a quarry closer to the village. Just then, reported Bean, "behind the right rear, an uproar of shots and bombs resounded for five minutes" in Marcelcave. "Then out came the Canadians, to the admiration of all, advancing as if on parade to their objective on the knuckle beyond the village."[24]

With Marcelcave effectively secured, the 19th Battalion continued its advance about a half a mile east of the village, where it reached the Green Line at 6:55 AM. By that time, the German field guns, which the Australians had observed in front of Pieuret Wood, presumably had been neutralized or driven off (perhaps by counter-battery fire). Once they reached their objective, the men set to work consolidating the line and reorganizing their scattered companies. Capt. Bliss sent a message back to battalion headquarters reporting that Marcelcave had fallen and that consolidation of the objective line had already begun.[25]

Canadian troops digging in and waiting for the next wave to continue the advance during the Battle of Amiens. In the background is a British medium tank known as a Whippet. This type of tank was smaller and faster than the Mark IV and Mark V heavy tanks. (LAC PA-002926)

While its four battalions had worked well together, the 4th Brigade's experience in cooperation with other formations and arms was mixed in quality. Liaison with infantry of the 3rd Canadian Brigade on the right and the 7th Australian Brigade on the left was maintained throughout the morning, and cooperation among flanking battalions had been excellent. The Australians had given outstanding support to the 19th Battalion's B Company along the railway embankment, and they contributed materially to the capture of Marcelcave.[30] Perhaps to some degree, the effective cooperation between the Australians and the 19th Battalion was facilitated by the work of Maj. Hatch, who had been temporarily attached to 2nd Canadian Division headquarters during the battle to serve as liaison officer with the 2nd Australian Division. Sources are not clear about his precise role and activities, but the outgoing and feisty Hatch probably got along very well with the stereotypically pugnacious Australians.[31]

Unfortunately, the fog and the unfavourable topography had interfered with the efforts of Stokes mortar crews and tanks to advance along with the leading elements of the 4th Brigade. After-action reports from the 19th Battalion do not mention the mortars at all, nor do the tanks feature in these narratives until after the infantry had reached the Green Line. However, some tanks appear to have come into action earlier with the 18th Battalion, which judged their support as "one of the finest features of the day."[32] Therefore, as far as the 4th Brigade's share of the operation was

Tanks passing through a field during the Battle of Amiens. A dead body lies just to the right of the nearest tank. (LAC PA-002879)

concerned, the effectiveness of the tanks on 8 August could be described as mixed at best, and was in keeping with previous Canadian experiences with the machines. Brig.-Gen. Rennie's conservative attitude regarding the role of tanks did nothing to foster increased trust or closer cooperation between infantry and armour. But it did reflect the harsh fact that the vulnerable infantryman still had to depend on his own weapons and skills to deal with any opposition that survived the artillery barrages.

As with the mortars and tanks, reports from the 19th Battalion mention no notable assistance from the 2nd Battalion, CMGC, during the advance to the Green Line. However, other sources indicate that the officers and men of M Battery had been fully engaged in the attack along the railway embankment, where they captured "several" German machine-gun positions. In one incident, Cpl. C.J. Duffy noticed one gun holding up the infantry and rushed it from the rear, killing its two-man crew. As well, the battery commander, Capt. J.A. McCullough, "with three gunners rushed three German machine guns successively, the officer being twice wounded." The 18th Battalion also had obtained good support from the machine gunners of J Battery in its assault at Cancellette Wood Ravine. Crews from both batteries took up positions alongside the infantry on the Green Line, where they "further harried retreating Germans."[33] The machine-gun crews, bringing their weapons to bear on targets of opportunity, and occasionally tackling enemy positions in the style of the

Canadian infantry moving up during the Battle of Amiens. The quiet nature of this scene suggests they are from one of the later waves. Several French troops are in the right foreground. (LAC PA-002925)

infantry, played a far more active role in the attack than the 19th Battalion's records would lead us to believe.

Overall, the artillery had been the infantry's single most important source of support in the morning's advance. Starting at zero hour, the field artillery's creeping barrage, that ubiquitous feature of major assaults, screened the attacking ground forces and either suppressed or destroyed many of the German infantry's defensive positions. After the progress of the attack had exceeded the field guns' range, designated heavy artillery batteries continued to lay down suppressive barrages on key points of resistance such as Marcelcave. At the same time, German artillery batteries, most of which had been located and carefully plotted on Allied maps, were effectively smothered by counter-battery fire from other heavy artillery groups. This left the Canadians largely free from the threat of indirect fire from their opponents' artillery, although still vulnerable to the many hidden machine guns that had survived the creeping barrage.[34]

But not every aspect of the artillery plan proceeded like clockwork on the morning of 8 August. The actions of the 5th Brigade, Canadian Field Artillery, in furnishing close-fire support for the 4th Infantry Brigade were much less decisive. The 18th and 20th batteries, which were detailed to move up behind the 19th Battalion, were caught by the German artillery bombardment that had plagued the infantry in the period leading up to zero hour. This caused "rather severe casualties in men and horses," which, in combination with the fog, likely prevented the guns from catching up with the infantry. The divisional artillery's after-action report, failing to appreciate the difficulties posed by poor visibility, also complained that German machine-gun activity in the area west of Marcelcave had impeded the batteries' progress, and that casualties to artillery personnel and horses "might well have been avoided had the mopping up been done in a more speedy and thorough manner." On the other hand, the 17th and 23rd batteries seem to have had an easier time of it in following the 18th Battalion and, according to one narrative, "did some useful work."[35]

In the final analysis, the 4th Brigade's assault on the morning of 8 August 1918 relied mainly on the suppressive power of the artillery's creeping barrage and counter-battery fire, as well as the infantrymen's ability to fight their own way forward, capitalizing on the firepower of their Lewis guns, rifle grenades, rifles, and hand grenades.[36] That progress was maintained and that no dangerous degree of disorganization arose was a testament to the leadership and initiative of individual officers and other ranks who took charge of small groups and continued the advance, infiltrating through enemy positions without always knowing the degrees of success achieved by other groups.

The overall cohesion of the different attacking battalions appears even more impressive when the limited range of options for communication is considered. Because of the fog, communication forward of battalion headquarters was facilitated mainly by runners; it was only between battalion and brigade headquarters that telephones could be relied upon.[37] Apparently, the telephone links between the forward battalion report centres and battalion headquarters were severed during the fighting. As in previous battles, platoons were left largely on their own to achieve their objectives, while runners and company commanders did what they could to coordinate their efforts and maintain touch with units on either flank.

The early morning advance had been a spectacular one for the 19th Battalion and the other leading elements of the Canadian Corps. By the time Lt.-Col. Millen opened his headquarters in Marcelcave, his men had advanced two and a half to three miles beyond their jumping-off line and captured one field gun, twenty-nine machine guns, two *Minenwerfers*, and around 250 prisoners, the latter including a commanding officer and his staff, complete with medical officers and a chaplain. But the price in casualties was as grim as the results were impressive. All told, 4 officers were killed, 7 officers were wounded, and 147 other ranks were killed, wounded, or missing.[38] Almost three-quarters of the officers and over one-quarter of the other ranks in the four rifle companies became casualties that day.[39] The officers collectively suffered a tremendously high loss rate, and some of their wounds were fearsome in nature. To give just one example, Fred Stitt recalled A Company's Lt. William Herbert, who "was a buck private along with me in the Exhibition Grounds with the 19th. He lost his arm. The machine-gun blast took the arm right off his body. That was my company commander."[40] Others were much luckier. In a contribution to the post-war battalion association newsletter, Les Griffin asked his comrades:

> Were you ever wounded and didn't know it? Well, I was. It was the 8th of August, 1918, the start of the Big Push at Amiens. We had gone quite a distance when I walked over to Harry George (of the Soo) to tell him to pass the word to ease off to the right, and as I walked around a shell hole a German shell burst in the hole. The concussion knocked me off my feet, but I got up and walked to Harry and found he was wounded. I stopped to put bandages from his field dressing kit on his left wrist and forearm. While doing so I stopped to rub my left breast thinking it was cooties. When I stopped the second time to do this Harry said, "What's the matter with you?" I replied, "I'm moving the lice." I continued to scratch when suddenly Harry said, "You're hit! Your shoulder strap is hanging by a thread." After I'd finished bandaging Harry, I opened my tunic and found a lot of blood on my shirt and the wound still bleeding. Harry managed to get a bandage on me and we then headed for the dressing station which was manned by Australians … I still have the battered pay-book that probably saved my life.[41]

George was sent to Blighty, while Griffin was sent to a succession of French hospitals before rejoining the battalion.

Other wounded men were ministered to that morning by the battalion medical officer, Capt. Herbert ("Doc") Allison, and the battalion chaplain, Honorary Capt. ("Padre") Ewan Macdonald, both of whom accompanied the attacking troops all the way to the Green Line.[42] Allison moved his Regimental Aid Post (RAP) forward, keeping behind the attacking troops but close enough to render timely treatment. The task of locating the wounded, who were scattered over the battlefield, was made somewhat easier for the stretcher-bearers by the practice of driving a wounded man's rifle into the ground beside him, bayonet-first, and then placing his steel helmet atop the rifle butt.[43] Parts of the battlefield must have appeared an eerie sight to the stretcher-bearers and to follow-up forces, as they peered through the dissipating mist to find veritable "groves" of inverted rifles sprouting from the ground.

In capturing Marcelcave and securing the Green Line, the 4th Brigade as a whole sustained heavy casualties: 25 officers and an estimated 563 other ranks. On the positive side, the brigade had taken between 900 and 1,000 prisoners that morning (including those captured by the 19th Battalion), thus demonstrating that the quality of mercy had not been forgotten entirely by the Canadians.[44] However, mercy often was tempered by avarice as the Canadian troops remorselessly plundered prisoners for souvenirs, claiming caps, watches, buttons, badges, medals, daggers, pistols, postcards, and anything else that struck their fancy.[45] Just after the fall of Marcelcave, Capt. R.J. Renison, the chaplain of the 21st Battalion, beheld two men "with their helmets askew loaded with souvenirs and fortified with Hun refreshments simply eating up the town; the very personification of Canadian conquering spirit." Rather naively, Renison recounted that "every man was slung with all kinds of trophies, which symbolized, not material gain, but the victory of the

Canadian and French soldiers resting around a French 120mm Model 1878 gun, which has been recaptured from the Germans during the Battle of Amiens. (LAC PA-002907)

Spirit."[46] The more jaded Germans put it this way: "The British fight for glory, the Canadians for souvenirs."[47]

At 8:20 AM, the 24th and 26th Battalions of the 5th Infantry Brigade passed through the 4th Brigade's forward positions to carry out the second stage of the 2nd Canadian Division's attack. Around this time, G.D. Marshall observed a wounded officer of the 18th Battalion

> who true to school-book tradition raised his bloody head and counseled the troops to "give 'em hell boys!" Carrying out this officer, [the] stretcher party suddenly [was] surrounded by a wildly charging wave of the 22nd Battalion emerging from the mist at great speed, bayonets glistening in the early morning light, machine gun bullets nipping off the stalks of wheat about their knees. [The] 18th officer rose to his elbow – sank back on the stretcher – [and] said nothing. Probably felt [the] "Vandoos" needed no encouragement.[48]

That afternoon, at 2:15 PM, the 5th Brigade units reached their objectives along the Red Line, having forced their way through Pieuret Wood and taken the villages of Wiencourt and Guillaucourt. Although the fighting in this stage had moved well beyond the range of the massed field artillery barrage that had preceded and protected the 4th Brigade's effort, the surviving tanks and the mobile batteries of the 5th Brigade, CFA, were able to assume greater shares of the action. Also, several captured German field guns were turned around and put to good use by Canadian artillery crews trained to handle them. After 9:00 AM, conditions had cleared sufficiently for aerial operations to commence in earnest. Contact patrols, which had been unable to effectively monitor the progress of the 4th Brigade's troops, now ranged over the battlefield, while close-support squadrons strafed and bombed selected targets, harassed enemy reserves, and dropped smoke bombs to create screens for the ground forces. However, scattered German machine-gun and artillery positions continued to inflict damage on the attacking forces before succumbing to the onslaught.[49]

By 4:30 PM it was the 6th Infantry Brigade's turn, with the 29th and 31st Battalions sallying forth from the Red Line preceded by units of the British 1st Cavalry Division. Opposition to this third phase of the advance was weaker, and by 5:30 PM the 2nd Canadian Division had reached its share of the Blue Dotted Line, along the old outer Amiens defences. By 7:00 PM the 6th Brigade infantry was well established and supported by the 5th and 6th Brigades, CFA, and by one company of the 2nd Battalion, CMGC. The 1st, 3rd, and 4th Canadian Divisions had also fought their way forward throughout the day until most of the Blue Dotted Line was secured in the Canadian sector. Only on the far right, where the strongly defended village of Le Quesnel had rapidly filled with German reinforcements, did the Blue Line remain to be taken.[50]

Neither the Canadians nor the other Allied forces involved achieved total success on 8 August. Nevertheless, the attack by the British Fourth and French First Armies, spearheaded by the Canadian and Australian Corps, had inflicted the greatest single defeat on the German army since the beginning of the war. The Australian and Canadian Corps had driven forward to a maximum depth of between seven and eight miles, while the British III Corps, to the north of the Australians, and the French, to the south of the Canadians, had protected the flanks and advanced, respectively, two and five miles. Total casualties sustained by the British Fourth Army in delivering the main portion of the attack amounted to roughly 8,800 all ranks, of which the Canadian Corps incurred 3,868 (1,036 killed, 2,803 wounded, 29 taken prisoner). As for the Germans, their 2nd Army alone is said to have suffered losses of 650 to 700 officers and as many as 27,000 other ranks, two-thirds of whom had been rounded up as prisoners.[51]

The Germans still had large numbers of reserves, and the Allies had not achieved a breakthrough; even so, the effect of this first day of the battle on the morale of the German high command was catastrophic. In despair, Gen. Ludendorff pronounced 8 August "the black day of the German Army in the history of this war." Aside from the losses in men and materiel, what seems to have disturbed the German high command most was the eagerness with which large numbers of their troops gave themselves up to capture. Many German officers simply lost control of both the situation and their men. The shock of 8 August compounded the effects of the

Canadian stretcher-bearers moving past a tank during the Battle of Amiens. (LAC PA-002887)

failed German spring and summer offensives, along with the French counter-offensive on the Marne in July. For Ludendorff, meaningful offensive action against the Allies in the west would henceforth be a pipe dream. Even Kaiser Wilhelm bitterly conceded on 10 August that "we have reached the limits of our capacity. The war must be terminated."[52]

For their victory at Amiens, the Allies had massed strong resources against a comparatively weak portion of the German front. Skilled staff work and diligent intelligence gathering underpinned the two pillars on which the operation's success rested: the achievement of surprise, and effective artillery bombardments. These factors gave the infantry, tanks, and other arms the best chance of fighting their way forward through an enemy defensive network that, except for scattered points of tenacious resistance, was largely paralyzed. The mass use of tanks and other, even more novel, mechanized forces (such as the armoured cars of the Canadian Independent Force under Brig.-Gen. Raymond Brutinel)[53] were important ingredients for success, and the Battle of Amiens has sometimes been held up as a tank triumph. But success rates with mechanized forces were not uniform among the attacking formations, owing to differences in terrain, varying levels of experience in working with tanks, and inconsistent enemy resistance. Tanks had made a strong impact on the Australian front, but not so much on others, as the 4th Canadian Infantry Brigade's experience proved. Some individual Canadian battalions praised the tanks' work, but others, including the 19th Battalion, gave them little credit.

Overall, the victory at Amiens was, at least on the Canadian front, won mainly by the more traditional fighting arms – the artillery and infantry.[54]

During the afternoon and evening of 8 August, the 4th Brigade remained at the Green Line, its troops taking advantage of their increasingly quieter position to get some rest as the battle moved eastward. Earlier that morning, the 19th Battalion's rear details, including the transport and quartermaster's sections, had moved forward from Cagny over roads packed with all manner of horsed and mechanical transport, including ambulances conveying the wounded to clearing stations and hospitals farther to the rear. After resting for a few hours at Cachy, the rear details moved out again at 8:30 PM, reaching Marcelcave at midnight. A wagon park was established just outside the village, while the company field kitchens moved up and provided all ranks with their first hot meal of the day.[55] It had been a harrowing but ultimately satisfying day's work, and in spite of the considerable casualties, veterans like Fred Stitt could look back years later with a great deal of pride. "Oh it was a wonderful day the 8th of August, it sure was."[56]

Building on the "Black Day"

As spectacular as the first day's results were, the Battle of Amiens did not end at dusk on 8 August. Field Marshal Haig's ambition to achieve a breakthrough kept the Fourth Army pressing its attack against German positions that were rapidly being shored up with reserve forces that had been rushed in to stem the tide. As in earlier offensives, the attacking force at Amiens quickly ran out of steam. Surviving personnel in the assault formations were tired, often to the point of exhaustion, and infantry battalions needed to refill the gaps in their ranks left by casualties. Tank units had to repair or replace damaged and destroyed vehicles and get some rest for their overworked crews. Moreover, the advantage of surprise was completely gone.

In driving forward seven to eight miles, the Canadian and Australian Corps had left behind a large part of the artillery and logistical support networks from which their infantry and tanks had been able to spring forward on the morning of 8 August. To have any hope of repeating their achievement on subsequent days, they would need time to bring forward the full weight of field and heavy artillery resources, set up new battery positions and ammunition dumps, and establish telephone and other communication links over newly captured ground. Perhaps most important, the Allies required fresh intelligence on new German positions (especially for counter-battery purposes) and the numbers of divisions they now faced. On the night of 8–9 August, the Germans had brought up six divisions, or elements of divisions, to reinforce the formations that had been shattered on the opening day. Another three divisions arrived the next day.[57]

Just before midnight on 8 August, Gen. Rawlinson ordered the Canadian, Australian, and British III Corps to continue pressing their attacks on the following day. On the Canadian front, the goal was to reach the area stretching between Roye to the south and Chaulnes to the north. Most divisions slated to attack on 9 August, including all four Canadian divisions, were no longer fresh or up to full strength, having fought all through the previous day. They were to jump off from recently captured positions without the benefit of all the support and preparation that had backed them up on the morning of 8 August.

The operation began well on the Canadian Corps' right, where the 4th Canadian Division finished the job of capturing Le Quesnel in the early morning. But delays in getting the attacking forces properly assembled, coupled with communications problems, hampered the rest of the day's progress. The ground fighting in the Canadian and other sectors was correctly characterized by the British official history as being

> of a very disjoined nature; the attacks of various divisions and brigades started at different times and under different conditions. Some of them were covered by artillery, some supported by tanks, whilst others were carried out by infantry unaided. The German defence was similarly very uneven and without any serious attempt at counter-attack. In the result only a bare three-miles advance, half the way to Roye-Chaulnes, was accomplished.[58]

The Canadians, in common with other formations, had perfected the methods for breaking into enemy positions but had not yet mastered the complexities of more open fighting. Also, technical impediments, such as the vulnerability of telephone cables to the movements of follow-up units of infantry, tanks, cavalry, and artillery (which often ran over and accidentally severed lines between forward units and their headquarters), did much to undercut the attackers' cohesion. Sending messages by runner, mounted orderly, or motorcycle often proved the only reliable means by which units and formations could keep in touch. But these courier-type methods required time and were prone to delays along roadways crammed with all manner of combatant and support forces making their way forward to back up the troops at the forefront of the attack.[59]

On 9 August the 2nd Canadian Division's share of the attack was carried out by the 5th and 6th Brigades, which were tasked with capturing the villages of Rosières and Vrély before moving on to Méharicourt and Chilly. After a vicious afternoon of fighting, the division made it as far as Méharicourt before settling down to regroup for the next day. The infantry had fought their way around the ever-present and always stubborn machine-gun nests, eventually getting some help from surviving tanks and trench mortar detachments.[60]

The 4th Brigade, in the meantime, still held the Green Line on the morning of 9 August, with the 19th Battalion on the left, the 21st in the centre, the 18th on the right, and the 20th in reserve. While the 5th and 6th Brigades continued the division's attack, the 4th was held in reserve, under orders to move at a few minutes' notice. The men of the 19th Battalion, along with the rest of the brigade, moved forward later in the day while the other brigades continued pushing the Germans east. But Brig.-Gen. Rennie's units were not required to take part in the day's operations. Having moved some distance southeast of Marcelcave, with its transport section following immediately behind, the 19th Battalion settled into new positions in the late morning. There, all companies took advantage of the opportunity to rest up from the previous day's exertions. By early evening, Lt.-Col. Millen had received word that his men would not be required to move until the following morning at the earliest. The men then briefly set to work digging small, rough holes in which to shelter for the night. This proved to be a wise move, for German aircraft ranged over the area at night, occasionally dropping bombs. But no casualties were incurred from this aerial nuisance.[61]

On 10 August the Fourth Army again continued its advance, with orders to capture the unattained objectives of the previous day. In the Canadian sector, the 1st and 2nd Canadian Divisions were relieved and passed into corps reserve, while the 4th Canadian Division and the 32nd British Division (attached temporarily to the Canadian Corps) carried out the operation. Thus the 4th Brigade again had little to do for the rest of the day but take up new stations farther forward, while the battle line continued to inch its way painfully eastward in the face of continued German efforts to reinforce the front. The 19th Battalion moved up to the vicinity of the hamlet of Caix, leaving rear details and part of its transport behind under the control of the 4th Brigade's transport officer. The weather was sunny and hot as the troops trudged past dusty fields along roads littered with the material and human wreckage of battle. Vivian Thompson observed "a number of Germans lying around and all seemed to have fallen to the cavalry since they all showed the throat wound of saber or lance … The long columns of prisoners was another feature of these days. I never did see so many Germans."[62] Having reached the fields around Caix, Millen's men took up positions in old trenches and bivouacs, enduring again some nighttime bombing courtesy of the German air force, which was no more successful in inflicting casualties than it had been the previous night.[63]

Gains along the Canadian front had been minimal on 10 August. Efforts by the 4th Canadian and 32nd British Divisions to capitalize on progress made during the morning were stymied by German resistance later that day. The ground was increasingly difficult to move over and did not facilitate rapid advances. Meanwhile, the Canadians were rapidly running out of available tank support, with only 37 machines available for the four divisions out of an original strength of 162.[64]

The Canadian Corps, along with other formations of the British Fourth and French First Armies, was now entering a zone of old trenches and defensive positions dating from the period before the Germans had pulled back to the Hindenburg Line in early 1917. The landscape was overgrown with long grass that concealed ragged stretches of trench, countless shell holes, and fearsome thickets of rusted barbed wire. For the four relatively fresh German formations that had just

A column of German prisoners marching through Amiens, August 1918. (LAC PA-003725)

moved into the line opposite the Canadian Corps (the 221st Infantry Division, 121st Infantry Division, and 38th Infantry Division, and the single division of the Alpine Corps), this was ideal country for setting up concealed machine-gun nests and other strongpoints. Now that the Allies were pushing their way back into the zone of the old Somme battlefield, the fighting "suddenly reverted from open pursuit almost to the old pattern of trench warfare."[65] The amount of territory captured was steadily diminishing each day as Allied casualties mounted and German resistance stiffened along stretches of terrain that gave greater advantage to the defender.

Contention was growing among the Allied high command regarding the merits of continuing the offensive east of Amiens. Marshal Foch[66] was keen to maintain pressure on the Germans, and he browbeat Field Marshal Haig to press his Fourth Army forward without adequate time to prepare another full-scale set-piece attack on a broad front. The senior commanders in closer touch with the actual pace of operations, including Lt.-Gens. Currie and Monash, saw little point in hurling more men at stronger positions, and Currie presented an alternative plan to

Gen. Rawlinson. Based on solid intelligence reports and aerial photos of German defences, which indicated that further hastily organized infantry attacks east of Amiens would result only in heavier losses, Currie convinced Rawlinson that the battle should be terminated on this front and resumed elsewhere. The Canadian Corps, Currie argued, should be pulled out of this sector and moved north to help spearhead another surprise attack in the First Army zone. Given the results of the fighting after 8 August, Rawlinson and Haig already had misgivings about continuing the assault against the increasingly strong enemy opposition east of Amiens. They were quickly persuaded by the merits of Currie's idea, but Foch needed more convincing before he finally agreed to it on 15 August. Through the soundness of their performance to date, the Canadians had strengthened their voice in the councils of the Allied high command.[67]

Fighting at Fransart

With plans for further large-scale offensive efforts by the Fourth Army suspended for the immediate future, the Battle of Amiens effectively came to a close on 11 August. However, small-scale actions continued over the next week, and while these incidents usually do not rate much explanation in most historical accounts, they were significant and sometimes savage encounters for the units involved. The 19th Battalion's own particular trial would occur at a tiny hamlet named Fransart.

On 11 August the 4th Brigade was still in divisional reserve, occupying and improving positions along the old outer Amiens defence line. It then moved forward later in the day to relieve the 6th Brigade in the Rosières area. The companies of the 19th Battalion, followed by elements of its quartermaster and transport sections, moved up to an area on the northeastern outskirts of Rosières, where they relieved the 29th Battalion in brigade support positions.[68] G.D. Marshall had been in the desolate village two days earlier, working with an evacuation party looking for wounded. The "only living things in Rosieres" that he saw were "one kitten; several carrier pigeons."[69]

The next day, the 2nd Canadian Division was ordered to take over the southern portion of the sector held by the 4th Canadian Division as a preliminary move for future operations. Having been out of action the longest of the division's three brigades, it was the 4th Brigade's turn to take over the divisional front. As such, the 19th Battalion assumed control of the far right sub-section of the brigade front, with the 20th Battalion and several 4th Division units taking up positions to their left. The relief was concluded by the morning of the 13th. The 19th Battalion's C, D, and A Companies respectively occupied the right, centre, and left front-line positions, while B Company sat in support.[70] Vivian Thompson remembered that "one night a plane came over (it was quite light) and dropped a bomb on the trench on my immediate right burying Ernie Young. I remember how Ernie's teeth were chattering when he passed me."[71]

On 14 August, division headquarters received word that all proposed major offensive efforts on that front were postponed indefinitely.[72] But constant touch still had to be maintained with the Germans in order to discern their strength and intentions. Vicious little patrol encounters became the order of the day, and tensions only increased when the Canadians learned that they were up against one of the elite formations of the German army. "We are very tired," wrote Deward Barnes, who had just been appointed lance corporal. "Only three to four hours sleep a night … The German unit opposite was relieved by Alpine troops, Germany's raiders … We are looking for raids as the Alpines are all young fellows."[73]

In the front lines, uncertainty usually bred fear. The best way to combat uncertainty was to gain accurate intelligence. Accordingly, when word came in on 14 August that troops of the 3rd Canadian Division, on the right, had stolen into the village of La Chavatte and found it unoccupied, Lt.-Col. Millen decided to send out a daylight patrol to check out conditions in Fransart, the village facing his unit. Scout officer Lt. Richard H.L. Dinsmore was in overall charge of the enterprise, which also counted Lts. Walter H. Curry and William P. Venn, three battalion scouts, and forty other ranks drawn from C, B, and D Companies. Curry led the party from C Company, Dinsmore the B Company crew, and Venn the men from D Company.

The parties moved carefully down three separate trenches towards Fransart, with Curry's men creeping down Ogre Trench, Dinsmore's through Oracle Alley, and Venn's along Tomb Alley. All three groups encountered well-manned German posts or blocks. After hurling bouquets of grenades at their opponents, the Canadians hurried back to their own positions, suffering no casualties for their efforts. They determined that Fransart was still strongly occupied, and so were not surprised when it turned out that the earlier reports on the status of La Chavatte proved to be rather hasty. The Germans were still in possession of it as well and had mounted a vigorous defence in the face of the 3rd Canadian Division's efforts to capture the village of Parvillers, to the southwest.[74]

Increasingly better informed of what faced them, the men of the 19th Battalion spent a quieter day on 15 August, save for an early morning bombardment, with a heavy proportion of gas shells, of the area around Fouquescourt. For all of their anxieties about the Alpine Corps, no enemy raids were forthcoming. Millen's men now occupied the entire brigade frontage, with the 18th, 20th, and 21st Battalions disposed in depth immediately to their rear.[75] As a result, they found themselves in the forefront of a short, sharp action on the following day, which would mark their bitter farewell to the Amiens sector.

On 16 August the 1st Canadian Division moved into the line to the right of the 19th Battalion, taking over the sector held by the 3rd Canadian Division. That same day, on the 1st Division's right flank, French forces of the XXXI Corps mounted an attack on the village of Goyencourt. In cooperation with the French, Lt.-Gen.

Canadian stretcher-bearers bringing in wounded during the Battle of Amiens. Not everyone in the photo is wearing a gas mask, therefore they may be either entering or leaving an area where anti-gas precautions are in force. (LAC PA-002919)

Currie ordered the 1st Canadian Division to seize both Fresnoy-les-Roye and La Chavatte. The 2nd Canadian Division, in turn, was to assist on the left by taking Fransart. The order from Currie's headquarters landed on Maj.-Gen. Burstall's desk at 11:00 AM. Thirty minutes later, the division commander telephoned 4th and 5th Brigade headquarters, instructing Brig.-Gen. Rennie to advance on Fransart and Brig.-Gen. Thomas-Louis Tremblay to attack Hallu. Both brigades were ordered to "send forward strong patrols which, if they did not encounter strong resistance," were to make good their objectives and, if possible, secure a line along the railway that ran just east of Fransart. Burstall organized a covering bombardment, which was initially set for 2:00 PM but quickly modified to 3:15 PM.[76]

With brigade orders drawn up, Brig.-Gen. Rennie summoned Lt.-Col. Millen to meet him at a point between their respective headquarters. When the two met at noon, Rennie personally issued the operation order to Millen, outlining the objectives and timing of the attack and placing four additional companies, two from the 18th Battalion and two from the 20th, at his disposal. The operation would require the engagement of all four of the 19th Battalion's companies, hence the need for additional support. Millen immediately returned to his headquarters and called a meeting of all company commanders, including those of A and B Companies from the 18th Battalion and A and C Companies from the 20th Battalion. The news came as an unwelcome surprise to the officers, who had not expected that their units would be sent into action again before their scheduled relief by battalions of the 4th Canadian Division. After reading out Rennie's order to the assembled officers, Millen brought out a map and worked out the role and objectives of each company. Once everyone understood their mission, Millen and the company commanders pondered the feasibility of a 3:15 PM start and concluded that this did not give them enough time to get their troops into the most favourable jumping-off positions before zero hour. With both Rennie's and Burstall's subsequent approval of a 4:30 start, all arrangements for the pending attack were finalized.[77]

After Rennie had settled matters with division headquarters, he moved forward to keep in closer touch with events as they developed. He proceeded first to his own advanced headquarters, but, evidently deciding that this was not far enough forward, he moved on to 19th Battalion headquarters. By then, the attacking troops from all four companies of the 19th Battalion had begun filtering forward through old communication trenches to get as close as they could to the German front line in time for zero hour.[78] The men were unpleasantly surprised to learn that the initial bombardment would fall on Fransart itself and that there would be no creeping barrage to shield their movement all the way to the German front line. Why this arrangement was chosen is not explained in the surviving records. Perhaps the attack was deemed insufficiently large to warrant a creeping barrage; or there simply may not have been enough time to organize one. Whatever the reason, the infantry was left to make its own way forward. Deward Barnes wrote that

> we … crawled through fields. I crawled, dragging the Lewis gun after me. Three or four of our platoon got shot through the top of the head near me but we had to keep going. There was some barbed wire in front of us where we had to find the openings, which zigzagged through the belts of wire, and kept on crawling until we came to a trench. When we got to it, our officer looked his map over to see where he was. We split up the platoon, the officer took a party one way and I took the remainder the other way. We were to meet in the German front line.[79]

Millen's troops were disposed as follows: B Company (left flank); A Company (left centre); D Company (right centre); and C Company (right flank). The two companies from the 18th Battalion acted in support of D and C Companies while those of the 20th Battalion did the same for B and A Companies. In addition, Lt. C.W. Dawson of the 10th Battery, CFA, stood by as artillery liaison officer and prepared to deal with certain enemy positions that required special attention from the gunners supporting the operation. At Dawson's request, further arrangements were made for him and his signalling equipment to move forward with the attacking troops so that he could be in the best position to direct the supporting batteries.[80]

At 4:30 PM the 19th Battalion attackers sprang into action as the artillery barrage moved off from the village of Fransart and rolled on to the Chaulnes–Roye railway line. Things went reasonably well for B Company on the left flank, although a certain amount of bombing was required before it could achieve its objective. This took only a few minutes, and by 4:45 PM, a mere fifteen minutes after zero hour, B Company reported that it was already consolidating along its objective, adding a request for additional ammunition and bombs. Probably owing to unexpectedly heavy German resistance, A Company, in the left-centre position, took considerably longer to clear its objective, which it finally reported captured at 6:50 PM. At one point, some assistance was required from a platoon of the 20th Battalion, which was used to help clear up the situation between the 19th Battalion's B and A Companies. This platoon captured two machine guns and killed twelve Germans, indicating that the enemy had put up a fight at this point.[81]

Ever the survivor, Deward Barnes had made it to the objective along with the rest of his comrades in A Company. After his platoon had split up before entering the German front line, Deward's party

> found a half dozen or so dead Germans in the trench and then came upon a machine-gun post. We captured the crew and sent them back with a couple of men and kept on going. We finally got to the German front line with only a few casualties. The officer gave us the devil for not killing the German machine gun crew. As soon as we got to the front line we started to dig in, as it was 5:30 PM now.[82]

It is not clear why Deward and his companions started digging in along the German front line at 5:30 PM, considering that at 6:15 PM their company commander reported continued enemy opposition near the "junction of Quergraben and [their] objective." It took another thirty-five minutes before the objective was secured. That there may have been some confusion about where the men should begin consolidating is understandable, given that the entire operation was planned and executed at only a few hours' notice.[83]

While A Company was capturing its objective, B Company was forced to occupy and consolidate the position called Danzig Alley because troops from the 5th Brigade on their immediate left had been unable to make much headway in their section of the attack. In securing its own left flank, B Company called on the services of both supporting companies from the 20th Battalion. Telephone communication along the left portion of the 19th Battalion's attack remained good throughout the operation, thanks largely to the efforts of Capt. A.A. Smith of the 20th Battalion, who remained at B Company's headquarters and relayed all messages back to Lt.-Col. Millen. At 7:10 PM, shortly after the situation was stabilized along the left, it was reported that German troops had been seen massing for a counterattack in a nearby wood. The coordinates were relayed back to the gunners of the 3rd Brigade,

CFA, who quickly unleashed several salvoes on the suspected assembly point. No further problems were reported from that area.[84]

Along the right portion of the 19th Battalion assault, the situation was considerably rougher. "Casualties were heavy," reported 4th Brigade headquarters, and "the machine gun work of the enemy was very costly to us." Reinforcements were sent in

> from the two supporting companies of the 18th Canadian Battalion. The enemy put up stout resistance in the S.W. [southwest] of the village and "C" Company, 19th Canadian Battalion at one time was held up and had to fight for every foot of ground. As soon as this information was received, instructions were sent to the centre right company [D Company] to advance into the village. The determination with which this company pushed forward through the village, weakened the resistance on our right and the right company [C Company], reinforced by two platoons of the 18th Canadian Battalion, were again able to push on and clear the southern portion of Fransart.

Numerous machine guns and many prisoners were captured.

Just after 6:00 PM, the officer commanding D Company reported that he had successfully established his forward headquarters, indicating that the situation along his unit's section of the attack was secure. The Germans, he informed Millen, had been driven behind the Chaulnes–Roye railway line, but casualties in his company were heavy. Consequently, he requested that more reinforcements be sent up to strengthen his position. As for C Company on the far right, its commanding officer reported at 7:05 PM that his men had finally taken their objective in front of Fransart and were in touch with D Company on the left. However, the state of affairs on his right flank was a different story altogether. In the 1st Canadian Division's sector, the 13th Battalion of the 3rd Infantry Brigade had failed in three attempts to capture La Chavatte; nor could troops of the 2nd Brigade manage to force their way through strong German defences into Fresnoy-les-Roye. This left the 19th Battalion's right flank exposed. According to Lt.-Col. Millen, the only solution was send troops into the 3rd Brigade's territory. This was done, and soon Millen reported that the flank was secured. After several more hours and "repeated requests" for assistance, the 3rd Brigade finally took over the trenches in their section occupied by Millen's men and established a firm connection with the 4th Brigade along their mutual boundary.[85]

The 4th Brigade effort, carried out mainly by the 19th Battalion, was the most successful of the Canadian operations mounted on 16 August. In some areas along its 2,500-yard frontage, the brigade had advanced more than one mile and in the process captured about half of the village of Fransart, "7 machine guns, numerous rifles and stores, [and] 56 prisoners including an adjutant." The price of this extremely local success was 8 other ranks killed, 4 officers and 53 other ranks wounded, and 8 other ranks missing. Presumably, most of these came from the four companies of the 19th Battalion.[86] These losses seem reasonably light for an attack involving all four of the battalion's companies; however, without knowing how many men took part in the operation, it is difficult to say anything definitive on the subject of casualties. In any case, Fred Stitt declared that the operation at Fransart was "a nasty piece of work, darn nasty":

> We went across and straightened it out, gathered up a few prisoners and in the process, did a lot of damage to them, but I never forget it. When the word came around that we were going over at 4 o'clock in the afternoon in broad daylight with the sun shining and no barrage. We said, "What is this?" and my brother Herb ... he had a big can of beans in his haversack and he was going to save it for some future purpose when you might be wishing he had some rations. He looked at the can of beans, and he said [if] "we're going over at 4 o'clock, I might as well eat the beans now because I might not eat them after."[87]

Although there had been no rolling barrage preceding the troops all the way to the German front line, the artillery *was* active at Fransart, beginning with the initial covering barrage directed onto the village itself by the 3rd Brigade, CFA. Throughout the operation, Lt. Dawson of the 10th Battery worked from his forward observation post, identifying especially troublesome enemy strongpoints and machine-gun nests and communicating this information back to 19th Battalion headquarters by signal flag. These messages were relayed by telephone to the gunners, who directed their fire onto the coordinates specified by Dawson. "Without this fire by the artillery," the war diarist of the 3rd Brigade, CFA, wrote, "it is doubtful if the objective could have been reached without heavy loss of life."[88]

In his after-action report, Lt.-Col. Millen offered glowing praise of Lt. Dawson, the supporting artillery, and the officers and other ranks of the 18th and 20th Battalions.[89] In a rather curious contrast to their reports on the events of 8 August, both Millen and the battalion war diarist neglected to mention by name any members of their own battalion. Perhaps this was to make up for their comparative neglect of other arms and units in their reports for 8 August. Nevertheless, it was the officers and other ranks of the 19th Battalion who had done the bulk of the dirty work in seizing and holding their companies' objectives at Fransart. And as in all actions, when many of the officers involved became casualties, it was up to the other ranks to see the job through. Years after the event, Fred Stitt could still recall the heroism displayed by his company sergeant major:

> Let me tell you a little incident ... [at] Fransart. These little dog fights you know could lead to some really interesting stuff. We had [in] our company, [a] Sgt. Major in C Company of the 19th Battalion, by the name of Joe Thomas, a fellow from Sault Ste. Marie. He wasn't very big, he was only about 5 foot 6 but he was a real Sgt. Major. He carried a 45 revolver which is as big as himself almost you know. Away goes C Company along with the rest of us to this Fransart affair. They hadn't gone very far until they had lost every darn one of their officers, everyone of them hit, which left Joe in

> command of the company. Well Joe didn't know this of course, he didn't know that he'd lost his officers, because it was spread over a huge area … But Joe was in command whether he knew it or not and he kept on belting along towards Fransart. He finally jumps into a German trench at Fransart, and they were in Fransart Village. Oh there must have been 14 or 15 Germans in it and he just waved this gat at them and they all surrendered, and … with the other hand he's bringing his men forward you see, "Come on men," and he turns around and looks and the closest man is 100 yards away. In other words Joe is in there with 15 Heinies with a gat, but he gets them and his men eventually reach there and he establishes his company in that trench, fixes it up for a defence if necessary and then decides to load his gat again. So he brings his gat over and there's nothing in it but blanks. He had used the loading on the way over and hadn't kept track of it so he jumped into that confounded mob of Germans with an empty gat.[90]

As astonished as Sgt. Thomas must have been at his own luck, the Germans had some nasty surprises of their own for the Canadians. Lt.-Col. Millen reported that several of his casualties were caused by "light booby traps on wires," which were set up at various points in the trenches at Fransart. One of the victims of these devices was Vivian Thompson of D Company, who wrote:

> We moved to our right and then got on top and made a dash for it but were received with plenty of machine gun fire. We dropped into a deep trench and proceeded to work our way up it. It was well blocked with barbed wire but we made our way through it. In this trench there was a sudden bang and our officer left us with a number of cuts on his face, as far as I could tell, as the result of some sort of a trench mine going off. We collected ourselves from this and went forward again under Charlie Kinch who was our corporal. All at once some one shouted to "watch that wire[,]" there was a bang, I got a heck of a welt in the face, had visions of going to eternity and then had a mental picture of an illustration in "Life" in which a chap laid down on the railway, the train passed on the other track and he sat up and said "not so worse." Charlie had one leg blown off and the other practically off and died immediately. Doady Taylor was wounded and went back to the clearing station where he died several days later … Another lad got his hand and arm full of sand and shrapnel, another got a bayonet in his neck, another lad in front of me was said to have lost both his eyes and I was thought to have lost my right eye. I helped to fix up the lad with the damaged arm as Terry was busy with the others, and then I ditched my gear and turned back as I could not see out of my right eye and only partly out of my left one. On the way back down the trench I met a couple of staff officers, one of whom was a colonel of the Medical Corps, and the colonel took out my field dressing and fixed up my eye … Evidently the trench mines were made of potato mashers and had more kick than hard stuff in them so that I had received one and one-half black eyes with a small piece of tin cutting my right eyebrow and while it was not so bad it might have been worse if the tin had been a quarter or half an inch lower.[91]

Thompson was eventually taken to a casualty clearing station and then to a military hospital in Rouen. He fared far better than some of his comrades. After a period of convalescence, he would be back on duty with the 19th Battalion by 20 September.[92]

Although losses were not nearly as high as on 8 August, many 19th Battalion men likely thought that the fight at Fransart caused more trouble than the amount of ground gained was worth. But the 2nd Canadian Division could not sit idly by while the formations to its right pushed ahead and exposed their flanks. As was the case with numerous other operations carried out along the Western Front over the course of the war, the attack was made to "even out" the front line and to support the advance of neighbouring formations. If the 19th Battalion did not assault Fransart, some other Canadian unit would have had to.

From a historical perspective, the operation does give us a rare glimpse into the operational planning process from division down to battalion level. It also provides the clearest picture yet of Lt.-Col. Millen's role and influence. In his meeting with the company commanders, he exhibited an executive and collaborative style of command: he explained their tasks and entertained opinions on the feasibility of the start time mandated by division headquarters. Millen's request to postpone zero hour until 4:30 PM shows that he and his officers had a clearer grasp of the situation on his front than either Brig.-Gen. Rennie or Maj.-Gen. Burstall. This was, to some degree, only natural. But more significantly, Rennie's and Burstall's willingness to adjust their plans based on Millen's recommendations illustrates the level of confidence they had in his judgment. It shows that by 1918 an experienced and respected battalion commander could dictate the pace of his unit's operations in the context of brigade and division plans.

It is more difficult to account for Rennie's decision to station himself at 19th Battalion headquarters during the attack, especially since there is no reason to question his confidence in Millen's ability to direct it. This decision may have reflected the brigadier's simple desire "to keep in closer touch with the situation."[93] Politeness and protocol required Millen to acknowledge in his after-action report the beneficial presence of his superior throughout the operation. As he put it, in rather awkward fashion, "considerable of the success of the operation is due to the presence throughout of the Brigadier at Battalion Headquarters." However, Rennie's pronouncement in his own report to Burstall has a far greater ring of truth: "The success of the operation was due largely to Lieutenant-Colonel L.H. Millen ... who throughout had a thorough grasp of the situation, and to the dash and spirit of all ranks."[94]

A Brief Rest

The rude shock of having to attack Fransart with scarcely any advance notice convinced many in 4th Brigade that they would be retained in the front lines for even more such dirty work. Thus, the word "relief" took on a very literal meaning on the evening of 16 August when news came that, as originally promised, they would be withdrawn later that night. The 47th Battalion and two companies of the 50th Battalion arrived to take over the line from the 19th Battalion, the relief being completed by early morning on 17 August. By noon the entire 2nd Canadian Division had been pulled back into corps reserve, replaced by the 4th Canadian Division.[95]

Maj.-Gen. Robert Rennie, CB, CMG, DSO, MVO, VD. This portrait, by Lt. (Robert) Allan Barr, hangs in the Officers' Mess of the Queen's Own Rifles of Canada. Rennie served as an officer in the Queen's Own Rifles before the war and was Colonel Commandant of the regiment from June 1916 to March 1920. He was promoted Maj.-Gen. in 1921. From December 1936 to March 1939 he served as Honorary Lt.-Col. of the Queen's Own Rifles and then as Honorary Col. until his death in December 1949. (Portrait photograph by Christopher Lawson, used with permission)

Lt.-Gen. Currie inspects some of the German artillery captured during the Battle of Amiens. (LAC PA-003046)

The 19th Battalion moved back some six miles to bivouac near Caix. Along the way, many men availed themselves of a comforting mug of hot tea as they passed by a canteen set up by the YMCA in a valley between the villages of Vrély and Caix. Shortly after reaching Caix, orders came through for the battalion to move two miles farther back, to Wiencourt, where it would be joined by transport and rear details. Before setting out again, the men were given time to make use of local bathing facilities, after which they were issued with clean clothes. Then they moved off to Wiencourt, which they reached later in the day on 17 August. There, they would stay for the next two days, huddled in scattered cellars and bivouacs. Pay parades and further issues of clothing brought some added cheer to the weary men.[96]

Few members of the battalion could have been more relieved to be out of action than Lt.-Col. Millen. Since returning from his course on 3 August, he had presided over the most intense period of activity, uncertainty, and expectation that his men had yet experienced. To top it all off, on 8 August, the day of his battalion's biggest attack since the storming of Vimy Ridge over a year earlier, Millen received a double dose of tragic news. His terminally ill wife, Edith, had passed away, and a good friend, Lt.-Col. Elmer W. Jones of the 21st Battalion, had been fatally wounded in action. At last, with some time to collect his thoughts as he sat in his billet in Weincourt, Millen poured his heart out in a letter to his mother:

> It is I know some considerable time since I wrote last, but the papers will have informed you we have been busy and that to some purpose. We have every reason to be satisfied with our share, two villages stand to our credit, one indisputably ours. We have just come back, yesterday. I was all in, thought for awhile it was sickness, but figure now it was dead dog tiredness all over as I had not had a decent sleep for a considerable period. Am alright again today, and am glad as we understand we are moving again, not forward but back. It looks as though they figure we have done (I mean Canadians) [our] share here … I received the wire from Rex [his brother] about poor dear Edith Aug 8th, after we had settled down on our first objective. It came the night before but others thought they knew what it contained, so opened it and held it until this operation was over … I realize it was inevitable so the shock was not as great as it might have been. I also know it was for the best, as life could never have meant anything to her in her condition. Again as you can imagine life has been too strenuous since for me to permit myself to brood on her loss.[97]

Never was Millen's habit of putting on a brave face in his letters more pronounced than in this note. If discussing Edith's anticipated passing was difficult enough, it took another two weeks before he could bring himself to inform his mother about the death of his friend, Elmer Jones.[98] In that letter he also enclosed a touching note from Jones's wife, Isobel, in which she wrote of her profound grief and asked: "Dear Lionel if it is possible for you to ever get to Elmer's grave will you say a little prayer there for me – Do you know he said to me in his last letters written the day before he was killed 'Tomorrow will be Canada's day' – the words ought to be written on his cross."[99] Vivian Thompson later recalled hearing "some sort of a yarn about Colonel Millen doing a weep as he watched the men go past on the way back [from Fransart] as they were so few. This may be a cock and bull story, but we certainly were a changed outfit when I next saw it."[100]

Like Millen, many other men used this brief period of rest to write to family and friends who were anxiously awaiting word that they had come through the recent fighting in one piece. One of them was Pte. Frederick J. McNulty of Hamilton, who wrote the following to his sister Mary:

> I'll bet all of you are worrying yourselves these days wondering what has happened to me that I haven't written you a line sooner to let you know that I am O.K. Well Sis we have been so busy that writing was out of the Question altogether. I suppose you have seen in the papers that we have been at it again and say Sis we sure did spill the beans for Fritz this time and yours truly did his little bit as usual and came through it O.K. I managed to capture the odd prisoner and got a nice revolver and cap for a souvenir.[101]

McNulty was one of over seventy members of the 19th Battalion who would later receive decorations for their service during the month of August. Most of them, like McNulty, were awarded the Military Medal.[102]

The Canadians' time at Amiens had finally come to an end. On 19 August, as the 1st and 4th Canadian Divisions were fighting their final actions in the sector, the 2nd and 3rd Canadian Divisions began their journey north to First Army.[103] Between 8 and 20 August the Canadian Corps had advanced as much as fourteen miles and established a frontage of 10,000 yards. In the process, the Canadians had liberated twenty-seven villages in an area covering sixty-seven square miles; among their captures were over 9,000 prisoners, more than 1,000 machine guns and trench mortars, and almost 200 artillery pieces. They had encountered elements of fifteen German divisions, "completely routing" four of the ten they engaged directly. The cost, by 20 August, was 11,822 Canadian casualties, most of which (9,074) were sustained between 8 and 11 August.[104] As in earlier years of the war, battlefield successes remained extremely costly. However, the amount of territory liberated for the number of casualties incurred was far greater than in any previous operation of comparable scale. Lt.-Gen. Currie told his men that they had achieved a "magnificent victory," which was won "because your training was good, your discipline was good, your leadership was good. Given these three, success must always come."[105]

19

Arras: 19–31 August 1918

In accordance with Lt.-Gen. Currie's recommendations, the British high command pulled the Canadian Corps out of the Amiens sector, and on 19 August the corps began to move north in order to rejoin Gen. Sir Henry Horne's British First Army. In securing Marshal Foch's agreement to wind up the offensive east of Amiens, Field Marshal Haig committed his forces to a renewed effort elsewhere on the front. Accordingly, Gen. Byng's British Third Army, occupying a nineteen-mile stretch of front north of Albert, was ordered to attack in the direction of Bapaume, while to the south, Rawlinson's British Fourth Army regained its strength and prepared to follow up any further German withdrawals. North of Byng's forces, Horne's First Army would launch its assault in a southeasterly direction from the Arras front.

The offensive at Amiens had demonstrated that the German armies on the Western Front were more vulnerable than anticipated. Instead of conserving their strength and waiting for the arrival of more American divisions to deliver a decisive blow in 1919, the Allies decided to mount an all-out effort and reach a decision before the end of the year. Now was the time to execute Foch's vision of multiple attacks delivered in rapid succession along the Western Front. But the downside to denying the Germans any respite was that it meant much the same for experienced assault troops like the Canadians. With reinforcements rushed up to fill gaps in the ranks left by the fighting at Amiens, the Canadians would be thrown into action by the First Army just days after their return to the familiar Arras sector.[1]

The goal of their attack, which would be carried out in conjunction with the Third Army's efforts to the south, would be to break through the heavily defended German position known as the Drocourt–Quéant Line. If they could accomplish this, they would be able to outflank the Hindenburg Line from the north and jeopardize any German attempts to rally their forces behind that formidable defensive system to oppose the Third Army.[2]

The 2nd Canadian Division, in corps reserve, was among the first formations to make the move back to the First Army. On 19 August, Lt.-Col. Millen was ordered to move his men to the vicinity of Boves, some five miles southeast of Amiens, where they arrived the following day. "The men were very tired," commented the battalion war diarist, and they "had a good rest and sleep in the open field" before moving to the local railway station. At 11:30 AM on 20 August, all ranks clambered aboard a train, which would take them to Wavrans. Twelve hours later, they reached their destination. After piling out of the packed boxcars, they marched to Ecoivres, where they occupied scattered billets for the next two and a half days.[3]

Planning the Next Show

While the men rested and began recovering from their ordeal at Amiens, little did they know that they would have to reprise their performance in very short order. On the evening of 22 August, Currie convened a conference of divisional commanders at which he outlined his plans for the upcoming operations southeast of Arras, astride the highway between Arras and Cambrai. After announcing the intended starting date (26 August), Currie laid out the tasks assigned to each division and asked their commanders to draw up their own specific plans as quickly as possible. The corps would attack on a three-division front, leading off with the 2nd Canadian Division on the right, the 3rd Canadian Division in the centre, and the 51st (Highland) Division, temporarily attached to Currie's command, on the left. The main thrust would be delivered by the 2nd and 3rd Canadian Divisions. Meanwhile, the 51st Division, protecting the left flank, would advance just north of the Scarpe River, while the 52nd British Division of XVII Corps would press forward along the Canadian Corps' right flank. On the other side of no man's land, the German 48th Reserve Division sat north of the Scarpe, facing the 51st Division. Arrayed against the 3rd and 2nd Canadian Divisions, from the south bank of the Scarpe to a point just south of the Arras–Cambrai highway, was the 214th Division; the 39th Division also opposed the 2nd Canadian Division in the Neuville-Vitasse sector. These enemy formations "were ready for action," with infantry battalions stationed in their allotted battle positions and artillery batteries prepared to unleash a deadly counter-bombardment.[4]

The terrain facing the Canadian Corps had been heavily scarred during earlier battles in 1917 and 1918, and stretched over the slopes of the Artois Hills, through which snaked the Scarpe, Cojeul, and Sensée river valleys. The Germans had taken full advantage of the hilltops, old trenches, and countless shell holes to fashion a complex network of mutually supporting defensive positions. "Their organization was the last word in military engineering," wrote Currie. "Barbed wire entanglements were formidable, machine-gun positions innumerable, and large tunnels had been provided for the protection of the garrison." Facing the 2nd Canadian Division was a succession of ridges and an area of high ground astride the Arras–Cambrai highway called Chapel Hill. This feature, along with Orange Hill, sitting just to the north and in the 3rd Canadian Division's sector, dominated the approaches to the key village of Monchy-le-Preux, which lay atop its own hill, just north of the 2nd Division's left boundary. Fortunately, the plans drawn up in late July for the assault on Orange Hill, which Currie had ordered to mask his corps' preparations for the attack at Amiens, had been saved. These would prove very useful to the staffs as they prepared for this new operation.[5]

Through the Canadian sector stretched five successive German defence lines. First was the old British front-line system, which had been overrun by the Germans in March 1918, and then the old German front line. Two miles east of Monchy-le-Preux ran a southern extension of the Fresnes–Rouvroy Line, and a further mile eastward sat the Drocourt–Quéant Line, which was the single strongest position facing the Canadians. After the Drocourt–Quéant Line lay the unfinished Canal du Nord, which, although not yet heavily fortified, still presented a major obstacle to any future Canadian advance. The battalions of 2nd Canadian Division would have to cross not only their share of these positions but also the Cojeul and Sensée river valleys. The terrain they had faced on the morning of 8 August was a level racetrack compared with what awaited them at Arras.[6] It was a task that could have benefited from "at least a month of planning."[7]

In the opening stage of this offensive, the Canadian Corps' task was to seize a line extending north and south, just west of Monchy-le-Preux, and then exploit it eastward as far as possible. Supporting it would be fourteen brigades of field artillery and nine brigades of heavy artillery; air support would again come from No. 5 Squadron, RAF. Some tanks were also available, but only in small numbers. Many of these machines had been destroyed in the fighting at Amiens, or were damaged and awaiting repair, and many among the surviving crews were severely exhausted from the heat, fumes, and din that plagued the tanks' interiors. Consequently, only nine tanks from the 3rd Tank Brigade were available to cooperate with each Canadian division. To preserve these few vehicles and crews for as long as possible, the tanks were ordered not to proceed ahead of the infantry unless called upon to eliminate an obstacle that the infantry could not overcome.[8] The Canadian assault scheme thus revolved around the traditional combination of infantry supported by initial overwhelming artillery firepower.

Maj.-Gen. Burstall and his staff worked quickly to outline their division's own plans to contend with the enemy defences and terrain in their assigned sector on the Canadian Corps' southern flank. Burstall assembled his brigadiers and their brigade majors on 23 August and explained his proposal for the division's advance. It would be on a two-brigade front, with the 6th Brigade attacking on the right and the 4th Brigade on the left. The 4th Brigade would deliver the main thrust against Chapel Hill and then move against the German defences lying southwest of Monchy-le-Preux and west of the village of Guémappe. Upon securing the enemy positions in this area, the brigade was to continue its advance if conditions permitted. The 6th Brigade, on the right, would form a defensive flank, mop up the territory around Neuville-Vitasse, and maintain contact with the 52nd British Division to its right. The 5th Brigade, in reserve, would, if possible, undertake further exploitation, either north or south of the Cojeul River. The attack would be carried out under the cover of field artillery and machine-gun barrages, as well as counter-battery bombardments. Because the artillery at Burstall's disposal could not adequately cover the division's entire 4,000-yard front, he decided to use most of it to support the 4th Brigade's effort. To Brig.-Gen. Rennie, he also gave the division's entire allotment of tanks, possibly because the terrain was more uniform throughout much of his section of the attack. Although the division's "punch" at Arras was less concentrated than it had been at Amiens, Burstall did what he could to employ his strongest resources to support the main axis of attack, which lay over the ground he had assigned to Rennie.[9]

One might wonder whether the Canadian infantry was strong enough to pull off another full-scale attack just two weeks after the last one had drawn to a close. Losses at Amiens had been substantial, but large numbers of reinforcements, some of them conscripts, were rushed forward to fill the gaping holes left in the ranks of hard-hit battalions. At least on paper, the 19th Battalion did not have any serious deficiencies in either officers or other ranks. A statement dated 24 August gave the total battalion strength as 32 officers and 921 other ranks, of which 20 officers and 584 other ranks were available for front-line duty in the headquarters and rifle companies. The companies still were sent into the lines on a three-platoon basis, with remaining personnel being left out of battle in rear details. But while these numbers seemed healthy enough, Burstall wisely pointed out that "numbers alone afford no criterion of the fighting power of a unit … Of the two thousand odd reinforcements [recently absorbed by the division] about one thousand were only partially trained, while units had not had sufficient time to thoroughly absorb this large new element."[10] More recently, historian Desmond Morton has estimated that "a quarter to half the men in any battalion always faced their first battle," and he wonders how such men could "in a few days, weeks, or months, absorb the intuitive expectations that real teamwork in sports or in battle requires."[11]

Although the exact proportion of experienced men to "greenhorns" in the battalion trench strength is difficult to determine, there is enough evidence to make a rough appraisal of the battalion's collective experience level on the eve of operations at Arras. Records from the 2nd Canadian Division general staff indicate that the 19th Battalion received 7 officers and 277 other ranks as reinforcements between 8 and 24 August. This was more than enough, at least as far as other ranks were concerned, to replace the 15 officers and 216 other ranks of the battalion who had been killed or wounded on 8 and 16 August. Moreover, the number of reinforcements received between 8 and 24 August amounted to virtually all of the reinforcements that would arrive in the battalion during the entire month, which was 10 officers and 283 other ranks. Included in this total were 1 officer and 79 other ranks who had served previously in the battalion and were returning from periods of convalescence or temporary service with other commands. With respect to the other-rank reinforcements, given that 28 per cent of them already had seen some service in the battalion, and that a significant number of the men called up to replace the casualties of 8 and 16 August likely would have come from personnel left out of battle on those dates, we may conclude that the 19th Battalion was able to field a favourable percentage of men with some measure of experience for the upcoming operation.[12] Even if a quarter or more of them were absolute novices, there were more than enough veterans among the ranks to provide the necessary skills and leadership to see the majority through.[13]

While the division and brigade staffs planned, the troops of the 19th Battalion, as yet unaware of exactly what was in store for them, were on the move again on 23 August. In the late morning the men began marching from Ecoivres to Wavrans, arriving at their destination at 2:30 PM. An hour later, they boarded a train for Maroeuil, and from there they marched to Warlus. That same evening, while the men were in transit, Brig.-Gen. Rennie assembled his battalion commanders and discussed the proposed operations that had been outlined to him earlier that afternoon by Maj.-Gen. Burstall. It was during this meeting that the specific battalion dispositions for the attack were worked out.[14]

As at Amiens, the brigade would advance on a two-battalion front covering approximately 2,000 yards. This time, the 20th and 21st Battalions would lead off, on the left and right respectively. Having led the brigade's effort on 8 August, the 18th and 19th Battalions took their turn to serve as follow-up forces, the former acting in support; Millen's men, who had borne the brunt of the fighting at Fransart, would be in reserve. Assisting the 4th Brigade infantry were eight Stokes mortars from the 4th Canadian Trench Mortar Battery; eight tanks from B Company, 9th Battalion, 3rd Tank Brigade; machine gunners from Number 3 Company, 2nd Battalion, CMGC; and parties of engineers and sappers from the 6th Battalion, 2nd Brigade, CE.[15]

The first task of the 20th and 21st Battalions was to capture Minorca and Corsica trenches, approximately 3,000 yards from the Canadian front line. Next, they would proceed to their second objective some 1,500 yards farther, along Southern Avenue, Congo, and Columbus trenches, forming a line stretching from the

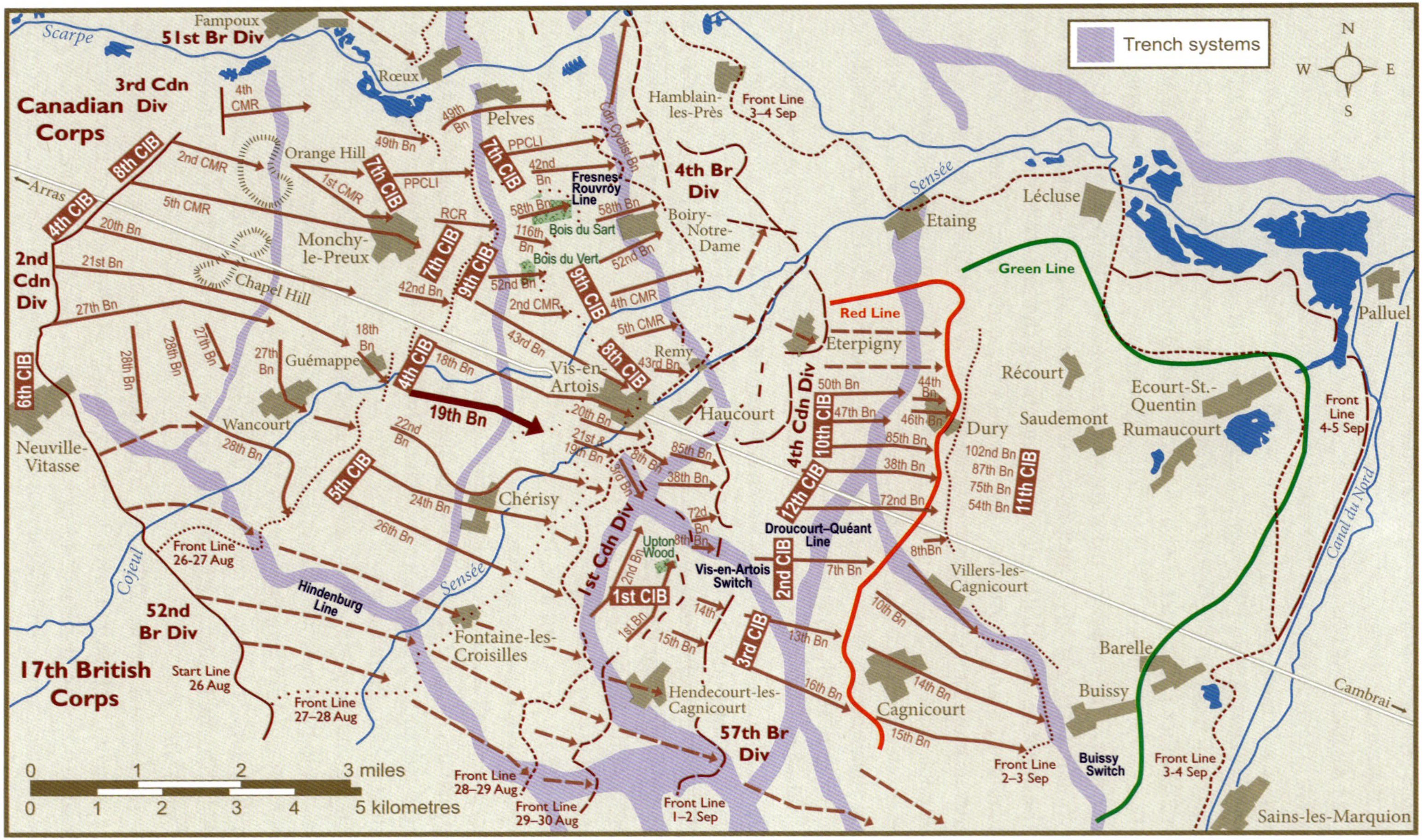

Map 19 – Arras 1918.

southern slopes of Monchy-le-Preux to a point just west of the village of Guémappe. There, they would consolidate and reorganize while the 18th Battalion prepared to leapfrog through and continue the advance, assaulting Guémappe and pushing on to the old British front line. This action by the support battalion could be carried out only if the 3rd Canadian Division succeeded in securing the heights of Monchy-le-Preux, which dominated the surrounding region. Meanwhile, the 19th Battalion, in reserve, would await orders to move up, if in fact that was necessary.[16]

Millen's men spent most of 24 August resting at Warlus until they were ordered to move out again later that evening. On the night of 24–25 August, the 4th Brigade moved into the lines in preparation for the attack. While the assault units filtered into the trench system between Telegraph Hill and Tilloy, the 19th Battalion moved forward into reserve positions in Arras itself. Meanwhile, the transport and quartermaster sections, along with LOB personnel and other rear details, proceeded to their assigned stations at Berneville, just south of Warlus. The following day, division headquarters issued warning orders to all brigades signalling the commencement of final preparations for action. Having received the go-ahead, Millen moved his battalion to its forward reserve position in the lines just west of Tilloy, which had been reconnoitred only a short time before.[17]

It was time for Millen to issue his final operation orders to all ranks. Although they did not yet know the exact time of zero hour, platoon and section commanders now at least had a clearer picture of what was expected of them. Companies were to begin their advance one hour after zero, with platoons disposed in artillery formation, until they reached the brigade's first objective line. A and B Companies were to occupy positions in Minorca and Corsica trenches while C and D Companies stood by in close support in Malta and Carlisle trenches. Any further movements would be subject to the situation on the battle line.[18]

At midnight on 25 August, division headquarters issued its final orders, including the announcement of zero hour, which was set for the unusual time of 3:00 AM the next morning. Lt.-Gen. Currie reasoned that, since the Germans knew an attack was imminent, the only way to achieve some measure of surprise was to commence the assault under a cloak of darkness that would restrict the defenders' visibility. Although his own troops would not be able to see well either, Currie reasoned that a night attack would give them a greater chance to "pass through the enemy's forward machine-gun defences by infiltration, and be in position to assault at dawn his line of resistance on the eastern slopes" of Orange Hill and Chapel Hill.[19]

This seemed a sound enough plan. But, as at Amiens, the weather threw in an added last-minute twist that threatened to make things more difficult for the Canadians. That night, as the assault battalions worked forward to their jumping-off lines, the sky grew increasingly overcast and rain began falling at intervals. The moonlight that Currie had banked on to guide his troops forward was completely obscured for a time. As raindrops pattered musically against thousands of steel-helmeted heads, many in the first waves wondered if this was an ill omen for the operation's success. Suddenly, as if on cue, the sky cleared at 2:00 AM, and by the radiant light of the late-August moon the troops were able to get into position in time. Just fifteen minutes before zero, all of the 4th Brigade's units were in position and ready to go.[20]

Day One: 26 August

At precisely 3:00 AM the artillery and heavy machine guns crashed forth in deadly chorus, and garish bursts of shellfire illuminated the darkness ahead of the infantry in strobe-light fashion. As the barrage line began its creep towards the German positions, it was followed by the dimmer glow of thousands of cigarettes, marking the movement of the foremost waves of attacking infantry. Currie's plan got off to a good start, for although the defending Germans were far better prepared than at Amiens, they were taken somewhat by surprise at the irregular timing of the assault. The Canadian and British troops encountered relatively little determined resistance in the opening stages of the operation. This was due partly to the timing of zero hour, but mainly to the German policy of pulling back most of their outpost garrisons in the face of a major attack, in order to conserve their strength to fight from their principal lines of resistance. On the far right of the Canadian Corps, Brig.-Gen. Arthur H. Bell's 6th Brigade cleared out the Neuville-Vitasse area and fanned out to present a strong right flank for the other formations advancing to its left. Brig.-Gen. Rennie's 4th Brigade, meanwhile, quickly pierced the German outpost zone and pushed onward to its objectives, with some of the men "slipping and sliding in mud" created by the overnight rain.[21]

Chapel Hill was in the 20th Battalion's hands soon after 6:00 AM, by which time daylight enabled both defenders and attackers to better observe each other and call down artillery fire. As usual, many German machine-gun crews fought to the bitter end, especially along Nova Scotia Trench, Minorca Trench, and Southern Avenue. There was no easy way to overcome this opposition except through disciplined section rushes covered by the fire of Lewis gunners and rifle grenadiers, with the help of an occasional tank. Sniper and machine-gun fire from the banks of the Arras–Cambrai highway proved troublesome and required some armoured support. One of the tanks did great service clearing an area on the south side of the road, but it was put out of action by a German shell while attempting to cross over to the north side. By 7:30 AM the 21st Battalion, with some tank assistance, had reached the outskirts of Guémappe and the 20th Battalion was consolidating on its second objective line. Along the way, each unit had captured three field guns, a number of machine guns, and several score of prisoners. There was no chance, however, for the men to savour their achievement. German observers, working from the higher ground around Monchy-le-Preux, skilfully directed their field artillery on the 4th

A tank advancing east of Arras, 1918. This image demonstrates the logic of the rhomboidal design of British heavy tanks when it came to negotiating embankments. (LAC PA-003152)

Brigade's newly captured positions, causing numerous casualties and knocking out several more tanks.[22]

While the leading battalions forged ahead to their objectives, the 19th Battalion sat in reserve, as per orders, until 4:00 AM. Then its companies moved out in artillery formation, following mainly in the wake of the 20th Battalion along the brigade's left sub-section. A Company took up position on the battalion right, and B Company on the left, with C and D Companies bringing up the rear. When they reached the Carlisle and Corsica trench systems, they halted and began to consolidate, while battalion headquarters moved up and established itself in a concrete pillbox a short distance behind Carlisle Trench. To that point, the battalion had suffered around 30 casualties, 9 of these from gas.[23]

To the left of the 4th Brigade, the 3rd Canadian Division had done very well that morning. Battalions of the 8th Brigade outflanked and captured Orange Hill before moving on to assault Monchy-le-Preux from the north and west. They secured the hilltop town by 7:40 AM, thereby relieving the 4th Brigade troops of a great deal of the enemy fire that had galled them as they were digging in.[24] Later that morning there was a shift in the divisional boundaries in response to changes on the Third Army's front. To accommodate this, the 2nd Canadian Division was ordered to shift its left boundary southward; this left the 3rd Canadian Division responsible for all of the frontage north of the Arras–Cambrai highway. This took some time to arrange, for the leading elements of both divisions were not yet in consistent contact with one another or with divisional headquarters. By the afternoon, the

20th Battalion was able to withdraw its troops south of the highway, and the 42nd Battalion of the 3rd Division took over the vacated area, cleaning out the remaining enemy positions just south of Monchy-le-Preux.[25]

Late afternoon finally saw the capture of Guémappe by the 18th Battalion, which had moved up from brigade support and had failed in an earlier attempt to take the hamlet around noon. Meanwhile, the 19th Battalion had hovered in reserve, along the brigade's first objective line, unable to move forward until the situation had been cleared up around Guémappe. After the 18th Battalion successfully pushed its troops ahead on both flanks of the village, Lt.-Col. Millen was called to brigade headquarters, which had moved up to Nova Scotia Trench. There, he received orders to send two of his companies forward to Panther and Egret trenches, where they would link up with the 18th Battalion on the left and forces of the 6th Brigade on the right. A and B Companies were detailed to make the advance starting at 4:45 PM; C and D Companies would shift to the right to cover more of Malta and Minorca trenches.[26]

A and B Companies made their move on time but suffered several casualties on the way, "being without any covered approach." Deward Barnes, by then a full corporal, remembered that "Sergeant Newell gave us each a drink of rum on the way over. He was feeling good."[27] At 6:50 PM, the officer commanding A Company sent a message back to battalion headquarters that his men had reached Curlew Trench, just west of Egret. There, they found the position already occupied by two companies of the 27th Battalion, which had been assigned the same objectives as the 19th Battalion. This illustrates the difficulties experienced by the 4th and 6th Brigades in coordinating their movements precisely. The 27th, having made it as far as Curlew (west of Egret), was checked in its attempt to move any farther by heavy German machine-gun fire. The commander of the 19th Battalion's A Company therefore decided to wait with his men at the junction of Shirker and Curlew trenches for further instructions. Eventually, A Company was ordered to withdraw back to Minorca Trench, while B Company was told to stay put for the time being. The men of B Company would come under the temporary command of the 18th Battalion, which transferred them to Southern Avenue, just north of Guémappe.[28]

Although the 19th Battalion had not yet been deeply involved in the battle, the first day had seen plenty of hard fighting all along the Canadian Corps front. By nightfall, the Canadians and the Highlanders of the 51st Division had advanced beyond the old German front-trench system and established a new line. In the 3rd and 2nd Canadian Divisions' sectors, this line ran from the wetland west of Pelves, on the south bank of the Scarpe, to a point 1,000 yards east of Monchy-le-Preux. It then extended southward, just east of Guémappe on the 4th Brigade's front and Wancourt Tower on the 6th Brigade's front. The Germans, determined to recapture Monchy-le-Preux, launched powerful counterattacks, which, although thrown back by the Canadians, succeeded in halting the Canadian advance.[29]

Day Two: 27 August

Lt.-Gen. Currie's goal for the second day was to break through the Fresnes–Rouvroy Line and continue on through the Drocourt–Quéant Line as far as Cagnicourt on the 2nd Canadian Division's front. This would entail an advance of over five miles through heavily defended territory. It was, in hindsight, a dangerously optimistic objective. But according to Maj.-Gen. Burstall, it was believed that "the enemy had been seriously disorganized by the attacks of the Third Army [to the south] and by the operations on August 26th." This prompted the high command, including Currie, to push divisions onward "as rapidly as possible." Unfortunately for the attacking divisions, the Germans were far less disoriented than expected. The attack in the 2nd Canadian Division's sector would again involve the 4th Brigade on the left, while the 5th Brigade moved up from reserve and passed through the 6th Brigade to take up the advance on the right. In the approach to their targeted sections of the Fresnes–Rouvroy system, the 4th and 5th Brigades would have to capture the villages of Vis-en-Artois and Chérisy before crossing the Sensée River and charging up the higher ground to the east – a daunting assignment, to say the least.[30]

Zero hour for the 2nd Canadian Division's operations on 27 August was set originally at 4:55 AM but was later moved to 10:00 AM. This was done to accommodate the 5th Brigade, which required extra time to get its units into position. At midnight, division headquarters issued its operation orders for the coming day, and at 5:00 AM on the morning of 27 August, Lt.-Col. Millen reported to brigade headquarters for discussions on the part his unit would play. After viewing the division orders and copying relevant extracts to formulate his own battalion orders, Millen hurried back to his headquarters and set to work. Having played a supporting role on the previous day, Millen's men now would leapfrog through the 20th and 21st Battalions and move to the forefront of the offensive. The 19th Battalion would attack along the right portion of the 4th Brigade's 1,600-yard frontage, with the 18th Battalion moving ahead on the left, with its own left flank resting on the south side of the Arras–Cambrai highway. The 20th Battalion would serve in support, and the 21st Battalion would move back into reserve. Principal support for the attacking units would come from an artillery barrage to be laid down 200 yards west of Egret, Panther, and Rake trenches. This barrage would then creep forward in 100-yard lifts every four minutes until it reached a line approximately 300 yards in front of the Sensée River, the limit of the stationary artillery's range. The gunners would maintain fire along this final line for a thirty-minute period, after which further artillery support would come from mobile batteries of the 1st Brigade, CFA, and one company of the 2nd Battalion, CMGC, which were detailed to move ahead with the 4th Infantry Brigade.[31]

Millen's orders were issued at 6:30 AM and were followed up by the broader brigade scheme, received at 8:00 AM. He assigned C and B Companies to lead off

Canadians advancing east of Arras through marshy ground near the River Sensée. Only the heads of several troops are visible just below the horizon on the left side of the image. In the foreground are what seem to be strands of barbed wire. (LAC PA-003043)

the attack on the right and left, followed up by A and D Companies in support. Overnight rain showers made for slippery ground conditions, which increased the difficulties of assembly; nevertheless, all units managed to get into position in time for zero hour.[32] Along the 4th Brigade's section, the advance began well enough. Following the barrage across the Cojeul River valley, the 18th and 19th Battalions pressed on in a southeasterly direction, parallel to the highway. The 19th Battalion's pace had been slowed somewhat by swampy ground in the Cojeul valley and by scattered enemy machine guns and snipers. Shortly before 10:30 AM, Capt. Gordon Applegath was killed leading B Company, and since the troops of B and D Companies had by now become quite intermingled, Capt. James Linton of D Company did his best to take effective charge of all the men he could muster.[33] Over with A Company, Cpl. Barnes and his men had gone

> over-the-top with a tank, but the Germans were using these anti-tank guns [cannons] and anti-tank rifles that have an immense cartridge. One of our fellows got shot by one of the rifles; it made a terrible hole – big enough to put your two fists in. But the guns! The shells from them burst just in front of the tank, close to the ground, and the shrapnel spread. Oh my! I dreaded them. You just heard the burst of the shell and then the shrapnel flew.[34]

In spite of such horrors, most of Vis-en-Artois, which lay astride the highway, fell without too much difficulty to troops of the 18th and 43rd Battalions, the latter

Allied air power was also active east of Arras. In the distance an airplane swoops over the battlefield, firing on German machine gunners. (LAC PA-003128)

occupying the portion of the village north of the highway, in the 3rd Canadian Division's sector. As on the previous day, the attackers inflicted many casualties and took numerous prisoners. As was typical, many of the prisoners were stripped of their personal belongings by souvenir-hungry Canadians. On rare occasions, this sort of pilfering could come back to haunt a man. One such collector was A Company's Sgt. Newell, who had gone out earlier that day to "investigate the enemy front lines." Deward Barnes observed that Newell and the private who accompanied him "had too much rum to drink." Later that day, as Barnes and his comrades struggled over the battlefield, they "found Sergeant Newell in the corner of a trench we had taken. He had been shot through the back of the head and his pockets were empty. The Germans let him get past them, then they ambushed him. When they captured him, they found his souvenirs, which were German photos of their families – and he had his pockets full of them."[35]

As both the 18th and 19th Battalions neared their initial objectives along the Sensée, they ran into much stiffer opposition. Their platoons were lacerated by intense machine-gun and rifle fire. A and C Companies of the 19th Battalion dove for shelter in Narrow Trench while B and D Companies took cover in Quarry Trench. An outpost of twenty men and two Lewis guns was pushed ahead down Ophir Trench, close to the riverbank.[36]

The brigade made its best effort to get across the Sensée in strength, but by 3:00 PM, division headquarters had received word that the advance had stalled. The

Canadians advancing east of Arras through swamps of the River Sensée, 200 yards from Remy. Given the location, these are most likely 3rd Division troops. But this image probably depicts similar conditions faced by men of the 19th Battalion and other units of the 4th Brigade in their part of the attack. Note the Lewis gunner leading the men in the foreground. (LAC PA-003033)

4th Brigade headquarters complained that the "artillery barrage failed and eventually subsided altogether" by the time its leading battalions had reached the river. Although a bridge on the highway spanning the river was secured, further attempts to reach the well-organized German defences beyond the east bank, such as Olive Trench and Ocean Work, generated heavy casualties. Adding to the brigade's misery, German aircraft swooped low over the battlefield, strafing and bombing the supporting units as they tried to move up to assist the leading battalions. Rather than incur crippling losses, the infantry was forced to dig in on a line established west of the Sensée.[37] Frustrated with the outcome of the day's operations, Lt.-Col. Millen reported that "throughout the advance the artillery barrage was very poor, the line of barrage was very irregular, and some guns were about 30 seconds after others in lifting, which caused many casualties. These operations were very costly to the Battalion, casualties were severe and at the end there were only five Company officers left."[38]

To the immediate south, the 5th Brigade was more successful in crossing the Sensée, probably owing to stronger tank support. The 26th Battalion, which was the first to cross, found the river valley to be mainly dry and established itself on the east bank by noon. It was later joined by the 24th and 22nd Battalions, which had captured the village of Chérisy before effecting their own crossings. As they pressed forward on the higher ground to the east, the 5th Brigade troops ran into a hail of fire similar to that which had stonewalled the 4th Brigade to the north. The German 26th and 21st Reserve Divisions, now blocking the 2nd Canadian Division's path, were putting up too strong a fight for the increasingly worn-out Canadians to overcome. Finally realizing this uncomfortable fact, Lt.-Gen. Currie instructed his subordinates "not to attempt too much in the face of heavy opposition." Consequently, Maj.-Gen. Burstall ordered the 4th and 5th Brigades to hold fast on their lines east and west of the Sensée, and operations after 5:45 PM were restricted to consolidation efforts.[39]

The 3rd Canadian, 51st (Highland), and 52nd British Divisions also made some gains that day but were no more successful than the 2nd Canadian Division in reaching the Fresnes–Rouvroy system, much less breaching it and pushing ahead to their more distant final objectives. What was required was more time to mount a carefully organized set-piece attack with sufficient artillery support. Compounding the deficiency in artillery, difficulties with communications and with getting fresh units and formations forward in time hampered coordination. With the Canadian infantry advancing beyond the effective range of much of their own artillery and the Germans pouring in reinforcements to their threatened sectors, Lt.-Gen. Currie's forces had little hope of overcoming the heavy weight of German firepower arrayed against them.

The strength of the 2nd and 3rd Canadian Divisions was virtually exhausted by nightfall on 27 August, and the time was ripe for fresh formations to be thrown into the fray, if any further meaningful progress was to be made. The 1st Canadian Division, having come north from the British Fourth Army front, was ready, but the 4th Canadian Division was still en route back to Currie's command. To make up for this shortfall, the 4th British Division was made available to the Canadians; however, delays in its arrival forestalled its use in any projected attack on 28 August. In the belief that relieving only one of his two most fatigued divisions would "create greater problems than it would solve," Currie decided to leave the 2nd and 3rd Canadian Divisions in the line for yet another day of fighting – a choice that has been pronounced "a rare mistake" on Currie's part.[40]

Day Three: 28 August

The Canadian Corps' goals for the third day remained the same as on the day before: punch through the Fresnes–Rouvroy Line and roll on to the villages of Cagnicourt (on the 2nd Canadian Division's front), Dury, and Étaing (on the 3rd Canadian Division's front). All of these villages were either incorporated within, or situated east of, the formidable Drocourt–Quéant Line, which meant that to attain their final objectives, each division would have to plough through two heavily defended trench systems. Given the events of the previous two days, and the state of the divisions making the attack, one wonders how Currie and his staff could have considered these to be achievable goals.[41]

The beleaguered 4th and 5th Brigades of the 2nd Canadian Division would lead off, with the 6th Brigade hovering in close support. The 4th Brigade, with its left flank still running along the Arras–Cambrai highway, saw its front narrowed to 700 yards. If Brig.-Gen. Rennie could secure no relief for his entire formation, at least he could rotate its spent units. The 20th and 21st Battalions moved to the van, on the left and right respectively, while the 19th Battalion was placed in support and the 18th Battalion in reserve. As on 27 August, the two attacking Canadian divisions were unable to coordinate their start times. The 3rd Division's assault commenced at 11:00 AM and the 2nd Division's at 12:30 PM.

On 28 August the loveliness of the weather contrasted sharply with the bitterness of the fighting. After enduring a night of heavy German shelling, the 2nd Canadian Division began its share of the attack on time, employing the usual rolling barrage. The leading battalions of the 4th Brigade, followed by the 19th Battalion in close support, succeeded in crossing the Sensée and pressed onward almost 2,200 yards to the southeast, towards enemy-held Olive Trench and Ocean Work. The Germans, fully prepared for another attack, and enjoying an excellent view from the higher ground around Ocean Work, poured withering machine-gun and artillery fire onto the struggling Canadians. The entire 4th Brigade was severely weakened from the previous two days of fighting, and its remaining troops were "tired and not fully equipped." Their predicament was made even worse by the thick belts of barbed wire that shielded the German lines. Attempts at bombing and cutting paths through the wire were met with pitiless streams of machine-gun bullets from the front and flanks.[42]

As the dead piled up amidst the wire, the artillery barrage, which according to Lt.-Col. Millen had "not … sufficiently dealt with strong opposition in Olive Trench and Ocean House [*sic*] and the ridge opposite," was called back to pound these positions some more. Meanwhile, the men of the 4th Brigade tried to establish a line among the shell–holes scattered over the approaches to the German wire. After holding these precarious positions for "many hours," the troops were finally withdrawn to a safer line of embankments and sunken roads closer to the east bank of the Sensée River. By this time, the few remaining officers of the 19th and 21st Battalions were forced to combine their decimated companies into a composite unit, which linked its posts up with those of the 18th and 20th Battalions to their left. So short was the brigade on men that its reserve by now consisted of little more than "Headquarters details, batmen, cooks, etc." Around 6:30 PM, Brig.-Gen. Rennie reported to division headquarters that his men "were absolutely unable to make any headway."[43]

The ferocity and chaos of the fighting on 28 August is well captured in Deward Barnes's journal entry for that date:

> We went over-the-top again with a barrage, but lost many men and could not make our objective ... held up by machine guns. We stayed in shell holes, then we got into a trench. It was a crime to stay here so we got ready for another attack, but we got word that the Germans were coming. I'm in charge of half a company here, there are no other NCOs. Everyone has to make steps so they can get up to fire over-the-top, as it is a deep trench. One or two of the draftees, although the majority were good men, refused and I threatened to shoot them if they didn't dig. We had only a few men left and everyone was needed to do their part. Some of us piled German dead on top of each other and stood on them so we could see over-the-top of the trench. I thought for sure we were gone. The Germans came on but at our particular part of the line they seemed to have slowed up. We had to retire again at 7:00 PM – to where we started from. At one point during the day, we were almost surrounded.[44]

Barnes's experience on 28 August highlights vividly the responsibility that devolved upon junior NCOs when most of a unit's officers were killed or wounded. Experienced and well-trained other ranks, like Barnes, were the very "glue" that held a battalion together. In a tight situation, such men spontaneously rose to the occasion and did what they could to accomplish the mission or to save the lives of their comrades without necessarily waiting for orders. As Desmond Morton has concluded, "most soldiers, laden down with weapons, ammunition, and kit, were supporting players for the minority of desperate fighters ... who determined success or failure."[45] Coolness under fire was an absolute prerequisite. Commenting further on the events of 28 August, Barnes recalled that

> there was a machine gun post we tried to get ... It played on a gap in the wire. There must have been forty men all heaped up dead in that gap. We had to get past the machine gun to get behind a bank for cover. A half dozen of us made it and we tried to plan to get the machine gun post. Unfortunately, we had no bombs ... so, we planned a rush ... some from the other side and us from where we were. We jumped into a kind of trench and rushed them. They killed the first four men and we saw that we couldn't make it. The Germans, however, started to jump out of the trench, but when they saw that we were beat they stopped, jumped back in the post, and started firing again.[46]

On the 4th Brigade's right flank, the 5th Brigade had attacked with the same three battalions as had been employed the day before. Despite their exhaustion, two of them, the 22nd and 24th Battalions, managed to force their way into the German front line during the afternoon. But the shattered remnants of these units were driven back almost to their own jumping-off line by a resolute German counterattack later that evening. The 22nd Battalion was terribly mauled, with all of its officers either killed or wounded. One of them was a future Canadian governor general, Maj. Georges Vanier, who lost his right leg as a result of wounds sustained that day.[47]

The Germans, not content with having driven off their assailants, bombarded the valley of the Sensée that evening, lacing their heavy barrage with deadly gas shells. Precise intelligence on the state of affairs facing the 4th Brigade was next to impossible to obtain, since the area "was continually swept by intense machine gun fire" that severely hampered movement and communication. Nevertheless, some observers caught glimpses of "large bodies of [Germans] … coming over the hill" to strengthen the local garrisons. Brig.-Gen. Rennie desperately needed reinforcements of his own. He got some, in the form of the 31st Battalion, which was temporarily detached from the 6th Brigade and placed under his orders. With the arrival of these relatively fresher troops, Lt.-Col. Millen immediately applied for the services of two companies to assist his own unit if it was expected to participate in any further attacks. The request was granted. But, luckily for all concerned, the 2nd Canadian Division's agony had finally come to an end: its units received word that they would be relieved at last by the 1st Canadian Division.[48]

The 3rd Canadian Division had fared better on 28 August, massing its artillery fire along a narrower portion of the divisional front to blast a path through the Fresnes–Rouvroy Line, first for one of its three attacking brigades, and then for another. But the division was unable to move much farther beyond this trench system, and in some areas its worn-out units could not even push entirely through it before they were relieved by the newly arrived 4th British Division and Brutinel's Brigade, a composite force of machine gunners, motor machine gunners, and cyclists. On the far left, north of the Scarpe, the Highlanders of the 51st Division had been unable to match even the diminishing progress of the 2nd and 3rd Canadian Divisions over the previous two days. As exhausted as the Canadian divisions were, the numerically weaker British divisions packed a smaller punch and had even less endurance in a protracted fight than their larger Canadian counterparts.[49]

Ending the Ordeal

On the night of 28–29 August, the 2nd Infantry Brigade relieved Brig.-Gen. Rennie's badly battered 4th Brigade, the latter moving to Wancourt before proceeding back to Arras later in the day. After resting in billets in the city, the 19th Battalion was moved about seven miles west on 30 August to new billets in Simencourt. There, Millen's men saw the end of what must have seemed like one of the longest months of their lives. The campaign to break the Fresnes–Rouvroy and Drocourt-Quéant lines would continue, but it would be left to other formations to complete the work started by the 2nd and 3rd Canadian Divisions in the Canadian Corps' sector. Owing to the incredible scale and intensity of operations during August, the 2nd Canadian Division, and many of its infantry battalions in particular, were ghosts of their former selves.[50]

Casualties for the 4th Brigade during its three full days of fighting at Arras totalled 60 officers and 1,366 other ranks – a huge loss for such a brief span of time. Among these were the 285 casualties suffered by the 19th Battalion (13 officers, 272

The archival description of this image reads: "Canadians advancing through a German barrage. Advance East of Arras." The barrage itself is not immediately apparent, but like many photos taken during the Allied offensives of 1918 it clearly shows how much more open the fighting has become. The contrast with more trench-bound conditions earlier in the war is obvious. (LAC PA-003130)

other ranks). When added to the losses sustained earlier in the month, especially during the fighting at Amiens, the 19th Battalion's total casualties for August sky-rocketed to 28 officers and 486 other ranks. This made August 1918 the battalion's costliest month of the war.[51]

What had been gained by this massive sacrifice? At Arras, the men of the 19th Battalion had participated in the 2nd Canadian Division's advance of over five miles through some of the most difficult and heavily defended territory on the Western Front. In the process, the battalion captured 9 German officers and 257 other ranks, contributing a good portion to the 4th Brigade's estimated bag of 900 prisoners, as well as numerous machine guns and one anti-tank gun.[52] Was this worth the price in life and limb? Probably not; at least not on the second and third days of the attack in the 2nd Canadian Division's sector. Earlier, at Amiens, the incredible amount of territory gained and the serious blow dealt to the Germans seemed to make the sacrifice worthwhile, even in the minds of many veterans looking back years later. But at Arras, the effort and the expenditure of human life might have been reduced if operations had not been so rushed and if worn-out formations had been replaced in a more timely fashion.

Canadians and prisoners take cover in a trench during the advance east of Arras. August 1918. (LAC PA-003127)

Historian Shane Schreiber, normally highly supportive of Lt.-Gen. Currie, admits that the corps commander "was simply pushing too hard" during the first three days of fighting at Arras. But he qualifies the criticism by pointing out that Currie "had little choice," given the pressure exerted by the Allied high command on all formation commanders to drive the Germans back in rapid and relentless fashion. Since "high casualty rates were inevitable" when tackling enemy positions that were as well prepared and strongly defended as those southeast of Arras, Currie felt that "it was probably better to take them on quickly in a successful engagement, rather than slow the tempo of the advance and give the Germans the time and opportunity to turn their formidable defences along the Arras–Cambrai road into a *schlacthaus* [slaughterhouse]."[53] Indeed, Currie's mindset during this battle was effectively revealed in his special order to the corps on 26 August, in which he exhorted his men to "keep constantly in mind Stonewall Jackson's motto 'Press forward.'"[54]

Given the exceedingly heavy casualties suffered in a number of units, especially those in the 4th and 5th Brigades, it is difficult to see how events could have turned out much worse if more time had been taken to prepare follow-up attacks after 26 August. As in earlier operations at the Somme and Passchendaele, GHQ's conviction that the enemy was on the verge of collapse propelled operations with a sense of urgency that resulted in more blood being spilled than might have been necessary. The Battle of Arras was considered by Currie to be "the hardest battle" in the Canadian Corps' history,[55] and it encapsulated the Allied experience during the final hundred days of the First World War: unrelenting, grinding struggle, with ultimate success gained through the expenditure of titanic amounts of human and material resources.

20

Cambrai and Iwuy: 1 September–13 October 1918

During the final two days of August, the 2nd Canadian Division remained in corps reserve while the much fresher 1st Canadian and 4th British Divisions, along with Brutinel's Brigade,[1] completed the job of driving through the Fresnes–Rouvroy defences and a portion of the Vis-en-Artois Switch. Then they cleared the approaches to the Drocourt–Quéant Line, the assault of which was scheduled to commence on 2 September.[2]

After the bloodletting undergone by the 2nd and 3rd Canadian Divisions, Lt.-Gen. Currie decided to take enough time to organize strong artillery support and to blast paths through the forest of wire that shielded the enemy positions. When the assault began on the morning of 2 September, the 4th British, 4th Canadian, and 1st Canadian Divisions, supported by fifty tanks, broke through the Drocourt–Quéant defences on a four-mile front and made good progress behind the barrages laid down by 762 pieces of artillery. However, once the leading brigades outran their artillery support, German machine guns, artillery, and gas wrought terrible vengeance. The advance of the 4th British and 4th Canadian Divisions eventually stalled, but the 1st Canadian Division, on the right, managed to push through to take Cagnicourt and the woods to the east. By evening, units of the 1st Division had battled their way through the Buissy Switch and outflanked enemy positions to the north. This compelled the Germans to mount a fighting retreat to a defensive line behind the Canal du Nord on the night of 2–3 September. After the Germans' main

A large concrete and iron reinforced machine-gun post. The archival description locates the captured German structure in "the Quéant line." It demonstrates the formidable strength of the German defences faced by Allied troops during September 1918. (LAC PA-003460)

force had made its way across the canal to the east bank, it destroyed the crossings to block the Canadian advance. The following day the Canadians surged across the largely open ground west of the canal. Opposed only by German artillery, they established a new line facing the canal's west bank between the Sensée River to the north and a point opposite the German-occupied village of Sains-lès-Marquion to the south.[3]

The Watch on the Canal

Meanwhile, the 19th Battalion, with the rest of 2nd Canadian Division, had taken advantage of a desperately needed breather to rest and refit. On 1–2 September the battalion remained in reserve at Simencourt. The next day, 3 September, saw the battalion move forward again, in accordance with brigade orders, to the Cherisy–Wancourt area. The weather was, for the most part, fine and seasonably warm, making the break all the more pleasant.[4] "We are still living in stirring times as the papers must show you," wrote Lt.-Col. Millen to his mother. "We are still moving but … in the right direction … During our journey from one place to another we rested near an aerodrome and I got a flight. Was up about 3/4 hr and traveled part of the time at 100 miles per hour at height of 4000 feet. I enjoyed the whole trip."[5]

After what they had been through during August, veterans of the recent fighting needed time to soothe their frayed nerves, while newcomers to the battalion required more practice on the training grounds to learn how to work with the section and platoon teams in which they would be operating on the battlefield. All ranks would have benefited from an extended period of relatively quiet time in which to get to know one another and cultivate a spirit of real teamwork. This was not to be, however; the high command's refusal to reduce the pressure on the Germans would keep the Canadians more or less constantly engaged for the remainder of the war.

Starting on the night of 3 September and concluding on the morning of the 5th, the 2nd Canadian Division relieved the 1st Canadian Division in the right sector of the corps' front, just west of the Canal du Nord. The 6th Brigade was sent up to hold the entire division front, while the 4th Brigade was ordered forward to the Cagnicourt area, a short distance east of the captured Drocourt–Quéant Line, where its units would be in divisional support. This left the 5th Brigade to occupy positions in reserve. In the support positions near Cagnicourt, the principal feature was "an old disused German trench," in which the men of the 19th Battalion scooped out new funkholes for themselves, covering them with whatever sheltering materials came to hand.[6] Cpl. John R. Gaetz, recently returned to the battalion after a period of convalescence, described his own rudimentary accommodations in a letter to his mother. For one who had served so long at the front, Gaetz maintained a surprisingly idealistic outlook (at least in his letters), although this attitude was tinged by now with a perceptible degree of fatalism: "As long as I am in France, and especially these days, I feel that this is my place … I wouldn't mind getting over to blighty for the winter but anything short of that I would sooner be here … Far better than on a bed or to wither away sitting around a kitchen stove as I have seen some old men."[7]

After a day of rest on 5 September, the battalion spent the following week training and cleaning up the area. On 12 September the 6th Brigade was due for relief in the front lines, and as the 4th Brigade was in support, the job fell to it. The day was a memorable one for two reasons. First, the 19th Battalion received a cruel awakening from the quiet it had enjoyed over the previous week. Millen's men were assigned to take over the right section of the divisional front from the 28th Battalion, and as they proceeded up the line by platoons, the German artillery opened fire. During the "strafe," which ranged deep into Canadian positions, two of Millen's platoons received direct hits, causing several casualties. Weather conditions worsened and a cold rain and occasional showers of hail whipped up, adding insult to the injury inflicted by the German guns. Nevertheless, the men stuck it out and successfully carried off the relief, wiring brigade headquarters at 11:50 PM that everyone was in position.[8]

The second significant event on 12 September was the departure of Brig.-Gen. Robert Rennie from 4th Brigade headquarters to take up command of Canadian troops stationed at Bramshott in England. Having led the brigade since mid-November 1915, Rennie was worn out and in need of a break from front-line command responsibilities. Chosen to replace Rennie was George E. McCuaig, a newly promoted brigadier who had commanded the 13th Battalion in the 1st Canadian Division. McCuaig would arrive to take over the 4th Brigade on 14 September, so an interim commander was needed immediately after Rennie's departure. Selected to fill that role was none other than Lt.-Col. Lionel Millen.[9] Millen's skills as a battalion commander evidently had marked him in the eyes of his superiors as one who was worthy of grooming for higher responsibilities in the Canadian Corps. His stint at brigade headquarters lasted less than two days; however, it would not be the last time he would sit in the brigadier's chair.

While Millen kept things running at brigade headquarters, Maj. Hatch filled in for him in command of the 19th Battalion. The men, having run the gauntlet of enemy bombardments on their way into the front lines, faced an additional trial in the early morning hours of 13 September, when the Germans drenched the area with gas shells. No casualties were reported from this gas attack, which testified to the coolness and discipline of all ranks in following the prescribed precautions and donning their respirators in time. Use of gas by both sides would be a depressingly regular feature of hostilities along this front for the rest of the month.[10]

During these days, Lt. Joe O'Neill paid tribute to the role of luck, but also to the importance of experience, in keeping veterans alive. "Some people are very lucky," he explained:

> So we were walking along in the dark, when all of a sudden I heard something coming, and you know it's a peculiar thing ... It took three months to develop it, anybody that was over two or three months in the line will tell you, that he could sense or hear something was coming right at him or where it was way up or down or close. Well I heard this thing coming, I knew it was coming and I dove for the ground, and the fellow behind me[,] the fellow who was carrying these Lewis gun pans[,] he didn't hear it, and the base of a six inch shell caught him right square where those pans were and knocked him right down on his back. Oh boy, we thought he was dead. We grabbed him and pulled him in an old trench, and pulled his clothes off and there [was] ... just a little scratch on him. The jagged edges of that shell went clean through two one-eighth steel pans of the Lewis gun, through two lots each pan – forty-nine rounds – it went right through all those rounds and knocked the wind out of him, of course, and shook him up a bit. The boy was able to carry on all right for the rest of the trip. That's the kind of luck you know some people have, and other people are unlucky.[11]

After it relieved the 1st Canadian Division, the 2nd Canadian Division's job was to dig in and form a main line of resistance. Because the enemy had an excellent view over much of the western approaches to the Canal du Nord, Maj.-Gen. Burstall decided to use only a light screen of outposts in the forward area. The bulk of his forces would be pulled back to the rear areas where the ground gave better cover and the troops could get more rest. There was little scope for territorial gains to the east. The canal itself was virtually "impassable for more than a few men at any point along the whole" of the 2nd Canadian Division's front. There were "remains of bridges, portions of the Canal which were not completed, and swamps, across which it was possible for a small body of troops to work their way." But there was no scope for any major incursions across the canal without recourse to a full-scale set-piece attack.[12]

When the units of the 4th Brigade relieved the 6th Brigade in the forward positions facing the west bank of the canal, they found themselves occupying a stretch of low ground that encompassed the villages of Buissy and Baralle, near the latter of which was a sizable swamp. As the brigades of the 2nd Canadian Division took their turns occupying the front line, they eventually forced the Germans to keep mainly to the east side of the canal. Maj. Hatch and his men quickly learned that patrol work or any other movement in this area during daylight hours was extremely hazardous, given the favourable vantage points occupied by the Germans east of the canal. The danger from shelling and machine-gun fire was even too much to permit the use of runners for communication between battalion headquarters and the companies. Fortunately, this was an occasion when telephone communication with the companies held out, obviating the need for men to risk their lives carrying messages.

After dark, it was a different story. Burstall warned all his battalion commanders that "the front must be energetically patrolled during the hours of darkness and all possible information obtained in regard to the location and strength of enemy posts."[13] Taking this injunction to heart, the 19th Battalion came alive at night, and multiple patrols ranged across its frontage looking for any signs of the enemy.[14] No German patrols or outposts were encountered along the canal's west bank on the night of 13–14 September, but enemy machine-gun fire wounded one man and prevented one of the 19th Battalion's patrols from reaching the canal. Things got even hotter on the following night. At 2:40 AM on 15 September, Lt. Herbert Addison and Cpl. Thomas Nodwell were visiting posts manned by their platoon when they noticed several figures crouched on the remains of a nearby bridge. Realizing that they were not his own men, but Germans, Addison "immediately pulled his revolver and fired four shots." The Germans responded in kind "and then rushed, three or four tackling the Officer, and another three or four tackling the N.C.O. Lieut. Addison was borne down, and fired two shots into the body of one Hun who was underneath him. He then managed to kick himself free and got up, whereupon all his assailants ran." Having shaken off his attackers, Addison ran over to Nodwell and found the NCO locked in a similar struggle. At the officer's approach, all but one of Nodwell's attackers fled. The corporal managed to keep a tight grip on this remaining German, and both he and Addison beat him "into submission with their revolver butts." From having nearly been killed or captured themselves, the two men instead managed to secure a prisoner of their own, who was soon identified as a member of the 189th Infantry Regiment.[15]

Based on intelligence extracted from this captive, Lts. Arthur Duncan and George Annand and eight other ranks went out at 11:50 PM on 15 September to locate a suspected enemy post on the west side of the canal, opposite Sains-lès-Marquion. Although they were unable to find any evidence of the post, the party did run into a German patrol, which was driven off after a brief scuffle. In the process, Lt. Annand and Pte. Young dashed after the nearest German to take him prisoner. As they did so, another member of B Company's patrol hurled a Mills grenade, which wounded not only the German but Annand and Young as well. Having debunked the reported existence of a German post in the area, Duncan collected his party, including the wounded and their new prisoner, and together they returned safely to their own lines.[16]

The action continued on the following day. Just before noon on 16 September, two patrolling British officers, from units on the 19th Battalion's right flank, were ambushed by a German party that had concealed itself in some bushes approximately 200 yards in front of the 19th Battalion's southernmost Lewis gun post. Although initial attempts to rescue the fallen officers failed in the face of heavy fire from German machine guns on a nearby canal lock, Lt. Addison and four other ranks, along with the Lewis gunners in Post no. 1, managed to drive the Germans out of the bushes after a brief firefight. But the intruders made good their escape after hurling some smoke bombs to give them additional cover. Early in the afternoon, Lts. Duncan and Addison stole out to investigate the scene. After locating the bodies of the two British officers, they determined that the grove where the Germans had been hiding was still unoccupied. More important, they discovered that the Germans had been accessing this position by using a path hidden from the Canadians' view. This led to the establishment of standing nighttime patrols in this area to keep the enemy from gaining any sort of lodgement along the 19th Battalion's right flank.

Later in the evening of that same day, after its relief by the 20th Battalion, the 19th Battalion proceeded back to positions in brigade support. The tour it had just completed would have been familiar in flavour to long-time veterans of the battalion, dominated as it was by vigorous patrol and outpost work – hallmarks of the trench war.[17] The battalion remained in support until the evening of 20 September, when it was rotated back to the front line to relieve the 20th Battalion. Earlier that day, its strength was augmented by the addition of twenty-seven other ranks returning from convalescence or from temporary assignments to other units or staffs.[18] The renewal of old friendships was always a boon to morale, and each draft of reinforcements was scrutinized upon arrival for familiar and friendly faces.

Lt.-Col. Millen's men moved back into their old positions in the right subsection of the divisional front, close to the Canal du Nord. Much to their chagrin, they found that the Germans had stepped up efforts to shell the forward area, which made even routine tasks risky. In addition, although German patrol activities seemed to decline in frequency, their parties were strong in numbers and aggressive in attitude. One enemy patrol numbering around fifteen men was encountered on the night of 22 September by a patrol of twelve other ranks from A Company under Lt. Harold S. Forbes. In the ensuing struggle, the Germans hurled their cylindrical stick bombs (nicknamed "potato mashers"), wounding three of the Canadians. But Forbes's men retaliated and managed to drive the Germans off.[19] This was most likely the same incident mentioned by Fred Stitt in a story he told after the war about a patrol encounter near the Canal du Nord in which he was seriously wounded by a German grenade.[20]

This turned out to be the only notable action of a brief tour, as the 20th Battalion moved back into the lines on the evening of 23 September. Patrols from the outgoing 19th Battalion fanned out along the front to cover the relief, which was completed at 10:15 PM. The 19th, having suffered ten non-fatal casualties over the previous three days, then moved back to the western outskirts of Cagnicourt, where the men rested on the following day before moving farther west to the area between Hendecourt and Chérisy. There they remained through 27 September. [21]

À la Bataille!

Earlier in the month, Marshal Foch, Field Marshal Haig, and the other Allied commanders had agreed to broaden the scope of their offensive efforts to prevent the Germans from massing their reserves along key portions of the front, such as the Hindenburg Line. They devised four great blows, to be delivered against important German positions along a huge front stretching from the Meuse River to the English Channel. By 22 September, the timetable for these joint offensive operations was set. It would begin on the 26th, with a combined attack by the US First and French Fourth Armies between the Suippe and Meuse rivers. Then, on 27 September, the British First and Third Armies would strike out towards the crucial communications centre of Cambrai. The next day, the Flanders Group of Armies, including British, Belgian, and French forces, would advance between the Lys River and the Channel coast. Finally, on 29 September, the British Fourth and French First Armies would assault the main portion of the Hindenburg Line, advancing in the direction of Busigny, some thirteen miles southeast of Cambrai. Once this series of operations began, Foch wanted to ensure that no momentum was lost and that the Germans were allowed no respite. *Tout le monde à la bataille!* became his motto for this grand offensive.[22]

The seizure of Cambrai was vitally important for the success of British operations against the Hindenburg Line, which was the "last fully-developed line of defence" facing the British armies. Cambrai was a main rail hub for the German armies, and its retention would facilitate the transport of men, munitions, and supplies to other

Canadian infantry and German prisoners in a shallow trench, September 1918. (LAC PA-003226)

important sectors. Moreover, the defensive positions shielding the city – the Marquion Line, the forbidding heights of Bourlon Wood, and the Marcoing Line – also guarded the northern flank of the Hindenburg Line. Field Marshal Haig assigned the British Third Army the task of capturing Cambrai itself; meanwhile, the First Army would form a defensive flank by taking Bourlon Wood and sweeping around the northeastern outskirts of the city. The First Army's commander, Gen. Horne, once more picked the battered but still powerful Canadian Corps to lead this cooperative effort with the Third Army. But in order to reach Bourlon Wood and the outskirts of Cambrai, the Canadians would have to cross the Canal du Nord.[23] This was a major operation in itself and was carried out on 27 September by the 1st and 4th Canadian Divisions, in conjunction with a diversionary attack by XXII Corps to the north and the advance of the Third Army to the south. Lt.-Gen. Currie's plan to cross the canal was as audacious as it was risky, dependent as it was on funnelling his attacking divisions over a dry stretch of the canal 2,600 yards wide situated between Sains-lès-Marquion and Moeuvres. Despite the concerns of his superiors, the gamble paid off. By nightfall on the 27th, the two Canadian divisions, preceded by a massive and complex artillery bombardment, had crossed the canal, broken through the defences on its east bank, fanned out to roll up the northern part of the Marquion Line, and secured Bourlon Wood. They were joined on the left by the

11th British Division, temporarily attached to the Canadians, which assisted the 1st Canadian Division in pushing onward as far as the approaches to the Marcoing Line, east of the villages of Épinoy and Haynecourt. There, and along positions just east of Bourlon Wood, the Canadian Corps' advance finally ground to a temporary halt in the face of strong German counterattacks.[24]

The breach of the Canal du Nord and its associated defences was a remarkable feat of planning and engineering on the Canadian Corps' part. From a strategic standpoint, the gains made on 27 September and in subsequent days "unhinged" the German high command's "plan for a last stand on the Hindenburg Line." The Germans rushed in reserve divisions to stem the British and Canadian tide threatening to engulf Cambrai, which soon was rendered almost useless to them as a strategic railhead. In doing so, they weakened their capacity to counter the punch that would be delivered shortly against the Hindenburg Line by the Fourth Army.[25]

The Canadian Corps continued fighting for the next four days (28 September–1 October), with the 3rd Canadian Division taking up the advance on the right of the 4th Canadian, 1st Canadian, and 11th British Divisions. The German 17th Army mounted a fierce resistance, with its artillery and machine-gun companies exacting a fearsome toll on the Canadians and British, while its infantry regiments delivered determined counterattacks. But in spite of the Germans' efforts, the Canadian Corps breached the Marcoing Line and reached Neuville-Saint-Rémy (on the northwestern outskirts of Cambrai), as well as the high ground east of the village of Tilloy. In doing so, the corps suffered heavy casualties for daily territorial gains that were dwarfed by the achievement of 27 September. Nevertheless, Currie drove his forces onward until their exhaustion made it clear that fresh formations were needed to reach the banks of the Canal de l'Escaut and the area northeast of Cambrai.[26]

The Return of the 2nd Canadian Division

Throughout the operations to cross the Canal du Nord and encircle Cambrai, the 2nd Canadian Division was held in corps reserve, with the 4th Brigade, in turn, situated in divisional reserve. All troops were held in readiness for the potential exploitation of successes gained by the attacking divisions. On 28 September the 6th Brigade, taking the lead for the 2nd Division, moved up to the area just north of Bourlon Wood. Behind it, the 5th Brigade crossed to the east bank of the Canal du Nord, while the 4th Brigade was stationed in "the vicinity of Moeuvres."[27]

Amidst the preparations, with imminent action anticipated, Lt.-Col. Millen found a few moments to dash off a few lines to his mother. As usual, he tried to put the situation in the best possible light:

> The battalion is in old trenches, I have a tent, but quite comfy to what I have had. I have had the earth dry out for about 3 feet beneath and this keeps it somewhat warmer. Have my camp bed and am sleeping in pyjamas. You would be surprised how cozy the

Map 20 – Canal du Nord and Cambrai.

A casually dressed Millen (seated) enjoys a laugh with fellow officers in this undated photo. (ASH, Argyll Regimental Foundation)

> men make themselves by digging holes in the ground and covering the entrance with a rubber sheet and the top with any old material they can find. I suppose you must all feel tremendously bucked at the news that comes through from all fronts now-a-days, we do and it certainly looks at last as if the end is in sight sometime.[28]

In the early afternoon of 28 September, Millen led his men into positions in the Buissy Switch and the Hindenburg Support Line. All ranks anticipated their imminent involvement in the current round of fighting. The war diarist pronounced their morale as "excellent," with officers and men alike "keen for attack after being freshened by baths and [a] short rest period." While the other Canadian divisions clawed their way eastward, Millen's men took the opportunity on 29–30 September to visit sections of the Canal du Nord that they had defended recently, revelling in their ability to walk the ground without the imminent threat of sniper or machine-gun fire.[29]

The previous month had not been overly hard on the 19th Battalion in terms of casualties, which numbered 3 officers and 61 other ranks in total, with only 8 men killed. But there still had been shortfalls to make up because of the heavy losses in August. Before September drew to a close, another 10 officers and 204 other ranks were taken on strength from the Canadian Corps Reinforcement Camp, while an additional officer and 109 other ranks rejoined the unit from periods of convalescence or duties outside the battalion.[30] A draft of 70 of the new reinforcements was inspected by Capt. Robert Bliss, who had been stationed in rear details during mid-September. Bliss rated the men's physique and morale as "good," adding that they "have never been out before and are very keen."[31]

On 30 September the 2nd Canadian Division was ordered to move forward in close support of the 3rd Canadian Division, and to pass through it after it had secured bridgeheads over the portion of the Canal de l'Escaut running just north of Cambrai. From there, the 2nd Division was to take over the advance and swing northeast, heading for the Erclin River and the village of Iwuy. On the morning of 1 October, the 4th Brigade was finally ordered across to the east side of the Canal du Nord, into positions formerly occupied by the Germans in the Marquion Line. Later that day, the exhausted 3rd Canadian Division proved unable to reach the Canal de l'Escaut, and operations by the 1st and 4th Canadian Divisions likewise stalled in the face of heavy German fire. As a result, Lt.-Gen. Currie ordered the 2nd Canadian Division to take over a broad front of 5,000 to 6,000 yards between the Cambrai–Arras railway and the outskirts of the village of Blécourt. The division thus relieved the entire 4th Canadian Division and part of the 1st and 3rd Canadian Divisions on the night of 1–2 October.[32]

While Currie and his staff made arrangements for the next stage of the offensive, which would open in a week and feature the crossing of the Canal de l'Escaut, Maj.-Gen. Burstall decided to organize his defences on a two-brigade front, with the 5th Brigade on the right and the 6th on the left. The 4th Brigade remained in reserve, having been moved up to an area west of the Marcoing Line on the afternoon of 1 October. From 2 to 4 October, the Germans launched attacks on the 5th and 6th Brigades' fronts but were driven back. The 2nd Canadian Division continued to hold the line through 6 October, "working hard … in gaining control of 'No Man's Land' and pushing back the enemy's outposts and patrols." The 19th Battalion, stationed near the village of Sailly, dug in and waited for word of its role in the coming storm. In preparation, all ranks were put through a brisk round of training in Lewis gunnery. These weapons were so integral to a platoon's tactical potency that no man could afford to be ignorant of their use. Personnel regularly engaged in the Lewis gun sections were, of course, the most familiar with the weapon, but in light of the heavy casualties, all men had to know at least how to load and fire it.[33]

Owing to the recent success of the British Third Army in crossing the Canal de l'Escaut south of Cambrai, the opportunity to seize the city by envelopment was at last at hand. It would involve close cooperation between the Canadian and XVII Corps (the flanking formations of the British First and Third Armies) and would be carried out in two principal phases. First, XVII Corps would encircle Cambrai from the south and capture the Niergnies–Awoingt Ridge overlooking the city from the south and east. Second, the Canadian Corps would circle around the northern outskirts of Cambrai, cross the Canal de l'Escaut, capture the village of Escaudoeuvres, and fan out to the northeast, where it would join hands with the left flank of XVII Corps. The task of executing this northern envelopment would fall to the brigades of the 2nd Canadian Division, while the 3rd Canadian Division endeavoured to cross the canal and enter Cambrai itself. Lt.-Gen. Currie also ensured that the cavalry and motor machine-gun units of Brutinel's Brigade were on hand to seize any opportunity to exploit territorial gains farther east.[34]

The western approaches of the Canal de l'Escaut gave practically no cover to an attacking force, and the German machine gunners would guarantee that any daylight attempt to cross the open ground sloping down to the canal would meet with heavy losses. Consequently, Maj.-Gen. Burstall determined that a night attack presented the only feasible means of capturing the bridgeheads he needed.[35] On the afternoon of 6 October, Burstall called his brigadiers and their chiefs of staff together for a conference at which he explained the proposed operations to cross the Canal de l'Escaut and join forces with troops of Gen. Byng's Third Army northeast of Cambrai. Advancing on the 2nd Canadian Division's right flank would be the 7th Brigade of the 3rd Canadian Division; the 11th British Division would secure the left. That evening, Brig.-Gen. McCuaig relayed the plans to his battalion commanders at 4th Brigade headquarters.[36]

On the night of 8 October, the British First Army, led by the 2nd Canadian Division, would attack in conjunction with an advance begun earlier that morning by the Third Army south of Cambrai. The 6th Brigade, now commanded by Brig.-Gen. Alex Ross, would form a defensive flank on the left portion of the divisional front, between Blécourt and Ramillies; meanwhile, Brig.-Gen. T.L. Tremblay's 5th Brigade would secure bridgeheads across the Canal de l'Escaut at Morenchies, Pont d'Aire, and Ramillies. After crossing the canal, Tremblay's men would force their way through to the railway line running south and east of the village of Escaudoeuvres, on the northeastern outskirts of Cambrai. Upon receiving word of the 5th Brigade's success, the 4th Brigade, led by the 18th and 19th Battalions, would move from its assembly area just north of Tilloy, cross the canal, and reassemble behind the railway. From this area, the 4th Brigade would launch its own share of the attack on the early morning of 9 October, with the 19th Battalion on the right, the 18th Battalion on the left, the 20th Battalion in support, and the 21st Battalion in reserve, west of the railway. In addition, one mortar team from the 4th Canadian Trench Mortar Battery would be attached to each of the two leading battalions. Night attacks always entailed the risk of troops becoming confused and firing on one another, so in order to make it easier to identify friend from foe, all ranks in each of the 2nd Canadian Division's three brigades were ordered to wear white calico armbands. In preparation for the impending struggle, the 19th Battalion received some additional reinforcements from rear details, to the tune of one officer and forty-six other ranks.[37]

Lt.-Col. Millen, who had just recently been notified that his services had merited a bar to his DSO, elected to remain out of battle during his unit's next tour. A few days before operations began in earnest, he wrote his mother: "Am living at present back at our transport lines. The battalion is not at present in the line but is forward of here and should go in in a few days. C.O.s are supposed to go fifty-fifty with their second in commands in tours. So I am letting Hatch take this one."[38]

Cambrai, Naves, and Open Warfare

The Third Army's attack south of Cambrai kicked off as planned on the morning of 8 October, but the progress of XVII Corps, on the Canadian Corps' right, was hampered by strong German opposition. Although the situation was uncertain on their right, the Canadians were ordered to stick to their plan and prepare to cross the Canal de l'Escaut that night. Since the delays experienced by the neighbouring British troops had slowed the Canadian preparations, the attack would have to begin after midnight instead of at 9:30 PM, as originally planned. Worried that this would not give the 4th Brigade enough hours of darkness in which to move across the canal and assemble for its proposed attack on the morning of 9 October, Maj.-Gen. Burstall decided to carry out only the 5th and 6th Brigades' phases of the operation. He would hold off on committing the 4th Brigade until the situation became clearer.[39]

While the supporting artillery fired "a series of short crashes and rolling barrages" over the German forward defences, the 5th and 6th Brigades began their advance at 1:30 AM on 9 October. Lashed by intermittent rain squalls, the Canadians punched through a network of rifle pits that marked the German outpost line. The Germans were already in the midst of preparations for a withdrawal, so the attack caught them completely by surprise. The 6th Brigade secured the situation on the left and pushed patrols out towards the villages of Cuvillers and Bantigny, while the 5th Brigade, in cooperation with parties of engineers, rushed the bridges at Pont d'Aire, saving the main span before it could be destroyed by the fleeing Germans. By 3:30 AM the infantry were well situated on the east bank of the Canal de l'Escaut and had begun mopping up remaining pockets of German troops in the village of Escaudoeuvres and the northern outskirts of Cambrai.[40]

After sunrise on 9 October, the 4th Brigade, concentrated just north of Tilloy, was ordered to move to the Morenchies–Ramillies area along the west bank of the Canal de l'Escaut. The first unit to move was the 19th Battalion, which at 9:15 AM was placed temporarily under the orders of the 5th Brigade. By 4:00 PM the rest of the brigade had moved up to the canal through some heavy German shelling, and the 19th Battalion reverted to 4th Brigade control. The Germans appeared to be retreating all along the Canadian front, and Lt.-Gen. Currie urged his subordinate commanders to pursue them "relentlessly." Accordingly, the 5th Brigade was ordered to continue its advance and capture the village of Naves, while the 6th Brigade advanced along the eastern bank of the canal. The 4th Brigade, meanwhile, was to ready itself to pass through the 5th Brigade and push on to the Erclin River and the higher ground to the northeast.[41]

The 5th Brigade, by now very tired, gamely attempted the advance, but it was held up by German wire and defensive posts west of Naves and south of Thun-Saint-Martin. German machine-gun and artillery fire checked any further progress, and even with assistance from the 2nd Battalion, CMGC, and units of cavalry and machine guns from Brutinel's Brigade, the 5th Brigade could not force its way through to Naves. A fresher formation was needed, so the task of taking the village was transferred to the 4th Brigade. At 5:30 PM, verbal orders came through from division headquarters for the 4th Brigade to move across the Canal de l'Escaut and assemble near Escaudoeuvres in preparation to resume the attack. The assembly was a tricky one, for the area around Escaudoeuvres was heavily bombarded by the Germans, who unleashed high explosive, gas, and incendiary shells at the incoming Canadians. In spite of this, all units managed to get into position by 9:00 PM. For the commander of the First Army, it was imperative that the Canadians continue to press their advance in order to support the efforts of the Third Army on their right.[42]

At 2:00 AM on 10 October the 4th Brigade was ordered to pass through the 5th Brigade, attack Naves, and occupy the higher ground across the Erclin River. Battalion dispositions remained as set on 7 October, with the 19th Battalion on the right, the 18th on the left, the 20th in support on the right, and the 21st in reserve on the left. The men of the 19th Battalion, backed up by those of the 20th, would begin their attack at 6:00 AM. Their job was to clear Naves, which was held by elements of the German 10th Ersatz Division, and capture a spur of higher ground about 1,000 yards northeast of the village. This ground would give good observation over the area to the north and east, including the valley of the Erclin River. As such, it would form an ideal springboard from which to launch the next stage of the advance, the objective of which was the commanding ridge known as the "Iwuy Spur," about a mile and a half northeast of the Erclin and defended by Prussian regulars of the 6th Infantry Division. The 18th Battalion, on the left, would begin its assault an hour later than the 19th's, press forward across the Erclin River, and attempt to seize a stretch of ground southeast of the village of Iwuy. To the left of the 18th Battalion, units of the 6th Infantry Brigade were to advance along the Canal de l'Escaut, secure Thun-l'Évêque and Thun-Saint-Martin, and capture Iwuy itself.[43]

Beyond the urban sprawl of Cambrai and its suburbs, the gently rising ground facing the 4th Brigade was "ideal country for open warfare." North and east of Naves, the ground fell away into the valley of the Erclin but then rose again gradually to an elevation of some 260 feet along the Iwuy Spur. The villages in this area, such as Naves and Iwuy, "had not been so severely shelled that they were to any extent demolished and beyond them there was practically no cover either natural or artificial."[44]

At 3:30 AM the 19th Battalion was instructed to assemble at its jumping-off line along the railway northeast of Escaudoeuvres and west of Naves. A and B Companies were earmarked to lead the attack, with C Company acting in close support and in charge of mopping up the village. D Company was held back in reserve along the railway to await further orders. The men were exhausted even before the attack began. "We have had no sleep for three days," remarked Deward Barnes.[45] The day's operations commenced at 5:30 AM when the 24th Division of the Third Army, on the Canadian Corps' right, began its advance against Cagnoncles. At the same time, the 6th Brigade entered and cleared the village of Thun-l'Évêque as a preliminary to its main effort against Iwuy. Then, at 6:00 AM, amidst showers of rain, the 4th Brigade's attack began with artillery and machine-gun barrages. Observers from the 19th Battalion judged the barrage to be "very light." Indeed, it posed little problem for the attacking infantry; opposition from German artillery and machine guns was "only spasmodic." The 10th Ersatz Division, which had been "rated by Allied intelligence as being third-class," did not put up a concerted effort to hold Naves. Attacking in artillery formation, the troops of the 19th Battalion, followed by those of the 20th, swept forward through the village, suffering "only ten casualties" before reaching their initial objective on the higher ground to the northeast by 8:35 AM.[46]

The German resistance at Naves had been spasmodic; even so, it posed some temporary difficulties for those sections and platoons of Canadians that happened to be in the fields of fire of scattered enemy machine-gun posts. "There are no trenches here," wrote Deward Barnes,

> just shell holes. We ... had no trouble until we got into a hollow before the town. [The Germans] opened up a fire and we sent up our SOS flares ... but the artillery could not see them for rain and mist and did not open fire. We wasted time there under whatever protection we could get, then received orders to advance. But, in the meantime, the Germans had retired and all we did was just go through the town, shooting into houses and looking into barnyards. We went over a bridge that had a mine under it but it did not work ... We dug in on the other side of town, into a ridge.[47]

Pte. Vivian Thompson, who had returned to the 19th Battalion on 20 September, after recovering from the wound he received at Fransart, also recalled some tense moments during the advance to Naves:

> We started off at a slow walk down the hillside and increased our pace as things began to get hotter. I remember getting into a deep ditch and wondering if I would be able to get out fast enough to avoid getting raked. I also remember how I would have given anything to run back but considered that while I might get shot going forward I was almost certain to be shot if I turned the other way. There were machine guns on the ridge in front, in a church tower on our left and an aeroplane above us all trying to make things pleasant. I can remember the bullets spitting up under my nose as I lay on the ground between rushes and thinking that it was lucky that I was not a little longer as they might have found a resting place in my head. I had been pushed into the Lewis gun crew and was carrying the container of pans plus the usual extra two bandoliers of S.A.A. and had on my greatcoat which was too long and to make matters worse we

> were going over a beetroot field which was heavy going. I remember wishing that I was dead and at the same time doing my best to remain alive. Finally we made a final rush and over to a lone house on my left where we took shelter.[48]

As far as attacks went, this one came off rather well for the 19th Battalion, with all initial objectives secured and few casualties. On the left, the 18th Battalion, which had gotten under way as scheduled at 7:00 AM, was not as lucky. Its advance, along with that of the right portion of the 6th Brigade, was held up by heavy machine-gun fire from German positions along the Erclin River south of Iwuy. There the 10th Ersatz Division had chosen to make its stand, and it proved more stubborn than the intelligence analysts had anticipated.[49]

Meanwhile, the 19th Battalion was busy making good its gains, and upon the lighting of a prearranged signal flare, its headquarters moved from the battered village of Escaudoeuvres up to Naves. Maj. Hatch, in command of the battalion during this operation, then went up to his positions on the high ground northeast of the village and dispatched two patrols to explore the possibility of crossing the Erclin River. The right patrol, under Lt. H.A. Lowe, scrambled 1,500 yards forward and secured a bridgehead over the river at 11:00 AM. Although the Germans had destroyed the bridge on the Cambrai–Saulzoir road, Hatch's men, along with elements of the Canadian Corps Cyclist Battalion, managed to cross the river and establish defensive strongpoints. The 19th Battalion's left patrol also succeeded in getting across the Erclin, aided by its discovery of a dry stretch of river bed some 500 yards northwest of the wrecked bridge. These actions occurred around the same time that British troops of the 24th Division captured the village of Rieux, just southeast of Lt. Lowe's bridgehead.[50]

Battling beyond the Erclin

Upon receiving word of his patrols' progress, Maj. Hatch contacted brigade headquarters, and it was decided that the 19th Battalion should continue its advance in short order. This was well in line with the division commander's wishes, since, having heard that the British were making good progress on his right, he wanted his brigades to "force the crossings of the River Erclin if at all possible." Accordingly, the 19th Battalion made ready to cross, its objective being a sunken road approximately 500 yards northeast of the river. This next stage of the attack was carried out by C and D Companies, which had been in support and reserve earlier that morning. Both companies were supported by covering fire from the 2nd Battalion, CMGC, and succeeded in crossing the Erclin shortly after 1:15 PM. Although C Company, operating on the right, reached its objective with relatively minimal losses, D Company, on the left, "met with very heavy machine gun fire" from the Prussians occupying the high ground to the northeast. Undaunted, D Company forged ahead, spurred on by the example of its commander, Lt. Robert O. Spreckley, who carried on with his duties in spite of his wounds. By 2:30 PM, both companies had attained their objectives in the sunken road and had pushed out strong patrols to reconnoitre the ground ahead.[51]

On the left, at 2:00 PM, the 18th Battalion had managed to establish a post in the railway embankment just east of the Erclin River, but it was unable to make any further progress in the face of heavy machine-gun fire from the left flank. The 6th Brigade was still stalled south of Iwuy, leaving the left flank of the 4th Brigade vulnerable to vicious enfilade fire. At this time, the 19th Battalion, in cooperation with A and C Squadrons of the Canadian Light Horse (from Brutinel's Brigade), attempted to clear up the situation on the left by outflanking the enemy-occupied high ground. But this manoeuvre, which featured the last charge ever made by Canadian horse cavalry, was unsuccessful, and was especially costly for the cavalrymen involved.[52] The sight of the cavalry galloping across the bed of the Erclin River and up the eastern slopes to engage the enemy was a stirring spectacle, but also a tragic one, for the 19th Battalion men who observed them. "The cavalry went forward," stated Deward Barnes, "the horses ringing wet [with sweat]. My, but it is a pretty sight as they dashed down the hill and over the creek … Then the Germans opened up on them. It was a shame. They could not help but hit them with machine guns … That attack was a failure. Cavalry were not much good in this war."[53] The fact that the infantry and cavalry were by this time operating outside the effective range of their supporting field artillery did not augur well for the effectiveness of the mounted men in particular, who presented splendid targets for the German machine gunners.[54] But the 19th Battalion had by no means gotten away scot-free either, having suffered casualties estimated at three officers and seventy other ranks by 4:00 PM.[55]

The 19th Battalion had suffered setbacks on the left, but its position on the right had been strengthened by its contact with the Northampton Regiment of the 24th Division, XVII Corps. Thus the time was considered ripe for some further exploitation. Leapfrogging through C and D Companies, A and B Companies jumped off at 5:15 PM to take the high ground at a point roughly 500 yards northwest of the Cambrai–Saulzoir road, north of Rieux. Although the troops were "subjected to heavy M.G. fire" and had to fight "for every foot of ground, the enemy opposition was overcome," and objectives along the southern portion of another sunken road were captured by 7:45 PM. The lack of artillery cover for this attack was mitigated somewhat by fact that it was launched at twilight and concluded in darkness. This was the 19th Battalion's third consecutive attack of the day. By the time it was completed, the unit had advanced a total distance of 6,000 yards from its starting point earlier that morning.[56]

Captain Arthur Duncan.
(MUA RC 0835)

The perfunctory official after-action reports make this final advance appear easier than it actually was for the men carrying it out. "We started," remarked A Company's Deward Barnes, with

> no artillery and pitch dark. We extended out in line just far enough so as you could see the man next to you. We went very slowly, orders passing down the line so as not to get one flank too far ahead of the other. An officer was on each end. We kept going, no shelling, but nice and quiet. I judged we had been going nearly two hours when we

> heard the Germans talking and clicking [cocking] their guns to get ready. We were practically on them. Their trench was only a few yards from us. They heard us. I got down quick. Their machine guns opened up but as luck had it, no one opened up in front of me. When they swept I was down close to the ground. The second fellow from me got it and was groaning. I passed the word along to try and stop if he could. He did.
>
> I don't know how many men we lost. Some were shot through the heels and most through the head while getting down. We waited for orders and they came. Crawl to the next man and retire to the road again! We went back … and when we were told about so many getting killed and wounded we all had to go back and get (and bring out) all the wounded we could.
>
> We spent most of the rest of the dark hours going back and forward getting the boys. We stayed on this main road [most likely Cambrai–Saulzoir] in funk holes. Cecil Arnold and several more were killed that were pals of mine.[57]

Although Barnes's account appears to depict a reverse, all official reports claim that the battalion's objectives were met. Men who had lost friends probably did not care much about the fact that they had secured favourable jumping-off points for the next day's advance.

That night, A and B Companies continued to probe the area in front of their advance posts but encountered heavy machine-gun fire from a railway line farther ahead. One of the officers out on patrol, Arthur Duncan (recently appointed Acting Captain), was wounded and reported missing at 3:15 AM on 11 October. As if this was not bad enough, an hour and a half later, Capt. Robert Shiell of A Company anxiously reported that not only was Duncan still missing but also he may have been carrying a copy of the orders for the coming day's operations.[58]

Having attacked three times over an impressive distance on the previous day, the 19th Battalion was due for relief. When the 4th Brigade drew up its plans for a resumption of the offensive on 11 October, it relegated the 19th Battalion to reserve status. The 20th and 21st Battalions would now move into the forefront of the advance, with the 18th Battalion placed in support. This rotation of battalions was not the only change, however. As part of the preliminaries for a planned relief of the Canadian Corps on its present front, the 146th and 147th Brigades of the 49th British Division (brought up from GHQ Reserve) took over a sizable portion of the line facing the Iwuy Spur, thus relieving the 19th Battalion of its share of the front. Maj. Hatch's men continued to hold their positions until the British troops arrived later that morning to carry on the operation.[59]

The main event on 11 October would commence at 9:00 AM. The 4th Brigade, now on a much narrower front, was charged with advancing on Avesnes-le-Sec, northeast of Iwuy. To its right, the British 146th and 147th Brigades would attempt to finish the job of taking the Iwuy Spur, while to the left, the 6th Brigade would try again to capture Iwuy itself before proceeding on to the villages of Hordain and Lieu-Saint-Amand. By this time, the field artillery had had a chance to move far enough forward to offer effective support. In addition, engineers had repaired the bridge over the Erclin on the Cambrai–Saulzoir road, so that by 3:30 that morning it was fit for heavy traffic.[60]

"The West Yorks went over us at 9:00 AM," reported Deward Barnes, who watched as a battalion of the West Yorkshire Regiment, from the 146th Brigade, passed through the 19th Battalion's positions to take up the advance. "The Imperials are so much different from us," he noted. "Their non-commissioned officers kept them in dead straight lines, there must have been six waves of them as far as you could see both ways. (The Canadians may go over in bunches any old way, but they always get there.) They passed us and kept going and reached their objective about 10:00 AM."[61]

The operation had begun on time and proceeded well enough at first, despite the rigid and outmoded tactical deployment executed by the unit Barnes observed. On the far left, with some timely assistance from a detachment of the 20th Battalion, the 6th Brigade finally forced its way into Iwuy by 10:45 AM, by which time reports from other sectors of the front indicated that the Germans had begun a general retirement throughout the region.[62] However, this broader assessment proved to be premature. Commanders and staffs at brigade and division headquarters barely had time to savour the sweet smell of success before the Germans administered a rude shock. Starting at around 10:30 AM, the German artillery opened up a brutal barrage along the British and Canadian front.[63] The 19th Battalion, sheltering along what seems to have been the Cambrai–Saulzoir road, came under heavy fire. "It was awful," Barnes recalled:

> This was a hard road. I had no funk hole, so got into the gutter. My back was on a level with the road. The shells would come straight down the road. Overhead [there were exploding] shells and shells that did not explode until they hit [the ground], making only a small hole and bouncing down the road, sometimes half a shell. It would make an awful noise twisting through the air. Men were cut to pieces in the funk holes which were higher than the road. A shell lit a foot … from me but I missed the blast.[64]

Between 10:30 and 11:00 AM, as the men of the 19th Battalion scrambled to find whatever meagre cover they could, five battalions of the German 370th and 371st Infantry Regiments (10th Ersatz Division) defied the expectations of Allied intelligence and mounted a spirited counterattack, the brunt of which fell upon the 146th and 147th British Brigades. But there was more to this surprise riposte than charging infantry. Heralded by one Canadian's cry of, "My God, look at them houses moving!" two detachments of German tanks came lumbering over the ridgeline from the direction of Avesnes-le-Sec. This was the first and only time that Canadian troops would face enemy tanks during the First World War.

Three monstrous, square, ungainly German A7V tanks of the 1st Panzer Detachment, supported by three captured British Mark IV tanks of the 13th Panzer Detachment, were pitted primarily against the 20th and 21st Battalions, southeast of Iwuy, while two more A7Vs attacked the British near Rieux. On the left, as the three A7Vs of the 1st Panzer Detachment bore down on the Canadian positions, elements of the German 18th Reserve Division suddenly joined them and "indulged in a spontaneous charge."[65] Meanwhile, on the right, a significant portion of the attacking British troops broke and ran back through the huddled ranks of the 19th Battalion. "We saw the Imperials coming back on the mad tear," Deward Barnes testified. "We got in position and waited and they finally came back to where we were, all in a panic. Down the road and through the fields as far as you could see saying 'for God's sake get out of here, they are coming tanks and all.' I never saw a more frightened crowd."[66] In some places, particularly on the right, the British and Canadian line had fallen back as much as a mile; elements of the 21st and 20th battalions likewise had to retreat to conform to the retirement on their right.[67]

Given their reaction to the counterattack and the parade ground style in which they had earlier advanced, the British units probably contained a high percentage of new and inexperienced men. What many of them needed was solid leadership, or at least a jolt of inspiration, and some of them found both with the 19th Battalion. "Col. Hatch [*sic*] sure had guts that afternoon," remembered veteran Sam Carpenter. When the German counterattack began, "Hatch and his batman got on their horses and rode forward with shells bursting all around to see what was wrong."[68] Although the major and his aide had made themselves foolishly conspicuous, their bravery encouraged many to stand and face the onslaught. Other officers wasted no time in rallying any troops they could gather to fight back. "Our officers began to figure it out," wrote Deward Barnes, and they "yelled 'come on Canadians.' We went and the Imperials as well, we were all mixed up, and the rally was followed up all along the line. It was in the open and there were thousands of men." Capt. Shiell, in charge of A Company, gathered the Lewis gun sections from both his own company and C Company and led them to a stretch of commanding ground on their left. From this position, they poured a remorseless fire into the oncoming enemy.[69]

"The Germans were thick too," reported Barnes, who was in the forefront of the action with his fellow Lewis gunners. "They had two tanks on our front. Great big square tanks. We went on to meet them and about halfways several of the tanks were shot by bullets."[70] Vivian Thompson, who also was manning a Lewis gun, later recalled that he "was ordered to shoot if I saw the tank coming over on us. I thought that a Lewis gun versus a tank was a rather onesided affair."[71] While Shiell was busy directing the Lewis gun teams, Lt. Vincent Crombie of the 19th Battalion's C Company found a discarded German anti-tank rifle and opened fire on the leading tank – an A7V. The massive rifle's 13.2-mm (.519-inch) armour-piercing rounds damaged one of the tank's treads and put it out of action. Groups of German infantry accompanying the tanks collapsed amidst the hail of Lewis gun and rifle fire, and the remaining machines circled around and headed back in the direction from which they had come. The tide irrevocably turned in the Canadians' favour when a battery of field artillery galloped onto the scene and, in concert with Vickers guns of the 2nd Canadian Motor Machine Gun Brigade, poured heavy fire into the wavering ranks of enemy infantry and any tanks that remained within range.[72] The surviving Germans were by now in full retreat in the face of a bowed but unbroken British and Canadian line. Seeing that the situation was well under control, Capt. Shiell, along with Lts. Earl Croft and Vincent Crombie, left others in charge of their forward detachments and proceeded back to assist in reorganizing the British units fighting alongside them.[73]

By shortly after noon, mopping-up operations in the village of Iwuy were completed by the 6th Brigade. Following the failure of the German counterattack, plans were made to resume the joint Canadian/British advance at 3:30 PM. By zero hour the 49th British Division had effectively recovered much of the ground it had given up earlier in the day and was ready to attack alongside the 4th and 6th Brigades of the 2nd Canadian Division. German machine-gun and artillery fire thwarted this later effort, however, and by 6:00 PM. Maj.-Gen. Burstall was informed that the assault "had practically failed." The 4th Brigade did manage to reach the top of the Iwuy Spur, suffering heavy casualties in the process. By evening, the Canadians had made it only 1,000 yards beyond Iwuy to the north and northeast, where they were situated on the forward slope of the Iwuy Spur. There, they faced the intact German defences along the Selle River, some four to five miles distant.[74]

The 19th Battalion remained in reserve for the rest of the day and was not involved in the afternoon attack. Having done more than their fair share between the previous day's fighting and in helping to throw back the German counterattack that morning, the dog-tired men of the 19th were pulled back by Maj. Hatch to a line along the sunken road just beyond the Erclin River. The measure of their exhaustion was amply demonstrated by a plaintive message sent by Capt. Shiell to battalion headquarters at 5:15 PM: "We are absolutely played out and the officers and men incapable of further action or marching." Fortunately, Shiell's men and the rest of the battalion were relieved later that night (11–12 October) by the 6th Seaforth Highlanders of the 51st (Highland) Division. The Canadian Corps was slated for relief as well, and the process of exchanging frontages with XXII Corps had already begun by the time the 19th Battalion finally departed the lines northeast of Cambrai.[75] It had been a hard tour, and although there was a strong sense that the Germans were at last on the run, no one knew that they would have to endure just one more month of fighting.

For the dead and seriously wounded, the struggle was already over. Casualties in the fighting northeast of Cambrai had cost the 19th Battalion a total of 4 officers wounded, 1 officer (Capt. A.J. Duncan) missing, and 139 other ranks killed or wounded. This amounted to almost all of the casualties that the unit would sustain

A Canadian leaving a dugout in Cambrai with German spiked helmets, October 1918. (LAC PA-003421)

during the month of October.[76] One of the injured other ranks was the faithful diarist Deward Barnes, who was hit at 2:00 PM on 11 October while rushing for cover with Capt. Shiell. Barnes recounted that he was

> not any more than seventy-five yards from the Germans when I got hit … My rifle was slung over my shoulder and the bullet went through the butt and through my right thigh. I yelled and reeled a couple of times, then went down. I ditched all I had and drank all my water but had no cigarettes. I had no field dressing and was bleeding, my leg was numb. I dragged myself along to a sunken road and got in. An Imperial man saw me and told me to come into a square cutting alongside of the road with him. He says, "You'll be alright here." … In the meantime the battalion had gone back to their original place, the main road. Captain Shiell sent two men up to take me out and with help I got back to our battalion Dressing Station, a couple of miles back.[77]

Barnes was warned that, because of persistent German shelling, it might take as long as three days before ambulances could be brought up to evacuate the survivors. He needed more help than the dressing station could provide, so he was forced to walk three miles to the rear before he managed to hitch a ride on a truck back to a mobile hospital run by a field ambulance unit. Eventually, he was evacuated to England. There, he would see out the remainder of the war, recovering in hospital, from which he would be discharged on 23 November. After being transferred to a reserve battalion at Kinmel Park, Wales, he embarked for Canada on 1 February 1919. For Barnes, the war effectively ended on 11 October 1918. But, as would be the case with many other veterans, chilling memories of his long experience at the front would haunt him for the rest of his life.[78]

In the hours before his battalion was relieved in the lines near the Erclin River, Lt.-Col. Millen took some opportunity to bask in the glow of the Canadians' latest success. Writing obviously of Cambrai, which had been evacuated, pillaged, and partly razed by the retreating Germans,[79] he informed his mother that "we are still keeping on the job as you can gather, to us it seems absolutely wonderful to walk around country that has been denied us so long, country that is miles inside of the old German lines."[80]

After being relieved by the Highlanders, the 19th Battalion moved back, first to Escaudoeuvres, where hot meals were dished out to the weary men, who had endured "no sleep … in four days and nights." By 13 October they had been moved west of the Canal de l'Escaut, where they were reunited with rear details and transport, and settled into billets in the nearby villages of Bantigny and Cuvillers.[81] When presented with a measure of "down time" on the heels of a rough period of fighting, some men did their best to put the recent past behind them and indulged in whichever recreational pursuits they had recourse to enjoy (i.e., sports, drinking, gambling). Others found a reliable form of catharsis in letter writing, and typically were rather modest about any honours awarded or special achievements ascribed to them. Cpl. John Gaetz informed his sister Daisy that he and his friends had been

> very busy this fall having had some very long days and gone through some trying times, however it can't last forever and there seems to be a brighter sky ahead of us now than ever before. The fighting is of a much different type now as we are quite in the open and moving practically all the time. I have been over the top again since I wrote you last and came through O.K. … On coming back from my sojourn to the hospital the Captain of my Company congratulated me on receiving the Military Medal. I haven't been officially presented with it yet though. Don't think that I did anything very wonderful but just devotion to duty.[82]

21

Long Road to Mons: 14 October–11 November 1918

Upon exchanging fronts with XXII Corps, the Canadian Corps occupied the central sector of the British First Army, still facing the formations of the German 17th Army. Also still in the Canadians' path were the Escaut and Sensée canals, both of which were surrounded by occasional stretches of marshy or flooded terrain. Being situated in the corps' right-hand sector, the 2nd Canadian Division had to contend with both waterways. After receiving word late in the evening of 13 October that the German forces in the area might execute a general withdrawal, Maj.-Gen. Burstall told his brigades to make ready to cross the canals and keep in touch with the enemy's movements. The 4th Brigade's section of front was situated west of the Canal de l'Escaut and faced the Sensée marshes. Owing to the generally exhausted state of the brigade, the 25th Battalion from 5th Brigade was temporarily attached and took over the entire 4th Brigade frontage while the other battalions got an additional day of rest.[1]

On 14 October the 4th Brigade was ordered to relieve the 5th Brigade. In the process, it would side-slip to the right and straddle the Canal de l'Escaut, while the 6th Brigade took over a portion of its former front on the left. This was accomplished on the night of 14–15 October. The 25th Battalion was relieved and returned to its parent formation, while the 18th and 19th Battalions took over 4th Brigade's right and left sub-sections. With the Canal de l'Escaut as the boundary between the two units, the 18th Battalion occupied Hordain, east of the canal and 2,000 yards north of Iwuy, while the 19th Battalion proceeded to the villages of Estrun and Paillencourt.[2]

Once again under the command of Lt.-Col. Millen, the 19th Battalion moved into Paillencourt, on the southern bank of the Canal de la Sensée. After the recent fighting at Naves and near Iwuy, its trench strength was down to 17 officers and 442 other ranks. While Millen established his headquarters in the local chateau, he dispatched patrols and set up strongpoints along a ditch on the reverse side of the canal's southern bank. Contact was maintained with the enemy along the canal, and, despite some periodic harassing fire from machine-gun nests along the north bank, the situation remained reasonably quiet throughout the night and into the morning of 15 October. When not on patrol or manning posts, the men were able to find very comfortable quarters in Paillencourt, the houses and buildings of which remained virtually untouched by the ravages of war. An even more pleasant discovery was the abundance of small vegetable gardens scattered throughout the village, which the men cheerfully raided to supplement their own tedious army fare. According to the battalion war diarist, opinion was unanimous that this was "the greatest front line trip in the history of the Battalion" so far.[3]

Conditions remained stable through to the evening of 17 October, when word came that patrols from the 1st Canadian Division, in the Canadian Corps' left sector, had advanced into Douai. In addition, the 4th Canadian Division, in the centre sector between the 1st and 2nd Divisions, had entered the village of Cantin and encountered no enemy opposition. The Germans at last had begun their anticipated withdrawal, spurred by advances across the Lys River two days earlier by Allied forces in Flanders. This compelled the German 6th and 17th Armies to retire to a new and as yet incomplete defensive system known as the Hermann Line, which opened the way for the British Fifth and First Armies to continue their advances.[4]

In spite of these movements, opposition along the 2nd Canadian Division's frontage remained stubborn, with the Germans unleashing fusillades of machine-gun and artillery fire in an attempt to cover their retreat and keep their Canadian pursuers at a distance. But around 8:00 PM, the enemy fire suddenly ceased along the 6th Brigade's front, in the division's left section, allowing patrols to filter across the Canal de la Sensée and establish bridgeheads on the north bank. It was time now for parties of engineers to come up and begin work on the canal bridges, which had been demolished earlier by the retreating Germans.[5]

By 5:45 AM on 18 October, the engineers managed to construct a pontoon bridge for foot traffic over the canal between Paillencourt and Estrun, enabling the 19th Battalion to get into action on the far side. One platoon from C Company managed to get across before the work was completed and provided cover for the sappers as they feverishly continued their work. As soon as the bridge was ready, the rest of C Company, under Lt. Harold Stuart, crossed the canal but found that the bridge across the Sensée River had been wrecked. So once again, the engineers were summoned to begin work anew. Light pontoon bridges were fine for infantry, but heavier, more permanent structures had to be erected to permit the movement of transport and supplies. While the engineers toiled, C Company pressed onward, followed by B Company in close support. D Company, on the battalion right, was also on the move, but it was held up by marshy ground that in some places submerged the men up to their knees. As if this was not frustrating enough, D Company also encountered heavy fire from German machine-gun posts on the east bank of the Canal de l'Escaut. However, the timely intervention of some trench mortar units silenced this opposition, and D Company was able to move up and establish its positions in line with those of B and C Companies. By early afternoon, it had caught up with German units on the outskirts of the village of Bouchain. Here, the Canadians dug in and waited for artillery support before launching a concerted attack. In the meantime, Lt.-Col. Millen brought up his headquarters, the reserve troops of A Company, and part of the battalion transport as far as Wavrechain, where he awaited further orders. The day's activity so far had cost the battalion only a single casualty – one man slightly wounded.[6]

During the night of 18–19 October, little solid intelligence could be gained about the enemy positions. But with the exception of some minor gas shelling, the time passed with no significant incident. By 6:30 AM, 19th Battalion patrols determined that the Germans had withdrawn altogether, under cover of darkness and the firepower of their remaining rearguard machine gunners. The enemy had also vacated other sectors of the front facing the Canadians, and by 9:20 AM the 6th Brigade had succeeded in reaching positions on the Bouchain Spur. An hour later, Maj.-Gen. Burstall ordered the 4th Brigade to push ahead, capture the village of Bouchain, and proceed towards Boucheneuil and Neuville-sur-l'Escaut.[7]

Liberation

The men of B Company were the first to reach Neuville-sur-l'Escaut, at around 4:00 PM, and when they did so they were "agreeably surprised to see hundreds of old men, women and children on the opposite side [of the canal] waving frantic welcomes to their liberators … Coffee, cognac, kisses and hugs were showered on the troops by the populace who were frantic with joy after having suffered 4 years of slavery under the ruthless rule of Hun masters."[8] This was the first real experience that the men of the 19th Battalion had as liberators. They already had passed through numerous French and Belgian towns that had been occupied by the Germans, but these had been mostly destroyed or deserted and their populations evacuated. Most of the civilians they had previously encountered lived in communities behind Allied lines. Now that they were freeing masses of people who had been living under German occupation, many men began to realize that their own suffering and hardship had a purpose. According to Wilfred Macklin,

> although there were times when we were extremely weary and very exhausted, we were nearly all very young people and we recovered from those things, and the thing that began to raise the morale as much as anything was the entry of our troops into inhabited villages and towns. You have to remember that we had been fighting for nearly a year in a devastated area where every village had been destroyed and there were no civilians at all. The city of Arras with forty thousand people had its population reduced to three or four hundred who were living in cellars with the rats. It was a ghost city and there were no people in it to speak of. But when we got forward beyond the city of Douai in the general direction of say, of Valenciennes, there we found cities like Denain with thousands of people in them and these people came out and greeted us with the greatest possible enthusiasm and this in itself was a great raiser of morale. The soldier felt that, after all, they've been telling us that we're fighting for freedom and there are the people that we are liberating and the very reception that the soldier got was enough to convince him that this was, in fact, true.[9]

As uplifting as the liberation of Neuville-sur-l'Escaut was, there was a dark side to it as well, as testified by veteran Ernie Knott, then the 19th Battalion's assistant adjutant. Knott, along with the battalion's new medical officer, Capt. Fred Schlanker Parney,[10] observed countless civilians who had been brutalized under the German occupation. "We made our way across the canal," Knott remembered,

> and were immediately greeted by hundreds of French civilians who had been confined there for four years. The town itself presented a clean, orderly appearance on the surface including the usual "Prisoners Cage," which was heavily charged with electricity to prevent escape. The civilian population all bore unmistakable evidence of much suffering and privation, and their first requests after greeting us profusely as their liberators, was to solicit aid from "Monsieur le docteur." I found Fritz Parney who was M.O. at the time, and accompanied him and his staff through a maze of underground passages, not even fit to designate as cellars. We then knew to some extent how these civilians had suffered at the hands of a Town Commandant of the most ruthless type.
>
> Vermin-infested, blind, ravaged by venereal disease and bearing little resemblance to humanity, these poor creatures were slowly being starved in darkness. Children born in these rat infested caverns were blind … were never permitted to come up into fresh air or daylight. Doc Parney worked like a Trojan trying to alleviate the suffering and disease so rampant, but it was quite evident that the poor wrecks which had once lived the vivacious, carefree life of the French Peasant could only hope to end their days in some Insane Asylum. They were all demented maniacs robbed of all reason by the continuous sufferings they had been so ruthlessly forced to endure.[11]

The 19th Battalion was not the only unit to enter Neuville-sur-l'Escaut. The village actually lay within the operational boundaries of the 20th Battalion, which had just relieved the 18th Battalion on the right portion of the brigade front. Personnel from the 20th Battalion's scouts and B Company entered Neuville-sur-l'Escaut at roughly the same time as, or soon after, the 19th Battalion, and witnessed the same spectacle of joy, relief, and sorrow.[12] "The plight of the civilians was sad indeed," wrote Maj. D.J. Corrigall:

> Only old men, women and children were about: families had been separated and where the able-bodied men were, those remaining knew not. Soon the roads were crowded by people moving back to Cambrai and towns in rear; on foot pushing hand carts piled high with their few belongings they trudged their weary way, picking their route past shell holes and craters blown in the road junctions, toward they knew not what. Many had not seen their homes since 1914 and little knew in what sad condition they would find them.[13]

Several days after liberating Neuville-sur-l'Escaut, Lt.-Col. Millen provided his mother with a synopsis of the battalion's adventures to date:

> Have really been enjoying the war the past week or so … I went into the line with the battalion. Took over as my headquarters one of the finest chateaus I have seen. It was pretty well knocked about but has some fine cellars and we had all kinds of good furniture, ate off of splendid china and gathered all kinds of vegetables. Our cook had the time of his life. He was giving us 5 or 6 different vegetables at dinner. After a couple of days we bridged a canal and river opposite us and went forward again. I took over another chateau as headquarters. The next morning we found the enemy had evacuated again, so started following and by afternoon my battalion had reached the divisional objective where we were supposed to be squeezed out by other divisions coming up on both flanks. I was on my way up forward to see how things were going when I met a message to me stating our objective had been gained and civilians could be seen across the canal … I immediately hiked back to my headquarters to phone the news back and then went forward again. The Bosch has blown up all bridges in his retirement, but I found the boys had discovered a small boat and a few of them had got across to the village opposite. I at once got a seat and went over and I don't think I will ever forget the day. The civilians were crazy glad and I suppose I was as bad. It all was certainly the most wonderful experience in this war to me. It was 6 or 7 weeks since I had seen civilians of any sort and the first time we had ever taken a place occupied by them and there were about 1500 in this place. It was a continuous performance of handshaking and kissing, children and grownups. One woman rushed down the street and thrust a large bunch of pansies and leaves into my hands. I had to go and visit the Maire and receive an address. Though this village was out of our area I left a company there all night.[14]

On the evening of 19 October, in accordance with the high command's plans, the paths of the 4th Canadian and 51st (Highland) Divisions converged just beyond Neuville-sur-l'Escaut, thereby pinching out the frontages of the 4th Brigade and the rest of the 2nd Canadian Division. The 2nd Canadian Division thus withdrew from the forefront of the action, its units retiring to billets scattered among the various communities they just had liberated. This was fine for the men of the 19th Battalion, who were well contented with their lodgings in Bouchain (battalion headquarters, A and C Companies), Boucheneuil (D Company), and Neuville-sur-l'Escaut (B Company).[15] The next day, Bouchain became the principal concentration point for the battalion. B Company was recalled to billets there, and rear details, transport, and quartermasters' stores were summoned from Paillencourt. After securing their lodgings, all ranks were set to work cleaning the streets and repairing roads, many of which were badly cratered by mine explosions set off by the retreating Germans to slow the Allied pursuit. Cleaning efforts then moved indoors to the men's own quarters, for the "fleeing Hun" had left the billets "in a very dirty condition."[16]

Ed Youngman, who still was with the battalion transport section, offered his assessment of the character of operations during the final hundred days of the war: "You would push on and somebody would leapfrog you and you would go on again … Of course there was plenty of casualties and lots of ground taken and all that but the fact is that we kept on a steady progress toward Germany. For the first time in four years, we had the Germans on the run which was quite a treat."[17] But while the men were happy to have the Germans "on the run," and equally pleased to be out of the fetid zone of the trenches, their wariness of the dangers posed by "booby traps" grew exponentially. As Cpl. Gaetz informed his mother:

> We are not in the most forward position just now and today I was out on fatigue with a party fixing up roads that had been blown up with mines. Now and again one comes across a "booby trap" but not often. When taking this billet over just shortly after the Hun pulled on[,] going down stairs we saw a hat sitting just at the foot of the stairs. We were suspicious and started throwing sticks and bricks at it. It turned out to be nothing however and we started fixing up our bunks.[18]

Anxious to relax and enjoy the fruits of their labours in Bouchain, the men were understandably disgruntled when orders came through on 21 October instructing the 19th Battalion to relocate to the town of Auberchicourt. This was part of a move by the 4th Brigade to the area around Aniche and Auberchicourt, some four miles northwest of Bouchain. When the 19th Battalion arrived at its destination on 22 October, the men's disappointment at moving from freshly cleaned quarters in Bouchain was allayed by the excellent state of the billets they found waiting for them in Auberchicourt.[19] By this time, Lt. Col. Millen had undergone not only a change in quarters but also an increase in responsibilities. Two days earlier, on 20 October, he had been summoned to brigade headquarters, where he learned that he was to take over command in the absence of Brig.-Gen. McCuaig, who had just departed for a well-earned stretch of leave. Pleased with his earlier flirtation with higher command, Millen was excited at the prospect of a longer period at the helm of the brigade. "I will be [in command of the brigade] … for about another two weeks," he proudly informed his mother:

> Naturally I am not sorry and the [brigade] staff and I always got on well together. We are quite a happy little family. We have moved again and are in rest in quite a comfortable town [Aniche]. I am in a chateau with large grounds, if you could see me now in my room you would not consider I was much in need of sympathy. This room is bigger than any at home, I am writing this at a very nice desk, there is a carpet on the floor, pictures on the wall, two big wardrobes, and bureau, a fine big bed, marble topped wash [basin] and a dandy fire in the grate. I have ordinary chairs and easy chairs, and

> big mirrors. I am planning for a big brigade church parade on Sunday, and in the afternoon tea and a band concert for all officers of the brigade out on the lawn. Just think how wonderful it all appears to us. This place just about a week ago was well in German hands and now they are ten miles away.[20]

In Millen's absence, the redoubtable and popular Maj. Hatch once again took over command of the 19th Battalion. Not one to let standards slip while Millen was gone, Hatch declared 23 October to be "Cleaning up Day." This time, it was not the men's quarters that required attention but the men themselves. Company commanders were ordered to "make it their personal duty" to see that the men were well scrubbed and their uniforms and equipment "put into the best possible shape" before the commencement of regular training exercises.[21]

While the men were busy scrubbing, repairing, or replacing damaged uniform and kit, Millen summoned all battalion commanders to brigade headquarters to discuss a program of training. They decided to concentrate first on the basics, concluding that "much attention should be given to smartening up the men with drill and physical training."[22] Fatigue and a degree of cockiness, both owing to recent operational successes, along with considerable numbers of reinforcements absorbed since August, had bred a certain level of slackness in the battalions' appearance and bearing. In the 19th Battalion, Maj. Hatch reminded all ranks in no uncertain terms of the protocols of saluting, the observance of which he found to be entirely too lax.[23]

But physical training and parade ground drills were not all that was required to "smarten the men up." In the increasingly fluid, mobile, and rapid pace of operations, greenhorns and grizzled veterans long schooled in trench fighting needed more practice in the arts of open warfare. They had to improve their capacity to think quickly and to make intelligent use of cover, either natural or man-made, in order to outflank and infiltrate enemy positions. Moreover, the infantry had to know how to do this both in cooperation with other arms (such as field artillery, heavy machine guns, and mortar teams) and independently, relying strictly on their own firepower. No longer could the infantry always count on the artillery to blast a path through for them because now they were fighting in a region where towns and villages contained large numbers of civilians, whose lives the Allies were doing their best to spare. Accordingly, Lt.-Col. Millen encouraged all battalion officers to institute regular platoon schemes in their training programs to "allow troops to [learn how to] encircle a spot," and to teach them "the use of ground" to gain cover when approaching enemy positions.[24] Attention was also devoted, in a training document circulated to battalions by 4th Brigade Headquarters, to a key element of infiltration, namely, the exploitation of a successful breach in enemy defences through constant movement and offensive tactics, supplemented by smoke screens and, when available, tanks.[25] Additionally, all NCOs were given refresher training in map reading, battalion and company scouts were intensively exercised in their

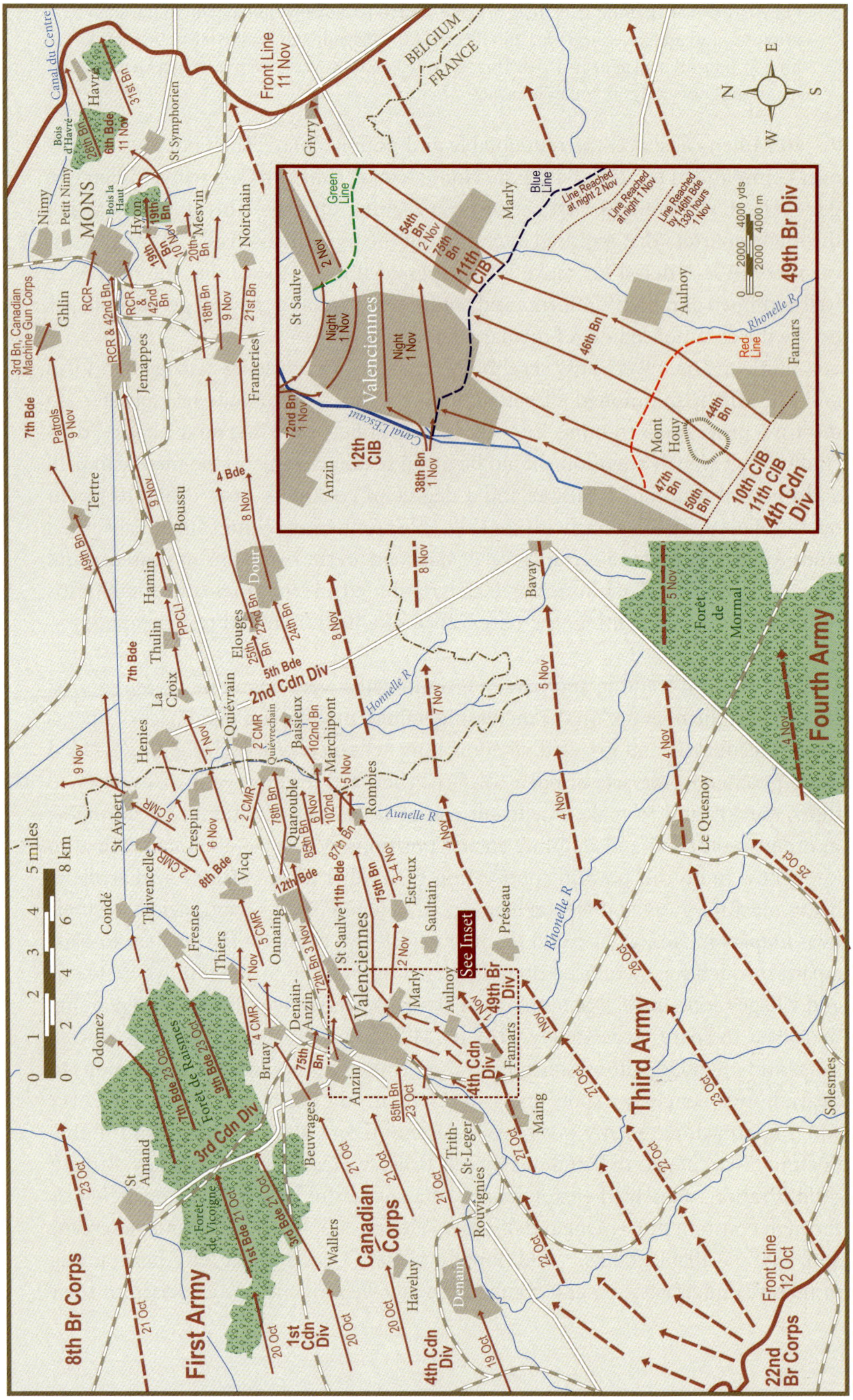

Map 21 – Final advance.

duties, and efforts were stepped up to ensure that all ranks were proficient in using each weapon integral to the platoon, especially the Lewis gun.[26]

Training was the 19th Battalion's chief activity for the remainder of October. It was carried out mainly during the morning hours, interrupted only by church parades on 27 October and, on the previous day, a move to new billets in Aniche. Afternoons were given over to clothing and equipment repair parades, concerts by the battalion brass band, and sporting activities. For the officers, there were additional social events, such as an afternoon tea party on 28 October that was made even more diverting by the presence of several nurses from nearby No. 1 Casualty Clearing Station.[27]

While the 4th Brigade rested, reorganized, and trained, the retreating German armies staggered closer to final capitulation. The heart of the Hindenburg Line had been pierced by the British Fourth Army at the end of September, and this, combined with gains along other sectors of the Western Front by British, French, American, and Belgian forces during October, accelerated the pace of the Germans' withdrawal and placed them in a situation from which they could not recover. Nevertheless, as they pulled back towards their homeland, stubborn German rear guards made the Allies pay in blood for every mile of French and Belgian territory that they liberated.

In the meantime, Germany's allies were, if anything, in even worse shape. Bulgaria had already signed an armistice with the Allies on 30 September, the Austro-Hungarian high command decided to request armistice terms on 28 October, and Turkey finally capitulated on 30 October. On the German home front, morale plummeted when official censors could no longer hide the scope of the armed forces' predicament, and profound war-weariness helped fuel a growing and irresistible movement for peace. Social unrest, hunger, and deepening economic crisis stalked the land, and were made worse by the Allied naval blockade. Parts of the German army were rife with desertion, and at the end of October, sailors of the High Seas Fleet rose in revolt against their officers. Gen. Ludendorff was dismissed on 26 October and fled to temporary self-imposed exile in Sweden. Even street posters in German towns and cities angrily proclaimed, "Down with the Kaiser!" The end was at hand, delayed only by the wrangling of Allied and German military officials and politicians as they hashed out armistice terms.[28]

The Final Pursuit

Through much of October, the Canadian Corps had maintained an average pace of approximately three miles per day. Lt.-Gen. Currie would have preferred to move even more quickly, but the stubbornness of German rear guards, an aversion to suffering more casualties than necessary, and the difficulties encountered by logistical services in keeping up with the advance over sabotaged road and rail links conspired to limit the Canadians' progress. The speed of the advance slowed even more as it approached the city of Valenciennes, where the German forces facing the Canadians were concentrating for what would be essentially their last stand.[29]

The strong defences around Valenciennes, the most important of which were the heavily fortified heights of Mont Houy to the south, were key components of the Germans' last major line of defence, the Hermann Line. Breaching these positions would be the Canadian Corps' next great task, and Currie was determined to carry it out at minimal risk to the lives of his men. Preceded by a complex artillery barrage so heavy that the expenditure of shells approached the tonnage fired during the entire South African War, the 10th Infantry Brigade of the 4th Canadian Division captured Mont Houy on 1 November, sweeping aside the remnants of its decimated garrisons. The loss of this key feature precipitated a rapid German withdrawal from defences in and around Valenciennes, so that by the morning of 2 November, the Canadians were in possession of the city and its environs. The capture of Mont Houy and the advance on Valenciennes would be the last major set-piece attack launched by the Canadian Corps.[30]

From this time onward, the "morale of the soldiers during the advance was extremely high," remembered Wilfred Macklin:

> We knew that we were winning this battle and we could see the effects of it. We could see the prisoners in the cages and we could see the German soldiers in the trenches surrendering. They'd had enough … And when a soldier thinks that his army is better than anybody else's and his Division is better than the other Divisions and his platoon's the best in the Battalion, well obviously he's the best soldier in the world and that's it. His morale must be high. Everybody believed that the Canadian Corps, all by itself and single-handed, was actually flogging the hide off the German Army and winning the war, and you could see it.[31]

With the fall of Valenciennes, Field Marshal Haig planned to launch a concerted assault on the rest of the Hermann Line, but this was pre-empted by a major German withdrawal to the east. From then on, the Germans had no more recourse to prearranged defensive positions in the zone facing the British First Army, and the Canadian Corps once more engaged in a general pursuit. This was carried out on a two-division front, with the 3rd Canadian Division on the left and the 4th on the right. The 2nd Canadian Division, which had been out of the forefront of the action since the night of 19 October, was slated to move forward during the first week of November and relieve the 4th Canadian Division.[32]

While the Canadian operations at Mont Houy and Valenciennes unfolded, the 19th Battalion remained in Aniche. The men by now had developed quite a taste for comfort in their billets – a taste that got out of hand when many of them began rummaging through neighbouring vacant houses and buildings to scrounge for better furniture to spruce up their lodgings. According to Vivian Thompson, "I remember that the troops made a devil of a mess by carting furniture from place to place until the citizens must have had a heck of a time in locating their possessions."[33] Such behaviour constituted a "grave disobedience of orders" and was sufficiently widespread to bring down an injunction from the high command, which feared that the "fair name of the British army" would be brought "into disrepute."[34] Lt.-Col. Millen, still in charge at brigade headquarters, found other ways to keep the men out of trouble and ensure that they did not become too relaxed. In order to maintain their physical endurance – a quality badly needed when following up a retreating enemy over long distances – he called for all units to devote an hour per day to route marching in full marching order with packs.[35]

Happily for the men, their next move towards the battlefront would be made not on foot but by bus. On 3 November, warning orders came through informing all ranks that the 2nd Canadian Division was making ready to relieve the 4th Canadian Division on the night of 5–6 November. For the first leg of the journey, the 4th Brigade would move to the area around Aubry and Hersin, with the 19th Battalion taking up billets in the latter village. After an advance party was dispatched to make arrangements for quartering the troops, the men of the 19th boarded buses on 4 November and rolled on to Hersin.[36]

Farther ahead, the leading Canadian divisions were following the Germans in an easterly direction, towards the cities of Dour and Mons. The Canadians found that their daily operations had assumed a predictable pattern. The Germans tended to fall back at night, and the Canadians usually did not regain contact with them until around noon on the following day. Once the Canadian advance patrols encountered the German rear guards, fighting generally escalated until evening, when a major effort would be required if the Canadians were to make any further progress. Knowing that the Germans would simply retreat again, the Canadians avoided getting entangled in a major battle, and so the cycle began again later each night.[37]

On 5 November, the 19th Battalion remained at Hersin and the other battalions of 4th Brigade likewise stayed put in their respective billets. Meanwhile, the 5th Brigade was ordered to follow the 4th Canadian Division closely and to relieve it on the evening of 6 November. Maj.-Gen. Burstall planned to use his brigades in relay fashion, leading off with 5th Brigade, followed in succession by the 4th and 6th Brigades. As the lines moved steadily eastward on 6 November, the entire 4th Brigade moved up to St-Saulve, just northeast of Valenciennes, where battalions were instructed to prepare to support the 5th Brigade as it assumed control of the division front. In addition, on this day Brig.-Gen. McCuaig returned from leave and Lt.-Col. Millen once more resumed command of the 19th Battalion. But it was to be a brief stay only, for Millen himself had also already applied for leave, which would come through on 8 November. Although he knew the Germans were on the run, he could not have known that the end of the fighting was only days away. Thus, it would be left to Maj. Hatch to see the 19th Battalion through the last day of battle on the Western Front.[38]

The 5th Brigade pressed onward to Élouges and Dour on 7–8 November, engaging in periodic bouts of bitter street fighting and enduring occasional squalls of rain. The poor weather, which reduced visibility, combined with the already bad state of the cratered roads and the fragility of ever-lengthening telephone links to make communication between the foremost units and brigade and division staffs increasingly difficult. The 4th Brigade followed along, proceeding first to the Quiévrechain–Marchipont area on 7 November and then to the area between Élouges and Quiévrain on the following day. As part of these movements, the 19th Battalion first took up stations in Quiévrechain and then moved on to Quiévrain on 8 November. Maj.-Gen. Burstall ordered the 4th Brigade to keep in close touch with the 5th Brigade and to be ready to take over the advance on 9 November. Once it did so, it was to maintain pressure on the Germans and advance as far as possible.[39]

But Burstall did not want forward battalions to rush bullheaded into the waiting machine guns of the German rear guards. In following up the enemy, battalions were instructed to employ as few troops forward as possible, so as to minimize casualties. The main force would be kept well back, but in positions from which it could easily be moved forward to carry out an attack in strength, if need be. Advanced batteries of field artillery would be pushed as far ahead as possible to offer heavy fire support, while Vickers gun teams would fan out to cover the infantry's flanks and offer close support in head-on clashes with their German counterparts.[40]

As planned, the 4th Brigade passed through the ranks of the 5th Brigade and assumed control of the 2nd Division's front at 8:00 AM on 9 November, the 21st Battalion taking up the advance on the right and the 18th Battalion on the left. Supporting them were two companies of the 2nd Battalion, CMGC, batteries of the 2nd Canadian Division Artillery and the 311th Army Brigade, RFA, and a mobile independent force consisting of the 2nd Canadian Motor Machine Gun Brigade, one company of the Canadian Corps Cyclist Battalion, and two squadrons of the Canadian Light Horse. These had all been attached to 5th Brigade and now came under the 4th Brigade's orders as it took over the advance. The 4th Brigade's job was to advance in a northeasterly direction, encircle the city of Mons from the south, and capture the dominating heights of Bois la Haut 2,000 yards southeast of the city. The fall of Bois-la-Haut might force the Germans to evacuate Mons without any need for a full-scale frontal assault by the 3rd Canadian Division, in whose sector the city lay.[41] The tremendous symbolic importance of Mons and the surrounding territory was not lost on the Canadians, for it was there that British and German forces first clashed in August 1914.

The 19th and 20th Battalions were kept in brigade support, backing up the 18th and 21st Battalions respectively. At around 6:00 AM, two hours before the forward units leapfrogged through the 5th Brigade's outpost line, the 19th and 20th Battalions, having already moved up to Élouges, formed up again and marched out in column of fours, heading for Warquignies. When they arrived in the "Grand Place" of the village at mid-morning, the men were permitted to obtain a bite of lunch from field kitchens that had been set up for the purpose. Later, both battalions moved out again, in accordance with brigade orders, and marched on to La Bouverie, which the 19th Battalion reached just after 5:00 PM.[42]

The 18th and 21st Battalions had progressed well throughout the morning and afternoon. Their advance was not contested severely, although they did sustain some losses from enemy machine-gun and artillery fire. The town of Frameries, three miles southwest of Mons, was entered in the morning, and despite the assurances of enthusiastic civilians that the Germans were not putting up a fight, heavier resistance was encountered east of the town during the afternoon. This did not completely stop the Canadians, however, and by dark, advance patrols from the 18th Battalion were pushing forward in the direction of Ciply and Hyon.[43]

It had been a good day for the 19th Battalion too. On its march to La Bouverie, it had met "a fine reception" when passing through the city of Dour, "where the civilian population cheered continually as the Battalion, headed by the Brass Band, moved forward." Upon reaching La Bouverie, the men were met by the mayor who, as a token of his people's great gratitude, went out of his way to see to it that all ranks were billeted comfortably for the night. As they settled in with their ebullient hosts, Maj. Hatch examined the latest orders from brigade, which informed him that the 19th and 20th Battalions would relieve the 18th and 21st on the following morning. The 19th Battalion would take up the advance on the left portion of the brigade frontage, relieving the 18th Battalion, which had established itself along a rail line 2,000 yards northeast of Frameries, facing the city of Mons. Hatch's objective for 10 November was the village of Hyon and a stretch of higher ground behind it, just 600 yards southeast of Mons. Opposing his men in this area were rear guards of the German 206th Infantry Division.[44] These men would not retire without a fight, for the German 17th Army had been ordered to hold off the British and Canadians long enough to permit the escape of German forces farther north. At Mons "and immediately north and south of the town," the German rear guards would fight "stubbornly, the rearmost parties of machine gunners having orders to fight to a finish."[45]

The Last Action

Sunday, 10 November 1918, dawned clear and fine, a seemingly positive harbinger for what would be the last full day of fighting on the Western Front. The men of the 19th Battalion fell in as ordered at 5:45 AM and began their march forward. Just after 8:00 AM, they passed through the 18th Battalion's forward outposts and, with the 20th Battalion on their right flank and the 3rd Canadian Division on their left, took up the offensive one last time. B and D Companies forged ahead in artillery formation, on the left and right, with C Company following 300 yards behind in support and A Company moving in reserve, 600 yards farther back. The rifle companies were not alone. Attached to the battalion was one troop of the Canadian Light Horse and one mobile battery of 18-pounder field guns, offering added mobility and firepower.[46]

The leading companies of the 19th Battalion met little opposition until they approached Mont Erebus. There, at 10:30 AM, they were raked by heavy machine-gun fire, both from the outskirts of Mons and from the high ground behind Hyon.[47] "As we came up there was a burst of machine-gun fire and we spotted some houses on our left and dived for them," remembered Vivian Thompson. "Through this farm we went out on to the road where we came on a 3rd Division machine gun. As we made the dash to this house I noticed that our stretcher-bearer fell and I suppose that he was killed but I really know nothing of this and I cannot even remember his name."[48] "We dropped flat in some cabbages," stated John Gaetz, "and after a short wait we advanced in rushes up to some cover. This was just an advanced post of the Hun and they did not stay long before falling back."[49]

B and D Companies responded to these initial machine-gun bursts by charging a number of enemy positions scattered around the vicinity of Chasse Royale, a road stretching north into Mons. Once these were cleaned up, the two leading companies established themselves along the road and sent patrols to ferret out further opposition ahead. On the left, B Company's patrol made good progress, up to 300 yards in front of the road. On the right, however, it was a different story. The houses in Hyon concealed a number of machine-gun nests, which swept the approaches to the village with streams of lead. At the same time, a number of German artillery batteries also opened fire on the 19th Battalion's positions, and the combined efforts of these two threats resulted in mounting casualties for the Canadians. Despite Currie's orders to avoid losses, it would not be a bloodless day for the 19th Battalion.[50]

"The Germans were fighting that morning from one position to another as well as any troops we had ever seen in the old line days," declared Joe O'Neill, who, having recovered from wounds suffered at Amiens, was back in charge of C Company. "They were also supported by a peculiar fact that this Mons had been a machine-gun school. All these fellows had been trained over this ground. We found machine gun bullets coming from cabbage patches, housetops, all sorts of fancy positions, and it certainly made a tough proposition."[51] In the face of all this enemy fire, John Gaetz and some companions dashed to the nearest houses to find better cover. After reaching their destination, he and his companions unexpectedly obtained some "liquid courage" to bolster their rattled nerves:

> In passing through the street the civilians having come out of the cellars crowded in the doorways and held out the odd stone jar of cognac. The one man that was following me like myself partook of several good drinks and carried on. In a short time we fell in with one of the Company officers and half a dozen men. We were just passing through

> the last screen of houses and saw some men dodging across a street some distance in front of us. Thinking they were our own men we continued towards them and just got nicely in the open when we were serenaded with two machine guns. Once again we flopped in the cabbages. This time we weren't left alone but the gunners continued to search the ground where we were. I could see bits of cabbages fly in the air around about me and I could tell by the cracking above my head that it was pretty good shooting. First one of the men near me was hit rather badly in the shoulder and then the officer muttered something and lay still. To make matters worse there was a field gun firing point blank at our position and this was decidedly uncomfortable. So one by one we ran back behind a building. I helped fix up the wounded man and then got some of our machine gunners posted [and] for a while we had some good shooting and made it pretty hot for the odd Hun who forgot that we carried guns.[52]

Elements of D Company, stalled in front of Hyon, made four successive attempts to work their way forward, but to no avail. Then, somehow, a fifth attempt managed to make headway, resulting in the capture of a strongly fortified machine-gun post situated in a cemetery, which had been causing considerable grief throughout the day.[53] Support from the guns of the 5th Brigade, CFA, which swung into action and bombarded various targets in the area around noon, likely suppressed the enemy machine-gunners long enough for members of D Company to get into the cemetery.[54]

Maj. Hatch, anxious to keep his finger on the pulse of events, quickly moved up to the Chasse Royale and set up a forward report centre. From there, he and Capt. John Harstone monitored the progress of the two leading companies and directed the actions of the support and reserve units. The intervening stretch of ground between Chasse Royale and Hyon was too flat and open to permit the battalion to advance in strength. So, finally heeding Lt.-Gen. Currie's orders to "stop until nightfall" if they encountered trouble, Hatch decided to wait until dark before ordering his companies forward again.[55] As dusk descended, Maj. Hatch sent out three patrols from C Company to work their way forward into Hyon. These small groups moved out, in the face of continued heavy bursts of machine-gun fire, and successfully slipped into Hyon at 1:45 on the morning of 11 November. It was not long before Lt. Harold Stuart, in charge of No. 2 patrol, discovered that the Germans had already begun to evacuate the village, and he immediately sent word back to Hatch. Now the time seemed ripe for Hatch to commit his reserve. Accordingly, he sent A Company forward, ordering it to filter through Hyon and take the high ground along the western side of Bois la Haut, which lay in the 20th Battalion's zone. In the meantime, the rest of C Company hurried forward to occupy Hyon itself.[56]

The main obstacle facing the entire 4th Brigade had been Bois la Haut, the garrison of which had stymied the efforts of the 20th Battalion to approach it during daylight hours on 10 November. But a half-hour bombardment of the position by heavy artillery shook the Germans' resolve sufficiently that they began to evacuate the hill that night. This allowed the 20th Battalion to press onward past the hill to the town of St-Symphorien, nearly three miles east of Mons, which they reached and occupied by 2:00 AM the next morning.[57]

The petering out of German resistance on Bois la Haut similarly opened the way for the 19th Battalion to move into Hyon and push beyond the village towards the great hill to the east. At 2:30 AM on 11 November, C Company completed its move into Hyon while A Company followed up the retreating Germans to Bois la Haut and eventually established outposts along Mont Pallisel. Between 3:30 and 4:00 AM, the 19th and 20th Battalions effectively snuffed out German resistance north of Bois la Haut, and troops were able to enter the wood itself and systematically clear it from the south.[58] At about 5:30 AM, forward elements of the 3rd Division gained contact with the 4th Brigade east of Mons, with the latter formation's front line now running along the road linking Mons and St-Symphorien.[59]

After C Company had gone through Hyon, Lt. Joe O'Neill moved his men out, well beyond the village, towards a point just east of Mons, where the roads leading to Charleroi and Beaumont intersected. There, they were joined by troops from the 5th (Royal Irish) Lancers of the 3rd Cavalry Brigade.[60] The 5th Lancers had been the last British cavalry regiment to withdraw from Mons during the Great Retreat of 1914, and as fate would have it, it was the first British unit to return to the area in 1918.[61] At 5:45 AM, just ahead of the advancing lancers and infantry, an eighteen-year-old Belgian named Georges Licope stole out of his home near the crossroads and gathered to chat with other wary neighbours in the silence following the German retreat earlier that night. "Suddenly," Licope later wrote, at "exactly five minutes to six – we saw at one hundred yards at front of us, the shadow of an horseman wearing a flat steel helmet and a lance, progressing cautiously along the side of the road from Mons." He continued:

> As soon as he saw civilians the scout approached and, in broken French, asked us: "A quelle heure boches partis?" Whilst I attempted to use my best English to explain [to] him that they had left at midnight towards [the] East, some among our neighbours presented some chrysanthemums to the scout and pricked some more in the harness of the horse, whilst other people brought some hot drinks. He had been hailed by some sounding: "Vivent les Anglais." In the meantime, two or three other horsemen did approach and were welcomed as the first one. Suddenly, someone among them took a whistle and whistled sharply. As soon, one dozen or so of infantrymen climbed on the road from the ditches in which they were crawling … They were welcomed also by the traditional: "Vivent les Anglais" but they replied fiercely: "No English, we are Canadians," pointing [at] their brass curved shoulder titles with the word "Canada" … No words can describe our surprise to hear that our liberators did belong to a genuine Canadian force, the existence of which was practically unknown for us … At that time, and in spite of the fact that training in Belgian schools was one among the most complete in the world, we did imagine that the uniforms of the Canadian Forces were very similar to those of the trappers of Hudson Bay, or, at least that their hat was similar to

it of the Canadian Mounted Police, fairly well known in Belgium yet before 1914 as the best police in the world.

So, all these boys had enlisted freely and they came from so long from overseas to help the Allies, and fate would [have it] that they brought freedom to us. We could find no words to express our gratitude to them, unfortunately practically no one among them could speak French, and I was alone at this spot to speak some broken English …

Just at front of home, two young and very smart lieutenants were talking together. I approached them, and, the best I could, did invite them to enter home. They looked pleased to accept, sat down and drunk the hot drink called pompously "coffee" but in which there was everything except coffee which was practically impossible to find anywhere in Belgium in November 1918. Immediately, I asked them their name and address. One of them was Lieutenant Joe O'Neill, M.C., from Lindsay near Toronto and acted as Company Commander. The second one was Lieutenant Harold Stuart from Sault-Sainte-Marie … Then, we took the breakfast, but when mother showed the black bread we had only to offer, Lieut. O'Neill took one from his bag and presented it to mother. It was nearly as round as a sphere and as white as snow, so white that our eyes were nearly injured. I believe that that breakfast has been the most memorable one in my life …

A third officer: Lieutenant Charlie Mitchell from Saint-Catharines close by Niagara Falls arrived home … As soon as he heard that I spoke some rough English, he insisted so much to use me as his interpreter, that I did accompany him outside. We followed the road to Mons along some two hundred yards, then, we entered in a large park then belonging to Mr. Gendebien … In these grounds, there were two castles: the smallest, completely burned on the 23rd August 1914 by German shells, in spite of the fact that it had been transformed in[to a] British ambulance and that several large flags with a red cross were waving at every window and even on the roof. Several wounded officers and soldiers of the 4th Middlesex, 2nd Royal Irish Regiment and 1st Gordon Highlanders had been attended there by Major Long, the medical officer of the 2nd Royal Irish, and [were] carried to the other chateau, some two hundred yards further in the middle of the park when the ambulance began to burn. Unfortunately, Major Maidlow, commanding the 49th Battery (XL Brigade) of the R.F.A., mortally wounded, could not be evacuated and was burned with the castle. So, Mr. Gendebien, the landlord had resolved to remember that sad event by a small cross in granite erected on a ruined wall.

As soon as we reached that spot, Lieutenant Mitchell asked me the signification of that small cross. So, one may imagine how hard for me was the explanation. That explanation was, of course, delivered in a language very far of it of Shakespeare. Mitchell understood by chance: he faced the cross, joined the heels, and, formally, saluted … I am sure that this silent tribute was the very first from the whole Canadian Corps to the "Old Contemptibles," and from those of 1918 to those of 1914. Never, did I forget that simple and so fine gesture.[62]

At 7:00 AM, with its outpost line secure, the 19th Battalion formally entered Hyon and established itself in the eastern outskirts of the village. Maj. Hatch also moved his headquarters forward and set up shop in the local chateau. An hour later, word came through from 4th Brigade headquarters that the 28th Battalion of the 6th Brigade would soon pass through the 19th's positions and resume the advance. After that, the 19th Battalion would temporarily serve in a reserve capacity to the 6th Brigade. But, far more important, the message also informed all ranks that an armistice had been signed between Germany and the Allied powers. Hostilities would officially cease at 11:00 AM that day. Canadian forces were to hold fast at the positions they reached at that time, where they would await further orders.[63]

Between 8:30 and 9:00 AM, Georges Licope and Lt. Mitchell were on their way back to the Licope household when they encountered the 28th Battalion moving up ahead of the 19th Battalion. "Among them," Licope later wrote, "was Private George L. Price who should be killed the very last of the whole Canadian Corps at less than 4 miles [east-northeast] from us at 10:58 AM, on the territory of the village of Ville-sur-Haine, at some 50 yards after crossing the 'Canal du Centre,' along the road from Mons to Le Roeulx." Licope then continued: "We were at home since a short time, when Lieut. O'Neill rushed in the room and, kissing mother as if she had been his own one, said to her: 'Madame, 11 heures, guerre finie.' He got these news from a motorcyclist dispatcher."[64]

Earlier that morning, while Licope and his neighbours had their first encounters with British and Canadian troops, Vivian Thompson and a few comrades, who were holed up for the night in the cellars of a row of houses on the outskirts of Mons, awoke to some unusual sounds:

> About six AM we heard a fuss above and also a violin and went up to find the Montreal Highlanders [the 42nd Battalion] on their way through the city ... We had something to eat and I had a shave and wash ... I saw General Currie and the P.P.C.L.I. [Princess Patricia Canadian Light Infantry] on their famous entry of the city and I remember how the folks all went wild and danced like the dickens.[65]

Armistice at Last

Shortly after 11:00 AM, Maj. Hatch called up the pipe band to lead a triumphal procession through the streets of Hyon to celebrate the armistice. Although the battalion diarist maintained that the "remainder of the day was spent rejoicing," with "impromptu celebrations" being thrown by the local population, many men were still numb from the effects of the previous twenty-four hours of fighting.[66] "As we were ready to push forward the news of the armistice came through," wrote John Gaetz, "and of course it was welcome but there was not the enthusiasm that one might expect."[67] "It was sprung on us so suddenly we couldn't realize it," recalled Lt. Charles H. Mitchell:

> We kind of stood around and didn't know what to make of it. The Armistice was on and the war was over and you couldn't realize that anything like that could happen. You were hypnotized. You just couldn't realize anything. I mean you were wondering what it was all about. You were fighting the day before, and men being killed, and the next day the war is all finished. Things went through your mind like that. It was impossible to realize that the war was over.[68]

Rumours of an armistice had rippled through the army during the previous weeks, and when the fighting still continued, hardened veterans turned a jaundiced ear to any further such talk. Even during the early morning of 11 November, most men had found the prospect hard to believe. Wilfred Macklin was cooking his breakfast in a courtyard in Hyon when he noticed "a little [Sopwith] Camel aircraft, [which] came and dived over us waving a Union Jack, and shortly thereafter the cavalry unit received an armistice order, and it was received by everybody with the greatest of skepticism."[69] "No one believed it," declared Joe O'Neill:

> Eventually, though, we began to wonder whether there was something to it. I saw a staff officer coming up the Mons–Namur Road, so I went over and stopped him to find out if there was anything to this because the rumours had been getting stronger. Well he hadn't heard it either so, while we were talking, a runner came along and he told us that it really was true. The war was over.[70]

"We were cynical, the fellows that had been there so long," admitted Ed Youngman,

> and we said that we were from Missouri, we had to be shown, and finally the armistice did happen. Even then we wouldn't believe and I can recall very well on the morning of November 11th, General Burstall … rode his horse into the square at Frameries. We all snapped to attention and saluted and General Burstall said, "No, you've been saluting me long enough … I will salute you this time." Well, then the mayor of the town of Frameries, with his gold chain of office, mounted the steps, and as did General Burstall, the proclamation was read and that was the first time that we knew that the war was ended. Although the French people that morning had been quite effusive in saying, "Finis le guerre," and we thought they meant that the war was ended for them because we had liberated their town, but when … General Burstall read out the proclamation, I turned to Jock Fisher and said, "What do you think?" Jock said, "I don't believe a word of it." And instead of throwing our hats in the air and going out and getting drunk or something, we just waited for another order to start moving.[71]

On the home front, crowds erupted with joy at the news, sweeping any servicemen they could find into the revelry. Felix Cullen, who had been invalided to England with pleurisy in February 1917, penned the following succinct, yet evocative, note in his diary on 11 November: "Germany throws up the sponge and surrenders uncondishionally [*sic*] every one goes mad with joy myself included."[72] Fred Stitt was still recovering from the wounds he had received at the Canal du Nord when he heard the news, and the occasion was made all the more memorable by the presence of his brother Herb – also a 19th Battalion man – who had just arrived in England on leave. Herb recounted that, while visiting Fred in hospital, a nurse entered the room

> and told us the war was over! In spite of the fact that Fred was covered in bandages, having been severely wounded at the Canal du Nord while out on patrol, he got out of bed and sneaked out of hospital and we both made our way to London where the

> real action was taking place. What a day that was! Everything was free and the people were mad with joy after the long nightmare they had come through. Poor old Fred was pretty tired and weak towards the end of the day, so he decided to return to the hospital. I saw him safely on the bus, and then resumed my merry-making 'til early next morning.[73]

Fred Stitt told his own story of the occasion. "Boy did we get a reception in London," he said with a grin, "especially the fellow in the blues, that was me." Sporting the blue service uniform reserved for convalescents, Fred dived into the frolic in downtown London along with his brother Herb:

> We got on a bus, and went down in Picadilly and there was a typical old English London flower girl on the bus and as soon as we appeared in the doorway, me in the blue suit, she says, "Here is one of the bloody heroes, have a drink my hero," and she reached down her petticoat and dragged out a bottle of gin … If my doctor had of seen me there he'd have hung me … She was a great old character; my brother pictures her to this day: "Do you remember the old biddy in the London bus with a bottle of gin on Armistice Day?"[74]

Lt.-Col. Millen had missed his battalion's final action and was still enjoying his leave in England when the armistice was declared. Several days later, he recorded his impressions of the ensuing jubilation. He informed his mother:

> Dear staid old England, you would not know it this week. Within half an hour of the news coming through last Monday the streets were absolutely crowded with yelling flag waving people and it has practically been going ever since. It lets up somewhat in the daytime but every night has been quite wild … I wonder how long it will be before I am crossing the ocean again.[75]

Across the Atlantic, crowds were no less joyous when news of the armistice broke. It was 2:30 AM local time when wire services first flashed the news to Toronto, touching off a gigantic celebration. In the middle of the night,

> church bells peeled, factory whistles wailed, and Extras were printed. Fire trucks drove through the streets sounding their sirens. Awakened from sleep, tens of thousands of Torontonians headed downtown. Many traveled in nightclothes and slippers: propriety demanded only that a winter coat be thrown overtop. Hanging off streetcars, or piling on the running boards of automobiles, people flooded to the core … Yonge Street was packed with revelers. The crowds were so thick that dozens of people walked over roofs to get to the party. Coal scuttles, tin cans, and garbage lids were grabbed – anything to add to the din. Bonfires were set to ward off the predawn chill. Cheering, patriotic songs, and skirling bagpipes filled the air. Fireworks lit up the night sky. Conversation was impossible – and unnecessary. A twenty-four hour victory party, 1,567 days in the making, had begun.[76]

Such fantastic scenes were repeated in countless communities across Ontario and the rest of the nation. In Hamilton on 11 November,

Captain Maurice Cameron Roberts, M.C., was another member of the 19th Battalion who lost his life in the action on 10 November 1918. This photo of Roberts, a native of Hamilton, was taken before his promotion to captain. (ASH Regimental collection)

> great crowds moved to the heart of the city where Mayor Booker declared a holiday – a superfluous formality. Floats, which had been built in the previous weeks for the Victory Loan Parade, turned out again in a mile-long procession that swelled with decorated cars. On the Gore, Bandmaster Harry Stares' Band played the National Anthem, "O God Our Help In Ages Past" and "Rule Britannia." Everyone joined in. Twenty-two prisoners were released without sentence by Magistrate George F. Jelfs, and doctors gave prescriptions to all who applied, that everyone might celebrate fittingly.[77]

At noon, the cheering throng was treated to the added spectacle of Harry H. Gardiner, better known as "The Human Fly," scaling the Bank of Hamilton Building to celebrate the end of the war.[78]

While crowds of soldiers and civilians rejoiced, others mourned the deaths of comrades whose loss seemed harder to bear because they were struck down so close to the end. The 19th Battalion had sustained a total of 52 casualties in its final action, including 3 officers and 9 other ranks killed and 1 officer and 2 other ranks who later died of their wounds.[79] One of the slain officers was Lt. Wesley Clarence McFaul, who was a close friend of Lt. Charles Mitchell. "This chap, Clarence McFaul, he and I chummed together," said Mitchell, "and I married his sister after I came back. Well, I'd just got word that he'd been killed and it was very sad. You lose your best pal and you didn't feel like celebrating. There was something about it that morning. It wasn't jubilant to me."[80]

"The 19th Battalion will ever be acclaimed as liberators of Hyon on the dawn of armistice morning," declared the battalion diarist, and special care was taken to honour those who were killed in the process. Later, on 13 November, the dead were buried in the village cemetery, where German machine gunners had temporarily checked the 19th Battalion's advance. According to Maj. Hatch, "the civilian population of Hyon turned out to a man to pay their last tribute of respect to those who had laid down their lives in freeing their country from the oppressors."[81] During the simple but moving ceremony, one of the local officials made the following address:

> Officers and Soldiers: Gentlemen: Allow me, in the name of the inhabitants of Hyon, to give a last homage to the valourous Captain and Soldiers who fell on the field of honour in this Commune.
>
> Never shall we forget the courageous Canadians of the 19th Battalion of the 2nd Division, who came from the other side of the Ocean to defend the right against the force. An indissoluble bond that is to perpetuate from generation to generation shall now unite our Country with Canada.
>
> Valourous Soldiers rest here in peace. Farewell.'[82]

In a further gesture of gratitude and perpetual remembrance, the people of Hyon later erected a memorial tablet to these men in their parish church.[83]

After the war, Lt.-Gen. Currie was criticized harshly by some who felt he had squandered Canadian lives needlessly in a vainglorious effort to wrest Mons from the enemy before the armistice took effect. There were individual political figures, members of the public, and even some veterans of the CEF who felt that the fight for Mons in particular could, and should, have been avoided. The former minister of militia, Sir Sam Hughes, mounted the most vitriolic attacks, bitter as he was that Currie's star had eclipsed his own and that the corps commander had refused to appoint his son Garnet to command the 1st Canadian Division.[84]

The grumbling died down until 1927, six years after Hughes's death, when a small Ontario newspaper took up the assault on Currie's reputation. The *Port Hope Evening Guide* accused Currie of attacking Mons for his own glory and condemned what it saw as the "deliberate and useless waste of human life" that resulted. Currie eventually sued the paper for libel, and in the spectacular trial that followed, scores of Canadian Corps veterans turned out to support their old commander. The trial rightly exonerated Currie; it also showed him that the majority of Canadians supported his wartime actions.[85] Nevertheless, some individuals continued to question the necessity of risking casualties in the war's final days. When asked his opinion almost fifty years after the war ended, Ed Youngman responded with a measured and realistic assessment:

> I think General Currie was severely criticized by an endless lot of people back home here, who possibly knew nothing about it, but he was also criticized … by quite a lot of people that was in the army. Now, I'm not going to say that the criticism was justified … I never was a general never expect to be and so I must confess that he knew

> what he was doing. But the fact does remain that on the last day of the war, that is the last day of fighting on the 10th … the 19th Battalion lost ten men [*sic*], three of those men had been with the battalion right from 1914 and while it was sad to lose any men … we did particularly feel it very keenly those three going all through the war and getting snapped off the last few hours. It was argued that General Currie could have refrained from too much fighting but the idea was that you never knew what the enemy was going to do. They could be treacherous, and you had to keep pounding and if you were going to keep pounding him, he was going to pound back.[86]

From 8 August to 11 November 1918, the 19th Battalion suffered 785 casualties (38 officers and 747 other ranks), including 15 officers and 157 other ranks killed.[87] This was by far the worst four-month period in the battalion's history, due mainly to the unprecedented number of casualties (over 500) sustained during August alone. This was true also for the Canadian Corps as a whole, which suffered 51,538 casualties from all causes – roughly two and a half divisions' worth of officers and other ranks – in the same period.[88] But, just as these losses were unparalleled in the corps' experience, so were the accomplishments. During the final "Hundred Days" campaign, the Canadian Corps had liberated over 500 square miles of French and Belgian territory containing 228 cities, towns, and villages. In the process, the corps had engaged at least 47 German divisions, in whole or in part, and captured 31,537 prisoners, 623 pieces of heavy and field artillery, 2,842 machine guns, and 336 heavy and light trench mortars.[89]

In this amazing effort, by a corps of only four Canadian divisions,[90] the 19th Battalion had played a full part, helping to capture or liberate a number of villages and towns, including Marcelcave, Fransart, Naves, Bouchain, Neuville-sur-l'Escaut, and Hyon. With its capture of the latter village, and its participation in the clearing of Bois la Haut, the battalion also played an important role in forcing the Germans to evacuate Mons and the surrounding countryside. During August and September the 19th Battalion had captured over 570 prisoners, a field gun, an anti-tank gun, two mortars, and well over 36 machine guns.[91]

Sorrow for the battalion's losses was mixed with pride of accomplishment, and the spirits of many were uplifted further by the generosity and warmth of the appreciative Belgians. Numerous celebratory gatherings convened throughout the day and well into the evening on 11 November as local civilians fêted their Canadian liberators. One particular party involved "practically the whole of the 19th Battalion's transport section," which tried its best to squeeze into the crowded venue. The "Belgians rolled out some horrible stuff that they called beer," remembered Ed Youngman, "and I never learned to dance but when I saw a buxom lass there, I had an eye on the future and I decided to learn to dance right there. I did know the tune that the band was playing and I had a pair of hob-nailed boots with spurs on and I was perfectly sober and I didn't care whether the girl could dance or not, I just wanted to whisper in her ear and it paid off. We had a good time."[92]

Canadians marching through the streets of Mons on the morning of 11 November 1918. (LAC PA-003547)

The Mayor of Mons calls for three cheers for Canadians, November 1918. (LAC PA-003592)

While the men of the transport section caroused, Wilfred Macklin hurried into Mons to see the huge festivities that were gaining momentum there:

> As the day went along everybody in the whole city of Mons began to celebrate. Every single house and every building was decorated with a flag or flags, and all the civilians turned out and all the pubs opened up and served free beer and free cognac and free everything else, and there was a tremendous outburst of rejoicing and celebration in the whole city of Mons which went on far into the night and all the soldiers participated in this …
>
> The people went through the city in parties, with civilians and soldiers arm-in-arm, roaring through the streets singing songs at the top of their voices and they would turn and invade one estaminet and everybody would have a drink and then they'd all come out in a file and go down to the next place. It was a spontaneous and unorganized celebration.[93]

For the 19th Battalion, the fighting at last was over. But their adventures in Europe were not. After battling their way to and beyond the outskirts of Mons, they soon would face a long march – not westward, towards the English Channel and the embarkation ports for home, but eastward, to Germany.

22

Going Home – Eventually: 12 November 1918–25 May 1919

"I have just unloaded my rifle," wrote John Gaetz to his mother on 13 November:

> I guess the last .303 cartridge I will ever fire was fired the day before yesterday when we had a hard days encounter with 'his' rear guard … Even yet although everything is peaceful and quiet except for the enthusiastic civilians, one cannot realize that the fighting is over. I am so used [to] surprises and disappointments that I don't believe I would bat an eye if they told us to stand to, [because] Heinie was counter attacking. I guess I would utter the odd oath though.[1]

Like Cpl. Gaetz, countless individuals on both sides of no man's land could scarcely imagine daily life outside the realities of the conflict that had gripped them in its bloody maw. Yet once the shock of disbelief began to wear off, many Canadian troops would have felt a sense of victorious exultation, a sense that *they* had prevailed, mingled with elation at the prospect of finally going home. Others would bear scars and anguish, both physical and mental, for some time to come, if not the rest of their lives. Amazingly, there even were some who were outraged that the fighting had been brought to a halt. "Bloody fools," grumbled Brig.-Gen. Andrew McNaughton, then commanding the Canadian Corps Heavy Artillery. "We have them on the run. That means that we shall have to do it all over again in another twenty-five years."[2]

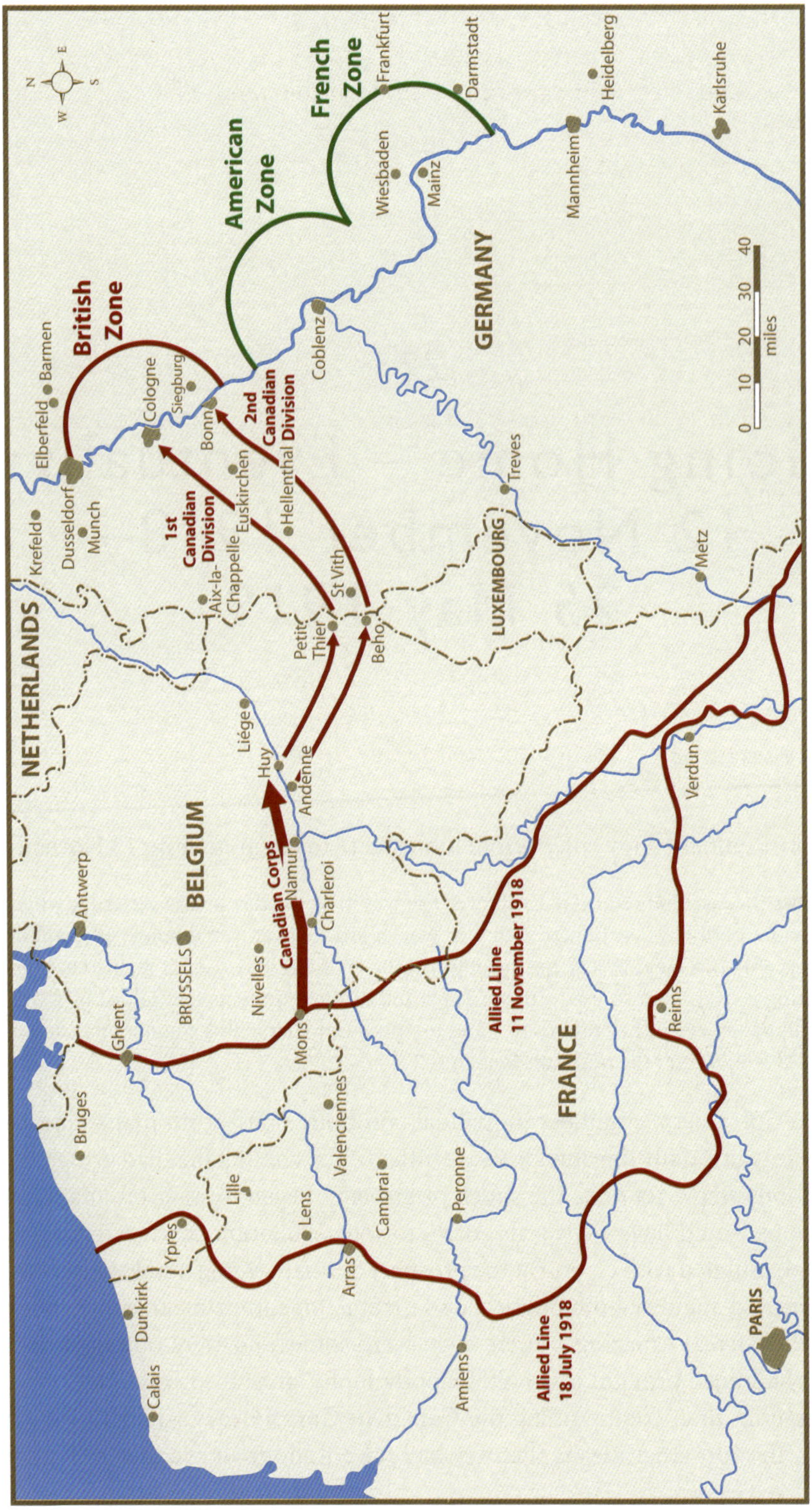

Map 22 – Advance to the Rhine.

McNaughton's frighteningly prescient remark boded ill, especially for the children of those who served in the Canadian Expeditionary Force. But the grim prospect of a second Great War was the last thing on the minds of most people in the immediate afterglow of 11 November. On the one hand, there were still civic and private celebrations to enjoy; on the other, there was a long march to Germany to prepare for.

On to Germany

In accordance with the terms of the armistice, the Allied forces would occupy a number of bridgeheads on the eastern bank of the Rhine, each having a radius of eighteen miles. The zone assigned to the British extended from Düsseldorf to a point southeast of Bonn and was centred on the city of Cologne. The Second and Fourth Armies were selected to occupy the British zone, and the Canadian Corps was chosen to be among the lead formations on the march with the Second Army. It was decided that the corps would proceed on a two-division front, with the two senior divisions, the 1st and 2nd, taking the lead, to be followed later by the 3rd and 4th.[3] This arrangement was changed when it soon became apparent that the existing road and rail networks were insufficient to permit the movement and supply of both armies while maintaining services for local civilian populations. Consequently, the Second Army would proceed to Germany alone, with the Canadian contribution to the occupation reduced to the 1st and 2nd Divisions. The 3rd and 4th Divisions would remain in Belgium with the Fourth Army.[4] From the humble foot soldier's perspective, the cessation of open hostilities did not, unfortunately, entail the end of military routine and discipline. The 19th Battalion remained at Hyon from 12 through 17 November, and most of its activities during this period resembled those carried out during its regular sojourns in reserve during the previous thirty-eight months of service in Western Europe. Once the first flush of victory had begun to cool, guards were mounted, clothing and pay parades were held, inspections were conducted by battalion and brigade commanders, and, of course, physical and weapons drills were carried out. Moreover, 4th Brigade headquarters exhorted all units to carry out "daily route marches in order to get men's feet in good condition." With the rigours of a 250-mile march to the Rhine ahead of them, the men needed to be in top physical condition.[5]

Before departing for Germany, there remained some official ceremonies – both solemn and celebratory – for the men to take in. The public funeral in Hyon for members of the 19th Battalion who were killed in the final hours of the war was held at 3:00 PM on 13 November, with the population of the village bringing generous floral tributes to place on the deceased's graves. Ten men were buried in the village cemetery, attended by a firing party of five men selected from each company.[6] That same day, an even larger funeral was held in Mons to commemorate the dead of the Canadian Corps. Two days later, the First Army staged its official triumphal entry into Mons, and the "stars of the show" – at least as far as the local population was concerned – were members of the Canadian Corps. Representing the 19th Battalion in the march past was a party of sixty-six other ranks led by two officers, Lts. Charles Mitchell and Arthur J. Anderson.[7]

One hazard inherent in such public gatherings was the spread of influenza. The worldwide pandemic, which had swept over Europe earlier in the spring, returned that autumn in an even more virulent form, casting a pall over societies already ravaged by the war itself. Men who contracted the illness, which was marked by initial symptoms of fever, aching limbs and back, headache, and sore throat, were isolated and attended to by medical personnel, who did their best to protect themselves with gowns and gauze masks.[8] The precise impact of influenza on the health of the 19th Battalion at this time is not clear. Although the causes were not specified in battalion records, reported cases of illness in the unit during November (sixty-four among the other ranks) were more than double the numbers reported in each of the previous two months. The vast majority of men, it is true, carried on with their duties as before, and the unit's overall efficiency does not appear to have been impaired.[9] Still, the affliction was bad enough for those who contracted it. Lt.-Col. Millen was still on leave in England when he "had a lovely attack of flu," as he put it. "Think I am getting better now," he wrote to his mother near the end of November. "Yesterday I stayed in bed practically all day. I got a weeks extension on account of it and go back in a couple of days."[10]

On 16 November the 19th Battalion at last received instructions for the march to the German frontier. The Canadian Corps would begin its advance on 18 November, led by the 2nd Canadian Division on the right and the 1st Canadian Division on the left. The 2nd Division organized itself in three brigade groups, each featuring a mix of infantry and other arms. The 4th Canadian Infantry Brigade Group consisted of the battalions of 4th Brigade, one troop of Canadian Light Horse, one field artillery brigade, one platoon of cyclists, one company of the 2nd Battalion, CMGC, the 4th Battalion, CE, the 4th Field Ambulance, and No. 2 Company, 2nd Canadian Divisional Train. Each brigade group would be essentially a miniature army, with all of the major types of combatant units and support services, thus giving it some degree of independence and flexibility.[11]

Leading off the 4th Brigade Group, as part of the advance guard, would be none other than the 19th Battalion. The march began in the frosty early morning hours of 18 November. At 5:45 AM the 19th Battalion formed up in column of fours, and at around 9:00 AM they passed through the Canadian outpost line along the Canal du Centre. The 4th Brigade Group's first destination was the area around the town of Roeulx, where the 19th Battalion was billeted at the end of the day's march. Led by the Canadian Light Horse, the battalion marched to the town square in Roeulx, where it was given "a most enthusiastic welcome by the Burgomeister" and a dense crowd of excited citizens. Maj. Hatch graciously returned the compliment, thanking the people for their kindness and hospitality.[12]

The region through which the Allies advanced was divided into zones, and the German armies were required to withdraw from each successive zone on the day before Allied forces entered it. A "safety zone" six miles deep was arranged between the Allied advance forces and German rearguards to prevent any accidents or incidents of violence between the two sides.[13] Although the landscape had generally been spared artillery bombardment and trench excavation, it nonetheless bore harsh witness to the waste of war. Along the journey to Germany,

> deserted aerodromes with machines still standing in the hangers were passed, and large parks of guns, wagons, lorries and motor cars, mostly damaged, were to be seen; and the ditches along the roadway, the valleys and the hillsides, were littered with pieces of equipment, damaged arms, steel helmets and even clothing. Here and there lay the carcass of a horse which had died from exhaustion caused by lack of feed and the strain of the rapid retirement of the Germans.[14]

The men of the 19th Battalion departed Roeulx and arrived at Trazegnies on the afternoon of 21 November. On the 24th it was time to move again, and over the next three days the troops marched through Lambusart, Spy, and the city of Namur to the town of Jambes, just across the Meuse River from Namur.[15] After a brief rest, the advance resumed again on the morning of 29 November. From Mons to Namur, the 19th Battalion had followed a generally eastward line of advance. Now the Canadians turned southeast in order to give British divisions to the north enough room to march around the southern extension of the Dutch province of Limburg. Having remained neutral during the war, the Netherlands could not be crossed by any of the European armies. This forced the Canadians to march over the sparsely inhabited Ardennes hills, a difficult but normally picturesque route. However, the views from the hilltops were marred by leaden skies and continued rain, which cast the region into a depressing gloom. The 1st and 2nd Canadian Divisions now moved in single columns, with each successive brigade group separated by a day's march and covering eight to ten miles of road space.[16]

Over the next several days, the footsore men of the 19th Battalion marched through Ohey, Somme-Leuze, Mormont, and Regne–Hebronval, reaching Beho on 5 December. This would be their last stop in Belgium before the German frontier. As they marched into Beho, the troops met with a frosty reception, the reason for which became apparent once they learned that the local population was of predominantly German descent. For the first time, the billeting officer, Capt. Gershom Carpenter, had to demand accommodation for his men from some of the local inhabitants.[17]

The weary monotony of the previous days gave way on 6 December to the thrill of anticipation as the 19th Battalion prepared to march across the German border.

Even the weather was cooperative for a change, with the mainly rainy conditions at last giving way to a fine day. A "bunting flag" that had been acquired previously was unfurled for the first time to serve as the battalion standard.[18] With bayonets fixed, pipes skirling, and the standard proudly borne aloft by Capt. James E. Johnson, the battalion column set out from Beho at 8:50 AM. Twenty minutes later, the men of the 19th Battalion, who again found themselves at the head of the 4th Brigade Group, passed the boundary post marking the border and took their first steps on German soil. At last they knew how it felt to be part of a conquering army.[19]

They continued on towards their next billeting points, in the area of Setz-Atsorath and Mackenbach. On the way, they passed through St-Vith, just outside of which was a hill where Lt.-Gen. Currie reviewed the brigade group on its march. The tired men did their best to straighten their backs and raise their heads while under the watchful eyes of the corps commander. Currie had circulated a special order exhorting his men to project the image of "a close-knitted army in grim, deadly earnest … In short, you must continue to be, and appear to be, that powerful hitting force which has won the fear and respect of your foes and the admiration of the world."[20] Local Germans responded to the Canadians with "curiosity but no applause," their attitude generally being "stoical … formally polite but not friendly."[21]

At 9:00 AM on 7 December, the 19th Battalion moved on to the next leg of its journey, having already turned northeast towards the Rhine crossing at Bonn. The destination that day was the town of Hallschlag, where the men found more comfortable billets than those they had enjoyed in recent days. The local population, however, "appeared to be very much afraid at our entrance," remarked the battalion war diarist, "evidently expecting that they would be treated as their troops had treated the people of France and Belgium."[22]

The battalion departed Hallschlag on 9 December and moved to new billets in Blankenheim. From there, the men marched to the neighbouring towns of Arloff and Kirspenich, and thence to Miel on 11 December. At the latter destination, Lt.-Col. Millen finally rejoined the battalion from his extended period of leave in England, and he led his troops into Lengsdorf on the 12th. All ranks were encouraged to learn that their long trek was nearly over, for the city of Bonn and the Rhine lay only three miles away, to the northeast.[23] The next day, after crossing to the east bank of the Rhine, they would proceed to their destination, the town of Neunkirchen, where they would take up stations as part of the army of occupation. The march across the Rhine would be the ceremonial climax of the entire journey from Belgium. The 1st Canadian Division would cross the river via South Bridge at Cologne, where it would be reviewed by the GOC Second Army, Gen. Sir Herbert Plumer. The 2nd Canadian Division would take the Bonn Bridge, where Lt.-Gen. Currie would receive the salute.[24]

The 19th Battalion passing Lt.-Gen. Currie on the Bonn Bridge, December 1918. Note the view of the battalion brass and pipe bands. The pipe band has fallen out to play the battalion past the corps commander. Mounted officers lead the rest of the troops. (LAC PA-003782)

The 19th Battalion passing the Canadian Corps commander on the Bonn Bridge, December 1918. (LAC PA-003776)

The 13th of December was a Friday, which some felt to be an ill omen. Indeed, the weather was exactly what one would not want for a grand parade – dark, overcast, and pouring rain. This dampened spirits but did not alter the day's planned events. After spending the previous day shining up their arms, equipment, and uniforms, the men of the 19th Battalion formed up and moved out of Lengsdorf at 8:20 AM. Again, the privilege of leading the 4th Brigade would fall to them, and because the three infantry brigades of the 2nd Canadian Division were marching in numerical order, they had the additional honour of being the first infantry battalion of the division to cross the Rhine.[25]

Led by the Headquarters Company and followed, in order, by the pipe band, A Company, B Company, the colour party bearing a new silk Union flag, the brass band, C Company, D Company, and transport, the 19th Battalion tramped through rain-slick streets towards the Bonn Bridge. The men presented an impressive, albeit drenched, sight, equipped in battle order, wearing steel helmets, and with bayonets fixed on their sloped rifles. "At long last we got going," said Vivian Thompson, "and marched into Bonn and through the streets of that city to show them just what fine soldiers we were, bayonets and all."[26] In spite of the weather, the spectacle in Bonn was impressive as the 2nd Canadian Division, in a column some eighteen miles long, marched past the reviewing stand on the east end of the Bonn Bridge. Upon reaching the saluting point, the 19th Battalion's pipe band fell out to the left and piped the men past Lt.-Gen. Currie, who proudly returned the salute.[27] The display put on by the sodden troops was, in Currie's words, "magnificent. The smart, sturdy Infantry, with bayonets fixed, marching perfectly, with colours flying and bands playing our national airs, was an impressive sight, which did not fail to bring home to the German population the great potential strength of our Army."[28]

The 19th Battalion crossed the Rhine at 11 AM, displaying excellent march discipline to the reviewing officers and the crowds of mainly silent and sullen civilian onlookers. Yet not everyone in the 1st or 2nd Canadian Divisions felt honoured to participate in the occupation force; some would far rather have marched to the nearest port and taken the first ship bound for Canada. Frustration at the prolongation of their military service, mixed with the gruelling effects of the long march to Germany, and topped off by the discomfort of parading for review in such dismal weather, must have sorely tried the patience of many Canadians.

When questioned about the state of the 19th Battalion's morale at this time, Ed Youngman maintained that it remained "high," even though thoughts of home were uppermost in most men's minds. "Naturally … we hadn't seen what they called home since the end of April 1915," said Youngman, who had been with the battalion since the beginning, "and here we were the 13th of December 1918, and we had got in the habit of calling a funk hole home."[29] Youngman was not the only "old original" still serving with the 19th Battalion in the post-armistice period.

Right: Pte. Alex Munro, 19th Battalion pipes and drums.

Below: Alex Munro's bagpipes. Munro played these pipes on the Bonn Bridge in 1918. (Ken Munro Collection)

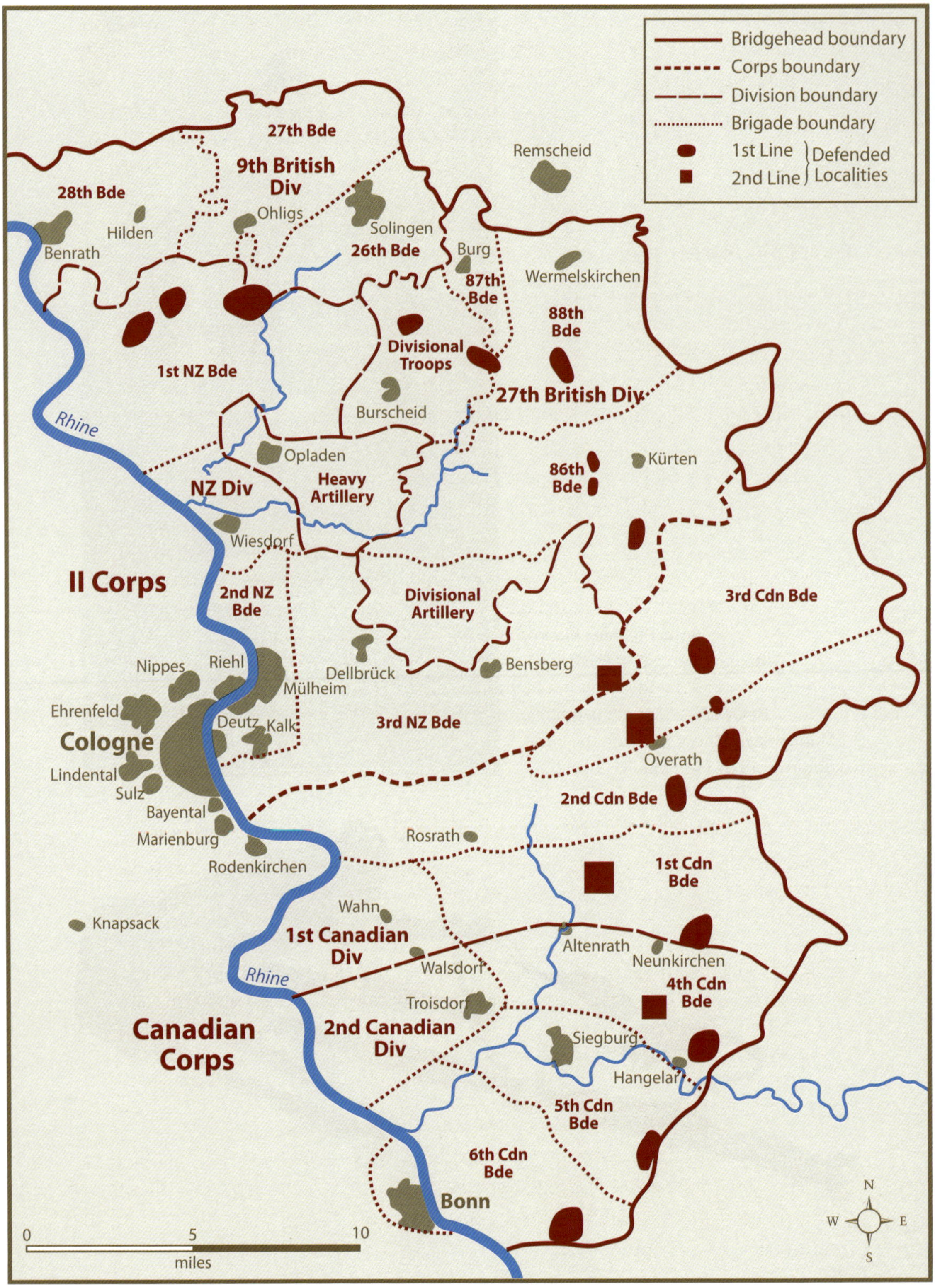

Map 23 – Rhine bridgehead.

Amazingly, there were 19 officers and 105 other ranks who had landed in France with the battalion in September 1915 who also participated in the march past on the Bonn Bridge in December 1918. This amounted to 12 percent of the total number of personnel who departed England for France in September 1915. Some of these originals would have spent considerable amounts of time away from the unit convalescing from wounds or seconded to other commands; even so, this was a noteworthy survival rate over such a long period of time.[30]

Occupation Duty

After crossing to the east bank of the Rhine, the 19th Battalion proceeded on to the city of Siegburg and then to the town of Neunkirchen. In accordance with the general defence scheme for the occupied territory, Lt.-Col. Millen established a series of outposts south and east of the town, which were to guard the roads and approaches from unoccupied Germany. Behind this outpost line, a main line of resistance was established, supported by machine-gun and artillery units. This main line featured a series of strongpoints, or "defended localities," and was to be held "at all costs."[31] "Today we crossed the Rhine," wrote Millen to his mother,

> and while I am not quite certain, I think my battalion is now further east than any other British troops … My Headquarters are in the home of the Burgomaster of the district and I have two wonderful rooms, beautifully furnished, practically the whole right-side of the downstairs. Beautiful furniture, rugs, pictures and electric lights, the desk I am writing this at would cost several hundred dollars. At the moment I am just waiting till they get the water hot in the bathroom to have a bath. We were on the road for about 8 hrs and it was raining most of the time. A bath and a change will be most acceptable.[32]

As for the internal affairs of the occupied territory, the Canadians, in common with other Allied forces, were to

> disturb as little as possible the existing conditions, unless those conditions menaced the safety of the troops or the general plan of the Allied command. The military occupation was to be essentially police work. The German local gendarmerie was to be used, but under Allied supervision, and all appointees of the Berlin Government were to be turned out of office. No Germans were to be permitted in the streets between the hours of 8 PM and 6 AM. The use of telephones was to be forbidden the inhabitants and the mails and press censored and controlled. No public meetings, except church services, were to be tolerated. Transportation services and trade between occupied and unoccupied Germany was to be forbidden, except under extreme circumstances approved by an Allied commission.[33]

Given the considerable restrictions, it is difficult to see how the local population could possibly be disturbed "as little as possible." The disruption to daily life must have been great, and would have been more difficult for those with family or other interests in the unoccupied territories.

In addition to these practical restrictions on German liberty, regulations required that proper respects be paid to the occupying Allied forces. German men were supposed to doff their hats when addressing Canadian or British officers, and all citizens had to bare their heads whenever the British national anthem was played in public. Local men were even expected to give up their seats on tram cars to Allied officers and other ranks.[34] For a people whose armies had only recently overrun huge stretches of Europe, these regulations must have seemed specially calculated to offend their already wounded pride. Some Canadians quickly recognized this and determined to make the best of a bad situation. In Lt.-Col. Millen's estimation, although his men and the locals were "getting along very well, it of course must be awfully galling to the people to have to doff their hats to our officers as we pass. My idea is to leave a good impression, so that when we leave they will feel that we their conquerors are a decent people."[35]

For all their power and privileges, Allied soldiers were not free to do as they pleased with local citizens and property. The 19th Battalion's standing orders declared that "severe punishment will be given if men ill-treat the civilian population."[36] On the other hand, the troops were not to become too friendly with locals. Open fraternization was strictly *verboten*, and any man seen walking with a German woman could have been arrested.[37] That such orders continued to be published from time to time indicates that they were honoured more in the breach than in the observance. In fact, it was almost impossible for men billeted in private homes to avoid some degree of fraternization. Vivian Thompson enjoyed card games with the family where he was billeted and recalled that "apart from the mud and the cold, I rather enjoyed this place."[38] Just a few days before Christmas, Millen informed his mother that "the people here will be sorry to see us go, as they say other troops may not be as nice. The burgomaster's wife's remark when she realized she would have another officer was 'I hope he is a nice man too.'"[39]

Owing to garrison and patrol duties, almost no training (other than physical drills) was carried out during the 19th Battalion's time in the Neunkirchen area – something that pleased the other ranks greatly. When not on duty, the men could relax at a nearby canteen set up by the YMCA or at one of the *estaminets* established in each company area.[40] Until Christmas, there was little to break the pattern of ordinary routine, save for a ceremony held at the YMCA hall on 18 December. During this gathering, the senior chaplain of the 2nd Canadian Division consecrated the silk Union flag recently received by the battalion; henceforth, the flag was to be accorded all the respect and honours due to Regimental Colours.[41] During the dark days of operations on the Western Front, little thought had been given to such totemic emblems of traditional regimental culture. Now, the somewhat more relaxed climate of the post-armistice period permitted the battalion – or at least its officers – to indulge in some of the rituals and customs observed by older, established units.

Maj.-Gen. Henry Burstall (right) with Field Marshal Sir Douglas Haig. (LAC PA-002498)

Christmas Day, 1918, was the most festive holiday since the battalion departed Canada. All ranks were certain that it would be their final one away from home. The day "was spent in joyous revelry," remarked the battalion diarist, and in "many of the Officers' Messes and billets gaily decorated Xmas trees were installed by the civilians."[42] Three days later, the 21st Battalion relieved the 19th Battalion on the outpost line and the latter moved back to the picturesque city of Siegburg. With a population of approximately 30,000, Siegburg was a sizable community. Situated sixteen miles southeast of Cologne, it offered ample accommodation. Other ranks were assigned barracks-style billets in a series of well-built wooden huts, while officers found billets in the surrounding neighbourhood. By New Year's Eve, all ranks were settled comfortably and finalizing preparations for a celebration that would dwarf the one held on Christmas Day.[43]

Ringing in the New Year

By coincidence, New Year's Day of 1919 happened to be the nineteenth day after the 19th Battalion had crossed the Rhine, and to mark the occasion Lt.-Col. Millen and Maj. Robert P. Saunders organized the grandest gathering yet staged by the battalion.[44] "Our battalion had a bit of money," explained Joe O'Neill. "It had originally come from the people of Hamilton, I believe, that was where it started

New Year's Dinner, 19th Battalion, Siegburg, Germany, January 1919. (LAC PA-004031)

and a big fund had been built up. They still had some of this money, and also from the canteen, they'd earned it."[45] With ample funds at his disposal, Millen authorized a lavish banquet for all ranks and secured the YMCA Hall in Siegburg as the venue. To ensure the attendance of as many battalion members as possible, Millen enlisted the aid of an old friend, Lt.-Col. Bert Hooper, the 19th Battalion's intrepid former bombing officer, who now commanded the 20th Battalion. Hooper graciously agreed to relieve all 19th Battalion personnel on guard duty with his own men, and even went so far as to volunteer the services of the 20th Battalion's brass band for entertainment, thereby allowing the 19th Battalion's own band members to enjoy the feast.[46]

By 11:30 AM on 1 January, after Major Saunders and his committee had completed all arrangements for the affair, 754 officers and other ranks of the battalion formed up at their barracks and paraded to the YMCA Hall. There, they found seven long rows of tables stretching the length of the hall.[47] "The tables all had either white cloths or white crinkly paper on," remarked Millen, and "we hired dishes and glasses. The whole hall was decorated [and] we also had flowers or plants on the table." Under colourful banners and flags representing the victorious Allied powers, the men dined on "soup, turkey, pork, potatoes, carrots, corn, Xmas pudding, pie, beer, nuts, raisins, oranges, and apples." Millen noted that "we hired waiters instead of using our own men," which enhanced the dignity of the affair and ensured that all ranks were able to sit for the meal. "Oh what a celebration," remarked Joe O'Neill, "German waiters and dress suits, [they] threw on the dog."[48] "No pains or expense had been spared on the menu," enthused the battalion war diarist. "During the course of the Dinner the orchestra of the 2nd Divisional Concert Party and the band of the 20th Battalion dispensed all the latest and best strains of operatic music, while civilian waiters kept the plates well filled."[49]

The importance of the occasion was highlighted by the presence of several distinguished guests. These included the 4th Brigade commander, Brig.-Gen. McCuaig, several members of his staff, and the division commander himself, Maj.-Gen. Burstall. Burstall had become quite popular with the men of the 19th Battalion, and although he was delayed in getting to the banquet, he met with a rousing reception when he made his entrance. "Well General Burstall arrived a bit late," said Joe O'Neill,

> and the head table was up at the front of the hall you see, and he had to come in the main door which was at the opposite end. Well the boys down at the end recognized him, well I don't think any man could have such a standing ovation, as General Burstall received from the boys of the 19th … The boys hopped to their feet and they cheered and they yelled, and they just went wild, they fairly adored him.[50]

During the meal, Lt.-Col. Millen rose on behalf of the battalion and graciously thanked Burstall and McCuaig for sharing the occasion with them. In response, both generals "paid glowing tributes to the 19th Battalion throughout monotonous periods of trench holding, the hard campaigns, the final hours of the war, and the triumphant march to Germany, and expressed their gratitude for the sincere co-operation with which the 'Dix-neufs' at all times responded to all demands."[51] Upon conclusion of the dinner, everyone drew their chairs back from the tables and relaxed while the 2nd Canadian Divisional Concert Party, the "See-Twos," performed a hilarious musical sketch. In addition, a photographer from Canadian Corps headquarters was present to record the event for posterity. Once the photographer, working from the gallery of the hall, had completed his task, the men were permitted to smoke.[52]

In Millen's estimation, the affair "was without doubt the biggest thing of its kind ever pulled off on this side by any battalion and was a wonderful success."[53] But in spite of Millen's judgment, the apparent abundance of food, and the battalion diarist's insistence that "nothing was left to be desired," some men reportedly left the banquet hungry. Vivian Thompson complained that "those [seated] nearest the kitchen seemed to get two dinners, those in the centre of the hall got very little and those on the far side got nothing."[54] That this sort of thing could have happened seems inexplicable, and it is difficult to believe that men who had not received dinners would have silently accepted their lot, or that officers and NCOs who had worked so hard to organize the celebration would have permitted this to happen. Whatever the scale of this alleged oversight, it shows that in spite of the best intentions and the most assiduous planning, no event came off "without a

The 19th Battalion headquarters (date uncertain). (MUA RC 0835)

hitch." Nevertheless, most of the men doubtless agreed with Millen's assertion that it had been "one of the greatest days in the history of the Battalion."[55]

Once the seasonal festivities had wound down, the inexorable shadow of routine once more fell over the 19th Battalion. But there was more for the men to do in Siegburg beyond mounting guards, drilling, and occasionally fraternizing with locals. Passes were granted for short leaves to visit Bonn and Cologne, permitting some to take in such famous attractions as Cologne's breathtaking Gothic cathedral. In addition, by the end of December, educational classes had been established in the battalion's large mess hall. This was part of a broader education movement in the CEF that had begun well before the armistice and was designed to prepare the men for civilian life. Within the 19th Battalion, classes covered such subjects as agriculture, business, motor mechanics, and elementary reading and writing.[56] While unit-level classes were generally at an elementary level, the CEF as a whole offered a growing array of education and training opportunities, from elementary through to post-secondary levels, especially through an organization known as the Khaki University of Canada, which ran courses at various locations in France and England. One of the 19th Battalion officers, Capt. James Linton, would depart for England on 12 February 1919 to further his studies through the Khaki University.[57]

For most of the first two weeks of January, the 19th Battalion remained at Siegburg, where daily activities were dominated by fatigues, guard duty, and classroom instruction.[58] Then on 12 January the 19th Battalion relieved the 21st Battalion on the outpost line and "received a very hearty reception by the civilian population" of Neunkirchen.[59] The men resumed the same duties as before, patrolling the outposts, examining "the passes of any one traveling to and fro and enforc[ing] regulations affecting the civilians."[60] In flagrant contravention of orders against fraternization, the men of the 19th Battalion continued to cultivate sociable relations with local Germans. Given that Lt.-Col. Millen himself continued to be one of the most incorrigible "offenders," it is little wonder that other ranks found little to deter them. Millen admitted to his mother:

> I suppose you will hardly understand it, but we are really enjoying our stay in Germany. The people here all seemed so pleased to see us back ... Twice, (this is on the quiet) I have been out into the neutral zone to a summer hotel, the second time they insisted on entertaining us and it was very nice, tea and a most wonderful pumpkin pie. Yesterday I took a party into a town [called] Troisdorf to play indoor baseball with the M.G. Battalion, it was a good game but we were beaten. I would have liked to have won because then we would have played against an American team.[61]

Leaving Germany

The 19th Battalion's second stay in the Neunkirchen area would not be a long one, for battalion headquarters received a warning order on 17 January announcing their impending relief by troops from the 34th British Division, which was arriving to replace the 2nd Canadian Division.

The withdrawal of Canadian troops from the Army of Occupation had begun earlier in the month, and by 18 January the 1st Canadian Division had completed

Headquarters platoon, D Company, 19th Battalion. Photo taken in Fosses, Belgium, 1919. John Gaetz is in the back row, second from the left. (GMA NA-2214-14)

its move to Belgium. For the 2nd Canadian Division, the changeover began on 19 January, when units of the British 101st Brigade commenced relieving those of the 4th Brigade Group. At 1:30 PM, Lt.-Col. Millen's men set out once more for Siegburg, where they took over their old billets.[62] Although eager to head west towards the Atlantic ports and home, many men did not look forward to spending more time in the war-torn regions of Belgium or France. "We are quite comfortable here," remarked John Gaetz of the billets in Siegburg, "and I would much rather stay until it is time to go right through rather than be side tracked in some of the desolated places of France."[63]

On 20 January 1919, units of the 4th Brigade Group departed Siegburg and Troisdorf and travelled southwest, not to France but to Belgium. The 32 officers and 619 other ranks of the 19th Battalion formed up and boarded a train that took them to Auvelais, around ten miles west of Namur in the British Fourth Army area. From there, they moved on to their final destination, the Belgian town of Fosses, which they reached on the morning of 22 January.[64] "This place Fosses is not much," Lt.-Col. Millen complained. "We are no where near as comfy as we were in Germany and from present indications we are likely to stay here some time. There was a dance on here the night we arrived, I can't say much for the belles of the town."[65] The other ranks were not impressed either. Their new billets were "nothing like as good as those in Germany," claimed Cpl. John Gaetz. "The town we are in is very small and like most of the Belgian towns it is pretty well starved out. Not nearly as prosperous as those I have seen in Germany." Gaetz also sensed "a feeling of restlessness" among the men and knew "that this has caused the authorities some concern."[66] Apprehension over the morale and conduct of the men was widespread among most Canadian units. Many officers believed that simply tightening the disciplinary regime would make the situation worse. Tact and forbearance became crucial to maintaining a reasonably harmonious atmosphere as all ranks waited impatiently to be shipped home.

Design for Demobilization

Indeed, the questions of demobilization and return to civilian life had been uppermost on most men's minds ever since the armistice was declared. Now that the Canadians had finished their occupation duties in Germany, there seemed little point in delaying their return home.[67] But the ordinary rank and file had little understanding or appreciation of the difficulties facing Canadian military and civil authorities in repatriating more than a quarter of a million members of the CEF from their scattered positions in England, France, Belgium, and Germany.[68]

Rough weather at sea, workers' strikes, shortages in available shipping (partly owing to competing interests with British, American, Australian, and New Zealand forces), and limitations in the carrying capacity of Canadian railways through the Maritime provinces during the winter months prevented rapid repatriation of the

CEF. In addition, because a great many CEF personnel wished to visit friends and relations in the United Kingdom before sailing for Canada, it was decided that the troops would proceed home from English as opposed to French ports.

There had been considerable debate among officials about the best way to organize demobilization. The Canadian government wanted to ship men home under a complex system of categorization based on their occupations, skill levels, and geographic destinations in Canada. This would entail dissolving existing units of the Canadian Corps while they were still overseas and mingling their personnel with those who had served in CEF support and training units operating in England and behind the lines in France and Belgium. The corps commander, Lt.-Gen. Currie, strongly opposed this scheme. Currie argued that in order to maintain adequate levels of morale and discipline, the integrity of existing Canadian Corps units had to be upheld. Men who had lived and fought together would be happier and better behaved if they remained united under the leadership of their own officers. By returning to Canada as formed units, they would also showcase the pride and power of a corps that had done its nation proud on the world stage during four years of horrendous conflict. By the end of November 1918, a compromise was reached: the CEF would demobilize in two principal streams. In one stream, combatant units of the roughly 100,000-strong Canadian Corps, would remain intact, returning to Canada under the command of their own officers. In the other stream, the rest of the CEF would be reorganized into drafts based on length of service and geographical destination in Canada. In this second stream, those with the longest periods of service and those who were married would return home first.[69]

Within this overall scheme, individual members of Canadian Corps units (such as the infantry battalions) also had some measure of choice regarding their own demobilization. In Canada, regional dispersal areas were established, and men could apply to be demobilized in areas other than those to which their units were destined. If they received approval, these men would depart their units before shipment back to Canada and be attached to other units bound for the dispersal area of their choice. Also, men with overseas dependents would be permitted to leave their units and assemble with their families in England; from there they would be transported back to Canada under the auspices of the Department of Immigration and Colonization.[70]

Normally, the four divisions of the Canadian Corps would have proceeded from Belgium to England in order of seniority, beginning with the 1st Canadian Division, followed by the 2nd, 3rd, and 4th. This would have happened had the 3rd and 4th Canadian Divisions relieved the 1st and 2nd on occupation duty in Germany. But with the earlier reduction of Canadian participation in the Army of Occupation, the 3rd and 4th Canadian Divisions were left to languish in Belgium. Consequently, Lt.-Gen. Currie decided to speed the demobilization process along by permitting one of these divisions to depart for England in advance of the two senior formations. The 3rd Canadian Division was chosen for release from France first, and by 2 February 1919 its units would begin arriving at a special embarkation camp established for the Canadians at Le Havre. In departing the continent, the 3rd Canadian Division would be followed by the 1st, 2nd, and 4th Canadian Divisions, in that order. After landing in England, the units of each division would concentrate in camps at Witley or Bramshott, where their personnel would be processed, documented, and then permitted a two-week furlough. When their leave was over, the men would reassemble at the camps to wait for available shipping back to Canada.[71]

Waiting It Out

Sitting through the chill and damp of another European winter was not what the weary Canadians had hoped for. Thus, measures had to be taken quickly to amuse all ranks while they waited, in order to prevent the development of potentially dangerous currents of disaffection. In addition to concerts, films, evening dances, and a busy program of athletic competitions, educational classes were resumed. In the 19th Battalion this was aided by the eventual establishment of a battalion library.[72]

The regular program of drill, classes, and entertainment activities continued during most of the 19th Battalion's extended sojourn in Fosses. This was enlivened with periods of leave, usually lasting three days, during which many men took the opportunity to visit the Belgian capital, Brussels.[73] There was, however, an alarming interruption in late February and early March, when a wave of influenza swept through the region occupied by the British Fourth Army. During February, thirty-two men from the 19th Battalion were sent to hospital, some of whom likely were suffering from influenza. "It seems that the flu is cutting a wide swath once again," commented John Gaetz. Two battalion members died from their illness, one of whom, Pte. Alexander Thomas, succumbed to pneumonia, which was cited as a frequent complication of the flu.[74]

When the epidemic died down again, regular routine resumed, punctuated by inspections and occasional visits from senior officers, such as General Sir Henry Rawlinson, GOC Fourth Army.[75] Then, at long last, final preparations for departure from the continent began. One of the first orders of business was to determine at which dispersal station in Canada the men of the 19th Battalion would be demobilized. The two likeliest stations were Toronto and Hamilton, since most of the battalion's personnel came from these two cities and the surrounding districts. Lt.-Col. Millen was keen on bringing the battalion back to his home city of Hamilton for demobilization; but after sounding out the matter among his officers, he found that most favoured Toronto. Millen knew this would disappoint the people of Hamilton, who had come to regard the 19th Battalion as the city's most representative infantry unit at the front. Nevertheless, he followed the wishes of the majority and agreed to "fall the men out" in Toronto.[76]

To get to England, the 19th Battalion first had to get to the French port of Le Havre, which was the main embarkation point for Canadian units. The date set for this move was 31 March, and considerable care was taken to explain to the troops the procedures and time frames involved in moving and demobilization. Steps were also taken to provide them with comforts and amusements during each stage of the journey home. There was good reason for this. In late 1918 and early 1919 difficulties had arisen at some Canadian camps in England, where largely idle and ill-informed troops grew impatient with waiting for shipment back to Canada and engaged in several incidents of rioting. The worst of these disturbances occurred on 4 and 5 March at Kinmel Park, a staging camp thirty miles from the port of Liverpool. By the time the riots at Kinmel were quelled, five Canadians were dead and twenty-three were wounded. Military authorities on both sides of the English Channel were anxious to prevent the reoccurrence of such outbursts.[77]

All in all, 29 March was a busy day throughout the 4th Brigade. Remaining educational classes finally wrapped up, battalions continued their departure preparations, and Lt.-Gen. Currie stopped by to lunch with the brigade staff and pay a last visit to each unit.[78] After shaking hands with the officers and wishing them the very best of luck in their future endeavours, Currie reminded the assembled ranks that "each one has his duty to the nation in peace, just as in war, and expressed his trust that all would carry it out as well as they had done in the field."[79]

On 31 March, the 19th Battalion finally departed Fosses, marched to Auvelais station, and boarded the train for Le Havre. Like its sister units, the 19th Battalion was, by this time, virtually a shell of its former incarnation. Some of its personnel had been attached to other units for demobilization elsewhere in Ontario, or in other provinces, and its supply and transport sections had virtually ceased to exist. All animals, vehicles, and equipment had been collected by personnel from the 2nd Canadian Divisional Train for disposal by the British government. Even remaining surplus medical stores had been turned over to the divisional field ambulances. The battalions were effectively "stripped, retaining only [their] arms and [their] traditions." For the officers, grooms, and transport personnel, parting with their trusted animals was especially difficult. Great attachments had developed between men, horses, and mules, who had shared alike in the discomforts and dangers of military service. Most of the animals were turned over to the Belgians, whose own beasts had long ago been requisitioned by the Germans.[80]

At 12:30 PM, with Lt.-Gen. Currie and Maj.-Gen. Burstall on hand to bid a final farewell, the train slowly chugged out of Auvelais and rattled onward towards the French coast. The men were housed in the familiar boxcars, but this time they felt less like "freight," crammed together with little regard for comfort. The old loading adage, "Hommes 40, Chevaux 8," was mercifully disregarded, and the men luxuriated in the extra space conferred by the transport authorities' decision to allot only twenty-four men per car. Each car also boasted a stove, as well as enough straw to give some semblance of bedding for those who wished to lie down. Comfort was important, for this would be a rather slow journey, lasting longer than a day and a half.[81]

At 5:30 AM on 2 April, the train arrived at Le Havre. After all ranks had clambered out of the coaches and collected their baggage, the battalion moved to Canada Camp, a complex of reasonably comfortable huts around two miles from the docks. They would remain there for the next few days, cleaning up, delousing, and getting new clothes.[82]

After all arrangements had been made, including the compilation of personnel nominal rolls for embarkation, the 19th Battalion assembled to board ship on the evening of 5 April. The process commenced with a bugle call sounding "Fall In," and a brisk but orderly scramble ensued. According to the battalion diarist, "the record held for 'falling in,' distributing Embarkation Cards, and moving off was 14½ minutes. The battalion accomplished it in 6½ minutes, breaking all previous records." Well pleased with their feat and keen to get moving, 28 officers and 599 other ranks marched to the docks, where they boarded the SS *Prince George* at 9:00 PM. Thirty minutes later, the vessel steamed out into the English Channel, meeting calm seas and a tranquil, starlit sky.[83]

English Interlude

The ship reached Southampton at 6:00 AM on 6 April. Before disembarking the men were served a hot breakfast. At 10:30 AM they boarded a train bound for Milford Station, not far from their destination, which was Witley Camp. Upon arrival, they moved into wooden huts in a section of the camp designated "O" Wing. There, the 19th Battalion would remain for the next five weeks while its personnel waited their turn to re-embark for home.[84]

Fortunately, the men were not kept pent-up at Witley for the entire time. After three days of bathing and clothing parades, medical inspections, and filling out various pay and discharge forms, the men were granted leave from 10 to 18 April, with only minimal numbers of personnel remaining in camp to deal with routine work.[85] Officers and men made the most of their furlough, many taking advantage of the myriad attractions offered by the bustling metropolis of London. Reality then set in on 19–20 April, as the men trudged back to camp from their holidays. Battalion records give no indication of the prevalence of absence at this time, but officers must have expected that a certain percentage of men would be slow to return from leave.

Dissatisfied murmurings circulated among the men, many of whom were annoyed that some units with less time served in the field than their own had been shipped home earlier. To prevent such grumbling from escalating into acts of protest, "tact was necessary to maintain discipline," and a good many minor lapses

J. O'Neill, A.O. Thompson, C.H. Mitchell, A.R. Switzer, and R.H.L. Dinsmore. (MUA RC 0835)

in behaviour and deportment were tolerated by intelligent officers.[86] Even Lt.-Col. Millen did not know for certain when his unit's turn to embark would come. "Just got back from 8 days leave," he wrote his mother on 20 April. "Probably by the time you receive this we will be on the ocean. Have no definite date but a little better than 2 weeks should see us moving."[87] In the meantime, there was little that Millen and his officers could do to occupy their men but to fall back on the tried and true routines practised in France, Belgium, and Germany. Officers and NCOs spent most mornings leading their men on short route marches, being careful not to drive them too hard. The rest of the day was given over to sports and recreation.[88]

The bureaucracy of demobilization continued unabated. Additional medical examinations were conducted to help identify physical problems that might influence future pension benefits. They also served to uncover any lingering cases of venereal disease. Between May 1915 and April 1919, 264 cases of venereal disease were reported among 19th Battalion personnel.[89] This number represents 4 percent of the total cases (66,083) reported by the Canadian army overseas. But whereas the average Canadian rate of infection was estimated to be 158 cases per 1,000 troops, the 19th Battalion's was closer to 53 per 1,000. Whether this means that 19th Battalion men were more abstemious than average, more diligent in employing prophylactic precautions, or simply luckier is impossible to determine.[90]

Lt.-Col. Millen leading the 19th Battalion on parade in London, 1919. Although "Canada Day" is written on the photo, this is likely the victory parade of 3 May. (MUA RC 0835)

In addition to the threat of venereal disease, the insidious spectre of influenza still made its presence felt. By March, a considerable portion of the British population had been affected, and the epidemic continued to take lives through April. One of the 19th Battalion's officers, Lt. Albert Switzer of D Company, contracted the flu shortly after arrival in England, where he succumbed to its effects. The battalion furnished pallbearers for his funeral on 26 April at Bramshott, where he was laid to rest with full military honours.[91]

A happier break in the monotony of waiting occurred a week later, on 3 May, when a massive Victory Parade was held in the city of London. The event was a royal review, featuring representative contingents from all British Dominion and Colonial forces that were stationed in England at the time. Each Canadian battalion sent five officers and two hundred other ranks to take part. Equipped in drill order, the troops swung jauntily along the parade route, overlooked for miles by cheering mobs and by buildings bedecked with flags and flowers. Even the weather was picture-perfect for the occasion. "Fortunately we had a fine day," reported John Gaetz. "The Canadians headed the march and of the Canadians the Cavalry units were the first. Then the Infantry. Representatives of the 19th Battalion being the second unit. They marched and looked very smart. Following the Canadians were the Aussies, New Zealanders, South Africans and Newfoundlanders."[92] As the great parade proceeded "down Constitution Hill and wheeled to march past His Majesty, in front of Buckingham Palace, the sight was most impressive," enthused the 20th Battalion's Maj. Corrigall:

> With bayonets fixed and colours flying the troops moved by two battalions abreast, each in column of fours ... For the first time in history the steady tramp of all the sons

> of Britain, who had been fighting for their Empire, was heard in the streets of London; men from all parts of the Empire were there, marching past their King, and watched by thousands on thousands of their fellow subjects of the Motherland.[93]

The 19th Battalion's contingent returned from this giddily imperialistic celebration and settled once more into the spartan confines of camp life at Witley, where all ranks waited for their turn to embark for home. Most units were subjected to an average sojourn of one month from the time of their initial arrival in camp; so by the second week of May, the men of the 19th Battalion knew their time must come soon.[94] As had so often been the case for other drafts of men anxious to depart, there was great disappointment when expected sailings were delayed or cancelled. "Our sailing was cancelled for last Saturday," wrote a weary John Gaetz on 11 May, "so Friday morning we were paid a pound and granted leave until Sunday … We have a muster parade tomorrow and are looking to sail on Tuesday. Of course I will never feel sure until I feel the throb of the propellers on the boat."[95]

When word filtered through the ranks of the 4th Brigade units at Witley that units of the 5th Brigade were slated for departure before them, tempers finally reached the breaking point. Jealousy evidently combined with notions that the

A.O. Thompson, G.M. Bradfield, J. O'Neill, R.H. Bliss, H. Stuart, L. Millen, R.H.L. Dinsmore, R.P. Saunders, and W.F. Smith. The date and location of the photo are uncertain, but the façade of the building in the background bears a resemblance to Buckingham Palace. (MUA RC 0835)

The 19th Battalion band playing for a large group of soldiers on the deck of the SS *Caronia,* May 1919. (CWM Photo Archives 52A 2 77.67)

numerical precedence of brigades and battalions should have been applied to the order of embarkation. The result, on the evening of 8 May, was a series of raids on beer and tobacco supplies at several canteens and stores by approximately 100 rowdies, mainly from disgruntled 4th Brigade units, the 19th Battalion included. Satisfied with their loot, and the opportunity to smash some windows and doors, the riotous rabble gradually dispersed, encouraged by irate officers and nervous picket personnel to return to their quarters.[96] Fortunately the incident was in no way comparable to the Kinmel Park riots in early March; but it stood as yet another "black mark" on the collective reputation of the tired and frustrated Canadian troops cooped up in England. It is not known exactly how many men from the 19th Battalion may have been involved in the affair, but Lt.-Col. Millen and his officers likely treated offenders with considerable leniency to avoid provoking any further outbursts.

Conditions at Witley calmed down, and on 10 May the units of 5th Brigade marched off as expected, under the envious gaze of the remaining battalions. Three days later, the great moment finally arrived for the units of 4th Brigade. In the early morning of 13 May, the men of the 19th Battalion were ordered to fall in and march to the railway station at Milford – their destination Canada Dock, Liverpool. The train sped across the English countryside and eventually reached the great port city, where it disgorged its excited passengers into the care of the local Permanent Detraining Staff. These officials quickly took charge and marched the troops along the docks and to the waiting gangways of the RMS *Caronia*. By early afternoon, the

19th Battalion's 32 officers and 679 other ranks were all comfortably aboard, along with their comrades from the 18th Battalion. The 20th and 21st Battalions arrived later that day, thus reuniting aboard ship the Ontarians of the old 4th Brigade.[97]

Homeward Bound

Later that evening, the *Caronia* slipped its moorings and steamed out the mouth of the Mersey River towards the Irish Sea. By sheer coincidence it had been on 13 May, exactly four years earlier, that the 19th Battalion had shipped out of Montreal for England on the RMS *Scandinavian.* Unlike the earlier voyage, there were no enemy submarines to worry about, and no daily parades or drills to disturb the atmosphere of leisure.

The one constant was the discomfort brought on by heavy seas among those whose constitutions had never become habituated to rolling decks. According to Maj. D.J. Corrigall:

> All were free, more or less, to do what they pleased. Everyone enjoyed deck games and sports during the day and listened with interest and appreciation to the concerts, produced through the efforts of the Chaplain Services and the Y.M.C.A., during the evenings; that is, all enjoyed them who were not affected by the rough weather the ship encountered.
>
> On the afternoon of the 21st of May, word went round the ship that the rocky shore of Nova Scotia would soon be in view. The news seemed to quicken the spirit of each one, even of those still suffering from the two days of severe storm in mid-Atlantic, during which time none had been allowed on deck. Soon, against the rays of the setting sun, there could be seen a low streak on the distant horizon, the first glimpse of the homeland.
>
> Just as darkness was closing down the "Coronia" [*sic*] ... entered Halifax Harbour. Quickly the ship was taken in hand by three tugs and as quickly berthed.[98]

To many on board it seemed almost unbelievable that they were about to set foot back on Canadian soil, something that some of them had not done in four long years. It was 22 May 1919, and the men of the 19th Battalion were almost home.[99]

Before long, a steady stream of eager men filed down the gangways and onto the pier. From there they were shepherded by staff of the local clearing depot towards waiting troop trains that would carry them westward to their battalions' dispersal stations. Most battalions proceeded in two sections, one following the other. The units of 4th Brigade bade their final farewells as they headed off to their respective destinations. The 19th and 20th Battalions were both bound for dispersal in Toronto, while the 18th proceeded to London and the 21st to Kingston.[100] As the trains slowly made their way through Halifax, the city presented a final stark reminder of the horrors of war. Devastated neighbourhoods were still rebuilding in the wake of the cataclysmic explosion of the French munitions ship *Mont Blanc* in the harbour narrows back in December 1917.

Although the journey to Ontario would be an overnight one, the prospect of seeing loved ones and friends kept most of the men in a state of excited anticipation, making sleep all but impossible. It also occurred to them that this would be the last time that many of them would be together. The comradeship of army life was about to meet its end, to be rekindled only at future veterans' gatherings or in chance meetings of old friends. As the trains rolled onward, section and platoon mates took time to share a few last laughs and stories before dismissal sent them their separate ways.

On the afternoon of 24 May, Victoria Day, the trains bearing the 19th and 20th Battalions at last eased into the CPR's North Toronto station. The men quickly piled out of their cars, collected their rifles and bayonets for the last time, and formed up for one final route march. There to meet them were numerous veterans of both battalions who had returned to Canada over the previous four years. Those veterans who were able to march would accompany the units on their triumphal procession downtown.[101] Prominent among the sea of old familiar faces were former 19th Battalion commanders John I. McLaren and William Turnbull, together with senior officers such as Maj. Herb Fearman. It was especially gratifying for these men to witness the return of their old unit after it had performed so well on the grim battlefields of France and Flanders. Heartfelt accolades were accorded Lt.-Col. Millen and Maj. Hatch, both of whom had rendered sterling service in command of the battalion through many of the toughest battles of the war. Members and veterans of Hamilton's 91st Regiment were especially proud of the fact that formal command of the 19th Battalion had remained with one of their own.[102] In addition, the battalion had provided commanding officers for additional units, including the 18th and 20th Battalions (Lt.-Cols. G.F. Morrison and B.O. Hooper respectively).

When everyone had found his place, the parade marched off down Yonge Street with the 19th Battalion leading the way. As the column reached the downtown core, it wheeled right from Yonge onto Bloor Street, towards the designated place of assembly at the University of Toronto's Varsity Stadium. Battalion bands belted out the liveliest tunes in their repertoires; the troops could scarcely maintain their military decorum in the face of the wildly cheering crowds lining the route. Assembled in the stadium to meet them were the mayors of Toronto and Hamilton, Tommy Church and Charles Booker, along with numerous dignitaries and multitudes of expectant relatives and friends. Countless heads craned to catch sight of the column as it made its way into the stadium; children were hoisted aloft to get a first glimpse of returning fathers or older brothers. The "veterans marched in front," remembered Ed Youngman, "by that I mean … the men who had come home wounded and so forth, and they marched in front and the boys came behind. They were a beautiful sight as they marched into formation on the arena."[103]

The mayors had planned a formal civic welcome, with speeches and tributes to the courage of both battalions and the sacrifices they had made. But it was not to be. According to Ed Youngman, when the 19th Battalion had fully assembled in the stadium, Mayor Church rose to begin his address. By that time, "the whole arena was standing on its feet, and there was a quiet come over the audience and then somebody yelled something, I couldn't tell you today what that was. It was either 'Jack' or 'Dad,' somebody screamed it out, a female voice, and … the stands just erupted." The crowds "simply broke through the police barricade … and it is the only time that I ever saw the 19th waver and that was the end of the civic welcome."[104] The 20th Battalion was met with equal fervour. "Police were powerless to stem the rush," wrote Maj. Corrigall, "and the speeches of welcome were never delivered, but the meeting of husbands with wives, of sons with parents, were none the less spontaneous and genuine because they took place in the midst of a surging throng."[105] It may not have been what the city fathers had intended, but it was certainly the most dramatic and emotional welcome the newly returned soldiers could have received. The dismissal of both battalions was a fait accompli, for there was no chance of extricating the men from the tide of loved ones who had engulfed the assembled ranks.

Celebrations by the hundreds carried on into the evening. Most of the troops spent the night in Toronto with relatives or friends, while those without a place to stay were given billets for the night at the Exhibition Grounds. The next day, 25 May, saw the official demobilization of all ranks. The majority undertook this last duty at the Toronto dispersal station. But some Hamiltonians from the 19th Battalion, having already returned home on the midnight train, did so in their own city. On arriving at his dispersal station, each man turned in his rifle, bayonet, and equipment to ordnance personnel; his uniform and steel helmet were his to keep, if he wanted them. He then received his final paycheque, a $35.00 clothing allowance, and the first instalment of his War Service Gratuity. Well-drilled station staff, who by now were capable of processing up to six or seven men per minute, signed medical and dental sheets and issued to each man his discharge certificate, a War Service Badge, and, if needed, a transportation warrant for travel to his home community.[106] After departing the dispersal stations, the men returned to the civilian lives they had left behind, and their service in the 19th Battalion faded into memories both bitter and sweet.

Epilogue

> As far as I was concerned this war consisted of taking all that was thrown at me with never a chance to get back at any one. In fact it was simply a matter of being lucky enough to come through alive and being able to endure the strain of the life.
>
> – Vivian E. Thompson[1]

> There will have been friendship of the genuine sort built up and good times had out in France here that will be much appreciated afterward and never forgotten.
>
> – John R. Gaetz[2]

With the demobilization of its personnel, the 19th Battalion effectively ceased to exist as an operational unit in May 1919. However, its official disbandment would not be proclaimed until 15 September 1920, four years to the day after its members went over the top in their first full-scale attack at Courcelette, and exactly five years after they first landed in France.[3] In all, the battalion earned eighteen Battle Honours in operations stretching from spring 1916 to the end of the war. Ten of these honours were selected for emblazonment on the colours of the Argyll and Sutherland Highlanders of Canada (Princess Louise's), the militia regiment that proudly perpetuates the legacy of the 19th Battalion.[4]

From its mobilization in November 1914 to its demobilization in May 1919, 118 officers and between 4,731 and 5,004 other ranks passed through the 19th Battalion.[5] Of these men, 3,076 were casualties, including 737 fatalities (all ranks).[6] "The

The 19th Battalion Association Committee in 1960. In the photo are "Bunny" Heron, Bill Doran, Jim Wardlaw, Fred Stitt, Frank Griffiths, Barney Clendining, Ted Lang, and Jimmie Wild. (MUA RC 0835)

battalion had changed over in personnel, almost four and one half times," remarked Harry Neil. "But one thing … had not changed – it was the same old 19th."[7] It was the veteran officers and other ranks, particularly the long-serving officers and NCOs (many of them promoted from the ranks themselves), who set the tone and preserved the unit's culture, even when the faces of many of its members changed. Exactly what made the 19th Battalion a unique social organization can never again be fully appreciated, because its members are no longer with us. The intangibles of battalion life that bound men together – the shared experiences and hardships; the jokes and stock sayings; the force of personality and leadership; particular attitudes towards, and methods of, administration; various customs and "unwritten rules" – all of these factors, and more, formed what historian Ian McCulloch has termed the "shop culture" of the Canadian Corps,[8] a culture that ceased to exist when units formally disbanded after the war, and when their members passed away over the ensuing decades.

Many veterans attempted to preserve some measure of their unit's spirit after the war, and one of the main ways they did so was by organizing battalion associations and annual reunions. Writing in the early 1970s, Harry Neil maintained that

> the last parade at Varsity Stadium only ended the history of the 19th Battalion as a fighting Unit. Since 1920, as close to Armistice Day as possible, former members meet for dinner when old friendships are renewed and with each passing year, these bonds become firmer and firmer. At the [most recent] dinner in 1971, there were 67

> present, mostly from the Toronto and Hamilton areas, but some from far distant parts of Canada and the U.S.A. Indeed, there are former members, not many, living in England, Western Canada, and the U.S.A. who still keep in close touch with the Battalion Association. This will continue until the last five meet to open the bottle of whiskey that has stood on the President's dais at every dinner since 1954, and at that meeting we shall drink to the glorious memory of the 19th Battalion Canadian Infantry, C.E.F. 1914–19.[9]

Although it is not known exactly when (or if) the sacred bottle of whisky was finally consumed, we do know that the 19th Battalion Association soldiered on into the 1980s, with its devoted secretary, Ted Lang, still churning out periodic bulletins to dwindling numbers of comrades until at least the autumn of 1985. In addition to providing a forum for old soldiers to swap stories and memories of their military service, the Battalion Association newsletter publicized personal milestones in the lives of its members and highlighted the activities that many of them still carried out in their communities. In the spring 1980 issue, Lang offered

> warm greetings from us all to Sgt. Major Jimmy Kenyon, 307 John Street North, Hamilton, Ontario, by long odds our oldest member, who celebrated his 106th birthday on Feb. 9th of this year and is still going strong! "Yours truly" chalked up his 90th birthday on January 25th 1980, and received Greetings from Old Comrades-in-arms as far distant as Bristol, England. Recollections of experiences at the front are growing dim. Some of you are engaged in useful Community projects in your home towns. How about letting me have particulars of same for future bulletins?[10]

Aged veterans, with a lifetime of memories to cushion the painful experience of war, could often look back to remember only the more humorous or pleasant aspects of army life. However, survivors in the immediate aftermath of the Great War were less well equipped to deal with the fresh physical and emotional scars they had brought home with them. In addition to the often horrible legacies borne by physically injured veterans, some, such as Deward Barnes, would have to live with the psychological trauma induced by the unspeakable experiences they endured. "I can only say that War is an awful thing and the hardships are great," Barnes later wrote,

> and there is something wrong if a man has seen as much of it as I have and wishes to see another ... My nerves were always good until I had my last leave from France, September 1918. Maybe, on account of the War lasting so long and the thought of what was in front of us, I soon started to get very nervous and have never gotten over it. Since I came home I have always tried to work hard and steady and get over this three year experience, but could never do it. So I class myself as a war wreck, which people will never understand.[11]

Others, at least outwardly, looked back on their service in the 19th Battalion with pride and a sense that they and their comrades were a breed apart from those who had not served overseas on the battlefront. Even before he departed Europe for

Portrait of Lt.-Col. Lionel Millen, by Lorne Toews (ASH, Argyll Regimental Foundation)

Canada in 1919, John Gaetz found his mind wandering back to the battlefields and the part he had played in the recent struggle:

> It is good to think that the long cold hours of watching and the hardship in the trenches is gone forever. As I came past Arras not long ago, from leave, I looked over the old trench systems for something suggestive of the old trench routine. I could find nothing that was very suggestive, just shell holes, barb wire and ditches so that anybody who comes to look over an old battlefield to get an idea of what it was like in reality, or I should say what trench life was in reality, they are bound to be disappointed. Even suppose the trenches were intact one must have to realize the limitations and possibilities of that life in order to appreciate it. After I had been out here some time I realized that there would be a day for those of us who came through, when we would look back and I knew it would be a great satisfaction to know that I had always "faced the music." I feel now that I have a satisfaction of never shirking whether it was stumbling along at night on working parties or following our barrage.[12]

Although he was immensely proud to have commanded the 19th Battalion, and had enjoyed a good deal more "creature comforts" overseas than most of his men, Lt.-Col. Lionel Millen was clearly affected by the strain of responsibility he bore for the battalion and its personnel. He saw himself as the "father of a large family," and the "burden of command" showed in the personal photos he sent home to his parents and siblings.[13] Writing to his mother in 1919, Millen remarked,

> So you don't like my photo, if I am not as pleasingly plump as I was probably I am all the better for it. I certainly am not thin but have probably got rid of some that I could well spare. You think I look very sober, others say I look sad. I think it is just a desire not to put on a sickly smile that I always imagine I have for a photographer.[14]

Hand in hand with his determination to see it through to the finish, Millen constantly found himself longing for the war's end, and the anguish he felt at the death and injury of so many of his men, to say nothing of the loss of close personal friends such as Lt.-Col. Elmer Jones and of his beloved wife, Edith, left an indelible mark on both his face and his spirit. "It is small wonder," writes historian Robert Fraser, "that those closest to him noticed a difference in his facial expression. The war had taken its toll and, no matter how hard he tried not to show it, his face could not hide it."[15]

Still, Millen, like Deward Barnes, John Gaetz, and countless other veterans, was not completely broken by his war experience and managed to lead a rich and productive life in the postwar years. "The Colonel," as he was universally known around Hamilton, would remarry, raise a family, and resume his business and public service pursuits. He maintained an active profile within the community of 19th Battalion veterans and never missed a Battalion Association event. When he died in Port Nelson in 1956, veterans "turned out in 'unbelievable numbers'" to pay him their last respects.[16]

The original caption to this photo reads: "Badge, patches, etc. presented to town of Mons by Col. Millen, 1932." (MUA RC 0835)

Four old comrades at the Canadian Corps reunion, Toronto, 1934. Presumably from left to right: Dave McKenna, unidentified, Fred Stitt, "Wally" Wallis. (MUA RC 0835)

Because many of its members hailed from the urban centres of southern and central Ontario, the 19th Battalion could assemble respectable contingents of veterans on special occasions, such as the funeral of Lionel Millen, or, earlier, in 1934, the great Canadian Corps reunion that was held in Toronto to mark the twentieth anniversary of the war's outbreak. Over three days, 90,000 veterans from across Canada congregated in Toronto, and although the number of 19th Battalion attendees remains unknown, the unit must have been well represented. Special events, such as performances by the renowned Dumbells entertainment troupe and a sports day inspired by the huge corps athletic meet held at Tincques in 1918, proved popular draws. But perhaps nothing was as appreciated by the veterans as much as the mock French village that was constructed for the occasion, "complete with half a dozen licensed *estaminets* that attracted tens of thousands of reunion goers."[17] The fun and fellowship of *estaminet* life that helped sustain so many men during the years of struggle on the Western Front continued to draw veterans together at reunions both great and small and provided the necessary counterpoint to the solemn remembrance of fallen comrades that also marked such events.

Shortly after the 1934 Canadian Corps reunion, veteran officer Robert O. Spreckley composed the following verse dedicated to the 19th Battalion and its surviving members. It evokes something of the spirit of the 19th Battalion and its veterans during active service and the postwar decades, and it stands as a fitting tribute to a unit that played a full and honourable part in Canada's military effort during the First World War – a unit whose story has, until now, remained largely unknown outside of regimental tradition and family memory.

Fall-In

1. The Nineteenth Battalion
Falls in on parade
In mufti, with brassards
And berets arrayed;
No badges of ranks
In the front or the flanks,
No eyewash inspection
To note the defection
Of equipment or rifles
And other such trifles,
And S.A.A. pouches
No kicks and no grouches,
As privates and majors,
Draftees and old stagers,
Now grown somewhat older,
Rub shoulder to shoulder,
To fall-in once more
As in Flanders of yore.

Route March

2. The Nineteenth Battalion
Moves off from the right,
In column of fours,
A right pleasing sight,
As they all keep in step,
Still with plenty of pep,
Though you'll have to admit,
That a few years have flit,
Since the last time they hobbled,
O'er French streets be-cobbled,
Through ploughed fields and highways,
And sunk roads and byways;
And as arms are a-swinging,
Old memories come winging,
Of weary night marches,
And whiz-bangs and Archies,
Of C.T's and front trenches,
And queer Flemish stenches,
Of barb-wire they tripped on,
And bath-mats they slipped on,
Of bivvies they slept in,
And funk holes they leapt in,
When night promenading,
With Fritz serenading,
And the strafe at the dawning
Of "stand-to" the next morning.

Stand Easy

3. The Nineteenth Battalion,
It sits down to dine,
On rations it never could
Get in the line,
On prime turkeys roasted,
And crisp murphies toasted,
(With the trimmings and all,)
That made them recall
Those Flemish tit-bits
The "Bombadier Fritz,"
That the troops relished fully,
Much better than bully.

But needless to say
This is just by the way.
While the boys are all seated
Till with food they're repleted,
They the old times invoke
With a quip and a joke;
Forgotten the dangers
To which they weren't strangers,
The mud and the cooties,
And unpleasant duties,
Such as packing a lump
From the Engineers' dump,
Of "I" beams and planks,
Iron sheeting and tanks,
Digging trenches and wiring,
While Heinie's conspiring
With bombs and with mines,
Pip-squeaks and five-nines;
But I have to confess
That I somewhat digress,
For peace reigns over all
In the banqueting hall,
Where the speeches are brief,
To the troop's great relief.
Then as time quickly flies
While the boys fraternise,
Hands are gripped by the score
By the pals known of yore,
That were last seen at Mons,
Or at Arras or Lens,
At the base, up the line,
Or at Bonn on the Rhine.

Dismiss

4. The Nineteenth Battalion
Disbands once again,
And scatters afar by the
Car and the train,
To their homes and relations,
And their peaceful vocations,
While the troops all declare
Twas a nifty affair;
No guards and fatigues,
No foot slogging for leagues,
With packs heavy weighted,
And it need not be stated
No roads that were muddy,
No trenches all floody,
No fleas and no cooties,
No nocturnal duties,
No digging or wiring,
No bullets or firing,
No "Minnies" or Jerrys,
It sure was the berries,
And the best "show" I've seen
Since Nineteen-Eighteen.

Robert O. Spreckley[18]

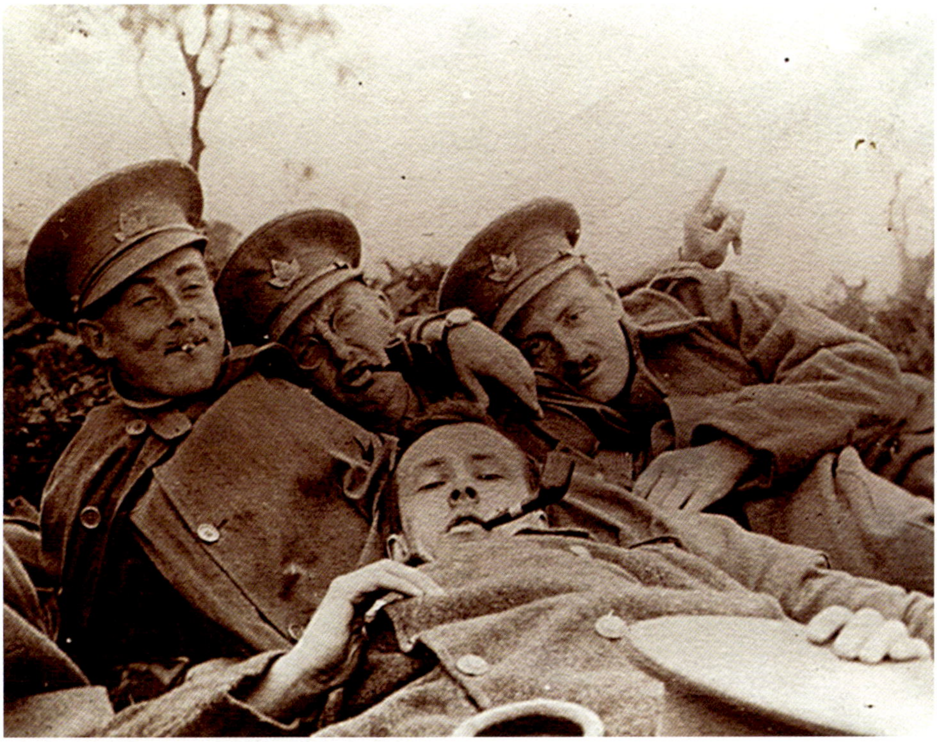

Four chums. (ASH, Lt.-Col. John I. McLaren Collection)

Plaque dedicated to the 19th Battalion in St. George's Memorial Church, Ypres. (Author's collection, 2015)

Appendix A

Monthly Casualties

Off = officers
OR = other ranks
POW = prisoners of war

Month	Battle casualties														Injuries, accidental and self-inflicted wounds								Grand total		
	Enemy fire (less POW and gas)				Prisoners of war						Gas				Injuries and accidental wounds				Wounds self-inflicted						
	Fatal		Non-fatal		Wounded fatal		Wounded non-fatal		Unwounded		Fatal		Non-fatal		Fatal		Non-fatal		Fatal		Non-fatal				
	Off.	OR	Off.	OR	Off.	OR	Off.	OR	Off.	OR	Off.	OR	Off.	OR	Off.	OR	Off.	OR	Off.	OR	Off.	OR	Off.	OR	All
1915																									
Sep			2	6														2					2	8	10
Oct		11		22														5						38	38
Nov		10		25														6						41	41
Dec		5		15														6						26	26
Total		26		68														19					2	113	115
1916																									
Jan		5		13														4						22	22
Feb		2	1	14														2					1	18	19
Mar	1	6		4														7					1	17	18
Apr		29	3	84										1			1	7					4	121	125
May		4		17														7						28	28
Jun		28		63				1										7						99	99
Jul		15	4	53														12					4	80	84
Aug	2	11	2	18														7					4	36	40
Sep	4	108	12	269														19					16	396	412
Oct		8		32												1		10				1		52	52
Nov		1		3														3						7	7
Dec		2		13														5				1		21	21
Total	7	219	22	583				1						1		1	1	90				2	30	897	927

Source: 1915 – LAC, RG 150, vols. 491–92; 1916 – LAC, RG 150, vols. 492–95

Month	Battle casualties																Injuries, accidental and self-inflicted wounds								Grand total		
	Enemy fire (less POW and gas)				Prisoners of war						Gas				Injuries and accidental wounds				Wounds self-inflicted						
	Fatal		Non-fatal		Wounded fatal		Wounded non-fatal		Unwounded		Fatal		Non-fatal		Fatal		Non-fatal		Fatal		Non-fatal				
	Off.	OR	Off.	OR	Off.	OR	Off.	OR	Off.	OR	Off.	OR	Off.	OR	Off.	OR	Off.	OR	Off.	OR	Off.	OR	Off.	OR	All
1917																									
Jan		7		12													1	4					1	23	24
Feb				4												1		1				1		7	7
Mar	1	1	1	17														3					2	21	23
Apr	4	55	6	186										3				6					10	250	260
May	6	83	2	129		2	1	7	1	8				9			1	14				1	11	253	264
Jun		1																7						8	8
Jul		8		14												1		3						26	26
Aug	3	44	3	111									2	18				9					8	182	190
Sep				3														8						11	11
Oct		3		11														3				1		18	18
Nov	3	44	1	93						1		1		17				4					4	160	164
Dec				6								1						2						9	9
Total	17	246	13	586		2	1	7	1	9		2	2	47		2	2	64				3	36	968	1004

Source: 1917 – LAC, RG 150, vols. 495–99

Month	Battle casualties														Injuries, accidental and self-inflicted wounds								Grand total		
	Enemy fire (less POW and gas)				Prisoners of war						Gas				Injuries and accidental wounds				Wounds self-inflicted						
	Fatal		Non-fatal		Wounded fatal		Wounded non-fatal		Unwounded		Fatal		Non-fatal		Fatal		Non-fatal		Fatal		Non-fatal				
	Off.	OR	Off.	OR	Off.	OR	Off.	OR	Off.	OR	Off.	OR	Off.	OR	Off.	OR	Off.	OR	Off.	OR	Off.	OR	Off.	OR	All
1918																									
Jan				5														7						12	12
Feb		2		8														3						13	13
Mar		2		7										1		1		2				1		14	14
Apr	1	21	4	49						3				2			1	11				1	6	87	93
May	1	3	1	38										2			2	4					4	47	51
Jun	1	11		26				3	1	2				2				3				1	2	48	50
Jul																		3						3	3
Aug	9	108	17	338									1	36			1	9					28	491	519
Sep		9	1	35										8		1	1	5		1		1	2	60	62
Oct	2	26	3	95						1				20				3				1	5	146	151
Nov	4	12		39														1					4	52	56
Dec																		4						4	4
Total	18	194	26	640				3	1	6			1	71		2	5	55		1		5	51	977	1028
1915–1919*																									
Grand Total	**42**	**685**	**63**	**1877**		**2**	**1**	**11**	**2**	**15**		**2**	**3**	**119**		**5**	**8**	**230**		**1**		**10**	**119**	**2957**	**3076**

* Grand total for 1915–1919 includes two other ranks, accidentally injured (non-fatally) during March 1919.

Source: 1918 – LAC, RG 150, Vols. 499-503; 1919 – LAC, RG 150, Vol. 504

Appendix B
Discipline in France and Flanders

Disciplinary Trends

The incidence of offences considered minor enough to be dealt with summarily by company or battalion commanders periodically rose and fell during the course of the war. Absence was the single most prevalent charge laid against other ranks. Others included drunkenness, disobedience, negligence, insubordination, and striking a superior (see Fig. 2). Field Punishment no. 1 was overwhelmingly the most common sentence awarded to individuals convicted of these offences, with fines and forfeitures of pay also levied frequently (see Fig. 1).

Overall, such cases of indiscipline generally declined within the 19th Battalion as the conflict wore on (see Fig. 3). Within this basic pattern, one might expect the incidence of offences to plummet during periods when the battalion was heavily engaged in battle, and numbers of infractions to peak during lulls in the fighting. Sometimes this is exactly what happened. In the 19th Battalion's experience, months marked by heavy operational activity, such as April and September 1916, April–May and November 1917, and March–June and September–October 1918, saw some of the lowest numbers of charges for minor offences. Simply put, the men were too busy fighting and surviving in engagements at St-Eloi, the Somme, Vimy, Fresnoy, Passchendaele, the 1918 German offensives, and the final Allied drives to get into much trouble.[1] During some of these months, the numbers of offences committed by personnel within the battalion were so low that they were exceeded by the numbers of offences committed by the minority of 19th Battalion personnel who were attached to other commands.[2]

Yet there also were "less active" months during which the 19th Battalion saw equally low, or even lower, numbers of charges for minor offences compared with periods marked by major operations. These included November 1915, February–March and June–July 1916, June and September 1917, and February 1918. Moreover, there were some periods of heavy fighting that saw moderate to sharp increases in numbers of charges for minor offences (such as absence and drunkenness), which may have been attributable to increased levels of stress among the troops. This was the case during August 1917, which featured the Battle of Hill 70, and August 1918, with the offensives at Amiens and Arras.[3] Except for the overarching trend towards decreasing incidence of offences as the war progressed, monthly rates of indiscipline could be quite variable.

One factor that often had a negative impact on discipline within units was the periodic influx of large numbers of reinforcements following periods of heavy casualties.[4] Significant shifts in the personnel composition of a unit, sometimes referred to as "personnel turbulence,"[5] could upset the established social and disciplinary climate within a unit. Casualties among experienced officers and NCOs were especially detrimental, since these individuals were the ones most responsible for promoting good discipline.

Historian Jean-Pierre Gagnon points out that the 22nd Battalion experienced acute disciplinary problems during periods of extreme personnel turbulence, especially in the aftermath of the Battle of the Somme, when rates of absence and desertion skyrocketed.[6] Increasing incidence of offences likewise occurred in the 19th Battalion when large numbers of reinforcements were absorbed into its ranks. From September through December 1916, the battalion took in between 660 and 712 other ranks and around 28 officers to replace losses suffered at the Somme.[7] During the same period, monthly numbers of minor offences within the 19th Battalion increased steadily from a low of ten in September 1916 to a peak of twenty-four in January 1917 (see Fig. 3). Although the absolute numbers of offences were relatively small, the change between September and January was still noticeable. Offences gradually trailed off again during February and March and then fell abruptly in April 1917, which saw the beginning of heavy fighting in the Vimy Ridge sector. A similar pattern occurred following the arrival of 378 other-rank reinforcements in late May 1917. The number of minor offences rose even more steeply, from a low of six in June to a peak of twenty-six in August, which saw heavy Canadian attacks at Hill 70 and the environs of Lens.[8]

It would be inaccurate, however, to associate acts of indiscipline in the 19th Battalion solely with reinforcement personnel. During 1916 the majority of minor offences were committed by original personnel who had enlisted in the battalion before it departed Canada. Naturally, this was the case because original men still comprised a majority of the battalion's personnel complement. But beginning in August 1916, reinforcement personnel began to marginally outnumber original men in the lists of minor offences appearing in Part II Orders.[9] By the end of the year, the split between original and reinforcement personnel receiving punishment was almost equal. Of a total of 185 19th Battalion men who were punished for minor offences during 1916, 96 were originals while 89 were reinforcements. As the ranks of original men were steadily whittled down during 1917, the vast majority of punishments for minor offences were meted out to men who had joined the battalion in England or France. Of 202 individuals who were convicted of committing minor offences during 1917, 36 were original men, while during 1918 only 10 cases of a total of 121 involved surviving original men.[10] Within the 2nd Canadian Division as a whole, given that many of its original personnel departed their units during and immediately after the Battle of the Somme (owing to death, injury, illness, or transfer), such ratios are not surprising.

Long-serving members of front-line units sometimes found their morale and their nerves so corroded by combat and stress that they were more prone to committing offences. Deward Barnes remembered the breakdown of a comrade who shared an advance post with him:

> May 27, 1917: Very quiet, not a shell coming. On duty from 12.15 a.m. to 2.15 a.m. Shelled for half an hour at about 1:00 a.m. very close too. A shell burst just in front of us and scattered earth over us. Horseman left our post. Our position is forty yards in front of [our] front line, not a healthy place, and a good thing it is quiet. You had to go over land to get to our post and only when it was dark.[11]

Abandoning one's post in the face of the enemy was a very serious offence – serious enough to draw a maximum penalty of death, according to British military law. That Horseman remained with the 19th Battalion and was not officially charged with either leaving his post or cowardice shows that the incident was not reported and that the man regained control of himself in relatively short order. Barnes's matter-of-fact comment on Horseman's act may indicate private sympathy or confidence that the mistake was only a temporary aberration. Horseman's reaction to the nearby exploding shell might well have been a manifestation of what was colloquially known as "shell shock" during the First World War and "battle exhaustion" during the Second World War.[12]

The incidence of shell shock in the 19th Battalion is extremely difficult to determine, owing to a scarcity of references to the condition in the unit's official records. However, those who generated such records may have indulged in some self-censorship, for the British high command, fearing that large numbers of soldiers looking for a quick way out of the strain and carnage of war would feign the condition if the term was legitimimized through regular official use, forbade mention of it starting in late 1916. More obscure-sounding diagnoses such as "neurasthenia" or the judgement "NYD(N)" ("not yet diagnosed [nervous]") were substituted in men's medical records, and patients were left uninformed of their condition until further assessed at special hospitals established to investigate such cases.[13]

Military psychiatry was not yet well developed, and regimental medical officers were under considerable pressure to ferret out malingerers and conserve manpower. Throughout the British armies, "it was almost a matter of chance whether a man with psychiatric illness was considered to be genuinely ill, a malingerer, or even a deserter."[14] Untold cases of psychological trauma may be hidden in numerous notations within 19th Battalion Part II Orders that refer to individual men as being simply "wounded" or "sick." For the CEF as a whole, "about 10,000 soldiers were treated or discharged for psychiatric reasons, about half of them labeled 'nervous.'"[15]

The strain of boredom and uncertainty that characterized much of routine trench warfare, punctuated by briefer periods of absolute chaos and terror during bombardments, battles, raids, or other operations, certainly took its toll on the nerves of countless men who were forced to endure situations unimaginable to any who have not gone through similar experiences. The sights, sounds, and smells of battle and death induced varying degrees of trauma that may have influenced innumerable instances of drunkenness, absence, desertion, disobedience, and other offences. The army, however, was not as concerned with underlying causes or conditions as it was with the actions and intentions of men brought up on charges. This was well illustrated in the handling of cases in which men were charged with wilfully wounding themselves in order to escape further service.

There can be little doubt that mental and emotional breakdown underpinned most incidents of self-inflicted wounds (SIWs). Only the most desperate or despondent men would place the muzzle of a loaded rifle or pistol against their hand, foot, or another body part and pull the trigger. The same was true of those who intentionally sickened themselves by drinking foul water or eating spoiled food.[16] However much one may sympathize with the fear or despair that motivated such acts, the army, at that time, treated self-inflicted injury as a crime to be investigated and, if the suspect was found guilty, punished severely. For senior military officials under constant pressure to conserve badly needed manpower, there seemed to be no alternative treatment for such cases. If one man in a unit were to escape service by intentionally injuring himself, others might do likewise. Therefore, examples had to be set through punishment, even though an accused man might already be suffering from a painful and debilitating wound.

Each suspected SIW case was subject to formal investigation, and it was up to a court martial to determine whether a suspected man's injury was caused by genuine accident, culpable negligence (such as cleaning a rifle before checking to see if it was still loaded), or wilful intent. Trials were held after the men had received medical treatment, with the most serious cases being sent to special segregated field hospitals or wards at base hospitals. Over the course of the war, twelve members of the 19th Battalion were tried for self-inflicted injuries, eleven of whom were found guilty. Two of these convicted men were sentenced to forfeitures of pay, indicating that their acts were comparatively minor. The remaining nine received sentences of FP 1 ranging in length from twenty-one to ninety days.[17]

Other SIW cases in the CEF received sentences of up to two years' imprisonment with hard labour for convicted other ranks, or dismissal from the service for convicted officers. By war's end, there were 582 cases of self-inflicted injury in the CEF in France and Belgium (including four officers), with a monthly average of eleven cases. The 19th Battalion's conviction of eleven men for SIWs was in line with the average number of cases in other front-line infantry units of the Canadian Corps, which stood at ten. Since roughly 5,000 officers and other ranks saw service in the 19th Battalion, this number may seem insignificant. But the importance attached to managing the problems posed by even small numbers of SIWs was by no means underestimated.[18]

Courts Martial

In the 19th Battalion, as in other units, most offenders were tried and summarily sentenced by company or battalion commanders. But serious cases warranting punishments that were beyond the purview of the battalion commander had to be tried by court martial. Under the British military judicial system there were several different types of court martial, each of which differed in its composition and scope of power. Regimental courts martial (RCMs) were the lowest variant and tried other ranks in cases where the offence was comparatively minor yet required punishment beyond the summary powers of the unit commander. The RCM's authority was carefully circumscribed: it could not try officers, and it was not employed on active service overseas. Accordingly, 19th Battalion personnel were subject to RCM only when stationed in Canada. In England, Canadian soldiers were tried by district courts martial (DCMs), which also were limited in their punitive powers. They could not try officers, but they could award sentences of up to two years' imprisonment to other ranks.[19]

The only military courts that had the power to try cases in which the accused might receive a sentence of penal servitude or death were the general courts martial (GCMs) and the field general courts martial (FGCMs).[20] On a GCM, between five and nine officers sat in judgment, and in Canada and England a GCM could try either officers or other ranks. When engaged in operations in France and Belgium,

Table 2
Minor offences, January 1917–December 1918[33]

Battalion	Absence without permission	Drunkenness	Other infractions	Total
19th	140	20	111	271
27th	71	26	145	242
28th	125	36	158	319
29th	149	69	187	405
31st	58	22	76	156

Only in the matter of court martial incidence do we have more comprehensive comparative data with all other battalions in the 2nd Canadian Division (see Table 3).[34]

Table 3
Number of courts martial by year[35]

Battalion	1915	1916	1917	1918	1919	Total
18th	5	16	32	24	8	85
19th	1	6	26	20	2	55
20th	3	7	35	38	8	91
21st	2	26	26	22	9	85
22nd	9	27	80	54	15	185
24th	2	19	29	37	22	109
25th	4	29	25	29	6	93
26th	1	10	26	33	6	76
27th	2	11	14	17	2	46
28th	7	13	19	16	10	65
29th	3	18	23	29	8	81
31st	8	5	8	7	6	34
Total	47	187	343	326	102	1,005

In terms of which units had the fewest courts martial, the 19th Battalion had the third-best record among the battalions of the 2nd Canadian Division. Exactly what this meant in terms of battalion discipline can only be surmised. Perhaps 19th Battalion men actually were better disciplined than those of most other battalions, or maybe the offences they committed tended to be less serious. Possibly their commanding officers simply chose to send fewer cases to trial. Whatever the case may have been, in a very general sense, these numbers do suggest that the 19th Battalion had fewer problems with discipline than most of the other battalions in the division.

One reason for this may have been the quality of leadership exhibited by battalion NCOs, officers, and especially commanding officers. In addition to exhibiting skill and courage in battle and proficiency in administrative matters, officers were supposed to minister to the other ranks' physical well-being and social needs, even before seeing to their own. In return, officers expected their men to show them due deference and obedience. This rather paternalistic dynamic underpinned relations between officers and other ranks in British military tradition and was well described in 1917 by the commander of the New Zealand Division, Maj.-Gen. A.H. Russell. He argued that officers could instill discipline in their troops "both by example and by looking after the men's comfort and food, by insisting on the men taking sufficient rest, by devising means of entertainment and amusement and by looking after their men at all times, but especially when off duty." Russell cautioned that punishment, although necessary, "must not be looked on as a means of prevention. The last resort, it is, after all, a confession of failure on our part to instill the right spirit."[36] To the officers fell the primary responsibility for creating and maintaining discipline, and they were assisted in this vital task by the NCOs. In fulfilling their responsibilities to their men, officers forged a bond of trust, confidence, and loyalty that usually minimized the development of discontent, which in turn might lead to breakdowns in discipline.[37]

Yet even though punishment was widely considered by senior officers to be a "last resort," if an officer, and especially a commanding officer, exhibited weakness in administering punishment, or failed to support and uphold the decisions and verdicts of his subordinate officers and NCOs, then he seriously risked losing their trust and support, without which command and control in the battalion would disintegrate. As W.F. Doolan of the 21st Battalion put it, "if an officer was not a good disciplinarian, he would lose the respect of his men. That is, he would lose the respect of the men who were worthwhile, sure as daylight."[38]

The importance of effective leadership, marked by both paternalistic beneficence and firm resolve, was recognized clearly in the 19th Battalion. According to Lt. Joe O'Neill,

> officers and N.C.O.s who could not handle the discipline in their own unit were considered misfits and very inefficient by their own unit, their own officers, and their own N.C.O.s ... Canadian officers, in general, had another rule that was if you treated men like men then you had men, but if you treated men like dogs well you just had a group of dogs and never no use. But if you treated men as men and that was standard through out the Canadian Corps ... there was an excellent feeling between the various ranks, and that was of great importance. [Still another rule] was never to tell a man or order a man to do anything that you could not or would not do yourself. Now a Canadian is a pretty independent guy, and I have seen cases of that, where ... if you wouldn't do it or couldn't do it yourself, well you were just useless from then on.[39]

Although Lt.-Col. Millen was said to have been a compassionate commander, he was no "soft touch" and did not hesitate to deal out punishment whenever he felt it was warranted, but without any malicious intent.[40] This was in keeping with the disciplinary tone set earlier by Lt.-Col. McLaren, who maintained that "underneath all the military discipline I always realized that I was dealing with men."[41]

As they steadily gained experience, senior officers like McLaren, Millen, and Maj. Hatch, along with their subordinate officers, got to know the men under their command and to recognize the most effective ways of keeping them in line without antagonizing them. Officers quickly learned that leading men required tact, finesse, and solid knowledge of what motivated them on an individual basis. As Joe O'Neill recalled, "above all things, it was up to that officer to know the men personally, and know that … one man would react to kindness and another man you had to crowd a bit and so on."[42] A good example of an officer who understood this principle was Lt. H.M. Harman, who demonstrated considerable skill in handling a difficult situation during the horrible fight at Fresnoy in May 1917. At one point Harman ordered a corporal and six men to go out under heavy fire and retrieve wounded comrades. One of the men was Pte. Deward Barnes, who was decidedly reluctant to obey. "He detailed me and I would not go," admitted Barnes.

> I told him I was a [Lewis] gunner and was not to leave my post (that was before I noticed who he was) and that was our training – which was all bosh. He sent me to get the Sergeant-Major, who was down a big dug-out. I got him and he told the Sergeant-Major that I was to go and lead the six men over the barricade and up to these wounded men. When I knew I had to go I was satisfied. I knew it was war and I never shirked once in any duty. It was about seven o'clock and he could see I was all in, but I had to go.[43]

According to Barnes's biographer, historian Bruce Cane,

> what Deward was experiencing was not cowardice, nor was it shirking, as he is afraid we will conclude. Rather, we are seeing a man on the brink of physical and emotional exhaustion … He had not slept in the previous thirty-six hours; he had marched more than six miles (ten kilometres) in a gas cloud over broken, soggy ground and under a ponderous load; he had fought in a desperate and confusing battle; experienced mass killing for the first time; prepared himself for death several times over; and had seen at least four of his closest comrades become casualties beside him in a matter of hours … To Harman's credit upon hearing Deward's reply to his order, he sent Deward to fetch the sergeant major (the most senior disciplinarian in the battalion), allowing Deward time to compose himself and consider the serious consequences of refusing an order. Harman's plan succeeded, and when Deward returned, with the sergeant major in tow, he realized that, despite being "all in," he must go.[44]

Officers adept at handling situations such as this exhibited leadership of the highest order and were instrumental in nipping potential disciplinary cases in the bud. Pte. Barnes was therefore spared from suffering the potential consequences of his momentary (and quite understandable) lapse and went on to become an outstanding soldier and leader in his own right.

Experience and effectiveness in leadership seems to have been the key component in keeping incidence of indiscipline to a minimum and probably accounts for the overall downturn in numbers of offences as the war progressed – even in the face of increasingly heavy operations and periodic bursts of extreme personnel turbulence. Skilled senior officers, who understood their own jobs, as well as those of their subordinates, were not as likely to put up with acts of indiscipline as less experienced or less confident men. Seasoned battalion commanders well knew the traditions and social customs of their units, along with the personalities and habits of many of the men they led. This knowledge underpinned a commander's success in taking care of his men's comfort and preserving what was best in his unit's culture. It also helped him recognize the best ways to deal with men whenever they found themselves in breach of military law. An officer had to know and understand the men he commanded in order to extract the best possible performance from them.[45]

After the Armistice took effect on 11 November 1918, there would be brief upsurges in the incidence of minor offences within the 19th Battalion. This likely stemmed from the relaxation of previous disciplinary standards, combined with the restlessness of men anxious to return home. But the numbers of men punished remained low, and battalion discipline in the post-armistice period did not pose any serious problems. Through the quality of their leadership, Lt.-Col. Millen, his officers, and the NCOs were able to maintain the high standard of discipline displayed by the 19th Battalion through the worst periods of the war.

Figure 1

Common Punishments for Minor Offences: 19th Battalion, 1915–1919

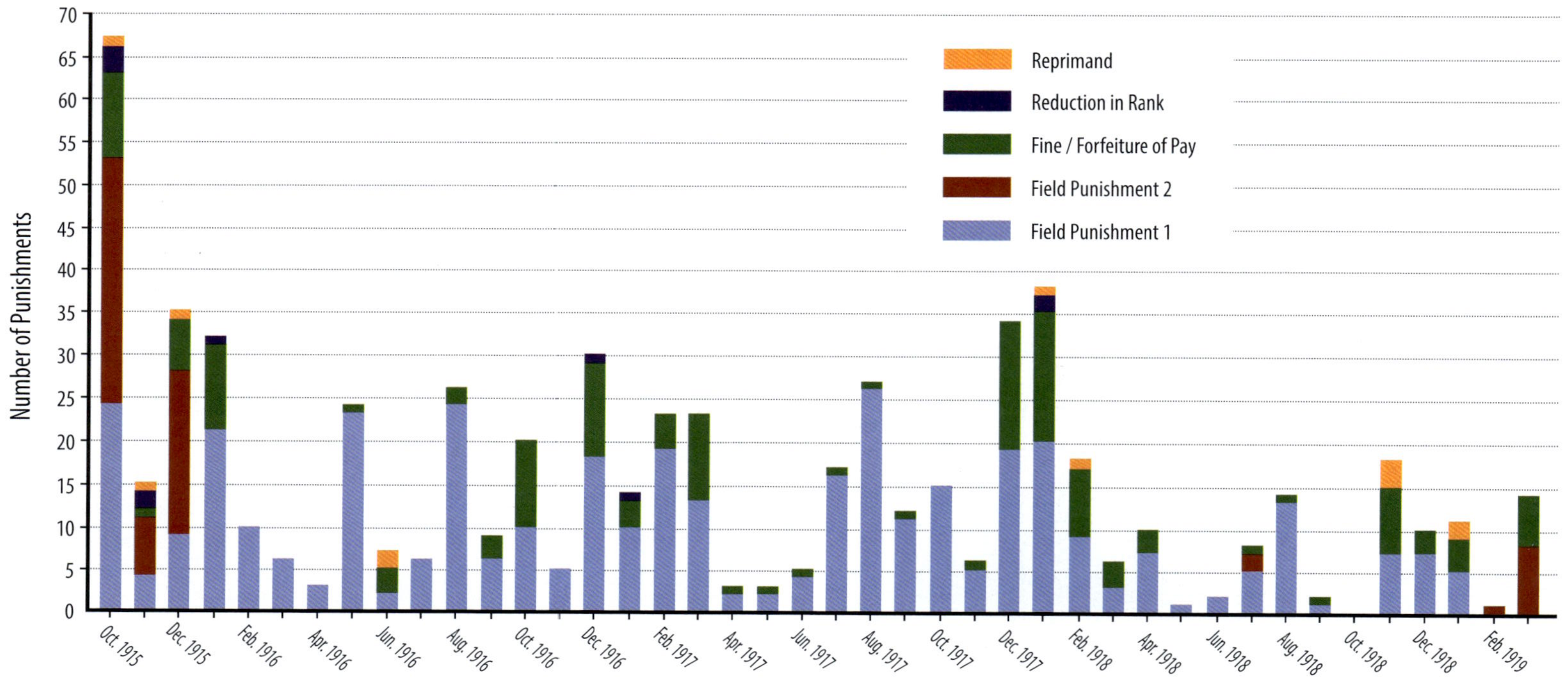

These numbers do not include punishments awarded to 19th Battalion personnel temporarily attached to other commands.
Source: NAC, RG 150, Series 1, Vol. 71, Files "19th Battalion (parts 1–5)," Part II Daily Orders, 1915–1919

Figure 2
Minor Offences: Numbers and Types of Charges, 19th Battalion, 1915–1919

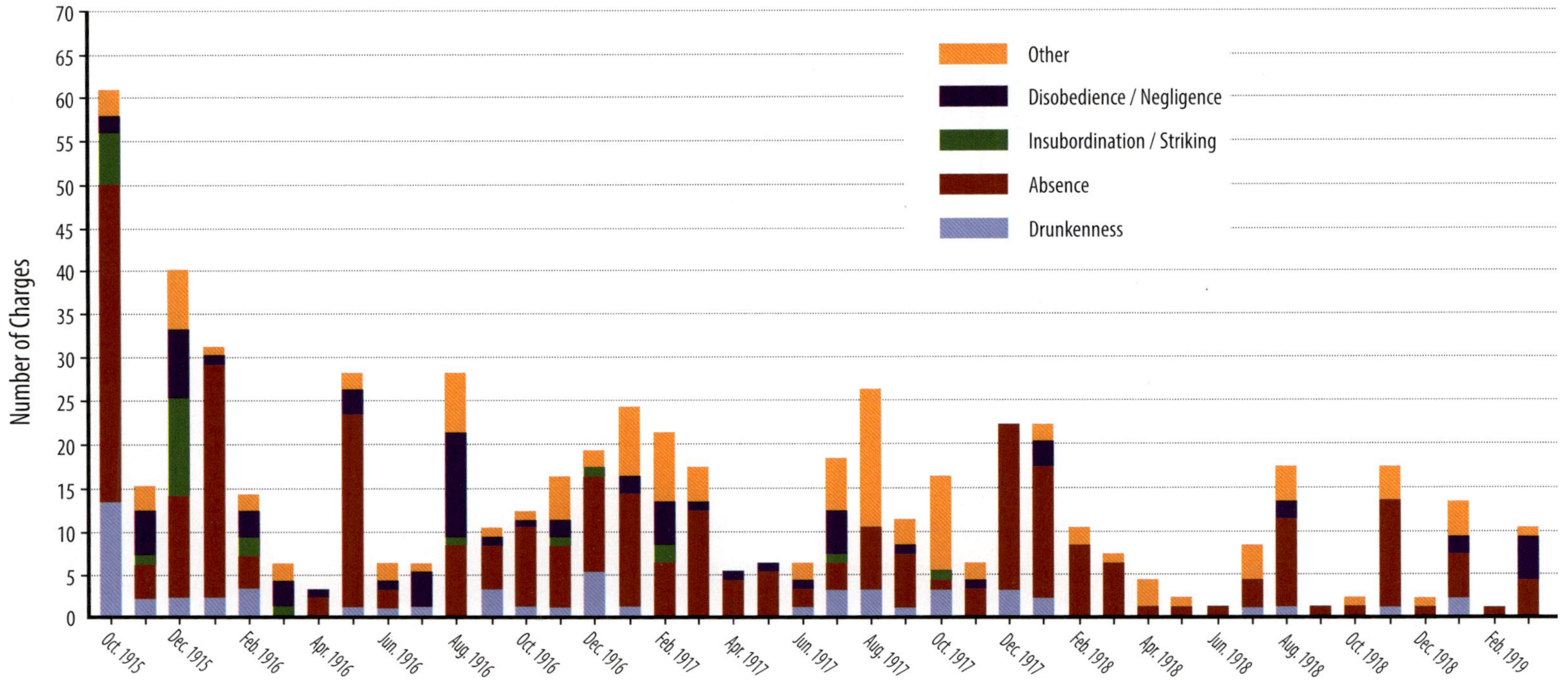

These numbers do not include charges against 19th Battalion personnel temporarily attached to other commands)
Source: NAC, RG 150, Series 1, Vol. 71, Files "19th Battalion (parts 1–5)," Part II Daily Orders, 1915–1919

Figure 3

Minor Offences: Total Charges by Month, 19th Battalion Personnel, 1915–1919

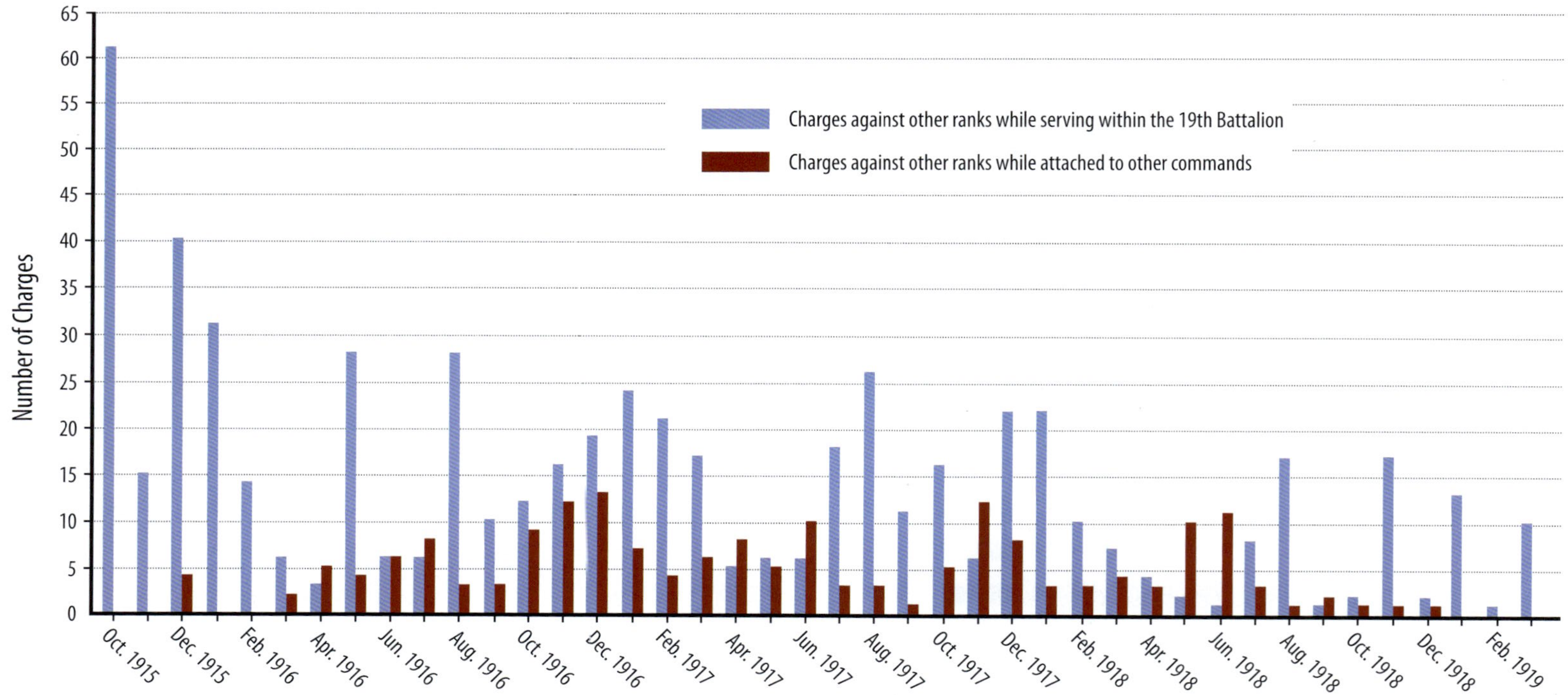

Source: NAC, RG 150, Series 1, Vol. 71, Files "19th Battalion (parts 1–5)," Part II Daily Orders, 1915–1919

Appendix C

Commanding Officers, 19th Battalion 1914–1919*

Lt.-Col. John I. McLaren	6 November 1914** to 18 July 1916
Lt.-Col. William R. Turnbull	18 July 1916 to 18 December 1916
Lt.-Col. Lionel H. Millen	18 December 1916 to 15 February 1918
Lt.-Col. (Acting) Harry C. Hatch	15 February 1918 to 22 June 1918
Lt.-Col. Lionel H. Millen	22 June 1918 to Demobilization

* This list does not include officers who periodically held temporary command of the battalion. The names of these officers, and the periods in which they held temporary command, are detailed in the text of the battalion history.

** Date of initial concentration of battalion personnel in Toronto. McLaren received his appointment to command the battalion on 20 October 1914. LAC, RG 9, III-D-1, Vol. 4692, Folder 51, File 11, "19th Canadian Battalion, Digest of Service."

Appendix D

Honours and Awards*

Bar to the Distinguished Service Order

Millen, Lt.-Col. L.H.

Distinguished Service Order

Bliss, Capt. R.H.
Burnham, Maj. S.S.
Fearman, Maj. H.D.
Hatch, Maj. H.C.
Kilmer, Capt. C.E.
Lindsay, Maj. C.B.
Millen, Lt.-Col. L.H.
Morrison, Lt.-Col. G.F.

Bar to the Military Cross

Saunders, Maj. R.P.
Shiell, Capt. R.
Trendell, Lt. E.A.
Waldrum, Lt. W.

* This list is based primarily on one that appears in the March 1919 war diary of the 19th Battalion. See LAC RG 9, III-D-3, Vol. 4930, War Diary, 19th Battalion, March 1919, diary text. Names were not listed alphabetically in the war diary, but they are listed alphabetically here to facilitate easier reference to individuals. In some cases, where the same name appears in the war diary list more than once (under different awards), and when such instances list that individual with different ranks, it is presumed that the rank in each case was the one held at the time that the award was given. As well, a number of additions and corrections to this list were made on the basis of information contained in Part II Orders. See LAC, RG 150, Series 1, Vol. 71, Files "19th Battalion (parts 1–5)," Part II Daily Orders, 1915–1920.

Military Cross

Allison, Capt. H.C., CAMC
Applegath, Lt. G.H.
Bell, Lt. A.G.
Bennett, 55752 RSM S.J.
Bennett, Lt. J.M.
Bradfield, Lt. G.M.
Cantlon, Lt. F.H.
Carmichael, Lt. C.
Catto, Capt. R.W.
Crombie, Lt. V.R.A.
Derbyshire, Lt. F.W.
Dinsmore, Lt. R.H.L.
Dunn, Lt. O.S.
Fitzgerald, Lt. J.P.
Gidley, Capt. W.G.
Greisenger, Capt. W.
Harstone, Capt. J.A.
Herbert, Lt. W.S.
Hooper, Lt. B.O.
Linton, Lt. J.A.
Lowe, Lt. H.A.
McDonald, Rev. (H. Capt.) E.J.
McLaren, Lt. J.A.
O'Neill, Lt. J.
Pepler, Lt. H.B.
Roberts, Capt. M.C.
Rogers, Capt. W.T.
Saunders, Capt. R.P.
Shiell, Capt. R.
Sinclair, Capt. C.E.
Smith, Lt. W.F.
Spendlove, Lt. A.E.
Spreckley, Lt. R.O.
Stuart, Lt. H.
Thompson, Lt. A.O.
Trendell, Lt. E.A.
Waldrum, Lt. W.
Weir, Capt. J.G.
Wittemore, Capt. W.L., CAMC

Bar to the Distinguished Conduct Medal

Thomas, 55723 CSM J.E.

Distinguished Conduct Medal

Cole, 55806 Sgt. S.F.
Craig, 799377 Cpl. A.
Dewar, 55821 CSM H.
Dumeresque, 416275 Cpl. J.
Dyball, 55414 CSM W.T.
Grayson, 799103 Pte. P.S.T.
Hollidge, 745086 Sgt. R.
Hutchinson, 55636 Pte. J.
Jackson, 55763 Sgt. L.
Jones, 213585 Sgt. G.
Jubin, 120814 Sgt. C.
Laing, 55540 CSM P.J.
Newton, 55914 Pte. J.
Ridley, 55696 CSM S.
Schwan, 407086 Pte. E.D.
Smith, 55710 Cpl. W.R.
Squibb, 55941 CSM W.J.
Thomas, 55723 CSM J.E.
Wilson, 55955 Pte. W.

Bar to the Military Medal

Bovineau, 210132 Sgt. L.
Clendining, 55394 Sgt. H.
Coomber, 757033 Sgt. J.
Flett, 853129 Cpl. C.J.
Graham, 55557 Sgt. D.
Heyburn, 55999 Cpl. W.T.
Hilborn, 862192 Cpl. F.L.
Jarvis, 56060 Sgt. J.H.
Newell, 55261 Sgt. S.
Robertson, 757420 Pte. J.
Thatcher, 402846 Pte. T.W.
Tousignant, 213453 Cpl. A.
Walley, 55956 Sgt. G.

Military Medal

Anderson, 273679 Pte. J.M.
Annand, 55359 Sgt. G.
Arbour, 644635 Pte. W.H.
Bacon, 408737 Pte. L.
Barber, 210097 Pte. B.W.
Barnes, 55152 Lance Cpl. J.
Barry, 853164 Pte. A.E.
Barter, 799268 Pte. C.W.
Bartlett, 642800 Lance Cpl. J.
Bash, 214298 Pte. H.R. D
Bate, 55146 Pte. E.J.
Bates, 699721 Cpl. T.J.
Beck, 213900 Pte. R.
Bernard, 55350 Lance Sgt. J.W.
Bickerstaff, 408750 Pte. H.W.
Black, 745019 Lance Cpl. J.C.
Blackie, 748000 Pte. W.
Blunt, 55787 Lance Cpl. R.
Bombard, 135643 Cpl. H.A.
Bourque, 814437 Pte. A.
Bovineau, 210132 Pte. L.
Brailsford, 210238 Pte. H.S.
Brisbin, 55162 Cpl. H.V.
Brooks, 121480 Pte. J.

on the home front, for services not in the face of the enemy and for services whilst prisoners of war. These were what came to be called 'A List' and was equivalent in all respects to a mention in despatches and the people on this list had their names published in the *London Gazette*." Edward H. Wigney, *Mentioned in Despatches of the Canadian Expeditionary Force including Names Brought to Notice to the Secretary of State for War A and B Lists* (Nepean, Ont.: Edward H. Wigney, 2000), v.

All four names appearing under the "Mentions" heading in the 19th Battalion war diary's list of awards are also found in Wigney's published list of Canadians who were mentioned in despatches or who appeared on this "A List." They are also listed in the *London Gazette*, 31089, 27 December 1918, page 15221. Because the two awards were considered equivalent, neither Wigney nor the *London Gazette* appear to distinguish those who were mentioned in despatches from those included on the "A List." On the basis of their separate listing under the "Mentions" heading in the war diary, it is my own presumption that the four individuals noted under that heading were among the "A List" personnel. My thanks to Col. John Boileau and to Chris McCreery for assistance in investigating this question.

Military Cross

Allison, Capt. H.C., CAMC
Applegath, Lt. G.H.
Bell, Lt. A.G.
Bennett, 55752 RSM S.J.
Bennett, Lt. J.M.
Bradfield, Lt. G.M.
Cantlon, Lt. F.H.
Carmichael, Lt. C.
Catto, Capt. R.W.
Crombie, Lt. V.R.A.
Derbyshire, Lt. F.W.
Dinsmore, Lt. R.H.L.
Dunn, Lt. O.S.
Fitzgerald, Lt. J.P.
Gidley, Capt. W.G.
Greisenger, Capt. W.
Harstone, Capt. J.A.
Herbert, Lt. W.S.
Hooper, Lt. B.O.
Linton, Lt. J.A.
Lowe, Lt. H.A.
McDonald, Rev. (H. Capt.) E.J.
McLaren, Lt. J.A.
O'Neill, Lt. J.
Pepler, Lt. H.B.
Roberts, Capt. M.C.
Rogers, Capt. W.T.
Saunders, Capt. R.P.
Shiell, Capt. R.
Sinclair, Capt. C.E.
Smith, Lt. W.F.
Spendlove, Lt. A.E.
Spreckley, Lt. R.O.
Stuart, Lt. H.
Thompson, Lt. A.O.
Trendell, Lt. E.A.
Waldrum, Lt. W.
Weir, Capt. J.G.
Wittemore, Capt. W.L., CAMC

Bar to the Distinguished Conduct Medal

Thomas, 55723 CSM J.E.

Distinguished Conduct Medal

Cole, 55806 Sgt. S.F.
Craig, 799377 Cpl. A.
Dewar, 55821 CSM H.
Dumeresque, 416275 Cpl. J.
Dyball, 55414 CSM W.T.
Grayson, 799103 Pte. P.S.T.
Hollidge, 745086 Sgt. R.
Hutchinson, 55636 Pte. J.
Jackson, 55763 Sgt. L.
Jones, 213585 Sgt. G.
Jubin, 120814 Sgt. C.
Laing, 55540 CSM P.J.
Newton, 55914 Pte. J.
Ridley, 55696 CSM S.
Schwan, 407086 Pte. E.D.
Smith, 55710 Cpl. W.R.
Squibb, 55941 CSM W.J.
Thomas, 55723 CSM J.E.
Wilson, 55955 Pte. W.

Bar to the Military Medal

Bovineau, 210132 Sgt. L.
Clendining, 55394 Sgt. H.
Coomber, 757033 Sgt. J.
Flett, 853129 Cpl. C.J.
Graham, 55557 Sgt. D.
Heyburn, 55999 Cpl. W.T.
Hilborn, 862192 Cpl. F.L.
Jarvis, 56060 Sgt. J.H.
Newell, 55261 Sgt. S.
Robertson, 757420 Pte. J.
Thatcher, 402846 Pte. T.W.
Tousignant, 213453 Cpl. A.
Walley, 55956 Sgt. G.

Military Medal

Anderson, 273679 Pte. J.M.
Annand, 55359 Sgt. G.
Arbour, 644635 Pte. W.H.
Bacon, 408737 Pte. L.
Barber, 210097 Pte. B.W.
Barnes, 55152 Lance Cpl. J.
Barry, 853164 Pte. A.E.
Barter, 799268 Pte. C.W.
Bartlett, 642800 Lance Cpl. J.
Bash, 214298 Pte. H.R. D
Bate, 55146 Pte. E.J.
Bates, 699721 Cpl. T.J.
Beck, 213900 Pte. R.
Bernard, 55350 Lance Sgt. J.W.
Bickerstaff, 408750 Pte. H.W.
Black, 745019 Lance Cpl. J.C.
Blackie, 748000 Pte. W.
Blunt, 55787 Lance Cpl. R.
Bombard, 135643 Cpl. H.A.
Bourque, 814437 Pte. A.
Bovineau, 210132 Pte. L.
Brailsford, 210238 Pte. H.S.
Brisbin, 55162 Cpl. H.V.
Brooks, 121480 Pte. J.

Military Medal (continued)

Brown, 56142 Pte. J.H.F.
Burnett, 55797 Sgt. R.
Burns, 55783 Pte. J.
Burton, 55793 Lance Cpl. J.
Cassidy, 214183 Pte. W.B.
Chatterton, 56151 Cpl. T.M.
Clarke, 862230 Pte. J.
Clendining, 55394 Sgt. H.
Cochrane, 192469 Cpl. J.B.
Coomber, 757033 Pte. J.
Cooper, 55175 Cpl. S.
Corris, 210219 Sgt. L.W.
Cowan, 211275 LCpl. J.M.
Cox, 55167 Sgt. A.H.
Cura, 214024 Pte. E.D.
Curbishley, 55813 Sgt. A.
Dalton, 3033435 Pte. G.D.
Davis, 767011 Pte. J.
Dewar, 55821 Sgt. H.
Dibble, 862186 Lance Cpl. H.
Dinner, 91539 Pte. F.C.
Dinsmore, 55407 Cpl. R.H.L.
Dove, 745286 Pte. A.E.
Dunnigan, 55603 Sgt. A.
(aka A. Dumigan)
Dyball, 55414 CSM W.T.
Falconer, 55420 Pte. A.
Finch, 757689 LSgt. R.A.
Finlayson, 799102 Pte. W.
Fitzgerald, 55551 Cpl. W.A.
Fleming, 853639 Pte. R.
Flett, 853129 Lance Cpl. C.J.
Ford, 745240 Pte. M.R.
Forrest, 745045 Pte. J.S.
Gaetz, 183711 Cpl. J.R.
Gagnon, 853255 Pte. E.
Gates, 757530 Pte. H.J.
Goodfellow, 55205 Pte. L.M.
Gore, 1027442 Sgt. J.
Gould, 1083104 Pte. P.J.L.
Gow, 408940 Pte. A.
Gower, 141329 Sgt. O.
Graham, 55557 Cpl. D.
Gray, 120399 Pte. O.
Habick, 803177 Pte. J.
Hall, 1063069 Pte. W.H.
Hall, 213250 Lance Cpl. L.
Harding, 55103 Cpl. R.G., CAMC
Harkness, 214135 LCpl. R.C.
Harlock, 55436 Lance Cpl. N.
Harold, 862297 Pte. E.M.
Harris, 124364 Pte. G.C.
Hart, 800152 Pte. S.H.
Hawker, 800025 Cpl. W.T.
Hayden, 55858 Sgt. B.
Healey, 925376 Pte. J.
Henderson, 228365 Pte. R.D.
Heyburn, 55999 Sgt. W.T.
Hilborn, 862192 Cpl. F.L.
Hobson, 405304 Pte. W.
Holk, 55766 Sgt. J.R.
Hollidge, 745086 Cpl. R.
Holtum, 55444 Pte. W.C.
Jarvis, 56060 Sgt. J.H.
Jones, 213585 Pte. G.
Kelly, 766412 Pte. A.
Kirk, 643370 Pte. D.H.
Klinck, 766236 Pte. N.R.
Laidlaw, 127464 Pte. R.J.
Landon, 157061 Pte. C.J.
Lang, 174322 Cpl. A.L.
Lasenby, 412494 LCpl. C.R.
Ling, 135776 Pte. W.
Lister, 758037 Cpl. J.
Lynch, 55088 Cpl. A.F.
Mabley, 213649 Cpl. W.J.
MacDonald, 657446 Pte. J.A.
MacFarlane, 55906 Cpl. R.
MacKenzie, 55252 Cpl. D.R.
Mackenzie, 56183 Sgt. R.
Mackintosh, 55109 Sgt. W.H.
McAuliffe, 214376 Cpl. W.
McGhee, 213550 Pte. H.
McKay, 408828 Sgt. I.
McLean, 55484 Pte. H.C.
McLellan, 193448 Pte. J.
McNulty, 757699 Pte. F.J.
Miller, 1006354 Pte. R.
Neilson, 55915 Lance Cpl. J.
Nichol, 799710 Pte. J.V.
O'Connell, 799068 LSgt. R.W.
O'Connor, 214282 Pte. J.P.
Pace, 406603 Pte. W.H.
Peddie, 745152 Pte. T.
Poynter, 55693 Sgt. C.R.
Price, 213145 Pte. J.
Pritchard, 657263 Cpl. M.W.
Pronouyh, 814969 Pte. A.
Quinn, 657740 Pte. C.
Ratcliffe, 55692 Pte. R.
Reid, 799571 Pte. W.
Reynolds, 55558 Sgt. J.
Richings, 55281 Sgt. G.
Richmond, 868208 Pte. H.H.
Riley, 799024 Sgt. H.
Robertson, 757420 Pte. J.
(aka F. Presnail)
Robinson, 405405 Cpl. J.H.
Robinson, 55048 Sgt. W.
Robinson, 55501 Sgt. S.H.
Rolland, 55326 Sgt. D.C.
Rootes, 195295 Pte. S.H.
Rose, 405109 Pte. F.
Routley, 56023 Pte. A.P.
Rowe, 228258 Pte. F.W.
Rule, 55500 Pte. C.J.
Scott, 408950 Pte. G.W.
Scott, 55936 Lance Cpl. W.C.
Scott, 56114 Sgt. G.
Serridge, 406619 Pte. J.
Shakell, 644841 Pte. G.
Shaw, 210866 Pte. F.
Shields, 55507 Lance Cpl. J.
Simcoe, 643967 Pte. B.
Simmons, 799732 Pte. E.A.
Simms, 657198 Lance Cpl. F.
Somerville, 642212 Pte. W.
Standish, 55711 Cpl. C.C.
Stephens, 800072 Pte. J.
Stewart, 56083Sgt. A.
Stitt, 55286 Cpl. F.
Strachan, 737011 Pte. R.
Summers, 401575 Lance Cpl. J.
Tapp, 56116 LSgt. W.
Tarr, 55521 Sgt. F.E.

Teale, 55519 Sgt. R.
Thatcher, 402848 Cpl. T.W.
Thompson, 799676 Pte. S.
Thomson, 56040 Cpl. D.
Thomson, 56065 Pte. T.C.
Thorn, 745209 Cpl. F.G.
Tousignant , 213453 Cpl. A.
Trendell, 55944 Sgt. E.A.
Venn, 55734 Sgt. W.P.
Walley, 55956 Sgt. G.
Wardlaw, 55313 LCpl. J.M.
Watson, 56048 Pte. A.B.
Webster, 56049 Pte. W.
Welsh, 228339 Cpl. W.F.
Wheadon, 55316 Pte. N.A.
White, 56051 Lance Cpl. T.J.
White, 757223 Pte. E.E.
Whittaker, 55051 LCpl. L.H.
Wilding, 767113 Pte. F.H.
Willan, 214211 Pte. R.H.
Willoughby, 56068 Sgt. F.
Wilson, 214297 Cpl. H.A.
Windover, 195402 Pte. J.
Windsor, 758038 LSgt. C.
Wright, 799912 Pte. V.J.
Young, 195554 Sgt. H.W.

Meritorious Service Medal

Bellgowan, 55012 Sgt. G.
Brown, 55577 Sgt. E.W.
Ferrell, 55351 Pte. G.C.
Griffiths, 56130 Pte. W.H.T.
Seymour, 55510 Sgt. J.J.
White, 55356 Cpl. J.A.

Montenegro Silver Medal

Newton, 55914 Pte. J.
Wilson, 55955 Pte. W.

Belgian Croix de Guerre

Currell, 55170 Pte. A.V.
Marshall, 55004 Sgt. W.F.

French Croix de Guerre

Ellis, Capt. A.W.
Milam, 120688 Pte. J.H.
Forteath, 799931 Sgt. S.

Mentioned in Despatches

Bernard, 55350 Cpl. J.W.
Bliss, Capt. R.H. (twice)
Bone, 907069 Pte. E.R.
Brown, 55577 Sgt. E.W.
Burnham, Maj. S.S. (twice)
Clendining, 55394 Sgt. H.
Dolman, 157122 Sgt. H.E.
Fearman, Maj. H.D.
Glen, 799429 Acting Sgt. C.E.
Hatch, Maj. H.C. (3 times)
Hooper, Capt. B.O.
Jones, 767143 A/RQMS H.B.
Kershaw, 55041 Cpl. H.
Kilmer, Capt. C.E.
Lindsay, Maj. C.B.
Marshall, 55004 Sgt. W.F.
McLaren, Lt.-Col. J.I.
Millen, Lt.-Col. L.H. (4 times)
Mitchell, 55900 Lance Cpl. G.
Morrison, Lt.-Col. G.F. (twice)
Trendell, 55944 Pte. E.A.
Turnbull, Lt.-Col. W.R.
Venn, 55734 Sgt. W.P.

Mentions**

McLoughlin, 214191 Sgt. C.
Robertson, Lt. V.K.
Saunders, Maj. R.P.
Sayer, Lt. G.

** The category termed "Mentions" appears at the end of the list in the battalion war diary. This most likely refers to personnel who were brought to the notice of the Secretary of State for War "for distinguished service in connection with the war." This was a new type of award initiated in January 1917. As described by historian Edward Wigney, it was awarded "generally for services on the home front, for services not in the face of the enemy and for services whilst prisoners of war. These were what came to be called 'A List' and was equivalent in all respects to a mention in despatches and the people on this list had their names published in the *London Gazette*." Edward H. Wigney, *Mentioned in Despatches of the Canadian Expeditionary Force including Names Brought to Notice to the Secretary of State for War A and B Lists* (Nepean, Ont.: Edward H. Wigney, 2000), v.

All four names appearing under the "Mentions" heading in the 19th Battalion war diary's list of awards are also found in Wigney's published list of Canadians who were mentioned in despatches or who appeared on this "A List." They are also listed in the *London Gazette*, 31089, 27 December 1918, page 15221. Because the two awards were considered equivalent, neither Wigney nor the *London Gazette* appear to distinguish those who were mentioned in despatches from those included on the "A List." On the basis of their separate listing under the "Mentions" heading in the war diary, it is my own presumption that the four individuals noted under that heading were among the "A List" personnel. My thanks to Col. John Boileau and to Chris McCreery for assistance in investigating this question.

Notes

Chapter 1 – Recruiting and Mobilization: 1914–15

1 For recent analyses of the war's outbreak, see Margaret MacMillan, *The War That Ended Peace: The Road to War, 1914* (Toronto: Allen Lane, 2013); Gordon Martel, *The Month That Changed the World, July 1914* (Oxford: Oxford University Press, 2014); and T.G. Otte, *July Crisis: The World's Descent into War, Summer 1914* (Cambridge: Cambridge University Press, 2014).

2 Desmond Morton and J.L. Granatstein, *Marching to Armageddon: Canadians and the Great War, 1914–1919* (Toronto: Lester and Orpen Dennys, 1989), 2; Barbara M. Wilson, ed., *Ontario and the First World War, 1914–1918: A Collection of Documents* (Toronto: Champlain Society, 1977), xxi; D.J. Goodspeed, *The Road Past Vimy: The Canadian Corps, 1914–1918* (Toronto: Macmillan, 1969), 3; Brian Douglas Tennyson, *Canada's Great War, 1914–1918: How Canada Helped Save the British Empire and Became a North American Nation* (Lanham: Rowman and Littlefield, 2015), 1–2.

3 Ronald Haycock, *Sam Hughes: The Public Career of a Controversial Canadian, 1885–1916*, Canadian War Museum Historical Publication no. 21 (Waterloo: Wilfrid Laurier University Press 1986), 124, 178, 180. See also Tim Cook, *The Madman and the Butcher: The Sensational Wars of Sam Hughes and General Arthur Currie* (Toronto: Allan Lane Canada, 2010).

4 In Canada the militia myth derived in part from the mistaken belief that Loyalist militiamen had played the primary role in saving the Canadas from American invasion during the War of 1812. In fact, that role had been played by officers and men of the British regular army and by warriors of allied First Nations. The militia myth fuelled the belief that well-armed and motivated volunteers made inherently better soldiers than long-serving professionals. David J. Bercuson and J.L. Granatstein, eds., *Dictionary of Canadian Military History* (Toronto: Oxford University Press 1992), 133; James Wood, *Militia Myths: Ideas of the Canadian Citizen Soldier, 1896–1921* (Vancouver: UBC Press, 2010), 24–26.

5 In military organization, the term "establishment" refers to the officially constituted strength and organization of a formation or unit of troops.

6 G.W.L. Nicholson, *Canadian Expeditionary Force, 1914–1919: The Official History of the Canadian Army in the First World War* (Ottawa: Queen's Printer, 1962), 12.

7 Ibid., 12.

8 Haycock, *Sam Hughes*, 181. The legal status of the putative expeditionary force was still debatable, even in 1914. The confusion was based on the status of the Canadian militia as set out in

section 69 of the Militia Act of 1904. See A.F. Duguid, *Official History of the Canadian Forces in the Great War 1914–1919, General Series*, vol. 1: *Chronicle: August 1914–September 1915* (Ottawa: King's Printer, 1938), 25; Desmond Morton, "Exerting Control: The Development of Canadian Authority over the Canadian Expeditionary Force, 1914–1919," in *Men at War: Politics, Technology, and Innovation in the Twentieth Century*, ed. Timothy Travers and Christon Archer (Chicago: Precedent, 1982), 9; Duguid, *Official History*, vol. 1, appendix 8; Richard A. Preston, *Canada and "Imperial Defence"* (Durham: Duke University Press, 1967), Ch. 15; Desmond Morton, *A Peculiar Kind of Politics: Canada's Overseas Ministry in the First World War* (Toronto: University of Toronto Press, 1982).

9 Qtd. in Stephen J. Harris, *Canadian Brass: The Making of a Professional Army, 1860–1939* (Toronto: University of Toronto Press, 1988), 92.

10 Divisional headquarters were established at London (1st Division), Toronto (2nd Division), Kingston (3rd Division), Montreal (4th Division), Quebec City (5th Division), and Halifax (6th Division). Western Canada was divided into three numbered Military Districts with headquarters in Winnipeg (no. 10), Victoria (no. 11), and Calgary (no. 13). Canada, House of Commons, Sessional Papers, 1913, no. 35, Report of the Militia Council for the Fiscal Year Ending March 31, 1912, 16.

11 Paul J. Maroney, "Recruiting the Canadian Expeditionary Force in Ontario, 1914–1917," MA thesis, Queen's University 1991, 14–16; Harris, *Canadian Brass*, 94–95. See also Daniel G. Dancocks, *Welcome to Flanders Fields: The First Canadian Battle of the Great War, Ypres, 1915* (Toronto: McClelland and Stewart, 1989), Chs. 2 and 3; and Nicholson, *Canadian Expeditionary Force*, 21–4, 39.

12 Duguid, *Official History*. vol. 1, appendix 133, "First Canadian Contingent – Detail of Units in Vessels," 118; Nicholson, *Canadian Expeditionary Force*, 29–30.

13 The established strength of the 1st Canadian Division on 10 February 1915 was 17,873. Along with accompanying Line of Communication units, this brought the total force up to 18,636, all ranks. Duguid, *Official History*, vol. 1, appendix 226, 158.

14 F.W. Perry, *The Commonwealth Armies: Manpower and Organisation in Two World Wars* (Manchester: Manchester University Press, 1988), 129–30. For analyses of the training and battlefield performance of the 1st Canadian Division in 1914 and 1915, see Andrew *Iarocci, Shoestring Soldiers: The 1st Canadian Division at War, 1914–1915* (Toronto: University of Toronto Press, 2008); Kenneth Radley, *We Lead Others Follow: First Canadian Division, 1914–1918* (St. Catharines: Vanwell, 2006); and Tim Cook, *At the Sharp End: Canadians Fighting the Great War, 1914–1916* (Toronto: Viking Canada, 2007), Chs. 2–22.

15 Nicholson, *Canadian Expeditionary Force*, 109.

16 Mobilization of the contingent was officially proclaimed by an order-in-council on 7 November. LAC, RG 24, C-6-e, vol. 1812, file G.A.Q. 4–1, "2nd Canadian Division," P.C. 2831, 7 November 1914.

17 Duguid, *Official History*, vol. 1, 424–25. For CEF recruiting, see David Campbell, "'The First 100,000 Came Easily': Recruiting the Canadian Expeditionary Force in the First World War," *Revue Internationale d'Histoire Militaire* 86 (2006): 62–87; and Richard Holt, "Filling the Ranks: Recruiting, Training, and Reinforcements in the Canadian Expeditionary Force, 1914–1919," PhD diss., University of Western Ontario, 2011.

18 George F.G. Stanley, *Canada's Soldiers: The Military History of an Unmilitary People*, 3rd ed. (Toronto: Macmillan, 1974), 308–9; Dancocks, *Welcome to Flanders Fields*, 44–45; Haycock, *Sam Hughes*, 178–79; Harris, *Canadian Brass*, 93–94.

19 Morton, *A Peculiar Kind of Politics*, 29; Nicholson, *Canadian Expeditionary Force*, 109.

20 LAC, RG 9, III-D-1, vol. 4692, folder 51, file 11, "19th Canadian Battalion, Digest of Service."

21 "McLaren, John Inglis," in Thomas Melville Bailey, ed., *Dictionary of Hamilton Biography*, vol. 4, 1940–70 (Hamilton: Dictionary of Hamilton Biography, 1999), 176. When it was authorized on 1 September 1903, the regiment was known simply as the 91st Highlanders. The official redesignation to "91st Regiment Canadian Highlanders" came on 2 July 1904. Directorate of History and Heritage (DHH), Department of National Defence, Kardex 145.2A3 (D1), "The Argyll and

Sutherland Highlanders of Canada (Princess Louise's), R.C.I.C. Organization, Perpetuations and Battle Honours."

22 Canadian War Museum (CWM), 19740071–017 58C 1 1.8, untitled file of letters, questionnaires, responses, and notes regarding 19th Battalion history and McLaren's background.

23 "McLaren, John Inglis," in Bailey, ed., *Dictionary of Hamilton Biography*, vol. 4, 176.

24 LAC, RG 150, 1992–93/166, box 7017–19, Personnel File, Lt.-Col. John Inglis McLaren.

25 This also was shown in Hughes's appointment of Arthur Currie to command the 2nd Infantry Brigade in the First Canadian Contingent. Currie, who would rise to command the 1st Canadian Division and later the Canadian Corps, was a known supporter of the Liberal Party.

26 Walter H. Bruce et al., *Historical Records of the Argyll and Sutherland Highlanders of Canada (Princess Louise's)* (Hamilton: Robert Duncan, 1928), 32–33.

27 LAC, "19th Canadian Battalion, Digest of Service." As a commanding officer, McLaren was "responsible for everybody and everything in the Battalion," although his primary responsibility was for the training, fighting efficiency, and discipline of the unit. *Report of the Ministry, Overseas Military Forces of Canada, 1918* (London: Minister, Overseas Military Forces of Canada, n.d.), 230–31.

28 LAC, RG 9, III-D-3, vol. 4926, War Diary, 19th Battalion, 6 November 1914.

29 LAC, "19th Canadian Battalion, Digest of Service"; Bruce et al., *Historical Records*, 9.

30 *Report of the Ministry*, 230.

31 Duguid, *Official History*, vol. 1, appendix 60, 43.

32 "More Brave Boys Leave for Front," *Hamilton Herald*, 7 November 1914.

33 The militia units contributing men to the unit were as follows: 2nd Battalion, Queen's Own Rifles (Toronto); 1st Battalion, Queen's Own Rifles (Toronto); 10th Regiment, Royal Grenadiers (Toronto); 48th Highlanders (Toronto); 38th Regiment (Brantford); 51st Regiment (Soo Rifles) (Sault Ste. Marie); 13th Royal Regiment (Hamilton); 91st Regiment (Canadian Highlanders) (Hamilton); 19th (Lincoln) Regiment (St. Catharines). LAC, War Diary, 19th Battalion, 6 November 1914; LAC, "19th Canadian Battalion, Digest of Service."

34 Among all ranks who joined the 19th Battalion between November 1914 and May 1915, prewar service was claimed by 420 men. LAC, RG 9, II-B-3, vol. 79, 19th Battalion, Nominal Roll of Officers, Non-Commissioned Officers and Men, Issued with Militia Orders, 1915 (hereafter LAC, Nominal Roll).

35 The distribution was as follows: 2nd Regiment, 7; 10th Regiment, 4; 48th Regiment, 4; 38th Regiment, 2; 51st Regiment, 3; 13th Regiment, 3; 91st Regiment, 11; 19th Regiment, 3; CAMC, 4; Corps of Guides, 1.

36 Over the course of the war, more than one-third of those who joined the CEF reported previous military experience. Desmond Morton, *When Your Number's Up: The Canadian Soldier in the First World War* (Toronto: Random House, 1993), 279.

37 LAC, "19th Canadian Battalion, Digest of Service"; LAC, War Diary, 19th Battalion, 9 November 1914.

38 John Herd Thompson, *The Harvests of War: The Prairie West, 1914–1918* (Toronto: McClelland and Stewart, 1978), 24. For a discussion of pay and allowances for members of the CEF, see Desmond Morton, *Fight or Pay: Soldiers' Families in the Great War* (Vancouver: UBC Press, 2004), Ch. 2.

39 Among the remaining twenty-eight 19th Battalion other ranks not born in either the British Isles or Canada, thirteen were born in other parts of the British Empire, twelve in the United States, one in Belgium, and one in Madagascar; one individual did not list his place of birth. LAC, Nominal Roll.

40 Duguid, *Official History*, vol. 1, appendix 86, 58.

41 Hamilton, 147; Toronto, 280; St. Catharines, 39; Brantford, 55; Sault Ste. Marie, 26; Other, Ontario, 97; Other, rest of Canada, 32.

42 LAC, Nominal Roll. According to a contemporary article in the press, "33 per cent of the rank and file" of the 19th Battalion hailed from Hamilton. "Toronto furnished 50 per cent of the strength, and the balance came from Brantford, St. Catharines, and Sault Ste. Marie." Archives

of the Argyll and Sutherland Highlanders (ASH) of Canada (Princess Louise's), large bound volume of papers and clippings belonging to W.R. Turnbull (hereafter Turnbull Papers), newspaper clipping, paper and date unknown, article on departure overseas of the 19th Battalion. These numbers are hard to verify, given the difficulty of establishing with certainty every man's place of residence at the time of enlisting. Upon attesting in 1914 and 1915, each man was requested to state his place of birth and the identity and address of his next of kin, but these would not have corresponded necessarily with his place of residence at that time.

43 Fraternal ties were determined by identifying pairs of men with identical surnames who provided the same addresses for next of kin. If not brothers in every case, such men would appear to have been related in some fashion. LAC, Nominal Roll.

44 LAC, Nominal Roll.

45 Robert Fraser, "Lt.-Col. Lionel Herbert Millen, DSO (1876–1956)," unpublished biographical sketch.

46 Tony Ashworth, *Trench Warfare, 1914–1918: The Live and Let Live System* (London: Macmillan, 1980), 7.

47 Public Record Office (PRO), War Office (WO), S.D.2, *War Establishments of the Canadian Division*, 27 January 1915, 16–20; WO 40/2564, *War Establishments Part VII. New Armies. 1915* (London: HMSO 1915), 1 August 1915, 20–4; WO, *War Establishments*, 3 September 1915. By 1916, the establishment was 35 officers and 998 other ranks, for a total of 1,033 all ranks, including attached personnel. *Canadian Expeditionary Force Units: Instructions Governing Organization and Administration* (Ottawa: Government Printing Bureau, 1916), 22–24. See also WO, *War Establishments. Part XVI. Canadian. Part II – France. 1917* (London: HMSO, December 1917), 203; LAC, RG 9, III-D-3, vol. 4891, War Diary, 6th Infantry Brigade, 1–31 July 1918, appendix 11, "Establishment of a Canadian Infantry Battalion. July, 1918."

48 Duguid, *Official History*, vol. 1, 427; Ian M. McCulloch, "The 'Fighting Seventh': The Evolution and Devolution of Tactical Command and Control in a Canadian Infantry Brigade in the Great War," MA thesis, Royal Military College of Canada, 1997, 33; LAC, War Diary, 19th Battalion, 4 January 1915; Shelford Bidwell and Dominick Graham, *Fire-Power, British Army Weapons and Theories of War, 1904–1945* (London: Allen and Unwin, 1982), 35.

49 WO, *War Establishments of the Canadian Division*, 27 January 1915, and *War Establishments Part VII*, 1 August 1915; LAC, RG 24, C-6-e, vol. 1833, file GAQ 8-16, "Notes Re Organization of Canadian Machine Gun Sections, Brigade Machine Gun Companies, Machine Gun Companies, and Machine Gun Battalions"; Bill Rawling, "Technology in Search of a Role: The Machine Gun and the CEF in the First World War," *Material History Review* 42 (Fall 1995): 88. The adoption of the four-gun establishment for battalion machine-gun sections came in February 1915. Radley, *We Lead Others Follow*, 63.

50 Ashworth, *Trench Warfare*, 8; McCulloch, "The 'Fighting Seventh,'" 28.

51 LAC, War Diary, 19th Battalion, 6 November 1914; CWM, 19740071-017 58C 1 1.8.

52 CWM, 19740071-017 58C 1 1.8, handwritten annotations to Questionnaire no. 1.

53 LAC, RG 41, B-III-1, Records of the CBC, *Flanders Fields*, vol. 10, 19th Battalion, transcript of interview with E. Youngman, tape 1, 1–2.

54 ASH, RG 4, series 3, World War 1, Chas. Henderson Donation, "First Impressions of 6th November 1914, and subsequently by Fred A. Stitt."

55 ASH, Henderson Donation, "First Impressions of 6th November 1914, and subsequently by Fred A. Stitt."

56 ASH, RG 4, series 3, World War I, Ted Lang Donation, R.H. (Harry) Neil, "A Brief History of the 19th Battalion C.E.F. 1914–18."

57 ASH, Henderson Donation, "First Impressions of 6th November 1914, and subsequently by Fred A. Stitt."

58 ASH, RG 4, series 3, World War 1, 19th Battalion Association, "Selections from the Mailbag," March 1966.

59 David W. Love, *A Nation in Making: The Organization and Administration of the Canadian Military during the First World War*, vol. 2 (Ottawa: Service Publications, 2012), 347; Mike

Chappell, *The Canadian Army at War* (London: Osprey 1985), 7–19; D.S.V. Fosten and R.J. Marrion, *The British Army, 1914–18* (London: Osprey, 1978), 26–27; "Canadian Expeditionary Force Tunic Patterns, 1903 to 1919," http://www.kaisersbunker.com/ceftp/ceftp.htm, 16 January 2004.

60 LAC, War Diary, 19th Battalion, 16–21 November, 7–12 December 1914.

61 Morton, *When Your Number's Up*, 18, 32. For an analysis of the development, use, and weaknesses of the Oliver equipment, see Jack L. Summers, *Tangled Web: Canadian Infantry Accoutrements, 1855–1985*, Canadian War Museum Historical Publication no. 26 (Bloomfield: Museum Restoration Service, 1992), Chs. 4 and 5.

62 LAC, *Flanders Fields*, transcript of interview with F.A. Stitt, tape 1, 2–3.

63 LAC, War Diary, 19th Battalion, 23–28 November, 30 December 1914.

64 Duguid, *Official History*, vol. 1, appendix 111, 76–77; Dancocks, *Welcome to Flanders Fields*, 9–15; Edward J. Anderson, Robert J. Dynes, et al., *The Military Arms of Canada* (Bloomfield: Museum Restoration Service, 1963), 40–41. Appendix 111 in vol. 1 of Duguid's *Official History* remains the best overall account of the Ross rifle story.

65 John Swettenham, *To Seize the Victory: The Canadian Corps in World War*, vol. 1 (Toronto: Ryerson, 1965), 59; Duguid, *Official History*, vol. 1, appendix 111, 82.

66 CWM, 19740071-017 58C 1 1.8, typed notes of D.G. Buckley.

67 ASH, RG 4, series 3, World War 1, 19th Battalion Association, newsletter, "Further Reflections of Some Army 'Brass,'" Spring 1967.

68 LAC, *Flanders Fields*, transcript of interview with E. Youngman, tape 1, 5.

69 Among the areas in which night manoeuvres were conducted were Cedarville and Richmond Hill. LAC, *Flanders Fields*, transcript of interview with F.A. Stitt, tape 1, 1–2.

70 LAC, War Diary, 19th Battalion, 7 November 1914.

71 ASH, Henderson Donation.

72 LAC, War Diary, 19th Battalion, 6 November 1914–31 January 1915, passim; ibid., 1 February–25 May 1915, passim; D.J. Corrigall, *The History of the Twentieth Canadian Battalion (Central Ontario Regiment) Canadian Expeditionary Force in the Great War, 1914–1918* (Toronto: Stone and Cox, 1935), 6; LAC, *Flanders Fields*, transcript of interview with E. Youngman, tape 1, 2.

73 LAC, War Diary, 19th Battalion, 6 November 1914–31 January 1915, passim; ibid., 1 February–25 May 1915, passim.

74 LAC, War Diary, 19th Battalion, 6 November 1914–31 January 1915, passim; Ibid., 1 February–25 May 1915, passim; LAC, *Flanders Fields*, transcript of interview with E. Youngman, tape 1, 3.

75 Corrigall, *The History of the Twentieth Canadian Battalion*, 6.

76 ASH, Henderson Donation.

77 CWM, 19740071-017 58C 1 1.8, typed notes of M.D. Sturgeon.

78 LAC, *Flanders Fields*, transcript of interview with E. Youngman, tape 1, p. 6.

79 Chris Madsen, *Another Kind of Justice: Canadian Military Law from Confederation to Somalia* (Vancouver: UBC Press, 1999), 13.

80 Ibid., 13.

81 LAC, RG 150, series 1, vol. 71, file "19th Battalion (part 1)," Part II Daily Orders, December 1914–March 1915.

82 LAC, "19th Battalion (part 1)," Part II Daily Orders, December 1914–March 1915.

83 LAC, RG 9, II-B-5, vol. 5, "C.E.F., 18th, 19th, 22nd, 24th–27th Bns," Examination of 19th Battalion, 29 January 1915.

84 Most infractions involved absence, and the bulk of punishments for this offence consisted of forfeitures of pay. LAC, Daily Orders.

85 Robert Craig Brown and Donald Loveridge, "Unrequited Faith: Recruiting the CEF, 1914–1918," *Revue Internationale d'Histoire Militaire* 51 (1982): 58.

86 LAC, Examination of 19th Battalion, 29 January 1915.

87 LAC, *Flanders Fields*, transcript of interview with E. Youngman, tape 1, 3–4.

88 Bruce et al., *Historical Records of the Argyll and Sutherland Highlanders*, 23.
89 ASH, Henderson Donation.
90 ASH, Henderson Donation.
91 CWM, 19740071-017 58C 1 1.9, Fred A. Hardman to W.S. Herbert, 30 October 1936.
92 CWM, Hardman to Herbert, 30 October 1936, untitled typed notes regarding mobilization and training of the battalion; ibid., Hardman to Herbert, 30 October 1936. On Hardman's letter, the word "Hamilton" is inserted in handwriting above the word "Toronto," thus indicating that Henri instead may have remained in Hamilton.
93 LAC, Examination of 19th Battalion, 29 January 1915.
94 LAC RG 9, II-B-5, vol. 5, Abridged Annual Report upon 19th Battalion, 25 February 1915.
95 LAC, War Diary, 19th Battalion, appendices, Report of OC, 19th Battalion to GOC, 2nd Division, 8 February 1915.
96 LAC, War Diary, 19th Battalion, 22, 28 February, 8, 15, 29 March 1915.
97 CWM, 19740071-017 58C 1 1.8, untitled typed draft description of events during the spring of 1915, 6; ASH, Henderson Donation, "The Two Voyages of the 19th Battalion"; LAC, War Diary, 19th Battalion, 10 April 1915.
98 ASH, Henderson Donation, "The Two Voyages of the 19th Battalion."
99 Corrigall, *The History of the Twentieth Canadian Battalion*, 9.
100 Sources are not consistent with respect to the precise number of personnel that departed Canada with the 19th Battalion. LAC, War Diary, 19th Battalion, 12 May 1915; LAC, Nominal Roll; LAC, RG 24, C-6-d, vol. 1884, file 58, Barbara Wilson, "Great War, 1914–1918: Notes on Units, Arms and Services of the Canadian Expeditionary Force Which Served in France and Flanders"; LAC, RG 9, III-D-3, War Diary, vol. 4842, 2nd Canadian Division Headquarters, May 1915; CWM, 19740071-017 58C 2 3.16, 19th Canadian Infantry Battalion Association, "First World War, 1914–1919: Composition of 19th Battalion, C.E.F., Original and Reinforcements," compiled by H. "Barney" Clendining. For the purpose of this study, it was decided to accept the battalion war diary's figure of 1,096 other ranks as the unit's strength upon departing Exhibition Camp for service overseas.
101 ASH, Turnbull Papers, diary notes, 12 May 1915.
102 ASH, Turnbull Papers, newspaper clipping, *Hamilton Spectator*, n.d., signed "Omar." This was the pen name used by Cpl. (later Lt.) Harry Adie, a former Canadian Press operator in Hamilton, in his letters to the newspapers at home. Adie later secured a commission with the Royal Flying Corps and died of wounds on 1 May 1916.
103 ASH, Turnbull Papers, newspaper clipping, *Hamilton Spectator*, n.d., signed "Omar."

Chapter 2 - Training in England: May–September 1915

1 LAC, RG 9, III-D-3, vol. 4926, War Diary, 19th Battalion, 12–13 May 1915; ASH, large bound volume of papers and clippings belonging to W.R. Turnbull (hereafter Turnbull Papers), diary notes, 13 May 1915; ibid., newspaper clipping, paper and date unknown, "19th Trip Across, Pte. H.W. Hunt Writes Entertainingly of His Experiences"; LAC, War Diary, 19th Battalion, February–May 1915, "Abstract of Log, R.M.S. 'Scandinavian.'"
2 ASH, Turnbull Papers, diary notes, 13–14 May 1915; ibid., "19th Trip Across."
3 ASH, Turnbull Papers, diary notes, 15 May 1915.
4 ASH, Turnbull Papers, "19th Trip Across"; ibid., newspaper clipping, *Hamilton Spectator*, n.d., signed "Omar" (pseudonym of Harry Adie). In early 1915, Canadian officials were nervous over rumours that U-boat activity might soon spread towards the western Atlantic. The possibility of U-boat activity in North American waters did not become an established reality until the second half of 1916. Marc Milner, *Canada's Navy: The First Century* (Toronto: University of Toronto Press, 1999), 46–50.
5 ASH, Turnbull Papers, "19th Trip Across"; ibid., *Hamilton Spectator*, "Omar" (Harry Adie).
6 ASH, Turnbull Papers, newspaper clipping, paper and date unknown, letter from Pte. Gladstone Ghent.

7 ASH, Turnbull Papers, *Hamilton Spectator*, "Omar" (Harry Adie).
8 ASH, Turnbull Papers, "19th Trip Across."
9 Personal collection of Mrs. Phyllis Douglas, letters of Lt.-Col. Lionel H. Millen (hereafter Millen Letters), Millen to his mother, 22 May 1915.
10 ASH, Turnbull Papers, diary notes, 17 May 1915.
11 ASH, Turnbull Papers, *Hamilton Spectator*, "Omar" (Harry Adie).
12 ASH, Turnbull Papers, diary notes, 21 May 1915.
13 ASH, Turnbull Papers, newspaper clipping, letter from Pte. Gladstone Ghent.
14 ASH, Turnbull Papers, diary notes, 21 May 1915. According to the German government, this zone encompassed, as of 18 February 1915, "all the waters surrounding Great Britain and Ireland." Michael L. Hadley and Roger Sarty, *Tin-Pots and Pirate Ships: Canadian Naval Forces and German Sea Raiders, 1880–1918* (Montreal and Kingston: McGill–Queen's University Press, 1991), 104.
15 ASH, RG 4, series 3, World War 1, 19th Battalion Association, Charles A. Henderson, "The Voyage Overseas – 19th Battalion," 19th Battalion Association newsletter, Fall 1976.
16 ASH, Turnbull Papers, diary notes, 18 May 1915.
17 ASH, "Selections from the Mail Bag," contribution by T.W. (Ted) Lang, 19th Battalion Association newsletter, Fall 1976.
18 ASH, Turnbull Papers, "19th Trip Across."
19 ASH, Turnbull Papers, diary notes, 22 May 1915; ibid., newspaper clipping, letter from Pte. Gladstone Ghent.
20 ASH, Turnbull Papers, *Hamilton Spectator*, "Omar" (Harry Adie).
21 ASH, 19th Battalion Association, Henderson, "The Voyage Overseas."
22 ASH, Turnbull Papers, diary notes, 23 May 1915.
23 ASH, Turnbull Papers, newspaper clipping, letter from Pte. Gladstone Ghent.
24 D.J. Corrigall, *The History of the Twentieth Canadian Battalion (Central Ontario Regiment) Canadian Expeditionary Force in the Great War, 1914–1918* (Toronto: Stone and Cox, 1935), 14.
25 Millen Letters, Millen to his mother, 27 May 1915.
26 ASH, Turnbull Papers, diary notes, 23 May 1915; ASH, 19th Battalion Association, Charles A. Henderson, "The Voyage Overseas – 19th Battalion."
27 ASH, "Selections from the Mail Bag," contribution by T.W. (Ted) Lang.
28 ASH, Turnbull Papers, newspaper clipping, paper and date unknown, "What 19th Men Are Doing at West Sandling," by "Omar" (Harry Adie).
29 ASH, Turnbull Papers, diary notes, 23 May 1915; LAC, War Diary, 19th Battalion, 23 May 1915.
30 ASH, 19th Battalion Association, "Selections from the Mail Bag," contribution by T.W. (Ted) Lang.
31 ASH, Turnbull Papers, newspaper clipping, letter from Pte. Gladstone Ghent; Millen Letters, Millen to his mother, 27 May 1915; Corrigall, *The History of the Twentieth Canadian Battalion*, 15.
32 ASH, Turnbull Papers, newspaper clipping, "What 19th Men Are Doing at West Sandling."
33 LAC, RG 41, B-III-1, Records of the CBC, *Flanders Fields*, transcript of interview with F.A. Stitt, tape 1, 6; ASH, Turnbull Papers, newspaper clipping, letter from Pte. Gladstone Ghent. The Canadian experience in Britain during the First World War has been examined in Jonathan F. Vance, *Maple Leaf Empire: Canada, Britain, and Two World Wars* (Toronto: Oxford University Press, 2012).
34 Corrigall, *The History of the Twentieth Canadian Battalion*, 15.
35 The established strength of the division's twelve infantry battalions was 12,348 all ranks. LAC, RG 24, C-6-k, vol. 22,003; WO 40/2564, *War Establishments, Part VII. New Armies, 1915*, 1 August 1915; ibid., S.D. 2, *2nd Canadian Division, War Establishments*, 3 September 1915. By 1918, a Canadian division contained more than 21,000 all ranks. The exact number of officers and men in the division varies according to source and ranges between 21,648 and 21,830 all ranks. LAC, RG 24, C-6-e, vol. 1831, file GAQ 8–11, Col. A.F. Duguid to Harold W. Timmins, 2 September 1925; LAC, RG 24, C-6-I, vol. 1874, file 22, vol. 2, J. Scanlon to W.L. Seely, 11

February 1930; LAC, RG 24, C-6-e, vol. 1815, file GAQ 4–27, Department of National Defence memorandum, 28 February 1940.

36 John Mochrie, "Training Hard," personal letter published in the *Hamilton Herald*, 24 August 1915.

37 LAC, War Diary, 19th Battalion, May–July 1915, passim; ASH, Turnbull Papers, diary notes, 19 June 1915.

38 There were some complaints that the "new larger peep sights" on the Ross Mk. III Rifles were "not true centre." Ibid., 7 June 1915.

39 Andrew Iarocci, *Shoestring Soldiers: The 1st Canadian Division at War, 1914–1915* (Toronto: University of Toronto Press, 2008), 10–12.

40 ASH, Turnbull Papers, diary notes, 19 June 1915.

41 LAC, War Diary, 19th Battalion, 18 June 1915.

42 ASH, Turnbull Papers, diary notes, 23 June 1915.

43 LAC, War Diary, 19th Battalion, May–July 1915, passim.

44 The approximate length of the Western Front was, of course, subject to considerable variation over the duration of the war. During the German offensives in the spring and summer of 1918, the front briefly reached a maximum length of roughly 600 miles. Robert Cowley, "The Unreal City," *MHQ: Quarterly Journal of Military History* 6, no. 2 (1994): 13; Gary Sheffield, *Forgotten Victory: The First World War, Myths and Realities* (London: Headline, 2001), 98–99.

45 LAC, War Diary, 19th Battalion, May–July 1915, passim.

46 LAC, RG 9, III-D-3, vol. 4930, War Diary, 20th Battalion, 13 July 1915.

47 LAC, War Diary, 19th Battalion, appendix 5, 4th Canadian Infantry Brigade order, 2 August 1915.

48 LAC, War Diary, 19th Battalion, appendix 7, "Some of the Principal Lessons to Be Learned from the Brigade Field Day of August 11th 1915."

49 ASH, Turnbull Papers, diary notes, 14 August 1915.

50 LAC, MG 30, D 150, Sir Andrew Macphail Papers, vol. 4, personal diary, vol. 1, 1914–1916, 26 August 1915.

51 ASH, Turnbull Papers, diary notes, 19 July 1915.

52 R.H. Roy, ed., *The Journal of Private Fraser* (Nepean: CEF Books, 1998), 23.

53 ASH, Turnbull Papers, diary notes, 10 July, 9 August 1915.

54 ASH, Turnbull Papers, 5 June 1915.

55 ASH, Turnbull Papers, 10 August 1915.

56 LAC, War Diary, 19th Battalion, 9–10 August 1915; ASH, Turnbull Papers, diary notes, 10, 17 August 1915.

57 ASH, Turnbull Papers, diary notes, 27 May, 2 June 1915.

58 Total absences in England during 1915 would have been higher than this, but to what degree is uncertain, owing to a lack of statistics for the period from 23 May to 5 June. LAC, RG 150, Series 1, vol. 71, file "19th Battalion (part 1)," Part II Daily Orders, December 1914–March 1915, June–September 1915.

59 LAC, "19th Battalion (part 1)," Part II Daily Orders, August–September 1915.

60 LAC, RG 9, III-D-3, vol. 5050, War Diary, APM, 2nd Canadian Division, 5–6 June 1915; Robert N. Clements, M.C., *Merry Hell: The Story of the 25th Battalion (Nova Scotia Regiment), Canadian Expeditionary Force, 1914–1919*, ed. Brian Douglas Tennyson (Toronto: University of Toronto Press, 2013), 43–5; Kenneth Radley, *Get Tough, Stay Tough: Shaping the Canadian Corps, 1914–1918* (Solihull: Helion & Company, 2014), 146.

61 In his war diary, the divisional APM criticized a number of 2nd Canadian Division units for laxity in discipline during the summer of 1915. By comparison, the 19th Battalion presumably had a good record in this respect, since it was hardly mentioned at all by Jarvis. See LAC, War Diary, APM, 2nd Canadian Division, June–September 1915.

62 "Rules for Field Punishment," in WO, *Manual of Military Law* (London: HMSO, 1914, repr. 1917), 721.

63 Denis Winter, *Death's Men: Soldiers of the Great War* (London: Penguin 1979), 43.
64 "Rules for Field Punishment," in War Office, *Manual of Military Law* (London: HMSO, 1914, repr. 1917), 721.
65 *The King's Regulations and Orders for the Army, 1912* (London: HMSO, repr. 1914), paras. 493–501, 112–15; Richard Holmes, *Tommy: The British Soldier on the Western Front, 1914–1918* (London: HarperCollins, 2004), 558.
66 ASH, Turnbull Papers, diary notes, 17 August 1915.
67 LAC, RG 9, III-D-3, vol. 4842, War Diary, 2nd Canadian Division Headquarters, 2 September 1915.
68 LAC, War Diary, 19th Battalion, 6 September 1915.
69 LAC, War Diary, 19th Battalion, 7 September 1915.
70 Desmond Morton, *When Your Number's Up: The Canadian Soldier in the First World War* (Toronto: Random House, 1993), 32; LAC, *Flanders Fields*, transcript of interview with E. Youngman, tape 1, 14. See also Jack L. Summers, *Tangled Web: Canadian Infantry Accoutrements, 1855–1955*, Canadian War Museum Historical Publication no. 26 (Bloomfield: Museum Restoration Service, 1992), Chs. 4 and 5.
71 Millen Letters, Millen to his mother, 12 September 1915.
72 A.F. Duguid, *Official History of the Canadian Forces in the Great War 1914–1919, General Series*, vol. 1: *Chronicle: August 1914–September, 1915* (Ottawa: King's Printer 1938), 545; Morton, *When Your Number's Up*, 32; John Ellis, *Eye-Deep in Hell: Trench Warfare in World War I* (New York: Pantheon, 1976), 36.
73 CEF Tunic Patterns, 1903 to 1919, http://www.kaisersbunker.com/ceftp/index.htm.
74 LAC, War Diary, 19th Battalion, 8–13 September 1915.
75 Millen Letters, Millen to his mother, 12 September 1915.
76 The 36th Battalion had been appointed to serve as the reserve unit for the 19th Battalion on 27 July.
77 Maj. Moors was the officer usually in command of B Company, which, according to the officers' nominal roll on 14 September, was then under the command of Capt. S.C.S. Kerr. LAC, War Diary, 19th Battalion, 12 September 1915.
78 LAC, War Diary, 19th Battalion, 14 September 1915, appendix 16; ASH, Turnbull Papers, "What 19th Men Are Doing at West Sandling."
79 ASH, "Selections from the Mail Bag," contribution by T.W. (Ted) Lang, 19th Battalion Association newsletter, October 1961.
80 "Crack Nineteenth Entering Trenches," *Hamilton Spectator*, 11 October 1915, likely written by "Omar" (Harry Adie).
81 The change in divisional command came about because the War Office decided that Maj.-Gen. Steele was too old and inexperienced. Turner, who assumed command of the division on 17 August, had previously commanded the 3rd Infantry Brigade in the 1st Canadian Division. Steele was shuffled to the post of GOC, Shorncliffe Command. Desmond Morton, *A Peculiar Kind of Politics: Canada's Overseas Ministry in the First World War* (Toronto: University of Toronto Press, 1982), 38, 40–41.

Chapter 3 – Life in the Trenches: September–December 1915

1 A.F. Duguid, *Official History of the Canadian Forces in the Great War 1914–1919, General Series*, vol. 1: *Chronicle: August 1914–September, 1915* (Ottawa: King's Printer, 1938), 545; D.J. Corrigall, *The History of the Twentieth Canadian Battalion (Central Ontario Regiment) Canadian Expeditionary Force in the Great War, 1914–1918* (Toronto: Stone and Cox, 1935), 21, 23.
2 LAC, RG 9, III-D-3, vol. 4926, War Diary, 19th Battalion, 15 September 1915; "Crack Nineteenth Entering Trenches," *Hamilton Spectator*, 11 October 1915, likely written by "Omar" (Harry Adie); LAC, War Diary, 19th Battalion, 15 September 1915; "Crack Nineteenth Entering Trenches;" Desmond Morton, *When Your Number's Up: The Canadian Soldier in the First World*

War (Toronto: Random House, 1993), 119; Corrigall, *The History of the Twentieth Canadian Battalion*, 24.

3 LAC, War Diary, 19th Battalion, 15 September 1915; CWM, 19740071–017 58C 1.8, untitled file of letters, questionnaires, responses, and notes regarding 19th Battalion history, handwritten annotation to section 23 of Questionnaire no. 1, and annotation to handwritten notes from 19th Battalion War Diary entry for 16 September 1915; LAC, MG 30, E 452, Felix J. Cullen Papers, personal diary, 14–15 September 1915.

4 LAC, War Diary, 19th Battalion, 16 September 1915; Corrigall, *History of the Twentieth Canadian Battalion*, 26.

5 "Crack Nineteenth Entering Trenches"; LAC, War Diary, 19th Battalion, 17–18 September 1915.

6 G.W.L. Nicholson, *Canadian Expeditionary Force, 1914–1919: The Official History of the Canadian Army in the First World War* (Ottawa: Queen's Printer, 1962), 114–15.

7 "Crack Nineteenth Entering Trenches."

8 Nicholson, *Canadian Expeditionary Force*, 113–14.

9 Ibid., 113–14, 120.

10 LAC, War Diary, 19th Battalion, 19 September 1915; LAC, RG 41, B-III-1, Records of the CBC, *Flanders Fields*, vol. 10, 19th Battalion, transcript of interview with F.A. Stitt, tape 1, 8.

11 LAC, War Diary, 19th Battalion, 20 September 1915.

12 Corrigall, *The History of the Twentieth Canadian Battalion*, 30.

13 ASH, RG 4, series 3, World War 1, Ted Lang Donation, "Now for a Bit of Battalion History by Yours Truly – Ted Lang," 19th Battalion Association newsletter, Fall 1984.

14 LAC, War Diary, 19th Battalion, 20–21 September 1915.

15 LAC, *Flanders Fields*, vol. 10, 19th Battalion, transcript of interview with E. Youngman, tape 2, 1–2.

16 Nicholson, *Canadian Expeditionary Force*, 115–16, sketch 17. The term *sector* was the official nomenclature applied to the portion of the line that was held by a division. A brigade front, in turn, was known as a "section," while a battalion front was termed a "sub-section." LAC, RG 9, III-C-3, vol. 4131, folder 10, file 11, First Army no. 669(G), to Canadian Corps, 18 November 1916.

17 LAC, War Diary, 19th Battalion, 20 September 1915, appendix 20, field messages, 19th Battalion to 4th Infantry Brigade, 22 September 1915; LAC, RG 150, 1992-93/166, Box 5208-40, personnel file for 56087 Charles Kisby. As a result of his wounds, Kisby's discharge from military service was approved in September 1916.

18 Nicholson, *Canadian Expeditionary Force*, 120–22.

19 Ibid., 120–22.

20 LAC, War Diary, 19th Battalion, 28 September–3 October 1915.

21 CWM, 19740071–017 58C 1 1.8, handwritten notes from 19th Battalion War Diary, entries for 22–28 September 1915 (vol. 4926). These notes may have been compiled by Robert Spreckley, a former lieutenant in the 19th Battalion, who was working on the unit's history in the postwar period. Unfortunately, the project was never completed.

22 Personal collection of Mrs. Phyllis Douglas, letters of Lt.-Col. Lionel H. Millen (hereafter Millen Letters), Millen to his mother, 28 September 1915.

23 Millen Letters, Millen to his mother, 28 September 1915; LAC, War Diary, 19th Battalion, appendix 32, field messages, 19th Battalion to 4th Infantry Brigade, 9:30 PM, 3 October 1915.

24 LAC, War Diary, 19th Battalion, 8–14 October 1915; LAC, Cullen Papers, personal diary, 2 November 1915.

25 LAC, *Flanders Fields*, transcript of interview with E. Youngman, tape 2, 2.

26 LAC, War Diary, 19th Battalion, 15 September 1915; "Crack Nineteenth Entering Trenches."

27 Robert Cowley, "The Unreal City," *MHQ: Quarterly Journal of Military History* 6, no. 2 (1994): 10–11.

28 John Ellis, *Eye-Deep in Hell: Trench Warfare in World War I* (New York: Pantheon, 1976), 12–13; Denis Winter, *Death's Men: Soldiers of the Great War* (London: Penguin, 1979), 80.

29 Ellis, *Eye-Deep in Hell*, 12; Cowley, "The Unreal City," 14.
30 Tony Ashworth, *Trench Warfare, 1914–1918: The Live and Let Live System* (London: Macmillan, 1980), 4–5; Ellis, *Eye-Deep in Hell*, 15; Cowley, "The Unreal City," 14; Winter, *Death's Men*, 81.
31 Ashworth, *Trench Warfare*, 5–6; Ellis, *Eye-Deep in Hell*, 14–16; Gordon Corrigan, *Mud, Blood, and Poppycock: Britain and the First World War* (London: Cassell, 2003), 84.
32 Ashworth, *Trench Warfare*, 5–6; Ellis, *Eye-Deep in Hell*, 14–16.
33 Ashworth, *Trench Warfare*, 5–6; Ellis, *Eye-Deep in Hell*, 16–17.
34 ASH, RG 4, series 3, World War 1, 19th Battalion Association, "Selections from the Mail Bag," contribution by T.W. (Ted) Lang, 19th Battalion Association newsletter, Fall 1969.
35 ASH, 19th Battalion Association, "Selections from the Mail Bag," contribution by T.W. (Ted) Lang.
36 Corrigan, *Mud, Blood, and Poppycock*, 88–9.
37 ASH, large bound volume of papers and clippings belonging to W.R. Turnbull (hereafter Turnbull Papers), "In the Trenches, Belgium, Sunday afternoon, November 28th, 1915."
38 LAC, *Flanders Fields*, transcript of interview with F.A. Stitt, tape 1, 8–9.
39 Millen Letters, Millen to his mother, 21 September 1915.
40 Ashworth, *Trench Warfare*, 5; Ellis, *Eye-Deep in Hell*, 24–25; Corrigan, *Mud, Blood, and Poppycock*, 84; Cowley, "The Unreal City," 13–14.
41 The established ration of rum was 1/64th of a gallon (1½ ounces) per man at one issue. LAC, RG 24, C-6-j, vol. 6992, "Chapter XII, Para 6," Liquor Restrictions in France; Tim Cook, "'More a Medicine Than a Beverage': 'Demon Rum' and the Canadian Trench Soldier of the First World War," Canadian Military History 9, no. 1 (2000): 6, 18; http://www.fjexpeditions.com/frameset/rumjar.htm; Tim Cook, *At the Sharp End: Canadians Fighting the Great War, 1914–1916* (Toronto: Viking, 2007), 242.
42 Millen Letters, Millen to his father, 27 October 1916. For an examination of the conflicting values of home front and battlefront over the subject of alcohol, see Cook, "'More a Medicine Than a Beverage.'"
43 Morton, *When Your Number's Up*, 123; Ellis, *Eye-Deep in Hell*, 38.
44 Morton, *When Your Number's Up*, 141; Desmond Morton and J.L Granatstein, *Marching to Armageddon: Canadians and the Great War, 1914–1919* (Toronto: Lester and Orpen Dennys, 1989), 54; Winter, *Death's Men*, 102; Ellis, *Eye-Deep in Hell*, 125–26, 130, 132–33.
45 Millen Letters, Millen to his mother, 21 September 1915.
46 Morton, *When Your Number's Up*, 125; Bruce Cane, *It Made You Think of Home: The Haunting Journal of Deward Barnes, Canadian Expeditionary Force: 1916–1919* (Toronto: Dundurn, 2004), 124.
47 Morton, *When Your Number's Up*, 140.
48 LAC, *Flanders Fields*, transcript of interview with Sid Smith, tape 1, 23–4.
49 Morton, *When Your Number's Up*, 125; Ellis, *Eye-Deep in Hell*, 38.
50 Millen Letters, Millen to his mother, 28 September 1915.
51 Ellis, *Eye-Deep in Hell*, 41–42.
52 Winter, *Death's Men*, 81.
53 Ellis, *Eye-Deep in Hell*, 27.
54 LAC, MG 53, John Taylor Fotheringham Papers, vol. 5, file 22, 2nd Canadian Division, Trench Relief Rosters; LAC, Fotheringham Papers, vol. 5, file 22, 2nd Canadian Division G. 237, 13 November 1915; see also LAC, RG 9, vols. 4926–7, War Diary, 19th Battalion, September 1915–March 1916.
55 LAC, *Flanders Fields*, transcript of interview with F.A. Stitt, tape 1, 13–14.
56 Barnes journal, appendix, as qtd. in Cane, *It Made You Think of Home*, 292–93.
57 Barnes journal, 10 February 1919, qtd. in Cane, *It Made You Think of Home*, 274.
58 CWM, 19740071-017 58C 1 1.8, "Questionnaire no. Two," para. 5, 14.
59 Corrigall, *The History of the Twentieth Canadian Battalion*, 35.
60 Millen Letters, Millen to his sister Gertie, 7 November 1915.
61 Corrigall, *The History of the Twentieth Canadian Battalion*, 43.

62 LAC, War Diary, 19th Battalion, 17 January 1916; R.E. Priestley, *The Signal Service in the European War of 1914 to 1918* (Chatham: W. and J. MacKay, 1921), 119; A.J. Kerry and W.A. McDill, *The History of the Corps of Royal Canadian Engineers,* vol. 1: *1749–1939* (Ottawa: Military Engineers Association of Canada, 1962), 237–38.
63 Millen Letters, Millen to his sister Gertie, 7 November 1915.
64 ASH, RG 4, series 3, World War 1, 19th Battalion Association, Charles A. Henderson, "Selections from the Mail Bag."
65 Morton, *When Your Number's Up*, 145–46.
66 CWM, 19740071-017 58C 1 1.8, "Questionnaire no. Two," para. 5; Morton, *When Your Number's Up*, 145.
67 Millen Letters, Millen to his mother, 3 October 1915.
68 Morton, *When Your Number's Up*, 140, 145; Winter, *Death's Men*, 97.
69 Sir Andrew Macphail, *Official History of the Canadian Forces in the Great War 1914–1919: The Medical Services* (Ottawa: King's Printer, 1925), 270; Robin Glen Keirstead, "The Canadian Military Medical Experience during the Great War, 1914–1918," MA thesis, Queen's University, 1982, 182–83; Corrigan, *Mud, Blood, and Poppycock*, 95–96.
70 LAC, RG 9, III-D-3, vol. 5024, War Diary, DDMS, Canadian Corps, December 1915, "Cases of 'Trench Feet' Admitted to Field Ambulances of Canadian Corps from October 15 to December 31, 1915;" LAC, War Diary, 19th Battalion, appendix 71, field message, 19th Battalion to 4th Infantry Brigade, 25 November 1915.
71 Millen Letters, Millen to his mother, 30 December 1915.
72 CWM, 19740071-017 58C 1 1.8, handwritten notes titled "Section #2."
73 LAC, Cullen Papers, personal diary, 25 December 1915.
74 Millen Letters, Millen to his father, 7 November 1915.

Chapter 4 – Waging Trench Warfare: September 1915–March 1916

1 LAC, RG 9, III-D-3, vols. 4926–27, War Diary, 19th Battalion, September 1915–March 1916, passim; LAC, MG 30, E 53, John Taylor Fotheringham Papers, vol. 5, file 22, 2nd Canadian Division Trench Relief Roster, November 1915–March 1916.
2 Martin Middlebrook, *The First Day on the Somme* (New York: W.W. Norton, 1972), 32.
3 Note that these numbers do not include those who were injured or wounded accidentally. For complete casualty statistics, see LAC, RG 150, vols. 491–92, "Casualties by Days—France and Belgium," 19th Battalion, September 1915–March 1916. LAC, RG 9, vols. 4926–27, War Diary, 19th Battalion, September 1915–March 1916.
4 Sir Andrew Macphail, *Official History of the Canadian Forces in the Great War, 1914–19: The Medical Services* (Ottawa: King's Printer, 1925), 105; Tim Cook, *At the Sharp End: Canadians Fighting the Great War, 1914–1916* (Toronto: Viking, 2007), 200; Nick Bosanquet, "Health Systems in Khaki: The British and American Medical Experience," in *Facing Armageddon: The First World War Experienced*, ed. Hugh Cecil and Peter Liddle (London: Leo Cooper, 1996), 459–60.
5 LAC, RG 41, B-III-1, Records of the CBC, *Flanders Fields*, vol. 11, 22nd Battalion, transcript of interview with G.U. Francoeur, tape 1, 5–6.
6 Harry Adie ("Omar"), "Courageous and Cool under Heavy Firing," *Hamilton Spectator*, 20 October 1915.
7 Personal collection of Mrs. Phyllis Douglas, letters of Lt.-Col. Lionel H. Millen (hereafter Millen Letters), Millen to his mother, 16 November 1915.
8 Millen Letters, Millen to his mother, 12 December 1915.
9 ASH, large bound volume of papers and clippings belonging to W.R. Turnbull (hereafter Turnbull Papers), typed draft of letter dated 5 December 1915, ostensibly from McLaren to the mayor of Hamilton but apparently written by "Omar" (Harry Adie). Handwritten at the top, presumably by Turnbull, is the comment, "another effusion of Omar's which he wrote for the Colonel."

10 "Lieut. Adie Killed," *Hamilton Herald*, 3 May 1916.

11 Wilfred Owen, "Anthem for Doomed Youth," in *Wilfred Owen: The War Poems*, ed. Jon Stallworthy (London: Chatto and Windus, 1994), 12.

12 Ian V. Hogg, *The Guns, 1914–18* (London: Ballantine, 1971), 57–72.

13 LAC, RG 9, vol. 4926, War Diary, 19th Battalion, October–December 1915, appendices, field messages, daily summaries.

14 See the glossary of slang and technical terms in John Brophy and Eric Partridge, *The Long Trail: What the British Soldier Sang and Said in the Great War of 1914–18* (London: Andre Deutsch, 1965).

15 Partridge, *The Long Trail*; Pierre Berton, *Vimy* (Toronto: Penguin, 1987), 81–82; Middlebrook, *The First Day on the Somme*, 31.

16 Tim Cook, *No Place to Run: The Canadian Corps and Gas Warfare in the First World War* (Vancouver: UBC Press, 2000), 41–44, 57–59.

17 See G.W.L. Nicholson, *The Gunners of Canada: The History of the Royal Regiment of Canadian Artillery*, vol. 1: *1534–1919* (Toronto: McClelland and Stewart, 1967); Leslie W.C. Barnes, *Canada's Guns: An Illustrated History of Artillery* (Ottawa: Canadian War Museum, 1979).

18 LAC, RG 24, C-6-j, vol. 6937, "Schools and Courses in the Field," xiii; Anthony Saunders, *Weapons of the Trench War, 1914–1918* (Phoenix Mill: Sutton, 1999), 129; G.W.L. Nicholson, *Canadian Expeditionary Force, 1914–1919: The Official History of the Canadian Army in the First World War* (Ottawa: Queen's Printer, 1962), 155, 568n87.

19 Tim Travers, *The Killing Ground: The British Army, the Western Front, and the Emergence of Modern Warfare, 1900–1918* (London: Unwin Hyman, 1987), 70; Paddy Griffith, *Battle Tactics of the Western Front: The British Army's Art of Attack, 1916–18* (New Haven: Yale University Press 1994), 67.

20 LAC, RG 24, C-6-k, vol. 22,004, *War Establishments, Part VII. New Armies, 1915* (London: HMSO, 1915), 21.

21 Nova Scotia Archives (NSA), UA 601 N42 M146, draft manuscript, S. Douglas MacGowan, Harry M. Heckbert, and Byron E. O'Leary, "New Brunswick's 'Fighting 26th': A Draft History of the 26th New Brunswick Battalion, C.E.F., 1914–1919," 53. The authors' work was published as *New Brunswick's "Fighting 26th": A History of the 26th New Brunswick Battalion, C.E.F., 1914–1919* (Saint John: Neptune Publishing, 1995). Earth-induction telegraph sets, known as "power buzzers," were also used but were not entirely satisfactory. Bill Rawling, "Communications in the Canadian Corps, 1915–1918: Wartime Technological Progress Revisited," *Canadian Military History* 3, no. 2 (1994): 7–21.

22 NSA, "New Brunswick's 'Fighting 26th,'" 12; LAC, *War Establishments, Part VII*, 21.

23 LAC, RG 150, 1992–93/166, box 4150–21, personnel file, Maj. H.C. Hatch; LAC, RG 9, III-D-1, vol. 4692, folder 51, file 11, "19th Canadian Battalion, Digest of Service."

24 In total, the section comprised thirty-one other ranks (who served as drivers), twenty-eight vehicles (carts and wagons), thirty-four draught horses, nine heavy draught horses, and nine pack mules. In carrying out its duties, the transport section was divided into two parts. The first part, known as "first line transport," comprised the majority of the section and accompanied the battalion at all times. It serviced the battalion during active operations and was divided among battalion headquarters, the machine-gun section, and each of the four rifle companies. The second part of the transport section, termed the "train," carried baggage, stores, and supplies and was generally kept well to the rear, out of harm's way. NSA, "New Brunswick's 'Fighting 26th,'" 12; LAC, *War Establishments, Part VII*, 21–24.

25 NSA, "New Brunswick's 'Fighting 26th,'" 13; LAC, *War Establishments, Part VII*, 21; John Ellis, *Eye-Deep in Hell: Trench Warfare in World War I* (New York: Pantheon, 1976), 106–10; Bill Rawling, *Death Their Enemy: Canadian Medical Practitioners and War* (Ottawa: Bill Rawling, 2001), 88; Denis Winter, *Death's Men: Soldiers of the Great War* (London: Penguin, 1979), 196–7; Desmond Morton, *When Your Number's Up: The Canadian Soldier in the First World War* (Toronto: Random House, 1993), 186–87, 190–91.

26 LAC, Records of the CBC, *Flanders Fields*, vol. 10, 19th Battalion, transcript of interview with E. Youngman, tape 2, 8.

27 Kenneth Radley, "First Canadian Division, C.E.F., 1914–1918: Ducimus (We Lead)," PhD diss., Carleton University, 2000, 54; Daniel G. Dancocks, *Welcome to Flanders Fields* (Toronto: McClelland and Stewart, 1989), 63–64; Bill Rawling, *Surviving Trench Warfare: Technology and the Canadian Corps, 1914–1918* (Toronto: University of Toronto Press, 1992), 38; and "Technology in Search of a Role: The Machine Gun and the CEF in the First World War," *Material History Review* 42 (Fall 1995): 88–90; Kenneth Macksey, *Vimy Ridge, 1914–18* (New York: Ballantine, 1972), 95.

28 Shelford Bidwell and Dominick Graham, *Fire-Power: British Army Weapons and Theories of War, 1904–1945* (London: Allen and Unwin, 1982), 122; Rawling, "Technology in Search of a Role," 89; LAC, RG 24, C-6-e, vol. 1833, GAQ 8–16, "Allotment of Machine Guns to Infantry Battalions" and "Notes Re Organization of Canadian Machine Gun Sections, Machine Gun Companies, and Machine Gun Battalions."

29 LAC, RG 9, III-C-3, vol. 4115, folder 1, file 17, Returns of Machine Guns, 1916, 1917, 19th Battalion. Griffith, *Battle Tactics of the Western Front*, 130; Rawling, *Surviving Trench Warfare*, 58–59, 72; Rawling, "Technology in Search of a Role," 90.

30 LAC, *War Establishments, Part VII*, 22.

31 LAC, RG 150, 1992–93/166, box 5150–1, personnel file, Lt. Charles Edward Kilmer.

32 LAC, MG 30, E 239, Edward Hilliam Papers, "Duties of Officers," 27 October 1915.

33 Winter, *Death's Men*, 112; Rawling, "Technology in Search of a Role," 91.

34 CWM, 19740071-017 58C 1 1.9, Ghent's typewritten answers to Questionnaire no. 1.

35 Orders to begin organizing and training battalion scout sections were issued in early August 1915. LAC, RG 9, III-C-3, vol. 4143, folder 8, file 8, Memorandum from Staff Captain, 6th Infantry Brigade to O.C., 29th Battalion, re "Organization and Training of Scouts," 3 August 1915.

36 During the First World War, the term "bomb" was often used as a synonym for "grenade," and those who specialized in their use were referred to as "bombers." The terms "grenade" and "bomb" will be used interchangeably throughout this work.

37 Gordon Corrigan, *Mud, Blood, and Poppycock: Britain and the First World War* (London: Cassell, 2003), 135–36.

38 Bernard Fitzsimons, ed., *The Illustrated Encyclopedia of 20th Century Weapons and Warfare*, vol. 17 (New York: Phoebus, 1971), 1895; Rawling, *Suriving Trench Warfare*, 58; Cook, *At the Sharp End*, 212.

39 Rawling, *Surviving Trench Warfare*, 48–49, 124; Griffith, *Battle Tactics of the Western Front*, 114–15; Saunders, *Weapons of the Trench War*, 96–9, 102, 112.

40 Winter, *Death's Men*, 110; Tony Ashworth, *Trench Warfare, 1914–1918: The Live and Let Live System* (London: Macmillan, 1980), 69.

41 For example, war diary entries for the periods 15–17 November 1915 and 4–9 January 1916 mention daily training activities of "Company and Battalion Bombers," or, alternatively, "Company and Battalion Grenade Sections."

42 LAC, RG 150, 1992–93/166, box 4482–28, personnel file, Lt.-Col. Bertram O. Hooper.

43 ASH, Turnbull Papers, diary notes, 23 June 1915.

44 ASH, RG 4, series 3, World War 1, 19th Battalion Association, "Selections from the Mail Bag," contribution by Phil Collins, 19th Battalion Association newsletter, Fall 1969.

45 Dan Jenkins, "Winning Trench Warfare: Battlefield Intelligence in the Canadian Corps, 1914–18," PhD thesis, Carleton University, 1999, 127–29.

46 Dan Jenkins, "The Other Side of the Hill: Combat Intelligence in the Canadian Corps, 1914–18," *Canadian Military History* 10, no. 2 (2000): 15.

47 Ibid., 134–35.

48 LAC, Edward Hilliam Papers, Field Messages, "Various Duties of Officers," 27 October 1915.

49 LAC, RG 9, III-C-3, vol. 4143, folder 8, file 8, "Organization and Training of Battalion Scouts, 2nd Canadian Division"; LAC, RG 24, C-6-j, vol. 6935, CEF historian's files, notes, and draft material on the "Canadian Intelligence Service." LAC, RG 9, vol. 4926, War Diary, 19th Battalion, 18–23 January, 27 March 1915.

50 LAC, MG 30, E 50, Elmer Jones Papers, file 3, Canadian Corps Officers' School, 1916, "Organization and System of Training Scouts and Patrols for Trench Warfare."

51 LAC, RG 150, 1992–93/166, box 1297–14, personnel file, Maj. Sydney Smith Burnham; LAC, RG 9, III-C-3, vol. 4117, folder 8, file 7, "19th Canadian Battalion, Nominal Roll of Original Scout Section"; Jenkins, "Winning Trench Warfare," 128.

52 Ian McCulloch, "The 'Fighting Seventh': The Evolution and Devolution of Tactical Command and Control in a Canadian Infantry Brigade of the Great War," MA thesis, Royal Military College of Canada, 1997, 37–38; Jenkins, "Winning Trench Warfare," 130.

53 Ashworth, *Trench Warfare*, 70; LAC, *Flanders Fields*, vol. 10, transcript of interview with F.A. Stitt, 19th Battalion, tape 2, 17.

54 Winter, *Death's Men*, 87–8; John Laffin, *The Western Front Illustrated, 1914–1918* (London: Grange, 1997), 58.

55 CWM, 19740071–017 58C 1 1.9, Ghent's typewritten answers to Questionnaire no. 1.

56 CWM, 19740071–017 58C 1 1.8, handwritten notes titled "Section #2," dealing with the battalion's early trench experiences.

57 LAC, War Diary, 19th Battalion, appendix 42, field message, 19th Bn to 4th Infantry Bde, 16 October 1915.

58 ASH, RG 4, series 3, World War I, 19th Battalion Association, "Selections from the Mail Bag," contribution by Allan F. Lynch, 19th Battalion Association newsletter, Spring 1980.

59 Ellis, *Eye-Deep in Hell*, 73.

60 Winter, *Death's Men*, 87; LAC, Elmer Jones Papers, "Organization and System of Training Scouts and Patrols for Trench Warfare," n.d.

61 LAC, War Diary, 19th Battalion, appendix 115, 25 January 1916. Although the report in the war diary does not specify, the other ranks in the patrol were drawn probably from the battalion bombing and scout sections.

62 LAC, War Diary, 19th Battalion, app. 115, 25 January 1916, and diary text, 29 February 1916.

63 Nicholson, *Canadian Expeditionary Force*, 122.

64 Rawling, *Surviving Trench Warfare*, 47; John Keegan, *The First World War* (Toronto: Key Porter 1998), 182. Tim Cook remarks that "although the Canadians did not pioneer raiding, they elevated it into a grim art." Cook, *At the Sharp End*, 292.

65 Ashworth, *Trench Warfare*, 73; Nicholson, *Canadian Expeditionary Force*, 124.

66 Paul Fussell, *The Great War and Modern Memory* (Oxford: Oxford University Press, 1975), 75.

67 Nicholson, *Canadian Expeditionary Force*, 122; LAC, RG 9, III-D-3, vol. 4812, War Diary, Canadian Corps Headquarters, Summary of Operations, 1–7 November 1915.

68 LAC, RG 9, vols. 4926–27, War Diary, 19th Battalion, October 1915–March 1916, appendices, daily field messages, 19th Battalion to 4th Infantry Brigade.

69 LAC, War Diary, 19th Battalion, October 1915–March 1916, appendices, daily field messages, 19th Battalion to 4th Infantry Brigade.

70 "English Unit Relieved by Boys of 19th," *Hamilton Spectator*, 25 October 1915.

71 LAC, War Diary, 19th Battalion, appendix 27, field message, 19th Battalion to 4th Infantry Brigade, 27 September 1915.

72 LAC, War Diary, 19th Battalion, appendix 33, field message, 19th Battalion to 4th Infantry Brigade, 5 October 1915.

73 LAC, War Diary, 19th Battalion, appendix 43, field message, 19th Battalion to 4th Infantry Brigade, 17 October 1915.

74 CWM, 19740071–017 58C 1 1.9, "Trench Story," by W. Poppelwell #55268, A. Coy., 19th Battn.

75 LAC, War Diary, 19th Battalion, appendix 76, field message, 19th Battalion to 4th Infantry Brigade, 30 November 1915.

76 LAC, War Diary, 19th Battalion, appendix 12, field message, 19th Battalion to 4th Infantry Brigade, 18 February 1916.

77 Millen Letters, Millen to his mother, 19 February 1916.

78 LAC, War Diary, 19th Battalion, appendix 44, field message, 19th Battalion to 4th Infantry Brigade, 18 October 1915.

79 LAC, RG 9, III-D-3, vol. 4842, War Diary, 2nd Canadian Division Headquarters, "Summary of Operations, December 14–21."
80 Millen Letters, Millen to his sister "Kath," 15 October 1915.
81 LAC, War Diary, 19th Battalion, appendix 34, field message, 19th Battalion to 4th Infantry Brigade, 6 October 1915.

Chapter 5 – Trial by Fire: St-Eloi, April 1916

1 See J.A. English, "Great War 1914–18: The 'Riddle of the Trenches,'" *Canadian Defence Quarterly* 15, no. 2 (1985): 41–47.
2 John H. Morrow, Jr, *The Great War: An Imperial History* (New York: Routledge, 2004), 46, 74; Martin Middlebrook, *The First Day on the Somme* (New York: W.W. Norton, 1972), 43.
3 Charles Messenger, *Trench Fighting, 1914–18* (London: Ballantine, 1972), 26.
4 Sir James E. Edmonds, *History of the Great War: Military Operations, France and Belgium, 1916*, vol. l (London: Macmillan, 1932), 178; G.W.L. Nicholson, *Canadian Expeditionary Force, 1914–1919: The Official History of the Canadian Army in the First World War* (Ottawa: Queen's Printer, 1962), 136–37.
5 Nicholson, *Canadian Expeditionary Force*, 137–38; LAC, RG 24, C-6-j, vol. 6992, vol. 2, ch. 10, para. 11, of A.F. Duguid's unpublished Canadian Official History.
6 Nicholson, *Canadian Expeditionary Force*, 138; LAC, Duguid, unpublished Official History, vol. 2, ch. 11, handwritten notes titled "9th April 1916."
7 LAC, Duguid, Official History, vol. 2, ch. 11.
8 The battalions involved in the initial assault were the 1/Northumberland Fusiliers on the right and the 4/Royal Fusiliers on the left. Engulfed in the destruction of the German front line by mines 2 through 5 were two companies of the 18th Reserve Jäger Battalion. Edmonds, *Military Operations, France and Belgium, 1916,* vol. 1, 181; Nicholson, *Canadian Expeditionary Force*, 138–9.
9 Edmonds, *Military Operations, France and Belgium, 1916*, vol. 1, 182–85; Nicholson, *Canadian Expeditionary Force*, 139.
10 Edmonds, *Military Operations, France and Belgium, 1916*, vol. 1, 183; David Campbell, "The Divisional Experience in the C.E.F.: A Social and Operational History of the 2nd Canadian Division, 1915–1918," PhD diss., University of Calgary, 2003, 107–8.
11 LAC, RG 9, III-D-3, vol. 5073, file no. 1, "Summary of Operations—Second Army for the period 22nd–31st March, 1916," 4; ibid., vol. 5074, report on operations of 3rd British Division, 27 March–3 April 1916; and "Summary of Reports on the Operations at St-Eloi—March 27th to April 18th, 1916," 3–6.
12 Campbell, "The Divisional Experience in the C.E.F.," 118.
13 Reginald H. Roy, ed., *The Journal of Private Fraser, Canadian Expeditionary Force, 1914–1918* (Nepean: CEF Books 1998), 113.
14 Edmonds, *Military Operations, France and Belgium, 1916*, vol. 1, 185.
15 Nicholson, *Canadian Expeditionary Force*, 140; Campbell, "The Divisional Experience in the C.E.F.," 110–12, 117.
16 Lord Beaverbrook, *Canada in Flanders,* vol. 2 (London: Hodder and Stoughton, 1917), 126.
17 Campbell, "The Divisional Experience in the C.E.F.," 112, 118; Edmonds, *Military Operations, France and Belgium, 1916*, vol. 1, 191–93; LAC, RG 9, III-D-3, vol. 4843, War Diary, 2nd Canadian Division H, April 1916, appendix C, "Report on Operations of the 2nd Canadian Division after Arrival in the New Divisional Area St. Eloi. From April 3rd to April 7th 1916."
18 Nicholson, *Canadian Expeditionary Force*, 136.
19 CWM, 19740071-017 58C 1 1.8, file of letters, questionnaires, responses, and notes regarding 19th Battalion history, typed notes, "Nineteenth Battalion History. Questionnaire no. 2," para. 15.
20 CWM, "Nineteenth Battalion History. Questionnaire no. 2," paras. 16–18; Tim Cook, "The Blind Leading the Blind: The Battle of the St. Eloi Craters," *Canadian Military History* 5, no. 2 (1996): 25.

21 LAC, RG 9, III-D-3, vol. 4927, War Diary, 19th Battalion, 28 March–5 April 1916.
22 LAC, War Diary, 19th Battalion, 6 April 1916; LAC, RG 9, III-D-3, vol. 4880, War Diary, 4th Infantry Brigade, 7 April 1916.
23 During the autumn of 1915, Maj.-Gen. Turner had determined that Lord Brooke was not an effective brigadier. Rennie had enjoyed a successful pre-war militia career in the Queen's Own Rifles of Canada, in which he had served since 1881. Desmond Morton, *A Peculiar Kind of Politics: Canada's Overseas Ministry in the First World War* (Toronto: University of Toronto Press, 1982), 49; Campbell, "The Divisional Experience in the C.E.F.," 72–74; LAC, RG 41, B-III-1, Records of the CBC, *Flanders Fields*, vol. 10, transcript of interview with Charles Stevens, 20th Battalion, tape 1, 3; LAC, RG 9, III-D-1, vol. 4734, folder 144, file 9, biographical notes on Brig.-Gen. Robert Rennie.
24 LAC, *Flanders Fields*, vol. 10, transcript of interview with Joe O'Neill, 19th Battalion, tape 4, 5.
25 LAC, War Diary, 19th Battalion, 7 April 1916; ibid., appendix 28, field message, 4th Brigade to 18th, 19th, 20th, 21st Battalions, 4th Brigade Machine Gun Company, 6th Brigade, 7 April 1916; D.J. Corrigall, *The History of the Twentieth Canadian Battalion (Central Ontario Regiment) Canadian Expeditionary Force in the Great War, 1914–1918* (Toronto: Stone and Cox, 1935), 53.
26 LAC, War Diary, 19th Battalion, 8 April 1916.
27 LAC, RG 9, III-D-1, vol. 4679, folder 14, file 1, notes on St. Eloi Fighting, April 7–13, from conversation with Brig.-Gen. Rennie; LAC, RG 9, III-D-3, vol. 4812, War Diary, Canadian Corps Headquarters, 9 April 1916; LAC, War Diary, 4th Infantry Brigade, 9 April 1916.
28 LAC, War Diary, 4th Infantry Brigade, appendix 8, Report from Grenade Officer, 19th Battalion, to Officer Commanding (OC), 19th Battalion, 13 April 1916.
29 LAC, War Diary, 4th Infantry Brigade, Report from Grenade Officer, 19th Battalion, 13 April 1916; LAC, vol. 4679, Notes on St. Eloi Fighting, listings of officers and other ranks mentioned in reports from 19th Battalion to 4th Brigade.
30 LAC, RG 9, III-D-3, vol. 4843, War Diary, 2nd Canadian Division Headquarters, 10 April 1916; LAC, vol. 4679, Notes on St. Eloi Fighting: From Report by Lieut. S.S. Burnham, OC Patrols, 19th Battalion.
31 LAC, Duguid, Official History, vol. 2, ch. 11, Canadian Corps Operations Report, 10 April 1916.
32 LAC, Duguid, Official History, vol. 2, ch. 11, Canadian Corps Operations Report, 12 April 1916; Thomas P. Leppard, "Richard Turner and the Battle of St. Eloi," MA thesis, University of Calgary, 1994, 73.
33 LAC, War Diary, 4th Infantry Brigade, appendix 8, Report from Grenade Officer, 19th Battalion, to OC 19th Battalion, 13 April 1916; LAC, Canadian Corps Operations Report, 12 April 1916; LAC, War Diary, 2nd Canadian Division Headquarters, appendix C, "Report on 2nd Canadian Division's Operations at St. Eloi, April 3rd to April 16th"; Leppard, "Richard Turner and the Battle of St. Eloi," 73.
34 LAC, Duguid, Official History, vol. 2, ch. 11, Canadian Corps G.120 to Second Army, 11 April 1916.
35 LAC, Duguid, Official History, vol. 2, ch. 11, Canadian Corps Operations Report, 12 April 1916; LAC, War Diary, 2nd Canadian Division Headquarters, "Report on 2nd Canadian Division's Operations at St. Eloi, April 3rd to April 16th." Alderson took a sympathetic view of Rennie's plight. See LAC, Duguid, Official History, vol. 2, ch. 11, Canadian Corps G.120 to Second Army, 11 April 1916.
36 LAC, War Diary, 19th Battalion, appendix 32, field message, G. Morrison to OC, 11 April 1916.
37 LAC, *Flanders Fields*, vol. 10, 19th Battalion, transcript of interview with F.A. Stitt, tape 1, 14–16.
38 CWM, 19740071-017 58C 1 1.8, handwritten notes titled "Section #2," observations on the fighting at St-Eloi. The actions of these troops in temporarily withdrawing from their positions are not mentioned in the war diary text, nor do they appear to be described in the reports and field messages in the war diary's appendices.
39 LAC, Notes on St. Eloi Fighting; LAC, War Diary, 4th Infantry Brigade, 13 April 1916; LAC, Duguid, Official History, vol. 2, ch. 11, handwritten notes on events of 12 April; LAC, War

Diary, 19th Battalion, 12–22 April 1916; LAC, MG 30, E 452, Felix J. Cullen Papers, personal diary, 12 April 1916.

40 LAC, MG 30, E 241, D.E. Macintyre Papers, vol. 2, unpublished manuscript, "Men of Valour," 47, 56.

41 Historian Tim Cook suggests that Turner and his staff may not have examined the photo as rigorously as they should have "because they thought there was nothing to search for." Cook, "The Blind Leading the Blind," 31. By examining surviving records, one can appreciate why this may have been the case. A scan of references in the divisional war diary and daily intelligence summaries turns up more than twenty reports from the front lines between 7 and 15 April that claim Canadian possession of craters 4 and 5, with no clear intelligence to the contrary. Before 16 April, Turner simply did not have sufficient information to warrant seriously questioning the fact that his men held craters 4 and 5.

42 McLaren, qtd. in "Ten Months of Trench Warfare," *Hamilton Herald*, 1 August 1916. Turner likewise believed strongly that the original assault on the craters, as carried out by the 3rd British Division, would have been an easier task than the relief and consolidation effort, which was assigned to his own division. In a handwritten personal appraisal composed shortly after the fateful aerial photo was taken on 16 April, Turner remarked: "I did not originate the situation which developed and has cost 1600 men." LAC, RG 9 III-D-1, vol. 4679, folder 14, file 1.

43 PRO, WO 158/296, Canadian Corps G.265 to Second Army, 18 April 1916.

44 LAC, Macintyre Papers, vol. 1, personal diary, 4 April 1916, 142.

45 PRO, Cab 45/149, Postwar British *Official History* Correspondence and Accounts, St-Eloi, personal Account of Brig.-Gen. A.H. Bell, 6, 7.

46 LAC, War Diary, 2nd Canadian Division Headquarters, appendix C, R.E.W. Turner, "Report on 2nd Canadian Division's Operations at St. Eloi. April 3rd to April 16th," 18 April 1916, 3.

47 ASH, RG 4, series 3, World War One, Ted Lang Donation, R.H. (Harry) Neil, "A Brief History of the 19th Battalion C.E.F. 1914–18."

48 LAC, Macintyre Papers, vol. 2, "Men of Valour," 39. For more recent analyses of the fighting at St-Eloi and the fallout, see Tim Cook, *At the Sharp End: Canadians Fighting the Great War, 1914–1916* (Toronto: Viking, 2007), 323–42; David Campbell, "'A Leap in the Dark'—Intelligence and the Struggle for the St. Eloi Craters: Reassessing the Role of Major-General Richard Turner," in *Great War Commands: Historical Perspectives on Canadian Army Leadership, 1914–1918*, ed. Andrew B. Godefroy (Kingston: Canadian Defence Academy Press, 2010), 21–52; William F. Stewart, *The Embattled General: Sir Richard Turner and the First World War* (Montreal and Kingston: McGill–Queen's University Press, 2015), 82–111.

49 Personal collection of Mrs. Phyllis Douglas, letters of Lt.-Col. Lionel H. Millen, Millen to his mother, 14 April 1916.

50 LAC, Notes on St. Eloi Fighting, listings of officers and other ranks mentioned in reports from 19th Battalion to 4th Brigade. A number of these individuals and their accomplishments were also mentioned by Lord Beaverbrook in his published account *Canada in Flanders,* vol. 2, 139–40.

51 LAC, War Diary, 19th Battalion, 17 April 1916; LAC, War Diary, 2nd Canadian Division Headquarters, appendix 191, "Summary of Operations, 2nd Canadian Division, April 14th-21st"; ibid., appendix 198, "2nd Canadian Division, Monthly Report on Defences," 27 April 1916.

52 Cook, "The Blind Leading the Blind," 31–32; LAC, Turner Papers, "Report on Operations," and appendix 2 to this report; LAC, *Flanders Fields*, vol. 10, 19th Battalion, transcript of interview with F.A. Stitt, tape 1, 12.

53 According to German records, total German losses "in the recapture of the craters and fighting that followed were 66 killed, 299 wounded and 118 missing, the last mostly buried." Edmonds, *Military Operations, France and Belgium, 1916*, vol. 1, 193.

54 LAC, III-D-3, vol. 4848, War Diary, 2nd Canadian Division, Assistant Adjutant (AA) and Quartermaster General (QMG), April 1916, appendix 17, Casualties for the Month of April 1916; LAC, RG 150, vol. 493, "Casualties by Days—France and Belgium," 19th Battalion. As for the unfortunate victims of the "friendly fire" incident on the morning of 10 April, three were

killed and seven were wounded. LAC, War Diary, 19th Battalion, appendix 31, field message, 10 April 1916. See also LAC, War Diary, 4th Brigade, appendix 7, situation report regarding "Craters 4 and 5," 7–12 April 1916, submitted by Lt. Burnham, scout officer, and signed by Lts. Macdonald, Pepler, Thomson, and Cassels, 13 April 1916.

55 Although the Report of the Battles Nomenclature Committee in 1921 listed the "Actions of St. Eloi Craters" as having lasted from 27 March to 16 April, the fighting effectively continued until 4:35 a.m. on 20 April. At that time, the 2nd Canadian Division finally halted efforts to recapture craters 6 and 7, which had been lost on the previous evening. Nicholson, *Canadian Expeditionary Force*, appendix F, "Battles and Other Engagements in which Canadian Forces Participated," 554; LAC, Turner Papers, vol. 1, file 9, "Messages Received, General Staff, 2nd Canadian Div. April 19th/20th"; Leppard, "Richard Turner and the Battle of St. Eloi," 96.

56 LAC, War Diary, 2nd Canadian Division Headquarters, appendix 162, 2nd Canadian Division G.571 to 4th Brigade, 8 April 1916.

57 For interpretations that hold Turner primarily responsible for the confusion at St-Eloi, see the following: Thomas P. Leppard, "'The Dashing Subaltern': Sir Richard Turner in Retrospect," *Canadian Military History* 6, no. 2 (1997): 21–28; idem, "Richard Turner and the Battle of St. Eloi"; and Cook, "The Blind Leading the Blind." My own view is that Turner should not bear primary responsibility for the mistakes made during the operation. Instead, he was the victim of intractable circumstances and overwhelmingly faulty front-line intelligence. See Campbell, "The Divisional Experience in the C.E.F.," ch. 3.

58 PRO, WO 158/296, Canadian Corps G.265 to Second Army, 18 April 1916.

59 DHH, A.F. Duguid Papers, box 2, folder E, file 75, "Relations between General Turner and General Alderson."

60 Cook, "The Blind Leading the Blind," 32; Campbell, "The Divisional Experience in the C.E.F.," 131–35, 138. Alderson had already aroused Sam Hughes's wrath during numerous policy disagreements, the most notable of which was Alderson's public criticism of the Canadian-made Ross rifle. The militia minister saw in the fallout over St-Eloi a perfect opportunity to get rid of the corps commander. Morton, *A Peculiar Kind of Politics*, 72–74; Ronald G. Haycock, *Sam Hughes: The Public Career of a Controversial Canadian, 1885–1916* (Waterloo and Ottawa: Wilfrid Laurier University Press / Canadian War Museum, 1986), 296–300.

Notes to Chapter 6 – "Trying the Nerves": May–July 1916

1 LAC, RG 9, III-D-3, vol. 4843, War Diary, 2nd Canadian Division headquarters, daily observations on weather conditions, 1–31 May 1916.

2 Archives of Ontario (AO), MU 7662, John F. Mould Papers, file 4, personal diary, 29 April–8 May 1916.

3 Tim Cook, *No Place to Run: The Canadian Corps and Gas Warfare in the First World War* (Vancouver: UBC Press, 1999), 70.

4 AO, Mould Papers, file 4, personal diary, 29 April–8 May 1916.

5 LAC, RG 9, III-D-3, vol. 4927, War Diary, 19th Battalion, appendices 8–14, casualties reported in field messages, 9–15 May 1916.

6 LAC, War Diary, 19th Battalion, appendix 9, daily activity report, 10 May 1916.

7 Many of the patrols during this tour consisted of three NCOs and eighteen men. LAC, War Diary, 19th Battalion, appendices 9–14, field messages with nightly patrol reports, 10–15 May 1916.

8 AO, Mould Papers, file 4, personal diary, 16–22 May 1916.

9 Personal collection of Mrs. Phyllis Douglas, letters of Lt.-Col. Lionel H. Millen (hereafter Millen Letters), Millen to his mother, 25 March 1916.

10 LAC, War Diary, 19th Battalion, 16–27 May 1916; ibid., appendix 22, message to company commanders, 24 May 1916.

11 G.W.L. Nicholson, *Canadian Expeditionary Force, 1914–1919: The Official History of the Canadian Army in the First World War* (Ottawa: Queen's Printer, 1962), 140; LAC, RG 9, III-D-3,

vol. 4848, War Diary, AA & QMG, 2nd Canadian Division, 3 June 1916; David W. Love, *A Nation in Making: The Organization and Administration of the Canadian Military During the First World War*, vol. 2 (Ottawa: Service Publications, 2012), 347; LAC, RG 9, III-C-3, vol. 4140, folder 1, file 10, memorandum from the director of medical services, Second Army, on the protective qualities of the steel helmet, 7 March 1916.

12 AO, Mould Papers, file 4, personal diary, 27 May 1916.

13 LAC, War Diary, 19th Battalion, 27–31 May 1916.

14 D.J. Corrigall, *The History of the Twentieth Canadian Battalion (Central Ontario Regiment) Canadian Expeditionary Force in the Great War, 1914–1918* (Toronto: Stone and Cox, 1935), 63.

15 LAC, War Diary, 19th Battalion, May 1916, appendices, orders and instructions to companies regarding the provision of work parties and their assignments; Corrigall, *The History of the Twentieth Canadian Battalion*, 63.

16 LAC, RG 9, III-C-1, vol. 3870, folder 112, file 4, Canadian Corps G.526/1 to Second Army, 24 December 1915; LAC, RG 24, C-6-j, vol. 6937, "Schools and Courses in the Field," xii–xiv, xvi. See also David Campbell, "The Divisional Experience in the C.E.F.: A Social and Operational History of the 2nd Canadian Division, 1915–1918," PhD diss., University of Calgary, 2003, 80–2; and idem, "Schooling for War: Canadian Infantry Training, 1914–1917," in *Perspectives on War: Essays on Security, Society and the State*, ed. Chris Bullock and Jillian Dowding (Calgary: Society for Military and Strategic Studies, 2001), 15–30; LAC, War Diary, 19th Battalion, appendix 16, Adjutant, 19th Battalion to OC, A Company, 17 May 1916.

17 Millen Letters, Millen to his mother, 25 March 1916.

18 LAC, War Diary, 19th Battalion, 1–8, 16–22 May 1916; LAC, RG 9, III-C-3, vol. 4136, folder 24, file 3, schedule of training, 27th Battalion, 5 March 1916; ibid., vol. 4143, folder 9, file 1, 31st Battalion training syllabi, 7 October, 22 November, 9 December 1915, 9 May 1916.

19 Andrew Horrall, "'Keep-a-Fighting! Play the Game!' Baseball and the Canadian Forces during the First World War," *Canadian Military History* 10, no. 2 (2001): 30, 34.

20 Isabella Losinger, "Officer-Man Relations in the Canadian Expeditionary Force, 1914–1919," MA thesis, Carleton University, 1990, 65.

21 Millen Letters, Millen to his mother, 9 May 1916.

22 Bruce Cane, *It Made You Think of Home: The Haunting Journal of Deward Barnes, Canadian Expeditionary Force: 1916–1919* (Toronto: Dundurn, 2004), 102–3.

23 Jonathan F. Vance, *Death So Noble: Memory, Meaning, and the First World War* (Vancouver: UBC Press, 1997), 79–80.

24 Ibid., 84–5; see also J.G. Fuller, *Troop Morale and Popular Culture in the British and Dominion Armies, 1914–1918* (Oxford: Clarendon Press, 1990), 94–110.

25 Ed Youngman did remember a few of the performers as well as a boxing skit. LAC, RG 41, B-III-1, Records of the CBC, *Flanders Fields*, vol. 10, 19th Battalion, transcript of interview with E. Youngman, tape 5, 2–3.

26 Fuller, *Troop Morale and Popular Culture*, 110–13; Andrew Horrall, "Charlie Chaplin and the Canadian Expeditionary Force," in *Canada and the Great War: Western Front Association Papers*, ed. Briton C. Busch (Montreal and Kingston: McGill–Queen's University Press, 2003), 27–45; LAC, RG 9, III-C-3, vol. 4116, folder 6, file 1, "Cinema, 2nd Canadian Division."

27 The profits of these games did not always go to those who organized them. See ASH, H.D. Fearman Collection, "Selections from the Mailbag," contribution by T.W. (Ted) Lang, 19th Battalion Association newsletter, Fall 1974.

28 Millen Letters, Millen to his mother, 17 October 1915.

29 Robert N. Clements, *Merry Hell: The Story of the 25th Battalion (Nova Scotia Regiment), Canadian Expeditionary Force, 1914–1919*, ed. Brian Douglas Tennyson (Toronto: University of Toronto Press, 2012), 199–200.

30 One wonders whether the note from "Arthur" was a gag designed to get a reaction from the censoring officer. Clements, *Merry Hell*, 199–200.

31 Millen Letters, Millen to his mother, 12 December 1915.

32 Millen Letters, Millen to his sister Gertie, 7 November 1915.

33 Glenbow Museum Archives (GMA), M399, Gaetz Family Fonds, Letters of J.R. Gaetz, Gaetz to his father, 1 February 1917.
34 CWM, 19740071-017 58C 1 1.8, untitled file of letters, questionnaires, responses, and notes regarding 19th Battalion history, handwritten letter to R.O. Spreckley, from "Ralph," dated "Edmonton July 16," year unknown. This likely was Ralph Whitney, a 19th Battalion veteran who is mentioned by Spreckley in another item of correspondence.
35 See Jeffery Williams, *Byng of Vimy: General and Governor General* (Toronto: University of Toronto Press, 1985; orig. ed., Leo Cooper, 1983), Chs. 5–7; Nicholson, *Canadian Expeditionary Force*, 147.
36 LAC, MG 30, D 150, Sir Andrew Macphail Papers, vol. 4, personal diary, vol. 2, 23 July 1916.
37 Qtd. in Williams, *Byng of Vimy*, 130.
38 ASH, RG 4, series 3, World War 1, 19th Battalion Association, "Recollections of Some Army 'Brass,'" contribution by Ted Lang, 19th Battalion Association newsletter, Fall 1969.
39 ASH, RG 4, series 3, World War 1, 19th Battalion Association, "Recollections of Some Army 'Brass,'" contribution by Harry G. James, 19th Battalion Association newsletter, Fall 1969.
40 Nicholson, *Canadian Expeditionary Force*, 147; Norm Christie, *For King and Empire: The Canadians at Mont Sorrel, June 2nd–14th, 1916* (Ottawa: CEF Books, 2000), 17–19; Williams, *Byng of Vimy*, 117.
41 D.J. Goodspeed, "Prelude to the Somme: Mont Sorrel, June 1916," in *Policy by Other Means: Essays in Honour of C.P. Stacey*, ed. Michael Cross and Robert Bothwell (Toronto: Clarke, Irwin, 1972), 149–50; Nicholson, *Canadian Expeditionary Force*, 148–49; LAC, MG 30, E 100, Sir Arthur Currie Papers, vol. 42, "Canadian Expeditionary Force, Diary of Events, Canadian Corps, 1916," 10.
42 LAC, War Diary, 19th Battalion, 1–5 June 1916.
43 AO, Mould Papers, file 4, personal diary, 5 June 1916.
44 LAC, War Diary, 19th Battalion, 1–5 June 1916.
45 AO, Mould Papers, file 4, personal diary, 5 June 1916.
46 AO, Mould Papers, file 4, personal diary, 7 June 1916.
47 CWM, 19740071-017 58C 1 1.8, typewritten notes from an anonymous member of no. 4 Platoon.
48 LAC, War Diary, 19th Battalion, 1–5 June 1916.
49 LAC, RG 9, III-D-3, vol. 4888, War Diary, 6th Infantry Brigade, 6 June 1916; ibid., vol. 4935, War Diary, 28th Battalion, 6 June 1916; Goodspeed, "Prelude to the Somme," 154.
50 Ibid., 154; LAC, RG 150, vol. 493, "Casualties by Days, France and Belgium," June 1916.
51 J.A. Cooper, *History of Operations of 4th Canadian Infantry Brigade, 1915–1919* (London: Charles and Son, n.d.), 12. A copy of this privately circulated history was located in LAC, MG 30, E46, Sir Richard Turner Papers, vol. 12, file 94.
52 LAC, War Diary, 19th Battalion, appendix 5, activity report, 6 June 1916; LAC, RG 9, III-D-3, vol. 4926, War Diary, 18th Battalion, 6 June 1916.
53 AO, Mould Papers, file 4, personal diary, 6 June 1916.
54 AO, Mould Papers, file 4, personal diary, 9 June 1916.
55 AO, Mould Papers, file 4, personal diary, 7 June 1916.
56 AO, Mould Papers, file 4, personal diary, 16 July 1916.
57 AO, Mould Papers, file 4, personal diary, 9 June 1916.
58 From right to left, the assault units were the 3rd, 16th, 13th, and 58th battalions. Goodspeed, "Prelude to the Somme," 155; Christie, *The Canadians at Mont Sorrel*, 24, 27.
59 LAC, Currie Papers, vol. 42, Canadian Expeditionary Force, Diary of Events, Canadian Corps, 1916, 14–16; LAC, War Diary, 2nd Canadian Division Headquarters, appendix 272, "Report on Operations of 2nd Canadian Division, June 13, 1916."
60 AO, Mould Papers, file 4, personal diary, 13 June 1916.
61 AO, Mould Papers, file 4, personal diary, 13 June 1916.
62 Goodspeed, "Prelude to the Somme," 157.
63 Nicholson, *Canadian Expeditionary Force*, 153; Goodspeed, "Prelude to the Somme," 156.

64 Ibid., 157–58.
65 Campbell, "The Divisional Experience in the C.E.F.," 162.
66 Nicholson, *Canadian Expeditionary Force*, 154.
67 AO, Mould Papers, file 4, personal diary, 18–23 June 1916.
68 LAC, War Diary, 19th Battalion, 17–29 June 1916.
69 LAC, War Diary, 19th Battalion, July 1916, appendix 1, message regarding intended artillery demonstration.
70 Gary Sheffield, *The Somme* (London: Cassell, 2003), 68; Tim Travers, "July 1, 1916: The Reason Why," *MHQ: Quarterly Journal of Military History* 7, no. 4 (1995): 62; Hew Strachan, *The First World War* (New York: Viking, 2004), 192. For a comprehensive study of all phases of the Somme offensive, including revealing panoramic photos of the battlefields, see Peter Barton, with Jeremy Banning, *The Somme: The Unseen Panoramas* (London: Constable, 2011).
71 LAC, War Diary, 19th Battalion, 5–15 July 1916; Cooper, *History of Operations*, 12.
72 AO, Mould Papers, file 4, personal diary, 5–15 July 1916.
73 LAC, War Diary, 19th Battalion, 5–15 July 1916.
74 LAC, RG 9, III-D-3, vol. 4880, War Diary, 4th Infantry Brigade, 8 July 1916; Cooper, *History of Operations*, 13.
75 AO, Mould Papers, file 4, personal diary, 16–18 July 1916; LAC, vol. 4927, War Diary, 19th Battalion, July 1916, appendices 7–9, daily activity and artillery reports.
76 DHH, A.F. Duguid Papers (Biog D), box 2, folder E, file 75, "Relations between General Turner and General Alderson; Notes on a Conversation between General Turner and D.H.S., 14th March, 1934"; LAC, War Diary, 2nd Canadian Division, AA & QMG, 17 July 1916.
77 The divisional GSO 1 (chief of staff for operations), Lt.-Col. C.A. Ker, also departed on 24 May to take up the same post in the Royal Naval Division. LAC, War Diary, 2nd Canadian Division Headquarters, 24 May 1916.
78 LAC, RG 9, III-C-3, vol. 4115, folder 3, file 11, field message reporting McLaren's impending departure, presumably dated 16 July 1916.
79 "Col. M'Laren Got Home from the Front Today," *Hamilton Herald*, 31 July 1916.
80 ASH, large bound volume of papers and clippings belonging to W.R. Turnbull (hereafter Turnbull Papers), newspaper clipping titled "McLaren's Bravery," *Hamilton Spectator*, date not known.
81 "Col. M'Laren Got Home From the Front Today."
82 Millen Letters, Millen to his mother, 30 October 1916.
83 ASH, Turnbull Papers, Report by 1st Canadian Division to Canadian Corps headquarters, 28 July 1916; ibid., handwritten note from Rennie to Turnbull, 30 July 1916.

Chapter 7 – A Daylight Coup and Departing Belgium: 29 July–August 1916

1 G.W.L. Nicholson, *Canadian Expeditionary Force, 1914–1919: The Official History of the Canadian Army in the First World War* (Ottawa: Queen's Printer, 1962), 136, 154.
2 David Campbell, "The Divisional Experience in the C.E.F.: A Social and Operational History of the 2nd Canadian Division, 1915–1918," PhD diss., University of Calgary, 2003, 168.
3 LAC, RG 9, III-D-3, vol. 4843, War Diary, 2nd Canadian Division Headquarters, appendix 331, Daily Intelligence Summary, 21 July 1916; LAC, RG 9, III-C-3, vol. 4091, folder 26, file 16, "Typical Patrol Enterprises Carried out by Canadian Corps, July 1st to August 18th 1916."
4 "19th Battalion Put on Famous Daylight Raid," *Hamilton Spectator*, 23 May 1919; J.A. Cooper, *History of Operations of 4th Canadian Infantry Brigade, 1915–1919* (London: Charles and Son, n.d.), 13.
5 "19th Battalion Put on Famous Daylight Raid."
6 Ibid.
7 LAC, RG 9, III-C-3, vol. 4116, folder 4, file 7, map, "Raid at Ypres-Comines Canal (4th Canadian Inf. Brigade, July 29th 1916"; see also LAC, RG 9, III-D-3, vol. 4880, War Diary, 4th Infantry Brigade, April 1916, appendix 24, map.

8 LAC, RG 9, III-D-1, vol. 4692, folder 51, file 15, Lt.-Col. W.R. Turnbull, "Report on Raid by 19th Battalion 29th July 1916," 30 July 1916 (hereafter Turnbull, "Report on Raid").

9 The 17th, 19th, 25th, 26th, and 27th Batteries under the command of Lt.-Col. J.S. Stewart were the field artillery units supporting the raid. LAC, RG 9, III-C-3, vol. 4106, folder 23, file 7, 19th Battalion Operation Order, 28 July 1916; ibid., Lt.-Col. J.S. Stewart, "Raiding Operation Carried out by 19th Canadian Battalion, 29th July 1916, Supported by 'Stewarts Group C.F.A.'" (hereafter Stewart Report); ibid., nominal roll of "Officers, Non-Commissioned Officers and men of the 19th Battalion Who Participated in the Raid on 29th July." A different copy of the operation orders, also dated 28 July, appears in the battalion war diary. It states that four officers and thirty-eight other ranks from the battalion would take part in the raid. LAC, RG 9, III-D-3, vol. 4927, War Diary, 19th Battalion, appendix 21, "Operation Orders by Lt. Colonel W.R. Turnbull Commanding," 28 July 1916. Because after-action reports and a nominal roll listing those from the battalion who participated in the operation cite only four officers and thirty-four other ranks, it has been decided to accept the lower number as the actual figure.

10 LAC, RG 9, vol. 4106, 19th Battalion Operation Order, 28 July 1916; LAC, War Diary, 19th Battalion, "Operation Orders by Lt. Colonel W.R. Turnbull Commanding"; LAC, RG 9, vol. 4692, folder 51, file 15, Maj. F. Logie Armstrong for GOC, 4th Infantry Brigade, "Report on Raiding Operation Carried out by the 19th Canadian Battalion, 29th July, 1916," 30 July 1916 (hereafter Armstrong Report).

11 LAC, RG 9, vol. 4106, 19th Battalion Operation Order, 28 July 1916; LAC, Turnbull, "Report on Raid"; LAC, Armstrong Report.

12 LAC, RG 9, vol. 4106, 19th Battalion Operation Order, 28 July 1916.

13 LAC, RG 9, vol. 4106, 19th Battalion Operation Order, 28 July 1916.

14 "19th Battalion Put on Famous Daylight Raid."

15 LAC, Armstrong Report; LAC, RG 9, III-C-3, vol. 4116, folder 4, file 7, "Typical Trench Raids Carried out by Canadian Corps July 1st to August 20th 1916"; LAC, RG 9, vol. 4106, folder 23, file 7, statement by no. 55955 Lance Cpl. W. Wilson, scout.

16 LAC, RG 9, vol. 4106, statement by No. 55766, Sgt. J. Holk, D Company.

17 LAC, RG 9, vol. 4106, statement by no. 55894, Pte. R. Montgomery, bomber.

18 LAC, RG 9, vol. 4106, statement by no. 406781, Pte. W. Nettleton, scout.

19 LAC, RG 9, vol. 4106, statement by no. 55162, Cpl. H.V. Brisbin, A Company.

20 LAC, RG 9, vol. 4106, statement by no. 55407, Lance Cpl. R. Dinsmore, scout.

21 LAC, RG 9, vol. 4106, statement by no. 55506, Pte. C. Stephenson, bomber.

22 LAC, RG 9, vol. 4106, statement by no. 56021, Pte. G. Pattenden, B Company.

23 LAC, RG 9, vol. 4106, statement by no. 56068, Lance Cpl. F. Willoughby, bomber.

24 LAC, RG 9, vol. 4106, statement by no. 56116, Pte. W. Tapp, scout.

25 LAC, Turnbull, "Report on Raid"; "19th Battalion Put on Famous Daylight Raid"; LAC, Armstrong Report.

26 LAC, RG 9, vol. 4106, folder 23, file 7, statement by no. 55766, Sgt. J. Holk, D Company.

27 LAC, Turnbull, "Report on Raid."

28 LAC, Turnbull, "Report on Raid"; LAC, Stewart Report; LAC, RG 9, vol. 4106, "Report of 'Stuart' [*sic*] Group C.F.A.," Lt. T.H. O'Brien, 19th Battery CFA (hereafter O'Brien Report).

29 LAC, Armstrong Report.

30 LAC, Armstrong Report.

31 LAC, RG 9, vol. 4106, folder 23, file 7, statement by no. 55914, Pte. J. Newton, scout (hereafter Newton statement).

32 LAC, Newton statement.

33 LAC, O'Brien Report.

34 LAC, Stewart Report.

35 LAC, O'Brien Report.

36 LAC, Newton statement.

37 LAC, RG 41, B-III-1, Records of the CBC, *Flanders Fields*, vol. 10, 19th Battalion, transcript of interview with E. Youngman, tape 3, 4.

38 LAC, Newton statement.
39 LAC, Stewart Report.
40 LAC, RG 9, vol. 4106, folder 23, file 8, GOC, 4th Infantry Brigade to GOC, 2nd Canadian Division, 1 August 1916.
41 Nicholson, *Canadian Expeditionary Force*, 154; LAC, RG 9, vol. 4116, "Typical Trench Raids Carried out by Canadian Corps July 1st to August 20th 1916"; LAC, Armstrong Report; LAC, Turnbull, "Report on Raid"; LAC, RG 9, III-D-3, vol. 4813, War Diary, Canadian Corps Headquarters, appendix III/2, "Canadian Corps, Summary of Operations, July 28th to August 3rd 1916"; "19th Battalion Put on Famous Daylight Raid"; ASH, large bound volume of papers and clippings belonging to W.R. Turnbull (hereafter Turnbull Papers), "Report of Raiding Operations carried out by the 19th Canadian Battalion, July 29th 1916"; LAC, RG 150, vol. 493, "Casualties by Days – France and Belgium," July 1916.
42 ASH, Turnbull Papers, "Report of Raiding Operations carried out by the 19th Canadian Battalion, July 29th 1916"; "19th Battalion Put on Famous Daylight Raid." On Kilmer's condition, see LAC, RG 9, vol. 4116, folder 4, file 8, ADMS, 2nd Canadian Division, 30 July 1916.
43 LAC, RG 150, series 7, vol. 465, file, "List of Officers – 19th Battalion," September 1916, June 1918.
44 "19th Battalion Put on Famous Daylight Raid"; ASH, Turnbull Papers, newspaper clipping "Hamilton Man Risked Life, Saved Officer," paper and date not stated but the article was published before 1 May 1917 and is likely from the *Hamilton Spectator*. Ironically, after having risked so much to rescue Capt. Kilmer and come through unscathed, Pte. Joe Newton was wounded by shrapnel in both shoulders when the rest camp was bombed by German aircraft. He spent the following six months recovering in hospital in England and was granted furlough back to his home in Hamilton during 1917. Lance Cpl. Wilfred Wilson survived the air raid without injury but would be wounded in action six weeks later at the Somme. ASH, Turnbull Papers, "Hamilton Man Risked Life, Saved Officer."
45 Cooper, *History of Operations*, 13.
46 LAC, RG 9, III-C-3, vol. 4115, folder 1, file 5, Turner to Turnbull, 29 July 1916.
47 The Canadian Corps Officers' School was established by Lt.-Gen. Byng in July 1916 to improve the training of junior officers. LAC, MG 30, E 50, Elmer Jones Papers, file 3, "Canadian Corps Officers School 1916."
48 LAC, RG 9, vol. 4116, "Typical Trench Raids Carried out by Canadian Corps July 1st to August 20th 1916."
49 LAC, *Flanders Fields*, vol. 10, 19th Battalion, transcript of interview with E. Youngman, tape 3, 3.
50 LAC, *Flanders Fields*, vol. 10, 19th Battalion, transcript of interview with E. Youngman, tape 3, 2.
51 Bill Rawling, *Surviving Trench Warfare: Technology and the Canadian Corps, 1914–1918* (Toronto: University of Toronto Press, 1992), 47–48; Andrew B. Godefroy, "A Lesson in Success: The Calonne Trench Raid, 17 January 1917," *Canadian Military History* 8, no. 2 (1999): 33–34; Campbell, "The Divisional Experience in the C.E.F.," 97–98, 179–81.
52 LAC, War Diary, 19th Battalion, appendix 22, casualty report, 30 July 1916; ibid., appendix 2, casualty report, 1 August 1916; ASH, Turnbull Papers, newspaper clipping, "Gallant Officer Was Warmly Welcomed This Morning," paper and date not stated; LAC, RG 24, C-6-d, vol. 1886, file 85, Lists of Commanders and Staffs, Second Canadian Division.
53 CWM, 19740071-017 58C 1 1.8, untitled file of letters, questionnaires, responses, and notes regarding 19th Battalion history, typewritten notes by a member of no. 4 Platoon, name unknown.
54 Personal collection of Mrs. Phyllis Douglas, letters of Lt.-Col. Lionel H. Millen (hereafter Millen Letters), Millen to his mother, 10 August 1916.
55 LAC, War Diary, 19th Battalion, 12 August 1916.
56 Nicholson, *Canadian Expeditionary Force*, 154; LAC, War Diary, 4th Infantry Brigade, 14 August 1916.

57 LAC, War Diary, 19th Battalion, appendix 13, Daily Activity Report, 14 August 1916.
58 AO, MU 7662, John F. Mould Papers, file 4, personal diary, 14 August 1916.
59 LAC, War Diary, 4th Infantry Brigade, appendix 7, "19th Battalion Operation Order," 14 August 1916.
60 LAC, War Diary, 4th Infantry Brigade, appendix 7, "19th Battalion Operation Order," 14 August 1916; ibid., "Report on Dummy Raid, Aug 15th inst."
61 LAC, RG 9, III-D-3, vol. 4930, War Diary, 21st Battalion, 15 August 1916.
62 LAC, War Diary, 4th Infantry Brigade, 14 August 1916; LAC, War Diary, 19th Battalion, 14 August 1916.
63 LAC, MG 30, D 150, Sir Andrew Macphail Papers, vol. 4, personal diary, vol. 2, 1916, 18 August 1916.
64 Author's interview with Col. Ian Douglas and Phyllis Douglas, 8 December 2002.
65 Millen Letters, Millen to his mother, 21 August 1916.
66 LAC, War Diary, 19th Battalion, 20 August 1916; Nicholson, *Canadian Expeditionary Force*, 157–58.
67 Campbell, "The Divisional Experience in the C.E.F.," 148.
68 Ibid., 150–56.
69 LAC, Sir Richard Turner Papers, vol. 11, file 82, Responses to Ross rifle questionnaire, Maj. W.R. Turnbull, 4 May 1916.
70 LAC, Turner Papers, Responses to Ross rifle questionnaire, Maj. G. Morrison, OC, A Company, 19th Battalion.
71 LAC, Turner Papers, Responses to Ross rifle questionnaire, Maj. W. Moors, B Company, 19th Battalion.
72 LAC, Turner Papers, Responses to Ross rifle questionnaire, Capt. F.J. Buchanan, C Company, 19th Battalion.
73 LAC, Turner Papers, Responses to Ross rifle questionnaire, Maj. L. Millen, D Company, 19th Battalion.
74 LAC, War Diary, 19th Battalion, 20 August 1916; Nicholson, *Canadian Expeditionary Force*, 155–56, 158–59.
75 D.J. Corrigall, *The History of the Twentieth Canadian Battalion (Central Ontario Regiment) Canadian Expeditionary Force in the Great War, 1914–1918* (Toronto: Stone and Cox, 1935), 75.
76 CWM, 19740071–017 58C 1 1.8, typewriten notes by a member of no. 4 Platoon, name unknown.
77 CWM, 19740071–017 58C 1 1.8, typewriten notes by a member of no. 4 Platoon, name unknown.
78 Malcolm Brown, *The Imperial War Museum Book of the Somme* (London: Pan Books, 1997), 264.
79 LAC, War Diary, 19th Battalion, 16–23 August 1916.
80 LAC, War Diary, 19th Battalion, appendices 16 and 17, Operation Orders, 22 and 23 August 1916.
81 CWM, 19740071–017 58C 1 1.8, 28 August 1916.
82 AO, John F. Mould Papers, personal diary, entry beginning on 26 August 1916.
83 CWM, 119740071–017 58C 1.8, handwritten notes titled "Section #2," author unknown.
84 LAC, vols. 4926–7, War Diary, 19th Battalion, November 1915–August 1916.
85 LAC, "Casualties By Days – France and Belgium," 19th Battalion (for monthly summaries of these daily casualty statistics, see Appendix A).

Chapter 8 – Preparing for Battle: 28 August–15 September 1916

1 LAC, RG 9, III-D-3, vol. 4927, War Diary, 19th Battalion, 28–31 August 1916.
2 AO, MU 7662, John F. Mould Papers, file 4, personal diary, 29–30 August 1916.
3 LAC, War Diary, 19th Battalion, 1–3 September 1916; D.J. Corrigall, *The History of the Twentieth Canadian Battalion (Central Ontario Regiment), Canadian Expeditionary Force, in the Great*

War, 1914–1918 (Toronto: Stone and Cox, 1935), 75. The infantry would signal to observers in aircraft by flashing reflective disks, lighting flares, or arranging sheets or panels on the ground into predetermined shapes that indicated the desired message. The airmen would relay messages and reports to division and corps headquarters by wireless or by dropping weighted message bags at prearranged drop zones. Dan Jenkins, "Winning Trench Warfare: Battlefield Intelligence in the Canadian Corps, 1914–1918," PhD diss., Carleton University, 1999, 213.

4 LAC, RG 41, B-III-1, Records of the CBC, *Flanders Fields*, vol. 12, 28th Battalion, transcript of interview with Capt. J.F. McKay, tape 2, 1–2.

5 LAC, MG 30, E 46, Sir Richard Turner Papers, vol. 2, file 14, 2nd Canadian Division notes, 21 August 1916; LAC, RG 9, III-C-3, vol. 4114, folder 46, file 1, 2nd Canadian Division G. 930, 25 August 1916.

6 Bill Rawling, *Surviving Trench Warfare: Technology and the Canadian Corps, 1914–1918* (Toronto: University of Toronto Press, 1992), 72–74.

7 S.S. 109, *Training of Divisions for Offensive Action*, 8 May 1916, 2.

8 This was a term used in Britain to refer to units of volunteers raised in the United Kingdom after the war's outbreak, as distinguished from units of Britain's small professional regular army and units of Britain's volunteer reserve troops (known as the Territorial Force), which predated the war.

9 Rawling, *Surviving Trench Warfare*, 68–70; Shelford Bidwell and Dominick Graham, *Fire-Power: British Army Weapons and Theories of War, 1904–1945* (London: Allen and Unwin, 1982), 36–37, 120–21.

10 Ian F.W. Beckett, *The Great War, 1914–1918* (London: Longman, 2001), 164; Paddy Griffith, *Battle Tactics on the Western Front: The British Army's Art of Attack, 1916–18* (New Haven: Yale University Press, 1994), 58–59, 63–64; Gary Sheffield, *Forgotten Victory: The First World War, Myths and Realities* (London: Headline, 2001), 138–39.

11 Bidwell and Graham, *Fire-Power*, 83–85; Rawling, *Surviving Trench Warfare*, 69–70, 77–78.

12 LAC, vol. 4926, War Diary, 19th Battalion, appendix 92, field message outlining instructions for practice attack, 26 December 1915.

13 CWM, 58, A1, 9.1, 1971, 0147–001, Personal Diary of Sir Richard Turner, 99.

14 R.C. Fetherstonhaugh, *The 24th Battalion, C.E.F., Victoria Rifles of Canada 1914–1919* (Montreal: Gazette Printing Company, 1930), 80–81.

15 Corrigall, *The History of the Twentieth Canadian Battalion*, 76.

16 LAC, vol. 4927, War Diary, 19th Battalion, 4 September 1916; LAC, RG 9, III-D-3, vol. 4844, War Diary, 2nd Canadian Division Headquarters, 4 September 1916.

17 LAC, War Diary, 19th Battalion, 5 September 1916; CWM, 19740071–017 58C 1 1.8, untitled file of letters, questionnaires, responses, and notes regarding 19th Battalion history, typewritten notes from a member of no. 4 Platoon, name unknown.

18 LAC, War Diary, 19th Battalion, 6–9 September 1916.

19 H.C. Singer and A.A. Peebles, *History of the Thirty-First Battalion C.E.F.* (Calgary: privately printed, 1939), 141.

20 LAC, War Diary, 19th Battalion, 9 September 1916.

21 CWM, 19740071–017 58C 1.8, typewritten notes from a member of no. 4 Platoon, name unknown.

22 LAC, War Diary, 19th Battalion, 10 September 1916.

23 G.W.L. Nicholson, *Canadian Expeditionary Force, 1914–1919: The Official History of the Canadian Army in the First World War* (Ottawa: Queen's Printer 1962), 167; Gary Sheffield, *The Somme* (London: Cassell 2003), 113.

24 AO, Mould Papers, peronal diary, 10 September 1916.

25 Sheffield, *The Somme*, 19; ASH, RG 4, series 3, World War 1, Ted Lang Donation, "19th Battalion Oldtimers," 19th Battalion Association newsletter, Spring 1985. The statue was secured at its oblique angle by French engineers, but it eventually plummeted in April 1918 as a result of British artillery fire. A replica of the famous statue now crowns the restored basilica. Martin Marix Evans, *The Battles of the Somme* (Toronto: Little, Brown 1996), 14.

26 AO, Mould Papers, personal diary, 10 September 1916.
27 Sheffield, *The Somme*, 95; Martin Middlebrook, *The First Day on the Somme* (London: Penguin, 1984), 63; Nicholson, *Canadian Expeditionary Force*, 169.
28 AO, Mould Papers, personal diary, 10 September 1916.
29 CWM, 19740071–017 58C 1 1.8, typewritten notes from a member of no. 4 Platoon, name unknown.
30 Each of the platoons in the front line and support positions had an approximate strength of 45 men. The reserve company contained roughly 180 men. LAC, War Diary, 19th Battalion, 10 September 1916.
31 AO, Mould Papers, personal diary, 10 September 1916.
32 LAC, War Diary, 19th Battalion, 10–11 September 1916.
33 LAC, War Diary, 19th Battalion, 11 September 1916.
34 LAC, War Diary, 19th Battalion, 11 September 1916. Whittemore was wounded by shrapnel while on duty in his dressing station. He refused to leave until another medical officer arrived to take his place on the following afternoon. Some of the officers who tended to the 19th Battalion's medical needs until the appointment of Capt. Allison were: Capt. Ireland; Capt. H. Macdonald; Capt. J. Moore; and Capt. G.W. Treleaven. LAC, RG 9, III-D-1, vol. 4692, folder 51, file 17, 19th Battalion, report on operations, 10–17 September 1916; LAC, War Diary, 19th Battalion, 5, 8 October 1916; LAC, RG 150, vol. 465, 19th Battalion, List of Officers, 1 December 1916.
35 LAC, War Diary, 19th Battalion, 11–12 September 1916.
36 CWM, 19740071–017 58C 1 1.8, typewritten notes from a member of no. 4 Platoon, name unknown; AO, Mould Papers, personal diary, 11–13 September 1916.
37 AO, Mould Papers, personal diary, 13 September 1916.
38 LAC, War Diary, 19th Battalion, 13–14 September 1916.
39 There, he would distinguish himself with his efforts to improve training arrangements within the division, rising to command the school itself. Eventually, he would be called back to assume a battlefield command, as commanding officer of the 20th Battalion in July 1918. LAC, War Diary, 19th Battalion, 12–14 September 1916; LAC, 19th Battalion, report on operations, 10-17 September 1916; LAC, 19th Battalion, List of Officers; Corrigall, *The History of the Twentieth Canadian Battalion*, 210, 212.
40 CWM, 19740071–017 58C 1 1.8, typed notes on battalion's experience at the Somme; ibid., Personal Diary of Sir Richard Turner, 100; LAC, RG 9, III-D-3, vol. 4880, War Diary, 4th Canadian Infantry Brigade, report on "Operations of 4th Canadian Infantry Brigade at the Somme, September 10–17, 1916."
41 Nicholson, *Canadian Expeditionary Force*, 169; LAC, War Diary, 2nd Canadian Division Headquarters, appendix 400, 2nd Canadian Division G.S. 1166, 8 September 1916; LAC, Turner Papers, vol. 2, file 14, "Summary of Operations of 2nd Canadian Division, September 15th and 16th."
42 The artillery units were from Canadian, British, and Indian formations. Nicholson, *Canadian Expeditionary Force*, 168–69; LAC, RG 9, III-D-1, vol. 4679, folder 15, file 3, Maj. Frederick Davy, "The Capture of Courcelette," 5; LAC, Turner Papers, vol. 2, file 14, Canadian Corps, G.688, 9 September 1916; G.W.L. Nicholson, *The Gunners of Canada: The History of the Royal Regiment of Canadian Artillery*, vol. 1: *1534–1919* (Toronto: McClelland and Stewart, 1967), 261–62.
43 LAC, War Diary, 19th Battalion, 15 September 1916; LAC, RG 9, III-D-3, vol. 4957, War Diary, G.O.C.R.A., Canadian Corps, appendices, Operation Order No. 26, 13 September 1916; Nicholson, *The Gunners of Canada*, 264.
44 LAC, RG 9, III-C-3, vol. 4098, folder 44–1, 1st Canadian Motor Machine Gun Brigade, Operation Order no. 82, 14 September 1916; LAC, War Diary, 2nd Canadian Division Headquarters, appendix 408, 2nd Canadian Division Operation Order no. 78, 14 September 1916; C.S. Grafton, *The Canadian 'Emma Gees': A History of the Canadian Machine Gun Corps* (London: Canadian Machine Gun Corps Association, 1938), 50.

45 David Fletcher, *Landships: British Tanks in the First World War* (London: HMSO, 1984), 16; Nicholson, *Canadian Expeditionary Force*, 169.
46 LAC, RG 9, III-C-3, vol. 4098, folder 43–2, 2nd Canadian Division, G.S.1174, 11 September 1916; LAC, War Diary, 2nd Canadian Division Headquarters, appendix 408, 2nd Canadian Division Operation Order No. 78, 14 September 1916.
47 Martin Marix Evans, *The Battles of the Somme* (Toronto: Little, Brown, 1996), 47.
48 LAC, War Diary, 19th Battalion, September 1916, appendix 11, Diagram of 4th Brigade Formation; ibid., Operation Order, 19th Battalion, 14 September 1916; ibid., Operation Order no. 70, 4th Infantry Brigade, 14 September 1916.
49 LAC, War Diary, 19th Battalion, Operation Order no. 70, 4th Infantry Brigade, 14 September 1916.
50 AO, Mould Papers, personal diary, 14 September 1916.
51 CWM, 19740071–017 58C 1 1.8, typewritten notes from a member of no. 4 Platoon, name unknown. Pipe Major Charles Davidson Dunbar is a celebrated figure in the history of the 19th Battalion and of its perpetuating unit, the Argyll and Sutherland Highlanders of Canada. Born in 1870 in the small village of Halkirk in northern Scotland, he had served in the British regular army as a piper, first with the Seaforth Highlanders, then with the 3rd Royal Scots, and finally with both the 2nd and the 3rd Gordon Highlanders. After a brief period of service in India, he saw action in South Africa in 1899, where, at the battle of Elandslaagte, he piped the Gordons into battle. He was cited for bravery three times and won a number of honours and awards in South Africa, including a prize for piping awarded by Lord Kitchener himself. In 1911 he resigned from the army after twenty-five years of service and emigrated to Canada with his wife and children. After settling in Hamilton, Ontario, he worked for various firms until he was approached by senior officers from the 91st Highlanders and enlisted as their pipe major in December 1913. Upon the outbreak of war in 1914, Dunbar proceeded to Valcartier, Quebec, where he enlisted and joined the Canadian Remounts, serving as a staff sergeant. On 15 September 1915, the day the 2nd Canadian Division landed in France, he transferred to the 19th Battalion and took command of its pipe band. He was wounded in the stomach and left leg as a result of the unfortunate grenade accident on 14 September 1916 and eventually was sent back to Canada to recuperate. Although he was invalided out of the army altogether in July 1917, he had recovered his health sufficiently that he immediately rejoined the 91st Highlanders. In November 1917 he received the singular honour of being made an honorary lieutenant, thus becoming "the first pipe-major in the British and Canadian forces to hold a commission while retaining command of a pipe band." He continued working in this capacity until he finally retired in 1937, after having built up the regimental pipe band into an award-winning and internationally respected institution. He died in Hamilton in January 1939. *Dictionary of Hamilton Biography*, vol. 2, 1876–1924, 46.
52 Corrigall, *The History of the Twentieth Canadian Battalion*, 82; LAC, RG 9, III-C-3, vol. 4116, folder 4, file 4, Field Messages, Capt. W.T. Rogers to adjutant, 19th Battalion, time: 6:00 AM (message received 6:23 AM), 15 September 1916.
53 Reginald H. Roy, ed., *The Journal of Private Fraser, Canadian Expeditionary Force, 1914–1918* (Nepean: CEF Books, 1998), 203; Corrigall, *The History of the Twentieth Canadian Battalion*, 80.
54 CWM, 19740071–017 58C 1 1.8, typewritten notes from a member of no. 4 Platoon, name unknown.
55 Corrigall, *The History of the Twentieth Canadian Battalion*, 80; LAC, War Diary, 4th Infantry Brigade, "Operations of 4th Canadian Infantry Brigade at the Somme, September 10–17, 1916"; LAC, Maj. Frederick Davy, "The Capture of Courcelette," 7–8; LAC, RG 24, C-6-a, vol. 1739, file DHS 3-17, vol. 5, Comments by Sir Richard Turner on the British Official History of the Somme; CWM, Personal Diary of Sir Richard Turner, 101½.
56 Turner qtd. in CWM, 19740071–017 58C 1 1.8, notes from a member of no. 4 Platoon, name unknown.
57 LAC, War Diary, 19th Battalion, 15 September 1916.

58 LAC, RG 9, III-C-3, vol. 4116, folder 4, file 4, field messages, Capt. W.T. Rogers to adjutant, 19th Battalion, 6:00 AM (message received 6:23 AM), 15 September 1916.
59 Nicholson, *The Gunners of Canada*, 264–65.
60 AO, Mould Papers, personal diary, 14 September 1916.

Chapter 9 – Fighting at the Somme: 15 September–3 October 1916

1 Bill Rawling, *Surviving Trench Warfare: Technology and the Canadian Corps, 1914–1918* (Toronto: University of Toronto Press, 1992), 71. For a comprehensive study of Canadian operations during the Somme offensive, see William F. Stewart, *'Ghastly and Gruelling': Canada's Ignored Campaign, Somme 1916* (Solihull: Helion & Company, 2017) (forthcoming).
2 ASH, RG 4, series 3, World War 1, Ted Lang Donation, "Some Memories of the Somme – by Ted Lang," 19th Battalion Association newsletter, Fall 1985.
3 AO, MU 7662, John F. Mould Papers, file 5, personal diary, "The Story of the Somme Battles, September 15, 1916–October 16, 1916."
4 LAC, RG 9, III-D-3, vol. 4880, War Diary, 4th Infantry Brigade, 15 September 1916; LAC, RG 9, III-D-1, vol. 4692, folder 51, file 17, 19th Battalion, Report on Operations, 10–17 September 1916.
5 Corrigall, *The History of the Twentieth Canadian Battalion*, 83; LAC, RG 9, III-D-3, vol. 4930, War Diary, 20th Battalion, 15 September 1916; LAC, RG 9, III-C-3, vol. 4116, folder 4, file 4, field message, Capt. W.T. Rogers to adjutant, 19th Battalion, 8:40 AM, 15 September 1916.
6 ASH, Ted Lang Donation, "Some Memories of the Somme."
7 LAC, MG 30, E 46, Sir Richard Turner Papers, vol. 2, file 14, Brig.-Gen. Ketchen, "Report on Operations September 15–16," 20 September 1916; LAC, MG 30, E 50, Elmer W. Jones Papers, folder 2, Report on Operations, 15–16 September 1916; LAC, War Diary, 4th Infantry Brigade, "Operations of 4th Canadian Infantry Brigade at the Somme."
8 LAC, Turner Papers, Brig.-Gen. Ketchen, "Report on Operations September 15–16"; LAC, Jones Papers, Report on Operations, 15–16 September 1916; LAC, RG 9, III-D-1, vol. 4679, folder 15, file 3, Maj. Frederick Davy, "The Capture of Courcelette," 9.
9 LAC, War Diary, 4th Infantry Brigade, 15 September 1916; Corrigall, *The Twentieth Canadian Battalion*, 83; LAC, Turner Papers, Brig.-Gen. Ketchen, "Report on Operations September 15–16."
10 LAC, War Diary, 4th Infantry Brigade, "Operations of 4th Canadian Infantry Brigade at the Somme."
11 LAC, RG 9, III-C-3, vol. 4116, folder 4, file 4, field message, Lt. A.W. Macdonald to adjutant, 19th Battalion, 7:04 AM, 15 September 1916; LAC, RG 9, III-D-3, vol. 4927, War Diary, 19th Battalion, 15 September 1916; LAC, 19th Battalion, Report on Operations, 10–17 September 1916.
12 LAC, War Diary, 19th Battalion, 15 September 1916; LAC, 19th Battalion, Report on Operations, 10–17 September 1916.
13 LAC, War Diary, 19th Battalion, 15 September 1916; LAC, 19th Battalion, Report on Operations, 10–17 September 1916; LAC, RG 9, III-C-3, vol. 4116, folder 4, file 4, field message, Capt. W.T. Rogers to adjutant, 19th Battalion, 8:40 AM, 15 September 1916.
14 LAC, RG 9, vol. 4116, field message, Lt. A.W. Macdonald to OC, 19th Battalion, time unstated, 15 September 1916.
15 LAC, 19th Battalion, Report on Operations, 10–17 September 1916.
16 LAC, RG 9, vol. 4116, field message, Lt. A.W. Macdonald to OC, 19th Battalion, 2:20 PM, 15 September 1916.
17 LAC, RG 9, vol. 4116, field message, Lt H.D. Fearman to Lt A.W. Macdonald, 2:45 PM, 15 Sept. 1916.
18 LAC, War Diary, 4th Infantry Brigade, "Operations of 4th Canadian Infantry Brigade at the Somme"; LAC, Turner Papers, untitled report by Ketchen regarding 6th Brigade operations on 15 September 1916; ibid., Brig.-Gen. Ketchen, "Report on Operations September 15–16."

19 LAC, War Diary, 19th Battalion, 15 September 1916.
20 G.W.L. Nicholson, *Canadian Expeditionary Force, 1914–1919: The Official History of the Canadian Army in the First World War* (Ottawa: Queen's Printer 1962), 170–71.
21 LAC, RG 9, III-D-3, vol. 4884, War Diary, 5th Infantry Brigade, appendix 25, 5th Canadian Infantry Brigade B.M.L. 216, 20 September 1916. For an overview of the 2nd Division's attack at Courcelette, see David Campbell, "Courcelette: A Forgotten Victory, 15 September 1916," *Canadian Military History* 16, no. 2 (2007): 27–48.
22 LAC, War Diary, 19th Battalion, 16 September 1916; LAC, 19th Battalion, Report on Operations, 10–17 September 1916.
23 AO, Mould Papers, personal diary, "The Story of the Somme Battles."
24 LAC, 19th Battalion, Report on Operations, 10–17 September 1916.
25 LAC, RG 9, III-B-1, series 28, vol. 2226, file O-4-28, "Report of Operations of the Tanks of No. 1 Section, 'C' Company, H.S.M.G.C. 16–9–16."
26 Imperial War Museum (IWM), 76/169/1, transcript of interview with Magnus MacIntyre Hood, part III, 4.
27 LAC, War Diary, 4th Infantry Brigade, "Operations of 4th Canadian Infantry Brigade at the Somme"; LAC, Jones Papers, folder 2, "Operations, 21st Canadian Battalion."
28 LAC, RG 41, B-III-1, Records of the CBC, *Flanders Fields*, vol. 10, 21st Battalion, transcript of interview with [Charles B.?] Collupy, tape 1, 11; Martin Marix Evans, *The Battles of the Somme* (Toronto: Little, Brown 1996), 47.
29 LAC, 19th Battalion, Report on Operations, 10–17 September 1916.
30 LAC, RG 9, III-D-3, vol. 4813, War Diary, Canadian Corps Headquarters, appendix VII, 2nd Canadian Division G.345, 19 September 1916; ibid., Canadian Corps G.167, 21 September 1916. In a recent analysis, Andrew McEwen concludes: "In the Canadian experience, tanks performed exactly as expected: not depended upon for success but able to assist the infantry wherever they could." Andrew McEwen, "'A Useful Accessory to the Infantry, but Nothing More': Tanks at the Battle of Flers-Courcelette, September 1916," *Canadian Military History* 20, no. 4 (2011): 17.
31 LAC, *Flanders Fields*, transcript of interview with E. Youngman, tape 3, 7–8.
32 David Campbell, "The Divisional Experience in the C.E.F.: A Social and Operational History of the 2nd Canadian Division, 1915–1918," PhD diss, University of Calgary, 2003, 209–12.
33 LAC, Jones Papers, Report on Operations, 15–16 September 1916.
34 CWM, 58, A1, 9.1, 1971, 0147-001, Personal Diary of Sir Richard Turner, 102.
35 Campbell, "The Divisional Experience in the C.E.F.," 210–11.
36 Tim Cook, "The Politics of Surrender: Canadian Soldiers and the Killing of Prisoners in the Great War," *Journal of Military History* 70, no. 3 (July 2006): 665.
37 Nicholson, *Canadian Expeditionary Force*, 173; Gary Sheffield, *The Somme* (London: Cassell, 2003), 122, 124.
38 LAC, RG 9, III-C-3, vol. 4116, folder 4, file 4, O.A.D. 151/2, Haig to Gough, 17 September 1916.
39 LAC, War Diary, 19th Battalion, 16 September 1916.
40 LAC, 19th Battalion, Report on Operations, 10–17 September 1916.
41 LAC, War Diary, 19th Battalion, 16 Sept. 1916; LAC, 19th Battalion, Report on Operations, 10–17 Sept. 1916.
42 LAC, War Diary, 19th Battalion, 16–19 September 1916. Although these numbers, as listed in the war diary, do not match precisely the statistics for 10–17 September provided in the ledger of daily casualties in RG 150 at LAC, they do accord reasonably well with the ledger statistics for the period 10–18 September.
43 John Swettenham, *To Seize the Victory: The Canadian Corps in World War I* (Toronto: Ryerson, 1965), 119.
44 LAC, War Diary, 19th Battalion, 16–24 September 1916.
45 LAC, War Diary, 19th Battalion, 21–25 September 1916.
46 Nicholson, *Canadian Expeditionary Force*, 174.

47 Ibid., 176–79.
48 LAC, War Diary, 19th Battalion, 26–27 September 1916; LAC, RG 9, III-D-1, vol. 4692, folder 51, file 17, "19th Canadian Battalion, 2nd Trip to the Somme Battlefield."
49 LAC, "19th Canadian Battalion, 2nd Trip to the Somme Battlefield."
50 LAC, "19th Canadian Battalion, 2nd Trip to the Somme Battlefield"; ASH, large bound volume of papers and clippings belonging to W.R. Turnbull (hereafter Turnbull Papers), typed report, "19th Canadian Battalion, Our Second Trip into the Somme."
51 ASH, Turnbull Papers, "19th Canadian Battalion, Our Second Trip into the Somme."
52 LAC, "19th Canadian Battalion, 2nd Trip to the Somme Battlefield"; LAC, War Diary, 19th Battalion, 28 September 1916; ASH, Turnbull Papers, "19th Canadian Battalion, Our Second Trip into the Somme."
53 AO, Mould Papers, "The Story of the Somme Battles."
54 LAC, War Diary, 19th Battalion, 28 September 1916; Nicholson, *Canadian Expeditionary Force*, 178, sketch 31, 179.
55 ASH, Turnbull Papers, "19th Canadian Battalion, Our Second Trip into the Somme."
56 AO, Mould Papers, "The Story of the Somme Battles."
57 ASH, Turnbull Papers, "19th Canadian Battalion, Our Second Trip into the Somme"; AO, Mould Papers, "The Story of the Somme Battles."
58 AO, Mould Papers, "The Story of the Somme Battles."
59 LAC, War Diary, 4th Infantry Brigade, "Operations of 4th Canadian Infantry Brigade at the Somme"; ASH, Turnbull Papers, "19th Canadian Battalion, Our Second Trip into the Somme."
60 LAC, War Diary, 4th Infantry Brigade, "Operations of 4th Canadian Infantry Brigade at the Somme"; ASH, Turnbull Papers, "19th Canadian Battalion, Our Second Trip into the Somme."
61 LAC, Turner Papers, vol. 2, file 14, 5th Infantry Brigade, "Summary of Operations," 26 September–2 October 1916.
62 LAC, War Diary, 4th Infantry Brigade, "Operations of 4th Canadian Infantry Brigade at the Somme."
63 AO, Mould Papers, "The Story of the Somme Battles."
64 ASH, Turnbull Papers, "19th Canadian Battalion, Our Second Trip into the Somme."
65 ASH, Turnbull Papers, "19th Canadian Battalion, Our Second Trip into the Somme"; LAC, War Diary, 19th Battalion, 29 September 1916.
66 LAC, War Diary, 19th Battalion, 29 September 1916; LAC, War Diary, 4th Infantry Brigade, "Operations of 4th Canadian Infantry Brigade at the Somme"; AO, Mould Papers, "The Story of the Somme Battles."
67 The battalion war diary erroneously refers to Gun Pit Road as "Sunken Road." LAC, War Diary, 19th Battalion, 30 September 1916; LAC, War Diary, 4th Infantry Brigade, "Operations of 4th Canadian Infantry Brigade at the Somme"; ASH, Turnbull Papers, "19th Canadian Battalion, Our Second Trip into the Somme."
68 Wilfrid Miles, *History of the Great War: Military Operations, France and Belgium, 1916, 2nd July 1916 to the End of the Battles of the Somme* (London: Macmillan 1938), 449, sketch 43.
69 Nicholson, *Canadian Expeditionary Force*, 180–83; LAC, Turner Papers, vol. 2, file 14, 5th Brigade B.M.L. 330, "Summary of Operations," from night of 26–27 September to night of 1–2 October 1916, dated 7 October 1916; Campbell, "The Divisional Experience in the C.E.F.," 218–21.
70 LAC, War Diary, 19th Battalion, 2 October 1916.
71 AO, Mould Papers, "The Story of the Somme Battles."
72 LAC, War Diary, 19th Battalion, 3 October 1916.
73 AO, Mould Papers, "The Story of the Somme Battles."
74 LAC, War Diary, 19th Battalion, 4–6 October 1916; Patricia Giesler, *Valour Remembered: Canada and the First World War* (Ottawa: Minister of Supply and Services Canada, 1982), 10; LAC, MG 30, E 100, Sir Arthur Currie Papers, vol. 42, "Canadian Expeditionary Force, Diary of Events, 1916," 27; LAC, RG 24, C-6-e, vol. 1844, GAQ 11-11B, notes on Canadian battles and casualties on the Western Front; Nicholson, *Canadian Expeditionary Force*, 198.

75 During the 19th Battalion's first tour at the Somme (10–17 September), casualty rates were roughly four times higher among the officers and just over three times higher among the other ranks than during the second tour (25 September–3 October). The number of sick during each tour remained rather consistent. LAC, War Diary, 19th Battalion, 3 October 1916. As with the casualty statistics for the first tour, the casualty figures listed in the daily casualty ledger (in LAC RG 150) for the dates corresponding to the battalion's second tour do not match those given in the war diary exactly. However, the ledger statistics for the period 25 September–7 October accord more closely with the war diary figures.

76 LAC, War Diary, 19th Battalion, 16–19 September–3 October 1916; LAC, RG 150, vols. 491–4, "Casualties by Days – France and Belgium," 19th Battalion. For monthly summaries of these daily casualty ledgers, see Appendix A.

77 British casualties for the entire year of 1916 would amount to approximately 660,000. Sheffield, *The Somme*, 151–52; Holger H. Herwig, *The First World War: Germany and Austria-Hungary, 1914–1918* (London: Arnold, 1997), 204.

78 In addition, Prior and Wilson raise the estimate of British casualties between 1 July and mid-November 1916 to 432,000. Robin Prior and Trevor Wilson, *The Somme* (New Haven: Yale University Press 2005), 300–1.

79 Hew Strachan, *The First World War* (New York: Viking 2004), 195.

80 Herwig, *The First World War*, 204.

81 Sheffield, *The Somme*, 155–56.

82 Ibid., 157. The British official historian offers a slightly different figure, stating that fifty-five British divisions had been engaged at the Somme. Sir James Edmonds, *A Short History of World War I* (London: Oxford University Press, 1951), 194.

83 For example, Sheffield, *The Somme*.

84 Tim Travers, "The Army and the Challenge of War, 1914–1918," in *The Oxford Illustrated History of the British Army*, ed. David Chandler and Ian Beckett (Oxford: Oxford University Press, 1994), 226, 230.

85 Strachan, *The First World War*, 193.

86 Personal collection of Mrs. Phyllis Douglas, letters of Lt.-Col. Lionel H. Millen (hereafter Millen Letters), Millen to his mother, 14 October 1916. Maj. Morrison, who had led the 19th Battalion until Lt.-Col. Turnbull's return on 20 September, was transferred to take command of the 18th Battalion on 6 October 1916. LAC, RG 9, III-D-3, vol. 4926, War Diary, 18th Battalion, 6 October 1916.

87 Millen Letters, Millen to his father, 27 October 1916.

88 LAC, *Flanders Fields*, transcript of interview with F.A. Stitt, tape 1, 10.

Chapter 10 – A "Most Uneventful Tour": October 1916–March 1917

1 G.W.L. Nicholson, *Canadian Expeditionary Force, 1914–1919: The Official History of the Canadian Army in the First World War* (Ottawa: Queen's Printer, 1962), 233.

2 LAC, RG 9, III-D-3, vol. 4927, War Diary, 19th Battalion, 4–14 October 1916; AO, MU 7662, John F. Mould Papers, file 5, personal diary, 14 October 1916.

3 LAC, War Diary, 19th Battalion, 17–23 October 1916.

4 Personal collection of Mrs. Phyllis Douglas, letters of Lt.-Col. Lionel H. Millen (hereafter Millen Letters), Millen to his mother, 24 October 1916.

5 CWM, 19740071-017 58C 1 1.8, untitled file of letters, questionnaires, responses, and notes regarding 19th Battalion history, 19th Battalion History, Questionnaire no. 4; Nicholson, *Canadian Expeditionary Force*, 233; ASH, RG 4, series 3, World War 1, Ted Lang Donation, R.H. (Harry Neil), "A Brief History of the 19th Battalion C.E.F. 1914–18."

6 LAC, War Diary, 19th Battalion, appendix 12, field message to OCs of A, B, C, D Companies from Lt. H.D. Fearman, 16 October 1916.

7 Desmond Morton and J.L. Granatstein, *Marching to Armageddon: Canadians and the Great War, 1914–1919* (Toronto: Lester and Orpen Dennys, 1989), 138. The 2nd Canadian Division as a whole absorbed a grand total of 8,007 reinforcements in span of only four months between 1 September and 31 December 1916. LAC, RG 9, III-D-3, vols. 4848–9, War Diary, 2nd Canadian Division, AA & QMG, September– December 1916, monthly summaries of casualties.
8 LAC, RG 9, III-C-3, vol. 4098, folder 43, file 2, 2nd Canadian Division, G.S.1176, 13 September 1916; S.S. 135, *Instructions for the Training of Divisions for Offensive Action* (London: Harrison and Sons, December 1916), 58. Different units likely employed varying methods of selecting LOB men. See David Campbell, "The Divisional Experience in the C.E.F.: A Social and Operational History of the 2nd Canadian Division, 1915–1918," PhD diss., University of Calgary, 2003, 244–45; Bruce Cane, *It Made You Think of Home: The Haunting Journal of Deward Barnes, Canadian Expeditionary Force: 1916–1919* (Toronto: Dundurn, 2004), 284.
9 LAC, RG 150, vols. 494–45, "Casualties by Days – France and Belgium," 19th Battalion; LAC, War Diary, 19th Battalion, October 1916–January 1917, appendices, field messages for daily reports of numbers sick.
10 Although the percentage of returned men quoted is based on statistics from British casualties, it should be reasonably representative of the Canadian experience as well. Nick Bosanquet, "Health Systems in Khaki: The British and American Medical Experience," in *Facing Armageddon: The First World War Experienced*, ed. Hugh Cecil and Peter Liddle (London: Leo Cooper, 1996), 459.
11 AO, Mould Papers, personal diary, 16, 20 November 1916; 12, 27 December 1917; 5, 7 January, 18 July, September 1918. See also LAC, RG 150, 1992–93/166, box 644–5, personnel file, John F. Mould, attestation paper.
12 GMA, M399, Gaetz Family Fonds, J.R. Gaetz to his father, 1 February 1917.
13 Patrick Brennan and Thomas Leppard, "How the Lessons Were Learned: Senior Commanders and the Moulding of the Canadian Corps after the Somme," in *Canadian Military History since the 17th Century*, ed. Yves Tremblay, Proceedings of the Canadian Military History Conference, Ottawa, 5–9 May 2000 (Ottawa: Department of National Defence, 2002), 135.
14 LAC, MG 30, E 46, Sir Richard Turner Papers, vol. 2, file 14, Canadian Corps G.428, 3 November 1916; LAC, RG 9, III-C-3, vol. 4089, folder 20, file 5, "19th Canadian Battalion, Answers to Canadian Corps G.428."
15 LAC, "19th Canadian Battalion, Answers to Canadian Corps G.428."
16 Bill Rawling, *Surviving Trench Warfare: Technology and the Canadian Corps, 1914–1918* (Toronto: University of Toronto Press, 1992), 84.
17 LAC, "19th Canadian Battalion, Answers to Canadian Corps G.428."
18 LAC, "19th Canadian Battalion, Answers to Canadian Corps G.428."
19 LAC, RG 9, III-D-3, vol. 4814, War Diary, Canadian Corps Headquarters, November 1916, appendices VII/3, VII/4.
20 LAC, War Diary, Canadian Corps Headquarters, appendices VII/3, VII/4; William Stewart, "Attack Doctrine in the Canadian Corps, 1916–1918," MA thesis, University of New Brunswick, 1982, 110–11.
21 Jeffrey Williams, *Byng of Vimy: General and Governor General* (Toronto: University of Toronto Press, 1992; orig. ed., Leo Cooper, 1983), 147.
22 Campbell, "The Divisional Experience in the C.E.F.," 290.
23 Millen Letters, Millen to his mother, 29 November 1916.
24 ASH, large bound volume of papers and clippings belonging to W.R. Turnbull (hereafter Turnbull Papers), press clippings, "Gallant Officer Welcomed This Morning," newspaper title not indicated, 6 January 1917, and "Lt.-Col. Turnbull Home to Recuperate," newspaper title not indicated, 8 January 1917; LAC, RG 24, C-6-d, vol. 1886, file 85, 2nd Canadian Division, lists of commanders and staffs.
25 Millen Letters, Millen to his mother, 20 December 1916.
26 ASH, Turnbull Papers, "Gallant Officer Was Warmly Welcomed This Morning."

27 Millen Letters, Millen to Gertie, 5 January 1917.

28 ASH, Turnbull Papers, 2MD 34–6–2–1, OC, 3rd Infantry Brigade, to Turnbull, 12 February 1917.

29 Millen Letters, Millen to his mother, 3 December 1916.

30 LAC, RG 150, 1992–93/166, box 4150–2, personnel file, Maj. H.C. Hatch.

31 Millen Letters, Millen to his mother, 20 October 1916.

32 LAC, RG 41, B-III-1, Records of the CBC, *Flanders Fields*, vol. 10, 19th Battalion, transcript of interview with Joe O'Neill, tape 4, 4–5.

33 Brereton Greenhous and Stephen J. Harris, *Canada and the Battle of Vimy Ridge, 9–12 April, 1917* (Ottawa: Minister of Supply and Services, 1992), 50, 52; Ronald Haycock, *Sam Hughes: The Public Career of a Controversial Canadian, 1885–1916* (Waterloo: Wilfrid Laurier University Press / Canadian War Museum, 1986), Chs. 14, 15; Stephen J. Harris, *Canadian Brass: The Making of a Professinal Army, 1860–1939* (Toronto: University of Toronto Press, 1988), Chs. 6, 7. For a detailed examination of the administration of the Canadian forces overseas, see Desmond Morton, *A Peculiar Kind of Politics: Canada's Overseas Ministry in the First World War* (Toronto: University of Toronto Press, 1982).

34 Albert P. Palazzo, "The British Army's Counter-Battery Staff Office and Control of the Enemy in World War I," *Journal of Military History* 63 (January 1999): 56–57; John Swettenham, *McNaughton*, vol. 1: *1887–1939* (Toronto: Ryerson, 1968), Ch. 4; Rawling, *Surviving Trench Warfare*, 93–95, 108–11; Shelford Bidwell and Dominick Graham, *Fire-Power: British Army Weapons and Theories of War, 1904–1945* (London: Allen and Unwin, 1982), 108–11; A.G.L. McNaughton, "The Development of Artillery in the Great War," *Canadian Defence Quarterly* 6, no. 2 (January 1929): 160–71; Greenhous and Harris, *Canada and the Battle of Vimy Ridge*, 60–61.

35 LAC, RG 24, C-6-e, vol. 1833, file GAQ 8–16, "Notes re Organization of Canadian Machine Gun Sections, Brigade Machine Gun Companies, Machine Gun Companies, and Machine Gun Battalions"; Greenhous and Harris, *Canada and the Battle of Vimy Ridge*, 58, 60.

36 Ibid., 56; "An Infantry Battalion War Establishment," in *Canadian Expeditionary Force Units: Instructions Governing Organization and Administration* (Ottawa: Ministry of Militia and Defence, 1916), 22–23; Bill Rawling, "Technology in Search of a Role: The Machine Gun and the C.E.F. in the First World War," *Material History Review*, Fall 1995, 92.

37 LAC, RG 9, III-C-3, vol. 4136, folder 24, file 3, Canadian Corps G.340, 27 December 1916; Bidwell and Graham, *Fire-Power*, 36–37, 120–21; Nicholson, *Canadian Expeditionary Force*, 240; Bruce Gudmundsson, *Stormtroop Tactics: Innovation in the German Army, 1914–1918* (Westport: Praeger, 1989), 93–94; Martin Samuels, *Command or Control? Command, Training, and Tactics in the British and German Armies, 1888–1918* (London: Cass, 1995), 180; Rawling, *Surviving Trench Warfare*, 91–92; Williams, *Byng of Vimy*, 146–47; LAC, RG 9, III-C-3, vol. 4091, folder 26, file 11, Maj.-Gen. A.W. Currie, "Notes on French Attacks, North-East of Verdun in October and December 1916," 23 January 1917; Tim Cook, *At the Sharp End: Canadians Fighting the Great War, 1914–1916* (Toronto: Viking, 2007), 420–21; Mark Osborne Humphries, "The Myth of the Learning Curve: Tactics and Training in the 12th Canadian Infantry Brigade, 1916–1918," *Canadian Military History* 14, no. 4 (Autumn 2005), 15–30. For an analysis of the operation and intellectual underpinnings of minor tactics in the British Army before and during the First World War, see M.A. Ramsay, *Command and Cohesion: The Citizen Soldier and Minor Tactics in the British Army, 1870–1918* (Westport: Praeger, 2002).

38 LAC, MG 30, E 61, C.H. Mitchell Papers, vol. 16, file "Western Front Orders and Instructions, 1916–1918," Canadian Corps G. 499, S/109/1, 10 January 1917; LAC, RG 9, III-C-3, vol. 4084, folder 7, file 9, 2nd Canadian Division G.S. 1378, 28 December 1916; LAC, RG 9, III-D-3, vol. 4844, War Diary, 2nd Canadian Division headquarters, 19 January 1917.

39 Campbell, "The Divisional Experience in the C.E.F.," 284–85, 286–87.

40 LAC, War Diary, 19th Battalion, 19–21 January 1917.

41 LAC, War Diary, 19th Battalion, 22–29 January 1917.
42 LAC, War Diary, 19th Battalion, 30 January–10 February 1917, appendix 1, "19th Canadian Battalion, Schedule of Daily Training, Week Ending 9/2/17"; General Staff, S.S. 143, *Instructions for the Training of Platoons for Offensive Action, 1917* (GHQ: February 1917), 3.
43 This particular formation had been proposed earlier by Maj.-Gen. Burstall. LAC, RG 9, III-C-3, vol. 4084, folder 7, file 9, 2nd Canadian Division G.S. 1378, 28 December 1916.
44 S.S. 143, *Instructions for the Training of Platoons for Offensive Action*, 3.
45 LAC, War Diary, 19th Battalion, appendix 1, Battalion Orders no. 21, 2 February 1917.
46 LAC, War Diary, 19th Battalion, 8 February 1917.
47 John Swettenham, *To Seize the Victory: The Canadian Corps in World War I* (Toronto: Ryerson, 1965), 146.
48 GMA, Gaetz Family Fonds, J.R. Gaetz to his brother Dick, 4 February 1917.
49 LAC, War Diary, 19th Battalion, 10–18 February 1917.
50 Nicholson, *Canadian Expeditionary Force*, 237, 245.
51 Nicholson, *Canadian Expeditionary Force*, 244–45; D.J. Goodspeed, *The Road Past Vimy: The Canadian Corps, 1914–1918* (Toronto: Macmillan, 1969), 81; Morton and Granatstein, *Marching to Armageddon*, 139–40; Stephen Pope and Elizabeth-Anne Wheal, eds., *The Macmillan Dictionary of the First World War* (London: Macmillan, 1995), 498.
52 Morton and Granatstein, *Marching to Armageddon*, 140; Nicholson, *Canadian Expeditionary Force*, 246; Greenhous and Harris, *Canada and the Battle of Vimy Ridge*, 68, 70.
53 Shane B. Schreiber, *Shock Army of the British Empire: The Canadian Corps in the Last 100 Days of the Great War* (Westport: Praeger, 1997), 9–11; Holger H. Herwig, *The First World War: Germany and Austria-Hungary, 1914–1918* (London: Arnold, 1997), 247–48; Paddy Griffith, *Fortifications of the Western Front, 1914–18* (Oxford: Osprey, 2004), 3–34.
54 Greenhous and Harris, *Canada and the Battle of Vimy Ridge*, 68, 70.
55 D.E. Macintyre, *Canada at Vimy* (Toronto: Peter Martin, 1967), 61–62.
56 Ibid., 62.
57 GMA, Gaetz Family Fonds, J.R. Gaetz to his mother, 21 February 1917.
58 LAC, RG 9, III-C-3, vol. 4091, folder 26, file 16, "Summary of Raids by Canadian Corps during the Period November 1, 1916–April 1, 1917."
59 Nicholson, *Canadian Expeditionary Force*, 233; Andrew Godefroy, "A Lesson in Success: The Calonne Trench Raid, 17 January 1917," *Canadian Military History* 8, no. 2 (1999): 25–34.
60 LAC, RG 9, III-D-3, vol. 4928, War Diary, 19th Battalion, appendix 15, "Report on Raid by 19th Canadian Battalion," 20 March 1917; ibid., appendix 14, "19th Canadian Battalion Orders No. 27," 19 March 1917; ibid., appendix 15, notes on artillery program in support of the raid; Paddy Griffith, *Battle Tactics of the Western Front: The British Army's Art of Attack, 1916–18* (New Haven: Yale University Press, 1994), 114.
61 LAC, War Diary, 19th Battalion, appendix 15, "Report on Raid by 19th Canadian Battalion," 20 March 1917; ibid., appendix 14, "19th Canadian Battalion Orders No. 27," 19 March 1917.
62 LAC, War Diary, 19th Battalion, appendix 15, "Report on Raid by 19th Canadian Battalion," 20 March 1917; ibid., appendix 14, "19th Canadian Battalion Orders No. 27," 19 March 1917.
63 Millen Letters, Millen to his mother, 24 March 1917.
64 Sgt. R.H. Ross and Pte. Madden were killed and Ptes. W. Harvey, T.W. Raddish, F.T. Downs, and J.B. Guillot were wounded. LAC, vol. 4927, War Diary, 19th Battalion, Dec. 1916, app. 15, "19th Canadian Battalion, Report on German Raid on Morning of December 21st 1916."
65 LAC, vol. 4928, War Diary, 19th Battalion, March 1917, appendix 15, "Report on Attempted Raid by the Enemy on Our Front Line Defences on the Morning of March 21st 1917"; ibid., appendix 16, Report by Lt. H.M. Harman, OC, B Company, 21 March 1917, and Report by Maj. R.B. Thomson, OC, D Company, 21 March 1917.
66 LAC, War Diary, 19th Battalion, 21–25 March 1917.
67 GMA, Gaetz Family Fonds, J.R. Gaetz to his father, 1 March 1917.

Chapter 11 – "An Easter Gift"—Vimy Ridge: 25 March–9 April 1917

1 Brereton Greenhous and Stephen J. Harris, *Canada and the Battle of Vimy Ridge, 9–12 April, 1917* (Ottawa: Minister of Supply and Services, 1992), 72; G.W.L. Nicholson, *Canadian Expeditionary Force, 1914–1919: The Official History of the Canadian Army in the First World War* (Ottawa: Queen's Printer, 1962), 236–37, 240.

2 Greenhous and Harris, *Canada and the Battle of Vimy Ridge*, 74.

3 A. Fortescue Duguid, "The Significance of Vimy," *Canadian Defence Quarterly* 12, no. 4 (1935): 399; Nicholson, *Canadian Expeditionary Force*, 245, 248; D.E. Macintyre, *Canada at Vimy* (Toronto: Peter Martin, 1967), 94–95.

4 Nicholson, *Canadian Expeditionary Force*, 247.

5 Macintyre, *Canada at Vimy*, 77. See also Cyril Falls, *Military Operations: France and Belgium, 1917*, vol. 1 (London: Macmillan, 1940), 303.

6 G.W.L. Nicholson, *The Gunners of Canada: The History of the Royal Regiment of Canadian Artillery*, vol. 1 (Toronto: McClelland and Stewart, 1967), 283; Nicholson, *Canadian Expeditionary Force*, 247–48.

7 For brigade and battalion dispositions at Vimy, see Nicholson, *Canadian Expeditionary Force*, map 7.

8 Tim Cook, *Shock Troops: Canadians Fighting the Great War, 1917–1918* (Toronto: Viking, 2008), 83.

9 Mark Osborne Humphries, "'Old Wine in New Bottles': A Comparison of British and Canadian Preparations for the Battle of Arras," in *Vimy Ridge: A Canadian Reassessment*, ed. Geoffrey Hayes, Andrew Iarocci, and Mike Bechthold (Waterloo: Laurier Centre for Military Strategic and Disarmament Studies / Wilfrid Laurier University Press, 2007), 65–85.

10 Nicholson, *Canadian Expeditionary Force*, 249–50; Greenhous and Harris, *Canada and the Battle of Vimy Ridge*, 74. For a comprehensive analysis of the artillery's efforts before and during the battle at Vimy, see Tim Cook, "The Gunners at Vimy: 'We Are Hammering Fritz to Pieces,'" in *Vimy Ridge*, ed. Hayes et al., 105–24.

11 Greenhous and Harris, *Canada and the Battle of Vimy Ridge*, 74; Macintyre, *Canada at Vimy*, 91.

12 Tim Cook admits that "official records vary on the number" of tunnels, with estimates ranging "from eleven to thirteen." See Nicholson, *Canadian Expeditionary Force*, 250; Pierre Berton, *Vimy* (Toronto: McClelland and Stewart, 1986), 149; Greenhous and Harris, *Canada and the Battle of Vimy Ridge*, 15; Cook, *Shock Troops*, 88, 661n53.

13 D.J. Goodspeed, *The Road Past Vimy: The Canadian Corps, 1914–1918* (Toronto: Macmillan, 1969), 86; Nicholson, *Canadian Expeditionary Force*, 250.

14 Greenhous and Harris, *Canada and the Battle of Vimy Ridge*, 75; Duguid, "The Significance of Vimy," 398; Bill Rawling, *Surviving Trench Warfare: Technology and the Canadian Corps, 1914–1918* (Toronto: University of Toronto Press, 1992), 112; Macintyre, *Canada at Vimy*, 100.

15 Rawling, *Surviving Trench Warfare*, 111–12; Nicholson, *Canadian Expeditionary Force*, 251; Greenhous and Harris, *Canada and the Battle of Vimy Ridge*, 78.

16 Macintyre, *Canada at Vimy*, 84; D.J. Corrigall, *The History of the Twentieth Canadian Battalion (Central Ontario Regiment) Canadian Expeditionary Force in the Great War, 1914–1918* (Toronto: Stone and Cox, 1935), 114; LAC, RG 150, 1992–93/166, box 6170–36, personnel file, Lt.-Col. Lionel Herbert Millen; Macintyre, *Canada at Vimy*, 82–84.

17 Macintyre, *Canada at Vimy*, 84–85.

18 ASH, RG 4, series 3, World War 1, Ted Lang Donation, R.H. (Harry) Neil, "A Brief History of the 19th Battalion C.E.F. 1914–18."

19 Corrigall, *The History of the Twentieth Canadian Battalion*, 114.

20 Falls, *Military* Operations, 305; Byng qtd. in Berton, *Vimy*, 162.

21 Jeffrey Williams, *Byng of Vimy: General and Governor General* (Toronto: University of Toronto Press, 1992; orig. ed., Leo Cooper, 1983), 153. According to official historian A.F. Duguid, "over

40,000 specially drawn maps were required by the Canadian Corps." Duguid, "The Significance of Vimy," 399; Patrick Brennan, "Julian Byng and Leadership in the Canadian Corps," in Hayes et al., *Vimy Ridge*, 87–104.

22 LAC, RG 9, III-D-3, vol. 4928, War Diary, 19th Battalion, 1–3 April 1917; LAC, RG 9, III-D-3, vol. 4845, War Diary, 2nd Canadian Division headquarters, 1 April 1917.

23 LAC, War Diary, 19th Battalion, 4 April 1917.

24 LAC, War Diary, 19th Battalion, 5 April 1917; LAC, vol. 4927, War Diary, 19th Battalion, 4–10 November 1916; Tim Cook, *No Place to Run: The Canadian Corps and Gas Warfare in the First World War* (Vancouver: UBC Press, 1999), 87–88. Lt. W.J. Wright was appointed the 19th Battalion's first gas officer. See LAC, MG 30, E 521, William Jonathan Wright Papers, personal letter dated 13 November 1916; LAC, vol. 4927, War Diary, 19th Battalion, 11 November 1916.

25 LAC, vol. 4928, War Diary, 19th Battalion, 5 April 1917; Greenhous and Harris, *Canada and the Battle of Vimy Ridge*, 78; Rawling, *Suriviving Trench Warfare*, 117; Serge Bernier, *Canadian Military Heritage*, vol. 3: *1872–2000* (Montreal: Art Global, 2000), 108.

26 LAC, War Diary, 19th Battalion, 5 April 1917.

27 LAC, RG 24, C-6-d, vol. 1886, file 85, Commanders and Staffs, 19th Canadian Infantry Battalion; Macintyre, *Canada at Vimy*, 91.

28 Greenhous and Harris, *Canada and the Battle of Vimy Ridge*, 78; LAC, War Diary, 19th Battalion, 6 April 1917.

29 Rawling, *Surviving Trench Warfare*, 108–10.

30 S.F. Wise, *Canadian Airmen and the First World War: The Official History of the Royal Canadian Air Force*, vol. 1 (Toronto: University of Toronto Press, 1980), 400–2, 404.

31 LAC, War Diary, 19th Battalion, 8 April 1917; ibid., appendix I, Preparations for the Offensive on Vimy Ridge, 4th Canadian Infantry Brigade Instructions, 4th Brigade Instructions for the Offensive no. 6, 6 April 1917.

32 ASH, RG 4, series 3, World War 1, 19th Battalion Association, "Selections from the Mail Bag," 19th Battalion Association newsletter, October 1967.

33 Corrigall, *The History of the Twentieth Canadian Battalion*, 109.

34 Rawling, *Surviving Trench Warfare*, 92.

35 LAC, War Diary, 19th Battalion, 9 April 1917; ibid., appendix 2, field messages, 9 April 1917; ibid., appendix I, Preparations for the Offensive on Vimy Ridge, 4th Canadian Infantry Brigade Instructions, 4th Brigade Instructions for the Offensive no. 3, 12 March 1917.

36 Nicholson, *Canadian Expeditionary Force*, map 7.

37 Greenhous and Harris, *Canada and the Battle of Vimy Ridge*, 70. For the operations at Vimy, Lt.-Gen. Byng had under his command a total approximate strength of 170,000 all ranks, of whom 97,184 were Canadians. The remainder were supporting British units and formations, including the attached 5th British Division, whose 13th Brigade would participate in the attack. Nicholson, *Canadian Expeditionary Force*, 252.

38 Andrew Godefroy, "The German Army at Vimy Ridge," in Hayes et al., *Vimy Ridge*, 227–29; Cook, *Shock Troops*, 78; Greenhous and Harris, *Canada and the Battle of Vimy Ridge*, 70.

39 LAC, War Diary, 19th Battalion, 9 April 1917; Nicholson, *Canadian Expeditionary Force*, 252; ASH, Neil, "A Brief History of the 19th Battalion C.E.F. 1914–18."

40 Corrigall, *The History of the Twentieth Canadian Battalion*, 116, 118.

41 ASH, 19th Battalion Association, "Selections from the Mail Bag," 19th Battalion Association newsletter, October 1967.

42 ASH, RG 4, series 3, World War 1, Chas. Henderson Donation, "The Battle of Vimy Ridge – April 9, 1917," as recounted by Cpl. C.A. Henderson, #55439, 19th Battalion.

43 Cook, *Shock Troops*, 99.

44 Corrigall, *The History of the Twentieth Canadian Battalion*, 118.

45 Nicholson, *Canadian Expeditionary Force*; Berton, *Vimy*, 18–19.

46 Rawling, *Surviving Trench Warfare*, 111; Cook, "The Gunners at Vimy," in Hayes et al., *Vimy Ridge*, 117–18. For the vital development of counter-battery tactics, see A.G.L. McNaughton, "Counter Battery Work," *Canadian Defence Quarterly* 3, no. 4 (1926): 380–91.

47 Corrigall, *The History of the Twentieth Canadian Battalion*, 118; LAC, RG 9, III-D-3, vol. 4881, War Diary, 4th Infantry Brigade, 9 April 1916.
48 Nicholson, *Canadian Expeditionary Force*, 248–49; Rawling, *Surviving Trench Warfare*, 115–16; Berton, *Vimy*, 18.
49 The three infantry regiments of the 79th Reserve Division were disposed along the ridge from the vicinity of Givenchy-en-Gohelle to the road linking Thélus with Neuville-Saint-Vaast. Falls, *Military* Operations, 353; Alfred Dieterich, "The German 79th Reserve Infantry Division in the Battle of Vimy Ridge, April 1917," trans. Christopher and Ute Wilde-Linnell, *Canadian Military History* 15, no. 1 (2006): 69–70, 72.
50 ASH, RG 4, Series 3, World War 1, 19th Battalion Association, "Selections from the Mail Bag," 19th Battalion Association newsletter, October 1967.
51 LAC, War Diary, 4th Infantry Brigade, 9 April 1916; Corrigall, *The History of the Twentieth Canadian Battalion*, 118–19.
52 Corrigall, *The History of the Twentieth Canadian Battalion*, 118–19; A. Fortescue Duguid, "The Significance of Vimy," 400.
53 LAC, War Diary, 19th Battalion, 9 April 1917; Nicholson, *Canadian Expeditionary Force*, 254.
54 Greenhous and Harris, *Canada and the Battle of Vimy Ridge*, 96, 98; LAC, War Diary, 2nd Canadian Division headquarters, 9 April 1917.
55 LAC, War Diary, 4th Infantry Brigade, 9 April 1916; ibid., vol. 4928, 19th Battalion, 9 April 1917; Greenhous and Harris, *Canada and the Battle of Vimy Ridge*, 96, 98; Goodspeed, *The Road Past Vimy*, 89–90; LAC, War Diary, 6th Infantry Brigade, appendix 10a, "6th Canadian Infantry Brigade, Narrative of Offensive Operations on 9th and 10th April 1917."
56 For an overview of the 2nd Canadian Division's role in the capture of Vimy Ridge, see David Campbell, "The 2nd Canadian Division: A 'Most Spectacular Battle,'" in Hayes et al., *Vimy Ridge*, 171–91.
57 "Fish tail" was the Canadian nickname for a type of German mortar projectile. Nicholson, *Canadian Expeditionary Force*, 256–57; LAC, War Diary, 19th Battalion, 9 April 1917; LAC, War Diary, 4th Infantry Brigade, April 1917, 9 April 1916. From 9 to 14 April, the Canadian Corps would advance 4,500 yards, capture more than 4,000 prisoners, and seize 54 guns, 104 trench mortars, and 124 machine guns. Nicholson, *Canadian Expeditionary Force*, 265.
58 GMA, M399, Gaetz Family Fonds, John Gaetz to his mother, 28 April 1917.
59 Personal collection of Mrs. Phyllis Douglas, letters of Lt.-Col. Lionel H. Millen (hereafter Millen Letters), Millen to his mother, 16 April 1917.
60 Cook, *Shock Troops*, 143–44.
61 Nicholson, *Canadian Expeditionary Force*, 265; Greenhous and Harris, *Canada and the Battle of Vimy Ridge*, 134. According to Tim Cook, "The records for two German divisions, the 79th Reserve and 1st Bavarian Reserve, indicated total losses up to April 11 of 6,604 soldiers, and likely another 1,000 men were killed, wounded, or captured on the 12th." Tim Cook, *Vimy: The Battle and the Legend* (Toronto: Allen Lane, 2017), 140–41.
62 Henderson was eventually transferred to the King George Hospital in London, where he was operated on and remained for six months. Stays at other hospitals followed before he reached Halifax. A hospital train then took him to Toronto, where he again was moved from hospital to hospital, his last stop being, on Armistice Day, 1918, Whitby Military Hospital. ASH, Henderson Donation, "The Battle of Vimy Ridge – April 9, 1917."
63 Corrigall, *The History of the Twentieth Canadian Battalion*, 120.
64 Macintyre, *Canada at Vimy*, 112.
65 LAC, RG 41, B-III-1, Records of the CBC, *Flanders Fields*, vol. 10, 19th Battalion, transcript of interview with E. Youngman, tape 2, 7.
66 Macintyre, *Canada at Vimy*, 112.
67 Millen Letters, Millen to his mother, 16 April 1917.
68 According to historian Bill Rawling, German machine guns "inflicted the great majority of assault casualties on Vimy Ridge." Rawling, *Surviving Trench Warfare*, 123.
69 Macintyre, *Canada at Vimy*, 112.

70 LAC, *Flanders Fields*, vol. 10, 19th Battalion, transcript of interview with E. Youngman, tape 2, 12–14.

71 LAC, *Flanders Fields*, vol. 10, 19th Battalion, transcript of interview with E. Youngman, tape 4, 16–17. The skilled stretcher-bearer's real name was Frederick Presnail, who was indeed a resident of Hamilton. Although he had not been a practising "skilled surgeon," as Youngman claimed, he had studied medicine at Queen's University and claimed to be twenty-eight years old at the time of his enlistment in 1915. He joined the 120th City of Hamilton Battalion under the pseudonym James Robertson (remembered erroneously by Youngman as "Robinson") and eventually was sent to the 19th Battalion in a reinforcement draft in December 1916. For his exceptional service at Vimy, Presnail would win the Military Medal. Although the details of his personal life as reported by Youngman can only be considered hearsay, there must have been some reason why Presnail enlisted under an assumed name. In any event, he would distinguish himself yet again, winning a bar to his Military Medal during Canadian operations at Hill 70 in August 1917. Presnail remained with the 19th Battalion until the end of April 1918, when he was transferred to the 2nd Battalion, CMGC. In early August 1918 he was sent back to England pending his return to Canada to resume his medical studies. On 16 November he was discharged in Toronto, still serving at the rank of private. ASH, large bound volume of papers and clippings belonging to W.R. Turnbull (hereafter Turnbull Papers), press clipping, "Hero Honored," paper and date not stated; LAC, RG 150, 1992–93/166, box 7963, personnel file, Frederick Presnail (a.k.a. James Robertson).

72 Tim Cook notes that "more than half of the 983 guns" backing the attack at Vimy were crewed by "British, Australian, or other Dominion forces." Tim Cook, "Storm Troops: Combat Effectiveness and the Canadian Corps in 1917," in *1917: Tactics, Training and Technology*, ed. Peter Dennis and Jeffrey Grey (Canberra: Australian History Military Publications, 2007), 51.

73 Recollecting his feelings fifty years after he first stood on the crest of Vimy Ridge, Gregory Clark, then a lieutenant in the 4th Canadian Mounted Rifles (3rd Canadian Division), wrote: "As far as I could see, south, north along the miles of the Ridge, there were the Canadians. And I experienced my first full sense of nationhood." Gregory Clark, *Weekend Magazine*, 4 April 1967, qtd. in Berton, *Vimy*, 4. Similarly, Brig.-Gen. Alex Ross, who commanded the 28th Battalion (2nd Canadian Division) at Vimy, wrote in 1967 of the advance: "It was Canada from the Atlantic to the Pacific on parade. I thought then, and I think today, that in those few minutes I witnessed the birth of a nation." Alex Ross, "Preface," in Macintyre, *Canada at Vimy*, viii.

74 Qtd. in Goodspeed, *The Road Past Vimy*, 92.

75 Andrew Godefroy, "The German Army at Vimy Ridge," in Hayes et al., *Vimy Ridge*, 229–34; Greenhous and Harris, *Canada and the Battle of Vimy Ridge*, 68, 70.

76 Greenhous and Harris, *Canada and the Battle of Vimy Ridge*, 70; Goodspeed, *The Road Past Vimy*, 92–93.

77 Cook, *Shock Troops*, 142.

78 Nicholson, *Canadian Expeditionary Force*, 263.

79 Nicholson, *Canadian Expeditionary Force*, 263; Greenhous and Harris, *Canada and the Battle of Vimy Ridge*, 134–35.

80 Desmond Morton and J.L. Granatstein, *Marching to Armageddon: Canadians and the Great War, 1914–1919* (Toronto: Lester and Orpen Dennys, 1989), 146–47; Greenhous and Harris, *Canada and the Battle of Vimy Ridge*, 134–35; Trevor Wilson, *The Myriad Faces of War: Britain and the Great War, 1914–1918* (Cambridge: Polity, 1986), 454; Nicholson, *Canadian Expeditionary Force*, 272, 278; Cook, *Shock Troops*, 145; James E. Edmonds, *A Short History of World War I* (London: Oxford University Press, 1951), 238; Spencer C. Tucker, *The Great War, 1914–18* (Bloomington: Indiana University Press, 1998), 129. In spite of its significance, the Battle of Arras has received much less historical attention than other offensives. Two studies that help remedy this situation are Jonathan Nicholls, *Cheerful Sacrifice: The Battle of Arras, 1917* (Barnsley: Pen and Sword, 2005); and Peter Barton with Jeremy Banning, *Arras: The Spring 1917 Offensive in Panoramas, Including Vimy Ridge and Bullecourt* (London: Constable, 2010).

81 John Swettenham, *To Seize the Victory: The Canadian Corps in World War I* (Toronto: Ryerson, 1965), 162–63; Gary Sheffield, *Forgotten Victory: The First World War, Myths and Realities* (London: Headline, 2001), 165.

Chapter 12 – A Bloody Setback: 10 April–1 July 1917

1 LAC, RG 9, III-D-3, vol. 4928, War Diary, 19th Battalion, 10–12 April 1917.
2 LAC, War Diary, 19th Battalion, 14 April 1917; ibid., appendix 5, field message, 13 April 1917.
3 This new position was different from the old "Observation Line" in the Thélus sector before the attack on 9 April. LAC, War Diary, 19th Battalion, 14–21 April 1917.
4 LAC, War Diary, 19th Battalion, reinforcement statement. From 15 to 30 April, the 19th Battalion would suffer additional casualties to the tune of thirty-nine other ranks, eleven of whom were killed. LAC, RG 150, vol. 496, "Casualties by Days – France and Belgium," 19th Battalion, April 1917.
5 Bruce Cane, *It Made You Think of Home: The Haunting Journal of Deward Barnes, Canadian Expeditionary Force: 1916–1919* (Toronto: Dundurn, 2004), 14, 58, 61; David W. Love, *A Nation in Making: The Organization and Administration of the Canadian Military during the First World War*, vol. 1 (Ottawa: Service Publications, 2012), 111, 195.
6 Barnes journal, 17 April 1917, qtd. in Cane, *It Made You Think of Home*, 67.
7 LAC, War Diary, 19th Battalion, 21 April 1917; D.E. Macintyre, *Canada at Vimy* (Toronto: Peter Martin, 1967), 129.
8 Haig's promotion to field marshal was announced by King George V at the beginning of 1917. The king regarded it "as a New Year's gift from myself and the country." Qtd. in G.W.L. Nicholson, *Canadian Expeditionary Force, 1914–1919: The Official History of the Canadian Army in the First World War* (Ottawa: Queen's Printer, 1962), 238.
9 John Swettenham, *To Seize the Victory: The Canadian Corps in World War I* (Toronto: Ryerson, 1965), 168.
10 LAC, War Diary, 19th Battalion, 22–26 April 1917; G.W.L. Nicholson, *The Gunners of Canada: The History of the Royal Regiment of Canadian Artillery*, vol. 1 (Toronto: McClelland and Stewart, 1967), 288–89.
11 LAC, War Diary, 19th Battalion, 26 April 1917; Swettenham, *To Seize the Victory*, 168.
12 LAC, War Diary, 19th Battalion, 27 April–2 May 1917.
13 GMA, Gaetz Family Fonds, John Gaetz to his mother, 1 May 1917.
14 LAC, War Diary, 19th Battalion, 27 April–2 May 1917. A detailed "Disposition State" drawn up for the battalion on 2 May gives a slightly different strength (19 officers and 668 other ranks) than that quoted in the war diary. In the former document, locations are provided for only three platoons in each company; the remaining platoons presumably were LOB. Ibid., appendix 1, "Disposition State, 19th Canadian Battalion," 2 May 1917.
15 Personal collection of Mrs. Phyllis Douglas, letters of Lt.-Col. Lionel H. Millen (hereafter Millen Letters), Millen to his mother, 3 May 1917.
16 GMA, Gaetz Family Fonds, John Gaetz to his mother, 1 May 1917.
17 Barnes journal, 3 May 1917, qtd. in Cane, *It Made You Think of Home*, 72.
18 CWM, 19740071-017 58C 1 1.8, untitled file of letters, questionnaires, responses, and notes regarding 19th Battalion history, typed comments by C.A. Gordon. Gordon (Regimental number 862958) had enlisted originally in the 180th Sportsmen's Battalion.
19 Nicholson, *Canadian Expeditionary Force*, 275–78; Cyril Falls, *Military Operations: France and Belgium, 1917*, vol. 1 (London: Macmillan, 1940), 520.
20 Macintyre, *Canada at Vimy*, 135; Cane, *It Made You Think of Home*, 78; LAC, War Diary, 19th Battalion, 6–7 May 1917; ibid., appendix 2, Report by Maj. H.D. Fearman, "19th Canadian Battalion, on the Left of Fresnoy, May 8th, 9th, & 10th, 1917" (hereafter Fearman Report).
21 LAC, War Diary, 19th Battalion, 6–7 May 1917; ibid., Fearman Report.
22 LAC, War Diary, 19th Battalion, 6–7 May 1917.

23 LAC, War Diary, 19th Battalion, 8 May 1917; Falls, *Military Operations:* 520–21; Nicholson, *Canadian Expeditionary Force*, 278.
24 Barnes journal, 8 May 1917, qtd. in Cane, *It Made You Think of Home*, 78–80.
25 CWM, 19740071-017 58C 1 1.8, typed comments and typed narrative by C.A. Gordon.
26 LAC, War Diary, 19th Battalion, 8 May 1917; RG 9, III-D-3, vol. 4936, War Diary, 29th Battalion, 7 May 1917; Barnes journal, 8 May 1917, qtd. in Cane, *It Made You Think of Home*, 82.
27 Gordon would survive the tribulations of life as a prisoner of war and return to Canada after the war. CWM, 19740071-017 58C 1 1.8, typed comments and typed narrative by C.A. Gordon.
28 Lt. Bridge was "wounded, unconscious and left for dead." He was "captured, spent 7½ months in solitary confinement, had a finger amputated, had a bad wound on his nose which took several years to heal, shrapnel scars to his arms and legs, and suffered from PTSD for a while. He weighed 121 lbs when he was demobbed [meaning demobilized]. Harold Edward Bridge died in BC in 1967." Dr. Robert Fraser, personal communication, 22 March 2015. See also Harold Bridge's personnel record in LAC, RG 150, Accession 1992-93/166, Box 1056–37.
29 LAC, War Diary, 19th Battalion, Fearman Report.
30 LAC, War Diary, 19th Battalion, 8 May 1917; ibid., Fearman Report.
31 LAC, War Diary, 19th Battalion, 8 May 1917; Nicholson, *Canadian Expeditionary Force*, 278; D.J. Corrigall, *The History of the Twentieth Canadian Battalion (Central Ontario Regiment) Canadian Expeditionary Force in the Great War, 1914–1918* (Toronto: Stone and Cox, 1935), 126; Cane, *It Made You Think of Home*, 82; LAC, War Diary, 19th Battalion, Fearman Report.
32 Barnes journal, 8 May 1917, qtd. in Cane, *It Made You Think of Home*, 83.
33 LAC, War Diary, 19th Battalion, 9–12 May 1917; ibid., Fearman Report; Corrigall, *History of the Twentieth Canadian Battalion*, 126; LAC, RG 9, III-D-3, vol. 4881, War Diary, 4th Infantry Brigade, 9 May 1917.
34 Nicholson, *Canadian Expeditionary Force*, 278.
35 Among the officers, Maj. G.T. Denison and Lt. E.D. Zoller were killed in the line, while Lt. F.G. Lawson was listed as missing. The battalion adjutant at that time, Lt. R. Williams, was killed in front of battalion headquarters, and Lts. C.C. Standish and J.G. Laurie were killed in Winnipeg Road. Lts. S.H. Johnston, A.F. Lynch, R.G. Washburn, and C.E. Cole were all wounded in action. In his after-action report, Maj. Fearman gives Johnston's rank as captain. Perhaps this was an acting or temporary rank when he was in charge of C Company. LAC, War Diary, 19th Battalion, Fearman Report. More than sixty years later, one of the wounded lieutenants, Allan Lynch, penned a vivid recollection of his experience at Fresnoy. See ASH, RG 4, series 3, World War 1, 19th Battalion Association, Allan F. Lynch, "Recollections of Fresnoy, May 1917," 19th Battalion Association newsletter, Fall 1981.
36 LAC, "Casualties by Days – France and Belgium," 19th Battalion, May 1917. Lt. Lawson, reported as missing in Fearman's report, likely was one of the two officers captured. The other was Lt. H.E. Bridge (see note 29above). In all, 3,842 Canadian troops were held in German prison camps during the First World War. For studies of prisoners' experiences, see Desmond Morton, *Silent Battle: Canadian Prisoners of War in Germany, 1914–1919* (Toronto: Lester Publishing, 1992); and Jonathan F. Vance, *Objects of Concern: Canadian Prisoners of War through the Twentieth Century* (Vancouver: UBC Press, 1994).
37 LAC, War Diary, 19th Battalion, 13–19 May 1917; Cane, *It Made You Think of Home*, 91.
38 GMA, Gaetz Family Fonds, John Gaetz to his mother, 15 May 1917.
39 GMA, Gaetz Family Fonds, John Gaetz to his brother Ted, 22 May 1917.
40 LAC, War Diary, 19th Battalion, 19 May 1917.
41 LAC, War Diary, 19th Battalion, 19–26 May 1917.
42 GMA, Gaetz Family Fonds, John Gaetz to his brother Ted, 22 May 1917.
43 This must have been the trench strength and not the unit's full complement. Only a week earlier (on 19 May) the battalion's strength had been reported as 25 officers and 677 other ranks. LAC, War Diary, 19th Battalion, 26 May 1917.

44 LAC, War Diary, 19th Battalion, 29 May 1917; Cane, *It Made You Think of Home*, 96.
45 Millen Letters, Millen to his mother, 30 May 1917.
46 LAC, War Diary, 19th Battalion, 29 May–3 June 1917.
47 Nicholson, *Canadian Expeditionary Force*, 278–79, 299; Ian F.W. Beckett, "Operational Command: The Plans and the Conduct of Battle," in *Passchendaele in Perspective: The Third Battle of* Ypres, ed. Peter Liddle (London: Leo Cooper, 1997), 103–6; Robin Prior and Trevor Wilson, *Passchendaele: The Untold Story* (New Haven: Yale University Press 1996), 45; Robin Prior and Trevor Wilson, *The First World War* (London: Cassell, 2000), 145, 147.
48 Nicholson, *Canadian Expeditionary Force*, 282.
49 Nicholson, *Canadian Expeditionary Force*, 282; Swettenham, *To Seize the Victory*, 170.
50 Nicholson, *Canadian Expeditionary Force*, 283–84, 540.
51 Tim Cook, "The Madman and the Butcher: Sir Sam Hughes, Sir Arthur Currie, and Their War of Reputations," *Canadian Historical Review* 85, no. 4 (2004): 699–700; see also A.M.J. Hyatt, *General Sir Arthur Currie: A Military Biography* (Toronto: University of Toronto Press / Canadian War Museum, 1987), Chs. 1–5.
52 ASH, RG 4, series 3, World War 1, 19th Battalion Association, "Recollections of Some Army 'Brass,'" 19th Battalion Association newsletter, Spring 1970.
53 The only major command change that would occur in the 2nd Canadian Division's infantry brigades during 1917 would be Brig.-Gen. A.H. Macdonell's replacement as GOC 5th Brigade by Brig.-Gen. J.M. Ross on 23 July. Nicholson, *Canadian Expeditionary Force*, 283–84, 541.
54 Nicholson, *Canadian Expeditionary Force*, 284–85.
55 LAC, War Diary, 19th Battalion, May 1917, list of casualties.
56 LAC, War Diary, 19th Battalion, May 1917, list of reinforcements.
57 LAC, War Diary, 19th Battalion, June 1917, list of reinforcements.
58 Love, *A Nation in Making*, vol. 1, 111; John F. Meek, *Over the Top!: The Canadian Infantry in the First World War* (privately printed, 1971), 99. Regarding the battalion substitutions in 3rd and 4th Canadian Divisions, the 60th Battalion was replaced by the 116th and the 73rd by the 85th during April 1917. See Nicholson, *Canadian Expeditionary Force*, Appendix D, 550.
59 LAC, RG 41, B-III-1, Records of the CBC, *Flanders Fields*, vol. 10, 19th Battalion, transcript of interview with Joe O'Neill, tape 1, 8–9, 12. O'Neill had another, distinctly friendlier, encounter with the corps commander when, on being separated temporarily from his battalion, he came across a cook tent. Not having eaten for some time, he asked the cook for some food. The cook replied testily, and an argument ensued. An officer then approached and, on being apprised of the situation, said to the cook, "Well now cook you've got some bacon here and some bread, how about putting a pot of tea on. Give these boys something to eat, they're really hungry, they've got a tough walk ahead of them." After the cook complied, he said to O'Neill, "You must have a great deal with the old man." O'Neill told him he didn't know what he meant, to which the cook responded, "Don't you know who that was you were talking to?" O'Neill said he had no idea. "Why," said the cook, "that's General Currie." The corps commander had stopped by "in his shirtsleeves," and O'Neill apparently failed to recognize him. Ibid., 12–13.
60 LAC, RG 9, III-C-1, vol. 3868, folder 109, file 3, 2nd Canadian Division, G.33/664, "Training While in Reserve," 26 May 1917; David Campbell, "The Divisional Experience in the C.E.F.: A Social and Operational History of the 2nd Canadian Division, 1915–1918," PhD diss., University of Calgary, 2003, 306–7; LAC, War Diary, 19th Battalion, June 1917, appendix 2, 4th Brigade training instructions, 31 May 1917; ibid., "19th Canadian Battalion, Training While in Reserve Area"; ibid., appendix 4, "19th Canadian Battalion, Training Schedule for Week Ending June 23rd, 1917."
61 LAC, RG 9, III-C-3, vol. 4112, folder 42, file 4, 2nd Canadian Division, G. 42/663, 19 May 1917; S.S. 143, *Instructions for the Training of Platoons for Offensive Action, 1917* (G.H.Q.: February 1917), 6–7; Campbell, "The Divisional Experience in the C.E.F.," 307–8.
62 Barnes journal, 3 June 1917, qtd. in Cane, *It Made You Think of Home*, 97.
63 Millen Letters, Millen to his mother, 11 June 1917.

64 LAC, War Diary, 19th Battalion, June 1917, appendix 4, list of winners of brigade sports competition; CWM, 19740071-017 58C 1 1.8, untitled file of letters, questionnaires, responses, and notes regarding 19th Battalion history, "Nineteenth Battalion History, Questionnaire No. 5, Verdrel – Hill 70 – Passchendeale," 4.

65 LAC, RG 9, III-D-3, vol. 4885, War Diary, 5th Infantry Brigade, June 1917, appendix 6, results of the 2nd Canadian Divisional Athletic Meet, 23 June 1917.

66 GMA, M399, Gaetz Family Fonds, John Gaetz to his mother, 30 June 1917.

67 LAC, War Diary, 19th Battalion, 1–7 July 1917; Cane, *It Made You Think of Home*, 101–2.

Chapter 13 – "The Worst Ever": July–August 1917 and the Battle for Hill 70

1 The French word *fosse* refers to a mining pit. Bruce Cane, *It Made You Think of Home: The Haunting Journal of Deward Barnes, Canadian Expeditionary Force: 1916–1919* (Toronto: Dundurn, 2004), 101–2.

2 In all, 8 officers and 244 other ranks were left back at Noulette Wood. The total battalion strength on 10 July was therefore 32 officers and 909 other ranks. LAC, RG 9, III-D-3, vol. 4928, War Diary, 19th Battalion, 8–11 July 1917.

3 LAC, War Diary, 19th Battalion, 12–17 July 1917; Barnes journal, 16 July 1917, qtd. in Cane, *It Made You Think of Home*, 105.

4 D.J. Corrigall, *The History of the Twentieth Canadian Battalion (Central Ontario Regiment), Canadian Expeditionary Force in the Great War, 1914–1918* (Toronto: Stone and Cox, 1935), 136.

5 G.W.L. Nicholson, *Canadian Expeditionary Force, 1914–1919: The Official History of the Canadian Army in the First World War* (Ottawa: Queen's Printer, 1962), 284–86. For recent studies of the operation at Hill 70, see Geoff Jackson, "'Anything But Lovely': The Canadian Corps at Lens in the Summer of 1917," *Canadian Military History* 17, no. 1 (Winter 2008): 5–20; Matthew Walthert, "Neglected Victory: The Canadian Corps at Hill 70," *Canadian Military History* 19, no. 1 (Winter 2010): 21–36. See also Geoffrey Jackson, "Hill 70 and Lens, the Forgotten Battles: The Canadian Corps in the Summer of 1917," MA thesis, University of Calgary, 2006; Trevor Harvey, "The Battle of Hill 70 – 15–25 August 1917: A Study of the Battle, with Particular Reference to the Role of Sir Arthur Currie in His First Action as Commander of the Canadian Corps," MA thesis, University of Birmingham, 2006. The most recent and comprehensive analyses of Hill 70 may be found in Douglas E. Delaney and Serge Marc Durflinger, eds., *Capturing Hill 70: Canada's Forgotten Battle of the First World War* (Vancouver: UBC Press, 2016).

6 LAC, War Diary, 19th Battalion, 23 July–5 August 1917; Corrigall, *The History of the Twentieth Canadian Battalion*, 136.

7 Barnes journal, 22 July 1917, qtd. in Cane, *It Made You Think of Home*, 106.

8 LAC, MG 30, E 488, William Clement Morgan Papers, personal diary, 28 July 1917.

9 Corrigall, *The History of the Twentieth Canadian Battalion*, 137.

10 It is doubtful that this number constituted the entire strength of the battalion, considering that it had boasted in excess of 30 officers and 900 other ranks during early July. July's casualties had, in fact, amounted to only twenty-one other ranks, of which seven were fatal. These losses were offset by the absorption of thirty reinforcements during the same month. It seems more likely that a portion of the battalion was again left out of the front lines as a reserve force on 5 August, but not as large a number as was usually the case. LAC, War Diary, 19th Battalion, 23 July–6 August 1917; ibid., July 1917, notes on reinforcements and casualties.

11 LAC, War Diary, 19th Battalion, 6 August 1917.

12 Barnes journal, 7 August 1917, qtd. in Cane, *It Made You Think of Home*, 108.

13 Tim Cook, *No Place to Run: The Canadian Corps and Gas Warfare in the First World War* (Vancouver: UBC Press, 1999), 119–21.

14 Cook, *No Place to Run*, 121–24.

15 LAC, War Diary, 19th Battalion, 8–13 August 1917.

16 LAC, War Diary, 19th Battalion, August 1917, 4th Canadian Infantry Brigade, Instructions for the Offensive no. 3, 29 July 1917; ibid., 19th Canadian Battalion, Operation Orders no. 46, 31 July 1917.
17 Bill Rawling, *Surviving Trench Warfare: Technology and the Canadian Corps, 1914–1918* (Toronto: University of Toronto Press, 1992), 139.
18 Corrigall, *The History of the Twentieth Canadian Battalion*, 135–36; James E. Edmonds, *Military Operations: France and Belgium, 1917*, vol. 2 (London: HMSO, 1948), 223.
19 J.A. Cooper, *History of Operations of 4th Canadian Infantry Brigade, 1915–1919* (London: Charles and Son, n.d.), 24. The northern suburbs of Lens consisted of rows of brick houses built by mining companies to accommodate their workers. On 15 August the 2nd Canadian Division would have to advance through four of these communities: Cité Saint-Edouard, Cité St-Laurent, Cité St-Emile, and Cité St-Elisabeth. Previous months of artillery shelling had already reduced these suburbs "to a fantastic maze of ruins across which trenches now meandered." Nicholson, *Canadian Expeditionary Force*, 286.
20 LAC, War Diary, 19th Battalion, 14–15 August 1917; ibid., appendix 4, 4th Canadian Infantry Brigade B.2-1, 14 August 1917.
21 LAC, RG 9, III-D-1, vol. 4692, folder 51, file 18, "Notes on Attack: N.W. Lens," 19th Battalion, C Company report, 15–17 August 1917.
22 LAC, RG 9, III-C-1, vol. 3868, folder 109, file 6, Canadian Corps, G. 869/14-3, 10 August 1917.
23 Nicholson, *Canadian Expeditionary Force*, 286.
24 Swettenham, *To Seize the Victory*, 176.
25 Barnes journal, 15 August 1917, qtd. in Cane, *It Made You Think of Home*, 111.
26 Corrigall, *The History of the Twentieth Canadian Battalion*, 141.
27 LAC, War Diary, 19th Battalion, August 1917, appendix 5, "Report on the Operations of 'C' Coy. 19th Can. Bn. during Attack on Hill 70," 15–17 August 1917.
28 LAC, War Diary, 19th Battalion, 15 August 1917; LAC, RG 9, III-D-1, vol. 4692, folder 51, file 18, "Notes on Attack: N.W. Lens," C Company report; LAC, RG 9, III-D-3, vol. 4930, War Diary, 20th Battalion, 15 August 1917.
29 LAC, "Notes on Attack: N.W. Lens," C Company report.
30 LAC, "Notes on Attack: N.W. Lens," C Company report; LAC, War Diary, 19th Battalion, "Report on the Operations of 'C' Coy. 19th Can. Bn."
31 Nicholson, *Canadian Expeditionary Force*, 288; Edmonds, *Military Operations*, vol. 2, 223–24; Rawling, *Surviving Trench Warfare*, 141.
32 LAC, "Report on the Operations of 'C' Coy. 19th Can. Bn."
33 LAC, "Report on the Operations of 'C' Coy. 19th Can. Bn."; LAC, "Notes on Attack: N.W. Lens," C Company report.
34 Rawling, *Surviving Trench Warfare*, 141; Swettenham, *To Seize the Victory*, 177; Nicholson, *Canadian Expeditionary Force*, 290.
35 Nicholson, *Canadian Expeditionary Force*, 289–90, map 8; LAC, RG 9, III-D-3, vol. 4931, War Diary, 21st Battalion, August 1917, appendices, report on operations at Hill 70.
36 LAC, "Notes on Attack: N.W. Lens," A Company report.
37 Barnes journal, 15 August 1917, qtd. in Cane, *It Made You Think of Home*, 113.
38 LAC, "Notes on Attack: N.W. Lens," A Company report; LAC, War Diary, 19th Battalion, August 1917, appendix 5, Lt. J.M. Bennett, A Company, "Report on Tour in Front Line."
39 LAC, "Notes on Attack: N.W. Lens," A Company report; LAC, Bennett, "Report on Tour in Front Line."
40 Barnes journal, 15 August 1917, qtd. in Cane, *It Made You Think of Home*, 113.
41 LAC, "Notes on Attack: N.W. Lens," A Company report; LAC, Bennett, "Report on Tour in Front Line."
42 Barnes journal, 15 August 1917, qtd. in Cane, *It Made You Think of Home*, 114–15.
43 LAC, "Notes on Attack: N.W. Lens," A Company report; LAC, Bennett, "Report on Tour in Front Line."

44 Andrew Borrowman was an accountant from Calgary. LAC, "Notes on Attack: N.W. Lens," A Company report; LAC, Bennett, "Report on Tour in Front Line"; Cane, *It Made You Think of Home*, 115.
45 LAC, "Notes on Attack: N.W. Lens," A Company report.
46 LAC, "Notes on Attack: N.W. Lens," A Company report; Ibid.; LAC, Bennett, "Report on Tour in Front Line."
47 LAC, "Notes on Attack: N.W. Lens," C Company report.
48 Cook, *No Place to Run*, 130; Nicholson, *Canadian Expeditionary Force*, p. 291.
49 Adye never returned to front-line duty with the 19th Battalion. Instead he remained in England, where he graduated from a senior NCOs' course and helped train conscripts. By war's end, he had been accepted as a cadet for officers' training but decided not to go through with it after the armistice took effect. He returned to Canada and later entered the ministry. LAC, *Flanders Fields*, vol. 10, transcript of interview with Canon E.R. Adye, tape 2, 23, 25–9, 34.
50 Barnes journal, 18 August 1917, quoted in Cane, *It Made You Think of Home*, 119; LAC, War Diary, 19th Battalion, 16–17 August 1917.
51 LAC, War Diary, 19th Battalion, August 1917, appendix 5, "Summary of Operations, D Coy, 19th Bn while att'd to 21 Bn."
52 Casualties sustained on the morning of 18 August included Acting CSM A. Catton ("one of the old originals"), who was killed, as was an attached officer, Lt. P.J.S. Laing. Capt. Linton "was blown down a dugout," and B Company's sergeant major "was also badly wounded." Laing was a former NCO in the 19th Battalion who was granted a commission and had served since December 1916 as an instructor at the Canadian Base Depot. He rejoined the 19th Battalion, being attached from the Canadian Base at Havre on 12 August 1917. LAC, "Summary of Operations, D Coy"; LAC, "Notes on Attack: N.W. Lens," D Company report; LAC, RG 150, vol. 465, "List of Officers, 19th Battalion"; CWM, 19740071-017 58C 1 1.8, handwritten list of other ranks from the 19th Battalion who were granted commissions.
53 LAC, War Diary, 19th Battalion, 18–21 August 1917; LAC, "Notes on Attack: N.W. Lens," D Company report.
54 Rawling, *Surviving Trench Warfare*, 142.
55 Swettenham, *To Seize the Victory*, 178.
56 LAC, War Diary, 19th Battalion, August 1917, list of casualties; LAC, RG 150, vol. 497, "Casualties by Days – France and Belgium," 19th Battalion, August 1917.
57 LAC, vol. 4928, War Diary, 19th Battalion, August 1917, list of reinforcements.
58 LAC, "Casualties by Days – France and Belgium," 18th, 19th, 20th, 21st Battalions.
59 On 15 August alone, the Canadian Corps lost 1,056 killed, 2,432 wounded, and 39 taken prisoner. Nicholson, *Canadian Expeditionary Force*, 290, 297; Walthert, "Neglected Victory," 36n82; LAC, "Casualties by Days – France and Belgium," Canadian Corps casualties, August 1917; Tim Cook, *Shock Troops: Canadians Fighting the Great War, 1917–1918* (Toronto: Viking, 2008), 305–6; Daniel G. Dancocks, *Sir Arthur Currie: A Biography* (Toronto: Methuen 1985), 107; Swettenham, *To Seize the Victory*, 178.
60 Gardner, qtd. in J.L. Granatstein, *Canada's Army: Waging War and Keeping the Peace* (Toronto: University of Toronto Press, 2002), 120–21.

Chapter 14 – "A Dirty, Dirty Country": Sep–Nov 1917 and the Battle for Passchendaele

1 GMA, M399, Gaetz Family Fonds, J.R. Gaetz to his mother, 26 August 1917.
2 LAC, RG 9, III-D-3, vol. 4928, War Diary, 19th Battalion, 24–31 August 1917.
3 GMA, Gaetz Family Fonds, J.R. Gaetz to his mother, 26 August 1917.
4 Four officers (Acting Capt. R.W. Catto and Lts. J.M. Bennett, W. Waldrum, and F.H. Cantlon) were awarded the Military Cross; one other rank (Lance Cpl. J. Dumaresque) was awarded the Distinguished Conduct Medal; two other ranks (Sgt. D. Graham and Pte. J. Robertson) were awarded bars to the Military Medal; and sixteen other ranks were awarded the Military Medal

(Sgt. G. Annand, Lance Cpl. J. Shields, Sgt. O. Gower, Acting Cpl. H. Dibble, Pte. L. Bovineau, Pte. L. Bacon, Pte. J. Coomber, Acting Sgt. I. McKay, Pte. C. London, Pte. W.H. Summerville, Sgt. H. Dewar, Sgt. S.H. Robinson, Acting Cpl. J. McP. Cowan, Sgt. R. McKenzie, Acting Lance Cpl. J. Barnes, Pte. S.H. Rootes). LAC, War Diary, 19th Battalion, 7, 9 September 1917 and list of honours and awards.

5 GMA, Gaetz Family Fonds, J.R. Gaetz to his father, 11 September 1917.

6 LAC, War Diary, 19th Battalion, 8–12 September 1917; ibid., appendix 1, 19th Canadian Battalion Orders, no. 292, 11 September 1917.

7 H.C. Singer and A.A. Peebles, *History of Thirty-First Battalion C.E.F. from Its Organization, November, 1914 to Its Demobilization, June, 1919* (Calgary: privately printed, 1939), 247; LAC, RG 9, III-C-1, vol. 3867, folder 107, file 1, "Notes on the Result of the Platoon Competition Held at the Corps Rifle Meeting"; David Campbell, "The Divisional Experience in the C.E.F.: A Social and Operational History of the 2nd Canadian Division, 1915–1918," PhD diss., University of Calgary, 2003, 320. At the corps platoon competition each competing platoon advanced over a specially constructed range on which targets would appear and disappear at varying intervals, the targets being engaged with rifle and Lewis gun fire. Points were allocated for each hit scored on a target, the method by which the platoon commander disposed his sections, the conduct of the advance, the direction of covering fire, and the overall turnout of the platoon.

8 Company positions were altered the following day, when the elements of the battalion stationed in the Bois-de-la-Folie were ordered to move farther forward to make room for the 20th Battalion. LAC, War Diary, 19th Battalion, 14, 17 September 1917; ibid., appendix 5, sketch map of 4th Infantry Brigade forward area; ibid., appendix 5, 19th Battalion Orders no. 55, 15 Sep. 1917.

9 Although the war diary reports no casualties from 15 to 19 September, postwar records indicate that one other rank was wounded by enemy fire and three other ranks were accidentally injured during this period. LAC, War Diary, 19th Battalion, 15–19 September 1917; LAC, RG 150, vol. 497, "Casualties by Days – France and Belgium," 19th Battalion, September 1917.

10 LAC, War Diary, 19th Battalion, 20–25 September 1917.

11 Daniel G. Dancocks, *Legacy of Valour: The Canadians at Passchendaele* (Edmonton: Hurtig, 1986), 95–96.

12 Three other ranks were killed (two on 3 October and one on 5 October), and one other rank was wounded (on 4 October). Two more other ranks were injured accidentally. LAC, "Casualties by Days – France and Belgium," 19th Battalion, October 1917; LAC, vol. 4928, War Diary, 19th Battalion, 1–7 October 1917.

13 Personal collection of Mrs. Phyllis Douglas, letters of Lt.-Col. Lionel H. Millen (hereafter Millen Letters), Millen to his mother, 10–11 October 1917

14 LAC, War Diary, 19th Battalion, 15–20 October 1917.

15 Ian M. Brown, "Not Glamorous, but Effective: The Canadian Corps and the Set-Piece Attack, 1917–1918," *Journal of Military History* 58, no. 3 (1994): 421–44.

16 Tim Travers, *How The War Was Won: Command and Technology in the British Army on the Western Front, 1917–1918* (London: Routledge, 1992), 11–12; Gary Sheffield, *Forgotten Victory: The First World War, Myths and Realities* (London: Headline, 2001), 171–80; Robin Prior and Trevor Wilson, *The First World War* (London: Cassell, 1999), 147, 150; John Lee, "The British Divisions at Third Ypres," in *Passchendaele in Perspective: The Third Battle of Ypres*, ed. Peter Liddle (London: Leo Cooper, 1997), 220–23. For a comprehensive analysis of the complexities and course of the Passchendaele offensive, see Robin Prior and Trevor Wilson, *Passchendaele: The Untold Story* (New Haven: Yale University Press, 1996), and the excellent collection of essays in Liddle, *Passchendaele in Perspective*.

17 Tim Cook, *Shock Troops: Canadians Fighting the Great War, 1917–1918* (Toronto: Viking, 2008), 316–17. Haig's view of French resilience was pessimistic, since in fact "the worst phase of the mutinies clearly had passed by early June." Robert Doughty, "How Did France Weather the Troubles of 1917?" in *1917: Tactics, Training, and Technology*, ed. Peter Dennis and Jeffrey Grey (Canberra: Australian Military History Publications, 2007), 91. In this same collection, Robin Prior's critical assessment of Haig's goal to capture Passchendaele Ridge includes this gem: "In

the prevailing conditions an announcement to capture the Sea of Tranquility on the Moon would have been just as sensible." Robin Prior, "The British High Command at Passchendaele," in Dennis and Grey, *1917: Tactics, Training and Technology*, 134.

18 Campbell, "The Divisional Experience in the C.E.F.," 341–42. For an excellent analytical overview, see Dean Oliver, "The Canadians at Passchendaele," in Liddle, *Passchendaele in Perspective*, 255–71.

19 LAC, Sir Arthur Currie Papers, vol. 43, file 192, "Diary of Events, Canadian Corps, 1917."

20 G.W.L. Nicholson, *Canadian Expeditionary Force, 1914–1919: The Official History of the Canadian Army in the First World War* (Ottawa: Queen's Printer, 1962), 312–13, map 9.

21 LAC, War Diary, 19th Battalion, 25 October 1917.

22 LAC, War Diary, 19th Battalion, 26–28 October 1917.

23 Dancocks, *Legacy of Valour*, 106–7, 156–57; G.W.L. Nicholson, *The Gunners of Canada: The History of the Royal Regiment of Canadian Artillery*, vol. 1: *1534–1919* (Toronto: McClelland and Stewart, 1967), 309.

24 LAC, RG 150, vol. 465, "List of Officers – 19th Infantry Battalion," 30 November 1917.

25 LAC, RG 41, B-III-1, Records of the CBC, *Flanders Fields*, vol. 10, 19th Battalion, transcript of interview with Joe O'Neill, tape 2, 14–15.

26 Nicholson, *Canadian Expeditionary Force*, 318–23; Bill Rawling, *Surviving Trench Warfare: Technology and the Canadian Corps, 1914–1918* (Toronto: University of Toronto Press, 1992), 152–59.

27 LAC, RG 9, III-D-3, vol. 4846, War Diary, 2nd Canadian Division headquarters, 2–3 November 1917; LAC, RG 9, III-D-3, vol. 4833, War Diary, 1st Canadian Division headquarters, "1st Canadian Division, Report on the Passchendaele Ridge Operations, November 4–12, 1917," 1, 2.

28 J.A. Cooper, *History of Operations of 4th Canadian Infantry Brigade, 1915–1919* (London: Charles and Son, n.d.), 26; Nicholson, *Canadian Expeditionary Force*, 324.

29 LAC, War Diary, 19th Battalion, 2 November 1917; Bruce Cane, *It Made You Think of Home: The Haunting Journal of Deward Barnes, Canadian Expeditionary Force: 1916–1919* (Toronto: Dundurn, 2004), 128.

30 The company commanders at this time were as follows: A Company, Capt. J.A. Harstone; B Company, Lt. G.H. Applegath; C Company, Lt. M.C. Roberts; D Company, Capt. J.A. Linton. LAC, vol. 4928, War Diary, 19th Battalion, 2 November 1917.

31 Pte. F.J. McNulty to Pte. James McNulty, Welland Canal Force, Merritton, Ontario, 27 October 1917, courtesy of Helen Sluis, forwarded by Fred Sherriff.

32 LAC, *Flanders Fields*, vol. 10, 19th Battalion, transcript of interview with Joe O'Neill, tape 2, 12.

33 Barnes journal, 6 November 1917, qtd. in Cane, *It Made You Think of Home*, 130–31.

34 LAC, *Flanders Fields*, vol. 10, 19th Battalion, transcript of interview with E. Youngman, tape 4, 3.

35 LAC, *Flanders Fields*, vol. 6, transcript of Episode 10, "The Battle of Passchendaele," quote from L.R. Fennel, 27th Battalion, 22.

36 LAC, *Flanders Fields*, vol. 12, 31st Battalion, transcript of interview with R. Ferrie, tape 2, 6.

37 Qtd. in Dancocks, *Legacy of Valour*, 119.

38 LAC, *Flanders Fields*, vol. 10, 19th Battalion, transcript of interview with E. Youngman, tape 4, 2.

39 LAC, *Flanders Fields*, vol. 10, 19th Battalion, transcript of interview with Joe O'Neill, tape 3, 2.

40 LAC, RG 9, III-C-3, vol. 4116, folder 4, file 5, "19th Canadian Battalion, Narrative of Operations, Night 2nd/3rd to 4th/5th" November 1917."

41 LAC, 19th Battalion Narrative of Operations, 2–5 November 1917.

42 LAC, War Diary, 19th Battalion, 3 November 1917; LAC, RG 9, III-D-3, vol. 4931, War Diary, 21st Battalion, November 1917, appendix D, "Report of Enemy Attack on Morning of November 3rd in front of Passchendaele."

43 LAC, War Diary, 19th Battalion, 3 November 1917; LAC, 19th Battalion Narrative of Operations, 2–5 November 1917.

44 The officer in charge of C Company, M.C. Roberts, was at that time a lieutenant and not a captain as O'Neill maintained. LAC, *Flanders Fields*, vol. 10, 19th Battalion, transcript of interview with Joe O'Neill, tape 2, 15–16; LAC, War Diary, 19th Battalion, November 1917, appendix 1, field message signed by Lt. M.C. Roberts, OC, C Company, 2 November 1917.
45 LAC, *Flanders Fields*, vol. 10, 19th Battalion, transcript of interview with Joe O'Neill, tape 2, 16–17; ibid., tape 3, 1.
46 LAC, War Diary, 19th Battalion, 3–5 November 1917; LAC, 19th Battalion Narrative of Operations, 2–5 November 1917; D.J. Corrigall, *The History of the Twentieth Canadian Battalion (Central Ontario Regiment), Canadian Expeditionary Force in the Great War, 1914–1918* (Toronto: Stone and Cox, 1935), 158.
47 LAC, War Diary, 19th Battalion, 3–4 November 1917; LAC, 19th Battalion Narrative of Operations, 2–5 November 1917.
48 LAC, *Flanders Fields*, vol. 10, 19th Battalion, transcript of interview with Joe O'Neill, tape 3, 1–2.
49 LAC, War Diary, 19th Battalion, 3–4 November 1917; LAC, 19th Battalion Narrative of Operations, 2–5 November 1917.
50 *London Gazette*, 24 April 1917, 8; ibid., 17 July 1917, 11.
51 LAC, *Flanders Fields*, vol. 10, 19th Battalion, transcript of interview with Joe O'Neill, tape 3, 2–4.
52 LAC, RG 150, 1992–93/166, box 1793–28, personnel file, Hamilton Clendining; LAC, War Diary, 19th Battalion, January 1918, list of reinforcements.
53 Barnes journal, 6 November 1917, qtd. in Cane, *It Made You Think of Home*, 129–32.
54 LAC, War Diary, 19th Battalion, 8 November 1917; LAC, RG 9, III-C-3, vol. 4116, folder 4, file 5, "19th Canadian Battalion, Narrative of Operations, November 8th–12th 1917."
55 LAC, War Diary, 19th Battalion, 8–9 Nov. 1917.
56 Cooper, *History of Operations of* 4th *Canadian Infantry Brigade*, 26–7.
57 LAC, War Diary, 19th Battalion, 9–10 November 1917.
58 LAC, War Diary, 19th Battalion, 10 November 1917.
59 LAC, War Diary, 19th Battalion, 11–12 November 1917.
60 Barnes journal, 11 November 1917, qtd. in Cane, *It Made You Think of Home*, 133.
61 LAC, War Diary, 19th Battalion, 11–12 November 1917. Possibly, fewer men would have died of their wounds if there had not been a shortage of supplies at the Regimental Aid Post. LAC, "19th Canadian Battalion, Narrative of Operations, November 8th–12th 1917"; LAC, RG 9, III-D-3, vol. 4882, War Diary, 4th Infantry Brigade, November 1917, appendix 8, "Report on the Operations of the 4th Canadian Infantry Brigade from November 8th/9th 1917 to November 12th/13th 1917."
62 Nicholson, *Canadian Expeditionary Force*, 327.
63 Holger Herwig, *The First World War: Germany and Austria-Hungary, 1914–1918* (London: Arnold, 1997), 332; William Philpott, *War of Attrition: Fighting the First World War* (New York: Overlook Press, 2014), 278. Others have argued for greater parity in casualties, to the tune of approximately 260,000 for each side. Sheffield, *Forgotten Victory*, 180; Richard Holmes, *The Western Front: Ordinary Soldiers and the Defining Battles of World War I* (New York: TV Books, 2000), 174. Historians Robin Prior and Trevor Wilson place British casualties at around 275,000 (of whom 70,000 were killed) and German casualties at "just under 200,000." Prior and Wilson, *Passchendaele*, 195.
64 Holmes, *The Western Front*, 172; Prior and Wilson, *Passchendaele*, 195–200; Sheffield, *Forgotten Victory*, 180; Robin Prior, "The British High Command at Passchendaele," in Dennis and Grey, *1917: Tactics, Training and Technology*, 132–33.
65 Corrigall, *The History of the Twentieth Canadian Battalion*, 167.
66 LAC, War Diary, 19th Battalion, 13–17 November 1917.
67 Millen Letters, Millen to his mother, 18 November 1917.

Chapter 15- Days of Uncertainty: November 1917–March 1918

1 J.P. Harris and Niall Barr, *Amiens to the Armistice: The BEF in the Hundred Days' Campaign, 8 August–11 November 1918* (London: Brassey's, 1998), 44–45; Bill Rawling, *Surviving Trench Warfare: Technology and the Canadian Corps, 1914–1918* (Toronto: University of Toronto Press, 1992), 168. For more information on technical developments in artillery, see Harris and Barr, *Amiens to the Armistice*, 38–46; Shelford Bidwell and Dominick Graham, *Fire-Power: British Army Weapons and Theories of War, 1904–1945* (London: Allen and Unwin, 1982), 107–11, 134; and Lawrence Bragg, A.H. Dowson, and H.H. Hemming, *Artillery Survey in the First World War* (London: Field Survey Association, 1971).

2 See Bryn Hammond, *Cambrai 1917: The Myth of the First Great Tank Battle* (London: Weidenfeld and Nicolson, 2008).

3 Gary Sheffield, *Forgotten Victory: The First World War, Myths and Realities* (London: Headline, 2001), 181–83; Spencer C. Tucker, *The Great War, 1914–18* (Bloomington: Indiana University Press, 1998), 141–43.

4 G.W.L. Nicholson, *Canadian Expeditionary Force, 1914–1919: The Official History of the Canadian Army in the First World War* (Ottawa: Queen's Printer, 1962), 338.

5 LAC, RG 9, III-D-3, vol. 4928, War Diary, 19th Battalion, 17 November 1917; ibid., appendix 4, 19th Battalion Orders, no. 317, 17 November 1917; Bruce Cane, *It Made You Think of Home: The Haunting Journal of Deward Barnes, Canadian Expeditionary Force: 1916–1919* (Toronto: Dundurn, 2004), 38; D.J. Corrigall, *The History of the Twentieth Canadian Battalion (Central Ontario Regiment), Canadian Expeditionary Force in the Great War, 1914–1918* (Toronto: Stone and Cox, 1935), 168.

6 LAC, War Diary, 19th Battalion, 29 November 1917; LAC, RG 150, 1992–93/166, box 4150–2, personnel file, Maj. H.C. Hatch.

7 LAC, War Diary, 19th Battalion, 30 November 1917; ibid., appendix 4, Report on Enemy Raid, 30 November 1917.

8 LAC, War Diary, 19th Battalion, list of casualties, November 1917; ibid., 3 December 1917.

9 LAC, RG 41, B-III-1, Records of the CBC, *Flanders Fields*, vol. 10, 19th Battalion, transcript of interview with F.A. Stitt, tape 1, 25.

10 Nicholson, *Canadian Expeditionary Force*, 345–46; LAC, War Diary, 19th Battalion, December 1917; Cane, *It Made You Think of Home*, 142.

11 For analyses of the issues surrounding conscription in Canada during the First World War, see J.L. Granatstein and J.M. Hitsman, *Broken Promises: A History of Conscription in Canada* (Toronto: Oxford University Press, 1977), Chs. 2–3; Robert Craig Brown, *Robert Laird Borden: A Biography*, vol. 2: *1914–1937* (Toronto: Macmillan, 1980), Chs. 8–11; J.L. Granatstein, "Conscription in the Great War," in *Canada and the First World War: Essays in Honour of Robert Craig Brown*, ed. David MacKenzie (Toronto: University of Toronto Press, 2005), 62–75; Andrew Theobald, *The Bitter Harvest of War: New Brunswick and the Conscription Crisis of 1917* (Fredericton: Goose Lane Editions / New Brunswick Military Heritage Project, 2008); and Tim Cook, *Warlords: Borden, Mackenzie King, and Canada's World Wars* (Toronto: Allen Lane, 2012), Chs. 6–8.

12 LAC, War Diary, 19th Battalion, 10–13 December 1917.

13 LAC, War Diary, 19th Battalion, 13–18 December 1917; Corrigall, *The History of the Twentieth Canadian Battalion*.

14 J.A. Cooper, *History of Operations of 4th Canadian Infantry Brigade, 1915–1919* (London: Charles and Son, n.d.), 27; LAC, War Diary, 19th Battalion, 19 December 1917; David Campbell, "The Divisional Experience in the C.E.F.: A Social and Operational History of the 2nd Canadian Division, 1915–1918," PhD diss., University of Calgary, 2003, 378.

15 LAC, War Diary, 19th Battalion, 19–20 December 1917; Cane, *It Made You Think of Home*, 144.

16 LAC, RG 9, III-C-3, vol. 4136, folder 25, file 1, 2nd Canadian Division G.33/436, 14 December 1917; LAC, War Diary, 19th Battalion, appendix 4, 19th Battalion syllabus of training, 21 December 1917–5 January 1918.

17 LAC, RG 9, III-C-3, vol. 4064, folder 15, file 6, Canadian Corps, "Notes on Training," 27 November 1917; Shane B. Schreiber, *Shock Army of the British Empire: The Canadian Corps in the Last 100 Days of the Great War* (Westport: Praeger 1997), 26–27, 31n35.
18 LAC, RG 9, III-C-3, vol. 4092, folder 27, file 15, Report by Lt.-Col. L.H. Millen to 4th Brigade, 24 November 1917.
19 LAC, Hatch Personnel File; LAC, RG 24, C-6-d, vol. 1886, file 85, Commanders and Staffs, 19th Canadian Infantry Battalion.
20 Barnes journal, 25 December 1917, qtd. in Cane, *It Made You Think of Home*, 145.
21 LAC, *Flanders Fields*, vol. 10, 19th Battalion, transcript of interview with F.A. Stitt, tape 1, 26–27.
22 LAC, RG 150, vol. 465, List of Officers, 19th Infantry Battalion, 31 January 1918.
23 Personal collection of Mrs. Phyllis Douglas, letters of Lt.-Col. Lionel H. Millen (hereafter Millen Letters), Millen to his mother, 5 January 1918.
24 LAC, War Diary, 19th Battalion, 12 January 1918 and list of decorations awarded.
25 LAC, War Diary, 19th Battalion, 14–15 January 1918, and list of reinforcements; ibid., list of reinforcements, December 1917. According to postwar records, the 19th Battalion suffered only nine casualties during December 1917. All of these were among the other ranks, one of which was a fatality (from gas). LAC, RG 150, vol. 499, "Casualties by Days – France and Belgium," 19th Battalion, December 1917.
26 CWM, 19740071–017 58C 1 1.8, untitled file of letters, questionnaires, responses, and notes regarding 19th Battalion history, handwritten notes titled "Granted Commissions from the Ranks." This list was compiled in the postwar period; if not completely accurate, it should be a reasonable approximation of the actual number of men commissioned from the ranks.
27 LAC, *Flanders Fields*, vol. 10, 19th Battalion, transcript of interview with Joe O'Neill, tape 4, 1–2.
28 LAC, *Flanders Fields*, vol. 10, 19th Battalion, transcript of interview with Joe O'Neill, tape 4, 3.
29 LAC, War Diary, 19th Battalion, 15–28 January 1917; ibid., vol. 4929, War Diary, 19th Battalion, 2–15 February 1918.
30 LAC, vol. 4929, War Diary, 19th Battalion, 16 February 1918. Château-de-la-Haie was owned by world-renowned actress Sarah Bernhardt, who turned its grounds over for use as a camp and training area. LAC, War Diary, 19th Battalion, 16–27 February 1918.
31 LAC, RG 150, 1992–93/166, box 6170–36, personnel file, Lt.-Col. L.H. Millen; Robert Fraser, "Lt.-Col. Lionel Herbert Millen, DSO (1876–1956)," unpublished biographical sketch; LAC, Hatch personnel file.
32 Lt.-Gen. Sir A.W. Currie, "Interim Report on the Operations of the Canadian Corps during the Year 1918," in *Report of the Ministry, Overseas Military Forces of Canada, 1918* (London: Minister, Overseas Military Forces of Canada, n.d.), 104–5.
33 Currie, "Interim Report," 105–7; Nicholson, *Canadian Expeditionary Force*, 378.
34 Stephen J. Harris, *Canadian Brass: The Making of a Professional Army, 1860–1939* (Toronto: University of Toronto Press, 1988), 128; William Stewart, "Attack Doctrine in the Canadian Corps, 1916–1918," MA thesis, University of New Brunswick, 1982, 132; LAC, MG 30, E 100, Arthur Currie Papers, vol. 50, Army Council Instruction, no. 1230 of 1917, "Training of Infantry Recruits," WO, 6 August 1917.
35 The 3rd Canadian Reserve Battalion was the reserve unit in England that supplied the 19th Battalion with most of its reinforcements. Nicholson, *Canadian Expeditionary Force*, 231–32, 363; Schreiber, *Shock Army of the British Empire*, 19–21; John F. Meek, *Over the Top! The Canadian Infantry in the First World War* (privately published, 1971), 41–44, 126; David W. Love, *A Nation in Making: The Organization and Administration of the Canadian Military during the First World War* (Ottawa: Service Publications, 2012), 110-11, 196; LAC, RG 150, vol. 71, "19th Cdn Bttn (4)," Part II Orders no. 18, 8 March 1918; LAC, "Guide to Sources Relating to Units of the Canadian Expeditionary Force: Infantry Battalions," 589, http://www.collectionscanada.gc.ca/obj/005/f2/005-1142.29.022-e.pdf.
36 Christoph Mick, "1918: Endgame," in *The Cambridge History of the First World War*, vol. 1: *Global War*, ed. Jay Winter (Cambridge: Cambridge University Press, 2014), 145. See also

David Stevenson, *With Our Backs to the Wall: Victory and Defeat in 1918* (Cambridge, MA: Belknap Press, 2011), 36.

37 Sheffield, *Forgotten Victory*, 185, 187.

38 LAC, War Diary, 19th Battalion, 3–4 March 1918; ibid., appendix 2, 19th Battalion Operation Order no. 48, 2 March 1918; LAC, RG 9, III-D-3, vol. 4882, War Diary, 4th Infantry Brigade, 4 March 1918.

39 LAC, vol. 4929, War Diary, 19th Battalion, 6–14 March 1918.

40 For comprehensive examinations of executions in the Canadian Expeditionary Force, see A.B. Godefroy, *For Freedom and Honour? The Story of the 25 Canadian Volunteers Executed in the First World War* (Nepean: CEF Books, 1998); and Teresa Iacobelli, *Death or Deliverance: Canadian Courts Martial in the Great War* (Vancouver: UBC Press, 2013).

41 LAC, RG 150, 1992–93/166, box 5709–28, personnel file, H.E.J. Lodge, attestation paper; Godefroy, *For Freedom and Honour?*, 61, 86.

42 Ibid., 86; LAC, RG 24, C-1-b, mfm. reel C-5053, 649-L-2727, Lodge, H.E.J. – Private, 19th Battalion.

43 LAC, reel C-5053, Lodge, H.E.J. – Private, 19th Battalion.

44 Godefroy, *For Freedom and Honour?*, 86; LAC, Part II Daily Orders, no. 3, 12 January 1918.

45 Godefroy, *For Freedom and Honour?*, 62, 86.

46 Iacobelli, *Death or Deliverance*, 90.

47 James Pedley, qtd. in Cane, *It Made You Think of Home*, 171.

48 Barnes journal, 13 March 1918, qtd. in ibid., 171–72.

49 LAC, War Diary, 19th Battalion, appendix 3, chart outlining program of movement and training, 11–17 March 1918; ibid., Schedule of Training, 15–21 March 1918.

50 GMA, Gaetz Family Fonds, J.R. Gaetz to his mother, 21 March 1918.

51 LAC, vols. 4928–9, War Diary, 19th Battalion, January–March 1918, listings of reinforcements and casualties; ibid., vol. 4929, appendix 4, Trench Strength, 20 March 1918.

Chapter 16 – "It Was Pretty Lively": 21 March–June 1918

1 Holger H. Herwig, *The First World War: Germany and Austria-Hungary, 1914–1918* (London: Arnold, 1997), 392; Gary Sheffield, *Forgotten Victory: The First World War, Myths and Realities* (London: Headline, 2001), 187–8.

2 Laurence V. Moyer, *Victory Must Be Ours: Germany in the Great War, 1914–1918* (New York: Hippocrene, 1995), 242, 380; Herwig, *The First World War*, 406; Sheffield, *Forgotten Victory*, 189; Richard Holmes, *The Western Front: Ordinary Soldiers and the Defining Battles of World War I* (New York: TV Books, 2000), 198; Tim Travers, *How the War Was Won: Command and Technology in the British Army on the Western Front, 1917–1918* (London: Routledge, 1992), 86–89.

3 Herwig, *The First World War*, 407; Holger H. Herwig, "The German Victories, 1917–1918," in *World War I: A History*, ed. Hew Strachan (Oxford: Oxford University Press, 1998), 260–62; Martin Marix Evans, *The Battles of the Somme* (Toronto: Little, Brown, 1996), 71.

4 LAC, RG 9, III-D-3, vol. 4882, War Diary, 4th Infantry Brigade, 21 March 1918; LAC, RG 9, III-D-3, vol. 4929, War Diary, 19th Battalion, 21 March 1918.

5 The 19th Battalion moved from Noeux-les-Mines on 23 March to Gouy Servins, and then to Ecurie. LAC, War Diary, 19th Battalion, 22–23 March 1918; ibid., appendix 5, Operation Order no. 12, 23 March 1918; ibid., 23–24 March 1918; David Campbell, "The Divisional Experience in the C.E.F.: A Social and Operational History of the 2nd Canadian Division, 1915–1918," PhD diss., University of Calgary, 2003, 383–85.

6 LAC, War Diary, 19th Battalion, 25 March 1918; ibid., appendix 5, J. 405, 25 March 1918.

7 Kenneth Radley, *We Lead Others Follow: First Canadian Division, 1914-1918* (St. Catharines: Vanwell, 2006), 114–15; Campbell, "The Divisional Experience in the C.E.F.," 373; Bill Rawling, *Surviving Trench Warfare: Technology and the Canadian Corps, 1914–1918* (Toronto: University of Toronto Press, 1992), 175–76.

8 LAC, War Diary, 19th Battalion, 26 March 1918.
9 CWM, 19740071-017 58C 1 1.8, untitled file of letters, questionnaires, responses, and notes regarding 19th Battalion history, Questionnaire no. 6, notes on events of 26 March 1918.
10 Barnes journal, 27 March 1918, qtd. in Bruce Cane, *It Made You Think of Home: The Haunting Journal of Deward Barnes, Canadian Expeditionary Force: 1916–1919* (Toronto: Dundurn, 2004), 177. Barnes is off in his dating by one day. The move to Bailleulmont actually occurred on 26 March.
11 LAC, RG 41, B-III-1, Records of the CBC, *Flanders Fields*, vol. 10, 19th Battalion, transcript of interview with F.A. Stitt, tape 2, 2.
12 CWM, 19740071-017 58C 1 1.8, Questionnaire no. 6, notes on events of 26 March 1918.
13 Lt.-Gen. Sir A.W. Currie, "Interim Report on the Operations of the Canadian Corps during the Year 1918," in *Report of the Ministry, Overseas Military Forces of Canada, 1918* (London: Minister, Overseas Military Forces of Canada, n.d.), 110–16, sketch no. 6; G.W.L. Nicholson, *Canadian Expeditionary Force, 1914–1919: The Official History of the Canadian Army in the First World War* (Ottawa: Queen's Printer, 1962), 368, 379–80; J.P. Harris and Niall Barr, *Amiens to the Armistice: The BEF in the Hundred Days' Campaign, 8 August–11 November 1918* (London: Brassey's, 1998), 13.
14 Nicholson, *Canadian Expeditionary Force*, 372, 379–80.
15 Haig, qtd. in John Terraine, *Ordeal of Victory* (Philadelphia: J.B. Lippincott, 1963), 433. This book was published in England under the title *Douglas Haig: The Educated Soldier*.
16 Currie, qtd. in Daniel G. Dancocks, *Sir Arthur Currie: A Biography* (Toronto: Methuen, 1985), 134.
17 LAC, War Diary, 19th Battalion, appendix 6, 2nd Canadian Division memo G. 45/274, 28 March 1918; ibid., 4th Brigade memo B. 2–4/928, 28 March 1918.
18 LAC, War Diary, 19th Battalion, 29–31 March 1918; LAC, War Diary, 4th Infantry Brigade, 30 March 1918; Campbell, "The Divisional Experience in the C.E.F.," 387–88; D.J. Corrigall, *The History of the Twentieth Canadian Battalion (Central Ontario Regiment), Canadian Expeditionary Force in the Great War, 1914–1918* (Toronto: Stone and Cox, 1935), 189–90.
19 LAC, War Diary, 19th Battalion, 29 March, 1–4 April 1918.
20 LAC, War Diary, 19th Battalion, 5 April 1918.
21 Barnes journal, 5 April 1918, qtd. in Cane, *It Made You Think of Home*, 179.
22 LAC, War Diary, 19th Battalion, 9 April 1918.
23 LAC, War Diary, 19th Battalion, 14 April 1918; Cane, *It Made You Think of Home*, 182.
24 LAC, War Diary, 19th Battalion, 14–16 April 1918.
25 LAC, War Diary, 19th Battalion, 17–19 April 1918.
26 LAC, War Diary, 19th Battalion, 20–28 April 1918.
27 LAC, War Diary, 19th Battalion, 28 April 1918. According to Deward Barnes, the three missing men were Ben Moore, Nick Carter, and George Morrison. Barnes journal, 28 April 1918, qtd. in Cane, *It Made You Think of Home*, 190.
28 LAC, War Diary, 19th Battalion, 29 April 1918.
29 LAC, War Diary, 19th Battalion, 29–30 April 1918.
30 LAC, War Diary, 19th Battalion, 1–15 May 1918.
31 Rawling, *Surviving Trench Warfare*, 175–76; Radley, *We Lead Others Follow*, 115.
32 LAC, War Diary, 19th Battalion, 15–20 May 1918; ibid., appendix 3, memo regarding company reorganization, 18 May 1918.
33 LAC, War Diary, 19th Battalion, 22 May–3 June 1918.
34 LAC, War Diary, 19th Battalion, 3–9 June 1918.
35 LAC, War Diary, 19th Battalion, 9–15 June 1918.
36 LAC, RG 150, vol. 465, "List of Officers – 19th Infantry Battalion," 31 May 1918; John F. Meek, *Over the Top! The Canadian Infantry in the First World War* (privately published, 1971), 42, 105; Cane, *It Made You Think of Home*, 208.
37 "Archies" was military slang for anti-aircraft guns. AO, MU 8113, Armour A. and Alexander J. Miller Papers, Miller to his wife, 15 June 1918.

38 LAC, War Diary, 19th Battalion, 15–19 June 1918.
39 LAC, War Diary, 19th Battalion, appendix 5, 19th Battalion memo H. 219, 18 June 1918; ibid., 19th Battalion Operation Order, n.d.
40 Campbell, "The Divisional Experience in the C.E.F.," 395–96.
41 Holk was a former NCO and a veteran of the 19th Battalion's famous daylight raid on 29 July 1916.
42 LAC, War Diary, 19th Battalion, 21 June 1918; ibid., appendix 5, 19th Battalion Operation Order, n.d.
43 LAC, War Diary, 19th Battalion, 21 June 1918; ibid., appendix 5, 19th Battalion Operation Order, n.d.; CWM, 19740071-017 58C 1 1.8, Ralph Whitney to R.O. Spreckley, 16 July (year not stated).
44 LAC, War Diary, 19th Battalion, 21 June 1918; ibid., appendix 5, "Report on Raid by 19th Canadian Battalion, morning of June 21st, 1918, at 1:40 AM"; ibid., "Statement of three witnesses re killing of three Huns by No. 55813 Sgt. Curbishley A."
45 LAC, War Diary, 19th Battalion, 21 June 1918; ibid., appendix 5, "Statement by Lieut. J.P. Fitzgerald"; ibid., "Report on Raid."
46 LAC, War Diary, 19th Battalion, appendix 5, "Statement by Lieut. J.P. Fitzgerald"; ibid., 19th Battalion, memo H. 306, 21 June 1918 (statement to 4th Brigade on presumed fates of missing men); ibid., "Statements made by Major Miller to Capt. Allison, M.C. and Lieut. McLaren"; AO, Miller Papers, Maj. Robert Shiell to Mrs. Helen B. Miller, 25 June 1918; LAC, *Flanders Fields*, vol. 10, 19th Battalion, transcript of interview with Joe O'Neill, tape 3, 13.
47 LAC, War Diary, 19th Battalion, 21 June 1918; ibid., appendix 5, "Statement by Lieut. J.P. Fitzgerald."
48 LAC, War Diary, 19th Battalion, "Report on Raid"; ibid., "Statement regarding missing men"; ibid., 19th Battalion, memo H. 306, 21 June 1918.
49 LAC, *Flanders Fields*, vol. 10, 19th Battalion, transcript of interview with Joe O'Neill, tape 3, 13.
50 LAC, War Diary, 19th Battalion, 21 June 1918; ibid., appendix 5, "Statement by Lieut. A.J. Duncan."
51 LAC, War Diary, 19th Battalion, 21 June 1918; AO, Miller Papers, Shiell to Mrs. Helen B. Miller, 25 June 1918.
52 LAC, *Flanders Fields*, vol. 10, 19th Battalion, transcript of interview with Joe O'Neill, tape 3, 13–14.
53 AO, Miller Papers, Shiell to Mrs Helen B. Miller, 25 June 1918; LAC, War Diary, 19th Battalion, 21 June 1918; ibid., appendix 5, "Statement by Lieut. A.J. Duncan."
54 AO, Miller Papers, Shiell to Mrs. Helen B. Miller, 25 June 1918.
55 LAC, *Flanders Fields*, vol. 10, transcript of interview with Joe O'Neill, tape 3, 14.
56 LAC, *Flanders Fields*, vol. 10, transcript of interview with Joe O'Neill, tape 3, 15.
57 LAC, War Diary, 19th Battalion, 21 June 1918; ibid., appendix 5, "Statement by Lieut. A.J. Duncan"; ibid., 19th Battalion, memo H. 306, 21 June 1918.
58 LAC, War Diary, 19th Battalion, 21 June 1918; ibid., appendix 5, "Statements made by Major Miller to Capt. Allison, M.C. and Lieut. McLaren"; AO, Miller Papers, Shiell to Mrs Helen B. Miller, 25 June 1918.
59 Cane, *It Made You Think of Home*, 208–9; LAC, RG 150, vol. 501, "Casualties by Days – France and Belgium," 19th Battalion, June 1918. This postwar statistical ledger lists one officer and five other ranks captured on 21 June 1918. Three of the captured other ranks were listed as having been wounded.
60 LAC, War Diary, 19th Battalion, 21 June 1918.
61 LAC, War Diary, 19th Battalion, appendix 5, "Report on Raid."
62 The total number of casualties inflicted on the Germans during the operation is not known. There were three men shot by Sgt. Curbishley, and four other men appear to have been killed or wounded by the Canadian barrage. The Germans may have suffered additional casualties from the supporting barrage.

63 LAC, War Diary, 19th Battalion, June 1918, appendix 5, Roster of Number 13 Platoon, Party no. 1; CWM, 19740071-017 58C 1 1.8, Ralph Whitney to R.O. Spreckley, 16 July.
64 LAC, War Diary, 19th Battalion, appendix 5, "Report on Raid."
65 LAC, War Diary, 19th Battalion, 21 June 1918; LAC, War Diary, 4th Infantry Brigade, 21–22 June 1918.
66 Personal collection of Mrs. Phyllis Douglas, letters of Lt.-Col. Lionel H. Millen, Millen to his mother, 18 June 1918.
67 LAC, War Diary, 19th Battalion, 23–27 June 1918.
68 Sheffield, *Forgotten Victory*, 188–96.
69 Hew Strachan, *The First World War* (New York: Viking 2004), 298; Travers, *How the War Was Won*, 108; Robin Prior and Trevor Wilson, *The First World War* (London: Cassell 1999), 180–81.
70 LAC, War Diary, 19th Battalion, 28–30 June 1918; Cane, *It Made You Think of Home*, 210–11; Henry Borden and Heath MacQuarrie, eds., *Robert Laird Borden: His Memoirs*, vol. 2 (Toronto: McClelland and Stewart, 1969), 141.
71 LAC, War Diary, 19th Battalion, June 1918, lists of casualties and reinforcements.
72 Campbell, "The Divisional Experience in the C.E.F.," 397–98.
73 LAC, *Flanders Fields*, vol. 6, transcript of Episode 13, "The German Drive," interview with E. Youngman, 19th Battalion, 20.
74 LAC, MG 30, E 6, Sir Henry Burstall Papers, vol. 3, file 21, Maj.-Gen. H.E. Burstall, "2nd Canadian Division, Narrative of Operations from March 13th to Nov. 11th, 1918," 2.
75 Tim Cook, *Shock Troops: Canadians Fighting the Great War, 1917–1918* (Toronto: Viking 2008), 400.
76 LAC, *Flanders Fields*, vol. 10, 19th Battalion, transcript of interview with F.A. Stitt, tape 2, 3–4.
77 LAC, *Flanders Fields*, vol. 10, 19th Battalion, transcript of interview with Joe O'Neill, tape 1, 5–6.
78 James H. Pedley, *Only This: A War Retrospect, 1917–1918* (Nepean: CEF Books 1999; repr.), 190–91.

Chapter 17 – Prelude to Victory: July–7 August 1918

1 Gary Sheffield, *Forgotten Victory: The First World War, Myths and Realities* (London: Headline, 2001), 69, 190; Tim Travers, *How the War Was Won: Command and Technology in the British Army on the Western Front, 1917–1918* (London: Routledge, 1992), 131–32; T.M. Hunter, *Marshal Foch: A Study in Leadership* (Ottawa: Queen's Printer, 1961), 186–87.
2 G.W.L. Nicholson, *Canadian Expeditionary Force, 1914–1919: The Official History of the Canadian Army in the First World War* (Ottawa: Queen's Printer, 1962), 383–84; Lt.-Gen. Sir A.W. Currie, "Interim Report on the Operations of the Canadian Corps during the Year 1918," in *Report of the Ministry, Overseas Military Forces of Canada, 1918* (London: Minister, Overseas Military Forces of Canada, n.d.), 121. See also H.F.H. Hertzberg, "The Reorganization of the Engineering Troops of a Canadian Division – Great War, 1914–18," *Canadian Defence Quarterly*, July 1924.
3 LAC, RG 24, C-6-e, vol. 1833, GAQ 8-16, "Notes re Organization of Canadian Machine Gun Sections, Brigade Machine Gun Companies, Machine Gun Companies, and Machine Gun Battalions"; Nicholson, *Canadian Expeditionary Force*, 382–83.
4 LAC, RG 9, III-D-3, vol. 4821, War Diary, Canadian Corps, A. & Q. Branch, 11 May 1918; William Stewart, "Attack Doctrine in the Canadian Corps, 1916–1918," MA thesis, University of New Brunswick, 1982, 186–87; Bill Rawling, *Surviving Trench Warfare: Technology and the Canadian Corps, 1914–1918* (Toronto: University of Toronto Press, 1992), 175–76.
5 British divisions featured nine infantry battalions and sixty-four heavy machine guns, while many German divisions were severely weakened after the failed spring offensives, especially in manpower. Nicholson, *Canadian Expeditionary Force*, 383; Holger H. Herwig, *The First World War: Germany and Austria-Hungary, 1914–1918* (London: Arnold, 1997), 421; Tim Cook,

"Bloody Victory: The Canadian Corps in the Hundred Days Campaign," in *1918, Year of Victory: The End of the Great War and the Shaping of History*, ed. Ashley Ekins (Auckland: Exisle Publishing, 2010), 165–66.

6 Nicholson, *Canadian Expeditionary Force*, 384.

7 LAC, RG 9, III-D-3, vol. 4929, War Diary, 19th Battalion, 1, 4, 11 July 1918; Personal collection of Mrs. Phyllis Douglas, letters of Lt.-Col. Lionel H. Millen (hereafter Millen Letters), Millen to his mother, 3 July 1918.

8 Mark Osborne Humphries, "Paths of Infection: The First World War and the Origins of the 1918 Influenza Pandemic," *War in History* 21, no. 1 (2013): 55–81.

9 Among the labourers were 140,000 Chinese men contracted by the British and French governments to work behind Allied lines in western Europe. Xu Guoqi, *Strangers on the Western Front: Chinese Workers in the Great War* (Cambridge, MA: Harvard University Press, 2011), 1, 5, Ch. 3.

10 Ian F.W. Beckett, *The Great War, 1914–1918* (London: Longman, 2001), 310–11; Ian Hugh Maclean Miller, *Our Glory and Our Grief: Torontonians and the Great War* (Toronto: University of Toronto Press, 2002), 185; Bruce Cane, *It Made You Think of Home: The Haunting Journal of Deward Barnes, Canadian Expeditionary Force: 1916–1919* (Toronto: Dundurn, 2004), 213; John Keegan, *The First World War* (Toronto: Key Porter, 1998), 408; www.stanford.edu/group/virus/uda/index.html; Mark Osborne Humphries, "The Horror at Home: The Canadian Military and the 'Great' Influenza Pandemic of 1918," Journal of the *Canadian Historical Association* 16 (2005): 236–39.

11 CWM, 19740071-017 58C 1 1.8, handwritten comments by Ralph Whitney.

12 Bill Rawling, *Death Their Enemy: Canadian Medical Practitioners and War* (Ottawa: privately published, 2001), 100–1; CWM, 19740071-017 58C 1 1.8, Whitney comments.

13 LAC, War Diary, 19th Battalion, appendix 1, Syllabus of Training, 1–7 July 1918.

14 Currie, "Interim Report," 123–24.

15 LAC, MG 30, E 6, Sir Henry Burstall Papers, vol. 3, file 21, Maj.-Gen. H.E. Burstall, "2nd Canadian Division, Narrative of Operations from March 13th to Nov. 11th, 1918," 4 (hereafter "2nd Division Narrative").

16 Tim Cook, *Shock Troops: Canadians Fighting the Great War, 1917–1918* (Toronto: Viking 2008), 406.

17 Rawling, *Surviving Trench Warfare*, 182–84; J.P. Harris and Niall Barr, *Amiens to the Armistice: The BEF in the Hundred Days' Campaign, 8 August–11 November 1918* (London: Brassey's, 1998), 56–57; Ross Mallett, "The Interplay between Technology, Tactics and Organisation in the First AIF," MA thesis, Australian Defence Force Academy, 1999, 182–87; Travers, *How the War Was Won*, 112; Shane B. Schreiber, *Shock Army of the British Empire: The Canadian Corps in the Last 100 Days of the Great War* (Westport: Praeger 1997), 35–36.

18 D.J. Corrigall, *The History of the Twentieth Canadian Battalion (Central Ontario Regiment), Canadian Expeditionary Force in the Great War, 1914–1918* (Toronto: Stone and Cox, 1935), 209; Barnes journal, 11 July 1918, qtd. in Cane, *It Made You Think of Home*, 215.

19 Ibid., 217–18; LAC, War Diary, 19th Battalion, 12–14 July 1918.

20 CWM, 19740071-017 58C 1 1.9, Marshall diary, 16 July 1918.

21 Barnes journal, 17 July 1918, qtd. in Cane, *It Made You Think of Home*, 218.

22 Barnes journal, 18 July 1918, qtd. in Cane, *It Made You Think of Home*, 219.

23 CWM, 19740071-017 58C 1 1.9, Marshall diary, 26 July 1918.

24 LAC, War Diary, 19th Battalion, 18–19 July 1918; Burstall, "2nd Division Narrative," 4.

25 LAC, War Diary, 19th Battalion, 20–29 July 1918; ibid., appendices 2 and 3, training syllabi; LAC, RG 9, III-D-3, vol. 4883, War Diary, 4th Infantry Brigade, 23 July 1918; Corrigall, *The History of the Twentieth Canadian Battalion*, 210.

26 LAC, War Diary, 19th Battalion, appendix 1, training syllabus, week ending 13 July 1918; ibid., appendix 2, training syllabus, 22 July 1918; J.L. Granatstein, *Canada's Army: Waging War and Keeping the Peace* (Toronto: University of Toronto Press, 2002), 135; Tim Cook, *No Place to Run: The Canadian Corps and Gas Warfare in the First World War* (Vancouver: UBC Press, 1999), 184–85.

27 LAC, War Diary, 19th Battalion, 27 July 1918; Millen Letters, Millen to his mother, 31 July 1918.
28 Tim Travers, "The Allied Victories, 1918," in *The Oxford Illustrated History of the First World War*, new ed., ed. Hew Strachan (Oxford: Oxford University Press, 2014), 278–80.
29 Travers, "The Allied Victories, 1918," 279; Sheffield, *Forgotten Victory*, 196; Spencer C. Tucker, *The Great War, 1914–18* (Bloomington: Indiana University Press, 1998), 169–70.
30 Robin Prior and Trevor Wilson, *The First World War* (London: Cassell, 1999), 182; Richard Holmes, *The Western Front: Ordinary Soldiers and the Defining Battles of World War I* (New York: TV Books, 2000), 207; Harris and Barr, *Amiens to the Armistice*, 62–63; S.F. Wise, *Canadian Airmen and the First World War: The Official History of the Royal Canadian Air Force*, vol. 1 (Toronto: University of Toronto Press, 1980), 518–19.
31 S.F. Wise, "The Black Day of the German Army: Australians and Canadians at Amiens, August 1918," in *1918: Defining Victory*, ed. Peter Dennis and Jeffrey Grey (Canberra: Army History Unit, Department of Defence, 1999), 4–5; C.E.W. Bean, *The Official History of Australia in the War of 1914–1918*, vol. 6: *The A.I.F. in France: May 1918–the Armistice* (Sydney: Angus and Robertson, 1942), 464.
32 Currie, "Interim Report," 127–28; Schreiber, *Shock Army of the British Empire*, 35.
33 Nicholson, *Canadian Expeditionary Force*, 385; A.M.J. Hyatt, *General Sir Arthur Currie: A Military Biography* (Toronto: University of Toronto Press, 1987), 115; Currie, "Interim Report," 130.
34 Harris and Barr, *Amiens to the Armistice*, 66; James McWilliams and R. James Steel, *Amiens: Dawn of Victory* (Toronto: Dundurn, 2001), 21.
35 These units would rejoin the Canadian Corps at Amiens two days before the attack. Nicholson, *Canadian Expeditionary Force*, 385, 389–90; Currie, "Interim Report," 129; McWilliams and Steel, *Amiens*, 42; Daniel G. Dancocks, *Spearhead to Victory: Canada and the Great War* (Edmonton: Hurtig, 1987), 29–30; Schreiber, *Shock Army of the British Empire*, 36.
36 LAC, War Diary, 19th Battalion, 29–30 July 1918; Barnes journal, 30 July 1918, qtd. in Cane, *It Made You Think of Home*, 221.
37 LAC, RG 41, B-III-1, Records of the CBC, *Flanders Fields*, vol. 10, 19th Battalion, transcript of interview with Joe O'Neill, tape 2, 4–8.
38 LAC, War Diary, 19th Battalion, 30 July 1918; LAC, War Diary, 4th Infantry Brigade, 29–31 July 1918.
39 LAC, War Diary, 19th Battalion, 1 Aug. 1918; LAC, 4th Infantry Brigade, 1 August 1918.
40 Bill Rawling, "A Resource Not to Be Squandered: The Canadian Corps on the 1918 Battlefield," in Peter Dennis and Jeffrey Grey, eds., *1918: Defining Victory* (Canberra: Army History Unit, Department of Defence, 1999), 49; Dean Chappelle, "The Canadian Attack at Amiens, 8–11 August 1918," *Canadian Military History* 2, no. 2 (1993): 92–93.
41 LAC, War Diary, 4th Infantry Brigade, 1 August 1918; Corrigall, *The History of the Twentieth Canadian Battalion*, 214.
42 Dancocks, *Spearhead to Victory*, facing 118.
43 LAC, War Diary, 4th Infantry Brigade, 1 August 1918; Burstall, "2nd Division Narrative," 5; Currie, "Interim Report," 130–31; Dancocks, *Spearhead to Victory*, 35.
44 McWilliams and Steel, *Amiens*, 45.
45 LAC, War Diary, 19th Battalion, 3 August 1918.
46 LAC, War Diary, 4th Infantry Brigade, 4 August 1918; McWilliams and Steel, *Amiens*, 55.
47 G.D. Sheffield, *The Pictorial History of World War I* (London: Bison, 1987), 210; John Swettenham, *McNaughton*, vol. 1: *1887–1939* (Toronto: Ryerson, 1968), 135–36; Nicholson, *Canadian Expeditionary Force*, 392, 394; Cyril Falls, *The Great War, 1914–1918* (New York: Putnam, 1959), 373–74.
48 Harris and Barr, *Amiens to the Armistice*, 64–66; Robin Prior and Trevor Wilson, *Command on the Western Front: The Military Career of Sir Henry Rawlinson, 1914–1918* (Barnsley: Pen and Sword, 2004; orig. ed., Blackwell, 1992), 305.
49 Currie, "Interim Report," 134–35; Nicholson, *Canadian Expeditionary Force*, 395–96.

50 Wise, *Canadian Airmen and the First World War*, 520; Nicholson, *Canadian Expeditionary Force*, 395–96.
51 Burstall, "2nd Division Narrative," 7–8; Nicholson, *Canadian Expeditionary Force*, 402, map 11; Corrigall, *The History of the Twentieth Canadian Battalion*, 217.
52 Nicholson, *Canadian Expeditionary Force*, 396; Bean, *The A.I.F. in France*, 606; Harris and Barr, *Amiens to the Armistice*, 106; G.W.L. Nicholson, *The Gunners of Canada: The History of the Royal Regiment of Canadian Artillery*, vol. 1 (Toronto: McClelland and Stewart, 1967), 339; Stewart, "Attack Doctrine in the Canadian Corps," 205.
53 Nicholson, *Canadian Expeditionary Force*, 393, 396–97; Schreiber, *Shock Army of the British Empire*, 44–45. During the Battle of Amiens, the 19th Battalion infantry arranged to communicate with tanks by using smoke grenades to identify strong points and give direction to the tank drivers. In addition, a helmet raised on an infantryman's rifle indicated, "Tank assistance required." LAC, War Diary, 19th Battalion, appendix 2, "Notes in Regard to Pending Operations," 6 August 1918.
54 The RAF was born on 1 April 1918, from the union of the Royal Flying Corps and the Royal Naval Air Service. Number 5 Squadron was equipped with lumbering RE8 two-seater aircraft. Wise, *Canadian Airmen and the First World War*, 521–22; Schreiber, *Shock Army of the British Empire*, 46; Nicholson, *Canadian Expeditionary Force*, 393, 397.
55 Nicholson, *Canadian Expeditionary Force*, 395, map 11; McWilliams and Steel, *Amiens*, 99.
56 C.P. Stacey, "The Battle of Amiens, 1918," in *Introduction to the Study of Military History for Canadian Students*, 4th ed., ed. Stacey (Ottawa: Queen's Printer, 1965), 101; Nicholson, *Canadian Expeditionary Force*, 394–95, map 11.
57 Nicholson, *Canadian Expeditionary Force*, 394–95; Schreiber, *Shock Army of the British Empire*, 41, 43; McWilliams and Steel, *Amiens*, 99.
58 Dancocks, *Spearhead to Victory*, 33; Travers, *How the War Was Won*, 119–20; Bean, *The A.I.F. in France*, 511–12, 607.
59 LAC, War Diary, 4th Infantry Brigade, 6 August 1918; John Swettenham, *To Seize the Victory: The Canadian Corps in World War I* (Toronto: Ryerson, 1965), 206; Harris and Barr, *Amiens to the Armistice*, 67; McWilliams and Steel, *Amiens*, 59.
60 LAC, War Diary, 4th Infantry Brigade, 6 August 1918; LAC, War Diary, 19th Battalion, appendix 2, 19th Battalion Order no. 90, 7 August 1918.
61 LAC, War Diary, 19th Battalion, 19th Battalion Order no. 90; LAC, War Diary, 4th Infantry Brigade, appendix 6, 4th Infantry Brigade Instructions, 6 August. 1918; Burstall, "2nd Division Narrative," 8; Corrigall, *The History of the Twentieth Canadian Battalion*, 218.
62 LAC, War Diary, 19th Battalion, 19th Battalion Order no. 90; LAC, War Diary, 4th Infantry Brigade, 4th Infantry Brigade Instructions; Corrigall, *The History of the Twentieth Canadian Battalion*, 218; C.S. Grafton, *The Canadian "Emma Gees": A History of the Canadian Machine Gun Corps* (London: Canadian Machine Gun Corps Association, 1938), 144.
63 Corrigall, *The History of the Twentieth Battalion*, 218; LAC, War Diary, 4th Infantry Brigade, 4th Infantry Brigade Instructions; Burstall, "2nd Division Narrative," 8.
64 James E. Edmonds, *Military Operations, France and Belgium, 1918*, vol. 4: *8th August–26th September* (London: HMSO, 1947), 50; LAC, War Diary, 19th Battalion, 19th Battalion Order no. 90; LAC, War Diary, 4th Infantry Brigade, 4th Infantry Brigade Instructions; Grafton, *The Canadian "Emma Gees,"* 144.
65 LAC, War Diary, 19th Battalion, 19th Battalion Order no. 90.
66 Nicholson, *Canadian Expeditionary Force*, 398; LAC, War Diary, 19th Battalion, 19th Battalion Order no. 90.
67 LAC, War Diary, 19th Battalion, 19th Battalion Order no. 90; LAC, War Diary, 4th Infantry Brigade, 4th Infantry Brigade Instructions; Edmonds, *Military Operations*, 50.
68 LAC, War Diary, 19th Battalion, 19th Battalion Order no. 90.
69 Burstall, "2nd Division Narrative," 5; McWilliams and Steel, *Amiens*, 63; Corrigall, *The History of the Twentieth Canadian Battalion*, 219.
70 LAC, *Flanders Fields*, vol. 10, 19th Battalion, transcript of interview with F.A. Stitt, tape 2, 6.

71 LAC, War Diary, 19th Battalion, appendix 1, 4th Infantry Brigade, Memo G.4/16, 7 August 1918; McWilliams and Steel, *Amiens*, 63; LAC, War Diary, 19th Battalion, appendix 2, "Notes for Offensive," 3 August 1918.
72 CWM, 19740071–017 58C 1 1.9, "The World War of 1914–18 and the 19th Battalion as They Affected Me, by #228421, Pte. V.E.Thompson, Rear Rank," 2–3, 6, 21 (hereafter "Thompson Narrative").
73 LAC, *Flanders Fields*, vol. 6, transcript of Episode 14, "Amiens and Arras," 5.
74 LAC, *Flanders Fields*, vol. 6, transcript of Episode 14, "Amiens and Arras," 5–6.
75 Qtd. in Dancocks, *Spearhead to Victory*, 37.
76 LAC, War Diary, 19th Battalion, appendix 2, 4th Infantry Brigade Operation Order no. 235/2, 6 August 1918.
77 McWilliams and Steel, *Amiens*, 58–68.
78 LAC, War Diary, 19th Battalion, appendix 1, 19th Battalion Warning Order, 4 August 1918; ibid., appendix 2, "Notes for Offensive," 3 August 1918.
79 LAC, War Diary, 19th Battalion, appendix 2, "Notes for Offensive," 3 August 1918.
80 Dancocks, *Spearhead to Victory*, 36; Desmond Morton and J.L. Granatstein, *Marching to Armageddon: Canadians and the Great War, 1914–1919* (Toronto: Lester and Orpen Dennys, 1989), 200; Tuxford, qtd. in McWilliams and Steel, *Amiens*, 31.
81 Barnes journal, 12 July 1918, qtd. in Cane, *It Made You Think of Home*, 215–16.
82 LAC, War Diary, 19th Battalion, 8 August 1918; Cane, *It Made You Think of Home*, 226; Bean, *The A.I.F. in France*, 527; "Thompson Narrative," 22.
83 O'Neill was invalided to England on 11 August and returned to the battalion later that autumn. LAC, *Flanders Fields*, vol. 10, 19th Battalion, transcript of interview with Joe O'Neill, tape 2, 8; LAC, RG 150, vol. 465, List of Officers, 19th Infantry Battalion, listings for 31 August 1918.
84 LAC, War Diary, 19th Battalion, 8 August 1918; Burstall, "2nd Division Narrative," 9.
85 Barnes journal, 8 August 1918, qtd. in Cane, *It Made You Think of Home*, 226.
86 Bean, *The A.I.F. in France*, 526.
87 Nicholson, *Canadian Expeditionary Force*, 398; McWilliams and Steel, *Amiens*, 74–75.

Chapter 18 – The Battle of Amiens and Its Aftermath: 8–18 August 1918

1 LAC, RG 41, B-III-1, Records of the CBC, *Flanders Fields*, vol. 10, 19th Battalion, transcript of interview with Joe O'Neill, tape 2, 7.
2 LAC, *Flanders Fields*, vol.10, transcript of interview with F.A. Stitt, tape 2, 7–8.
3 LAC, *Flanders Fields*, vol. 6, transcript of Episode 14, "Amiens and Arras," 9. Macklin came to the 19th Battalion in March 1918 with a reinforcement draft from the 198th Battalion.
4 LAC, RG 9, III-D-3, vol. 4929, War Diary, 19th Battalion, 8 August 1918.
5 CWM, 19740071–017 58C 1 1.9, untitled file of correspondence and notes regarding 19th Battalion history, "The World War of 1914–18 and the 19th Battalion as They Affected Me, by #228421, Pte. V.E. Thompson, Rear Rank," 22 (hereafter "Thompson Narrative").
6 G.W.L. Nicholson, *Canadian Expeditionary Force, 1914–1919: The Official History of the Canadian Army in the First World War* (Ottawa: Queen's Printer, 1962), 398; LAC, War Diary, 19th Battalion, appendix 2, "Notes for the Offensive," 3 August 1918.
7 C.E.W. Bean, *The Official History of Australia in the War of 1914–1918*, vol. 6: *The A.I.F. in France: May 1918–the Armistice* (Sydney: Angus and Robertson, 1942), 530; Daniel G. Dancocks, *Spearhead to Victory: Canada and the Great War* (Edmonton: Hurtig, 1987), 39.
8 Ibid., 39.
9 Bean, *The A.I.F. in France*, 531.
10 Barnes journal, 8 August 1918, qtd. in Bruce Cane, *It Made You Think of Home: The Haunting Journal of Deward Barnes, Canadian Expeditionary Force: 1916–1919* (Toronto: Dundurn, 2004), 228.
11 "Thompson Narrative," 23.

12 Barnes journal, 8 August 1918, qtd. in Cane, *It Made You Think of Home*, 231.

13 Nicholson, *Canadian Expeditionary Force*, 404; LAC, MG 30, E 6, Sir Henry Burstall Papers, vol. 3, file 21, Maj.-Gen. H.E. Burstall, "2nd Canadian Division, Narrative of Operations from March 13th to Nov. 11th, 1918," 7 (hereafter "2nd Division Narrative").

14 LAC, War Diary, 19th Battalion, 8 August 1918; LAC, RG 9, III-D-3, vol. 4883, War Diary, 4th Infantry Brigade, appendix 10, "Narrative of Operations by 4th Canadian Infantry Brigade on 8th August, 1918."

15 LAC, War Diary, 19th Battalion, appendix 2, "Brief Report on Capture of Marcelcave by 19th Canadian Battalion, August 8th 1918"; LAC, War Diary, 4th Infantry Brigade, "Narrative of Operations"; Burstall, "2nd Division Narrative," 9.

16 LAC, War Diary, 19th Battalion, "Brief Report"; Bean, *The A.I.F. in France*, 532–33.

17 LAC, War Diary, 19th Battalion, 8 August 1918.

18 Bean, *The A.I.F. in France*, 533.

19 LAC, War Diary, 19th Battalion, 8 August 1918; ibid., "Brief Report"; LAC, War Diary, 4th Infantry Brigade, "Narrative of Operations"; Burstall, "2nd Division Narrative," 9.

20 LAC, *Flanders Fields*, vol. 10, 19th Battalion, transcript of interview with F.A. Stitt, tape 2, 8.

21 "Thompson Narrative," 23.

22 Barnes journal, 8 August 1918, qtd. in Cane, *It Made You Think of Home*, 229.

23 LAC, *Flanders Fields*, vol. 10, 19th Battalion, transcript of interview with F.A. Stitt, tape 2, 7, 9.

24 Bean, *The A.I.F. in France*, 541.

25 Burstall, "2nd Division Narrative," 10; LAC, War Diary, 19th Battalion, 8 August 1918; ibid., "Brief Report."

26 Barnes journal, 8 August 1918, qtd. in Cane, *It Made You Think of Home*, 229.

27 LAC, War Diary, 19th Battalion, 8 August 1918; Barnes journal, 8 August 1918, qtd. in Cane, *It Made You Think of Home*, 230.

28 LAC, RG 9, III-D-3, vol. 4931, War Diary, 21st Battalion, 8 August 1918; LAC, War Diary, 4th Infantry Brigade, "Narrative of Operations"; C.S. Grafton, *The Canadian "Emma Gees": A History of the Canadian Machine Gun Corps* (London: Canadian Machine Gun Corps Association 1938), 144.

29 LAC, RG 9, III-D-3, vol. 4930, War Diary, 20th Battalion, 8 August 1918; LAC, War Diary, 4th Infantry Brigade, "Narrative of Operations"; D.J. Corrigall, *The History of the Twentieth Canadian Battalion (Central Ontario Regiment) Canadian Expeditionary Force in the Great War, 1914–1918* (Toronto: Stone and Cox, 1935), 220.

30 LAC, War Diary, 4th Infantry Brigade, "Narrative of Operations."

31 LAC, RG 9, III-D-3, vol. 4847, War Diary, 2nd Canadian Division headquarters, 8 August 1918; LAC, War Diary, 19th Battalion, 8 August 1918.

32 LAC, RG 9, III-D-3, vol. 4926, War Diary, 18th Battalion, 8 August 1918.

33 Grafton, *The Canadian "Emma Gees,"* 144; see also LAC, RG 9, III-D-3, vol. 4985, War Diary, 2nd Canadian Machine Gun Battalion, 8 August 1918.

34 Shane B. Schreiber, *Shock Army of the British Empire: The Canadian Corps in the Last 100 Days of the Great War* (Westport: Praeger, 1997), 44. It is estimated that 95 per cent of the German guns facing the Fourth Army were accurately located before the attack commenced. J.P. Harris and Niall Barr, *Amiens to the Armistice: The BEF in the Hundred Days' Campaign, 8 August–11 November 1918* (London: Brassey's, 1998), 106.

35 Royal Military College of Canada Archives, 255, Maj.-Gen. H.A. Panet Papers, box 2, World War I, "Official Record of the 5th Canadian Field Artillery Brigade"; ibid., "2nd Canadian Divisional Artillery Report on Operations," 8 August 1918.

36 Corrigall, *The History of the Twentieth Canadian Battalion*, 223.

37 LAC, War Diary, 4th Infantry Brigade, 8 August 1918.

38 The following officers of the 19th Battalion were listed as casualties on 8 August: Lts. J.L. Burton, G.H. Coghlan, H. Dibble, and T.A. Allan (all killed); and Lts. W.S. Herbert, A.G. Bell, A.P. Fletcher, J.R. Buller, J.R. Holk, C.E.G. Robertson, and B. Moon (all wounded). LAC, War Diary, 19th Battalion, 8 August 1918, list of casualties.

39 The strength of D Company is not provided in the 19th Battalion's war diary text on 8 August. Based on the strengths given for the other three companies, we may assume that D Company advanced with 4 officers and around 130 other ranks.
40 LAC, *Flanders Fields*, vol. 10, 19th Battalion, transcript of interview with F.A. Stitt, tape 2, 8.
41 ASH, RG 4, Series 3, World War 1, 19th Battalion Association, "Selections from the Mail Bag," 19th Battalion Association newsletter, date uncertain. Similarly, Charles Henderson wrote that at Vimy Ridge a Bible that he carried in the lower left pocket of his tunic had taken a bullet and thereby likely saved his life. Ibid., "Selections from the Mail Bag," Spring 1970.
42 LAC, War Diary, 19th Battalion, 8 August 1918; CWM, 19740071–017 58C 1 1.8, "19th Battalion History, Memo to W.S. Herbert."
43 LAC, War Diary, 19th Battalion, appendix 2, 19th Canadian Battalion, Order no. 90, 7 August 1918.
44 LAC, War Diary, 4th Infantry Brigade, "Narrative of Operations."
45 Barnes journal, 9 August 1918, qtd. in Cane, *It Made You Think of Home*, 233.
46 LAC, War Diary, 21st Battalion, August 1918, appendix Z, "The Battle of Amiens: A Graphic Canadian Story by Captain R.J. Renison, Canadian Chaplain Services."
47 Qtd. in Pierre Berton, *Vimy* (Toronto: McClelland and Stewart, 1986), 255.
48 Nicholson, *Canadian Expeditionary Force*, 403; CWM, 19740071–017 58C 1 1.9, typed extracts from the diary of G.D. Marshall, 8 August 1918.
49 Nicholson, *Canadian Expeditionary Force*, 403; S.F. Wise, *Canadian Airmen and the First World War: The Official History of the Royal Canadian Air Force*, vol. 1 (Toronto: University of Toronto Press, 1980), 526–27; C.P. Stacey, "The Battle of Amiens, 1918," in *Introduction to the Study of Military History for Canadian Students*, 4th ed., ed. Stacey (Ottawa: Queen's Printer, 1965), 103.
50 Nicholson, *Canadian Expeditionary Force*, 403–4; Burstall, "2nd Division Narrative," 11.
51 The Canadian Corps claimed 5,033 prisoners and 161 guns captured on 8 August. Nicholson, *Canadian Expeditionary Force*, 407.
52 Harris and Barr, *Amiens to the Armistice*, 103–4; Holger H. Herwig, *The First World War: Germany and Austria-Hungary, 1914–1918* (London: Arnold 1997), 419, 424; Nicholson, *Canadian Expeditionary Force*, 407–8.
53 This force consisted of armoured cars equipped with machine guns, additional truck-mounted machine guns and mortars, motorcycles, and ancillary vehicles. Its core elements were the 1st and 2nd Canadian Motor Machine Gun Brigades. Cameron Pulsifer, "Canada's First Armoured Unit: Raymond Brutinel and the Canadian Motor Machine Gun Brigades of the First World War," *Canadian Military History* 10, no. 1 (2001): 51–52; Tim Cook, *Shock Troops: Canadians Fighting the Great War, 1917–1918* (Toronto: Viking, 2008), 392.
54 Harris and Barr, *Amiens to the Armistice*, 104–7; Dean Chappelle, "The Canadian Attack at Amiens, 8–11 August 1918," *Canadian Military History* 2, no. 2 (1993): 92, 100; Tim Travers, "Could the Tanks of 1918 Have Been War-Winners for the British Expeditionary Force?," *Journal of Contemporary History* 27 (1992): 398–99; Tim Travers, *How the War Was Won: Command and Technology in the British Army on the Western Front, 1917–1918* (London: Routledge, 1992), 122–24.
55 LAC, War Diary, 19th Battalion, 8 August 1918.
56 LAC, *Flanders Fields*, vol. 10, 19th Battalion, transcript of interview with F.A. Stitt, tape 2, 8.
57 Harris and Barr, *Amiens to the Armistice*, 111; Nicholson, *Canadian Expeditionary Force*, 108.
58 Stacey, "The Battle of Amiens, 1918," 105; James E. Edmonds, *Military Operations, France and Belgium, 1918*, vol. 4: *8th August–26th September* (London: HMSO, 1947), 95.
59 Edmonds, *Military Operations*, 102.
60 Nicholson, *Canadian Expeditionary Force*, 411–12.
61 LAC, War Diary, 4th Infantry Brigade, 9 August 1918; LAC, War Diary, 19th Battalion, 9 August 1918.
62 "Thompson Narrative," 25.

63 Nicholson, *Canadian Expeditionary Force*, 414–15; LAC, War Diary, 19th Battalion, 10 August 1918.
64 Schreiber, *Shock Army of the British Empire*, 67n89; Nicholson, *Canadian Expeditionary Force*, 396–97.
65 Lt.-Gen. Sir A.W. Currie, "Interim Report on the Operations of the Canadian Corps during the Year 1918," in *Report of the Ministry, Overseas Military Forces of Canada, 1918* (London: Minister, Overseas Military Forces of Canada, n.d.), 138–39; Nicholson, *Canadian Expeditionary Force*, 414–15; Schreiber, *Shock Army of the British Empire*, 55.
66 Foch was appointed a marshal of France as of 7 August 1918. T.M. Hunter, *Marshal Foch: A Study in Leadership* (Ottawa: Queen's Printer, 1961), 188.
67 Nicholson, *Canadian Expeditionary Force*, 417; Currie, "Interim Report," 140; Schreiber, *Shock Army of the British Empire*, 55; Cook, *Shock Troops*, 448.
68 LAC, War Diary, 4th Infantry Brigade, 11 August 1918; LAC, War Diary, 19th Battalion, 11 August 1918; ibid., appendix 3, 4th Brigade Operation Order no. 242, 11 August 1918; ibid., appendix 3, battalion disposition sketch.
69 CWM, 19740071-017 58C 1 1.9, Marshall diary, 9 August 1918.
70 Burstall, "2nd Division Narrative," 17; LAC, War Diary, 19th Battalion, 12–13 August 1918.
71 "Thompson Narrative," 26.
72 Burstall, "2nd Division Narrative," 17.
73 Barnes journal, 15–16 August 1918, qtd. in Cane, *It Made You Think of Home*, 234–35.
74 LAC, War Diary, 19th Battalion, 14 August 1918; LAC, War Diary, 4th Infantry Brigade, 14 August 1918.
75 LAC, War Diary, 19th Battalion, 15 August 1918.
76 Nicholson, *Canadian Expeditionary Force*, 419; Burstall, "2nd Division Narrative," 17.
77 LAC, Burstall Papers, vol. 1, file 7, "4th Canadian Infantry Brigade, Narrative of Operation, 16th August 1918"; LAC, War Diary, 19th Battalion, appendix 5, "Account of Operation August 16th, 1918, by 19th Canadian Battalion," 18 August 1918; Corrigall, *The History of the Twentieth Canadian Battalion*, 227.
78 LAC, Burstall Papers, "4th Canadian Infantry Brigade, Narrative of Operation"; LAC, War Diary, 19th Battalion, "Account of Operation August 16th, 1918."
79 Barnes journal, 16 August 1918, qtd. in Cane, *It Made You Think of Home*, 235–36.
80 LAC, Burstall Papers, "4th Canadian Infantry Brigade, Narrative of Operation"; LAC, War Diary, 19th Battalion, "Account of Operation."
81 LAC, RG 9, III-D-3, vol. 4966, War Diary, 3rd Brigade, CFA, 16 August 1918; LAC, Burstall Papers, "4th Canadian Infantry Brigade, Narrative of Operation"; LAC, War Diary, 19th Battalion, "Account of Operation."
82 Barnes journal, 16 August 1918, qtd. in Cane, *It Made You Think of Home*, 236.
83 LAC, War Diary, 19th Battalion, "Account of Operation"; Cane, *It Made You Think of Home*, 236.
84 LAC, Burstall Papers, "4th Canadian Infantry Brigade, Narrative of Operation"; LAC, War Diary, 19th Battalion, "Account of Operation."
85 LAC, Burstall Papers, "4th Canadian Infantry Brigade, Narrative of Operation"; LAC, War Diary, 19th Battalion, "Account of Operation."
86 The 19th Battalion's war diary entry for 16 August gives a slightly different breakdown of casualties. According to it, four officers (Capt. W. Waldrum and Lts. W.C. McFaul, V.K. Robertson, and W.B. Venn) were wounded. As for the other ranks, ten were reported killed, six died of wounds, fifty-two were wounded, and one was missing. This gives a total of sixty-nine other ranks, the same number reported in both the battalion and brigade after-action reports. In the above text, it was decided to quote the figures provided in the after-action reports because these were presumably compiled after the war diary entry was written and so are probably more accurate. LAC, Burstall Papers, "4th Canadian Infantry Brigade, Narrative of Operation";

LAC, War Diary, 19th Battalion, "Account of Operation"; Corrigall, *The History of the Twentieth Canadian Battalion*, 227; Nicholson, *Canadian Expeditionary Force*, Map 11.

87 LAC, *Flanders Fields*, vol. 10, 19th Battalion, transcript of interview with F.A. Stitt, tape 2, 10–11.

88 LAC, War Diary, 19th Battalion, "Account of Operation"; LAC, War Diary, 3rd Brigade, CFA, 16 August 1918.

89 LAC, War Diary, 19th Battalion, "Account of Operation." Millen also sent a letter of appreciation to the 20th Battalion, thanking them for their assistance, praising the work of Capt. A.A. Smith, and concluding warmly, "This co-operation throughout was of the greatest help, and something I can never forget." Qtd. in Corrigall, *The History of the Twentieth Canadian Battalion*, 227. Millen most likely sent a similar letter to the 18th Battalion.

90 Stitt must have been transferred over to C Company by this time, because on 8 August he had been serving in A Company. LAC, *Flanders Fields*, vol. 10, 19th Battalion, transcript of interview with F.A. Stitt, tape 2, 11–13.

91 "Thompson Narrative," 26–27.

92 "Thompson Narrative," 28.

93 LAC, War Diary, 19th Battalion, "Account of Operation."

94 LAC, Burstall Papers, "4th Canadian Infantry Brigade, Narrative of Operation."

95 Corrigall, *The History of the Twentieth Canadian Battalion*, 227; LAC, War Diary, 19th Battalion, 16 August 1918; Burstall, "2nd Division Narrative," 18.

96 LAC, War Diary, 19th Battalion, 17–19 August 1918.

97 Personal collection of Mrs. Phyllis Douglas, letters of Lt.-Col. Lionel H. Millen (hereafter Millen Letters), Millen to his mother, 19 August 1918.

98 Millen Letters, Millen to his mother, 4 September 1918. Jones had been mortally wounded by machine-gun fire as he led his headquarters forward over the battlefield on 8 August. LAC, War Diary, 21st Battalion, 4–8 August 1918.

99 Millen Letters, Isobel Jones to Millen, 18 August 1918.

100 CWM, 19740071-017 58C 1 1.9, typed response from V.E. Thompson regarding his group's discussion of Questionnaire no. 7, 3.

101 Pte. F.J. McNulty to his sister Mary (also known as "Min"), 19 August 1918, qtd. from http://www.kingandempire.com/fmcnulty2.html. Letter contributed by Sean McNulty.

102 The circumstances for which Fred McNulty was awarded his Military Medal are not known, but family members suspect that it was due to his capture of several prisoners, as described in his letter to his sister. Like many veterans, McNulty rarely discussed his wartime experiences with family. According to grandson Sean McNulty, one of Fred's sons overheard a conversation in which a cousin asked Fred how he had won the medal. Fred told the cousin that he "rounded a corner and found himself face to face with a party of Germans ... Fred said they were more surprised than he was, and he managed to take them prisoner." Quotations from http://www.kingandempire.com/fmcnulty1.html, contributed by Sean McNulty. Another McNulty relative, Fred Sherriff, suspects that the action in question may have occurred after 8 August, possibly at Fransart. Personal communication, 31 January 2005. I am grateful to Fred Sherriff for bringing the story of Pte. Fred McNulty and his family to my attention.

Fred Stitt was another recipient of the Military Medal for his work on 8 August. When asked what he had done to earn it, he responded evasively: "Well we don't know how they work these things, I just as well not say nothing about it." But he did surmise that he was awarded it "possibly because I was one of the senior NCO's to arrive at the objective." This modesty was typical of many decorated veterans and probably stemmed from an acute awareness that many other men also deserved honours and awards but never received any. LAC, *Flanders Fields*, vol. 10, 19th Battalion, transcript of interview with F.A. Stitt, tape 2, 9.

103 Currie, "Interim Report," 141–42.

104 Nicholson, *Canadian Expeditionary Force*, 419; Currie, "Interim Report," 141.

105 LAC, RG 9, III-D-3, vol. 4861, War Diary, 4th Canadian Division, appendix 3, Special Order by Lt.-Gen. Sir Arthur W. Currie, 13 August 1918.

Chapter 19 - Arras: 19–31 August 1918

1 G.W.L. Nicholson, *Canadian Expeditionary Force, 1914–1919: The Official History of the Canadian Army in the First World War* (Ottawa: Queen's Printer, 1962), 423–26.
2 Lt.-Gen. Sir A.W. Currie, "Interim Report on the Operations of the Canadian Corps during the Year 1918," in *Report of the Ministry, Overseas Military Forces of Canada, 1918* (London: Minister, Overseas Military Forces of Canada, n.d.), 143–44; Nicholson, *Canadian Expeditionary Force*, 426.
3 LAC, RG 9, III-D-3, vol. 4929, War Diary, 19th Battalion, 19–23 August 1918; D.J. Corrigall, *The History of the Twentieth Canadian Battalion (Central Ontario Regiment) Canadian Expeditionary Force in the Great War, 1914–1918* (Toronto: Stone and Cox, 1935), 228.
4 LAC, MG 30, E 6, Sir Henry Burstall Papers, vol. 3, file 21, Maj.-Gen. H.E. Burstall, "2nd Canadian Division, Narrative of Operations from March 13th to Nov. 11th, 1918," 21 (hereafter "2nd Division Narrative"); Currie, "Interim Report," 144; Nicholson, *Canadian Expeditionary Force*, 427–28.
5 Nicholson, *Canadian Expeditionary Force*, 426; Burstall, "2nd Division Narrative," 21–22; Currie, "Interim Report," 144; Shane B. Schreiber, *Shock Army of the British Empire: The Canadian Corps in the Last 100 Days of the Great War* (Westport: Praeger 1997), 73.
6 Nicholson, *Canadian Expeditionary Force*, 426.
7 Tim Cook, *Shock Troops: Canadians Fighting the Great War, 1917–1918* (Toronto: Viking, 2008), 458.
8 Cook, *Shock Troops*, 426–27; Burstall, "2nd Division Narrative," 23.
9 Burstall, "2nd Division Narrative," 22–23; Nicholson, *Canadian Expeditionary Force*, 429, map 12.
10 Burstall, "2nd Division Narrative," 22; LAC, War Diary, 19th Battalion, appendix 5, "Strength of Bn. by Platoons," 24 August 1918.
11 Desmond Morton, *When Your Number's Up: The Canadian Soldier in the First World War* (Toronto: Random House, 1993), 180.
12 LAC, RG 9, III-D-3, vol. 4850, War Diary, AA & QMG, 2nd Canadian Division, appendix 1, Nominal Roll of Reinforcements for August 1918. See also LAC, War Diary, 19th Battalion, August 1918, list of officers and numbers of other ranks received as reinforcements.
13 G.D. Marshall noted the presence of returned men in a group of reinforcements that he observed on 13 August. CWM, 19740071-017 58C 1 1.9, untitled file of correspondence and notes regarding 19th Battalion history, typed extracts from the diary of G.D. Marshall, 13 August 1918.
14 LAC, War Diary, 19th Battalion, 23 August 1918; LAC, RG 9, III-D-3, vol. 4883, War Diary, 4th Infantry Brigade, appendix 31, "Narrative of Operations South of Scarpe, 26th, 27th, and 28th August, 1918."
15 LAC, War Diary, 4th Infantry Brigade, "Narrative of Operations South of Scarpe."
16 Corrigall, *The History of the Twentieth Canadian Battalion*, 235; LAC, War Diary, 19th Battalion, appendix 5, 4th Brigade Operation Order no. 254, 25 August 1918; LAC, War Diary, 4th Infantry Brigade, "Narrative of Operations South of Scarpe."
17 LAC, War Diary, 19th Battalion, 24–25 August 1918; LAC, War Diary, 4th Infantry Brigade, 24 August 1918.
18 LAC, War Diary, 19th Battalion, appendix 5, 19th Battalion Order no. 95, 25 August 1918.
19 LAC, RG 9, III-D-3, vol. 4847, War Diary, 2nd Canadian Division headquarters, appendix 205, 2nd Canadian Division Operation Order no. 246, 25 August 1918; Currie, "Interim Report," 146–47.
20 LAC, War Diary, 4th Infantry Brigade, "Narrative of Operations South of Scarpe."
21 Corrigall, *The History of the Twentieth Canadian Battalion*, 236; LAC, War Diary, 4th Infantry Brigade, "Narrative of Operations South of Scarpe"; Nicholson, *Canadian Expeditionary Force*, 428; CWM, 19740071-017 58C 1 1.9, Marshall Diary, 26 August 1918.
22 LAC, War Diary, 4th Infantry Brigade, "Narrative of Operations South of Scarpe"; Nicholson, *Canadian Expeditionary Force*, 428.

23 LAC, War Diary, 19th Battalion, appendix 6, "Operations by the 19th Canadian Battalion, August 25th–29th 1918"; ibid., report by Capt. J.A. Linton, OC, D Company.
24 Nicholson, *Canadian Expeditionary Force*, 429.
25 Ibid., 428–29; Burstall, "2nd Division Narrative," 26.
26 LAC, War Diary, 4th Infantry Brigade, "Narrative of Operations South of Scarpe"; Burstall, "2nd Division Narrative," 27.
27 LAC, War Diary, 19th Battalion, "Operations by the 19th Canadian Battalion"; Barnes journal, 26 August 1918, qtd. in Bruce Cane, *It Made You Think of Home: The Haunting Journal of Deward Barnes, Canadian Expeditionary Force: 1916–1919* (Toronto: Dundurn, 2004), 241–42.
28 LAC, War Diary, 19th Battalion, "Operations by the 19th Canadian Battalion."
29 Nicholson, *Canadian Expeditionary Force*, 429, Map 12.
30 Ibid., 430; Burstall, "2nd Division Narrative," 29.
31 LAC, War Diary, 19th Battalion, "Operations by the 19th Canadian Battalion"; ibid., 19th Battalion X.33 to all companies, 27 August 1918; LAC, War Diary, 4th Infantry Brigade, "Narrative of Operations South of Scarpe"; Burstall, "2nd Division Narrative," 29.
32 LAC, War Diary, 19th Battalion, "Operations by the 19th Canadian Battalion"; ibid., 19th Battalion X.33 to all companies, 27 August 1918.
33 Nicholson, *Canadian Expeditionary Force*, 430; LAC, War Diary, 4th Infantry Brigade, "Narrative of Operations South of Scarpe"; LAC, War Diary, 19th Battalion, August 1918, appendix 6, report by Capt. Linton.
34 Barnes journal, 27 August 1918, qtd. in Cane, *It Made You Think of Home*, 242.
35 Nicholson, *Canadian Expeditionary Force*, 430; Barnes journal, 27 August 1918, qtd. in Cane, *It Made You Think of Home*, 243.
36 Nicholson, *Canadian Expeditionary Force*, 430; LAC, War Diary, 19th Battalion, report by Capt. Linton.
37 Nicholson, *Canadian Expeditionary Force*, 430; LAC, War Diary, 4th Infantry Brigade, "Narrative of Operations South of Scarpe."
38 LAC, War Diary, 19th Battalion, "Operations by the 19th Canadian Battalion."
39 Nicholson, *Canadian Expeditionary Force*, 430; Currie, "Interim Report," 148–49; Burstall, "2nd Division Narrative," 30; LAC, RG 9, III-D-3, vol. 4934, War Diary, 26th Battalion, appendix B7, after-action report, C Company, covering operations 26–28 August 1918.
40 Schreiber, *Shock Army of the British Empire*, 76.
41 Nicholson, *Canadian Expeditionary Force*, 431.
42 Ibid., 431; LAC, War Diary, 4th Infantry Brigade, "Narrative of Operations South of Scarpe"; LAC, War Diary, 19th Battalion, "Operations by the 19th Canadian Battalion"; ibid., appendix 6, "C Company, Report on Operations of Aug 26, 27, 28."
43 LAC, War Diary, 4th Infantry Brigade, "Narrative of Operations South of Scarpe"; LAC, War Diary, 19th Battalion, "Operations by the 19th Canadian Battalion"; Burstall, "2nd Division Narrative," 33.
44 Barnes journal, 28 August 1918, qtd. in Cane, *It Made You Think of Home*, 245.
45 Morton, *When Your Number's Up*, 180.
46 Barnes journal, 28 August 1918, qtd. in Cane, *It Made You Think of Home*, 246, 248.
47 Nicholson, *Canadian Expeditionary Force*, 431–32.
48 LAC, War Diary, 4th Infantry Brigade, "Narrative of Operations South of Scarpe"; LAC, War Diary, 19th Battalion, "Operations by the 19th Canadian Battalion."
49 Nicholson, *Canadian Expeditionary Force*, 431–32, map 12; Currie, "Interim Report," 149–50; Schreiber, *Shock Army of the British Empire*, 76–77.
50 Both the 19th and the 21st Battalions were relieved by the 8th Battalion of 2nd Brigade. LAC, War Diary, 4th Infantry Brigade, "Narrative of Operations South of Scarpe"; LAC, War Diary, 19th Battalion, 29–31 August 1918; ibid., "Operations by the 19th Canadian Battalion"; Corrigall, *The History of the Twentieth Canadian Battalion*, 243.
51 During its tour at Arras, the 19th Battalion lost 5 officers killed, 7 wounded, and 1 gassed. Among the other ranks, there were 25 killed, 180 wounded, 26 gassed, 40 missing, and 1

wounded and missing. LAC, War Diary, 19th Battalion, "Operations by the 19th Canadian Battalion." For the month as a whole, 9 officers were killed, 18 wounded, and 1 gassed. As for the other ranks, the breakdown was as follows: 56 killed; 29 died of wounds; 346 wounded; 31 gassed; 24 missing. LAC, War Diary, 19th Battalion, August 1918, casualty statistics. As usual, the statistics provided in the postwar records of daily casualties differ somewhat from the war diary, but only to a minor degree.

52 LAC, War Diary, 19th Battalion, 26–28 August 1918; ibid., "Operations by the 19th Canadian Battalion."

53 Schreiber, *Shock Army of the British Empire*, 78.

54 LAC, War Diary, 19th Battalion, appendix 6, "Special Order by Lieutenant-General Sir Arthur W. Currie," 26 August 1918.

55 Currie, "Interim Report," 144; Cook, *Shock Troops*, 458.

Chapter 20 – Cambrai and Iwuy: 1 September–13 October 1918

1 For information on changes in the nomenclature and organization of Brutinel's mobile forces during the Hundred Days, see G.W.L. Nicholson, *Canadian Expeditionary Force, 1914–1919: The Official History of the Canadian Army in the First World War* (Ottawa: Queen's Printer, 1962), 397, 432, 435, 448.

2 Ibid., 433; Shane B. Schreiber, *Shock Army of the British Empire: The Canadian Corps in the Last 100 Days of the Great War* (Westport: Praeger, 1997), 78–79.

3 Ibid., 79–83; Lt.-Gen. Sir A.W. Currie, "Interim Report on the Operations of the Canadian Corps during the Year 1918," in *Report of the Ministry, Overseas Military Forces of Canada, 1918* (London: Minister, Overseas Military Forces of Canada, n.d.), 152–54; Nicholson, *Canadian Expeditionary Force*, 438, map 12.

4 LAC, RG 9, III-D-3, vol. 4929, War Diary, 19th Battalion, 1–3 September 1918.

5 Personal collection of Mrs. Phyllis Douglas, letters of Lt.-Col. Lionel H. Millen (hereafter Millen Letters), Millen to his mother, 4 September 1918.

6 LAC, RG 9, III-D-3, vol. 4847, War Diary, 2nd Canadian Division headquarters, 3 September 1918; LAC, War Diary, 19th Battalion, 4 September 1918; LAC, RG 9, III-D-3, vol. 4883, War Diary, 4th Infantry Brigade, 4 September 1918.

7 GMA, M399, Gaetz Family Fonds, J.R. Gaetz to his mother, 7 September 1918.

8 LAC, War Diary, 19th Battalion, 12 September 1918.

9 LAC, War Diary, 4th Infantry Brigade, 12 September 1918; Patrick H. Brennan, "Byng's and Currie's Commanders: A Still Untold Story of the Canadian Corps," *Canadian Military History* 11, no. 2 (2002): 7; LAC, RG 9, III-D-1, vol. 4734, folder 144, file 9, Biographical Summary of Brig.-Gen. George Eric McCuaig; LAC, RG 24, C-6-d, vol. 1886, file 85, Lists of Commanders and Staffs, 2nd Canadian Division.

10 LAC, War Diary, 19th Battalion, 12–13 September 1918; ibid., appendix 1, 4th Brigade Memo G.183 to all battalions, 10 September 1918; LAC, MG 30, E 6, Sir Henry Burstall Papers, vol. 3, file 21, Maj.-Gen. H.E. Burstall, "2nd Canadian Division, Narrative of Operations from March 13th to Nov. 11th, 1918," 39 (hereafter "2nd Division Narrative").

11 LAC, RG 41, B-III-1, Records of the CBC, *Flanders Fields*, vol. 10, 19th Battalion, transcript of interview with Joe O'Neill, tape 4, 12–13.

12 Burstall, "2nd Division Narrative," 38–9.

13 LAC, War Diary, 19th Battalion, 13 September 1918; ibid., appendix 2, 19th Battalion A. 53 to all companies and scout officers, 14 September 1918.

14 Fred Stitt of A Company had a good deal of patrol experience along the Canal du Nord front during September. See LAC, *Flanders Fields*, vol. 10, 19th Battalion, transcript of interview with F.A. Stitt, tape 2, 15–16.

15 LAC, War Diary, 19th Battalion, 14 September 1918; ibid., appendix 2, 19th Battalion, Patrol Report, 14 September 1918; ibid., 19th Battalion, M.68 to 4th Brigade, 15 September 1918; ibid., message from B Company regarding capture of prisoner, 15 September 1918.

16 LAC, War Diary, 19th Battalion, 15 September 1918; ibid., appendix 2, patrol report by Lt A.J. Duncan, 16 September 1918.
17 LAC, War Diary, 19th Battalion, appendix 2, patrol report by Lt. A.J. Duncan, 16 September 1918.
18 During this period in brigade support, there were several casualties among the other ranks. One was killed, one died of wounds, two were wounded, and five were gassed. The two fatalities occurred on 19 September, when a stray shell burst near battalion headquarters, killing one signaller and mortally wounding another. LAC, War Diary, 19th Battalion, 20 Sept. 1918.
19 LAC, War Diary, 19th Battalion, 21–23 September 1918; ibid., appendix 4, 19th Battalion patrol report, 22 September 1918.
20 Because the patrol encounter on 22 September involved men from A Company (Stitt's company), and because 22 September was a Sunday (the day of the week mentioned by Stitt in his story), it seems likely that Stitt's anecdote refers to the same action as the one described in the official patrol report dated 22 September. LAC, *Flanders Fields*, vol. 10, 19th Battalion, transcript of interview with F.A. Stitt, tape 2, 16–18; LAC, War Diary, 19th Battalion, 21–23 September 1918; ibid., appendix 4, 19th Battalion Patrol Report, 22 September 1918.
21 LAC, War Diary, 19th Battalion, 23–27 September 1918.
22 T.M. Hunter, *Marshal Foch: A Study in Leadership* (Ottawa: Queen's Printer, 1961), 200; Tim Travers, *How the War Was Won: Command and Technology in the British Army on the Western Front, 1917–1918* (London: Routledge, 1992), 157; Nicholson, *Canadian Expeditionary Force*, 441–42; Gary Sheffield, *Forgotten Victory: The First World War, Myths and Realities* (London: Headline, 2001), 207–8.
23 Schreiber, *Shock Army of the British Empire*, 95–96; Nicholson, *Canadian Expeditionary Force*, 442.
24 Ibid., 442–44; Schreiber, *Shock Army of the British Empire*, 98–103; Currie, "Interim Report," 159–60.
25 Schreiber, *Shock Army of the British Empire*, 110; J.P. Harris and Niall Barr, *Amiens to the Armistice: The BEF in the Hundred Days' Campaign, 8 August–11 November 1918* (London: Brassey's, 1998), 197.
26 Ibid., 188, 231; Schreiber, *Shock Army of the British Empire*, 104–7; Nicholson, *Canadian Expeditionary Force*, 448–53.
27 Burstall, "2nd Division Narrative," 41.
28 Millen Letters, Millen to his mother, 27 September 1918.
29 LAC, War Diary, 19th Battalion, 28–30 September 1918.
30 LAC, War Diary, 19th Battalion, September 1918, numbers of reinforcements received and casualties sustained.
31 LAC, War Diary, 19th Battalion, appendix 2, memo from Capt. R.H. Bliss to battalion adjutant, 13 September 1918.
32 Burstall, "2nd Division Narrative," 42–44; LAC, War Diary, 4th Infantry Brigade, October 1918, appendix 8, "Report on Operations, Cambrai–Iwuy"; Nicholson, *Canadian Expeditionary Force*, 453.
33 Burstall, "2nd Division Narrative," 42–44; LAC, War Diary, 4th Infantry Brigade, "Report on Operations"; ibid., vol. 4929, 19th Battalion, 1–6 October 1918; ibid., appendix 1, "Report on Recent Operations, Oct 7th to Oct 13th."
34 Currie, "Interim Report," 164; Nicholson, *Canadian Expeditionary Force*, 456.
35 Burstall, "2nd Division Narrative," 45.
36 LAC, War Diary, 4th Infantry Brigade, "Report on Operations."
37 LAC, War Diary, 19th Battalion, 7 October 1918; ibid., appendix 1, 4th Brigade G. 285, "Instructions for Offensive," 7 October 1918; ibid., 19th Battalion, Operation Order no. 102, 7 October 1918; Burstall, "2nd Division Narrative," 47.
38 Millen Letters, Millen to his mother, 5 October 1918.
39 Burstall, "2nd Division Narrative," 46–47.

40 Burstall, "2nd Division Narrative," 48–49; Nicholson, *Canadian Expeditionary Force*, 457.
41 Burstall, "2nd Division Narrative," 49; LAC, War Diary, 19th Battalion, "Report on Recent Operations."
42 Burstall, "2nd Division Narrative," 49–50; LAC, War Diary, 4th Infantry Brigade, 9 October 1918; ibid., "Report on Operations"; LAC, War Diary, 19th Battalion, "Report on Recent Operations"; Nicholson, *Canadian Expeditionary Force*, 458.
43 LAC, War Diary, 4th Infantry Brigade, "Report on Operations"; ibid., appendix 9, 4th Brigade Operation Order no. 23, 10 October 1918; LAC, War Diary, 19th Battalion, 10 October 1918; Michael R. McNorgan, "'My God, Look at Them Houses Moving!' Combined Arms Action at Iwuy, 10–11 October 1918," in *More Fighting for Canada: Five Battles, 1760–1944*, ed. Donald E. Graves (Toronto: Robin Brass, 2004), 215–16; Burstall, "2nd Division Narrative," 51.
44 D.J. Corrigall, *The History of the Twentieth Canadian Battalion (Central Ontario Regiment) Canadian Expeditionary Force in the Great War, 1914–1918* (Toronto: Stone and Cox, 1935), 257; Burstall, "2nd Division Narrative," 50; Nicholson, *Canadian Expeditionary Force*, map 13, facing 458.
45 LAC, War Diary, 19th Battalion, 10 October 1918; Barnes journal, 9 October 1918, qtd. in Bruce Cane, *It Made You Think of Home: The Haunting Journal of Deward Barnes, Canadian Expeditionary Force: 1916–1919* (Toronto: Dundurn, 2004), 259.
46 LAC, War Diary, 19th Battalion, 10 October 1918; ibid., "Report on Recent Operations"; LAC, War Diary, 4th Infantry Brigade, "Report on Operations"; McNorgan, "Combined Arms Action at Iwuy," 215; Burstall, "2nd Division Narrative," 51; Corrigall, *The History of the Twentieth Canadian Battalion*, 258.
47 Barnes journal, 10 October 1918, qtd. in Cane, *It Made You Think of Home*, 259–60.
48 CWM, 19740071-017 58C 1 1.9, untitled file of correspondence and notes regarding 19th Battalion history, "The World War of 1914–18 and the 19th Battalion as They Affected Me, by #228421, Pte. V.E. Thompson, Rear Rank," 29 (hereafter "Thompson Narrative").
49 Burstall, "2nd Division Narrative," 51.
50 LAC, War Diary, 19th Battalion, "Report on Recent Operations"; LAC, War Diary, 4th Infantry Brigade, "Report on Operations"; LAC, RG 9, III-D-3, vol. 4956, War Diary, Canadian Corps Cyclist Battalion, appendix Y, Report on Operations, 9–12 October 1918; LAC, RG 9, III-D-3, vol. 4891, War Diary, 6th Infantry Brigade, appendix 33, map of operations, 9–10 October 1918; Burstall, "2nd Division Narrative, 51.
51 LAC, War Diary, 19th Battalion, "Report on Recent Operation"; ibid., field message announcing zero hour of 1:15 PM for next stage of advance; Nicholson, *Canadian Expeditionary Force*, 458–59; Burstall, "2nd Division Narrative," 52; McNorgan, "Combined Arms Action at Iwuy," 213; Corrigall, *The History of the Twentieth Canadian Battalion*, 258.
52 LAC, RG 9, III-D-3, vol. 4926, War Diary, 18th Battalion, 10 October 1918; Burstall, "2nd Division Narrative," 52; Cane, *It Made You Think of Home*, 261.
53 Although the troopers of the Canadian Light Horse sustained only twenty-two casualties (five killed, seventeen wounded), the unfortunate horses suffered far more heavily (seventy-one animals became casualties, of which sixty-six were killed). Barnes journal, 10 October 1918, qtd. in Cane, *It Made You Think of Home*, 260–61.
54 LAC, War Diary, 18th Battalion, 10 October 1918; Burstall, "2nd Division Narrative," 52.
55 LAC, War Diary, 19th Battalion, appendix 1, field message, 4:30 PM, 10 October 1918.
56 LAC, War Diary, 19th Battalion, "Report on Recent Operations"; ibid., field message from A and B Companies, 19:45, 10 October 1918; LAC, War Diary, 4th Infantry Brigade, "Report on Operations."
57 Barnes journal, 10 October 1918, qtd. in Cane, *It Made You Think of Home*, 261–62.
58 Captain Duncan later died of his wounds while being held as a prisoner of war. LAC, War Diary, 19th Battalion, field messages, 3:15, 4:45 AM, 11 October 1918; Cane, *It Made You Think of Home*, 263. The field messages refer to Duncan as "Lieutenant," but the list of officers dated 31 October in LAC, RG 150, vol. 465 gives his rank as captain. His personnel file indicates that

he was appointed Acting Captain in September. In his file the notation of this appointment was dated 29 September, with the appointment itself being backdated to 12 September. LAC RG 150, 1992-93/166, box 2728-8.

59 LAC, War Diary, 19th Battalion, "Report on Recent Operations"; LAC, War Diary, 4th Infantry Brigade, "Report on Operations"; Nicholson, *Canadian Expeditionary Force*, map 13, facing 458; James E. Edmonds and R. Maxwell-Hyslop, *Military Operations: France and Belgium, 1918*, vol. 5 (London: HMSO, 1947), 254.

60 Burstall, "2nd Division Narrative," 53.

61 Barnes journal, 11 October 1918, qtd. in Cane, *It Made You Think of Home*, 263.

62 Burstall, "2nd Division Narrative," 54. The detachment from the 20th Battalion was led by Lt. W.L. Algie, who took his men across the inter-brigade boundary, rushed two German machine-gun nests, and then began clearing out the east end of Iwuy. Shortly after, Algie was killed while bringing up reinforcements, but his deeds would earn him a posthumous Victoria Cross. Nicholson, *Canadian Expeditionary Force*, 459.

63 McNorgan, "Combined Arms Action at Iwuy," 226.

64 Barnes journal, 11 October 1918, qtd. in Cane, *It Made You Think of Home*, 264.

65 McNorgan, "Combined Arms Action at Iwuy," 228, 230–32. The *Sturmpanzerwagen* A7V was the only German-designed tank produced during the war. Box-like in its basic design (10' 10" inches high, 24' long, 10' wide) and weighing 32 tons, it is little wonder that many Canadian and British troops at first mistook the machines for "moving armoured houses." Overall, the design was not a success, and only twenty machines were ever produced. The designation "A7V" stood for *Allgemeine Kriegsdepartment 7 Abteilung Verkehrwesen* ("General War Department Division 7 Transport"), a form of "verbal camouflage," much like the more succinct British use of the term "tank." Ibid., 226–30.

66 Barnes journal, 11 October 1918, qtd. in Cane, *It Made You Think of Home*, 264.

67 Nicholson, *Canadian Expeditionary Force*, 459; Edmonds and Maxwell-Hyslop, *Military Operations*, vol. 5, 256.

68 ASH, RG 4, series 3, World War 1, 19th Battalion Association, "Selections from the Mailbag," 19th Battalion Association newsletter, Fall 1968.

69 Barnes journal, 11 October 1918, qtd. in Cane, *It Made You Think of Home*, 264; LAC, War Diary, 19th Battalion, "Report on Recent Operations."

70 Barnes journal, 11 October 1918, quoted in Cane, *It Made You Think of Home*, 264–65.

71 "Thompson Narrative," 31.

72 LAC, War Diary, 19th Battalion, "Report on Recent Operations"; McNorgan, "Combined Arms Action at Iwuy," 232; Barnes journal, 11 October 1918, qtd. in Cane, *It Made You Think of Home*, 265; Burstall, "2nd Division Narrative," 54. Both the 20th Battalion's published history and the analysis of the fighting at Iwuy by Michael McNorgan erroneously identify Lt. Crombie as an officer in the 21st Battalion. Corrigall, *The History of the Twentieth Canadian Battalion*, 261; McNorgan, "Combined Arms Action at Iwuy," 232.

73 Crombie was wounded in action later in the day on 11 October and succumbed to his injuries in hospital on 26 October. Cane, *It Made You Think of Home*, 265; LAC, RG 150, vol. 465, "List of Officers, 19th Infantry Battalion," 31 October 1918.

74 Burstall, "2nd Division Narrative," 55; Nicholson, *Canadian Expeditionary Force*, 45, map 15.

75 LAC, War Diary, 19th Battalion, "Report on Recent Operations"; ibid., field message, Shiell to headquarters, 11 October 1918; Currie, "Interim Report," 167–68.

76 The four wounded officers were Lts. R.O. Spreckley, W.A. Fitzgerald, W.P. Venn, and V.R.A. Crombie. During this month, the total casualties for other ranks listed in the battalion war diary (15 killed, 3 died of wounds, and 106 wounded; 124 in total) do not make sense in light of figures quoted in the same document for the fighting around Cambrai during the first half of the month (139 other ranks killed or wounded). Assuming that the figures quoted for the fighting around Cambrai are reasonably accurate, then the total casualties for October given in the war diary are in error. The actual total is probably more in line with the monthly casualty figures given in postwar records (5 officers and 146 other ranks during October 1918; see

Appendix A). LAC, War Diary, 19th Battalion, "Report on Recent Operations." See also ibid., 11 October 1918; LAC, RG 150, vol. 502, "Casualties by Days–France and Belgium," 19th Battalion, October 1918. The 19th Battalion actually fared the best of the infantry units in the 4th Brigade. The casualties suffered by the other battalions during the fighting near Cambrai and Iwuy were as follows: 18th Battalion – 7 officers, 167 other ranks; 20th Battalion – 11 officers, 319 other ranks; 21st Battalion, 12 officers, 310 other ranks. LAC, vol. 4883, War Diary, 4th Infantry Brigade, "Report of Operations."

77 Barnes journal, 11 October 1918, qtd. in Cane, *It Made You Think of Home*, 266–67.

78 Ibid., 267–73.

79 Laurence V. Moyer, *Victory Must Be Ours: Germany in the Great War, 1914–1918* (New York: Hippocrene, 1995), 279.

80 Millen Letters, Millen to his mother, 11 October 1918.

81 LAC, War Diary, 19th Battalion, appendix 1, "Report on Recent Operations, Oct 7th to Oct 13th"; ibid., 12–13 October 1918.

82 GMA, M399, Gaetz Family Fonds, J.R. Gaetz to his sister Daisy, 15 October 1918.

Chapter 21 – Long Road to Mons: 14 October–11 November 1918

1 G.W.L. Nicholson, *Canadian Expeditionary Force, 1914–1919: The Official History of the Canadian Army in the First World War* (Ottawa: Queen's Printer, 1962), 465, 467; LAC, MG 30, E 6, Sir Henry Burstall Papers, vol. 3, file 21, Maj.-Gen. H.E. Burstall, "2nd Canadian Division, Narrative of Operations from March 13th to Nov. 11th, 1918," 58 (hereafter "2nd Division Narrative"); LAC, RG 9, III-D-3, vol. 4883, War Diary, 4th Infantry Brigade, 12–13 October 1918.

2 Burstall, "2nd Division Narrative," 58; LAC, War Diary, 4th Infantry Brigade, 14 October 1918; ibid., appendix 10, 4th Brigade Operation Order no. 25, 14 October 1918; J.A. Cooper, *History of Operations of 4th Canadian Infantry Brigade, 1915–1919* (London: Charles and Son, n.d.), 40; D.J. Corrigall, *The History of the Twentieth Canadian Battalion (Central Ontario Regiment) Canadian Expeditionary Force in the Great War, 1914–1918* (Toronto: Stone and Cox, 1935), 266.

3 LAC, RG 9, III-D-3, vol. 4929, War Diary, 19th Battalion, 14–15 October 1918; ibid., appendix 2, "Trench State," 14 October 1918; LAC, War Diary, 4th Infantry Brigade, 15 October 1918.

4 LAC, War Diary, 19th Battalion, 16–17 October 1918; Nicholson, *Canadian Expeditionary Force*, 468; Burstall, "2nd Division Narrative," 58.

5 Ibid.," 57–58.

6 LAC, War Diary, 19th Battalion, 18 October 1918; Burstall, "2nd Division Narrative," 59.

7 Corrigall, *The History of the Twentieth Canadian Battalion*, 266, 269; Burstall, "2nd Division Narrative," 59.

8 LAC, War Diary, 19th Battalion, 19 October 1918. The timing of B Company's arrival in Neuville-sur-l'Escaut is inferred from the text of the 4th Brigade's war diary entry for 19 October 1918.

9 LAC, RG 41, B-III-1, Records of the CBC, *Flanders Fields*, vol. 6, transcript of Episode 15, "The Last Push," 23. The city of Denain was located less than two miles northeast of Neuville-sur-l'Escaut. Corrigall, *The History of the Twentieth Canadian Battalion*, map, 255.

10 At some point after 30 September, Capt. H.C. Allison left the battalion and Capt. Parney took over as medical officer. Due to his German middle name he was sometimes referred to as "Fritz" Parney. His attestation paper also lists his Christian name as "Fred" and not "Frederick." LAC, RG 150, vol. 465, List of Officers, 19th Battalion, September and October 1918.

11 CWM, 19740071-017 58C 1 1.9, untitled file of correspondence and notes regarding 19th Battalion history, handwritten memories from Ernie Knott.

12 Corrigall, *The History of the Twentieth Canadian Battalion*, 266, 270; LAC, War Diary, 4th Infantry Brigade, 19 October 1918.

13 Corrigall, *The History of the Twentieth Canadian Battalion*, 271.

14 Personal collection of Mrs. Phyllis Douglas, letters of Lt.-Col. Lionel H. Millen (hereafter Millen Letters), Millen to his mother, 23 October 1918.
15 Burstall, "2nd Division Narrative," 60; LAC, War Diary, 19th Battalion, 19 October 1918.
16 LAC, War Diary, 19th Battalion, 20–21 October 1918.
17 LAC, *Flanders Fields*, vol. 10, 19th Battalion, transcript of interview with E. Youngman, tape 4, 6–7.
18 GMA, M399, Gaetz Family Fonds, J.R. Gaetz to his mother, 21 October 1918.
19 LAC, War Diary, 19th Battalion, 21–22 October 1918; LAC, War Diary, 4th Infantry Brigade, 22 October 1918.
20 Millen Letters, Millen to his mother, 23 October 1918.
21 LAC, War Diary, 19th Battalion, 22–23 October 1918; ibid., appendix 3, memorandum O.B. 160, 22 October 1918.
22 LAC, War Diary, 4th Infantry Brigade, 23 October 1918.
23 LAC, War Diary, 19th Battalion, appendix 3, Battalion Order no. 102, 23 October 1918.
24 LAC, War Diary, 19th Battalion, battalion memorandum D.A. 158, 23 October 1918; Shane B. Schreiber, *Shock Army of the British Empire: The Canadian Corps in the Last 100 Days of the Great War* (Westport: Praeger, 1997), 116.
25 LAC, War Diary, 19th Battalion, appendix 3, 4th Brigade G. 626, 25 October 1918.
26 LAC, War Diary, 19th Battalion, battalion memorandum D.A. 158, 23 October 1918.
27 LAC, War Diary, 19th Battalion, 24–31 October 1918; LAC, War Diary, 4th Infantry Brigade, 24–31 October 1918.
28 Tim Travers, "The Allied Victories, 1918," in *World War I: A History*, ed. Hew Strachan (Oxford: Oxford University Press, 1998), 288; Holger H. Herwig, *The First World War: Germany and Austria-Hungary, 1914–1918* (London: Arnold, 1997), 428, 433, 437, 440–45; Robert B. Asprey, *The German High Command at War: Hindenburg and Ludendorff Conduct World War I* (New York: Quill, 1991), 484; Laurence V. Moyer, *Victory Must Be Ours: Germany in the Great War, 1914–1918* (New York: Hippocrene, 1995), Chs. 9–10; Alexander Watson, *Ring of Steel: Germany and Austria-Hungary at War, 1914–1918* (London: Allen Lane, 2014), 551–56.
29 Schreiber, *Shock Army of the British Empire*, 119–20.
30 Nicholson, *Canadian Expeditionary Force*, 471–75; A.G.L. McNaughton, "The Development of Artillery in the Great War," *Canadian Defence Quarterly* 6, no. 2 (1929): 170–71.
31 LAC, *Flanders Fields*, vol. 6, transcript of Episode 15, "The Last Push," 29, 30.
32 Nicholson, *Canadian Expeditionary Force*, 475; Schreiber, *Shock Army of the British Empire*, 126; Burstall, "2nd Division Narrative," 61.
33 CWM, 19740071-017 58C 1 1.9, untitled file of correspondence and notes regarding 19th Battalion history, "The World War of 1914–18 and the 19th Battalion as They Affected Me, by #228421, Pte. V.E. Thompson, Rear Rank," 32 (hereafter "Thompson Narrative").
34 LAC, War Diary, 19th Battalion, appendix 3, Battalion Order no. 106, 29 October 1918.
35 LAC, War Diary, 19th Battalion, 4th Brigade G. 637, 31 October 1918.
36 LAC, War Diary, 19th Battalion, 1–4 November 1918; ibid., appendix 2, 19th Battalion Embussing Strength, 4 November 1918.
37 Tim Travers, *How the War Was Won: Command and Technology in the British Army on the Western Front, 1917–1918* (London: Routledge, 1992), 172–73.
38 LAC, War Diary, 19th Battalion, 5–6 November 1918; Burstall, "2nd Division Narrative," 62; LAC, RG 24,C-6-d, vol. 1886, file 85, Commanders and Staffs, 19th Canadian Infantry Battalion.
39 Burstall, "2nd Division Narrative," 63–64; LAC, War Diary, 19th Battalion, 7–8 November 1918; LAC, RG 9, III-C-3, vol. 4091, folder 26, file 7, "Narrative of Operations Carried Out by 4th Canadian Infantry Brigade, 9th, 10th, 11th November 1918" (hereafter "4th Brigade Narrative, 9–11 November 1918").
40 Burstall, "2nd Division Narrative," 61.
41 At that time, the population of Mons was nearly 30,000. Corrigall, *The History of the Twentieth Canadian Battalion*, 277, 284.

42 Ibid., 276; LAC, War Diary, 19th Battalion, 9 November 1918; LAC, War Diary, 4th Infantry Brigade, appendix 7, 4th Brigade Operation Order no. 34, 9 November 1918; LAC, War Diary, 19th Battalion, appendix 2, "Report on Operations of 19th Canadian Battalion Involving the Capture of Hyon, November 11th 1918" (hereafter, "19th Battalion Report, 11 November 1918").
43 Burstall, "2nd Division Narrative," 65; "4th Brigade Narrative, 9–11 Nov. 1918"; Corrigall, *The History of the Twentieth Canadian Battalion*, 277.
44 "19th Battalion Report, 11 Nov. 1918"; "4th Brigade Narrative, 9–11 Nov. 1918"; Nicholson, *Canadian Expeditionary Force*, 481.
45 James E. Edmonds and R. Maxwell-Hyslop, *Military Operations: France and Belgium, 1918*, vol. 5 (London: HMSO, 1947), 535.
46 "19th Battalion Report, 11 Nov. 1918"; LAC, War Diary, 19th Battalion, appendix 2, 19th Battalion, Operation Order no. 107, 9 November 1918.
47 LAC, War Diary, 19th Battalion, 10 November 1918.
48 "Thompson Narrative," 33–34.
49 GMA, Gaetz Family Fonds, J.R. Gaetz to his mother, 19 November 1918.
50 "19th Battalion Report, 11 Nov. 1918"; "4th Brigade Narrative, 9–11 Nov. 1918."
51 LAC, *Flanders Fields*, vol. 6, transcript of Episode 16, "Victory," 5.
52 GMA, Gaetz Family Fonds, J.R. Gaetz to his mother, 19 November 1918.
53 "19th Battalion Report, 11 Nov. 1918"; "4th Brigade Narrative, 9–11 Nov. 1918."
54 LAC, RG 9, III-D-3, vol. 4969, War Diary, 5th Brigade, CFA, 10 November 1918; "19th Battalion Report, 11 Nov. 1918"; "4th Brigade Narrative, 9–11 Nov. 1918."
55 "19th Battalion Report, 11 Nov. 1918"; "4th Brigade Narrative, 9–11 Nov. 1918"; GMA, Gaetz Family Fonds, J.R. Gaetz to his mother, 19 November 1918.
56 "19th Battalion Report, 11 Nov. 1918"; "4th Brigade Narrative, 9–11 Nov. 1918."
57 Corrigall, *The History of the Twentieth Canadian Battalion*, 280.
58 "19th Battalion Report, 11 Nov. 1918"; Burstall, "2nd Division Narrative," 68; "4th Brigade Narrative, 9–11 Nov. 1918"; John Swettenham, *To Seize the Victory: The Canadian Corps in World War I* (Toronto: Ryerson, 1965), 13.
59 Burstall, "2nd Division Narrative," 68; Corrigall, *The History of the Twentieth Canadian Battalion*, 281; "4th Brigade Narrative, 9–11 Nov. 1918."
60 One squadron of the 5th Lancers was assigned to work with the 2nd Canadian Division. Edmonds and Maxwell-Hyslop, *Military Operations*, 554; LAC, RG 9, III-D-3, vol. 4847, War Diary, 2nd Canadian Division headquarters, 9 November 1918; LAC, *Flanders Fields*, vol. 10, 19th Battalion, transcript of interview with Joe O'Neill, tape 2, 10.
61 http://www.qrl.uk.com/h_5.html, history of the 5th Royal Irish Lancers.
62 LAC, MG 30, E 249, John Smith Stewart Papers, World War I Accounts, "My Own Souvenirs of the Battle of Mons 9–11th November 1918, and of Our Liberation by the 'C' Company the 19th C.I.B. [*sic*]." Georges Licope, who later served as chief of cabinet for the burgomaster of Mons and curator of the local war museum, maintained a lifelong friendship with the 19th Battalion. ASH, RG 4, series 3, World War 1, 19th Battalion Association, "Selections from the Mailbag," 19th Battalion Association newsletter, Spring 1975.
63 LAC, War Diary, 19th Battalion, 11 November 1918.
64 LAC, Stewart Papers, "My Own Souvenirs." Pte. George L. Price of the 28th Battalion was leading a patrol across the Canal du Centre, between the villages of Havre and Ville-sur-Haine, when he was shot in the chest by a German sniper just two minutes before the armistice came into effect. He was the last Canadian killed in action in the First World War. Daniel G. Dancocks, *Spearhead to Victory: Canada and the Great War* (Edmonton: Hurtig, 1987), 205.
65 "Thompson Narrative," 35. Other groups of 19th Battalion men also apparently made their way into Mons. W.H.S. Macklin maintained that "it's true that my particular platoon got lost and actually entered the city and went through the city in the early hours of the morning." LAC, *Flanders Fields*, vol. 6, transcript of Episode 16, "Victory," 8.

66 LAC, War Diary, 19th Battalion, 1 November 1918. The official wire received at 4th Brigade headquarters from division at 7:20 AM read as follows: "Hostilities will cease at 1100 hours November 11th 1918. Troops will stand fast on the line reached at that time which will be reported to Divisional Headquarters immediately. Defensive precautions will be maintained. There will be no intercourse of any description with the enemy. Further instructions will follow." "4th Brigade Narrative, 9–11 Nov. 1918."

67 GMA, Gaetz Family Fonds, J.R. Gaetz to his mother, 19 November 1918.

68 LAC, *Flanders Fields*, vol. 6, transcript of Episode 16, "Victory," 15.

69 LAC, *Flanders Fields*, vol. 6, transcript of Episode 16, "Victory," 10.

70 LAC, *Flanders Fields*, vol. 6, transcript of Episode 16, "Victory," 10.

71 LAC, *Flanders Fields*, vol. 10, 19th Battalion, transcript of interview with E. Youngman, tape 4, 7–8.

72 LAC, MG 30, E 452, Felix J. Cullen Papers, personal diary, 11 November 1918.

73 ASH, RG 4, series 3, World War 1, 19th Battalion Association, "Selections from the Mailbag," 19th Battalion Association newsletter, Fall 1969.

74 Another happy day was in store for Fred when he married his sweetheart in London in January 1919. LAC, *Flanders Fields*, vol. 10, 19th Battalion, transcript of interview with F.A. Stitt, tape 2, 21–22.

75 Millen Letters, Millen to his mother, 15 November 1918.

76 Ian Hugh MacLean Miller, *Our Glory and Our Grief: Torontonians and the Great War* (Toronto: University of Toronto Press, 2002), 190.

77 "The Heart of the City: A Virtual Tour of Downtown Hamilton, General History," http://collections.ic.gc.ca/hamilton_tour/history.html. By 1917, every Canadian province except Quebec had enacted prohibition legislation; and in 1918, with the federal Union government's imposition of national prohibition, even Quebec had gone officially "dry." As a result, people could legally obtain alcohol only with a medical prescription. Robert Craig Brown and Ramsay Cook, *Canada, 1896–1921: A Nation Transformed* (Toronto: McClelland and Stewart, 1974), 300–1; Robert Bothwell, Ian Drummond, and John English, *Canada: 1900–1945* (Toronto: University of Toronto Press, 1987), 156–57.

78 "The Heart of the City."

79 Numbers derived from Part II Orders located in LAC 150, vol. 71, "19th Canadian Battalion (Part 4)." The three officers killed in action on 10 November were Capt. M.C. Roberts, Lt. C.E.G. Robertson, and Lt. W.C. McFaul. In addition, Lt. W.W. Copeland was wounded in action on the same date and died of his injuries on 23 December. Other ranks killed in action were Pte. J.C. Buttimer, Pte. W. Chowns, Pte. P.J. Cronin, Pte. W. Curry, Pte. W. Hales, Pte. H. Howard, Pte. C. Jennings, Pte. G. Shewfelt, and Cpl. J.A. Simon. Two more other ranks, Pte. J.S. Malzard and Sgt. A. Craig, died of wounds received in action on 10 November. Maj. Hatch's after-action report counts only seven fatalities on 10 November (three officers and four other ranks): "19th Battalion Report, 11 Nov. 1918." This number is too low as far as the other ranks are concerned. As for total monthly casualties, both the war diary and the postwar statistics outlined in Appendix A agree that the 19th Battalion suffered fifty-six casualties (four officers, fifty-two other ranks) in November 1918.

80 LAC, *Flanders Fields*, vol. 6, transcript of Episode 16, "Victory," 16.

81 "19th Battalion Report, 11 Nov. 1918."

82 The captain referred to was Maurice C. Roberts. CWM, 19740071–020, 58C 2 3.16, 19th Canadian Infantry Battalion Association, file of correspondence, anecdotes, and drafts of material for the battalion association newsletter, statement by Leopold de Hem contributed by Herb Addison. During the fighting, Capt. Roberts had been assisted in his efforts to connect A and B Companies by Frank ("Chubby") Rowe, a runner from B Company. According to Walter Charles, Rowe won the Military Medal for his work in "guiding Captain Roberts across the cabbage patch." Roberts, unfortunately, was "riddled with machine gun bullets. Chubby Rowe tried to pull him back to lower ground but couldn't make it and just barely made it himself." ASH,

RG 4, Series 3, World War 1, 19th Battalion Association, "Selections from the Mailbag," 19th Battalion Association newsletter, October 1967.

83 Cooper, *History of Operations of 4th Canadian Infantry Brigade*, 42.

84 For a thorough analysis of Currie's and Hughes's respective public images and the battle that erupted between them, see Tim Cook, *The Madman and the Butcher: The Sensational Wars of Sam Hughes and General Arthur Currie* (Toronto: Allen Lane, 2010). See also Tim Cook, "The Madman and the Butcher: Sir Sam Hughes, Sir Arthur Currie, and Their War of Reputations," *Canadian Historical Review* 85, no. 4 (2004): 693–719.

85 Nicholson, *Canadian Expeditionary Force*, 482; Swettenham, *To Seize the Victory*, 1–2; Desmond Morton, *When Your Number's Up: The Canadian Soldier in the First World War* (Toronto: Random House, 1993), 272. Despite the prevalence on 10 November of fresh rumours of the war's impending termination, the armistice was not actually signed until 5 AM on 11 November, and it was not scheduled to take effect for a further six hours. At the libel trial that commenced in April 1928, "responsible and informed testimony established that the attack on Mons was both justifiable and necessary, the Corps Commander's task being to press the enemy as hard as he could until ordered to stop." Documentary evidence was brought to bear showing that official news of the armistice did not arrive at Canadian Corps headquarters until 6:30 AM on 11 November, thirty minutes after the Germans had been effectively cleared from Mons. Hence, the Canadian Corps' actions on 10–11 November were squarely in accordance with the high command's orders to keep pushing the Germans back until the very end. Moreover, Currie himself had given clear orders that advancing units were to avoid taking casualties if at all possible. In addition to exonerating Sir Arthur Currie of wanton recklessness, the court awarded him damages and costs. Edmonds and Maxwell-Hyslop, *Military Operations*, 537; Nicholson, *Canadian Expeditionary Force*, 482. See also Robert J. Sharpe, *The Last Day, The Last Hour: The Currie Libel Trial* (Toronto: Osgoode Society for Canadian Legal History / University of Toronto Press, 2009).

86 LAC, *Flanders Fields*, vol. 10, 19th Battalion, transcript of interview with E. Youngman, tape 4, 9.

87 Numbers include prisoners captured, accidental injuries, and self-inflicted wounds. For a complete breakdown of casualties during each calendar month, see Appendix A. See also LAC, RG 150, vols. 502–3, "Casualties by Days – France and Belgium," 19th Battalion, August–November 1918. Because of the error in the casualty figures listed in the war diary for the month of October, it was decided to rely on the postwar record of daily casualties.

88 By 1918, a Canadian division numbered over 21,000 all ranks. LAC, "Casualties by Days – France and Belgium," Canadian Corps, August–November 1918; LAC, RG 24, C-6-I, Scanlon Files, vol. 1874, file 22, vol. 2, J. Scanlon to W.L. Seely, 11 February 1930.

89 Lt.-Gen. Sir A.W. Currie, "Interim Report on the Operations of the Canadian Corps during the Year 1918," in *Report of the Ministry, Overseas Military Forces of Canada, 1918* (London: Minister, Overseas Military Forces of Canada, n.d.), 184.

90 Plus corps troops and temporarily attached British divisions, artillery brigades, and other units.

91 Numbers of prisoners and weapons captured are taken from the battalion war diary and after-action reports.

92 LAC, *Flanders Fields*, vol. 10, 19th Battalion, transcript of interview with E. Youngman, tape 4, 8.

93 LAC, *Flanders Fields*, vol. 6, transcript of Episode 16, "Victory," 19.

Chapter 22 – Going Home – Eventually: 12 November 1918–25 May 1919

1 GMA, M399, Gaetz Family Fonds, J.R. Gaetz to his mother, 13 November 1918.

2 McNaughton, qtd. in John Swettenham, *McNaughton*, vol. 1: *1887–1939* (Toronto: Ryerson, 1968), 168.

3 Nicholson, *Canadian Expeditionary Force, 1914–1919: The Official History of the Canadian Army in the First World War* (Ottawa: Queen's Printer, 1962), 524; Lt.-Gen. Sir A.W. Currie, "Interim Report on the Operations of the Canadian Corps during the Year 1918," in *Report of*

the Ministry, Overseas Military Forces of Canada, 1918 (London: Minister, Overseas Military Forces of Canada, n.d.), 185 (hereafter "Interim Report").

4 LAC, RG 9, III-D-3, vol. 4929, War Diary, 19th Battalion, November 1918, appendix 4, 4th Brigade Instructions no. 2 "for Advance to German Frontier," 18 November 1918; Nicholson, *Canadian Expeditionary Force*, 525.

5 LAC, War Diary, 19th Battalion, 12–17 November 1918; ibid., appendix 3, 4th Brigade G. 703, 12 November 1918; ibid., 19th Battalion, Battalion Order no. 112, 12 November 1918; Nicholson, *Canadian Expeditionary Force*, 525.

6 LAC, War Diary, 19th Battalion, 13 November 1918; ibid., appendix 3, 19th Battalion, memo D.A. 19, 12 November 1918.

7 LAC, War Diary, 19th Battalion, 13, 15 November 1918.

8 LAC, 4929, War Diary, 19th Battalion, Battalion Orders no. 112, 12 November 1918.

9 LAC, War Diary, 19th Battalion, number of other ranks listed as sick, November 1918.

10 Personal collection of Mrs. Phyllis Douglas, letters of Lt.-Col. Lionel H. Millen (hereafter Millen Letters), Millen to his mother, 28 November 1918.

11 LAC, War Diary, 19th Battalion, 16 November 1918; ibid., appendix 3, 4th Canadian Infantry Brigade Instructions no. 1, "for Advance to German Frontier," 16 November 1918.

12 The 19th Battalion formed part of the brigade group's advance guard in concert with the light-horsemen, cyclists, one section of engineers, and one battery of the 13th Brigade, CFA. LAC, War Diary, 19th Battalion, appendix 4, 4th Brigade, Operation Order no. 37, 17 November 1918; ibid., 19th Battalion Operation Order no. 110, 17 November 1918; ibid., appendix 3, "4th Canadian Infantry Brigade Instructions No. 1," 16 November 1918; D.J. Corrigall, *The History of the Twentieth Canadian Battalion (Central Ontario Regiment) Canadian Expeditionary Force in the Great War, 1914–1918* (Toronto: Stone and Cox, 1935), 285; LAC, War Diary, 19th Battalion, 18 November 1918; Nicholson, *Canadian Expeditionary Force*, 525; Toronto *Daily Star*, "Canadian Soldiers Greeted as the Liberators of Belgium," 18 December 1918.

13 LAC, War Diary, 19th Battalion, 19–21 November 1918; Currie, "Interim Report," 186–87; Corrigall, *The History of the Twentieth Canadian Battalion*, 283.

14 Ibid., 289.

15 LAC, War Diary, 19th Battalion, 24–27 November 1918; LAC, RG 9, III-D-3, vol. 4883, War Diary, 4th Infantry Brigade, 25 November 1918.

16 LAC, War Diary, 19th Battalion, 27–29 November 1918; Corrigall, *The History of the Twentieth Canadian Battalion*, 287; Nicholson, *Canadian Expeditionary Force*, 526.

17 LAC, RG 9, III-D-3, vols. 4929-4930, War Diary, 19th Battalion, 29 November–5 December 1918.

18 LAC, RG 24, C-1, vol. 1518, HQ 683-35-5, Maj.-Gen. W. Turnbull to secretary, Militia Council, Ottawa, 30 June 1920.

19 LAC, RG 9, III-D-3, vol. 4930, War Diary, 19th Battalion, 6 December 1918; ibid., appendix 1, 19th Battalion, Operation Order 123, 5 December 1918.

20 LAC, War Diary, 19th Battalion, 6 December 1918; Currie qtd. in Nicholson, *Canadian Expeditionary Force*, 526.

21 LAC, War Diary, 4th Infantry Brigade, 6 December 1918.

22 Currie, "Interim Report," sketch 13; LAC, War Diary, 19th Battalion, 7 December 1918.

23 LAC, War Diary, 19th Battalion, 9–12 December 1918; Corrigall, *The History of the Twentieth Canadian Battalion*, 291.

24 Nicholson, *Canadian Expeditionary Force*, 527.

25 LAC, War Diary, 19th Battalion, 13 December 1918; Corrigall, *The History of the Twentieth Canadian Battalion*, 292.

26 LAC, War Diary, 19th Battalion, appendix 1, 19th Battalion Operation Order, 12 December 1918; CWM, 19740071–017 58C 1 1.9, untitled file of correspondence and notes regarding 19th Battalion history, "The World War of 1914–18 and the 19th Battalion as They Affected Me, by #228421, Pte. V.E. Thompson, Rear Rank," 37 (hereafter "Thompson Narrative"). Shortly after arriving in Germany, the 19th Battalion acquired a silk Union flag. According to a battalion

memo dated 11 December, battalions for which colours had not "hitherto been authorized" (such as the 19th Battalion) would be "presented with a Silk Union Flag to take the place of the King's Colour." LAC, War Diary, 19th Battalion, appendix 1, 19th Battalion memo, D. 111, 11 December 1918.

27 Nicholson, *Canadian Expeditionary Force*, 527; LAC, War Diary, 4th Infantry Brigade, 13 December 1918.

28 Currie, "Interim Report," 192.

29 LAC, RG 41, B-III-1, Records of the CBC, *Flanders Fields*, vol. 10, 19th Battalion, transcript of interview with E. Youngman (hereafter "Youngman interview"), tape 4, 14.

30 LAC, War Diary, 19th Battalion, appendix 2, 19th Battalion memo, D.A. 130, 17 December 1918; LAC, RG 9, III-D-3, vol. 4850, AA & QMG, 2nd Canadian Division, appendix 8, "Nominal Roll of Officers and Other Ranks Who Came to France in September 1915 with the 2nd Canadian Division and Who Were in the 'March Past' on the Bonn Bridge December 13, 1918." In all, 32 officers and 1,002 other ranks left England in September 1915 (see Ch. 2).

31 LAC, War Diary, 19th Battalion, 13 December 1918; LAC, War Diary, 4th Infantry Brigade, appendix 9, Addenda to 4th Brigade Operation Order no. 53, 12 December 1918; ibid., 4th Infantry Brigade Provisional Defence Scheme, 18 December 1918; ibid., 4th Brigade Defence Scheme, 30 December 1918; Corrigall, *The History of the Twentieth Canadian Battalion*, 294.

32 Millen Letters, Millen to his mother, 13–14 December 1918.

33 Corrigall, *The History of the Twentieth Canadian Battalion*, 288.

34 LAC, War Diary, 4th Infantry Brigade, appendix 11, 4th Brigade memo, G. 969, 24 December 1918; LAC, War Diary, 19th Battalion, appendix 1, Routine Orders no. 3, 4 January 1919.

35 Millen Letters, Millen to his mother, 13–14 December 1918.

36 LAC, War Diary, 19th Battalion, appendix 2, 19th Battalion Orders as of 14 December 1918.

37 LAC, War Diary, 19th Battalion, Routine Orders no. 122, 18 December 1918.

38 "Thompson Narrative," 37–38.

39 Millen Letters, Millen to his mother, 22 December 1918.

40 LAC, War Diary, 19th Battalion, 15, 21–24 December 1918; ibid., appendix 2, 19th Battalion Orders as of 14 December 1918.

41 LAC, War Diary, 19th Battalion, 18 December 1918; ibid., appendix 1, 19th Battalion memo D. 111, 11 December 1918.

42 LAC, War Diary, 19th Battalion, 25 December 1918; LAC, War Diary, 4th Infantry Brigade, 25 December 1918.

43 Also stationed in Siegburg at that time were the 4th Brigade headquarters, the 20th Battalion, the 13th Brigade, CFA, and the 6th Canadian Field Ambulance. LAC, War Diary, 19th Battalion, 28 December 1918; ibid., appendix 3, 19th Battalion Routine Orders no. 131, 29 December 1918; "Thompson Narrative," 39; LAC, War Diary, 4th Infantry Brigade, 1 January 1919.

44 Millen Letters, Millen to his mother, 2 January 1919.

45 LAC, *Flanders Fields*, vol. 10, 19th Battalion, transcript of interview with Joe O'Neill, tape 2, 2–3.

46 LAC, War Diary, 19th Battalion, 1 January 1919.

47 LAC, War Diary, 19th Battalion, 1 January 1919; CWM, 19740071-016, W 3.2, oversize photo of "19th Canadian Infantry Battalion, New Year's Dinner Held at Siegburg, Germany, 1 January 1919."

48 Millen Letters, Millen to his mother, 2 January 1919; LAC, *Flanders Fields*, vol. 10, 19th Battalion, transcript of interview with Joe O'Neill, tape 2, 3.

49 LAC, War Diary, 19th Battalion, 1 January 1919.

50 LAC, *Flanders Fields*, vol. 10, 19th Battalion, transcript of interview with Joe O'Neill, tape 2, 2–3. Burstall's concern for the ordinary soldier's needs and his genuine respect for the men under his command made him popular among the other ranks. See David Campbell, "The Divisional Experience in the C.E.F.: A Social and Operational History of the 2nd Canadian Division, 1915–1918," PhD diss., University of Calgary, 2003, 275–77.

51 LAC, War Diary, 19th Battalion, 1 January 1919.

52 LAC, War Diary, 19th Battalion, 1 January 1919; ibid., appendix 3, 19th Battalion memo, D.A. 120, 31 December 1918.
53 Millen Letters, Millen to his mother, 2 January 1919.
54 "Thompson Narrative," 39.
55 Millen Letters, Millen to his mother, 2 January 1919.
56 LAC, War Diary, 19th Battalion, appendix 1, 19th Battalion Routine Order no. 3, 4 January 1919; Corrigall, *The History of the Twentieth Canadian Battalion*, 295; LAC, War Diary, 19th Battalion, 31 December 1918; ibid., appendix 1, Syllabus of Training and Education, 3 January 1919.
57 Nicholson, *Canadian Expeditionary Force*, 527–28; "The Khaki University of Canada," in *Report of the Ministry, Overseas Military Forces of Canada, 1918*, 473–81; LAC, RG 150, vol. 465, "List of Officers, 19th Infantry Battalion," 28 February 1919. One other rank also proceeded to England on 17 February in order to continue his studies at university. LAC, RG 150, vol. 71, "19th Battalion (part 5)," Part II Orders, no. 17, 6 March 1919. For a more recent analysis of the Khaki University and its significance, see Tim Cook, "From Destruction to Construction: The Khaki University of Canada, 1917–1919," *Journal of Canadian Studies* 37, no. 1 (Spring 2002): 109–43.
58 LAC, War Diary, 19th Battalion, 2–11 January 1919.
59 LAC, War Diary, 19th Battalion, 12 January 1919.
60 GMA, Gaetz Family Fonds, J.R. Gaetz to his father, 9 January 1919.
61 Millen Letters, Millen to his mother, 19 January 1919.
62 LAC, War Diary, 19th Battalion, 17–19 January 1919; Nicholson, *Canadian Expeditionary Force*, 529; J.A. *Cooper, History of Operations of 4th Canadian Infantry Brigade, 1915–1919* (London: Charles and Son, n.d.), 47.
63 GMA, Gaetz Family Fonds, J.R. Gaetz to his father, 9 January 1919.
64 LAC, War Diary, 19th Battalion, 20–22 January 1919; ibid., appendix 3, Field State, 19th Battalion, 20 January 1919; Nicholson, *Canadian Expeditionary Force*, 529.
65 Millen Letters, Millen to his mother, 25 January 1919.
66 GMA, M399, Gaetz Family Fonds, J.R. Gaetz to his mother, 26 January 1919.
67 Nicholson, *Canadian Expeditionary Force*, 529.
68 Desmond Morton, "'Kicking and Complaining': Demobilization Riots in the Canadian Expeditionary Force, 1918–19," *Canadian Historical Review* 61 (1980): 335.
69 Ibid., 335–37; Nicholson, *Canadian Expeditionary Force*, 528–30, 531; "Demobilization," in *Report of the Ministry, Overseas Military Forces of Canada, 1918*, 516–17.
70 In Canada, twenty-two dispersal stations, each servicing a certain dispersal area, were set up to facilitate demobilization. LAC, RG 24, C-6-e, vol. 1846, GAQ 11-43A, "General Demobilization – C.E.F., 1919," 1–4; Corrigall, *The History of the Twentieth Canadian Battalion*, 302–3.
71 Nicholson, *Canadian Expeditionary Force*, 529–30; Corrigall, *The History of the Twentieth Canadian Battalion*, 297–8; Morton, "'Kicking and Complaining,'" 342; LAC, "General Demobilization," 5–9.
72 The battalion library was opened on 27 February. LAC, War Diary, 19th Battalion, 27 February 1919.
73 The flavour of the officers' lives in Fosses is vividly portrayed in a letter written in 1945 by Lt.-Col. F.S. Parney, who had served as the 19th Battalion's medical officer. He also served in the Canadian Army Medical Corps in northwest Europe during the Second World War, and, as fate would have it, he found himself billeted again in the town of Fosses. See AO, F 970, Ewan Macdonald Fonds, Military Papers, 1915–1952, MS 444, reel 1; Corrigall, *The History of the Twentieth Canadian Battalion*, 300–1.
74 LAC, War Diary, 19th Battalion, battalion casualties, February 1919; ibid., appendix 1, Routine Orders no. 33, 7 February 1919; ibid., appendix 1, Routine Orders no. 57, 3 March 1919; GMA, M399, Gaetz Family Fonds, J.R. Gaetz to his mother, 25 February 1919.
75 LAC, War Diary, 4th Infantry Brigade, 12 March 1919; LAC, War Diary, 19th Battalion, 12 March 1919; ibid., appendix 1, Special Order, 10 March 1919.

76 Millen Letters, Millen to his mother, 11 March 1919. An article appearing in the *Hamilton Spectator* on 22 February 1918 lauded the 19th Battalion as the "Most Representative Hamilton Unit in France."

77 Nicholson, *Canadian Expeditionary Force*, 531–32; LAC, RG 24, C-6-e, vol. 1846, GAQ 11-43A, "Disturbances in Canadian Camps and Areas, 1918–1919"; Morton, "'Kicking and Complaining,'" 338, 342–51; Desmond Morton, *Winning the Second Battle: Canadian Veterans and the Return to Civilian Life, 1915–1930* (Toronto: University of Toronto Press, 1987), 110–12.

78 LAC, War Diary, 4th Infantry Brigade, 29 March 1919.

79 Corrigall, *The History of the Twentieth Canadian Battalion*, 302. Corrigall claims that Currie's visit occurred on 27 March, but according to the brigade war diary, it took place on 29 March. In addition, although the brigade diary claims that Currie visited "all battalions," the 19th Battalion's war diary makes no mention of his presence.

80 In actual fact, the 19th Battalion did not travel as a complete unit. One of its companies (C Company) remained behind for an extra day and began the journey to Le Havre on 1 April, under the temporary control of the 20th Battalion. LAC, War Diary, 19th Battalion, 31 March 1919; ibid., appendix 1, 19th Battalion, Operation Order no. 5, 30 March 1919; LAC, "General Demobilization," 4; Corrigall, *The History of the Twentieth Canadian Battalion*, 303.

81 LAC, War Diary, 19th Battalion, 31 March, 1 April 1919; LAC, RG 9, III-D-3, vol. 4926, War Diary, 18th Battalion, 31 March 1919; LAC, "General Demobilization."

82 LAC, War Diary, 19th Battalion, 2–4 April 1919; Corrigall, *The History of the Twentieth Canadian Battalion*, 303.

83 LAC, War Diary, 19th Battalion, 5 April 1919; LAC, RG 150, vol. 71, "19th Canadian Battalion (5)," Part II Orders no. 25, 7 April 1919.

84 LAC, War Diary, 19th Battalion, 6 April 1919; LAC, "General Demobilization," 6.

85 LAC, War Diary, 19th Battalion, 7–18 April 1919; Nicholson, *Canadian Expeditionary Force*, 531.

86 LAC, War Diary, 19th Battalion, 19–20 April 1919; Corigall, *The History of the Twentieth Canadian Battalion*, 304.

87 Millen Letters, Millen to his mother, 20 April 1919.

88 LAC, War Diary, 19th Battalion, 21–30 April 1919.

89 Determining exactly how many of these were new cases and how many were relapses requires more detailed investigation. The period from December 1914 to December 1915 saw the greatest incidence of venereal disease in the battalion, with 104 cases. LAC, RG 150, Series 1, vol. 71, "19th Battalion (Parts 1–5)," listings in Part II Orders, usually under the heading, "Hospital Stoppages (Venereal Diseases)." Venereal disease was considered by many military authorities to be a form of self-inflicted wound because it was deemed preventable and treatment usually necessitated hospitalization, rendering the victim unavailable for service in the field. Consequently, those who contracted venereal disease could be subject to punishment. While in hospital, they often were fined fifty cents per day and their field allowance was forfeit. Ibid.; Andrew Macphail, *Official History of the Canadian Forces in the Great War 1914–19: The Medical Services* (Ottawa: King's Printer 1925), 279, 289.

90 Macphail, *The Medical Services*, 293. The rate of infection among Canadians was dramatically higher than among British troops (24 cases per 1,000 men). Hospital-admission rates for venereal cases among Australian and New Zealand troops (128 and 130 cases per 1,000 respectively) also did not quite match the Canadian record. The Dominion troops' higher rates of pay and longer absence from home likely contributed to greater incidence of venereal disease. Richard Holmes, *Tommy: The British Soldier on the Western Front, 1914–1918* (London: HarperCollins, 2004), 483; Desmond Morton, *When Your Number's Up: The Canadian Soldier in the First World War* (Toronto: Random House, 1993), 200.

91 Morton, *Winning the Second Battle*, 110; LAC, War Diary, 19th Battalion, 26 April 1919; Bruce Cane, *It Made You Think of Home: The Haunting Journal of Deward Barnes, Canadian Expeditionary Force: 1916–1919* (Toronto: Dundurn, 2004), 164–5.

92 CWM, 19740071-017 58C 1 1.8, untitled file of letters, questionnaires, responses, and notes regarding 19th Battalion history, "Questionnaire No. 8, Mons to Demobilization," 3 May 1919; GMA, Gaetz Family Fonds, J.R. Gaetz to his mother, 4 May 1919.
93 Corrigall, *The History of the Twentieth Canadian Battalion*, 304–5.
94 Nicholson, *Canadian Expeditionary Force*, 531; LAC, "General Demobilization."
95 GMA, Gaetz Family Fonds, J.R. Gaetz to his mother, 11 May 1919.
96 Although the brigades had formally ceased to exist as such by the time their constituent units had returned to England, in popular discourse units often were collectively referenced in relation to their old formations. LAC, RG 24, C-1-a, vol. 6558, HQ 868-8-23, proceedings of court of inquiry regarding beer and tobacco raids at Witley Camp by units of the 2nd Division.
97 CWM, "Questionnaire No. 8, Mons to Demobilization," 13 May 1919; Corrigall, *The History of the Twentieth Canadian Battalion*, 305; LAC, RG 24, vol. 1884, C-6-d, 59, "Return of Second Canadian Division, Distribution of Units to their various Dispersal Stations." The strength reported for the 19th Battalion presumably included personnel from other units or commands who were attached for demobilization purposes. According to the battalion diarist's entry for 30 April, "during the month there were men of other Units attached for Demobilization. Practically all 4th Canadian Infantry Brigade Headquarters were taken on the strength for the same purpose." LAC, War Diary, 19th Battalion, 30 April 1919.
98 Corrigall, *The History of the Twentieth Canadian Battalion*, 305.
99 By coincidence, it was on 22 May 1915 that the 19th Battalion first arrived in Plymouth Sound aboard the RMS *Scandinavian*.
100 Nicholson, *Canadian Expeditionary Force*, 533; Corrigall, *The History of the Twentieth Canadian Battalion*, 305; LAC, "General Demobilization"; LAC, "Return of Second Canadian Division."
101 Corrigall, *The History of the Twentieth Canadian Battalion*, 306; LAC, RG 41, B-III-1, Records of the CBC, *Flanders Fields*, vol. 10, 19th Battalion, transcript of interview with E. Youngman, tape 4, 15.
102 "Lights of Home for Heroes of 19th Battalion," *Hamilton Spectator*, 26 May 1919. The only exception was the period in August and September 1916 when Maj. G.F. Morrison of Toronto assumed temporary command of the battalion while Lt.-Col. Turnbull recovered from his wound.
103 LAC, *Flanders Fields*, vol. 10, 19th Battalion, transcript of interview with E. Youngman, tape 4, 15.
104 LAC, *Flanders Fields*, vol. 10, 19th Battalion, transcript of interview with E. Youngman, tape 4, 14–15.
105 Corrigall, *The History of the Twentieth Canadian Battalion*, 306.
106 "Toronto Plans Big Welcome for 19th Battalion," *Hamilton Spectator*, 23 May 1919; "Lights of Home for Heroes of 19th Battalion"; Nicholson, *Canadian Expeditionary Force*, 533; LAC, "General Demobilization," 17. In December 1918 the Canadian government announced its plans to issue a War Service Gratuity. If a private soldier served for three or more years overseas, he was entitled "to six months' pay at a minimum rate of seventy dollars a month for a single man; a married private would have one hundred dollars. A year's service in Canada earned the minimum gratuity, seventy dollars." Men of higher rank would receive correspondingly higher rates of pay. Morton, *Winning the Second Battle*, 113; Nicholson, *Canadian Expeditionary Force*, 533.

Epilogue

1 CWM, 19740071-017 58C 1 1.9, untitled file of correspondence and notes regarding 19th Battalion history, "The World War of 1914–18 and the 19th Battalion as They Affected Me, by #228421, Pte. V.E. Thompson, Rear Rank," 25.
2 GMA, M399, Gaetz Family Fonds, J.R. Gaetz to his mother, 21 March 1918.

3 According to the Department of Militia and Defence, the 19th Battalion was "officially disbanded, vide General Order No. 149 of the 15th September, 1920." LAC, RG 24, C-1, vol. 1518, HQ 683-35-5, memo from Department of Militia and Defence, 14 October 1920.

4 Based in Hamilton, Ontario, the Argyll and Sutherland Highlanders of Canada trace their origins to Hamilton's 91st Regiment (Canadian Highlanders), the militia unit that contributed numerous recruits to the 19th Battalion as well as much of its cadre of senior officers. The Argylls also perpetuate the 173rd Battalion and the 3rd Canadian Machine Gun Battalion, both of the CEF. DHH, Kardex 145.2A3 (D1), "The Argyll and Sutherland Highlanders of Canada (Princess Louise's), R.C.I.C. Organization, Perpetuations and Battle Honours."

5 The figure of 4,731 other ranks was cited in the following sources: LAC, RG 24, C-6-e, vol. 1821, GAQ 5-16, "Comparative Statement Showing the Number of Other Ranks Passed through the Fighting Battalions of the Canadian Corps," April 1924; LAC, RG 24, C-6-d, vol. 1884, 58, "Notes on Units, Arms and Services of the Canadian Expeditionary Force Which Served in France and Flanders" (compiled by W. Davidson, Historical Section, Ottawa). The figures of 118 officers and 5,004 other ranks were derived from CWM, 19740071-020 58C 2 3.16, 19th Canadian Infantry Battalion Association, "First World War, 1914–1919: Composition of 19th Battalion, C.E.F., Original and Reinforcements," compiled by H. "Barney" Clendining, "with the help of the Historical Section of Army Headquarters, Ottawa, and the D.V.A. Toronto." Clendining lists numbers of original and reinforcement personnel and the different units that contributed them. He claims a total figure of 5,143 all ranks for the 19th Battalion. However, when the numbers in his list are added up, the total actually works out to be 5,122 all ranks. Without knowing the exact methodology through which the figures in the preceding sources were derived, it is difficult to determine which is the most accurate with respect to total numbers of other ranks.

6 These numbers include prisoners of war, self-inflicted wounds, and injuries and accidental wounds. LAC, RG 150, vol. 504, "Casualties, France and Belgium – Recapitulation," 19th Battalion. For full details on total battle casualties, injuries, and accidental and self-inflicted wounds from September 1915 to March 1919, see Appendix A. The souvenir program for the 19th Battalion Association's Golden Jubilee dinner claims that 785 officers and men of the 19th Battalion were killed in action or died of wounds.

7 ASH, RG 4, series 3, World War 1, Ted Lang Donation, R.H. (Harry) Neil, "A Brief History of the 19th Battalion C.E.F. 1914–18."

8 Ian M. McCulloch, "The 'Fighting Seventh': The Evolution and Devolution of Tactical Command and Control in a Canadian Infantry Brigade of the Great War," MA thesis, Royal Military College of Canada, 1997, 267.

9 ASH, Neil, "A Brief History of the 19th Battalion."

10 ASH, RG 4, Series 3, World War 1, 19th Battalion Association, 19th Battalion Association newsletter, Spring 1980.

11 Barnes journal, 10 February 1919, qtd. in Bruce Cane, *It Made You Think of Home: The Haunting Journal of Deward Barnes, Canadian Expeditionary Force: 1916–1919* (Toronto: Dundurn, 2004), 273–74, 275–76.

12 GMA, Gaetz Family Fonds, J.R. Gaetz to his father, 9 January 1919.

13 Personal interview, Col. Ian Douglas and Phyllis Douglas, 8 December 2002; Robert Fraser, "Lt.-Col. Lionel Herbert Millen, DSO (1876–1956)," unpublished biographical sketch.

14 Personal collection of Mrs. Phyllis Douglas, letters of Lt.-Col. Lionel H. Millen, Millen to his mother, 24 March 1919.

15 Fraser, "Lt.-Col. Lionel Herbert Millen."

16 Millen was especially interested in the scouting movement and served as provincial commissioner for Ontario during the 1930s. During the Second World War, he served as spice controller of Canada for the nominal sum of one dollar per annum. Fraser, "Lt.-Col. Lionel Herbert Millen"; personal interview, Col. Ian Douglas and Phyllis Douglas.

17 Jonathan Vance, *Death So Noble: Memory, Meaning, and the First World War* (Vancouver: UBC Press, 1997), 79.

18 This poem was found in a file containing numerous newsletters from the 19th Battalion Association. On the sheet of paper on which the verse appears is the heading, "Spring 1935. Lines written by R.O. Spreckley of Ottawa following the Canadian Corps Reunion, Toronto, July 1934." At the bottom of the page, after the verse, is the following note, presumably written by Ted Lang: "(R.O. Spreckley, 'Spreck,' came to the 19th Bn. as a combatant officer in 1917 from the 5th Field Ambulance. He is a retired Civil Servant and a free lance writer for various newspapers and magazines. T.W.L.)." ASH, RG 4, series 3, World War 1, 19th Battalion Association, poem dedicated to the 19th Battalion written by R.O. Spreckley.

Appendix B – Discipline in France and Flanders

1 See Fig. 3. In his study of the New Zealand Division, historian Christopher Pugsley notes that "disciplinary problems all but vanished during the [Battle of the] Somme: everybody was too concerned with the fighting ... It was more in the lull before and after battle that disciplinary matters became of concern." Christopher Pugsley, *On the Fringe of Hell: New Zealanders and Military Discpline in the First World War* (Toronto: Hodder and Stoughton 1991), 123.

2 See Fig. 3. In every battalion, there were varying numbers of men who served outside the unit but who were still carried on the battalion strength. Such men could be attached to other combatant or support units (e.g., trench mortar, machine gun, tunnelling, or railway companies) for short or long periods of service. They also might be stationed in convalescent camps, base depots, training camps, or other rear-echelon establishments following periods of illness or injury, or while serving limited terms as instructors or administrative staff.

3 See Fig. 3.

4 In June 1916, Maj. Arthur M. Jarvis, Assistant Provost Marshal (APM) of 2nd Canadian Division remarked: "The new drafts which are coming to the country are not nearly up to the standard of the original Canadian battalions either physically or in discipline and they are now the cause of nearly all our troubles." LAC, War Diary, vol. 5050, 2nd Canadian Division A.P.M., 19 June 1916. See also David Campbell, "The Divisional Experience in the C.E.F.: A Social and Operational History of the 2nd Canadian Division, 1915–1918," PhD thesis, University of Calgary, 2003, 443–45.

5 According to T.O. Jacobs, "personnel turbulence is endemic in military units. In war, it results from casualties. In peace it results from personnel movements." T.O. Jacobs, "Introduction to Section 4," in *Handbook of Military Psychology*, ed. Reuven Gal and A. David Mangelsdorff, (New York: John Wiley 1991), 391.

6 See Jean-Pierre Gagnon, *Le 22e Bataillon (Canadien-français), Étude socio-militaire* (Québec and Ottawa: Les Presses de l'Université Laval / Department of National Defence, 1986), Ch. 8.

7 Part II Daily Orders account for 660 other ranks taken on strength from 8 September to the end of December 1916. Statistics compiled after the war by the Directorate of Records, Department of National Defence, add up to 712 other ranks taken on strength from September through December. LAC, Part II Daily Orders, 1916; LAC, RG 24, C-6-i, vol. 1874, file 22, vol. 1, Other Ranks, Monthly Strength, Infantry, 2nd Division.

8 LAC, Part II Daily Orders, no. 42, 18 June 1917.

9 Part II Orders were administrative orders issued by a unit, sometimes on a daily basis. They addressed changes in personnel, including lists of men taken on the unit's strength; lists of those who were struck off strength owing to illness, injury, death, or transfer; lists of men promoted or decorated; and lists of men undergoing punishment.

10 These numbers include men who were attached to other units but who were still carried on the battalion strength. They also include repeat offenders. Many individuals committed multiple offences and were awarded multiple punishments (such as field punishment along with fines or forfeitures of pay). LAC, "19th Battalion (parts 2–4)," Part II Daily Orders, 1916–18. When examining cases of punishment or courts martial in unit Part II Orders, one may distinguish

between original personnel and personnel who joined the unit after its departure from Canada by looking at an individual's regimental number. This number is provided in the listings along with the individual's name and rank. Original other ranks from the 19th Battalion were issued regimental numbers within the range 55001 to 57000. Men with regimental numbers falling outside that range joined the battalion after its departure from Canada. For serial number blocks assigned to each unit of the CEF, see Edward H. Wigney, *Serial Numbers of the C.E.F.* (Nepean: published by author, 1996).

11 Barnes journal, 27 May 1917, qtd. in Bruce Cane, *It Made You Think of Home: The Haunting Journal of Deward Barnes, Canadian Expeditionary Force: 1916–1919* (Toronto: Dundurn, 2004), 95.

12 Ibid. The subject of shell shock during the First World War has received scrutiny from medical professionals and scholars, beginning during the war and continuing into the present day. For further discussion, see Campbell Meyers, "The Canadian Soldier and Shell Shock," *Hospital World*, February 1917, repr. ed. found in LAC, RG 24, C-8, vol. 4268, file 15-2-35; P.R. Bolus, "Some Notes on Shell Shock," *Canadian Defence Quarterly* 12, no. 3 (1935): 347–54; Desmond Morton, *When Your Number's Up: The Canadian Soldier in the First World War* (Toronto: Random House, 1993), 196–98; Cathryn Corns and John Hughes-Wilson, *Blindfold and Alone: British Military Executions in the Great War* (London: Cassell, 2001), Chs. 6–7, 25–26, 35; Robin Glen Keirstead, "The Canadian Military Medical Experience during the Great War, 1914–1918," MA thesis, Queen's University, 1982, 217–33; Special Issue: "Shell Shock," *Journal of Contemporary History* 35, no. 1 (2000); Tim Cook, *Shock Troops: Canadians Fighting the Great War, 1917–1918* (Toronto: Viking, 2008), Ch. 15. Terry Copp and Bill McAndrew, in *Battle Exhaustion: Soldiers and Psychiatrists in the Canadian Army, 1939–1945* (Montreal and Kingston: McGill–Queen's University Press, 1990), provide an excellent account of changing attitudes to psychiatric trauma in the Canadian Army during the Second World War. For a broader approach, see Terry Copp and Mark Osborne Humphries, *Combat Stress in the 20th Century: The Commonwealth Perspective* (Kingston: Canadian Defence Academy Press, 2010).

13 Morton, *When Your Number's Up*, 197; Corns and Hughes-Wilson, *Blindfold and Alone*, 309–10; LAC, RG 24, C-6-j, vol. 6992, Ch. VII, vol. 2, "Note on Self-Inflicted Injuries."

14 Richard Holmes, *Tommy: The British Soldier on the Western Front, 1914–1918* (London: HarperCollins, 2004), 484–5.

15 Morton, *When Your Number's Up*, 198. Tim Cook notes that "according to official records, at least 9,000 Canadians were diagnosed with shell shock, but one contemporary wartime CAMC doctor later claimed that there were at least 15,000 diagnosed cases, and this did not include all the men who were killed even before they made it out of the line to be diagnosed." Cook, *Shock Troops*, 243.

16 Gunshot wounds were not the only form of self-inflicted injury. According to historians Cathryn Corns and John Hughes-Wilson, "there were other, less obvious tricks: adding egg white to urine to mimic kidney disease ... eating cordite to cause an irregular heartbeat, eating picric acid to imitate jaundice, injecting turpentine under the skin to cause abscesses, rubbing horse manure onto the gums to mimic scurvy are but a few." Desmond Morton reports a case in which a man dug a hole, planted his foot and a live grenade, and blew his leg off to escape service. By 1917, those who contracted trench foot or failed to don a respirator during a gas alert were treated as SIW cases. Corns and Hughes-Wilson, *Blindfold and Alone*, 309; Morton, *When Your Number's Up*, 249.

17 LAC, "Note on Self-Inflicted Injuries"; LAC, Part II Daily Orders, 1916–18.

18 Among the Canadian SIW cases in France and Belgium, one officer and thirty-six other ranks died as a result of their injuries. LAC, "Note on Self-Inflicted Injuries." Numbers of SIWs in other battalions may be found in LAC, RG 38, vol. 443, "Casualties per Corps." All told, there were 729 cases of self-inflicted wounds among Canadian personnel serving in Canada and overseas during the war. Sir Andrew Macphail, *Official History of the Canadian Forces in the Great War, 1914–1919: The Medical Services* (Ottawa: King's Printer, 1925), 278–79.

19 Andrew Godefroy, *For Freedom and Honour? The Story of the 25 Canadian Volunteers Executed in the First World War* (Nepean: CEF Books, 1998), 9; Corns and Hughes-Wilson, *Blindfold and Alone*, 90; T.M. Hunter, *Some Aspects of Disciplinary Policy in the Canadian Services, 1914–1946* (Ottawa: Report no. 91, Historical Section, Army Headquarters, 1960), 7–8.

20 War Office, *Manual of Military* Law, 35. There was a distinction between the sentences of "imprisonment" and "penal servitude." The Army Act stipulated that imprisonment, with or without hard labour, was for terms "not exceeding two years," whereas penal servitude was awarded for terms "not less than three years." Army Act, s. 44, in ibid., 416.

21 Julian Putkowski, *British Army Mutineers, 1914–1922* (London: Francis Boutle, 1998), 10; Corns and Hughes-Wilson, *Blindfold and Alone*, 90; Hunter, *Some Aspects of Disciplinary Policy*, 8. Within the Canadian Corps, officers sitting on a FGCM were selected from the pool of officers stationed within the area in which the trial was held, and who were qualified to sit on the panel by dint of their experience and length of service. Selections were made by the officer who convened the court – usually the accused man's brigade commander. Ideally, an officer of field rank (a major or higher) acted as president of the court, with the other two panel members often being a captain and a lieutenant. To ensure that an accused man received as fair a trial as possible, regulations prevented his commanding officer from sitting on the panel. However, other officers from the accused's battalion sometimes sat, owing to the exigencies of the situation and the availability of officers from other units. LAC, "Discipline"; Corns and Hughes-Wilson, *Blindfold and Alone*, 90–91.

22 Records in 19th Battalion Part II Orders reveal fifty courts martial, while a finding aid for CEF courts martial holdings at LAC contains fifty-five listings for the 19th Battalion. See LAC, Part II Daily Orders, 1914–1920 (http://www.collectionscanada.ca/archivianet/020107_e.html). Determining which number is the most accurate requires more detailed investigation of each court martial in the proceedings and other documents held by LAC.

According to entries in battalion Part II Orders, four other ranks were tried in Canada between December 1914 and March 1915. These trials would have been RCMs. The offences in these cases included disobedience, drunkenness, and striking an NCO. Punishments ranged from seven to twenty-one days of detention – well within the powers of the CO to award summarily. Either the accused men elected not to take a summary punishment in favour of trial by court martial or the courts were disposed to be lenient. LAC, Part II Daily Orders, 1914–15.

23 Several individuals were tried for two or three offences (i.e., drunkenness and striking a superior officer): LAC, Part II Daily Orders, 1914–20. Sixteen of the fifty courts martial listed in Part II Orders were of original men who joined the battalion before it departed Canada. Seven of the men tried appear to have been attached to other commands at the time of their offences and/or trials. Confirmation of all specifics related to individual courts martial would require review of the trial proceedings in each case. These are held by LAC.

24 Ibid.

25 Teresa Iacobelli, *Death or Deliverance: Canadian Courts Martial in the Great War* (Vancouver: UBC Press, 2013), 137.

26 In six cases, the terms of FP 1 awarded were between ten and twenty-eight days – within a battalion commander's powers of summary punishment. Ibid.

27 Four other ranks were convicted by RCMs during 1914 and early 1915 and sentenced to periods of detention between seven and twenty-one days in length. Ibid.

28 Morton, *When Your Number's Up*, 106–7; LAC, Part II Daily Orders, no. 5, 21 January 1919. Connolly was suspended from duty until 19 December, when the sentence was finally promulgated.

29 Army Act, ss. 4–12, in War Office, *Manual of Military Law*, 378–90. For a detailed analysis of death sentences awarded in the CEF, and especially the majority of cases in which such sentences were commuted, see Iacobelli, *Death or Deliverance*.

30 There were twenty-two cases of desertion, one of cowardice, and two of murder. Godefroy, *For Freedom and Honour?*, 3. The twenty-five Canadians actually executed were a small percentage

of the total number of Canadians sentenced to death, which was 222. One of these condemned men was an officer, a lieutenant from the 72nd Battalion who was charged with disobedience. His sentence was commuted to ten years' penal servitude and cashiering. Similarly, the majority of other men sentenced to death had their punishments commuted, often to terms of imprisonment or penal servitude of varying length. For lists of more than 3,000 individuals sentenced to death in the British armies during the First World War, see Gerard Oram, *Death Sentences Passed by Military Courts of the British Army, 1914–1924* (London: Francis Boutle, 1998). Those who were actually executed numbered 346 (including the twenty-five Canadians).

31 Information in these tables was first published in Gagnon, *Le 22e Bataillon (Canadien-français)*, Table 24, 287; David Campbell, "Military Discipline, Punishment, and Leadership in the First World War: The Case of the 2nd Canadian Division," in *The Apathetic and the Defiant: Case Studies of Canadian Mutiny and Disobedience, 1812–1919*, ed. Craig L. Mantle (Kingston and Toronto: Canadian Defence Academy Press / Dundurn 2007), 470; Maxime Dagenais, "'Une Permission! C'est bon pour une recrue': Discipline and Illegal Absences in the 22nd (French-Canadian) Battalion, 1915–1919," *Canadian Military History* 18, no. 4 (2009): 7, 9.

32 Categories and timescale in this table are taken from Gagnon, *Le 22e Bataillon*, Table 24, 287; LAC, Part II Daily Orders, 1915–18. The numbers given here for the 19th Battalion do not include those offences committed by personnel when they were attached temporarily to other units or commands. Statistics for 24th Battalion cover the period October 1915 to November 1918; those for the 25th Battalion range from October 1915 to October 1918. Records for the remaining unit of the 5th Brigade, 26th Battalion, were incomplete, furnishing statistics only for the period between January 1917 and October 1918. These were as follows: absences, 332; drunkenness 54; other infractions, 229; total minor infractions, 615. Interestingly, these statistics for the 26th Battalion exceed or equal those of the 19th Battalion, even though they occurred in a much narrower time frame. Dagenais, "'Une Permission!'" 7, 9.

33 Figures from the 19th Battalion as taken from LAC, Part II Daily Orders, 1915–18; figures from 27th, 28th, 29th, and 31st Battalions taken from LAC, RG 9, III-C-3, vol. 4123, folder 1, "6th Canadian Infantry Brigade Headquarters. Discipline. From January 1917 to November 1918."

34 Information in this table first published in Campbell, "Military Discipline," 470.

35 Numbers derived from LAC online database Courts Martial of the First World War; see http://www.collectionscanada.ca/archivianet/020107_e.html. As noted earlier, the number of court martial listings found in this source, and the reported dating of the trials, differ somewhat from the listings found in the 19th Battalion Part II Orders.

36 Confidential letter from Maj.-Gen. Russell to brigadiers and battalion commanders of the New Zealand Division, 24 May 1917, qtd. in Pugsley, *On the Fringe of Hell*, 188.

37 For a detailed study of the function and role of paternalism among British officers and other ranks during the First World War, see G.D. Sheffield, *Leadership in the Trenches: Officer-Man Relations, Morale and Discipline in the British Army in the Era of the First World War* (London: Macmillan, 2000).

38 LAC, *Flanders Fields*, vol. 10, 21st Battalion, transcript of interview with W.F. Doolan, tape 1, 12. According to Maj.-Gen. Russell, GOC, New Zealand Division, it was a small minority (about 10 percent) of personnel who were consistently getting into trouble and giving platoon commanders and NCO's "all the headaches." Pugsley, *On the Fringe of Hell*, 206.

39 LAC, *Flanders Fields*, vol. 10, 19th Battalion, transcript of interview with Joe O'Neill, tape 1, 6–7.

40 Personal interview, Col. Ian and Phyllis Douglas, 8 December 2002.

41 McLaren, qtd. in LAC, *Flanders Fields*, vol. 10, 19th Battalion, transcript of interview with E. Youngman, tape 1, 6.

42 Ibid., vol. 10, 19th Battalion, transcript of interview with Joe O'Neill, tape 1, 9.

43 Barnes journal, 8 May 1917, qtd. in Cane, *It Made You Think of Home*, 85–86.

44 Ibid., 86.

45 Campbell, "Military Discipline," 326–9.

Index

Page numbers in *italics* indicate photos and maps.

Canadian Unit, Formation, and Command Histories series

Published by Wilfrid Laurier University Press

Loyal Gunners: 3rd Field Artillery Regiment (The Loyal Company) and the History of New Brunswick's Artillery, 1893 to 2012 | Lee Windsor, Roger Sarty, Marc Milner | 2016 | 978-1-77112-237-5

Toronto's Fighting 75th in the Great War 1915–1919: A Prehistory of the Toronto Scottish Regiment (Queen Elizabeth The Queen Mother's Own) | Timothy J. Stewart | 2017 | 978-1-77112-182-8

It Can't Last Forever: The 19th Battalion and the Canadian Corps in the First World War | David Campbell | 2017 | 978-1-77112-236-8